BANK MANAGEMENT
TEXT AND CASES

GEORGE H. HEMPEL
Southern Methodist University

ALAN B. COLEMAN
Southern Methodist University

DONALD G. SIMONSON
University of Oklahoma

JOHN WILEY & SONS
New York / Chichester / Brisbane / Toronto / Singapore

Library of Congress Cataloging in Publication Data:

Hempel, George H.
  Bank management.

  Includes index.
    1. Bank management.   2. Bank management—Case studies.
I. Coleman, Alan B.   II. Simonson, Donald G.   III. Title.
HG1615.H45   1983   332.1′068   83-3620
ISBN 0-471-87772-7

Printed in the United States of America

10 9 8 7 6 5

ABOUT THE AUTHORS

Dr. George H. Hempel is Professor of Finance and Associate Director of the South-western Graduate School of Banking at Southern Methodist University. He has written nine other books and numerous articles on various topics in banking and finance. Dr. Hempel has served on banking boards and as a consultant to banks and is involved in numerous banking professional educational programs. He is currently president of the Financial Management Association, a professional association whose over 5,000 members include approximately sixty percent of all U.S. finance professors.

Dr. Alan B. Coleman is Caruth Professor of Finance and President of the Southwestern Graduate School of Banking Foundation at Southern Methodist University. Dr. Coleman had previously served as president of two corporations and as Dean of Southern Methodist's School of Business. Dr. Coleman has been author of three other casebooks and has written numerous cases in banking and finance. He serves on the boards of and as consultant to several banks and businesses.

Dr. Donald G. Simonson is Oklahoma Bankers Professor of Finance at the University of Oklahoma. Prior to his academic career, he was employed at Martin Marietta and Mobil Oil. Dr. Simonson has extensive research published in banking and finance journals, and has served on the faculties of a number of regional and national schools of banking.

PREFACE

Managing a commercial bank in the 1980s has been—and promises to continue to be—a challenging task. A difficult economic environment, a changing regulatory environment, a rapid rate of technological development, an increasingly intense level of competition, and some worrisome trends in the banking industry have combined to create a demand for good bank management. The purpose of this book is to present the management concepts and techniques that will help current and potential managers to be successful in this challenging period. We have included twenty-six up-to-date cases in which bankers and students can test their abilities to solve problems in modern banking situations.

This book is divided into five parts. Each of the parts has three or more cases in which readers can apply the concepts and techniques discussed in the part. Part I is an introduction to bank management. In it, we review the dynamic nature of bank management and the banking structures (Chapter 1). Then in Chapter 2 we move to the basic measures of returns and risks in banking and examine how bank management should use such measures to evaluate bank performance.

In Part II we examine how a bank obtains funds. In Chapter 3, we evaluate methods for acquiring deposits and short-term borrowed liabilities, as well as the cost of these funds. We also examine the potential profit on the various types of deposits and short-term liabilities. Chapter 4 covers how a bank determines and obtains the appropriate amount and mix of capital funds.

Part III covers management of a bank's reserves, liquidity, and securities needs. In Chapter 5 of this part we demonstrate how bank reserve requirements are measured and met. We present methods for measuring short-term, seasonal, and long-term liquidity needs and then discuss methods for meeting such liquidity needs. In Chapter 6 we evaluate the ways the securities portfolio affects a bank's profitability and risk. We discuss several techniques for increasing returns without significantly increasing risks.

Part IV (Chapters 7 through 11) covers the lending function of commercial banks. The primary types of bank loans are described and the ways a bank may organize to compete successfully in lending are also discussed. In this part we present details on such topics as credit analysis, loan pricing, and structuring a loan for the primary types of bank loans.

The fifth and final part emphasizes integrative asset/liability management techniques. In Chapter 12 we introduce techniques for managing a bank's overall interest sensitivity position and for increasing the interest margin. Chapter 13 includes a method for determining actual and potential risk-return tradeoffs and a system for long-range planning.

A separate Instructor's Manual, which includes a summary, teaching objectives, analyses, and suggested questions for each case, is available for professors and bank training directors. Potential bank simulations that may be used with this book are also evaluated.

We are indebted to several professors and bankers. William S. Townsend of Banc-First Corporation helped with the initial formulation of the book and with ideas on how to incorporate cases with the text material. Harry Blythe of Ohio State University provided assistance and helpful comments throughout the book's preparation. In addition, we wish to thank Tim Sidley of InterFirst Bancshares, Dwight Crane of Harvard University, Dick Roberts of Wachovia National Bank, Don Wright of Allied Lakewood Bank, Gene Simonoff of Warren, Gorham, and Lamont, Gerry Czarnecki of Republic Bank, and Frank Schackelford of Indiana National Bank for their helpful comments.

Case materials were obtained from George Parker of Stanford University, Harry Blythe and David Cole of Ohio State University, and Jerry Darnell of The University of Colorado. Valuable research assistance on the cases was supplied by Joanne Gruber and Armando Gallegos, two Southern Methodist University graduate students. Secretarial assistance was provided by Janet Hardy, Kay McKee, Jane Girard, Sherri Phillips, and the Cox School of the Business Word Processing Center.

Helpful suggestions were also generated from those using this book in manuscript form at Wharton, Southern Methodist University, Texas Tech University, The University of Hawaii, Washington University, Oklahoma University, University of Missouri, The Southwestern Graduate School of Banking, and the Pacific Coast Banking School. In spite of the help received, deficiencies undoubtedly remain. For these, we take full responsibility and urge readers to call them to our attention.

GEORGE H. HEMPEL
ALAN B. COLEMAN
DONALD G. SIMONSON

CONTENTS

I

INTRODUCTION TO BANK MANAGEMENT

1
THE CHANGING NATURE OF BANK MANAGEMENT

Management of a commercial bank has become an increasingly challenging task. Concepts and techniques gainfully used only a few years ago now seem outdated. Protection from regulation and geographic and product constraints appears to be rapidly disappearing. To some managers the increasing complexity of banking decisions is worrisome, yet to many others this increasing challenge presents the opportunity for rewarding good management. The purpose of this book is to present up-to-date concepts and techniques that can help actual and prospective bank managers in this challenging period.

In this introductory chapter, we briefly discuss the economic role of commercial banks and the current structure of banking and its regulation. We then examine the dynamic and increasingly challenging nature of the banking environment and conclude with an outline of the primary topics of bank management covered in this book.

ROLE OF COMMERCIAL BANKING IN THE U.S. ECONOMY[1]

The primary economic role of commercial banks can be understood by looking at the financial flows in our economy over a time period. Figure 1-1 illustrates the three ways in which the business and household income for a period can be used. First, part of this income is taxed by government units. The remaining "disposable" amount is either spent or not spent by the unit earning the income. What happens to each of these three uses of income? Taxes paid to governments are typically spent by these units and con-

[1] The economic role of financial intermediaries is discussed in greater depth in *Two Faces of Debt* (Federal Reserve Bank of Chicago, 1978) and George H. Hempel and Jess B. Yawitz, *Financial Management of Financial Institutions* (Englewood Cliffs, N.J.: Prentice-Hall, 1977).

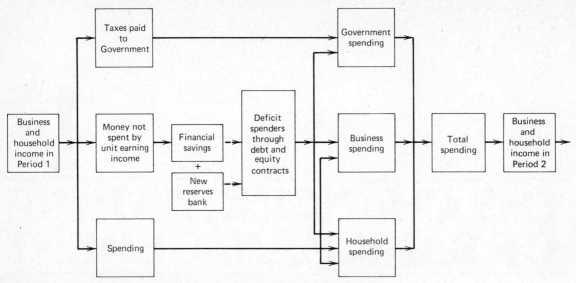

FIGURE 1-1   Simplified Graph of Financial Flows in the United States Economy

stitute a part of total spending and business and household income in the next period. Funds spent by the unit earning them find their way into the spending stream and provide household and business income for the following period. Money not spent by the unit earning the income, plus any new reserves provided from the Federal Reserve, are transferred for varying periods of time to units that want to spend more than they earned in that particular period. These "borrowed" funds are rapidly returned to the spending stream by deficit-spending governments, businesses, and households.

Although some of the transfers of funds from surplus units to deficit units are made directly through borrowing or equity contracts, the different desires of surplus and deficit units create the need for financial intermediaries. Such differences might include size, maturity, legal character, marketability, liquidity, divisibility, redeemability, and risk. For example, many surplus units have relatively small amounts and want to be able to convert to cash easily and to have relatively short maturities. On the other hand, deficit units often want large amounts, for long periods of time, and the assurance that they will not be forced to pay except when payments are scheduled. The intermediaries who try to meet the diverse desires of the surplus and deficit units are called financial intermediaries.[2] In facilitating the flow of funds between surplus and deficit units (see Figure 1-2), financial intermediaries create two separate markets. They purchase primary securities from deficit units and emit secondary, indirect liabilities to surplus units. In this way, a financial intermediary is able to tailor its assets and liability structure to satisfy the desires of both the ultimate borrowers and ultimate lenders in the economy. Financial intermediaries simply substitute their own more desirable (to

---

[2] Brokers or agents are also institutions that serve as go-betweens and receive commissions for their services. Typically, they do not hold financial assets for long periods themselves, and their services help match surplus and deficit units but do not overcome the differences that may exist between surplus and deficit units.

the surplus units) financial liabilities for the financial liabilities of the deficit unit. By holding a diversified portfolio of assets, many intermediaries can reduce risk beyond the reduction available to individual units. They also assist deficit units in finding funds in the desirable amount and form.

In the fully developed U.S. financial system, surplus units are able to choose from a wide variety of alternative financial assets—including primary securities of deficit units and the numerous secondary liabilities offered by financial intermediaries. Deficit units can usually acquire purchasing power in a desirable form, either directly from surplus units or, more commonly, from a financial intermediary. Liquidity and marketability of the securities created in the direct or indirect flows between surplus and deficit units are vastly improved by the existence of a secondary market (the New York Stock Exchange is an example) in which securities may be traded. Such a setting encourages economic efficiency since the allocation of financing is based on a unit's profitability and ability to pay rather than on the form of financing. This greater efficiency should stimulate both capital accumulation and growth in the economy.

Commercial banks are financial intermediaries that supply financial services to surplus and deficit units in the U.S. economy. Most bank assets are financial in nature, consisting primarily of money owed them by nonfinancial economic units such as households, businesses, and governments. Commercial banks issue contractual obligations, primarily in deposit or borrowing form, in order to obtain the funds to purchase these financial assets. A bank's capital results from the sale of stock or the accumulation of retained earnings and generally represents a relatively minor source of funds.

The role of commercial banking can, therefore, be stated very simply—to fill the diverse desires of both the ultimate borrowers and lenders in our economy. A commercial bank must obviously compete with other banks, with other financial intermediaries, with direct market transactions, and with any other organization that wishes to perform the task of filling the diverse desires of surplus and deficit units. A bank will be successful only if it performs its economic role as well as or better than its competition.

The difficulty of performing this role successfully can be understood by considering the problems banks have in balancing the diverse desires of the four groups affected

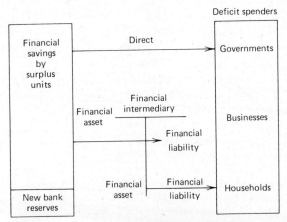

FIGURE 1-2 Financial Intermediaries in the Flow Between Surplus and Deficit Units

by their actions: surplus units, deficit units, bank owners, and bank regulators. Banks must not only issue liabilities in a form acceptable to surplus units, they must also pay a high enough return to outbid competitors. Virtually every surplus unit (be it a household, business, or government) will choose the highest return available in an acceptable form. A higher return to the surplus unit, of course, means a higher cost to the bank acquiring that unit's funds. Deficit units, on the other hand, want the bank to lend them money at the lowest cost available for the desirable form. What borrower would pay 15 percent for a loan when the same loan is available at 14 percent? Corporate and government treasurers tend to be even more sensitive to differences in interest costs. The problem is that the lower the cost to the borrower, the lower the return to the bank.

In addition to pleasing the surplus and deficit units, bank management must be concerned about a third group, the bank's owners. There must be an adequate difference between what the bank earns from the deficit units and what it pays surplus units for the funds (plus people and overhead costs) if it is to keep its owners satisfied. The owners would prefer to earn more for themselves by paying less to surplus units and charging more to deficit units, but competition limits both of these actions.

As if keeping surplus units, deficit units, and owners satisfied is not enough, bank management must also be concerned with a fourth group, bank regulators. In broad, general terms, these regulators are interested in limiting the risk a bank takes in obtaining and employing funds. Limiting risks, however, tends to limit the ability to pay a high return to surplus units, to lend to deficit units at low costs, and to earn an adequate difference between these costs (revenues for the bank) and the returns (expenses for the bank) for the shareholders. In a competitive environment, bank management that can keep these four economic groups satisfied has done a remarkable job.

CURRENT BANKING STRUCTURE AND REGULATION

The current banking structure and regulation of commercial banks in the United States defies logical explanation and is primarily the result of our historical development.[3] The purpose, here, is to briefly describe the current (as of early 1983) banking structure and bank regulation. Nearly all commercial banks in the United States are privately owned. Most banks can choose whether to be national or state banks and whether to be members of the Federal Reserve or not. Depending on the laws of the state in which they are located, banks can choose if they wish to be unit banks or part of a branch system, to be members of a holding company, and to seek correspondent relationships with other commercial banks. Available data on the banking structure as of mid-1982 are summarized in Table 1-1.

Since the passage of the National Banking Act in 1863, a bank has been able to choose between seeking a national charter from the Comptroller of the Currency or a

---

[3] The historical development of banks and bank regulation is covered in depth in D. R. Dewey, *Financial History of the United States* (New York: Longman Greens, 1934); Raymond W. Goldsmith, *Financial Intermediaries in the American Economy Since 1900* (Princeton, N.J.: Princeton University Press, 1958); Paul B. Trescott, *Financing American Enterprise* (New York: Harper & Row, 1963); and H. R. Kroos and M. R. Blyn, *A History of Financial Institutions* (New York: Random House, 1971).

TABLE 1-1
Data on Current Banking Structure, June 30, 1982[a]

Structure			Number of banks
National banks (examined by Comptroller of the Currency)			4,511
Federal member bank—national banks plan (examined by Federal Reserve)			1,032
Bank covered by FDIC—all federal members plan (examined by state and FDIC)			8,879
State non-FDIC banks (examined by state banking authority)			392
Total banks			14,814
Branch offices (of 6,418 banks)			41,450
Total banking offices			56,264

	Number	Banks controlled	Assets (billions of dollars)
One-bank holding companies	3,093	3,082[b]	$ 756
Multibank holding companies	407	2,607	$ 886
Total holding company banks	3,500	5,689	$1,642 (70.8%)

[a]Fifty states and District of Columbia
[b]A few banks are partially owned by two one-bank holding companies.
Source: Federal Reserve System

state charter under the supervision of its state's banking regulatory body. Since the formation of the Federal Reserve in 1913, national banks have had to become members of the Federal Reserve while state banks can choose whether to become members or not.

Unit Versus Branch Banking

Most banks in the United States have traditionally been unit banks—single-office institutions primarily serving their local communities. In mid-1982 there were 14,425 insured commercial banks in the United States. Of these, 8,399 were unit banks, down from 9,375 at the end of 1971. While still in the majority, especially in those few states that do not permit branch banking, the unit bank might well be placed on the "endangered species list." The tide toward multiple-office banking is running strong. The number of branch banking offices increased from 4,613 in 1948, to 10,605 in 1960, 23,362 at the end of 1971, and 41,450 in mid-1982.[4] This increase has resulted from both the establishment of new branches in growing communities and the absorption of previously independent banks through mergers. The pros and cons of multiple-office banking and bank mergers are still in the forefront of bank policy considerations today.

Branch banking has been a controversial subject since the earliest days of the

[4] *Annual Report of the Federal Deposit Insurance Corporation, 1981* (Washington, D.C.: Federal Deposit Insurance Corporation, 1982), pp. 176, 180.

United States. As early as 1790, Secretary of the Treasury Alexander Hamilton had grave doubts about it.[5] Nevertheless, both the First and Second Bank of the United States were branch-banking institutions.[6] In many instances, the early state banks also had branches. The 406 state banks existing in 1834 operated 100 branches. On the eve of the Civil War, there were 170 state bank branches in 11 states. However, the existence of over 1,500 banks by that time indicated a clear trend toward unit banking.

Opposition to branch banking arose from two directions. First, the remoteness of some branches (as well as of some unit banks) tended to facilitate some of the worst abuses of the note-issue privilege in the days of wildcat banking, so that banking reform and early attempts at bank supervision often led to the abolition of the branch-banking privilege.[7] Second, the Jacksonian campaign against the Second Bank of the United States and the subsequent Populist campaigns for cheap money were in a real sense directed against the concentration of monetary power in large Eastern banks, some of which were branch institutions. The resultant political furor helped to establish the emotional tone that is still evident in much of the popular and political opposition to branch banking.[8]

When the National Bank Act was passed in 1863, the question of branches was not even discussed. The Federal Reserve Act of 1913 extended the privilege of membership to state banks without prohibiting them from operating existing branches but did not accord the right to establish new branches to national banks, for whom membership was compulsory. Limited branch powers were gradually granted to national banks and subsequently extended until 1952, when all national banks were empowered to establish branches as freely as banks chartered by the respective states.

The history of banking in the United States, therefore, starts with branch banking, veers in the direction of unit banking, and is now quite rapidly swinging back again. Opposition to branch banking is still strong in some areas, however, and state laws concerning the establishment of branches vary from one part of the country to another. Statewide branching is permitted in 21 states (all of the Western states and a few Eastern states). Branching is prohibited or permitted in an extensively limited manner in 14 states (mainly the Middle states). The remaining 15 states allow limited branching.[9]

Against this background of diversity in law and tradition, those who are responsible for managing banks must attempt a logical assessment of the virtues and deficiencies of unit banking. The issues are obviously not clear-cut or they would have been resolved long ago. Nor is the available evidence entirely conclusive, even when weighed objectively. It is, nevertheless, incumbent on bank management and legislative bodies

---

[5] "Report on a National Bank" (December 13, 1790), in *Papers on Public Credit, Commerce and Finance*, ed. Samuel McKee, Jr. (New York: Columbia University Press, 1934).

[6] The Second Bank, organized in 1816, had established 19 offices in 14 states by October 1817.

[7] By the early 1840s, Massachusetts, New York, and Rhode Island had passed legislation providing that no one should conduct the business of banking except at his or her place of residence.

[8] In a court case, *Old Kent Bank and Trust Company* v. *William McC. Martin et al.*, Judge Washington, dissenting, said, "There has long been public hostility to the extension, by means of branches, of a bank's geographic area of operation. At one time branch banking was almost uniformly forbidden in the United States. Many persons feared, and still fear that, among other things, unrestrained bank operations would enable a few wealthy urban banks to extend their operations to a point where the independence and prosperity of the poorer banks . . . would be seriously jeopardized."

[9] *Annual Report of the Federal Deposit Insurance Corporation, 1981.*

regulating bankers to evaluate the banking structure, actual and prospective, in the light of economic reality and the expanding needs of a complex and dynamic economy.

The Bank Holding Company

Bank holding companies are also an integral part of our current banking structure. There are two general types of bank holding companies, the one-bank and the multibank. Prior to the 1970 amendments, one-bank holding companies did not fall within the definition of the Bank Holding Company Act of 1956 and were therefore not subject to the specific control of the Board of Governors of the Federal Reserve System. Under our current laws, a one-bank holding company is created when an existing bank organizes a holding company of which the bank became a subsidiary. Multibank holding companies own a controlling interest in the stock of two or more banks. Many smaller banks (with assets under $200 million) have formed one-bank holding companies to gain tax or capital-raising benefits, or both, from that form of organization. The holding company form of organization appeals to larger banks for two additional reasons. Multibank holding companies can be used to acquire additional banks (particularly important in states limiting branching), and either type can be used to form or acquire additional subsidiaries in financially related activities.

The Board of Governors, under the authority of the 1970 amendments, has established a "laundry list" of such permissible activities. According to this list:

> Bank holding companies could have mortgage, finance, credit card or factoring subsidiaries. They could have industrial bank or industrial loan company subsidiaries and subsidiaries that service loans, conduct fiduciary activities or lease personal and real property. They could have subsidiaries that make equity or debt investments in corporations designed to promote community welfare and subsidiaries that provide bookkeeping or data processing services or that furnish economic or financial information. Bank holding companies could also have insurance agency subsidiaries and subsidiaries that underwrite credit life and credit accident and health insurance and that act as investment or financial advisers to mutual funds and mortgage or real estate investment trusts, that provide portfolio investment advice to other persons or that offer financial advice to state and local governments on the issuing of securities. Finally, they could have subsidiaries that engage in the travelers check business, that trade and arbitrage gold and silver bullion, that operate courier services, and that provide management consulting services to nonaffiliated banks. All of these permissible activities were subject to certain conditions and limitations set forth in the Board's regulations and interpretations.

> By 1976, the Board's policy also prohibited bank holding companies from conducting a number of activities determined to be "not closely related to banking." Bank holding companies could not have subsidiaries engaged in insurance premium funding—that is, the combined sale of mutual funds and insurance. They could not have subsidiaries underwriting life insurance that is not sold in connection with one of its own credit transactions nor subsidiaries that engaged in real estate brokerage, land development, real estate syndication, general management consulting, property management services or mortgage guarantee insurance un-

derwriting. They could not have travel agency subsidiaries. And they could not have subsidiaries engaged exclusively in computer output microfilm services.

One of the most important results of the Bank Holding Company Act Amendments of 1970 and its implementation by the Board is that neither the law nor the Board's rules place any geographic limits on the activities of bank holding companies determined to be closely related to banking. Under the 1970 Act, a bank holding company still may acquire banks only in its home state unless another state, by an express authorization in its state law, allows bank acquisitions by an out-of-state holding company, but a bank holding company may carry on its closely related financial activities across state lines under the Bank Holding Company Act and the Federal Reserve Board's rules.[10]

As of June 30, 1982, bank holding companies controlled 5,689 subsidiaries engaged in, or authorized to engage in, these various activities. Not all of them are currently active. At that time, there were 3,500 holding company groups in the United States controlling 70.8 percent of the assets of all commercial banks. Of these, 3,093 were one-bank holding companies.[11]

Under the current legislative structure, the distinctive feature of any form of bank holding company lies in its ability to realize many of the benefits and render most of the services of widespread branch banking organizations while retaining the decentralization of management that can preserve the "local touch." Each banking unit of a holding company system typically is managed by a board of directors composed of local citizens who retain a substantial measure of autonomy in forming lending policies and dealing with local management problems. Without a substantial grant of local autonomy, the outstanding citizens and business leaders of the various communities could hardly be induced to serve as directors, because in most cases they hold only a nominal stock interest in the bank or the holding company. Given enough local authority, they will regard their directorships as a form of community service.

The relationship of the holding company to its subsidiary banks is largely that of an informed and helpful stockholder. This role combines many of the functions often rendered to country banks by their city correspondents with provision for effective group action in such fields as accounting, purchase of supplies, or investment analysis. The holding companies have, in short, developed as staff organizations for their constituent banks.

The holding company form of organization also tends to encourage a certain amount of healthy rivalry among its units. Such competition provides stimulus for experimentation and can lead to a diversity of approaches that is less likely to be found in a branch organization, where final management authority stems from one top-management team and a single board of directors.

Correspondent Banking in the United States

The correspondent banking system is an entirely informal arrangement whereby the smaller banks maintain deposit balances with larger banks in nearby cities and look to

---

[10] "Bank Holding Companies Today," (Washington, D.C.: Association of Registered Bank Holding Companies, November 1976).

[11] Board of Governors of the Federal Reserve System.

them for a wide variety of services and assistance. The city banks, in turn, keep correspondent balances with still larger banks in the principal money centers. Before the establishment of the Federal Reserve System, checks were collected entirely through this network of correspondent banks (often by roundabout routing), and, most important, the correspondent system served as a means of mobilizing the supply of credit and channeling it to areas where and when it was needed. Thus, correspondent banks provided liquidity and credit fluidity to a diverse economy. Country banks could deposit their idle funds with their correspondents, who invested them in money market loans (theoretically, at least); and then, at times of peak demand for seasonal agricultural credit, the country banks not only could draw down their balances but could borrow from their correspondents as well. The inadequacies of these arrangements, which did not include a central bank, were evident in recurring panics and finally led to the establishment of the Federal Reserve System. Nevertheless, without correspondent relationships, the early credit needs of the country could hardly have been met at all.

Correspondent banks are still active in the collection of checks and still supply credit to the smaller banks for the balances that the latter maintain. In addition, correspondent banks perform many services that would otherwise be unobtainable for smaller banks and their customers. They give investment advice, hold customers' securities in safekeeping, arrange for the purchase and sale of securities, arrange international financial transactions, trade in federal funds, participate in loans too large for the small banks, sell participation in large loans to small banks with surplus funds, and provide a wide range of other services.

The larger correspondent banks, nearly all of which are members of the Federal Reserve System, indirectly channel the benefits of that system to those banks that are not members and at the same time provide some services even to member banks (such as giving investment advice) that would be inappropriate for the central bank to perform.[12] The correspondent banking system tends to extend economies of scale to smaller banks. Smaller banks experience infrequent demands for some services, such as international financial transactions, but must generally be prepared to offer such services to customers. Returns would rarely compensate the initial investment required for small-scale production of these services. Larger banks, however, encounter sufficient demand from the public and from other commercial banks to provide these services profitably and at a lower unit cost to their customers. Aside from direct expenses incurred in providing these services or the fees required for data processing, correspondents rarely charge customer banks. The deposit balances a bank holds with its correspondent are expected to compensate for the services.[13]

The volume of interbank demand deposits provides some indication of the usage of correspondent services. In 1896, correspondent balances represented 10 percent of

[12] One of the primary advantages Federal Reserve membership gave larger banks was the ability to "pass on" many benefits of system membership to their smaller correspondents. The Depository Institution Regulation and Monetary Control Act of 1980, which requires the Federal Reserve to price its services to members, to allow nonmembers to receive some "Fed" services, and increasingly to encourage nonmember banks to hold reserves at the Fed, is changing this aspect of correspondent relationships.

[13] By far the largest share of these compensating correspondent balances is held as demand deposits. A recent survey found that fewer than 6 percent of the banks favored a fee arrangement. This general preference for demand deposits as compensation for correspondent services may be partly because nonmember banks can normally count correspondent balances toward reserve requirements. Many banks, however, charge fees for computer services.

total demand deposits in commercial banks. These balances climbed to 13 percent in 1913, just before the organization of the Federal Reserve System, and then fell gradually to 7 percent in 1928. They reached roughly 12 percent of total demand deposits in the late 1940s, declined to 9 percent by the early 1960s, and then rose back to approximately 11 percent by early 1976. The rather sharp increase in the late 1960s and 1970s appears to have been caused by the increasing need for correspondent services and the substantial increase in loan participation among correspondent banks. In 1981, this percentage dropped back to 9 percent. This drop-off probably results from the high levels of interest rates in 1980 and 1981, which have encouraged banks to economize on idle balances, and from the Depository Institution Regulation and Monetary Control Act of 1980, which will increasingly encourage nonmember banks to hold reserves at the Federal Reserve.[14]

The Regulatory Structure

Regulation of banking is currently divided among three federal agencies and 50 state agencies. Areas of responsibility overlap, yet the duties of the diverse regulatory agencies are generally carried out smoothly and efficiently. Indeed, the pluralism of bank regulatory authority in the United States may have led to a regulatory environment superior to one charted by a single authority.

Bank regulation encompasses a wide variety of technical functions relating to the operation of banks. These concern (1) the issuance and enforcement of regulations; (2) the chartering of banks; (3) the periodic examination of banks and the requirement that bank management take steps to correct unsatisfactory or unsound conditions found through such examinations; (4) the review and analysis of periodic reports of conditions, earnings, and expenses; (5) the rendering of counsel and advice, when requested, on bank operating problems, particularly in the case of smaller banks; (6) the approval of proposed changes in the scope of corporate functions exercised by individual banks and of proposed changes in their capital structures; (7) authorization for the establishment of branches and for the exercise of trust powers; (8) the approval of bank mergers and consolidations; (9) the organization and regulation of bank holding companies; (10) the regulation of bank service corporations; and (11) the liquidation of banks. All of these functions are not performed by each of the four types of supervisory agencies, but they are all the responsibility of at least one of the agencies. The purpose of this section is to summarize the broad aspects of the regulatory environment in which commercial banks must operate.[15]

The diffusion of bank regulatory authority does not mean that banks are not closely regulated. Banking is more closely regulated in the United States than in any other developed country in the world. At the same time, no other country has as many banks in relation to its population. These facts are not unrelated. On the contrary, the degree and character of bank regulation in the United States springs directly from the nature of our banking structure.

---

[14] *All Bank Statistics,* 1896–1955 (Washington, D.C.: U.S. Board of Governors of the Federal Reserve System, 1959); *Federal Reserve Bulletins,* 1956–1982.

[15] More complete descriptions of the regulatory structure for banks are contained in Part 10 of *The Bankers' Handbook,* ed. William H. Baughn and Charles E. Walker (Homewood, Ill.: Dow-Jones-Irwin, 1978), and in *Bank Supervision* (St. Louis: Federal Reserve Bank).

As noted in the preceding paragraphs, the diversity of U.S. banking structures developed in response to the often conflicting desires of different segments of the public. In spite of recent trends toward consolidation, there are still thousands of banks chartered by both state and federal governments and, for the most part, locally owned and operated. Left to their own and often inadequate devices in the past, hundreds of banks failed. Americans apparently wanted to preserve this diverse structure without sacrificing banking safety. The American system of bank regulation, therefore, has developed over the years in response to the desires for a sound banking system that is, at the same time, responsive to the credit needs of a dynamic economy. To ensure the continuance of such a system should be one of the basic responsibilities of bank regulatory authorities.

The limitation of banking activities through detailed provisions of regulation and law is a distinctive feature of banking in the United States. All banks derive their powers from the banking laws which are, in this sense, permissive. On the other hand, banking laws specifically limit the powers granted and are thus essentially restrictive. The restrictions are designed to prevent, if possible, U.S. banks from making the mistakes that led to widespread bank failures in the past.

The regulatory authorities, both state and federal, are concerned with regulation and supervision. They administer the banking laws, promulgate and interpret regulations issued thereunder, and exercise impersonal and objective judgments with respect to bank policies in order to further the public interest. They use the examination process to keep informed of both the legality and the soundness of an individual bank's operations.

As noted earlier, the historical development of the American banking structure has given rise to a multiplicity of regulatory agencies at both the state and federal levels. Under our concept of dual banking, national banks are chartered and supervised by the Office of the Comptroller of the Currency, while state banks are chartered and supervised primarily by the banking authorities of the respective states. Most state-chartered banks, however, have come under federal supervision and regulation of one kind or another. With the establishment of the Federal Reserve System, those state-chartered banks that became members submitted voluntarily to many of the restrictions imposed by law on national banks and to examination and supervision by the Board of Governors of the Federal Reserve System.

With the advent of federal deposit insurance, nearly all of the remaining state banks accepted supervision by the Federal Deposit Insurance Corporation (FDIC) as a condition of insurance. Fewer than 400 nonmember, noninsured commercial banks subject to no direct federal supervision remain.

Moreover, the jurisdictions of three federal regulatory agencies overlap, and individual banks are subject to the rules of more than one agency. National banks, for example, while chartered and supervised solely by the Comptroller of the Currency, are required to be members of the Federal Reserve System, and their deposits are insured by the Federal Deposit Insurance Corporation. Both of these latter agencies have the power to examine national banks—a power seldom exercised—but both review reports of examinations made by national bank examiners. National banks are also subject to some state laws such as those governing branching authority, legal holidays, and so on.

The crisscrossing of regulatory responsibility is further illustrated by the rules regarding changes in banking structure. All holding company transactions, including those involving nonmember banks, are subject to the jurisdiction of the Board of Governors of the Federal Reserve System. The establishment of *de novo* branches requires the approval of the chartering authority, state or national, and, for state banks, the additional approval of either the Board of Governors or the FDIC, depending on member- or nonmember-insured status. Merger applications follow the same course, except that each of the three federal agencies must seek the advice of the other two and the Department of Justice with respect to the competitive factors involved.

The three federal regulatory agencies and the state agencies are responsible for bank examination, the foundation of bank regulation. American banking is highly competitive because of the large number of banks in the country. In most communities there are two or more sources of banking services. Bank examinations in the United States are primarily designed to protect depositors from unsound banking practices rather than provide a substitute for competition. Bank examinations, by any of the four major types of regulatory agencies, emphasize review and appraisal of asset quality, capital adequacy, and the ability of management.

Two factors which give rise to the need for examination are inherent in banking. The first involves the bank's loans and investments, which lead to the creation of demand deposits. Since these demand deposits make up the major portion of the nation's money supply, the quality of bank credit underlies the value of money. The second factor is the nature of the financial intermediary role that banks fulfill in the economy. Banks receive savings and demand deposits that are highly liquid. The banks invest these deposits in other less-liquid assets. To prevent a liquidity crisis, banks must hold some liquid assets, have adequate capital, and maintain professional management.

The risks in banking have been particularly visible in the early 1980s. Large companies, such as Braniff and International Harvester, have failed or been unable to pay their debts. Foreign countries, such as Poland and Mexico, have delayed payments on their obligations to banks. The banking community was shocked in May, 1982 when Drysdale Government Securities, Inc., a small and aggressive New York securities dealer, defaulted on $160 million owed to other government securities' dealers. Chase Manhattan Bank and Manufacturers Hanover Trust, which acted as Drysdale's agent in the securities market, covered Drysdale's debts at an aftertax cost of $117 and $9 million, respectively. In July, federal regulators closed Penn Square Bank in Oklahoma. Much of that bank's $250 million in uninsured deposits are not likely to be recovered. In addition, Penn Square had packaged about $2 billion worth of poor-quality loans for other banks—including Continental Illinois Bank, Seattle First National Bank, and Chase Manhattan Bank. In August another small securities market fund, Lombard-Wall, was forced into bankruptcy. Several banks were its primary creditors. Forced acquisitions of problem banks and nonbank depository institutions continued during much of 1982 and early 1983.

Joint consideration of some problems by the various regulatory bodies has been a positive trend. For example, representatives from each of the major bank regulatory groups have met to consider bank capital requirements. And the Depository Institution Deregulation Committee (formed in 1980) has representatives from both the primary bank regulatory groups and the thrift regulatory bodies.

A CHALLENGING AND CHANGING ENVIRONMENT IN THE 1980s

Anticipating the environment in which commercial banks will make their management decisions during the next several years is clearly important. It is, of course, impossible to predict accurately all aspects of the future environment for bank management decisions. Some reasonable inferences, however, can be made about the future environment by studying economic trends, recent legislation, and developments in the banking industry. The following discussion of the future environment is divided into three parts: the economic environment, the regulatory environment, and trends in the banking industry.

The Economic Environment

The economic environment of the 1980s promises to be challenging for bank management. It appears likely that management decisions for the next few years may be made in an environment of relatively slow real economic growth. The primary causes of slow

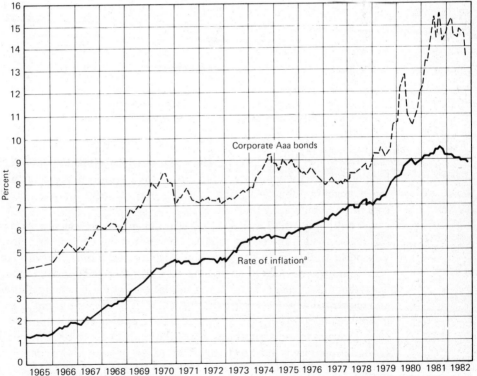

^a Rate of change for Consumer Price Index over five year periods. CPI for 1974 was adjusted for estimated effect of the oil price increase.

FIGURE 1-3 Inflation and Interest Rates

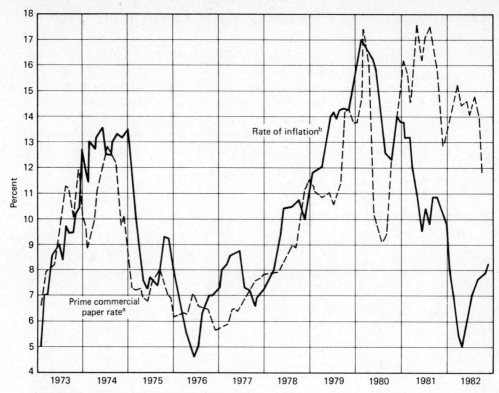

^a Yields on four to six month prime commercial paper
^b Rates of change in consumer prices over the previous six months

FIGURE 1-4   Inflation and Short-term Interest Rates

real growth include the low (in relation to other developed Western economics) capital base of our economy and the limited probability of productivity gains. Although positive changes in public and private policies may improve the rate of real growth, significant improvement may take a long time.

Continuing inflation may be cause for even greater concern for bank management. Figure 1-3, which traces the rates of change for the Consumer Price Index over five-year periods, clearly illustrates the increasing rates of inflation through early 1981. Figure 1-4 shows the rates of change in the Consumer Price Index for six-month periods. This figure illustrates that the rate of inflation has varied cyclically, with higher peaks and higher troughs occurring in each ensuing cycle. The six-month rates of change were in double digits throughout 1979 and 1980. Inflation rates fell in 1981 and 1982; however, progress in reducing the rate of inflation is likely to be slow because much of our economic activity is indexed to price increases. In spite of President Reagan's attempts, a balanced federal budget appears to be an illusory target. The cost of reducing inflation appears to be recession and high unemployment. Renewed price pressures in key areas, such as food and housing, appear likely in the next few years. Finally, it seems that the primary hope for reduced inflation—national monetary policy—may take several years to achieve significant results. Predicted continued inflation, but at below the double-digit level, should affect bank management decisions appreciably in the coming years.

Two other elements of the future American economic environment, high and fluctuating interest rates, are also likely to challenge bank managers in the next several years. Figures 1-3 and 1-4 illustrate the high correlation between interest rates and the rate of inflation. Numerous studies have concluded that longer term interest rates tend to exceed the expected rate of inflation by roughly 3 percent. Brief periods, such as mid-1981 through mid-1982, when long-term rates exceeded actual inflation by 6 or 7 percent, occur because people's expectation for inflation probably affects interest rates more than the reported level of inflation. Thus, a prediction of continued high levels of interest rates—although moderated by some improvement in the inflation rate—is consistent with a prediction of continued high levels of price inflation.

Wide and rapid fluctuation in interest rates also seems very likely in the 1980s. The increasing amplitude of interest rate fluctuations can be seen by observing the increasingly wide fluctuations in the rate on four- to six-month price commercial paper in Figure 1-4 and by the following data on changes in the prime lending rate charged by commercial banks:

Years	Number of changes
1950–54	6
1955–59	10
1960–64	1
1965–69	15
1970–74	65
1975–79	74
1980–82	98

Source: Federal Reserve Bulletins, various years.

The preceding data understate the magnitude of changes in the prime rate because changes were usually one-quarter of a percentage point prior to the late 1970s, whereas many prime rate changes in 1980 through 1982 were one-half or a full percentage point.

Continuation of these rapid and wide fluctuations in interest rates seems likely if the Federal Reserve sticks to its October 6, 1979, declaration. In essence, the Fed said it will place more emphasis on controlling reserves and monetary aggregates and will let interest rates seek their market levels consistent with reserve and monetary goals. The prime rate was 12 percent on October 6, 1979, and 20 percent two years later. During these two years, the prime rate had risen to 20 percent, fallen to 11 percent, and risen back to over 21 percent before falling to 17 percent and then rising to 20 percent. Since the rates discussed are fairly representative of the borrowing and lending rates on many other bank liabilities and assets, balance sheet management at a bank is likely to become more and more challenging.

One paradoxical result of the changing economic environment is that interest rate forecasting has become both more important and more challenging. It is more important because the stakes are higher for banks exposed to interest rate risks resulting from wider swings in interest rates. It is more challenging because these interest rate swings seem to defy some of the more familiar rules of thumb forecasters have traditionally used to predict interest rates.

The Regulatory Environment

Passage of HR 4986, the Depository Institutions Deregulation and Monetary Control Act of 1980 and HR 6267, the Garn-St. Germain Depository Institution Act of 1982, will probably lead to greater changes in bank management than any legislation since the 1930s. HR 4986 includes nine titles on far-reaching and diverse subjects including monetary control and reserve requirements, a phaseout of deposit interest rate ceilings, nationwide authorization of Negotiable Order of Withdrawal (NOW) accounts, expanded asset and liability powers for thrift institutions, fees for services provided by the Federal Reserve, preemption of state usury laws, and simplification of truth-in-lending regulations.

Table 1-2 summarizes the primary immediate and longer run impact on bank management of HR 4986. The primary objective of standardization and broader applicability of reserve requirements is better control of the money supply. The lower percentage requirements applied to more banks and the greater limitation in the types of deposits covered mean that most banks will have increased earning assets. The potential for increased earnings, *ceteris paribus*, as a result of these stair-step reductions, will be completed for banks and thrift institutions by 1988. A small number of banks, and most thrift institutions, will have higher reserves, which will reduce earning assets and hurt earnings. Longer run effects will probably include a more equitable competitive environment and decreased variation of relative growth rates among various types of deposits. The Federal Reserve still will not pay interest on reserves left with it; however, the door for that was partially opened. The Federal Reserve can pay a return up to what its securities portfolio earned during the previous calendar quarter on accounts above required reserves and on supplemental required reserves (up to 4 percent of transaction accounts) that the Federal Reserve is permitted to impose under certain situations.

HR 4986 required the Federal Reserve to price its services, such as check-clearing and collection, settlement, wire transfer, and float, at their estimated full cost plus a mark-up so that the resulting prices would be similar to those charged by private businesses. It is too early to know the results of this pricing—services are being initially priced over several years—but it appears certain that banks will have to pay increased explicit cost to the Fed for services. There is some chance that the demand for Federal Reserve services will rise because more bank and thrift institutions may use them, but most banks are investigating other sources that may provide the needed services more efficiently (i.e., will cost less). The longer run effects of Federal Reserve pricing will probably include changes in banks' "cash management" practices, further reduction in bank and Federal Reserve float, greater reliance by correspondent banks on explicit pricing than on balances, and realistic bank pricing of retail transaction deposit services. It is also believed that Federal Reserve pricing will provide additional stimuli to electronic banking, such as debit cards, direct deposits, automated teller machines (ATMs), and points of sales (POSs).

Nationwide approval of NOW accounts, which became effective at the beginning of 1981, has led to higher interest expense for transaction-type deposits. These higher interest expenses seem most likely to hurt smaller, retail-oriented banks whose profitability has been more dependent on having substantial amounts in low-cost demand deposits. In addition, the reserves on savings accounts that are switched to NOW ac-

TABLE 1-2
Immediate and Longer Run Effects of HR 4986 on Bank Management Decisions

Actions	Impact effects	Subsequent effects
Lower (higher) reserve requirements	Increased (decreased) earning assets and earnings	After transition period, more equitable competitive environment (less of a differential license fee based on size) Decreased variation of relative growth rates among various types of deposits Reduction in correspondent balances
Federal Reserve pricing	Increased explicit costs paid to Federal Reserve	Changes in retail checking services (truncation, pricing) Changes in "cash management" practices and float Reduction in correspondent balances Greater reliance on explicit pricing (fees, service charges) Stimulus to debit cards, EFTS, direct deposits, POS, ATMs
Nationwide NOW accounts	Higher interest expense of "core deposits"	Higher average "personal checking" balances Reduced NSF, overdrafts Higher reserve requirements on ATS balances that are switched to NOW accounts
Phaseout Regulation Q ceilings	Gradual increase in interest costs and pressures on margins	Greater discretion in product design of savings instruments Decreased variation in relative size and growth rates of various types of deposits Reliance on explicit interest instead of premiums; enhanced value of "one-stop banking"
Higher FDIC insurance level	Higher insurance fees	Potential for marketing distinction vis-à-vis money market funds, Sears, American Express, and Merrill Lynch
Expanded powers for thrifts	Costly entry of thrifts into several new markets	Greater competition for obtaining and profitably using bank funds Narrowing of spread between attracting and employing funds
Relaxation of many state usury laws	Loan rates more consistent with market	Enhancement of ability to hold interest margin stable over credit cycles Reduction of artificial barrier on fund allocation

counts will rise from 3 to 12 percent. Nevertheless, in the longer run, NOW accounts also offer positive opportunities to bank management. They should bring higher and more stable personal transaction balances and fewer unwanted returned checks and overdrafts. NOW accounts may be the forerunner of one-account banking. Setting the appropriate levels for NOW pricing factors, such as minimum balances and any fee and service charges, will be an important bank management decision in the 1980s.

The gradual phaseout of Regulation Q ceilings, if completed according to schedule, will probably have the most far-reaching effect on commercial banking. A gradual increase in the interest cost of many types of bank funds and an increase in pressures on bank margins will probably occur. The impact will be greatest on many retail banks, which will find the maximum interest they can pay on nearly all of their bank deposits, including NOW accounts, rising regularly. Intense competition from other banks and thrifts and predicted high interest rates in the economy are likely to keep most banks at these maximums. Furthermore, competition on the lending side is likely to prevent most banks from maintaining their interest margins. As time passes, the emphasis in funds acquisition is likely to shift from quantity to product design and pricing. Variation in the relative size and growth of various types of deposits will probably decline and more emphasis will be placed on explicit interest rather than on premiums.

Several other parts of HR 4986 will also affect bank management in the coming years. The increase in insurance coverage on private deposits from $40,000 to $100,000 will mean higher insurance fees but should improve the ability of banks to distinguish their deposit product from competitive nonbank products. Expanded deposit and lending powers for thrifts should increase competition for obtaining and profitably using bank funds. The interest spread between attracting and employing funds may narrow; banks, however, have several key advantages, such as greater experience and expertise and a more flexible asset structure. Finally, the section providing for relaxation of existing usury laws in many states means that lending rates can be more consistent with existing market rates. This relaxation should reduce artificial barriers to funds allocation and should enhance the ability of banks to hold interest margins stable over the business cycle.

Several regulatory and legislative changes that occurred between the passage of HR 4986 and of HR 6267 also deserve mention. The Depository Institutions Deregulation Committee exempted additional longer maturity CDs from Regulation Q interest ceilings. In addition, this committee established a new category of time deposits called all savers certificates. Permission for these certificates was included in the income tax reduction legislation passed by Congress in 1981. The certificates have one-year maturity, yield 70 percent of the one-year bill rate, and have tax-free interest up to $1,000 per individual. Another part of the 1981 income tax reduction legislation—permission to establish tax-free individual retirement accounts (IRAs) of up to $2,000 a year regardless of other pension coverage and not subject to Regulation Q—would appear to offer banks significant new product opportunities.

HR6267, The Garn-St. Germain Depository Institutions Act of 1982, was signed by President Reagan on October 15, 1982. HR6267 has eight titles or sections. Title 1 enhances the ability of the Federal Savings and Loan Insurance Corporation (FSLIC) and FDIC to merge failing thrift institutions of any size and failing commercial banks with assets of $500 million or higher. Title 2 permits capital infusion through the issuance of capital notes drawn from the assets of the FSLIC or FDIC for qualifying depository institutions. Qualifying rules include: capital of less than 3 percent of assets, above 20 percent of the loan portfolio in mortgages or mortgage-backed securities, and losses in the two previous quarters.

Title 3 mandates the phase-out by January 1, 1984, of all interest differentials on maximum rates among depository institutions. Title 3 also mandates the depository institutions deregulation committee (DIDC) to create a new depository instrument "equivalent to and competitive with" money market funds. The instrument will have the following characteristics: (1) no minimum maturity, (2) no interest rate ceiling, (3) a minimum denomination of $2,500, (4) only three preauthorized or automatic withdrawals and three drafts permitted in any month and reserve requirements of 0 percent for individual accounts and 3 percent for corporate accounts, (5) all types of depositors eligible, and (6) insurance up to $100,000 by the FSLIC or FDIC. These depository instruments were issued starting December 14, 1982. Title 3 of HR6267 also permits mutual savings banks and savings and loan associations to have more commercial and consumer loans (up to 10 and 30 percent, respectively, of assets by 1984) and to offer with restrictions demand deposits to commercial and agricultural customers.

Title 4 provides relief to national and member banks on provisions of banking laws that are obsolete or restrictive. For example, the legal lending limit was raised to 15 and 25 percent of capital for unsecured or secured borrowers, respectively. Title 5 provides greater operating flexibility to credit unions. Title 6 states that the sale of property, casualty, and life insurance (other than credit life, health, and accident) was not an activity closely related to banking. This wording will discourage bank holding companies from acquiring insurance agencies; however, acquisitions by small banks are permitted, acquisition are permitted in sparsely populated areas, and acquisitions prior to May 1, 1982, are grandfathered. Title 7 requires a study of the insurance system for deposits and contains miscellaneous amendments, such as clarification of Truth in Lending, permitting establishment of bank service corporations by one or more banks, and permitting NOWs to be issued to state and local governments. Title 8 requires that all nonfederally-chartered housing creditors be permitted to offer alternative mortgage transactions in accordance with federal regulations.

The new depository instruments permitted in HR6267, and by the DIDC, money market accounts and super NOW accounts, will probably have the most far reaching effects on bank management in the coming years. Banks will be able to compete freely with money market funds for the first time. However, at the same time, the pricing protection of Regulation Q will disappear. Banks will have to price (some for the first time) such accounts in a very competitive market. It is too early to tell the impact of these accounts at this time (1983); however, it seems likely that interest margins will come under increasing pressures.

Changes in banking as more of HR 4986 and HR 6267 becomes effective should be significant; but the laws have several important deficiencies that may or may not be resolved by future legislation or regulation. For example, there is no provision for removing the remaining constraints on interstate expansion by banks or bank holding companies. Restrictions now imposed under Glass-Steagall, such as those aimed at commingled investment accounts, were not addressed. The longer run implications of the fact that low-yielding, fixed-rate mortgages will remain a significant part of the portfolios of most thrift institutions and many banks for some years to come were not explicitly considered. These and similar issues cannot be ignored. The problem is that banking legislation and regulation tend to be following, not leading, influences on bank management. Legislation and regulation tend to validate or legitimize successful innovations in the banking industry.

Current trends indicate that some additional legislative or regulatory developments are likely in the near future. One possibility is some form of relaxation of state boundary constraints in providing financial services. These constraints are already partly overcome by Edge Act offices, loan production offices, and bank holding company subsidiaries, but using such loophole opportunities is not particularly efficient. Improved electronic technology and the need for domestic rather than international takeovers of "weakened" depository institutions should provide added incentives for some kind of legislative or regulatory action. Our prediction is that by the mid-1980s at least regional, and probably nationwide, banking will be permitted.

Legislative action in other areas in the near future is difficult to predict (in early

1983 as this book goes to press). Key areas in which some type of action may be forced on legislative or regulatory bodies include further definitions of the nontraditional financial services that banks will be allowed to provide; ground rules for how far money market funds, brokerage firms, and other nondepository firms can go in competing with depository institutions without constraint; payment of interest on reserves and some form of relief for institutions holding significant amounts of previously acquired, low-fixed-return mortgages.

Trends in the Banking Industry

Finally, in examining the environment for bank management decisions in the coming years, one needs to review the current status of the banking industry itself. How much flexibility will the industry have to face the challenging external and regulatory environment? Will future technology help or hurt the industry? Will competitive pressure be intra- or interindustry?

Table 1-3 shows that in 1950, as a result of the Depression and World War II, commercial banks held over 60 percent of their total assets in cash and due from bank accounts or in Treasury securities. At the same time, funds were acquired primarily through checking accounts. Demand deposits made up over 70 percent of the total liabilities and capital in 1950. The low average return of banking assets, caused by the bank asset mix and low interest rates, meant that banks paid relatively low returns on time and savings deposits and were often not aggressive in trying to obtain funds from such accounts.

The primary emphasis in bank management during the 1950s and early 1960s was

TABLE 1-3
Percentage Distribution of Assets and Liabilities of Commercial Banks

	1950	1964	1981
Assets			
Cash and due from banks	24	18	14
Treasury and agency securities	37	21	6
Other securities	7	10	11
Loans	31	49	64
Other assets	1	2	5
Total assets	100	100	100
Liabilities and Capital			
Transaction deposits	70	55	24
Time and savings	22	34	52
Borrowings	0	1	14
Other liabilities	1	2	4
Capital accounts	7	8	6
Total Liabilities and capital	100	100	100

Source: Selected *Federal Reserve Bulletins* and FDIC *Annual Reports*.

a shift from Treasury securities and cash and due from bank accounts to riskier assets with higher returns. Emphasis on time and savings deposits as sources of funds increased somewhat, but demand deposits still contributed well over half the total sources of funds for most banks. Furthermore, the total deposits and assets of all commercial banks grew at an annual rate of less than 5 percent from 1950 through 1964. During this period, the combined assets of nonbank financial intermediaries grew at an annual rate of roughly 12 percent. The causes of this low growth in banks vis-à-vis other financial institutions included (1) slow demand deposit growth as corporate treasurers began to utilize efficient cash management techniques, (2) significantly lower average rates paid on time and savings deposits than those paid by many other intermediaries, and (3) generally conservative attitudes toward attracting funds by bank managers.

The prevailing philosophy of bank managers and directors appeared to emphasize the profitable lending of attracted funds, at the cost of additional risk. The excess liquidity and low portfolio credit risk of banks during the immediate postwar period was substantially reduced. Table 1-3 illustrates that from 1950 to 1964 cash and due from bank accounts and Treasury securities fell from 61 to 39 percent of bank assets, while loans rose from 31 to 49 percent.

In the early and mid-1960s, banks responded to their relatively slow growth during the preceding decade by (1) requiring loan customers to keep larger demand deposit balances; (2) paying competitive rates on time and savings accounts within the confines of Regulation Q; and (3) aggressively offering certificates of deposit, savings certificates, and other old and new liability sources. The emphasis in management shifted from asset selection to the acquisition of funds—liability management. This more aggressive acquisition of funds was part of a shift in bank strategy away from the high margins and slow growth of the 1950s toward the lower margins with more rapid growth by the mid-1960s. This shift was encouraged by the gradual relaxation of Regulation Q, which set the minimum rates banks could pay on time and savings deposits, and by allowing banks to use certificates of deposit and other liability forms to compete more effectively for funds. The strong demand for credit from the mid-1960s through the 1970s allowed banks to employ the substantially larger amounts of funds they were able to attract.

The surge in asset and loan growth was pronounced—the rate of asset growth doubled to rates averaging nearly 11 percent annually from 1964 through 1981. By comparison, in this same period, the assets of nonbank financial intermediaries grew at an average annual rate of slightly less than 7 percent. It is noteworthy that this rapid growth may be slowing somewhat because of intensified competition with money market funds, brokerage houses, and other institutions offering banklike financial instruments or services. New liability innovations to compete with these institutions, such as money market certificates, longer term savings certificates not subject to Regulation Q, and the super NOW accounts, are proving costly and may lead to difficult liability management problems.

The change in the composition and financing of the rapid growth from 1964 through 1981 has many implications for the future. Transaction deposits declined from 55 percent of total liabilities and capital in the mid-1960s to 24 percent of total liabilities and capital in 1981. Time and savings deposits increased from 33 percent of total liabilities and capital in the early 1960s to 52 percent by 1981. Borrowing and other liabilities increased from a relatively small source of funds to roughly 18 percent of the total liabilities and capital in this same period. On the asset side, cash and due from bank accounts and Treasury securities declined absolutely as well as relatively, while loans continued their rapid growth (increasing from 49 to 64 percent of the total assets from 1964 through 1981), and other securities (nearly all of which are state and local issues) increased slightly from 10 to 11 percent of the total assets.

These broad trends indicate that banks will probably be exposed to greater risk in the early 1980s than they have been at any time since the early Depression years. Options, such as conversion from low-cost, core demand and savings deposits to interest-sensitive deposits and shifts from securities to higher earning, higher risk loans, have already been partially utilized. Flexibility of bank management is very limited in the challenging economic and regulatory environment predicted (in the preceding section) for the 1980s.

Technological changes in the 1980s complicate efforts to predict how many banks will fare in coming years. The pace of technological change for banks has been slower than many predicted in the last few years. On average, the industry is still dominated by a paper-based brick-and-mortar, customer-bank-employee-interaction delivery system. Recent developments, however, indicate that substantive movement away from this system is taking place. The technology exists to alter banks' delivery systems rapidly. This technology consists of advances in computer capabilities, which permit easy and inexpensive gathering, storing, analyzing, and retrieving of customer data and of advances in communication hardware and software which permit convenient access to customer records at great distances. There is a veritable revolution in the delivery system which has significant implications for bank management decisions.

By 1982, ATMs had become widely accepted in most areas of the country. By the mid-1980s, the vast majority of bank transactions probably will be by electronic impulse made away from the bank's physical location. With existing technology, automated clearinghouses, direct payroll crediting, direct bill paying, widespread use of debit cards and POS terminals, and disappearance of float appear very likely. The technology exists and is being implemented by larger firms and their banks. Furthermore, on a trial basis, some individuals already can sit at home and pay bills, make deposits, shift among types of deposits, shift from deposits to other financial assets, and so forth, all by electronic impulse. By the late 1980s, such home banking may be commonplace. To compete effectively on a cost basis, commercial banks must find this and other methods to significantly reduce the cost of most common transactions with all but their very large customers. The task may be literally to keep most customers away from the bank except for unusual transactions.

In the long run such technology will increase productivity and reduce costs in banking, however, the transition period will be difficult. This difficulty is compounded by the trying economic and regulatory environment predicted. Some banks will be willing and able to take the high costs and risks involved whereas others may still try to drag their feet. The feet-draggers may find themselves rapidly becoming noncompetitive.

The preceding statement leads to the final area of discussion concerning the status of banking—the competitive environment. There is disagreement over the major source of competition for a bank in the 1980s. Will it be other banks, other depository institutions, nondepository institutions (such as money market funds, brokerage firms, or insurance companies), or nonfinancial companies? Each of these possibilities is discussed in the following paragraphs. The answer to the question, however, is probably that all will provide significant competition in an increasingly competitive environment.

Competition with other banks will probably intensify for several reasons. One is the lack of product differentiation for some banking services. A second reason is the disappearance of Regulation Q, which prohibited rate competition for some categories of deposits. Another reason is the continuing decline in geographic constraints restricting banking competition. Finally, greater use of advanced technology may increase the ability of banks to compete with each other.

Competition with other depository institutions is also likely to increase. The prediction that other depository institutions will be unable to compete because of their inferior asset positions and lack of experience in many banking areas seem overoptimistic. The opposite will probably occur. Some large thrifts will be very competitive in both attracting and employing funds. By the end of 1982, thrifts had acquired permission to do most of the things a bank can do with the attraction and employment of funds. After some failures, consolidations, and restructuring, the surviving, aggressive thrifts may reappear as even more formidable competition than in the past.

Nondepository financial organizations appear likely to use their substantial competitive edge—fewer restrictions, no reserves, no capital requirements, less regulation—to offer more and more banklike financial services. Some of the nondepository organizations providing banklike services are known. For example, much has been written about money market funds and brokerage firms, like Merrill Lynch, which offer cash management accounts. The combination of financial giants, such as Bache with Prudential and American Express with Shearson in 1981, may be indicative of very competitive financial supermarkets in the near future. In addition, other nondepository financial organizations, such as life insurance companies and private pension funds, are looking carefully at segments of banking services they believe would be profitable for themselves.

Finally, more and more companies whose primary business activities are nonfinancial appear to be interested in starting to offer financial assets, liabilities, and services that will compete with many banking products and services. For example, Sears has opened 10 financial centers on a trial basis and has announced it will offer consumer savings certificates and a money market mutual fund in the near future. Penneys is reportedly considering offering "market" rates of interest to savers prepaying their charge accounts. National Steel Company already owns the seventh largest publicly held savings and loan holding company in the United States and has stated in its annual report that it is "looking for further possible ventures into related [financial] fields."[16] Nonfinancial companies are likely to prove formidable competition for banks in the coming years.

[16] This and numerous other examples of competition to banks from nonfinancial corporations are cited in *Financial Competition and the Public Interest* (New York: Citicorp).

AN APPROACH TO BANK MANAGEMENT IN THIS CHALLENGING ENVIRONMENT

Where does the combination of a difficult economic environment, a changing regulatory environment, a virtual technological revolution, increasingly sharp competition, and some worrisome trends in the banking industry leave the banking industry? The environment for bank management decisions is clearly going to be a challenging one in the coming years. Some banks, and probably a larger number of other depository institutions, will fail. There will be numerous acquisitions and mergers in the banking and depository industry. The number of banks will probably decline by 30 to 40 percent over the next decade, and the decline in other depository institutions may be even greater. Well-managed banks can and will be very successful during such times. The purpose of this book is to present the concepts and techniques that will help current and potential bank managers to be successful in this challenging period. Twenty-six case situations in which bankers can test their applications of these concepts and techniques are included.

This book is divided into five sections. In the first section (this chapter and Chapter 2) we deal with the changing nature of banking, the banking structure and return-risk tradeoffs in banking. In the second section (Chapters 3 and 4) we examine how and at what costs a bank obtains funds and manages its capital position. Subsequent sections cover many of the primary areas in which bank management decisions must be made in future years. The 26 selected cases that appear in the book illustrate most of the key ideas and techniques. In the authors' opinion, just reading the concepts and techniques espoused in this book is not enough. Bank managers and students of banking should reinforce their learning by applying the concepts and techniques to the case situations covered in this book. This will not only reinforce the learning process, it should indicate the applicability of the concepts and techniques to real-life situations as well.

Chapter 2 emphasizes techniques for evaluating how well a bank is performing. Included are a brief description of the similarities between basic concepts used in analysis of nonfinancial businesses and those used for commercial banks, a discussion of the key measures of banking returns and risks, and ideas for establishing criteria for evaluating bank performance. A sample bank is used to illustrate the risk-return tradeoffs in banking. The concepts developed are then applied to an actual commercial bank.

In Chapter 3 we examine trends in the acquisition and cost of bank funds. We evaluate methods for measuring the cost of and potential profits on bank funds. The risks associated with acquiring bank funds are discussed. Finally, we present specific strategies for acquiring funds, such as product development and market segmentations.

Chapter 4, on Financing the Bank's Capital Needs, covers four integrated steps in capital planning. Step 1 emphasizes the elements of an overall financial plan on which the capital plan is based. Consideration of how much capital is needed in a bank's financial structure is Step 2. Factors considered include the appropriate purposes of bank capital, the effects of financial leverage, and regulatory ideas on capital adequacy. The third step is determining the appropriate amount of internal generation of bank capital and the fourth step includes an evaluation of the primary forms of raising bank capital.

Chapter 5 covers measuring and providing reserves and liquidity. Techniques for managing the money position are evaluated. We present methods for measuring short-term, seasonal, and long-term liquidity needs and then discuss ways of meeting such liquidity needs. The chapter closes with a suggested integrative system for appropriate liquidity, recognizing both the risks and returns associated with a bank's liquidity position.

Management of a bank's securities portfolio is the topic of Chapter 6. We evaluate the ways which the securities portfolio affect a bank's profitability and risk. The fact that the securities portfolio is usually less personal and should be more flexible than the loan portfolio is emphasized in using the portfolio to attain desired liquidity and interest sensitivity. Finally, we discuss several techniques for increasing return without significantly increasing risks.

Chapters 7 through 11 cover the lending function of commercial banks in considerable detail. How a bank should organize to compete successfully in lending is discussed. The primary types of bank loans are described The chapters present details on credit analysis, loan pricing, and so on for these types of loans.

Chapter 12 emphasizes managing the interest sensitivity and increasing the interest margin. Techniques such as duration, immunization, financial futures, and gap management are utilized. We investigate causes of interest sensitivity and determine sources of such sensitivity through income statement analysis. We then examine vulnerability to future interest rate change. The chapter includes a technique for measuring the required returns from the loan portfolio, recognizing the methods employed to attract funds and the interest sensitivity of a bank's assets and liabilities.

The book concludes with Chapter 13, which covers techniques for tying together asset and liability management. Included in the chapter are a method for determining risk-return tradeoffs and a system for bank long-range planning.

2

EVALUATING BANK PERFORMANCE: MEASURING RETURNS AND RISKS

The primary purposes of this chapter are (1) to show how the basic concepts used in analysis of most businesses are appropriate for commercial banks, (2) to identify the key measures of returns made and of risks taken for a commercial bank, (3) to demonstrate the interrelationships between these returns and risks, and (4) to illustrate how the concepts developed can be applied to an actual commercial bank. The material covered in this chapter is particularly important for two reasons. First, it is likely that banks will have to take higher risks in the 1980s than in the 1970s in order to make acceptable returns. It will be increasingly important for a bank to be able to measure the risks taken to produce acceptable returns during the coming period of challenging external factors and deregulation. Second, although a bank cannot change its past performance, thorough evaluation of this performance is the necessary first step in planning for an acceptable future performance.

USING BASIC IDEAS FROM BUSINESS FINANCE

All too often bankers and students of banking seem to conclude that commercial banks are so different from nonfinancial businesses that most of the concepts developed in analyzing such businesses are not appropriate for commercial banks. Such a conclusion seems inappropriate. While certain characteristics are unique to banks, just as others are to steel companies or to grocery chains, most of the primary concepts developed for profit-oriented, private corporations are generally appropriate for commercial banks. Some of the primary concepts of business finance and their parallels with commercial banking are discussed in this chapter.

Attaining the Primary Objective by Balancing Returns and Risks

In simplified operating terms, a business firm buys raw materials, combines these raw materials with capital and labor to produce goods or services, which are then sold to others at prices high enough to yield returns above the cost of the raw materials, capital, and labor. In financial terms, the business obtains funds through creditor and ownership sources, spends funds for raw materials, labor and capital, and recovers funds, hopefully in excess of the amount spent. According to current financial theory, the basic objective of the management of the business should be to maximize the value of the owners' investment in the business. For larger, publicly held businesses operating in efficient capital markets, this objective is obtained by maximizing the market price per share. Efficient capital markets help management in seeking the highest returns for the appropriate risk level. The task is more difficult for smaller firms, some of which do not have actively traded shares. Nevertheless, the firm's management (which for smaller firms is also often its owners) tries to maximize the value of the owners' investment by seeking to achieve the highest returns for the risk level deemed appropriate by the owners. Unfortunately, there is no efficient market mechanism to assist the manager with his or her decisions on tradeoffs between returns and risks taken.

Interested parties look at return and risk measures, many of which can be developed from a firm's financial statements, to analyze whether or not management has been successful in achieving its objectives. A simplified situation illustrates some of the basic measures used in such an analysis. Table 2-1 presents a balance sheet, income statement, and beginning profitability analysis for the ABC Manufacturing Company. The simplified balance sheet includes typical assets such as cash, accounts receivable, inventory, and plant and equipment. Money was obtained from current liabilities, long-term debt, and either issued or retained common equity. The firm's revenues and expenses for the year are contained in its income statement. The introductory profitability analysis in the lower part of the table includes the beginning items in a typical return on equity model illustrated in Table 2-2.

Additional information is needed to analyze ABC's performance. A more in-depth profitability analysis is needed to evaluate the firm's returns. Risk measures, such as variability of sales, nature of costs, coverage of fixed operating and financial cost, and variability of the firm's returns versus returns on a diversified portfolio, need to be calculated. The firm's return and risk measures are often compared with those of similar businesses. Generally higher returns are available if higher risks are taken. Finally, the firm's management tries to balance the tradeoffs between returns and risks by maximizing the value of the owners' investment in the firm.

TABLE 2-1
ABC Manufacturing Company

Average Balance Sheet for 198X

Assets		Liabilities and Net Worth	
Cash	$ 500,000	Current liabilities	$ 3,000,000
Accounts receivable	3,000,000	Long-term debt	2,000,000
Inventory	2,000,000	Common stock	1,000,000
Plant and equipment	4,500,000	Retained earnings	4,000,000
	$10,000,000		$10,000,000

Income Statement for Year 198X

Sales	$20,000,000
Cost of goods sold	15,000,000
Gross operating income	5,000,000
Selling and administrative expenses	3,000,000
Net operating income	2,000,000
Interest	400,000
Taxable income	1,600,000
Taxes (50%)	800,000
Net Income	800,000

Profitability Analysis

Gross margin $= \dfrac{\text{Gross operating income}}{\text{Sales}} = \dfrac{5,000,000}{20,000,000} = 25\%$

Net margin (before) $= \dfrac{\text{Net operating income}}{\text{Sales}} = \dfrac{2,000,000}{20,000,000} = 10\%$

Net margin (after) $= \dfrac{\text{Net income}}{\text{Sales}} = \dfrac{800,000}{20,000,000} = 4\%$

Asset utilization $= \dfrac{\text{Sales}}{\text{Assets}} = \dfrac{20,000,000}{10,000,000} = 2\times$

Return on assets $= \dfrac{\text{Net income}}{\text{Assets}} = \dfrac{800,000}{10,000,000} = 8\%$

Leverage multiplier $= \dfrac{\text{Asset}}{\text{Equity}} = \dfrac{10,000,000}{5,000,000} = 2\times$

Return on equity $= \dfrac{\text{Net income}}{\text{Equity}} = \dfrac{800,000}{5,000,000} = 16\%$

TABLE 2-2
Return on Equity Model

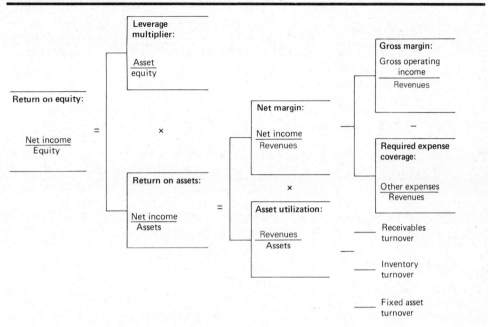

Parallels with Banking

Similar to a nonfinancial business, a commercial bank obtains funds from creditor and ownership sources; spends funds for its raw materials, labor, and capital; and recovers funds, hopefully in excess of the amount spent. The raw material purchased is funds instead of iron, cloth, or food, and the product sold is funds packaged in a usable form instead of steel, clothing, or groceries. As in a nonfinancial business, a bank management's basic objective should be to maximize the value of the owner's investment in the bank. Useful information on the appropriate tradeoffs between returns made and risk taken is obtained from relatively efficient markets for most publicly held banks. The management of smaller banks seeks to achieve the highest returns for the risk level deemed appropriate by the owners.

The simplified financial information on XYZ Commercial Bank in Table 2-3 illustrates some of these similarities. Note that, like ABC Manufacturing, XYZ Bank has short- and long-term assets and that funds were obtained from current liabilities, long-term liabilities, and either issued or retained common equity. The proportions of assets and liabilities are often different—compared with nonfinancial businesses, banks tend to have limited amounts in premise and equity capital and substantially larger amounts in short-term financial assets and liabilities. XYZ Bank's income statement included revenue and expense items similar to those of ABC Manufacturing. The same basic profitability analysis (see Table 2-2) can be applied to the XYZ Bank example. The

TABLE 2-3
XYZ Commercial Bank

Average Balance Sheet for 198X

Assets		Liabilities and Net Worth	
Cash and due from banks	$ 8,000,000	Current liabilities	$ 70,000,000
Short-term loans and securities	60,000,000	Long-term liabilities	23,000,000
Long-term loans and securities	30,000,000	Common stock	1,000,000
Premises and equipment	2,000,000	Undivided profits	6,000,000
	$100,000,000		$100,000,000

Income Statement for Year 198X

Revenues—interest	$15,000,000
Interest Expenses	10,000,000
Net interest income	5,000,000
Overhead—People and premises	3,000,000
Net operating income	2,000,000
Taxes (50%)	1,000,000
Net Income	1,000,000

Profitability Analysis

$$\text{Interest margin} \quad \frac{\text{Net interest income}}{\text{Earning assets}} = \frac{5,000,000}{90,000,000} = 5.5\%$$

$$\text{Net margin (after tax)} \quad \frac{\text{Net income}}{\text{Revenues}} = \frac{1,000,000}{15,000,000} = 6.6\%$$

$$\text{Asset utilization} \quad \frac{\text{Revenues}}{\text{Assets}} = \frac{15,000,000}{100,000,000} = 15\%$$

$$\text{Return on assets} \quad \frac{\text{Net income}}{\text{Assets}} = \frac{1,000,000}{100,000,000} = 1\%$$

$$\text{Leverage multiplier} \quad \frac{\text{Assets}}{\text{Equity}} = \frac{100,000,000}{7,000,000} = 14.3\times$$

$$\text{Return on capital} \quad \frac{\text{Net income}}{\text{Equity}} = \frac{1,000,000}{7,000,000} = 14.3\%$$

results indicate that the XYZ Bank had lower margins, asset utilization, and return on assets, but that the higher leverage multiplier tended to make the resulting return on equity competitive with ABC Manufacturing. This would, of course, have to be true if the two types of businesses are to compete in the markets for new equity capital.

Just as additional information is needed to analyze ABC's performance, more in-depth profitability analysis is necessary to evaluate the bank's returns. Risk measures, some like such measures for nonfinancial businesses and some specific to banks and similar financial institutions, should be calculated. The bank's return and risk measures should then be compared with those of similar banks. As with nonfinancial firms, generally higher returns are available if higher risks are taken. The bank's management tries to balance the tradeoffs between the risks and returns by maximizing the owners' investment in the bank. Bank management should keep such parallel concepts in mind when analyzing the key measures of returns made and risks taken by commercial banks.

KEY RETURN AND RISK MEASURES FOR BANKS

Financial Statements for a Sample Bank

An example of a commercial bank in a hypothesized environment will be used to further illustrate how to measure bank returns and risks and to evaluate the interrelationships between returns and risks. To keep this example basic, it is assumed that the bank can obtain funds in only five ways: (1) transaction deposits consisting of demand deposit (checking) and negotiable order of withdrawal (NOW) accounts, (2) short-term time and savings deposits consisting of passbook savings and time deposits maturing within 90 days, (3) long-term time deposits, which mature in over 90 days, (4) money borrowed from other sources, and (5) equity capital representing the owners' investment and earnings retained in the bank. Similarly, it is assumed that, after meeting its cash and premises requirements, the bank can employ the funds it has obtained in only five ways: (1) short-term high-quality debt securities maturing within 90 days, (2) longer term high-quality debt securities maturing in over 90 days, (3) good-quality loans whose rate varies with changes in interest rates, (4) medium-quality loans whose rate varies with changes in interest rates, (5) and good-quality fixed-rate loans.

Table 2-4 presents the basic conditions in the hypothesized environment in which the sample bank must operate. Although the hypothesized environment is not meant to be representative of any particular time period, the reserves, revenues, and expenses are not far from those that existed in the early 1980s. Furthermore, the relationships between rates are reasonably representative of many periods of time. Short-term securities yield 14 percent versus 16 percent on long-term securities because of the greater price fluctuations (interest rate risk) on the long-term securities. Loans tend to yield more than securities because of the greater credit risk on loans. Also, higher quality loans yield less than medium quality loans, and variable rate loans tend to yield less than fixed-rate loans. On the cost side, transaction deposits cost less than time deposits but have higher required reserves and may cause more liquidity pressures on assets. Long-term time deposits cost more than short-term ones.

The sample bank, Smithville Bank, is a $100 million-asset bank operating in this environment. The balance sheet and income statements for Smithville are summarized in Table 2-5. It is assumed that Smithville Bank has been able to obtain $40 million in transaction deposits (demand deposits and NOW accounts), $25 million in short-term time and savings deposits, and $25 million in longer term time deposits. Furthermore, the bank has chosen to borrow an additional $3 million and has equity capital totaling $7 million. In employing these funds, the bank has had to hold $8 million in reserves—

TABLE 2-4
Hypothesized Environment

	Rates
Reserve and cash requirements	
Transaction deposits	15%
Time deposits	4%
Potential earnings available	
Short-term securities	14%
Long-term securities (currently)	16%
Long-term securities (held)	10%
High-quality, variable-rate loans	17%
Medium-quality, variable-rate loans	19%
Fixed-rate loans (currently)	18%
Fixed-rate loans (held)	12%
Expenses in environment	
Transaction deposits	6%
Short-term time deposits	12%
Long-term time deposits	15%
Borrowings	13%
Other expenses	$2 million
Income tax rate	45%

TABLE 2-5
Smithville Bank

Balance Sheet (dollars in thousands)

Assets		Liabilities	
Cash and due from banks	$ 8,000	Transaction deposits	$ 40,000
Short-term securities	15,000	Short-term time deposits	25,000
Long-term securities	15,000	Long-term time deposits	25,000
High variable loans	20,000	Borrowings	3,000
Medium variable loans	20,000	Equity capital	7,000
Fixed-rate loans	20,000		$100,000
Premises	2,000		
	$100,000		

Income statement (dollars in thousands)

Revenues	$13,200
Interest expenses	−9,540
Other expenses	−2,000
Operating income	1,660
Taxes (45%)	747
Net income	$ 913

15 percent of $40 million of transaction deposits and 4 percent of $50 million of time deposits—and had premises of $2 million.[1] The bank's management chose to leave $15 million in liquid short-term securities and had lent $20 million, respectively, in high-quality variable-rate loans, low-quality variable-rate loans, and fixed-rate loans. The remaining $15 million had been invested in long-term securities. Unfortunately, the $15 million of long-term securities and $20 million of fixed-rate loans had been invested in lower rate environments and had average yields of 10 and 12 percent, respectively.

The income statement for Smithville Bank was calculated from the account balances and rates available in the environment. For example, revenues are as follows:

Category	Balance	×	Yield	=	Revenues
Cash and due from banks	$ 8,000		0%		$ 0
Short-term securities	15,000		14		2,100
Long-term securities	15,000		10		1,500
High variable loans	20,000		17		3,400
Medium variable loans	20,000		19		3,800
Fixed-rate loans	20,000		12		2,400
Premises	2,000		0		0
Total revenues					$13,200

Note that although returns on long-term securities and fixed-rate loans average 10 and 12 percent, respectively, increases in these accounts would earn 16 percent and 18 percent, respectively. Interest expenses are similarly calculated.

Category	Balance	×	Cost	=	Expense
Transaction deposits	$40,000		6%		$2,400
Short-term deposits	25,000		12		3,000
Long-term deposits	25,000		15		3,750
Borrowing	3,000		13		390
Total interest expenses					$9,540

The operating income is the total revenues less the total interest expenses and other expenses. The net income is the operating income less income taxes of 45 percent.

Measuring Returns and Risks

The key questions now are how well has this bank performed, has it earned acceptable returns, and what risks has it taken to achieve these returns? Table 2-6 defines and cal-

[1] The amount in cash and due from banks is set by regulation (required reserves might be thought of as the price of being a commercial bank), efficiency in the collection process, and need for correspondent services. *Premises* refers to the building and equipment necessary for a bank to provide its desired service level. Since there are no direct earnings on either of these asset categories, bank managers try to keep only the minimum necessary amounts in these categories.

TABLE 2-6
Introductory Return and Risk Measurements (Smithville Bank Figures)

Category	Equation	Calculations	Results
Interest margin	$\dfrac{\text{Interest income} - \text{Interest expenses}}{\text{Earning assets}} =$	$\dfrac{13{,}200 - 9{,}540}{90{,}000}$	4.07%
			- - -
Net margin	$\dfrac{\text{Net income}}{\text{Revenues}} =$	$\dfrac{913}{13{,}200}$	=6.92%
			×
Asset utilization	$\dfrac{\text{Revenues}}{\text{Assets}} =$	$\dfrac{13{,}200}{100{,}000}$	=13.20%
			‖
Return on assets	$\dfrac{\text{Net income}}{\text{Assets}} =$	$\dfrac{913}{100{,}000}$	=0.91%
			×
Leverage multiplier	$\dfrac{\text{Assets}}{\text{Equity}} =$	$\dfrac{100{,}000}{7{,}000}$	=14.29×
			‖
Return on capital	$\dfrac{\text{Net income}}{\text{Equity}} =$	$\dfrac{913}{7{,}000}$	=13.04%
	Risk Measures		
Liquidity risk	$\dfrac{\text{Short-term securities}}{\text{Deposits}} =$	$\dfrac{15{,}000}{90{,}000}$	=16.67%
Interest rate risk[a]	$\dfrac{\text{I.S. assets}}{\text{I.S. liabilities}} =$	$\dfrac{55{,}000}{68{,}000}$	=0.81
Credit risk	$\dfrac{\text{Medium loans}}{\text{Assets}} =$	$\dfrac{20{,}000}{100{,}000}$	=20.00%
Capital risk	$\dfrac{\text{Capital}}{\text{Risk assets}} =$	$\dfrac{7{,}000}{75{,}000}$	=9.33%

[a]Short-term securities and all variable-rate loans are interest-sensitive assets whereas transaction deposits, short-term time and savings deposits, and borrowings are treated as interest-sensitive liabilities. Transaction deposits are treated as interest sensitive because more and more of such deposits are interest-bearing deposits, which appear likely to be covered less and less by Regulation Q.

culates ten introductory return and risk measurements for Smithville Bank. The return measurements and their relationships are similar to those appearing in Table 2-2. The first return measurement is the interest margin in percentage terms, which is interest income minus interest expense divided by earning assets (all securities and loans). Interest income less both interest expense and other expenses divided by revenues is labeled the net margin. This net margin times asset utilization (revenues divided by assets) equals the return on assets. It is important to note that this asset utilization is strongly affected by how much a bank has in earning assets. When the return on assets is multiplied by the leverage multiplier (assets divided by equity) the result is the return on equity. This return on equity (net income divided by equity capital) is the most important measurement of banking returns because it is influenced by how well the bank has performed on all other return categories and indicates whether a bank can compete for private sources of capital in our economy.

The risk measurements are related to the return measurements, because a bank must take risks to earn adequate returns. Four basic categories of risk measurements are described in this section and introductory measurements for Smithville Bank are calculated in Table 2-6. The liquidity risk of a bank refers to a comparison of a bank's liquidity needs for deposit outflows and loan increases with its actual or potential sources of liquidity, from either selling an asset it holds or acquiring an additional liability. For the sample bank, this risk is approximated by comparing a proxy of the bank's liquidity needs, its deposits, with a proxy for the bank's liquidity sources, its short-term securities. Although both variables are only rough approximations—funding loans may be a major liquidity need and purchasing liabilities may be an important source of liquidity—this relationship is a beginning indicator of most bank's liquidity risk. The tradeoffs that generally exist between returns and risks are demonstrated by observing that a shift from short-term securities into long-term securities or loans would raise a bank's returns but would also increase its liquidity risk. The reverse results would be true if short-term securities were increased. Thus, a higher liquidity ratio for the sample bank would indicate a less risky and less profitable bank.

The interest-rate risk of a bank arises from the fact that asset returns and values versus liability costs and values may change at different magnitudes because of changes in market rates of interest. A beginning measurement of this risk is the ratio of interest-sensitive assets to interest-sensitive liabilities. Particularly in periods of wide interest-rate movements, this ratio reflects the risk the bank is willing to take that it can predict the direction of interest rates. If a bank has a ratio above 1.0, the bank's returns will generally be higher if interest rates increase and lower if interest rates decline. On the other hand, if its ratio is below 1.0, a bank's returns will be lower if interest rates increase and higher if they decline. Given the difficulty of predicting interest rates, at least some banks have concluded that the way to minimize interest-rate risk is to have an interest-sensitivity ratio of close to 1.0. Such a ratio may be hard for some banks to achieve and often may be reached only at the cost of lower returns on assets such as short-term securities or variable-rate loans.

The credit risk of a bank is defined as the risk that the interest or principal, or both, on securities and loans will not be paid as promised. In the Smithville Bank example, the credit risk is estimated by observing the proportion of assets that are medium-quality loans. The relative amount of past-due loans or loan losses would be a better measure, but such data are not available in this example. The credit risk is higher if the bank has more medium-quality loans, but returns are usually higher too. Returns tend to be lower if the bank chooses to lower its credit risk by having a smaller portion of its assets in medium-quality loans.

The capital risk of a bank indicates how much asset values may decline before the position of depositors and other creditors is jeopardized. Thus, a bank with 10 percent capital to assets could withstand greater declines in asset values than a bank with 5 percent capital. The capital risk of Smithville Bank is measured by examining what percentage of the bank's risk assets are covered by its capital. The capital risk is inversely related to the leverage mutiplier and, therefore, to the return on equity. When a bank chooses (assuming this is allowed by its regulators) to take more capital risk, its leverage multiplier and return on equity, *ceteris paribus*, are higher. If the bank chooses (or is forced to choose) lower capital risk, its leverage multiplier and return on equity are lower.

Setting Objectives for Returns and Risk

Clearly, returns are increased by adding to one or more of the four primary risks a bank may take. Obviously, bank management would prefer the highest returns for a given level of risks and the lowest risks for a given level of returns. Two questions remain for the bank manager. What degree of total risks should a bank take in order to increase returns? How much of which type of risk should a bank take? The answer to these questions are difficult and not exact. For assistance, a bank can look at its past performance and ask if it is satisfied with the returns obtained and risks taken. The bank can find return and risk measurements for similar individual banks or peer groups of banks and compare these with similar measurements for itself. If the bank's stock is actually traded, the bank can take actions that will maximize its market price. Exact answers are hard to come by. Constraints, such as the nature of a bank's market, the level of competition it faces, the areas in which it has special management expertise, and the stance of its regulators, mean that each bank has individual characteristics that affect its desired return-risk tradeoffs.

The following three steps should prove helpful. The first step for bank management is to look at how other similar individual banks and groupings of banks have made their risk-return decisions. Any bank can obtain such information on other individual banks or peer groupings from the Federal Deposit Insurance Corporation (FDIC), Federal Reserve, Comptroller's Office, or numerous private bank service companies. Many banks' regulatory reports include a comparison with peer-group banks. The second step is to compare a bank's performance (return and risk) measurements with those of selected similar banks. Significant variances in these measurements should be justified. There are many reasons for differences—different markets, different management philosophies, and so on—however, many banks may find one or several areas for improvement. The final step is to set reasonable (challenging but attainable) objectives, given a bank's past performance, the performance of its peers, and its environment.

Assume that after careful study of its past performance and that of its peers, Smithville Bank decided on the performance objectives in the first column in Table 2-7. These objectives should be compared with the bank's actual performance for the period being examined (see Table 2-6). Smithville Bank's return on equity was very close to its objective; however, the composition for achieving this target was slightly different from those objectives. The bank's interest margin (and resulting net margin and return on assets) was below its objective, but an above-target leverage multiplier brought the return on equity closer to, though still below, the objective.

An analysis of the risk measures showed that the bank's liquidity and interest-rate risks were substantially different from its objectives. Smithville Bank was able to obtain its return on equity objective only by taking higher risks than desired in these areas, as well as greater capital risk to provide a higher leverage multiplier. The bank appears to be vulnerable to substantial increases in interest rates or loan demand. Based

TABLE 2-7
Performance Objectives for Smithville Bank

	Objective	*Actual*
Return Measures		
Interest margin	4.20%	4.07%
Net margin	7.50%	6.92%
Asset utilization	13.33%	13.20%
Return of assets	1.00%	.91%
Leverage multiplier	14.00×	14.29×
Return on equity	14.00%	13.04%
Risk Measures		
Liquidity risk	23.00%	16.67%
Interest-rate risk	1.00	0.81
Credit risk	20.00%	20.00%
Capital risk	10.00%	9.33%

on the preceding analysis, Smithville Bank might set future goals such as increasing its net interest margin, increasing liquid assets, and balancing its interest-rate sensitivity position. Such action would be expected to increase the value of the shareholders' investment in the bank.

Examples of Return-Risk Tradeoffs

Two additional Smithville Bank examples illustrate the difficulty in obtaining conflicting goals and the tradeoffs between returns and risks taken by nearly every commercial bank. It is assumed that in the year following our initial example (see Table 2-5), Smithville's deposits grew $10 million and its capital grew $1 million. Available returns and expenses remained the same (see Table 2-4). The bank's management set its highest priorities on increasing the bank's liquidity position and on making the bank less vulnerable to interest-rate fluctuations. To achieve these objectives, the bank chose to place all the newly attracted funds, less those required as reserves and cash, into short-term securities. The resulting balance sheet, income statements, and return-risk measures are shown in Table 2-8.[2]

Smithville Bank's management decisions improved its risk position measurably. The bank's liquidity risk, credit risk, and capital risk were all better than the targeted objective. Its interest sensitivity position was moving from 0.81 to 0.90—toward its targeted goal of 1.00. However, the other side of the bank's performance, its returns, had deteriorated. Both the interest margin and the net margin declined appreciably because the bank's use of the funds obtained emphasized the more liquid, variable-return securities which had lower yields than other alternatives. The resulting return on assets and on capital fell to 0.89 percent and 12.34 percent, respectively, even further below

---

[2] Revenues and interest expenses were calculated, as in the initial example, by multiplying the assets and liability accounts by the rates as shown in Table 2-4. Rates on previously outstanding long-term securities and fixed-rate loans remained at 10 and 12 percent, respectively.

TABLE 2-8
Emphasis on Liquidity and Balanced Interest Sensitivity (For Smithville Bank)

Balance Sheet (dollars in thousands)

Assets		Liabilities	
Cash and due from banks	$ 8,400	Transaction deposits	$ 40,000
Short-term securities	25,600	Short-term time deposits	30,000
Long-term securities	15,000	Long-term time deposits	30,000
High-variable loans	20,000	Borrowings	3,000
Medium-variable loans	20,000	Equity capital	8,000
Fixed-rate loans	20,000		
Premises	2,000		
	$111,000		$111,000

Income Statement (dollars in thousands)

Revenues	$14,684
Interest expenses	10,890
Other expenses	2,000
Operating income	1,794
Taxes (45%)	807
Net income	$ 987

Introductory Return and Risk Measures

Return Measures	Objective	Previous	Emphasizing Liquidity
Interest margin	4.20%	4.07%	3.77%
Net margin	7.50%	6.92%	6.72%
Asset utilization	13.33%	13.20%	13.23%
Return on assets	1.00%	0.91%	0.89%
Leverage Multiplier	14.00×	14.29×	13.88×
Return on equity	14.00%	13.04%	12.34%
Risk Measures			
Liquidity risk	23.00%	16.67%	25.60%
Interest-rate risk	1.00	0.81	0.90
Credit risk	20.00%	20.00%	18.02%
Capital risk	10.00%	9.33%	10.66%

the bank's goals of 1.00 and 14.00 percent. Thus, Smithville Bank was unable to obtain its risk objectives without hurting its return performance significantly. The bank's owners would probably be unhappy with such management decisions.

Using the same figures—Smithville's deposits grew $10 million and its capital grew $1 million with returns and expenses as in Table 2-4—the second example assumes that the bank's management decided to emphasize increasing returns. The bank chose to invest the newly attracted funds, less those required as reserves, in the three asset catego-

TABLE 2-9
Emphasis on Profitability (For Smithville Bank)

Balance Sheet (dollars in thousands)

Assets		Liabilities	
Cash and due from banks	$ 8,400	Transaction deposits	$ 40,000
Short-term securities	15,000	Short-term time deposits	30,000
Long-term securities	18,600	Long-term time deposits	30,000
High-variable loans	20,000	Borrowings	3,000
Medium-variable loans	23,500	Equity capital	8,000
Fixed-rate loans	23,500		
Premises	2,000		
	$111,000		$111,000

Income Statement (dollars in thousands)

Revenues	$15,071
Interest expenses	10,890
Other expenses	2,000
Operating income	2,181
Taxes (45%)	981
Net income	$ 1,200

Introductory Return and Risk Measures

Return Measures	Objective	Previous	Emphasizing Returns
Interest margin	4.20%	4.07%	4.16%
Net margin	7.50%	6.92%	7.96%
Asset utilization	13.33%	13.20%	13.57%
Return on assets	1.00%	0.91%	1.08%
Leverage multiplier	14.00×	14.29×	13.88×
Return on equity	14.00%	13.04%	15.00%
Risk Measures			
Liquidity risk	23.00%	16.67%	15.00%
Interest-rate risk	1.00	0.81	0.80
Credit risk	20.00%	20.00%	21.17%
Capital risk	10.00%	9.33%	9.35%

ries that produced the highest returns. The resulting balance sheet, income statement, and return-risk measures are shown in Table 2-9.[3]

The new management decisions improved Smithville Bank's returns appreciably.

[3] Revenues and interest expenses were calculated, as in the initial example, by multiplying the asset and liability accounts by the rates shown in Table 2-4. Rates on previously-held long-term securities and fixed-rate loans remained at 10 and 12 percent, but newly acquired assets in these categories earned the current rates of 16 and 18 percent respectively.

The interest margin improved slightly, and the net margin and asset utilization improved significantly. The resulting return on assets and return on capital increased to 1.08 and 15.00 percent, respectively—well above the bank's objectives of 1.00 and 14.00 percent. The cost of obtaining these increased returns was taking risks considerably higher than in the previous year and than its objectives. Smithville's liquidity deteriorated further; its earnings were even more sensitive to interest-rate movements; and it had taken slightly above-average credit risk. The bank's capital risk improved slightly from the previous year; however, it was still significantly below the bank's objective. The bank's owners might be happy with the higher returns, but other parties, such as large depositors and regulators, might become concerned about the risks the bank was taking to obtain these returns.

With the aid of a computer, management can try many variations of the Smithville Bank example—changing the bank's liability structure, increasing or decreasing its capital position, varying the external environment so that rates are higher or lower, and so forth. Four such situations are summarized in Table 2-10. The results are always similar. To increase its returns, the bank must take additional risk. Lower risk means lower returns.

The first situation summarized in Table 2-10 is based on the assumption that regulatory authorities allow the liquid version of Smithville Bank (see Table 2-8) a lower capital position and, therefore, a higher leverage multiplier. It is assumed that the liquid Smithville Bank is required to hold $1 million less capital and obtains this $1 million through borrowing. Although return on assets is lower because of the cost of borrowing the additional $1 million, the return on equity is significantly higher than for

TABLE 2-10
Additional Risk–Return Situations for Smithville Bank

	Objective	(1) Liquid, low capital bank	(2) Profitable, high capital bank	(3) Shifting fund sources bank	(4) Rapid purchased growth bank
Return Measures					
Interest margin	4.20%	3.64%	4.28%	3.61%	4.01%
Net margin	7.50%	6.23%	8.43%	6.06%	7.00%
Asset utilization	13.33%	13.23%	13.58%	13.64%	13.79%
Return on assets	1.00%	0.83%	1.14%	0.83%	0.97%
Leverage multiplier	14.00×	15.86×	12.33×	13.88×	13.00×
Return on equity	14.00%	13.07%	14.12%	11.46%	12.55%
Risk Measures					
Liquidity risk	23.00%	25.60%	13.51%	17.70%	21.81%
Interest-rate risk	1.00	0.90	0.79	0.91	0.85
Credit risk	20.00%	18.02%	21.17%	19.82%	18.46%
Capital risk	10.00%	9.33%	10.51%	9.52%	10.50%

the liquid situation in Table 2-8 because of the higher leverage multiplier. Risks are the same except the capital risk is higher.

The second situation summarized in Table 2-10 assumes that the regulatory authorities require $1 million of additional capital for the higher profit, high-risk version of Smithville Bank (see Table 2-9). The asset structure is left the same, but borrowing falls $1 million and capital is raised by $1 million. With the lower leverage multiplier, the return on capital falls from 15.0 to 14.1 percent and, except for capital risk, the risk measures all remain high. Raising capital lowered profitability and did not improve the bank's liquidity, interest sensitivity, or credit-risk situation.

In the third situation, it is assumed that Smithville Bank's sources of funds changed appreciably. Transaction deposits fell to $30 million, and the bank was able to remain the same size by attracting $5 million more in short-term time and savings deposits and $5 million more in long-term time deposits. The attracted funds were invested approximately equally in five categories of earning assets. The results in this situation are scary (particularly when it may be close to what may happen in the mid-1980s). Profits decline appreciably—the return on equity is slightly under 11.5 percent and liquidity risk, interest-rate risk, and capital risk are above average.

The fourth and final situation depicts the case in which Smithvile Bank decides to grow rapidly from $111 million to $130 million in the following year. Funds are attracted by aggressively bidding to obtain $5 million in new short-term time and savings deposits, $5 million in new long-term time deposits, and $7 million in new borrowings. For this situation, capital is increased to $10 million and approximately equal amounts are invested in each of the five categories of earning assets. The results, as summarized in Table 2-10, indicate that Smithville Bank had below-average profits and slightly above-average liquidity and interest-rate risk. A bank having above-average growth clearly needs to consider the effects on its return-risk position of how the growth is financed and how the funds obtained are employed.

AN EXAMPLE OF EVALUATING A BANK'S PERFORMANCE

The principles in the preceding sections are now applied to a bank, Community National Bank. This section starts with a brief explanation of the primary items in a bank's balance sheet and income statement. Community National's statements are used as an example. The key return-risk measures from the preceding section are computed and analyzed for Community National Bank. A number of supporting ratios for the key return-risk measures are presented and computed for Community National Bank. Selected problems in analyzing a bank's performance are also discussed.

Understanding a Bank's Balance Sheet

Balance sheets for Community National Bank for 1979, 1980, and 1981 appear in Table 2-11. The balance sheets presented in Table 2-11 are average daily balances rather than end-of-the-year figures. End-of-the-year figures are useful in a few situations, but aver-

TABLE 2-11
Community National Bank—Average Balance Sheet (dollars in thousands) for Specified Year

	1979		1980		1981	
Assets						
Cash and due from banks	$ 17,898	13.4%	$ 23,205	14.2%	$ 23,831	13.1%
Short-term instruments:						
Fed funds sold	0	0	0	0	0	0
Other short-term instruments	0	0	0	0	0	0
Investment securities:						
Taxable securities	19,425	14.6%	26,925	16.5%	27,824	15.3%
Tax-exempt securities	6,330	4.8%	10,176	6.2%	15,676	8.6%
Trading account securities	0	0	0	0	0	0
Loans:						
Commercial loans	40,561	30.5%	48,817	29.9%	54,626	30.0%
Individual loans	31,938	24.0%	32,141	19.7%	34,983	19.2%
Real estate loans	10,869	8.2%	14,154	8.7%	15,438	8.5%
Other loans	1,262	0.9%	1,341	0.8%	2,351	1.3%
Total loans (gross)	84,630	63.6%	96,453	59.1%	107,398	59.9%
Less valuation reserve	486	0.4%	477	0.3%	931	0.5%
Net loans	84,144	63.2%	95,976	58.8%	106,467	58.5%
Direct lease financing	0	0	0	0	0	0
Bank premises and equipment	3,743	2.8%	3,984	2.4%	4,301	2.4%
Other real estate owned	0	0	0	0	0	0
Other assets	1,615	1.2%	3,057	1.9%	3,775	2.1%
Total assets	$133,155	100.0%	$163,326	100.0%	$181,874	100.0%
Liabilities and Net Worth						
Demand deposits, noninterest	$ 59,550	44.7%	$ 66,108	40.5%	$ 58,632	32.2%

age balances should usually be used for measuring a bank's performance because of possible distortions that may occur if balances on only one day are considered. In broad terms, Community National Bank's assets represent the bank's uses of funds it has been able to attract. The bank's liabilities and net worth record the specific sources of funds. Liabilities are nonowner claims on the bank's assets whereas net worth represents the book value of the shareholder's claims on the bank's assets. This net worth is the value of the bank's assets minus the value of its liabilities. Since most bank assets and liabilities are valued at cost or adjusted (toward their maturity value) cost rather than market values, many analysts worry about the usefulness of the resulting net worth.

The following paragraphs provide a brief description of the principal bank asset accounts.

Cash and due from banks generally included four categories of cash assets:

1 Currency and coin held in the bank's vault.

2 Deposits with the Federal Reserve Bank, which are used to meet legal reserve re-

TABLE 2-11 (continued)

	1979		1980		1981	
Demand deposits, interest-bearing	0	0	0	0	15,107	8.3%
Savings and time deposits:						
Passbook savings	16,710	12.6%	15,012	9.2%	12,347	6.8%
Savings certificates	7,185	5.4%	6,843	4.2%	6,971	3.8%
Money market certificates	10,425	7.8%	19,329	11.8%	23,389	12.9%
All savers certificates	0	0	0	0	3,181	1.7%
CDs, 100,000 and over	18,165	13.6%	24,078	14.7%	27,090	14.9%
Public and other time deposits	5,403	4.1%	8,664	5.3%	7,289	4.0%
Total savings and time	57,888	43.5%	73,926	45.2%	80,267	44.1%
Total deposits	$117,438	88.2%	$140,034	85.7%	$154,006	84.7%
Short-term borrowing						
Fed funds purchased	4,700	3.5%	6,900	4.2%	8,200	4.5%
Other short-term borrowing	147	0.1%	1,508	0.9%	2,890	1.6%
Other liabilities	2,925	2.2%	4,948	3.0%	5,795	3.2%
Long-term debt	0	0	0	0	0	0
Stockholder equity:						
Common stock (par $1.00)	963	0.7%	1,013	0.6%	1,013	0.6%
Surplus	1,348	1.0%	1,798	1.1%	1,798	1.0%
Undivided profits	5,634	4.2%	7,125	4.4%	8,172	4.5%
Equity reserves	0	0	0	0	0	0
Total equity	7,945	6.0%	9,936	6.1%	10,983	6.0%
Total liabilities and net worth	$133,155	100.0%	$163,326	100.0%	$181,874	100.0%

quirements and may also serve as a balancing account for checking clearance, transactions in Treasury securities, wire transfers, and so on.

3 Deposits with correspondent banks which Fed nonmember banks can use to help meet legal requirements and all banks can use to compensate their correspondents for services performed.

4 Cash items in process of collection, that is, checks deposited in the Federal Reserve or correspondent banks for which credit has not been received. Since a bank does not earn interest on any of these four categories of cash assets, they are labeled nonearning assets and banks generally exert considerable effort to minimize their cash assets.

Short-term instruments include interest-bearing short-term assets such as Fed Funds sold (excess reserves that one bank lends to another), securities purchased under agreement to resell, and other bank certificates of deposits. Such short-term instruments have obvious appeal to banks with extra funds for a short period; however, some banks use these short-term assets continuously as a way of employing attracted funds.

Investment securities are interest-bearing debt securities that a bank owns. These securities may be any maturity and they are usually valued at what the bank paid for them plus or minus an amortized adjustment toward the maturity value of the principal. The income on "taxable" securities is subject to federal income tax. The largest type of taxable securities held by most banks are securities of the U.S. government—Treasury bills, notes, and bonds. Many banks do have sizable holdings of securities of U.S. government agencies, such as the Federal National Mortgage Association, the Export-Import Bank, and the Federal Home Loan Bank. Some banks also hold either corporate debt or debts of foreign governments or businesses. Tax-exempt securities held by banks are general obligations or revenue bonds issued by states or their political subdivisions. The interest on such bonds is exempt from federal income taxes. Realized appreciation or depreciation on these bonds' principal value, however, is subject to such taxes. Banks are not permitted to buy corporate stocks.

Trading account securities are any of the preceding debt securities (usually Treasury securities), which are held primarily for resale within relatively short periods. These securities must be valued at market rather than book value, and appreciation or depreciation in value must be reported as an ordinary gain or loss on the income statement.

Loans are the primary earning assets of most banks in the United States. The bank lends funds to a customer and in return gets a note from the customer promising to pay interest, at either a fixed or a variable rate, and to repay the loan. Loans are usually categorized according to the type of user and how he or she plans to use the funds. The following are the three major categories for most banks:

1 Commercial loans, which are short- or intermediate-term loans to businesses typically for seasonal buildup of accounts receivable or inventory and for permanent working capital or plant and equipment.

2 Individual loans, which include automobile loans, other consumer durable loans, home modernization loans, credit card loans, and other installment and single-payment loans to finance personal expenditures.

3 Real estate loans, which include temporary construction financing as well as long-term loans to finance residences, office buildings, retail outlets, and factories. Most long-term loans were amortized and fixed-rate until 1980, however, many recent real estate loans have been variable-rate or renegotiable every few years.

Other types of loans might include agricultural loans, loans to banks and other financial institutions, loans to brokers and dealers, and any other loans that do not fit into the preceding loan categories.

The valuation reserve represents the balance in the valuation portion of a bank's bad debt reserve. A bank can build up this reserve according to strict Internal Revenue Service tax rules to absorb future loan losses. This reserve is increased by tax-deductible charges to income and decreased by charged-off loan losses. The valuation reserve is subtracted from total loans to arrive at a bank's net loans.

Direct-lease financing consists of the outstanding balances on all types of leases on property acquired by a bank for the purpose of lease financing.

Bank premises and equipment include all the bank's premises, facilities, equipment, furniture, fixtures, and leasehold improvements. These items are on the books at their depreciated book value and are classified as nonearning assets because they usually do not directly create an income stream.

Other real estate owned refers to all real estate actually owned by the bank, excluding bank premises and equipment. A major item included under this category is real estate acquired through foreclosure.

Other assets is a catchall category of other assets not large enough to warrant a separate account, such as customer liability to the bank on acceptances, prepaid expenses, and balances with savings and loan associations. If the items become significant, they will appear as a separate balance sheet item.

The liabilities and net worth side of a bank's balance sheet separates all the bank's sources of funds into appropriate categories. The categories used can be based on the form of the organization supplying the funds, such as individual, partnership, and corporate deposits versus public deposits, or on the form of the contract, such as passbook savings versus all savers certificates. The following paragraphs emphasize the form of the contract, but they include some of the principal forms of the organization using each contract.

Noninterest demand deposits are noninterest-bearing checking accounts of individuals, partnerships, corporations, and governmental units. The majority of these accounts generally come from businesses (partnerships or corporations) because (1) businesses are usually forced to leave compensating demand deposit balances with the bank in order to get loans, (2) individuals are usually eligible for interest-bearing checking accounts, and (3) governmental units keep most of their deposits in interest-bearing accounts.

Interest-bearing demand deposits are checking accounts of individuals that receive interest as long as they meet the specifications set by the bank. The proper legal title for these accounts are negotiable order of withdrawal (NOW) accounts, and they are subject to Regulation Q set by the Depository Institutions Deregulation Committee.

Passbook (or statement) savings are savings deposits that have no specified maturity, are subject to Regulation Q rate maximums set by the Depository Institutions Deregulation Committee, and do not have contractual provisions requiring the depositor to give written notice of an intention to withdraw funds. Businesses are usually not permitted to hold this type of deposit.

Savings certificates are time deposits evidenced by nonnegotiable instruments that specify the rate of interest to be paid and the maturity date, which must be 14 days or longer. Smaller and short-term certificates are generally subject to Regulation Q maximums, and there are interest penalities if the deposits are withdrawn prior to maturity.

Money market certificates are a special form of savings certificate. They have a fixed six-month maturity, require a minimum investment of $10,000 (which banks have found ways to get around), and receive a rate at the higher of the average six-month Treasury bill rate set at the previous week's sale of Treasury bills or the preceding four weeks' average rate for the same securities. The interest rate on new certificates fluctuates with the six-month Treasury bill rate; however, the rate is fixed for six months once the certificate is issued. At the end of six months, if the holder wants to renew a money market certificate, he or she must do so at the prevailing rate. There is a substantial penalty for withdrawal prior to maturity.

All savers certificates are special time deposits with a one-year maturity and minimum size of $500.00. The interest rate is 70 percent of the rate on one-year Treasury bills sold in the preceding month, and up to $1,000 of the interest received per person ($2,000 on a joint return) is exempt for federal income taxes. The cost of these funds is lower than that of money market certificates and most other time and savings deposits; however, the additional legislation required for these certificates to be issued beyond 1982 has not passed. These deposits will disappear by the end of 1983. Money market deposit accounts and super NOW accounts permitted in HR 6267 will appear on bank balance sheets starting in late 1982 or early 1983.

Certificates of deposit (CDs) of $100,000 and over are larger, usually negotiable, certificates with maturities of 14 days or over. Negotiable CDs are denominated in amounts ranging from $100,000 to $100 million, with $1 million the standard trading unit and six-months to one-year the most popular maturity range. Principal purchasers are treasurers of large businesses; however, states and local governments and wealthy individuals also have purchased significant amounts.

Public and other time deposits is a catchall category of time and saving deposit accounts. The primary category of public deposits are usually time deposits of state and local governments. In many states, securities must be pledged as collateral for such deposits. Other time deposits include time deposits of commercial banks, other financial intermediaries, and foreign governments and financial institutions.

Short-term borrowing of a commercial bank may consist of Federal Funds purchased and other forms of short-term borrowing. Federal Funds purchased are excess reserves of one bank which are purchased by another bank or possibly another institution. These purchases are often made on a daily basis but generally cannot be renewed easily. For the banking system, Federal Funds purchased are roughly equal to Federal Funds sold, and the rate on Federal Funds is determined by the amount of excess reserve available versus the desires of banks and others for this form of funding. Securities sold under agreement to repurchase are a short-term borrowing form representing a bank's obligation to buy back securities it has temporarily sold. Since the purchaser owns the securities during this period, these "repos" are, in effect, secured borrowing. Other short-term borrowing forms include discount borrowings from the Federal Reserve, Eurodollars, and commercial paper (by bank holding companies).

Other liabilities is a catchall category for remaining liabilities. Items usually found in this category include accrued taxes and expenses, dividends payable, liabilities on acceptances, trade payables, and other miscellaneous liabilities.

Long-term debt includes bank capital notes and debentures with maturities exceeding one year. These notes or debentures are not insured and may be either straight (nonconvertible) or convertible into the bank's common stock. Long-term debt is a source of funds and may also be treated as part of capital by some regulatory bodies (the Comptroller and Federal Reserve at the present time) if the debt meets certain requirements. The requirements usually include subordination to deposits and other liabilities, minimum average maturity when issued (usually eight to 10 years), and minimum remaining maturity.

Stockholder's equity represents the difference between the book value of a bank's assets and its liabilities. Included are up to five possible items—preferred stock, common stock, surplus, undivided profits, and equity reserves. Preferred stock pays a fixed dividend, which is not a tax-deductible expense; therefore, banks do not often use preferred stock. The common stock account is the total book value of all the bank's outstanding shares. The surplus account can be increased by sale of common stock at a premium above its par value and by transfers from the undivided profits account. The undivided profits account is similar to the retained earning account for most nonfinancial businesses. After-tax net income increases undivided profits while cash or stock dividends and capital transfers are paid from undivided profits. Equity reserves include contingency reserves (the emphasis generally on reserves that are not a tax-deductible expense), such as reserves for security losses and the contingency portion of provisions for possible loan losses.

Understanding a Bank's Income Statement

In Table 2-12, are the income statements for Community National Bank in 1979, 1980, and 1981. The primary items in a typical income statement will be discussed before this particular statement is analyzed. Interest income on a bank's earning assets is the primary source of bank income whereas the interest expense required to obtain the funds employed by the bank is usually the primary cost category for a bank. Other income items, such as service charges, fees, and net trust income are important to some banks. Other expenses, most notably the costs associated with the bank's employees and its premises and equipment, are usually significant expenditures for a bank.

Using the accounts in Table 2-12 as examples, we will briefly describe the income statement items.

Interest income on short-term instruments, taxable securities, tax-exempt securities, commercial loans, real estate loans, and other loans, is the interest the bank receives on each of these specific asset categories. All interest income, less associated expenses, is taxable with the exception of the interest income on tax-exempt securities. A method of calculating the tax equivalent interest income on such securities is discussed in the following section.

Service charges and fees includes income from maintenance fees and various activity fees that most banks charge on their demand deposit accounts under a certain size. Businesses usually receive a credit against these charges based on their average balances, whereas fees on individual deposits are often waived if a minimum balance requirement is met. Fees for originating loans or guaranteed lines are often included in this category.

Other noninterest income often includes the net income from the bank's trust area (if it has one), commissions on insurance premiums, income from direct lease financing, trading account income, safe deposit rental fees, and miscellaneous noninterest income sources.

Interest expense on interest-bearing demand deposits, passbook savings, savings certificates, money market certificates, all savers certificates, CDs of $100,000 and over, other time deposits, short-term borrowing, other liabilities, and long-term debt includes the interest expense on each of these specific deposit or liability categories.

TABLE 2-12
Community National Bank—Income Statement
(dollars in thousands) for Specified Years Ended December 31

	1979	1980	1981
Interest income on:			
Short-term instrument	$ 0	$ 0	$ 0
Taxable securities	2,214	3,701	3,964
Tax-exempt securities	330	634	1,081
Commercial loans	5,869	8,868	10,236
Individual loans	4,481	4,686	5,470
Real estate loans	1,320	2,019	2,297
Other loans	195	207	351
Total interest income	$14,409	$20,115	$23,399
Service charges and fees	657	747	861
Other noninterest income	309	249	286
Total operating income	$15,375	$21,111	$24,546
Interest expense on:			
Interest-bearing demand deposits	$ 0	$ 0	$ 789
Passbook savings	885	798	663
Savings certificates	875	932	1,006
Money market certificates	1,490	2,949	3,677
All savers certificates	0	0	388
CDs $100,000 and over	2,559	4,143	4,873
Other time deposits	674	992	968
Short-term borrowing	732	1,334	1,827
Other liabilities	150	280	412
Long-term debt	0	0	0
Total interest expense	$ 7,365	$11,418	$14,603
Provision for loan losses	297	303	517
Salaries and benefits	2,505	3,021	3,702
Occupancy expense	1,206	1,383	1,569
Other expenses	1,905	2,265	2,480
Total operating expense	$13,278	$18,390	$22,871
Net operating income before tax	2,097	2,721	1,675
Income taxes	819	1,005	307
Net operating income after taxes	$ 1,278	$ 1,716	$ 1,368
Security gains or losses (net)	−87	0	−21
Net income	$ 1,191	$ 1,716	$ 1,347
Cash dividends paid	180	225	300

Every category of interest expense is a deductible expense for determining a bank's income taxes.

Provision for loan losses is the amount charged against earnings to establish a reserve sufficient to absorb expected loan losses. Internal Revenue Service rules set the maximum amount that can be a tax-deductible expense and be placed in the valuation reserve account on the balance sheet. Management, based on its knowledge of the quality of the loan portfolio and the opinions of the regulatory authorities, may charge more or less than the maximum tax-deductible amount if it believes this amount is more appropriate for possible loan losses.

Salaries and benefits represent the total compensation paid to all officers and employees of the bank. This compensation includes not only salaries and wages but also unemployment and social security taxes paid, contributions to retirement or pension plans, cost of medical or health services, and other fringe benefits provided officers and employees.

Occupancy expense consists of depreciation on premises and equipment, the rental or leasing cost of offices or machines, and taxes on premises and equipment.

Other operating expense is a catchall category for a bank's remaining operating expenses. This account usually includes such expenses as advertising, premiums on deposit insurance and fidelity insurance, director's fees, supplies and postage, and costs associated with temporary employees.

Net operating income before taxes is the difference between total operating income and total operating expenses. Although banks pay the existing corporate income tax rates, net operating income usually must be adjusted to determine taxable income. The primary adjustment is usually to subtract the interest on tax-exempt securities from net operating income before taxes; however, other adjustment may be needed if the bank uses other tax avoidance techniques.

Net operating income after taxes includes the net operating income before taxes less the estimated federal, state, and local income taxes payable for that year assuming there are no security gains or losses on extraordinary items. Most bank regulators and analysts favor using net operating income after taxes as the primary dollar measure of a bank's income. Nonoperating events, such as significant gains or losses on the sale of securities or extraordinary items, are classified as unusual and nonrecurring events, which do not reflect normal, continuing income of the bank.

Security gains or losses are from the sale, exchange, redemption, or retirement of investment securities above or below the value these securities are carried on the bank's books. Sometimes extraordinary items, such as gains or losses from a major foreign currency revaluation on tax loss carry-forwards, are also included with this category. Gains or losses on sale of securities are subject to ordinary rather than capital gains taxes, and securities gains or losses are presented net of all tax effects.

Net income is the net operating income after taxes and after the net effect of all security gains or losses. Net income generally receives less attention than net operating income after taxes. The major inconsistency in the preference for net operating income is that a bank could take security losses in one year that would not affect its net operating income in that year in order to increase its interest income and net operating income in future years. Gains on sales of securities usually would not raise the net operating income in the year taken, but, when reinvested, they would tend to lower future net operating income.

Supplementary Information

Items from a bank's balance sheet and income statement are generally accompanied by other information that is useful in evaluating bank performance. Table 2-13 is an exam-

TABLE 2-13
Community National Bank—Supplementary Information (dollars in thousands)

	1979	1980	1981
Earning assets	$111,247	$135,716	$153,308
Risk assets	$105,115	$125,912	$141,188
Maturities of investment, securities:			
Under one year	$ 6,132	$ 9,804	$ 12,120
One to five years	9,867	12,218	14,372
Five to ten years	6,320	9,824	11,808
Over ten years	3,436	5,255	5,190
Market to book value of securities (%):			
Taxable securities	94.81%	90.17%	87.91%
Tax-exempt securities	93.04%	86.01%	80.18%
Past due loans:			
Commercial	$ 552	$ 481	$ 645
Individual	$ 964	$ 1,433	$ 1,688
Real estate	$ 251	$ 388	$ 436
Other	$ 18	$ 13	$ 13
Interest rate sensitivity (one year):			
Interest sensitive assets	$ 50,664	$ 59,766	$ 73,352
Interest sensitive liabilities	$ 46,741	$ 65,182	$ 91,749
Number of employees	129	142	156
Average market price per share (estimated)	$ 10	$ 12	$ 10
Tax equivalent interest income on tax-exempt securities	$ 611	$ 1,174	$ 2,002
Total tax equivalent interest income	$ 14,690	$ 20,655	$ 24,320
Total tax equivalent revenues	$ 15,656	$ 21,651	$ 55,467

ple of useful supplementary data that are usually available in a bank's annual report or its 10-K report. Following is a brief description of the supplementary items.

Earning assets refer to all assets earning an explicit interest return. Cash and due from banks and bank premises and equipment are the two major asset categories that are not earning assets.

Risk assets are earning assets subject to either credit risk or interest rate risk. Some banks still calculate risk assets as earning assets less all government securities, however, Community National Bank uses a more appropriate designation of earning assets less all short-term instruments and investment securities maturing within one year.

Maturity of investment securities classifies the book value of a bank's investment securities into selected maturity categories. This information is helpful in understanding the interest sensitivity of the securities portfolio and the potential appreciation or depreciation of this portfolio if interest rates decline or increase.

Market to book value of securities shows what percentage of the book value of a bank's securities, as shown on the bank's balance sheet, is represented by the market value of those securities. The difference between the market value (calculated by multiplying the book value by the market to book value percentage) and the book value of securities represents the unrealized appreciation or depreciation in the securities portfolio.

Past due loans are loans on which interest or principal payments or both have not been paid at the contracted time. Usually a bank allows a short grace period (for example, 15 or 30 days) before it classifies a loan as past due. Past due loans differ from classified loans, provisions for possible loan losses, and loan losses, although all of these categories give some idea of the credit quality of a bank's loan portfolio.

Interest rate sensitivity refers to the sensitivity of cash flows on either assets or liabilities to change in interest rates. Interest-sensitive assets are any category of assets on which interest income will change in the specified time period in response to rate change. Interest-sensitive liabilities are any category of liabilities on which interest expense will change in the specified time period in response to interest rate changes. The time period of this sensitivity should be identified. Many banks measure rate sensitivity for several time periods—for example, 30 days, 90 days, six months, and one year— because of sizable time differences in sensitivity between assets and liabilities. A dollar gap or difference between sensitive assets and sensitive liabilities as well as the ratio of sensitive assets to sensitive liabilities is often calculated.

Number of employees should be the number of full-time officers and employees plus the full-time equivalent of a bank's part-time employees. Temporary employees generally are not included.

Average market price per share is available for larger banks whose shares are usually actively traded. Problems may arise if a bank is the nondominant member of a bank holding company or if the bank is small and does not have an active market for its shares.

Tax equivalent interest income on tax-exempt securities is a hypothetical figure, which makes the income on tax-exempt securities comparable with the taxable income on most other bank earning assets. The formula for determining the taxable equivalent income on tax exempt securities is the tax-exempt interest income over 1 minus the bank's marginal tax rate or in equation form,

$$\frac{\text{Tax-exempt interest income}}{1-\text{Marginal tax rate}}$$

Total tax equivalent interest income is the total interest income from the balance sheet less the tax-exempt interest income plus tax equivalent interest income on tax-exempt securities. A 46 percent marginal federal income tax rate was used in this computation for Community National Bank.

Analysis of Key Return-Risk Ratios

Table 2-14 illustrates the calculation of the key ratios measuring the bank's returns and the risks it has taken to obtain these returns. Two risk measures are modified because more information is available than was available for the sample bank. Liquidity risk is measured by comparing the difference between liquid assets (short-term instruments and securities maturing within a year) and short-term borrowing (a proxy for how much of the bank's borrowing capacity is used) with total deposits. Credit risk is measured by dividing past-due loans by net loans.

TABLE 2-14
Community National Bank—Key Return-Risk Ratios

	Formula	1979	1980	1981
Interest margin (te)[a]	$\dfrac{\text{Interest income} - \text{Interest expense}}{\text{Earning assets}}$	$\dfrac{14{,}690 - 7{,}365}{111{,}247} = 6.58\%$	$\dfrac{20{,}655 - 11{,}418}{135{,}716} = 6.80\%$	$\dfrac{24{,}320 - 14{,}403}{153{,}308} = 6.46\%$
Net margin	$\dfrac{\text{Net operating income (at)[b]}}{\text{Revenues}}$	$\dfrac{1{,}278}{15{,}375} = 8.31\%$	$\dfrac{1{,}716}{21{,}111} = 8.12\%$	$\dfrac{1{,}368}{24{,}546} = 5.57\%$
Asset utilization	$\dfrac{\text{Revenues}}{\text{Assets}}$	$\dfrac{15{,}375}{133{,}155} = 11.55\%$	$\dfrac{21{,}111}{163{,}326} = 12.93\%$	$\dfrac{24{,}546}{181{,}874} = 13.50\%$
Return on assets	$\dfrac{\text{Net operating income (at)[b]}}{\text{Assets}}$	$\dfrac{1{,}278}{133{,}155} = 0.95\%$	$\dfrac{1{,}716}{163{,}326} = 1.05\%$	$\dfrac{1{,}368}{181{,}874} = 0.75\%$
Leverage multiplier	$\dfrac{\text{Assets}}{\text{Equity}}$	$\dfrac{133{,}155}{7{,}945} = 16.76\text{X}$	$\dfrac{163{,}326}{9{,}936} = 16.43\text{X}$	$\dfrac{181{,}874}{10{,}983} = 16.56\text{X}$
Return on equity	$\dfrac{\text{Net operating income (at)[b]}}{\text{Equity}}$	$\dfrac{1{,}278}{7{,}945} = 16.08\%$	$\dfrac{1{,}716}{9{,}936} = 17.27\%$	$\dfrac{1{,}368}{10{,}983} = 12.46\%$
Liquidity risk	$\dfrac{\text{Liquid assets} - \text{Short-term borrowing}}{\text{Total deposits}}$	$\dfrac{6{,}132 - 4{,}847}{117{,}438} = 1.09\%$	$\dfrac{9{,}804 - 8{,}408}{140{,}034} = 1.00\%$	$\dfrac{12{,}120 - 11{,}090}{154{,}006} = 0.67\%$
Interest rate risk	$\dfrac{\text{Interest sensitive assets}}{\text{Interest sensitive liabilities}}$	$\dfrac{50{,}664}{46{,}741} = 1.08$	$\dfrac{59{,}766}{65{,}182} = 0.92$	$\dfrac{73{,}352}{91{,}749} = 0.80$
Credit risk	$\dfrac{\text{Past due loans}}{\text{Net loans}}$	$\dfrac{1{,}785}{84{,}144} = 2.12\%$	$\dfrac{2{,}315}{95{,}976} = 2.41\%$	$\dfrac{2{,}782}{106{,}467} = 2.61\%$
Capital risk	$\dfrac{\text{Equity}}{\text{Risk assets}}$	$\dfrac{7{,}945}{105{,}115} = 7.55\%$	$\dfrac{9{,}936}{125{,}912} = 7.89\%$	$\dfrac{10{,}983}{141{,}188} = 7.78\%$

[a] (te) = tax equivalent.
[b] (at) = after tax.

Once such calculations are completed, the next concern is the interpretation of the resulting return-risk ratios. Several sources may serve as a beginning basis for comparison. First, trends in a bank's own return-risk measures over time often provide useful insights. Second, comparison of a bank's return-risk measures with the same measures for reasonably similar banks is helpful in identifying area of strength and weakness. Reasonably similar banks could include individual banks of like size and in comparable markets or a grouping of peer banks of similar size and in comparable markets. Averages and often various percentile grouping of return-risk measures for peer groupings are available from the three national regulatory agencies and numerous service companies. Finally, a bank can compare its return-risk measures with its own planned targets or objectives for such measures.

Care should be taken in interpreting comparisons with any of these sources. Even favorable trends in a bank's own return-risk ratios may still be at an undesired level. Totally identical individual banks or groupings of banks are difficult, if not impossible, to identify. A bank's planned objectives are typically based on its own and its peer grouping's performance in recent years—which may still be at an unacceptable level. In addition, the directors and top management of a bank may choose different strategies and tradeoffs between return and risk from peer banks to achieve an acceptable level of performance. Clearly comparative ratios are only the beginning step in analyzing a bank's key return-risk ratios.

The skill and complexities in analyzing a bank's key return-risk ratios can be illustrated by trying to interpret the trends in Table 2-14 and by comparing Community National Bank's key ratios with the average ratios for peer banks of similar size and in regions and markets similar to those of Community Bank, which appear in Table 2-15. In the case of its interest margin, Community National would probably be somewhat concerned with the decline in its interest margin from slightly above to slightly below average from 1980 to 1981. The slightly below average interest margin in 1981 might not be of much concern if the bank's other costs, such as salaries and occupancy costs, were below average. Often retail banks have high interest margins and high other costs, but wholesale banks often tend to have relatively lower margins but considerably lower other costs.[4]

Community National Bank's net margin, which reflects both its interest margin and its ability to cover all other costs including taxes, is clearly cause for considerable concern. The bank's net margin (appropriately using tax equivalent income) declined markedly from 1980 to 1981 and was about 2 percent under the average net margin of peer banks. Clearly, other costs in addition to interest expense had risen rapidly and were above average. Techniques for investigating this problem area will be discussed in the following section.

Community National's asset utilization was slightly above average and rising by a magnitude similar to that of its peer banks. This would tend to verify that Community's problem was expense control rather than failure to earn an adequate gross yield on assets. The return on assets which resulted from the low net margin and the average asset utilization fell from 1980 to 1981 and was significantly below that of peer banks in

---

[4] Retail banks are defined as emphasizing consumer deposits and loans; wholesale banks handle larger proportions of business deposits and loans to businesses.

TABLE 2-15
Key Return-Risk Ratios for Peer Banks of Community National Bank[a]

	1979	1980	1981
Interest margin (te)	6.74%	6.68%	6.59%
Net margin (te)	9.15%	8.83%	7.99%
Asset utilization (te)	11.91%	12.80%	13.19%
Return on assets	1.09%	1.13%	1.07%
Leverage multiplier	13.59×	13.82×	14.09×
Return on equity	14.78%	15.63%	15.08%
Liquidity risk	11.05%	9.87%	10.31%
Interest rate risk	1.06	1.04	1.01
Credit risk	1.29%	1.46%	1.84%
Capital risk	9.45%	9.26%	9.14%

[a]Based on banks with assets of from $100 million to $250 million in regions and markets similar to those of Community National Bank.

1981. An above-peer-average leverage multiplier helped Community National's return on equity; however, because of the low return on assets in 1981, the 1981 return on capital was nearly 3 percent below that of its peer banks.

Examination of the risk position of Community National Bank produced some surprising results. Because of its lower than average returns, it seems logical to expect the bank to be taking lower risks. The reverse proved true for the four primary risk categories. Community National Bank appeared to be taking substantial liquidity risk. Its liquid assets seem low and its short-term borrowings appeared high in relation to its deposits and the liquidity ratio recognizing these variables for its peer banks. Community National experienced a rapid growth in interest-sensitive liabilities in 1980 and 1981. By 1981 the bank's interest rate risk (interest-sensitive assets divided by interest-sensitive liabilities) had fallen to 0.80. This strong net liability sensitivity indicates that the bank is gambling on the rates falling. If they increase instead, the bank will be hurt by money costs rising faster than asset yields. Community National's credit risk (measured by past due loans) is also above the similar measurement for its peers. Finally, in spite of a small common stock issue in 1980, its capital risk is considerably higher, that is, the bank's equity capital is a smaller proportion of risk assets than it is for its peer banks.

In summary, analysis of the key risk-return ratios for Community National Bank indicate that the bank's low return on equity is primarily caused by higher-than-average expenses. Better control of such higher expenses should be a top priority in coming years. Of equal concern is the fact that the bank appears to be taking above-average risk in each of the four primary risk categories. Community National appears to be gambling that interest rates will fall and that the liquidity needs of the bank will be relatively small. The bank has no area of significant strength to give it flexibility if bad times come. Using the preceding analysis as a starting base, supplemental ratios can be developed to enable Community National to understand its performance in greater depth and to serve as a guide to specific future actions.

Supplemental Measures of Bank Performance

Once the key return-risk ratios have been used to spot the areas of greatest concern, supplemental measures of bank performance can be used to identify specific strengths and weaknesses. Table 2-16 contains an example of such supplemental ratios for Community National Bank. The emphasis at this time is on the types of supplemental measures a bank may use. Trends, targets, and peer group figures are helpful as a basis for evaluating such supplemental ratios, but these are not presented here.

The first four categories of supplemental measures are particularly useful for a detailed understanding of the factors underlying a bank's net margin and return on assets. The first category measures the yields on each type of earning asset. A bank like Community National is able to see the trends in yields on various earning assets, to examine how its gross returns compare with those of its peers on specific assets, and to identify assets on which yields might be improved. The second category looks at noninterest sources of income to examine a bank's performance in earnings income from sources other than interest on its earning assets. Although noninterest income is relatively small for most banks, adequate returns can be the margin of success for a bank. Furthermore, many bank analysts feel noninterest income will be a growing contributor to bank returns in future years. The other two categories emphasize the interest costs of a bank's various sources of funds and its cost efficiency in other areas, such as salaries and occupancy expenses. Rising or above-average costs can be indicative of potential problem areas that may be improved.

The composition of a bank's assets and liabilities often provides useful supplemental information to a bank's key return-risk ratios. The current environment and a bank's specific market will obviously affect a bank's mixture of assets and liabilities, however, bank management decisions also have an impact in this important area. Analysis of these compositions in conjunction with yields on assets and cost of fund sources often proves helpful. As an example, specific costs of fund sources for Community National Bank are generally at acceptable levels. It is the change in the composition of liabilities from low-cost sources, such as demand deposits and passbook savings, to high-cost sources, such as money market certificates, that has caused the bank's interest margin and net margin to deteriorate.

Examining the annual growth rates of selected items, the next category of supplemental measures, provides helpful insights on both returns and risks. For example, rapid growth in loans tends to lead to higher returns and higher risk. More rapid growth in assets than in deposits is indicative of a bank using borrowed sources of funds extensively. The growth rate of capital in relation to the growth rate of assets and loans often indicates the bank's future capital position (this is discussed in detail in the chapter on bank capital).

Finally, the four categories of supplemental risk ratios add greater depth to an understanding of the risks a bank is taking to try to obtain higher returns. For example, in the liquidity risk category, the sources of liquidity are estimated by looking at liquid assets in relation to total assets and at total borrowings as a percentage of stockholder equity. Volatile deposits (all savers certificates, large CDs, and public time deposits) as a percentage of total deposits and rate of growth in loans (from the preceding ratio category) serve as beginning approximations of liquidity needs.

TABLE 2-16
Community National Bank—Supplemental Measures

	1979	1980	1981
Yields on earning assets:			
Taxable securities	11.4%	13.7%	14.2%
Tax-exempt securities	5.2%	6.2%	6.9%
Tax-exempt securities (te)	9.7%	11.5%	12.8%
All investment securities (te)	11.0%	13.2%	13.7%
Commercial loans	14.5%	18.2%	18.7%
Individual loans	14.0%	14.6%	15.6%
Real estate loans	12.1%	14.2%	14.9%
Other loans	15.5%	15.4%	14.9%
All loans	14.0%	16.4%	17.1%
All earning assets (te)	13.2%	15.2%	15.9%
Noninterest income:			
Net trust income/revenues	—	—	—
Service charges and fees/revenues	4.3%	3.5%	3.5%
Other noninterest income/revenues	2.0%	1.2%	1.2%
Cost of fund sources:			
Interest-bearing demand deposits	—	—	5.2%
Passbook savings	5.3%	5.3%	5.4%
Savings certificates	12.2%	13.6%	14.4%
Money market certificates	14.3%	15.3%	15.7%
All savers certificates	—	—	12.2%
CDs $100,000 and over	14.1%	17.4%	18.0%
Other time deposits	12.5%	11.4%	13.3%
All interest-bearing deposits	11.2%	13.3%	13.0%
Short-term borrowing	15.1%	15.9%	16.5%
Other liabilities	5.1%	5.7%	7.1%
All interest-bearing funds	11.2%	13.1%	13.0%
Interest expenses/earning assets	6.6%	8.4%	9.5%
Cost efficiency:			
Provision for loan losses/revenues	1.9%	1.4%	2.1%
Salaries and benefits/revenues	16.3%	14.3%	15.1%
Salaries and benefits/employees	$19,419	$21,275	$23,731
Total assets (dollars in thousands)/employee	$ 1,032	$ 1,150	$ 1,166
Occupancy expense/revenues	7.8%	6.6%	6.4%
Occupancy expense/total assets	0.9%	0.8%	0.9%
Other expenses/revenues	12.4%	10.7%	10.1%
Taxes/operating income	39.1%	36.9%	18.3%
Taxes/operating income — tax-exempt income	46.3%	48.2%	51.7%
Total expenses/earning assets	11.9%	13.6%	14.9%
Composition of assets:			
Earning assets/total assets	83.5%	83.1%	84.3%
Details appear on balance sheet[a]			
Composition of liabilities:			
Details appear on balance sheet[a]			

TABLE 2-16 (continued)

	1979	1980	1981
Annual growth rates:			
Assets	—	22.7%	11.4%
Loans	—	14.1%	10.9%
Deposits	—	19.2%	10.0%
Capital	—	25.1%	10.5%
Supplemental liquidity ratios:			
Liquid assets/total assets	4.6%	6.0%	6.7%
Total borrowing/stockholder equity	97.8%	134.4%	153.7%
Volatile deposits/total deposits	20.1%	23.4%	24.4%
Supplemental interest sensitivity ratios:			
Interest-sensitive assets/assets	38.0%	36.6%	40.3%
Interest-sensitive liabilities/assets	35.1%	39.9%	50.4%
Net sensitive assets/assets	2.9%	−3.3%	−10.1%
Supplemental credit risk measures:			
Risk assets/total assets	78.9%	77.1%	77.6%
Provisions for loan losses/net loans	0.4%	0.3%	0.5%
Valuation reserves/net loans	0.6%	0.5%	0.9%
Supplemental capital ratios:			
Debt capital/total capital	0%	0%	0%
Capital/assets	6.0%	6.1%	6.0%
Capital/loans	9.4%	10.4%	10.3%

[a]See Table 2-11.

SUMMARY

This chapter has identified the key measures of returns made and risks taken for a commercial bank. A hypothetical bank was used to demonstrate the interrelationships between these returns and risks. These concepts were then applied to a commercial bank. To evaluate this bank, in addition to calculating and interpreting the key return and risk measures, it was necessary to examine trends in this bank's measures and to compare its measures with like measures for similar banks or peer groupings of banks and the bank's own return-risk targets. Supplemental ratios to enhance the evaluation of the commercial bank were then introduced. Later chapters will discuss more sophisticated supplemental measures, such as a liquidity analysis model, more sophisticated measures of interest sensitivity, and the use of break-even yield analysis. At this point, readers should be sufficiently prepared to tackle the cases at the end of this part.

CASE 1
Peninsula Cities Bank

In early April 1972, C. Ashley Brown read with interest an article describing the merger agreement between the Stanford Bank of Palo Alto, California, and Union Bank of Los Angeles. Brown recalled that the Stanford Bank had been formed as an independent bank sometime in 1963. It appeared to him that the merger terms as described in the article had resulted in a very attractive investment return to the original investors of the Stanford Bank. Moreover, whenever he read about bank mergers, the terms to the selling bank usually were cited as "significantly above book value."

At the time, Brown was 38 years old and held an appointment as associate professor in the department of industrial engineering at Stanford University. In addition to his academic duties, Brown had been quite active as a private investor. Even though he had done quite well for himself, he was becoming dissatisfied with the impersonal nature of investing through a broker. Brown felt that he was young enough and could devote a good part of several years and a substantial portion of his wealth to a venture that might prove satisfying both financially and personally. Since the Stanford Bank had been the only independent bank in the Palo Alto area, Brown began to wonder just what was involved in forming a new bank. He decided to spend a few days investigating that question.

Basic Information on Bank Formation

As a first step, Brown contacted his personal lawyer and asked him about the requirements for forming a new bank. His lawyer advised him that bank formation was a rather specialized area of law and that it would be best for Brown to consult one of several attorneys specializing in this field. Brown contacted one of these individuals and arranged for a consultation in order to find out about the legal requirements for bank formation and the probable costs and time involved.

The attorney proved extremely knowledgeable and helpful. Brown learned that before a bank can be started it must receive a "license to operate" from the regulatory authorities. The specific regulatory agency which would have jurisdiction would depend on whether the bank was to be a "national" or a "state" chartered institution. In either case, the application process was similar. First, an organizing group of at least five individuals would have to file an *application* for a license. If the application is approved, the organizing group must then provide substantial amounts of additional information to the regulatory authorities. The agency then decides whether to grant the *license to operate*. The time from initial application to the decision on the license varied, but it ran typically from five to seven months. Once the license is granted, the bank must open for business within a relatively short time (90 days in the case of a "state" bank) unless an extension is received. Failure to meet these requirements would cause the license to be revoked. The entire process may take about a year, depending on how fast the organizing group moved and on the sometimes unpredictable reactions of the regulatory authorities.

As far as costs of forming a bank were concerned, the attorney felt that these could be segregated into three parts. The first set of costs would be incurred in connection with the filing of the application. In the attorney's opinion, such costs should be kept to an absolute minimum because, even if the license were to be granted, the costs incurred during this phase would not be recoverable by the organizing group from any future issue of bank capital. The principal item of costs would be the application fee, amounting to either $2,500 if the group were to apply for a national charter, or $1,000 if the group sought a state charter. Minor additional expenses would be incurred to collect preliminary economic and financial information and to sponsor meetings of interested individuals who might become members of the organizing group. The attorney indicated that he would charge a fee only if the application were approved.

The second set of costs would be incurred once the initial application was approved. At that stage, the organizing group would have to commission a full-scale survey justifying the economic need for a new bank. Additional costs would include legal fees, the costs involved in searching for and selecting a president, possible travel expenses to Washington, D.C., a study for the Federal Deposit Insurance Corporation, and so on. All of these expenses would be necessary *before* a charter could be approved. The total of these expenses would amount to about $30,000 and none would be recoverable by the organizing group if the charter application were to be denied. If the charter were approved, these expenses could be capitalized and the organizing group could recover them either in cash or by receiving capital stock.

Brown learned that, if the charter were approved, an additional amount of approximately $35,000 would be spent on salaries and other expenses, *exclusive* of the costs of premises, before the bank could open. Of course, all of the latter would be proper expenses of the newly formed bank. None of these amounts make any allowance for Brown's own time, even though he was well aware that such a project may take as much as 30 to 40 percent of his available time for at least six months.

Collection of Preliminary Data

After his meeting with the attorney, Brown decided to collect some additional information before reaching a final decision on whether to go ahead with the idea of a new bank or forget the whole thing.

With the help of his broker, Brown compiled financial statistics for other independent banks that were started in northern California in the 1960s. The summary is shown in Exhibit 1. The performance of the different small banks seemed "mixed," and he was not quite sure what to make of this information.

Brown also contacted both federal and state regulatory agency officials. From them he received the application forms and the instructions on what information is required. Exhibit 2 contains the instructions for the federal application, and Exhibit 3 has the information for the state application. In addition, Brown collected some information on the principal operating differences under the two forms of charter. This information is summarized in Exhibit 4.

One of Brown's major worries was the ability to justify the new bank on "economic grounds." He was told by the attorney that the regulatory authorities were very sensitive to the possibility of bank failure when considering bank applications. An important factor in considering the charter application would be the ability to demonstrate that the new bank could become profitable "within reasonable time." The attorney had shown him a sample of the full-scale economic survey similar to the type that his group would have to commission—it was nearly 2 inches thick! It contained detailed census information on such factors as population, property values, average income, retail sales, employment in the area, traffic flows, and many other items. Without commissioning a detailed study, Brown with the help of one of his students collected some economic data so that he could get a preliminary evaluation of the "need" and "profit potential" for a new bank. The data are summarized in Exhibit 5. With the assistance of a friend, a retired banker, Brown projected the impact of the preliminary economic study on various key bank variables. Thus, he forecasted deposits, loans, revenues, and expenses. His forecasts are given in Exhibit 6.

Having collected all this information, Brown decided that the prospects for a new bank looked quite reasonable. At this stage, he felt that the time was right to form the "organizing group."

The Organizing Group

Brown felt very strongly that the composition of the organizing group would influence the chances of receiving a bank charter. In particular, he felt that the group should be composed of individuals with varied background so as to indicate to the authorities broad-based community support for a new bank. Also, such a diverse group of individuals could ensure the success of a new bank by providing helpful advice and attracting new business. A fairly large group of organizers would also limit the financial commitment of any one investor. On the other hand, the group could not be so large that they could not meet on relatively short notice to make the various decisions during the formation phase.

He knew that the regulatory authorities would scrutinize carefully the members of the organizing group. Each member would have to demonstrate a sizable net worth and a "clean" financial history. In addition, each member would have to provide complete information on the following items: place of birth, educational background, places of residence for the past 10 years, military service information, criminal offenses, income tax returns, employment, proposed stock acquisitions, directorships, and so on. In total, each investing member would have to complete some 11 pages of personal information.

On July 12, Brown held a meeting at his home to which he invited 16 individuals whom he considered as possible candidates for the organizing group. The meeting was held in order to discover the individuals' possible interest in applying for a bank charter, as well as to give Brown the opportunity to assess each of the attendees.

By July 19, Brown had narrowed the group to 10 members. In Brown's opinion this group could provide the capital to finance the application phase and would serve as the bank's board of directors if the charter were obtained. Also, the members of this group would be able to acquire on personal account a significant amount of the capital that the new bank would issue. Brown's choice was influenced by a number of factors. First, he desired a cross section of prominent local businessmen and businesswomen. Second, he wanted individuals who would actively contribute time to the bank should a charter be received. Third, he wanted a group of individuals who were relatively young and financially successful.

Personal highlights of the 10 individuals are summarized in Exhibit 7. This initial group had an average age of 40 years and an average net worth of $1 million, with a minimum net worth of $150,000. Brown anticipated that the organizers would ultimately own approximately 35 percent of the bank stock, if the charter were granted. He had made it clear to the group that the objective of the new bank would be to continue in operation as an independent bank and not to "make a quick buck" by merging in a few years. By maintaining a relatively large interest in capital in the hands of the organizers, it would facilitate the realization of such an objective.

Having received an indication of general interest from each of the 10 individuals, Brown sent to each of them the information summarized in the various exhibits. At the same time, he called another meeting for July 23, to discuss the following important questions:

1   Should the group go ahead and file an application for a bank charter?

2   If the answer to the first question is affirmative, should application be made for a federal charter or state charter?

3   How much capital stock should be planned for the initial capital offering?

4   How should the initial capital offering be allocated between the various members of the organizing group and the general market?

5   How should the group proceed to locate a president?

6   Where should the bank be located?

7   How should the organizing group share the workload and the expenses to be incurred during the organizing phase?

As he looked at the list of questions, Brown realized that he had a lot of work to do in preparation for the July 23 meeting.

EXHIBIT 1

Information Relating to Independent Banks Formed in Northern California

Bank	Date formed	Offering price	Date merged	Stock dividends	Merger price or present price if no merger
Stanford Bank	11/12/63	$20.00	5/19/72	None	17 shares UNIONAMERICA at $29 for 10 shares of Stanford Bank
Redwood National Bank	1/7/63	$20.00		2 for 1 1964 50% in 1971	$22
Commercial Nat'l Bank of San Leandro	12/21/64	$20.00	5/72	None	1.6 shares First National at $38 for each share Commercial
Commonwealth National Bank	6/4/64	$20.00	2/68	None	$31.50 cash plus 1/5 share Morris Plan selling at $30.00 (for each share of Commonwealth)
Bank of Sacramento	8/6/63	$20.00	1969	5% in 1968 25% in 1964	Share for share with Security Pacific at $32/share
First National of Daly City	5/3/63	$25.00		4 for 1 1968 5% each year 1967 thru 1971	$20
Bank of Marin[a]	11/9/62	$25.00			$52
Alameda First National Bank	6/26/64	$20.00			Merged into holding company of same name: 2 shares of holding co. for 1 of bank—price today of holding co. shares: $22
Peninsula National Bank	4/24/64	$20.00	5/69	5% in 1971 2 for 1 1971 4% in 1972	Merged share for share Exchange Central Bank Systems, price unknown
Tiburon National Bank		$20.00	Bank failed		
National Bank of Berkeley		$20.00	Bank failed		
San Francisco National Bank		$30.00	Bank failed		

[a]Twenty-five cent dividend paid each year.

Note: No dividends paid unless otherwise noted. Offering prices unadjusted.

EXHIBIT 2

Instructions Regarding
Application to Organize a National Bank
and Supplementary Forms (Sample)

_____

Mr._____

_____

_____

Dear Mr._____

You and your associates have expressed an interest in organizing a National Bank. Before undertaking action of _any nature_ to effectuate your purpose, including execution of the enclosed documents, you are urged to discuss your proposal with the following named Regional Administrator of National Banks for the National Bank Region in which you intend to locate the proposed bank.

_____

_____

_____

Such consultation will save you time and expense.

In developing your proposal for presentation to the Regional Administrator, bear in mind that the statutory minimum invested capital requirements for organization of a National Bank vary according to the population of the city, town, village, or other place in which the bank is to be located. In general, in a place having a population of not more than 6,000, capital of not less than $50,000 is required. In a place having a population in excess of 6,000 but less than 50,000, capital of not less than $100,000 is required. In a city the population of which is in excess of 50,000, a minimum capital of $200,000 is required. The Comptroller of the Currency, however, ordinarily requires a substantially larger amount of initial capital, depending upon the facts developed in an investigation.

In addition to paid-in capital, a National Bank is required to have an amount of paid-in surplus equal to not less than 20 percent of its capital. Moreover, the Comptroller of the Currency always requires an amount of paid-in undivided profits, over and above capital and paid-in surplus, adequate to meet organizational and other expenses and still provide a margin of safety until the operations of a new bank become profitable.

The following enclosed documents are to be executed and submitted to the Regional Administrator of National Banks in accordance with the instructions hereinafter set forth:

Application to Organize a National Bank and
Representations of Applicants (Three Copies)

Appointment of Agent (Three Copies)

Financial Report (Three Copies)

Biographical Report (Three Copies)

If additional copies of these documents are required, please advise the Regional Administrator. The purpose of these documents is to seek the preliminary approval of the Comptroller to organize the proposed bank.

The _Application to Organize a National Bank and Representations of Applicants_ must be completed and signed, in duplicate, by at least five adult natural persons and the _Appointment of Agent_ must be completed and

EXHIBIT 2 (continued)

signed, in duplicate, by the same persons who signed the application to organize. The latter document should also be signed, in duplicate, at the appropriate place by the person designated as agent for those signing the application to organize, whether or not the person designated as agent is one of those signing the application to organize.

A *Financial Report* and a *Biographical Report* must be completed and signed, in duplicate, by each person who signed the application to organize.

When properly executed, the application to organize, the appointment of agent, and financial and biographical reports for each applicant, all in duplicate, must be *mailed* to the Regional Administrator. Do not deliver them by hand or otherwise. If desired, an applicant may forward, *by mail*, his financial and biographical reports directly to the Regional Administrator so as to arrive at or about the same time as the other documents are delivered to the Regional Administrator. If all financial and biographical reports do not accompany the application to organize and appointment of agent, the application to organize will not be acted upon in any manner by the Regional Administrator until all such reports are received by the Regional Administrator.

The fee for filing an application to organize is $2,500. A check in this amount, payable to the Comptroller of the Currency, must be transmitted to the Regional Administrator with the application to organize. Refund with respect to this filing fee will be made only as follows:

1 If the application is withdrawn by you before a field investigation is undertaken by this Office, $2,000 will be refunded.

2 If the application is withdrawn by you after a field investigation is undertaken by this office but before the Comptroller renders a decision with respect to preliminary approval of the application, $500 will be refunded.

Your attention is particularly directed to the several representations and warranties set forth in the application to organize. Read these representations and warranties carefully. Be certain you understand them fully. Their importance cannot be overemphasized. The information set forth by you in the application to organize, and in the appointment of agent and biographical and financial reports is subject to verification through investigation. A misrepresentation in or omission of a material fact from these documents may subject you to severe criminal penalties, including those provided for by 18 U.S.C. 1001. Moreover, discovery of a misrepresentation or omission of a material fact will ordinarily result in no further action being taken by the Comptroller of the Currency in connection with the application or if discovered after the proposed bank has achieved corporate existence or has commenced the business of banking, may result in action to revoke the bank's corporate existence or its authority to do business.

Also enclosed is an outline of the minimum information which must be developed and submitted to the Regional Administrator of National Banks within 30 days after filing of the application. Failure to meet this requirement or to be otherwise prepared for personal interviews or to assist in the investigation may result in your application being considered as abandoned.

While ordinarily unnecessary, you may, if you choose, employ professional assistance such as attorneys, economic researchers, and other specialists, to aid you in connection with your application. You are, however, advised that *all* charges for organization expenses must be reasonable in amount. No such expense or charge except *minor* organizational expenses may be paid until full details, including dates, nature of services, and the charges therefor, are submitted to the Comptroller of the Currency and the Comptroller has expressly approved payment. Moreover, if the Comptroller of the Currency approves payment, payment shall ultimately be paid only out of bank funds and reflected on the books of the bank.

Funds to pay for organizational expenses should not be borrowed by the proposed bank or the applicants from any source. If necessary, *minor* organizational expenses incurred by you should be paid out of your personal funds subject to reimbursement by the bank and later approval by the Comptroller.

In no event shall the amount of or payment of an expense or charge be solely contingent upon any action, decision, or forbearance on the part of the Comptroller of the Currency. A contingent expense or charge will ordinarily result in the Comptroller of the Currency's refusal to grant preliminary approval, or the Comptroller's with-

EXHIBIT 2 (continued)

drawal of such approval if the same has already been granted. A contingent charge, however, is not one where an additional charge will be made to cover additional work resulting from action by the Comptroller of the Currency.

You will be notified by letter when your application has been accepted for filing. Within 15 days after receipt of such notification you must publish the proposals contained in the application and the names of the signatories to the application one time in a local newspaper of general circulation. Immediately thereafter, supply the Regional Administrator with a tearsheet or clipping evidencing such publication.

The acceptance for filing of your application to organize *should not* be construed as evidence that your application will receive the preliminary approval of the Comptroller of the Currency. In addition, the Comptroller of the Currency may grant preliminary approval and yet disapprove some persons who have participated in submitting the application to be shareholders in the bank or to be affiliated with the bank in any other way. Consequently, until you receive a written authorization from the Comptroller of the Currency, do not enter into any binding agreements written or oral, among yourselves or with any other person regarding subscriptions for or purchase of stock, in the proposed bank or regarding election of directors of the proposed bank.

Until further notice by the Comptroller of the Currency or the Regional Administrator of National Banks, *do not* take any other action of *any kind* with respect to organization of the bank. In the event preliminary approval is granted, complete additional instructions will be given to you at that time.

The Administrator of National Banks
The Comptroller of the Currency

Summary of Information to Be Submitted to the Regional Comptroller of the Currency within 30 Days after the Filing of an Application to Organize a National Bank

1 Population of city, town, county, village or municipality in which the proposed bank is to be located as of the last two decennial census and a present estimate.

2 (a) Estimated population of the service area, for the years 1950, 1960 and a present estimate, from which the proposed bank is expected to generate 75 percent or more of its loans and deposits.

(b) This area extends from the proposed bank location approximately

_____ miles north; _____ miles east; _____ miles south;

_____ miles west.
(Area must be outlined on the maps and aerial photographs submitted.)

3 Provide the following information with respect to each competitive bank and branches thereof located within the service area of the proposed bank (if complete branch figures are not available use consolidated figures). In nonpar, so indicate.
(a) Location marker number, names, and addresses[a]
(b) Distance by road mileage and direction from proposed bank
(c) Date established if within three years
(d) Interest rates paid on savings deposits and certificates of deposits
(e) Deposits
(f) Interest rates normally received on short-term business and installment loans
(g) Loans
(h) Rate of return on capital for previous three years
(i) Hours of business
(j) Estimate of commercial bank share of mortgage loan business
(k) Loan-deposit ratio

4 Provide handy-sized duplicate maps (with a scale of miles and compass points) of the city or area appropri-

EXHIBIT 2 (continued)

ately labeled to show the location of the proposed bank and the names and locations of all banks and branches, including applications pending and those approved but not opened. Aerial photographs of reasonable coverage, including expected service area are helpful, and if available, one so labeled should be submitted. The expected service area of the proposed bank should be clearly outlined on the maps and on aerial photographs.

5 Provide the following information with respect to Savings and Loan, Building and Loan, and Mutual Savings Banks located within the proposed service area.
   (a) Names and addresses
   (b) Date established, if within three years
   (c) Share accounts
   (d) Loans
   (e) Distance by road mileage and direction from proposed bank

6 Indicate the number of the following institutions within the proposed service area three years ago and the number of each at the present: credit unions, finance companies, insurance companies granting loans, and other institutions granting loans.

7 Indicate degree of intensity of competition in service area by savings and loan, mutual savings banks, credit banks, etc.

8 Provide a copy of any survey made preliminary to filing the application for the proposed bank and also the cost for any such survey.

9 Comment on the economic character of the area to be served.
   (a) If area is largely residential, state whether homes are generally owner-occupied, the extent of housing development, type, quality, price level, average age, number of unsold new homes, and prospect for continued development.
   (b) If primarily industrial or business, state the number and general types of business, and in the cases of principal employers, give the name of each company or firm, number of employees, and payroll, and comment on the consistency of employment and special skills required.
   (c) Shopping center locations should be fully described. State the number of units, size as to total land and building area, number of individual parking spaces, accessibility to surrounding communities, the extent to which signed leases have been obtained, the names of principal lessees, and provide information as to their financial responsibility, if not national concerns.
   (d) Provide information regarding population growth potential; new businesses recently established or planned, etc. Discuss the traffic pattern, the street and road facilities, and their adequacy. Describe geographical barriers, if any.

10 If no bank in community, where is banking business conducted by resident?

11 Past banking history of community.

12 Proposed ownership of stock: is it to be widely distributed or closely held? Amounts to be taken by organizers, proposed directors, officers and their families.

13 Financial position of city, town, village, school districts and county. Discuss tax collections, showing total levy, percentage collected and arrears, etc.

14 List the major types of loaning demands proposed bank expects to serve.

15 Give estimates of the volume of total deposits, showing the amount of public funds included in total and total loans expected at the end of the first year of operations, second and third year.

16 A detailed projection of earnings and expenses must be submitted showing the breakdown of income and expenses for each of the first three years of operations.

EXHIBIT 2 (continued)

17 Give the following information regarding banking house and equipment as it applies:
  (a) If to be purchased, the separate costs of land, building, furniture and fixtures, and vault.
  (b) If to be leased, give terms in brief and describe the quarters.
  (c) If property is to be purchased or leased from a director, officer, or large shareholder, state name and other pertinent data.
  (d) Give expiration date of any option to purchase or lease.
  (e) If new construction, furnish anticipated completion date.
  (f) If a temporary location is planned furnish exact address, distance and direction from permanent location, and period it will be occupied.
  (g) State the approximate period of time that will be required to place bank in operation in temporary and/or permanent site.

18 What plans have been made to obtain fidelity insurance covering all individuals authorized to collect, receive, or deposit funds from stock subscriptions?

Revised April 1965

ᵃInclude applications pending and those approved but not opened.

EXHIBIT 3
Banking Law of the State of California—Chapter 3: Organization of Banks

---

Article 1, Section 350—General

When authorized by the superintendent as provided in this chapter a corporation may be formed by three or more persons in accordance with the laws of this State for the purpose of conducting a commercial banking business, a savings banking business, a trust business, or any two or all of them. The articles of incorporation shall provide that the common shares of the corporation shall be subject to assessment by the board of directors upon order of the superintendent for the purposes of restoring an impairment or reduction of capital in the manner and to the extent provided in this code. They may also provide that such shares are subject to assessment by the board of directors in its discretion, but if such discretionary power is granted the articles shall provide that it may be exercised only with the approval of the superintendent and may provide other limitations thereon. The Corporate Securities Law shall not apply to securities issued by and representing an interest in or a direct obligation of a bank or trust company incorporated under the laws of this State.

Article 2, Section 360—Application

The request for authority to organize and establish a corporation to engage in the banking or trust business shall be set forth in an application in such form and containing such information as the superintendent may require and shall be accompanied by a fee of one thousand dollars ($1,000).

Section 361
Upon the filing of an application the superintendent shall make or cause to be made a careful investigation and examination relative to the following:

(a) The character, reputation, and financial standing of the organizers or incorporators and their motives in seeking to organize the proposed bank or trust company.

(b) The need for banking or trust facilities or additional banking or trust facilities, as the case may be, in the community where the proposed bank or trust company is to be located, giving particular consideration to the adequacy of existing banking or trust facilities and the need for further banking or trust facilities in the locality.

EXHIBIT 3 (continued)

(c) The ability of the community to support the proposed bank or trust company giving consideration to (1) the competition offered by existing banks or trust companies and other financial institutions; (2) the previous banking history of the community; (3) the opportunities for profitable employment of bank funds as indicated by the average demand for credit, the number of potential depositors, the volume of bank transactions, and the business and industries of the community with particular regard to their stability, diversification and size; and (4) as to trust companies, the opportunities for profitable employment of fiduciary services.

(d) The character, financial responsibility, banking or trust experience, and business qualifications of the proposed officers of the bank or trust company.

(e) The character, financial responsibility, business experience, and standing of the proposed stockholders and directors.

(f) Such other facts and circumstances bearing on the proposed bank or trust company and its relation to the locality as in the opinion of the superintendent may be relevant.

Section 362
The superintendent may give or withhold his approval of the application in his discretion but he shall not approve the application until he has ascertained to his satisfaction:

(a) That the public convenience and advantage will be promoted by the establishment of the proposed bank or trust company.

(b) That conditions in the locality in which the proposed bank or trust company will transact business afford reasonable promise of successful operation.

(c) That the bank is being formed for no other purpose than the legitimate objects contemplated by this division.

(d) That the proposed capital structure is adequate.

(e) That the proposed officers and directors have sufficient banking or trust experience, ability, and standing to afford reasonable promise of successful operation.

(f) That the name of the proposed bank or trust company does not resemble, so closely as to be likely to cause confusion, the name of any other bank or trust company transacting business in this State or which had previously transacted business in this State.

(g) That the applicant has complied with all of the applicable provisions of this division.

Article 3, Section 380—Capital
The paid-up capital of every bank hereafter organized shall not be less than the following amounts:

(a) Fifty thousand dollars ($50,000) if the population of the city or the locality in which the head office of the bank will be located does not exceed 10,000 persons.

(b) One hundred thousand dollars ($100,000) if the population of the city or the locality in which the head office of the bank will be located exceeds 10,000 persons but does not exceed 50,000 persons.

(c) Two hundred thousand dollars ($200,000) if the population of the city in which the head office of the bank will be located exceeds 50,000 persons but does not exceed 200,000 persons.

(d) Three hundred thousand dollars ($300,000) if the population of the city in which the head office of the bank will be located exceeds 200,000 persons. For the purposes of this article population means the population as determined by the latest federal census or other later information available to the superintendent.

Section 381
A bank hereafter authorized to exercise banking and trust powers shall have, in addition to the capital required by Section 380, paid-up capital allocated to the trust department as follows:

EXHIBIT 3 (continued)

(a) One hundred thousand dollars ($100,000) if the population of the city in which the head office of the bank will be located does not exceed 50,000 persons.

(b) Two hundred thousand dollars ($200,000) if the population of the city in which the head office of the bank will be located exceeds 50,000 persons.

Section 382
The paid-up capital of every trust company shall be not less than the following amounts:

(a) One hundred thousand dollars ($100,000) if the population of the city in which the head office of the trust company will be located does not exceed 50,000 persons.

(b) Two hundred thousand dollars ($200,000) if the population of the city in which the head office of the trust company will be located exceeds 50,000 persons.

Section 383
If the head office of the proposed bank or trust company will be situated in territory which by annexation or consolidation has become part of a city whose population according to the classification in Sections 380, 381, and 382 of this code calls for capital requirements larger than those which would have been called for if the territory had not been annexed or consolidated, the superintendent may in his discretion modify the requirements, and may permit the bank or trust company to be organized with paid-up capital in amount satisfactory to him but not less than the amount which would have been required if the territory had not been annexed or consolidated. No such bank or trust company shall establish any branch, or move its place of business, out of the territory embraced in the annexation or consolidation unless and until it has paid-up capital in amount not less than the minimum required for banks in the territory to which it proposes to move its place of business or in which it proposes to establish a branch.

Section 384
Every bank and trust company hereafter organized shall establish upon its organization in addition to the capital required by this code a paid-up surplus equal in amount to not less than 25 percent of its paid-up capital, a specified portion of which, with the written approval of the superintendent, may be designated as a contingent fund. No part of the paid-up capital or paid-in surplus except the contingent fund may be used to pay for organization expense without the prior written approval of the superintendent. Organization expense means all lawful expenses incurred before the commencement of business other than capital expenditures for land, buildings, and fixtures.

Article 4, Section 400—Authorization to Engage in Banking

The articles of incorporation of the proposed bank or trust company shall be submitted to the superintendent for his approval before they are filed with the Secretary of State pursuant to the Corporations Code. After the articles have been filed with the Secretary of State the proposed bank or trust company shall:

(a) File with the superintendent a copy of its articles of incorporation, certified by the Secretary of State, and, after the organization meeting of the directors, a copy of its by-laws certified by its secretary.

(b) File with the superintendent a statement in such form and with such supporting data as he may require showing that the entire capital and surplus have been fully paid in lawful money, unconditionally, and that the funds representing such capital and surplus, less sums spent as authorized by this code for organization expense and for land, buildings, and fixtures are on deposit in a state or national bank in this State, subject to withdrawal on demand.

(c) Pay to the superintendent a fee of one hundred dollars ($100) for each department.

Section 401
If the superintendent finds that the proposed bank or trust company has in good faith complied with all the requirements of law and fulfilled all the conditions precedent to commencing business imposed by this code or by regulation, he shall, within 30 days after the statement and supporting data specified in Section 400 have been filed with him, issue in duplicate a certificate of authorization to transact business as a bank or trust company, as the

EXHIBIT 3 (continued)

case may be, and shall transmit one copy to the bank or trust company and place one copy on file in the department. The certificate of authorization shall state that the corporation named therein has complied with all the provisions of this code governing organization of banks or trust companies and that it is authorized to transact the business specified therein.

Section 402

It shall be unlawful to accept payment of subscriptions for shares of any corporation proposing to engage in the banking or trust business unless authority to organize such corporation has been granted by the superintendent.

Section 403

No corporation organized to transact a commercial banking, savings banking or trust business shall transact any business until the superintendent has issued his certificate authorizing it to transact such business. No bank or trust company shall incur any indebtedness except that which is incidental to its organization until the amount of its capital and surplus has been fully paid in lawful money to the cashier or treasurer thereof.

Section 404

If the proposed bank or trust company fails to file evidence of incorporation and organization with the superintendent pursuant to Section 400 within six months after the approval of the application for authority to organize the bank or trust company, the right to organize the bank or trust company automatically terminates. The superintendent, however, for good cause on written application filed before the expiration of any such six months' period, may extend for additional periods not in excess of six months each the time within which the bank or trust company may be organized.

Section 405

If the proposed bank or trust company fails to open for business within 90 days after the issuance of the certificate of authorization, the right to transact business automatically terminates. The superintendent, however, for good cause on written application filed before the end of said 90-day period, may extend for one additional period of not to exceed 90 days the time within which the bank or trust company may open for business.

Section 406

It is unlawful to apply any part of the funds collected from subscribers or shareholders to the payment of commissions or fees for obtaining subscriptions or selling shares or to the payment of compensation for services in connection with the organization of a proposed bank or trust company or in connection with securing authority to transact business other than to the payment of fees for legal services and of other usual and ordinary expenses necessary for the organization of a bank or trust company.

EXHIBIT 4
Federal Versus State Charter

A federally chartered bank must operate under the control of the Board of Governors of the Federal Reserve System. Only federally chartered banks can use the word "national" as a part of the bank's name. Every national bank must hold stock in the Federal Reserve System equal to 3 percent of its capital and surplus. This stock yields a 6 percent cummulative dividend. Reserve requirements must be held in the form of either vault cash or deposits at the local Federal Reserve Bank. Such deposits yield no return. The privileges of membership in the Federal Reserve System include the free use of check-clearing facilities and the use of the "discount window."

A state charter permits a bank to count correspondent balances as a part of its reserve requirements. Since most small banks need correspondent balances anyway, the small state bank has an economic advantage over a small national bank because it can generally obtain services from correspondents in return for deposits. The most common correspondent services include the clearing of checks and investment advice. This particular advantage to the state bank lessens as the bank grows in size. Eventually, the value of the Federal Reserve's clearing facilities may outweigh the disadvantages of having nonearning funds tied up as reserves.

Under a state charter, a bank is permitted to lend on unimproved real estate. National banks are not permitted

EXHIBIT 4 (continued)

to do so. A state-chartered bank can make loans to a single customer up to a level equal to 20 percent of capital and surplus, whereas the limit for a national bank is 10 percent.

All national banks are automatically members of the Federal Deposit Insurance Corporation (FDIC). State chartered banks must elect membership and be approved by the FDIC.

As a general rule, a federal charter is somewhat easier to obtain. The banking authorities in the State of California have a reputation of being among the strictest in the nation.

EXHIBIT 5
Preliminary Economic Survey of Palo Alto Area

Facts reported below reflect both the primary and the secondary area of possible service to the proposed new bank. A primary service area is the one providing the bulk of the deposits. It normally includes the surrounding community, or the area within 2 to 3 miles in the case of a large city. The secondary area includes outlying area that can be expected to provide additional deposits or loans.

The primary service area has a population of 360,000; the secondary service area has a population of 250,000 people. In the primary service area, one banking facility exists for each 7,345 people, and the secondary area has one banking facility per 7,650 people. For the state as a whole, there is one banking facility for every 6,432 persons.

With the merger of the Stanford Bank, there are no independent banks left in the proposed primary area of service for Peninsula Cities Bank. For the state as a whole, 84 percent of all banks having 14 percent of all banking offices represent independent banks. Independent banks account for 6.5 percent of total deposits in the state. In the two neighboring counties, independent banks have approximately 8 percent of bank offices and 2.5 percent of deposits.

The last independent bank in the area, the Stanford Bank, had increased deposits from $10.4 million in 1965 to $21.3 million in 1970. Its net operating income had risen during that period from $127,000 to $579,000 while capital was rising from $2.3 million to $3 million.

The basic economy of the area is influenced by the presence of Stanford University. The surrounding area houses a heavy concentration of high technology industry, and this industry is expected to expand. One of the adjacent counties expects employment in the area to double by 1980. While this would not mean a greatly increased population in the primary service area of the bank, it would indicate that higher retail

Banking Structure of Commercial Banks within Santa Clara and San Mateo Counties Compared with the State of California, June 30, 1966–1970

	Percent of total	
	1966	1970
Number of Banks		
California	100.00	100.00
Independent banks	87.96	84.25
Chain-system and foreign banks	12.04	15.75
Santa Clara County	100.00	100.00
Independent banks	25.00	17.64
Chain-system and foreign banks	75.00	82.35
San Mateo County	100.00	100.00
Independent banks	30.77	20.00
Chain-system and foreign banks	69.23	80.00
Number of Offices		
California	100.00	100.00
Independent banks	13.75	14.00
Chain-system and foreign banks	86.25	86.00
Santa Clara County	100.00	100.00
Independent banks	7.47	1.94
Chain-system and foreign banks	92.53	98.06
San Mateo County	100.00	100.00
Independent banks	8.22	6.81
Chain-system and foreign banks	91.78	93.19
Amount of Deposits		
California	100.00	100.00
Independent banks	6.58	6.55
Chain-system and foreign banks	93.42	93.45
Santa Clara County	100.00	100.00
Independent banks	4.03	2.52
Chain-system and foreign banks	95.97	97.48

sales and a further strengthening of the entire local economy could be expected.

The demographic characteristics of the population indicate a banking market of high quality. The average annual income is exceptionally high compared with national standards. The total deposit potential for all commercial banks within the primary service area has been estimated at $640,000,000. In addition, the secondary market is estimated at $450,000,000.

If the new bank can capture 2.0 percent of the primary market (a target well within reason), this would lead to a deposit level of approximately $13 million. This estimate ignores any potential deposits from the secondary market.

EXHIBIT 6
Estimates of Deposit, Loan Volume, and Profits

End of:	1st year	2nd year	3rd year
Deposits:			
Demand	$4,200,000	$ 5,500,000	$ 6,500,000
Time	2,600,000	4,200,000	6,100,000
Public	200,000	300,000	400,000
Total	$7,000,000	$10,000,000	$13,000,000
Loans:			
Commercial	$1,680,000	$ 2,600,000	$ 3,640,000
Installment	2,100,000	3,250,000	4,550,000
Real estate	420,000	650,000	910,000
Total	$4,200,000	$ 6,500,000	$ 9,100,000
Revenue	$ 260,000	$ 670,000	$ 960,000
Expenses	345,000	555,000	710,000
Income before taxes	$ (85,000)	$ 115,000	$ 250,000
Taxes	0	2,000	110,000
Income (loss) after taxes	$ (85,000)	$ 113,000	$ 140,000

EXHIBIT 7
Personal Information About Members of the Organizing Group

MR. BARTON HUGO, president of a large European auto dealership. Mr. Hugo was also active in real estate development activities, had served as an international trade consultant and research executive, and was chairman of the board of a small holding company.

MR. DUANE HERMAN had a master's degree in electrical engineering from Stanford University, and was founder and president of a young, but highly successful electronic instrumentation company.

MR. FRED THORNE served as president and chairman of the board of a local company that designed and marketed highly advanced electronic calculators.

MR. MAXWELL WEYFIELD was extensively engaged in real estate development in the area and had served as the president of the county chamber of commerce.

DR. NATHAN ROYCE was one of the original founders of one of the area's largest and most successful semiconductor companies. He had since left the company to become president of another high-technology company.

MR. ROSS FRANKLIN had been active in the grocery and supermarket business since 1950 and currently was president of several corporations owning supermarkets in the area.

MR. SETH THOMPSON was a practicing attorney and founding partner of a prominent local law firm.

EXHIBIT 7 (continued)

MR. THEODORE CREIGHTON was employed by a large National Life Insurance Company in addition to serving as vice-president of an insurance benefit sales force company.

MR. WARREN JACKSON was president of a large construction company and was active in several real estate investment enterprises.

MRS. WENDY BERGAN had served as a financial accountant and supervisor for several major companies and presently maintains her own financial consulting service.

CASE 2
Imperial National Bank

Mr. Geoffrey Mellors, recently appointed president of Imperial National Bank of Alpine, Texas, decided in 1978 to invite an experienced independent consultant to review the overall organization and strategic policies of his bank. This comprehensive review was prompted by the concern expressed by two members of the board of directors at the new directions taken by the bank during the past year. The sudden accidental death of the late chairman of the board and president had caused the Imperial National to require an immediate change of leadership. That new leadership, in the person of Geoffrey Mellors, had also rather quickly brought substantial change in the bank's approach to business development and its traditional pattern of operations. Accordingly, at a recent board meeting two of the older and experienced board members politely but firmly suggested it might prove advisable for an independent consultant to evaluate the bank's total situation so that the board and the new president could jointly consider the new activities undertaken by the bank, as well as its problems and opportunities, based on an objective assessment.

Mellors agreed, although somewhat reluctantly, that such a review would be advisable, and he promised to make appropriate arrangements for consulting assistance. The material that follows summarizes the preliminary information gathered by a consultant, selected by Mellors, regarding the organization, liquidity, investments, loan activities, and personnel of Imperial National Bank of Alpine. The consultant

intended, after an initial survey of the situation and a study of these basic bank data, to determine which areas of management appeared to merit further detailed study and in which directions his appraisal of the bank should be carried. It was agreed by all concerned that the consultant would render a report to the board at a meeting in the near future.

The Imperial National Bank was founded in 1951, in the city of Alpine, Buck's County, Texas. It was organized by its former chairman who was the bank's dominant figure until his accidental death about two years earlier.

Imperial National Bank was located about 20 miles from Brownwood, a city of nearly 600,000 people. Alpine itself had a population totaling some 70,000, and Buck's County comprised of total population of nearly 800,000. Alpine's population had grown from less than 20,000 people 20 years ago. The county population had doubled in the same period. The city of Brownwood was a leading financial and distributing center with extensive commercial and financial operations which made the city a dominant economic factor for the entire area.

There were five commercial banks in Alpine with total deposits on December 31, 1977, of about $240 million. Three of these banks had been operating for between 20 and 40 years. The other two had been organized less than 10 years, one having been incorporated as recently as 4 years earlier. The largest bank in Alpine had deposits of about $112 million, the second largest had deposits of about $60 million, and the third largest was the Imperial National Bank with deposits at year-end 1977 of $46 million. The deposits of the remaining two banks totaled approximately $12 million each.

Alpine's largest bank had a stable, experienced management. Its common stock was widely held among local business and professional people. The second largest bank was managed by two brothers, one serving as president who was 62 years old, and the other as executive vice-president who was 59 years old. Between the two brothers and their immediate families, they owned 45.5 percent of the bank's stock. The remainder was broadly distributed among local residents. The largest single stockholder, other than the two executive officers, was an attorney in nearby Brownwood, who owned about 11 percent of the bank's stock. The two principal officers founded the bank and had been the dominant figures in management since its organization.

Imperial National Bank's stock was held by about 125 stockholders, with one, who was a director but not an officer, owning 25 percent of the outstanding stock. Cash dividends ranging between 10 and 15 percent of par value had been paid in recent years, as well as several stock dividends. Imperial's board of directors was composed of 15 members, all of whom had business interests in Alpine, although two lived in Brownwood. The board members were chosen more for their business ability than for their participation in community affairs. They included persons representing broadly diversified business activities, and several directors were quite wealthy. Their investments in Imperial National Bank were not, in any case, an important part of their financial holdings. The president and executive vice-president were the only two bank officers on the board. About two thirds of the directors were from 55 to 65 years old.

Imperial National was located in a three-story building which was about 20 years old and a part of which was rented as office space. The structure had been partly remodeled about 6 years ago and 3 drive-in windows were added. The bank's equipment was fairly efficient, but no effort had been made to acquire the most modern equipment.

Twenty years ago an important part of the bank's business was agricultural, but by 1977 only a modest part of the bank's volume involved agriculture. In fact, Alpine's growth had resulted primarily because its business was fairly well distributed between personal, retail, and commercial banking business. Local building and construction activity had also produced a considerable volume of construction loans on which the bank's past record had proven good.

Recently, Imperial National Bank had not found it necessary to buy Federal Funds or to borrow to any great extent. In the past, however, some borrowing had been necessary on a few occasions. Imperial National had been a net seller of Federal funds to a rather modest degree during the past few months. Imperial National did have an arrangement with City National Bank, their principal correspondent, to borrow Federal Funds up to $900,000, if needed. In this connection, City National Bank stipulated as a condition of this line, that total borrowings and Federal Fund purchases from all sources would not at any time exceed $900,000.

BANK OFFICERS AND ORGANIZATION

Late in August 1976, the Chairman of the Board and his son, who was president of the bank, were killed in an automobile accident. Shortly thereafter a new president and chief executive officer, Geoffrey Mellors, was elected by the board.

Mr. Mellors lived in Alpine and had served on the bank's board for several years. He owned about 5 percent of the bank's stock, which he inherited from his father. Mellors was a 40-year-old lawyer, having obtained a law degree at Southern Methodist University. He did not practice law, however, but rather occupied himself with looking after his personal wealth, which was substantial, and that of his wife who inherited a large amount of local urban property.

During the last 10 years Mellors had also been heavily engaged in real estate development and construction. Part of this activity involved the improvement of property which had long remained in his family. Mellors' construction experience largely centered on the commercial field. In 1978 he was still engaged in one local development project which had started three years previously and on which sales had moved slowly. This project was financed by Imperial's principal correspondent in Brownwood. Four warehouse buildings, which were completed from 9 to 24 months earlier, also remained unsold and were still being financed by City National. They were originally undertaken on a speculative basis, without commitments for permanent financing. In the aggregate these development and construction projects involved total financing of about $3 million and, although they had not sold as anticipated, Mellors was not unduly concerned.

Mellors had long believed that frequent use of substantial credit constituted "one of the best ways to make money." He felt that Imperial National Bank had not been as aggressive as it should have been in its loan policies and that over the years the bank had not taken advantage of many opportunities for business that would have proven quite profitable. Although he had mentioned this from time to time in the past as a board member, Mellors never pressed the matter with the bank's former management. He had made it clear to certain people, however, that he would be available to serve as the bank's chief executive should the necessity arise. Moreover, Mellors had increased his stock ownership by purchasing the holdings of the two former chief executives. He financed these stock purchases through a loan with the same correspondent who was handling his real estate financing.

Since he became president of Imperial National Bank, Mellors had devoted some of his time to reconsidering several loan proposals declined by prior management. A number of these transactions were subsequently approved, several from geographic regions outside the bank's normal service area. Some of these transactions were such that opportunities developed for participation on an equity basis. Mellors took advantage of some of these situations and made personal investments of some $100,000 representing an equity position. Mellors felt that his more aggressive approach to bank management would materially increase Imperial's profit performance.

Mellors participated actively in local civic matters; he was a very personable man who made friends readily, and over the years his many activities had caused him to be widely known. Following is a summary of the other members of management.

The executive vice-president, George Parrott, was 35 years of age. He had grown up in Alpine, was single, was graduated from the local high school, and had attended college for a year and a half. At that time he joined the bank, and during these years he had gained experience in most phases of bank operations except commercial loan and investment activities. During the past five years Parrott had served primarily in the bank's consumer loan division. He had always been alert and watchful in seeking ways to increase the bank's profitability.

Parrott had also exhibited a desire for further personal development and he had proven a hard worker. He enrolled in all American Institute of Banking courses locally available, and he also studied accounting at a junior college in nearby Brownwood. In the past he had exhibited great enthusiasm about his work, although since the death of the former chairman, he seemed somewhat less confident of his future and perhaps slightly less vigorous in his approach to his daily responsibilities.

Stephen Beard, vice-president, was 38 years old, married, and had two children. He had earned a B.A. degree from the University of New Mexico, majoring in social sciences.

Beard was a relative newcomer to Imperial National Bank, having held his present position since December 1976, at which time he was recommended to the board by Mellors. Previously, Beard had been employed for 13 years in various capacities by City National, Imperial National's principal correspondent in Brownwood. Beard had worked in various divisions at City National Bank including the credit department, but for the last 8 years he had served in the correspondent bank division, and one of his duties was to act as City National's contact officer for Imperial National Bank.

Steve Beard became acquainted with Mellors through the numerous loan participations City National Bank had made at the request of Imperial National. Over the years, Beard's loan experience had centered on handling loans and loan participations sent to City National by various correspondent banks in his area of responsibility. These loan participations had been of a widely varying nature; moreover, these lending activities by officers of City National Bank's correspondent division were rather closely supervised.

From the time Beard joined Imperial National Bank, he had worked closely with Mellors, particularly in handling the more important personal loans, many commercial loans, and numerous interim real estate construction transactions. Beard also worked closely with the new president in implementing his aggressive loan policy, even though he was not an entirely enthusiastic supporter of this new approach to business development. Beard felt he would probably be more conservative in his lending activities if left entirely to his own inclinations. Because he was not that thoroughly versed in credit fundamentals, however, he had "gone along" with Mellors' basically more aggressive strategies.

In addition to his duties relating to loans, Beard was given the responsibility of handling the bank's investment portfolio. To assist him in this activity he sought the continuing advice and guidance of Imperial National Bank's principal correspondent, which was well staffed with experienced investment management personnel. Thus far, at least, Steve Beard had been satisfied with this arrangement, feeling that he was steadily increasing his own knowledge in this important management area. He believed that with the large correspondent bank's assistance he would soon have sufficient knowledge to become more self-reliant in investment matters.

The bank employed two assistant vice-presidents, one of whom aided the executive vice-president in the consumer credit division while the other worked with the new vice-president, Steve Beard, in handling smaller personal and commercial loans. Each of these men was about 31 years old, neither of them had a college degree

although one had attended a nearby junior college for two years. They were both diligent, reliable employees who had worked in several departments of the bank. Neither had shown a great deal of initiative. Each required considerable guidance and leadership in his work.

The cashier of Imperial National, Henry Murar, has been employed since he was graduated from high school. He was 35 years of age, was married, and had one child. He was tall, quiet, and dignified. Usually dressed in conservative dark blue, he moved about briskly, yet smoothly, his manner suggesting a man who approached his work seriously and with a strong sense of responsibility. Though pleasant, he was by no means as approachable as the executive vice-president, George Parrott. One might doubt whether Murar would ever be elected, say, as president of the chamber of commerce, a position currently held by George Parrott. Watching him at work, depositors probably felt that this serious-minded young man was the personification of prudence. Although Murar had worked in numerous departments in the bank, for the past five years he had been in charge of paying and receiving tellers and the bookkeeping, proof, and transit departments.

There was an assistant cashier who assisted Murar in the teller's responsibilities and who served as head teller. Finally, another assistant cashier had charge of bookkeeping, proof, and transit activities. He was, however, quite young and needed close supervision from Murar.

Historically, Imperial National Bank had experienced few personnel problems. The bank's salary schedules were about average for comparable banks. Some problems had developed during the last few years, however, because of accessibility to higher paying jobs in nearby Brownwood, in part because of the increased ease of commuting between Alpine and Brownwood.

Imperial National had no formal training program although there had been modest encouragement for employees to study A.I.B. courses offered in Brownwood. Imperial National Bank made relatively little use of committees. The only really active committee was the loan committee, composed of three board members who were not officers, plus the president, executive vice-president, and vice-president. The committee met weekly and reviewed all loans above $1,000. It was charged with responsibility for decisions on all major loans or lines of credit, although there had not been a clear definition of these latter two terms since Mellors had assumed office.

In addition to holding the titles of assistant cashier and head teller, one of the assistant cashiers also performed some audit functions. The general ledger was maintained by an employee who had been with the bank for more than 20 years. The note and credit department was di-rected by an assistant cashier who had two employees to assist him. He, in turn, reported to the vice-president, Steven Beard. The bank had 47 employees, 9 of whom were officers.

The following exhibits include some of the initial study material gathered by the consultant as he began his review of Imperial National Bank. It was the consultant's intention to begin his analysis with these data and from them to gather ideas as to how this study should proceed. His "mandate" from Mellors was a broad one—simply that the consultant should examine the bank's policies and operations and comment on any problem areas revealed by his analysis with specific suggestions for improvement.

EXHIBIT 1

Imperial National Bank of Alpine—Population and Bank Data on Alpine

Year	Population	No. banks
1955	20,800	2
1960	36,800	3
1965	48,400	3
1970	58,600	4
Mid-1977	69,000	5

Total Bank Deposits—Imperial (in thousands of dollars)

	1973	1974	1975	1976	1977
Bank A	$ 79,856	$ 91,818	$ 94,420	$105,874	$111,684
Imperial National Bank	31,774	32,842	38,484	42,318	45,876
Bank B	47,710	50,442	67,216	56,332	59,746
Bank C	3,208	4,246	6,050	9,170	12,014
Bank D	3,016	4,466	7,912	9,874	12,298
Total deposits	$165,564	$183,814	$214,052	$223,568	$241,620

EXHIBIT 2

Imperial National Bank of Alpine (dollar figures in thousands)

	1975	1976		1977	
	12/31	6/30	12/31	6/30	12/31
Assets					
Cash and balances	$ 5,148	$ 4,908	$ 5,602	$ 6,190	$ 5,736
U.S. Treasury securities	2,234	2,900	3,764	2,646	2,310
Securities of U.S. government agencies	3,556	3,174	3,374	3,956	4,068
Obligations of state and political subdivisions	6,878	7,186	7,430	8,398	7,792
Other securities	314	50	56	56	56

EXHIBIT 2 (continued)

	1975	1976		1977	
	12/31	6/30	12/31	6/30	12/31
Trading account securities	0	0	0	0	0
Loans and discounts—grossa	22,752	24,636	25,182	26,932	29,684
Fixed assetsb	650	618	580	590	626
Investment in subsidiaries not consolidated	0	0	0	0	0
Customer liability to this bank acceptances outstanding	0	0	0	0	0
Other assets	86	236	218	310	334
Total assets	$41,618	$43,698	$46,206	$49,078	$50,606
Liabilities					
Demand deposits	$13,382	$14,180	$14,958	$15,954	$16,244
Time deposits	19,586	20,706	21,836	22,962	23,754
Deposits of U.S. government	324	280	568	670	478
Deposits of state and political subdivisions	4,528	4,126	4,086	4,238	4,730
Deposits of foreign governments and official institutions	0	0	0	0	0
Deposits of commercial banks	438	382	574	492	406
Certified and officers checks	196	180	296	306	264
Total deposits	$38,454	$39,854	$42,318	$44,622	$45,876
Federal funds purchased and other liabilities for borrowed money	0	0	0	0	0
Mortgage indebtedness	6	6	6	6	6
Acceptances executed and outstanding	0	0	0	0	0
Other liabilities	430	660	608	686	814
Total liabilities	$38,890	$40,520	$42,932	$45,314	$46,696
Reserves on Loans and Securities					
Reserves for bad debt loss on loans	82	68	174	170	254
Other reserves on loans	0	0	0	0	0
Reserves on securities	0	0	0	0	0
Total reserves on loans and securities	$ 82	$ 68	$ 174	$ 170	$ 254
Capital Accounts					
Capital	570	659	650	658	658
Surplusc	856	1,064	1,233	1,238	1,504
Undivided profitsc	1,184	1,396	1,210	1,698	1,446
Reserves	36	0	7	0	48
Total capital accounts	$ 2,646	$ 3,110	$ 3,100	$ 3,594	$ 3,656
Total liabilities, reserves, and capital accounts	$41,618	$43,698	$46,206	$49,078	$50,606

aIncludes Federal Funds sold.

bIncludes bank premises owned, real estate owned other than bank premises, and investments and other assets indirectly representing bank premises or other real estate.

cStock dividends declared in 1976 and 1977. Changes among capital accounts are not material in this case.

EXHIBIT 3

Imperial National Bank of Alpine (dollar figures in thousands)

	12/31/75	12/31/76	12/31/77
Operating Income:			
Income from loans (including income from sale of federal funds)	$2,070	$2,458	$3,139
Interest and dividends on investment (excluding trading account income)	592	692	896
Trust department income	0	0	0
Miscellaneous income	198	234	241
Total operating income	$2,860	$3,384	$4,276
Operating Expense:			
Employee compensation and benefits	562	694	775
Interest on deposits	1,368	1,382	1,703
Expense of federal funds purchased and securities sold under agreements to repurchase	20	10	0
Net operating expense of bank premises plus furniture, equipment depreciation, and rent	101	103	124
Provision for loan loss (or actual net loan loss)	108	127	205
Other operating expenses	312	544	677
Total operating expenses	$2,471	$2,860	$3,484
Income before income taxes and security, gains, or losses	389	524	792
Applicable income taxes	41	66	142
Income after taxes and before security gains or losses	348	458	650
Net security gains or losses	6	10	16
Net income before extraordinary items	354	468	666
Extraordinary charges or credits	0	0	0
Net income	354	468	666
Cash dividend declared on common stock	58	100	74

EXHIBIT 4

Imperial National Bank of Alpine (dollar figures in thousands)

	12/31/75	12/31/76	12/31/77
Schedule A—Loans and Discounts			
Real estate loans	$ 6,136	$ 7,566	$ 9,338
Loans to financial institutions[a]	1,111	914	1,357
Loans for purchasing or carrying securities	68	73	137
Loans to farmers	1,915	2,008	2,344
Commercial and industrial loans	5,768	6,487	7,685
Loans to individuals	7,486	7,847	8,450
All other loans	268	287	373
Total loans, gross	$22,752	$25,182	$29,684

[a]Includes Federal Funds sold of $200, 0, and $250, respectively.

EXHIBIT 5

Imperial National Bank of Alpine

Amount (dollars in thousands)	*Name*	*Coupon*	*Maturity*	*Book value*	*Market value (12/31/77)*	*Difference*
			List of U.S. Treasury Securities Owned[a]			
$ 400	4⅛ Treasury Bond		4/15/78	Par	99.00	$− 4,000
200	6¾ Treasury Bond		2/15/93	98.00	87.00	− 22,000
900	4% Treasury Bond		2/15/80	Par	85.50	−130,500
200	3¼ Treasury Bond		6/15/83	75.20	85.20	+ 20,000
800	3½ Treasury Bond		2/15/90	83.00	79.50	− 28,000
$2,500	(Total book value, $2,310)					$−164,500
			U.S. Agencies[a]			
$ 800	5.79 Debenture FNMA		7/10/78	Par	98.75	$− 10,000
800	6.20 Federal Land Bank		4/20/81	Par	95.90	− 32,000
1,268	7¼ Federal Land Bank		7/20/87	Par	89.00	−139,480
1,200	6¼ Debenture FNMA		6/11/84	Par	91.90	− 97,200
$4,068	(Total book value, $4,068)					$−279,480
			Obligations of States and Political Subdivisions[a]			
$2,432	Dallas G.O.	3	9/1/82	100.00	93.00	$−170,240
1,500	Terrebonne Parish	4	6/10/91	94.00	83.60	−156,000
500	Irving, Texas, G.O.	3.80	12/1/85	100.00	90.00	− 50,000
700	Baytown, Texas, G.O.	4.10	5/1/89	100.00	88.40	− 81,200
950	Port of Seattle	6	10/1/78	100.00	101.00	+ 9,500
350	State of Texas	3¼	3/1/83	100.00	93.00	− 24,500
700	Texarkana G.O.	3⅝	7/1/87	100.00	87.20	89,600
750	Albany Co., N.Y.	3¾	5/1/81	100.00	98.00	− 15,000
$7,882	(Book value, $7,792)					$−577,040

[a]Prices are shown in decimals. Market value and difference figures (+ is gain and − is loss) are as of 12/31/77.

EXHIBIT 6
Imperial National Bank of Alpine—Operating Ratios

	Your bank	
	1977	*1976*
Profitability		
Percentage of Equity Capital Including All Reserves:		
1. Income after taxes and before securities gains or losses	17.8	14.8
2. Net income	18.2	15.1
Percentage of Net Income:		
3. Cash dividends paid	11.1	21.4
Sources and Disposition of Income		
Percentage of Total Assets:		
4. Total operating income	8.4	7.3
5. Salaries, wages, and fringe benefits	1.2	1.3
6. Interest on deposits	4.1	3.6
7. Interest on borrowed money	0.0	0.1
8. Net occupancy expense of bank premises	0.7	0.7
9. All other operating expenses	0.6	0.4
10. Total operating expense	6.9	6.2
11. Income after taxes and before securities gains or losses	1.3	1.0
12. Net income	1.3	1.0
Percentage of Total Operating Income:		
13. Interest on U.S. Treasury securities	4.1	6.0
14. Interest on securities of U.S. government agencies and corporations	7.0	5.3
15. Interest on obligations of states and political subdivisions	9.8	9.0
16. Interest and dividends on all other securities	0.1	0.1
17. Interest and fees on loans	72.2	70.5
18. Interest on Federal Funds sold and repos	1.2	2.1
19. All other operating income	5.6	6.9
20. Total operating income	100.0	100.0
21. Trust department income (included in all other operating income)	0.0	0.0
22. Salaries and employee benefits	18.1	20.5
23. Interest on deposits	39.8	40.8
24. Interest on borrowed money	0.0	0.0
25. Interest on subordinated debt and debentures	0.0	0.0
26. Net occupancy expense of bank premises	2.9	3.0
27. Provision for loan losses	4.8	3.8
28. All other operating expenses	15.8	16.1
29. Total operating expense	81.5	84.5
30. Income before taxes and securities gains or losses	18.5	15.5
31. Income after income taxes and before securities gains or losses	15.2	13.5

EXHIBIT 6 (continued)

	Your bank	
	1977	*1976*
32. Net securities gains (+) or losses (−), after tax effect	0.3	0.3
33. Net income	15.5	13.8

Rates of Return on Securities and Loans

Return on Securities:

34. Interest on U.S. Treasury securities	6.0	6.4
35. Interest on securities of U.S. government agencies and corporations	6.9	6.3
36. Interest on obligations of states and political subdivisions	5.1	5.0
37. Interest and dividends on all other securities	2.9	2.9

Return on Loans:

38. Interest and fees on loans	10.6	9.7
39. Net losses (−) or recoveries (+) on loans	−0.4	−0.4

Distribution of Total Assets

Percentage of Total Assets (average balances):

40. Cash assets	12.0	11.9
41. U.S. Treasury securities	5.9	6.8
42. Securities of other U.S. government agencies and corporations	7.9	7.6
43. Obligations of states and political subdivisions	16.2	16.3
44. All other securities	0.1	0.3
45. Loans	56.1	55.2
46. Real estate	1.2	1.4
47. All other assets	0.6	0.4

Distribution of Loans

Percentage of Gross Loans (year end):

48. Real estate loans	31.5	30.0
49. Loans to farmers	7.9	8.0
50. Commercial and industrial loans	25.9	25.8
51. Consumer loans to individuals	28.5	31.2
52. Federal funds sold with agreements to repurchase	0.8	0.0
53. All other loans	5.4	5.1

Other Ratios

54. Total capital accounts and reserves to total assets	7.2	6.7
55. Time and savings deposits to total deposits	57.9	58.0
56. Interest on time and savings deposits to total time deposits	5.9	5.7
57. Interest on large CDs	n.a.	n.a.
58. Income taxes to net income plus income taxes	17.9	12.6
59. Interest and fees on loans to other loans	10.5	9.6

EXHIBIT 7
Imperial National Bank of Alpine—Operating Ratios

	Peer banks[a]	
	1977	*1976*

Profitability

Percentage of Equity Capital Including All Reserves:

1. Income after taxes and before securities gains or losses:	14.06	13.21
2. Net Income	14.51	13.66

Percentage of Net Income:

3. Cash dividends paid	26.13	27.08

Sources and Disposition of Income

Percentage of Total Assets:

4. Total Operating Income	7.67	7.54
5. Salaries, wages, and fringe benefits	1.45	1.44
6. Interest on deposits	3.10	3.05
7. Interest on borrowed money	.04	.05
8. Net occupancy expense of bank premises	.28	.29
9. All other operating expenses	1.47	1.57
10. Total Operating Expense	6.34	6.40
11. Income after taxes and before securities gains or losses	1.09	.99
12. Net income	1.12	1.04

Percentage of Total Operating Income:

13. Interest on U.S. Treasury securities	7.67	7.30
14. Interest on securities of U.S. Government agencies and corporations	5.04	4.97
15. Interest on obligations of states and political subdivisions	9.45	10.70
16. Interest and dividends on all other securities	.40	.43
17. Interest and fees on loans	63.97	62.86
18. Interest on Fed funds sold and repos	3.79	3.49
19. All other operating income	9.68	10.25
20. Total Operating Income	100.00	100.00
21. Trust department income (included in Item 19)	.61	.67
22. Salaries and employee benefits	18.89	19.03
23. Interest on deposits	40.68	40.78
24. Interest on borrowed money	.37	.48
25. Interest on subordinated debt and debentures	.21	.21
26. Net occupancy expense of bank premises	3.74	3.49
27. Provision for loan losses	3.46	4.51
28. All other operating expenses	15.63	15.98
29. Total Operating Expense	82.98	84.92
30. Income before taxes and securities gains or losses	17.02	15.08
31. Income after income taxes and before securities gains or losses	14.32	12.78
32. Net securities gains (+) or losses (−), after tax effect	.38	.60
33. Net income	14.72	13.45

EXHIBIT 7 (continued)

	Peer banks[a]	
	1977	1976

Rates of Return on Securities and Loans

Return on Securities:

34. Interest on U.S. Treasury securities	6.85	6.86
35. Interest on securities of U.S. Government agencies and corporations	7.28	7.53
36. Interest on obligations of states and political subdivisions	4.92	5.04
37. Interest and dividends on all other securities	6.07	6.51

Return on Loans:

38. Interest and fees on loans	9.68	9.62
39. Net losses (−) or recoveries (+) on loans	−.38	−.60

Distribution of Total Assets

Percentage of Total Assets (average balances):

40. Cash Assets	11.72	12.49
41. U.S. Treasury securities	8.67	8.15
42. Securities of other U.S. Government agencies and corporations	5.24	5.05
43. Obligations of states and political subdivisions	14.60	16.12
44. All other securities	.48	.46
45. Loans	53.36	53.67
46. Real estate	2.27	2.30
47. All other assets	1.66	1.76

Distribution of Loans

Percentage of Gross Loans (year end):

48. Real estate loans	21.14	19.87
49. Loans to farmers	8.60	8.20
50. Commercial and industrial loans	26.52	28.50
51. Consumer loans to individuals	31.87	30.79
52. Fed funds sold with agreements to repurchase	8.08	8.44
53. All other loans	3.79	4.26

Other Ratios

54. Total capital accounts and reserves to total assets	7.99	8.01
55. Time and savings deposits to total deposits	59.41	58.12
56. Interest on time and savings deposits to total time deposits	5.76	5.81
57. Interest on large CDs	6.42	6.35
58. Income taxes to net income plus income taxes	14.74	14.30
59. Interest and fees on loans to other loans	9.60	9.60

[a]Commercial banks in Eleventh Federal Reserve District with total deposits from $25,000,000 to $50,000,000.

CASE 3
Suburban National Bank*

Suburban National Bank was chartered and opened for business on October 1, 1963. By year-end 1975, it had total deposits of $31.3 million. The bank was located in a large shopping center with a wide variety of small retail and service establishments, typical of most modern shopping centers. The center included a major food retailer and an important nationally known department store among its tenants. The suburban community from which the bank drew most business had a population of about 25,000 in 1970 and nearly 30,000 by 1975.

The suburb was part of a large metropolitan area which contained approximately 1.7 million people in 1975. Since Suburban National was in a state that prohibited branch banking, there were some 90 individually chartered banks in the metropolitan area. State law permitted multibank holding companies, and therefore about 40 percent of the banks in the standard metropolitan statistical area (SMSA) belonged to a holding company. Holding company banks controlled some 70 percent of total SMSA deposits.

Both the state's economy and this metropolitan area were well diversified and had been growing rapidly in recent years. Manufacturing, trade, services, and the government sector accounted for the largest employment categories. Agriculture and tourism were also important state economic activities.

Suburban National Bank's service area was composed primarily of working-class families whose median family income was above the national average. The median level income of the metropolitan area was also substantially above that for the state as a whole.

In addition to the shopping center businesses in Suburban's immediate market area, there were "strip developments" with many small retail and service shops scattered throughout the district.

* This material has been adapted from a case written by Professor Jerome Darnell, University of Colorado (Boulder).

The shopping center was located on a major thoroughfare running through the length of the suburb. An interstate highway was only a few blocks away. There were no major employers (other than the shopping center) in the area. Several major companies, however, were concentrated within 5 to 10 minutes' driving time from Suburban's office.

COMPETITION

Even though it was the "oldest" bank in the immediate vicinity, a number of new banks had been chartered recently in Suburban's service area. These new banks were providing significant new competition. In particular, four commercial banks organized within the past five years were operating in the suburb's corporate limits. All of these banks were within 2 to 3 miles and 5 to 7 minutes' driving time from Suburban's office. These four banks ranged in size from $35 million (slightly larger than Suburban National Bank) down to $9 million in deposits for a new bank that had opened only two years ago. A charter for a fifth bank had been submitted to the Comptroller of the Currency's office and conceivably would be open in the next 12 months at a location very near Suburban. Three of the four currently competing banks each were members of multibank holding companies "anchored" by a large downtown bank. The fourth competitor was independent but had close director ties with another holding company. Suburban National Bank was, therefore, the only one of the five that was truly independent. In addition to competition furnished by commercial banks, three downtown savings and loan associations had branch offices in Suburban National's general vicinity.

The five banks in the suburb offered quite similar services and rates to their customers. They all maintained comparable hours of operation and none were open on Saturday. Four of the five provided bank-by-mail and telephone-transfer services. None of them had absolutely "free" checking accounts and all required some minimum deposit level to avoid monthly service charges. Only the newest of the five banks had a 24-hour automated teller machine.

All of the banks offered the usual variety of savings and time deposits, checking accounts, and other bank services. All paid the maximum rates on time deposits allowed under Regulation Q. Loan rates were probably about the same, although it was impossible to evaluate in a comparable way loan requests from such a wide variety of business, consumer, and real estate loans.

While the competitive climate had thus been strikingly stable in recent years, it was becoming increasingly clear that changes in the status quo would soon occur. The management of Suburban National Bank had recently learned that the largest bank in the area (a member of a multibank holding company) was planning a series of changes that could have a substantial competitive impact. It was rumored that this bank would soon open drive-up windows on Saturday mornings. At the same time it planned to set up a free-standing, 24-hour automated teller machine in the shopping center within 1,000 feet (the legal minimum) of Suburban Bank's location. And perhaps most significant of all—the bank would be offering completely free checking accounts with no minimum balances or other account limitations!

MANAGEMENT AND BOARD OF DIRECTORS

The management and board of directors at Suburban National Bank believed they had been operating a successful organization since the bank began in 1963, although profit performance had begun to slip recently, especially in 1975. The board was composed of 11 members, 5 of whom were original organizers. Three of these five were local business executives, one served as the bank's president, and the fifth was an investor from out of town. The remaining six board members had been added over the years, primarily from prominent persons in the business community.

Mr. David Henry was president of the bank. He owned a sizable amount of the bank's stock although four other shareholders, including the chairman of the board, held larger stock positions. The chairman of the board owned and managed a large General Motors dealership located near the bank.

Henry served first as executive vice-president and then was promoted by the board of directors to president about 10 years ago. He was 48 years old and had been employed previously in an out-of-state bank before becoming one of Suburban National Bank's organizers. Henry's sister-in-law was a senior vice-president at the bank in charge of operations. She also was a member of the board of directors.

Suburban National's employees totaled 68, including 16 officers. In addition to Henry's sister-in-law, three other women were bank officers. The officer and employee staff appeared to have a good blend of youthfulness and experience. The executive vice-president, Gordon Reed, was 36 and was familiar with most phases of bank operations. He was considered by the board as a very capable support to the president. Most board members believed he could fill the presidency if necessary. In fact, Gordon Reed had diplomatically made it known that he hoped to become a bank president before too much time passed. Reed had about concluded that he would have to wait several years before such an opportunity might occur at Suburban National Bank. Some board members had reluctantly concluded that he would soon be moving on, and they might need to find a new executive vice-president.

OPERATING PERFORMANCE OF SUBURBAN NATIONAL BANK

At the first board meeting following year-end 1975, a lively and at times harsh discussion ensued regarding Suburban National Bank's overall performance. Of particular worry to board members was the profitability decline in 1975. Board members were especially concerned that not only were profits down in 1975 but they had been trending downward since 1972. The board chairman noted that as recently as 1972 Suburban National Bank had earned 1.31 percent on average total assets, whereas in 1975 the earnings on average assets had declined to 0.75 percent. Each year between 1972 and 1975 had produced a steadily lower return on assets.

Another board member suggested that return on assets was not of as much concern as the return on his own invested capital. He had concluded that the bank was not doing so poorly when profitability was measured as a return on invested equity capital. He added, however, that he was not pleased with the dividends the bank had been paying and expressed the hope that the board would agree to pay higher dividends.

Henry commented that the bank must maintain a strong capital base, not only to satisfy regulatory authorities, but to be able to grow with the community and to offer better services. Henry observed that the larger the capital base, the larger the loans that Suburban National Bank could approve. And in regard to larger loans, Henry reported that he had found a growing reluctance on the part of its major correspondent bank to participate in overline loans.[1] Although none of these overline participations had ever been flatly turned down, on several occasions the correspondent bank officer had become much more selective about conditions under which overlines would be accepted. Henry wondered if this situation occurred because the correspondent bank also owned another bank in the same service area.

As the board discussion reviewing 1975 continued, the chairman expressed his conviction that Suburban National had been performing effectively in serving the community. As evidence, he pointed to the bank's deposit growth which had more than doubled since 1970. He also noted that Suburban National Bank had grown at a faster rate than almost any other bank in the region. Why was it, he asked, that a bank growing faster than most other banks should be lagging in profitability?

After further discussion, somewhat disorganized at times, it was agreed that the board needed better and more specific guidelines to monitor and evaluate performance. What should be the earmarks of a high-performance bank as opposed to a mediocre one? What should be examined in order to assess fairly a bank's performance? Henry promised to develop both general and quantitative guidelines to the board to sharpen the focus of these discussions.

Somewhat reluctantly, Henry agreed that Suburban National Bank did not have very clearly defined profit objectives from the board and the stockholders' point of view. Henry observed that, before the bank could be evaluated, the directors should agree among themselves on qualitative and quantitative goals that seemed appropriate. When asked what he had in mind, Henry replied that examples were return on equity capital, return on assets, growth in deposits, increases in loans, levels of customer service, employee salary levels, and other measures of expense controls.

Speaking of salaries, one of the founding board members observed that a few years earlier the bank had had only 15 employees and the total annual salaries had been less than $150,000. There were now, he noted, 68 employees with a payroll of over $500,000. In this director's mind, the bank had just not grown enough to warrant such an increase in payroll and employees. He wondered how these data would compare with other banks. Were other institutions controlling personnel costs better than Suburban National Bank, he asked pointedly!

Henry was also questioned about Suburban National Bank's lending policies and particularly whether, in his view, they were more conservative than the bank's competitors. One director reported that a few customers had indicated they had "shopped" loan rates and found competing banks offering lower rates. This same director questioned whether Suburban's loan policy should not be thoroughly reviewed as to loan mix, rate comparisons with other banks, and relative loan-to-deposit ratios. This director expressed the view that Suburban's loan to deposit

[1] Loans in excess of the bank's legal lending limit, as stipulated by law and government regulatory authorities.

ratio was low compared to other banks, which perhaps also explained the inadequate profit results.

Henry agreed that the quantity of Suburban National's loans might not be as high as that of some other banks, but he pointed with pride to the quality of the loan portfolio. He felt that there was very little potential for loss and that several problem loans recently had been repaid. Writeoffs of actual loan losses had, in fact, been moderate. Henry also observed that some banks maintained loan-to-deposit ratios of less than 50 percent, while still earning an attractive 1.4 to 1.5 percent return on assets. Furthermore, said Henry, as recently as 1972 Suburban National Bank had operated with a loan-to-deposit ratio of around 40 percent and yet it still earned 1.3 percent on assets in that year, the most profitable of the past five years.

Henry commented that low profitability was not related as much to a loan-to-deposit ratio as to the pricing of loans and the "spread" maintained between the cost of funds and the amount earned on those funds. In that regard, Henry believed that Suburban National's spread management could perhaps be improved.

Henry also added that one of Suburban's problems was that it did not have an organized promotional and marketing effort. He reminded the board that they had been very reluctant to authorize expenditures for advertising and promotion, feeling that much bank advertising was ill-conceived and its beneficial results, if any, were frequently very difficult to measure. Perhaps a concerted effort to promote the bank's services would be money well spent after all, declared Henry; but several directors promptly expressed real misgivings about bank promotional efforts, as they had in the past.

The discussion then shifted to the problems Suburban National Bank would face when and if other banks began opening on Saturday, offering free checking accounts, and utilizing automated teller machines. The savings and loan offices could also be expected to counter with their own competitive response of longer hours and automated tellers.

One director wondered aloud if the bank should explore the possibility of selling to a holding company. Henry commented that he had been cautiously approached recently by a major holding company that did not already own a bank in Suburban's area. Henry had not previously reported that "feeler" to the board since he was not sure it was a really serious inquiry.

There then followed some spirited discussion about whether the timing and circumstances of a possible sale were at all appropriate. The majority sentiment in the discussion was against any idea of a sale at this time, but several board members observed that "things just can't go on as they are" without running a serious risk of getting the bank into a position in which it was neither very profitable nor very salable!

The longer the meeting continued, the more uncomfortable Henry became. It was evident to him that the steady decline in profitability during the past year or two had aroused the board members much more than he had anticipated. He sensed that perhaps his own position could even be in jeopardy, since some of the comments had become quite pointed and a bit personal during the long and somewhat rambling board discussion. His nervousness was reinforced as he realized that Gordon Reed, the executive vice-president, who was listening to the entire discussion, was viewed by some board members as a well-qualified young banker who could take over as president.

Finally, the chairman of the board concluded that the meeting was becoming unproductive and more facts were needed about the bank's operation and relative performance. Accordingly, he suggested that a special board meeting should be convened in two weeks and that Henry and other members of the bank staff should prepare additional information and data which could be used to make a better assessment of the bank's total situation. Henry assured the board that he would assemble and analyze all the relevant data in order to assist the board. He was quite relieved when the meeting adjourned long after its scheduled time!

EXHIBIT 1
Suburban National Bank—Deposit Growth (dollar figures in thousands) 1970–1975

Year	State	Percent increase	SMSA	Percent increase	Suburban National Bank	Percent increase
1970	$4,330,039	—	$2,797,546	—	$15,574	—
1971	5,027,472	16.1	3,241,678	15.9	17,165	10.2
1972	5,976,933	18.9	3,883,475	19.8	20,729	20.8
1973	6,628,695	10.9	4,228,091	8.9	25,715	24.1
1974	6,988,495	5.4	4,413,765	4.4	25,662	−0.2
1975	7,392,596	5.8	4,587,637	3.9	31,324	22.1
5-year compound growth rate		11.3		10.4		15.0

EXHIBIT 2
Suburban National Bank—Report of Condition, December 31 (dollar figures in thousands)

	1975	1974	1973	1972
Assets				
Cash and due from banks	3,779	3,336	4,464	4,176
U.S. Treasury securities	3,804	4,308	5,489	6,340
Other U.S. government securities	149	359	499	—
States and other obligations	7,739	4,000	3,663	3,151
Other securities	27	27	27	27
Trading account securities	0	0	0	0
Federal funds sold	800	250	150	0
Other loans	17,325	15,624	13,480	8,610
Bank premises	1,282	1,233	1,154	1,172
Real estate other than bank	193	0	0	—
Customers liabilities	0	0	0	—
Other assets	306	367	317	—
Total assets	35,404	29,504	29,243	23,476
Liabilities				
Demand deposits (IPC)	11,265	10,923	11,210	—
Time and savings deposits (IPC)	12,394	9,913	9,294	—
Deposits of U.S. government	302	528	437	—
Deposits of states and others	6,716	3,842	4,208	—
Deposits of foreign governments and institutions	0	0	0	—
Deposits of commercial banks	0	0	0	—
Certified and officers checks	647	456	566	—
Total deposits	31,324	25,662	25,715	20,729
Demand	12,782	13,557	13,949	
Time	18,542	12,105	11,766	
Federal funds purchased	0	0	0	—
Other liabilities	0	0	0	—
Mortgage indebtedness	0	0	0	—

EXHIBIT 2 (continued)

	1975	1974	1973	1972
Acceptances	0	0	0	—
Other liabilities	1,083	1,052	862	360
Total liabilities	32,407	26,714	26,577	21,089
Reserves on Loans and Securities				
Reserve for bad debt losses	18	0	108	76
Other reserves on loans	0	0	0	0
Reserves on securities	0	0	0	0
Total reserves on loans and securities	18	0	108	76
Capital Accounts				
Capital notes and debentures	0	0	0	0
Equity capital	2,979	2,790	2,558	2,311
Preferred stock (par)	0	0	0	0
Common stock (par)	150	150	150	150
Surplus	750	750	750	750
Undivided profits	2,079	1,890	1,658	1,411
Reserves for contingencies and other	0	0	0	0
Total capital accounts	2,979	2,790	2,558	2,311
Total liabilities, reserves and capital accounts	35,404	29,504	29,243	23,476

EXHIBIT 3
Suburban National Bank—Schedule A: Loans and Discounts, December 31 (dollar figures in thousands)

	1975	1974	1973
Real Estate Loans:			
Secured by farm	239	17	20
By 1–4 family FHA	0	0	0
By 1–4 family VA	21	22	34
Conventionally financed	2,998	2,795	805
By 5+ family FHA	0	1,011	0
By 5+ conventionally fin.	0	117	121
By nonfarm nonresidential	2,744	0	2,572
Total real estate loans	6,002	3,962	3,552
Loans to Domestic and Foreign Banks	0	0	300
Loans to Other Financial Institutions	0	67	67
Loans to Buy and Carry Securities:			
To brokers	0	0	0
To others	307	13	19
Loans to Farmers	0	0	4
Commercial and Industrial Loans	2,969	2,307	2,717
Loans to Individuals:			
To buy private autos	5,973	5,496	3,999
Retail credit cards	254	331	233

EXHIBIT 3 (continued)

	1975	1974	1973
Check credit	218	58	0
Mobile homes	209	295	381
Other consumer goods	0	439	808
Installment loans on residence	88	215	237
Other installment loans	210	323	26
Single-payment loans	0	2,037	1,068
Total loans to individuals	6,952	9,194	6,752
All Other Loans	1,095	81	69
Total Loans and Discounts	17,325	15,624	13,480

EXHIBIT 4
Suburban National Bank—Report of Income (dollar figures in thousands)

	1975	1974	1973
Operating Income			
Interest and fees on loans	1,605	1,41	959
Income on federal funds sold	98	86	101
Interest and dividends on U.S. Treasury	300	354	352
Other U.S. government securities	30	21	35
States and political subsidies	284	195	162
Other securities	2	2	2
Trust department income	0	0	0
Service charges on deposit accounts	155	150	151
Other service charges	46	21	24
Other operating income	17	26	79
Total operating income	2,537	2,269	1,865
Operating Expense			
Number of employees	68	65	58
Salaries and wages	552	449	354
Pensions and other benefits	110	51	35
Interest on deposits	894	792	535
Expenses on Federal Funds purchased	2	5	1
Interest on other borrowed money	0	0	0
Interest on capital notes and debentures	0	0	0
Occupancy expenses of bank premises (net)	136	126	111
Furniture and equipment costs	161	134	123
Provision for loan losses	87	45	44
Other operating expense	314	289	232
Total operating expense	2,256	1,891	1,435
Tax and Security Items			
Income before taxes and security gains	281	378	430
Applicable income taxes	37	96	131

EXHIBIT 4 (continued)

	1975	1974	1973
Income before security gains and losses	244	282	299
Net securities gains and losses	5	10	2
Net income before extraordinary items	249	292	301
Extraordinary items	0	0	0
Net income	249	292	301
Cash dividends on common stock	60	60	54

II

OBTAINING THE NECESSARY FUNDS AND CAPITAL

3

TRENDS IN THE ACQUISITION AND COST OF BANK FUNDS

The ability to attract funds at a reasonable cost has become one of the key ingredients of commercial bank management in recent years. For many years after the Depression of the 1930s, banking could be labeled an industry that emphasized the use of funds. The focus of bank management was on how to lend and invest the surplus of funds that banks were easily able to attract. Although the use of attracted funds is still obviously important, changing conditions such as the shortage of savings, increased competition for these scarce savings, and increasing loan demands force banks to place increased emphasis on attracting funds. This shift is demonstrated by the more creative and intensive use of existing sources of funds and in the aggressive development of new sources of funds during the 1970s and early 1980s. Furthermore, under the banking environment forecast for the 1980s (see Chapter 1), it appears likely pressures will continue on banks to be able to attract adequate amounts of funds at a reasonable cost.

The four sections in this chapter address this challenging situation. First, we will examine trends in the total funds and primary types of funds that banks attract. Second, we will discuss techniques for measuring the cost of and resulting potential profit from these sources of funding. Third, the risks associated with acquiring the various types of bank funds will be assessed. Finally, strategies for acquiring funds that banks might use will be investigated.

TRENDS IN BANK SOURCES OF FUNDS

Commercial banks attracted less funds than competing financial intermediaries from the early 1900s to the mid-1960s. Funds attraction for the various financial intermedi-

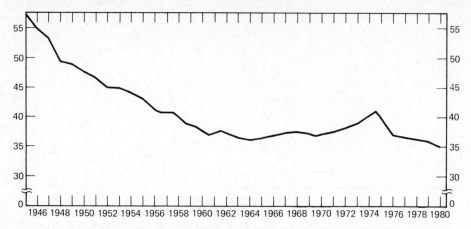

FIGURE 3-1   Commercial Bank Assets as Percentage of all Financial Institutions Assets

aries from 1900 through 1952 appears in Goldsmith's *Financial Intermediaries in the American Economy Since 1900.*[1] Figure 3-1 presents the trend of bank liabilities as a percentage of all financial intermediary liabilities from the end of the Second World War through 1980. The relative decline in bank liabilities in the 1930s and 1940s appears to have been caused primarily by the lack of adequate demand for bank loans. Because they felt profitable use of funds was restricted, many banks discouraged deposit growth by paying relatively low rates on interest-bearing deposits and by not making any marketing effort—for example, in advertising or with product development—to attract any funds.

The rapid growth of loan demand in the 1950s and 1960s led to an increased number of profitable uses for commercial bank funds. Nevertheless, the growth of bank funds remained slow in relation to the growth of most other financial intermediaries. Banks still limited their marketing effort and were content to have the rates on their deposits remain significantly below the rates of other financial intermediaries. In addition, rising interest rates during this period encouraged depositors, particularly businesses and governmental bodies, to hold their demand deposit balances to a minimum.

By the early 1960s banks finally became sufficiently concerned about their declining share of the financial intermediation market to begin taking positive actions to attract more funds. It could reasonably be stated that banks began using the marketing concept of developing financial products that consumers needed and wanted. Bank action came in several forms. First, banks began to emphasize the use of compensating deposit balances from most of their loan customers. Second, banks began to pay more competitive rates on their time and savings accounts. Although still 0.25 percent below other depository institutions, most banks paid the maximum allowable rate on deposits permitted by Regulation Q. When Regulation Q ceilings were removed on larger deposits, banks responded by paying rates as high as or higher than competing intermediaries. Third, commercial banks began the aggressive use of new types of deposits and nondeposit liability forms to attract consumer business and public deposits. For exam-

[1] Raymond W. Goldsmith, *Financial Intermediaries in the American Economy Since 1900* (Princeton, N.J.: Princeton University Press, 1958).

ple, larger banks, following the lead of Citicorp, began to use negotiable certificates of deposit to actively solicit the time deposits of their corporate customers who had previously invested their excess funds in money market instruments. They used longer term savings certificates and deposits with rates tied to market rates to attract funds from consumers. Nondeposit sources of funds, such as commercial paper, capital notes, and Eurodollars, began to be used extensively.

The results of these actions can be observed in Figure 3-1. Commercial bank funds began to grow more rapidly in the mid-1960s and remained approximately a constant proportion of the liabilities of all financial intermediaries during the late 1960s. The absolute growth of bank funds slowed somewhat in the credit crunch of 1969–1970 because of the disintermediation caused by market interest rates exceeding bank rates constrained by Regulation Q ceilings. Bank funds grew rapidly, both absolutely and in relation to other intermediaries, through the first half of the 1970s, but relative growth in bank funds was slower in the later 1970s and early 1980s. Although banks were less constrained by Regulation Q ceilings in the late 1970s, competition was severe from nondepository financial intermediaries, such as money market mutual funds, and from nonintermediaries, such as cash management accounts at brokerage firms. As this book is being published, it looks as though bank funds have continued to grow somewhat slower than other financial intermediaries in 1982. It appears that in the mid-1980s banks will need to reemphasize the marketing concept and to develop new financial products that appeal to a broader spectrum of savers. Recent legislation gives banks relatively broad abilities to try to achieve these objectives.

The Changing Composition of Bank Funds

The changing trends in total bank funds may provide future challenges to bank management; however, it is the marked and continuing changes in the composition of the sources of bank funds which have caused drastic changes in bank management in recent years. Table 3-1 categorizes the principal types of nonequity sources of funds for commercial banks according to primary ownership, nature of interest paid, and maturity. Table 3-2 shows the amount of funds in each of these categories of sources of funds as of July 1981. Table 3-3 indicates the net amount of funds in the major categories of funds in selected years from 1950 through 1981. Interbank sources of funds—deposits of other banks, deposits in process of collection, and Federal Funds transactions between banks—have been eliminated from the figures in Table 3-3. We will briefly describe each of the sources of bank funds and then discuss the overall pattern of bank funding and its implications for bank returns and risks.

Demand deposits are noninterest-bearing deposits that have no maturity and that must be paid by banks when a negotiable instrument, generally in the form of a check or an electronic impulse, is presented. Since demand deposits have no explicit interest cost, they are generally a bank's lowest cost source of funding; however, increasing costs of processing demand deposit transactions have raised the effective overall cost of demand deposits to close to, if not higher than, the cost of passbook savings.[2] Table 3-2

---

[2] The cost associated with servicing demand deposits is estimated in *Functional Cost Analysis: 1981 Average Banks* (Washington, D.C.: Board of Governors of the Federal Reserve System, 1982).

TABLE 3-1
Primary Sources of Funds for Commercial Banks (at the end of 1982)

Principal sources of bank funds	Primary ownership				Interest					Maturity
	Individuals	Business	Government	Interbank	Noninterest	Low-rate ceiling	Variable-rate ceiling	No-rate ceiling	None fixed	Typical range
Demand deposits	x	x	x	x	x				x	
NOW accounts	x					x			x	
Passbook or statement savings deposits	x	x				x			x	
Time deposits, under $100,000	x	x				x				90 days to 8 years
Money market certificates	x					x				6 months
Variable-rate certificates	x						x			2½ or more years
Super NOW accounts	x						x		x	
Individual retirement and Keogh time deposits	x							x		
Certificates of deposit	x	x	x					x		14 days to year
"High-fi" accounts	x	x	x					x	x	
Federal Funds				x				x		Day or term
Repurchase agreements	x	x	x	x				x		Day to year
Other borrowings (Eurodollars, bank's acceptances, etc.)	x	x		x				x		Day to 270 days
Capital notes	x	x		x				x		

TABLE 3-2
Major Noncapital Sources of Funds for All Insured
Commercial Banks in July 1981 (in billions of dollars)

Demand Deposits			
Individuals, partnerships, corporations	$292.8		
Held by others	102.7		
Total		$395.5	(26.3%)
NOW and Automatic Transfer Accounts		54.0	(3.6%)
Savings Deposits			
Held by individuals	$189.4		
Held by others	12.6		
Total		202.0	(13.4%)
Time Deposits			
Less than $100,000	$ 62.5		
Money market certificates	217.9		
Variable-ceiling time deposits	35.9		
Time deposits of $100,000 or more	272.2		
IRA and Keogh time deposits	6.7		
Total		595.2	(39.5%)
Miscellaneous Other Deposits		6.6	(0.4%)
Federal Funds purchased and repos.	$143.1		
Other borrowed money	30.8		
Mortgage indebtedness	2.3		
All other liabilities	77.0		
Total		253.3	(16.8%)
All Noncapital Sources of Funds		$1,506.6	(100.0%)

Source: *Federal Reserve Bulletin*, October 1981.

illustrates that total demand deposits were roughly over one-fourth of bank noncapital sources of funds at the end of 1981. Table 3-3 shows that the demand deposits net of interbank deposits and checks in process of collection fell from 63.3 percent of all commercial bank net sources of funds in 1950 to slightly over one-fifth of those sources in 1981. The reasons for the declining importance of demand deposits in the last three decades include more efficient cash management by individuals, businesses, and governmental units; significantly higher interest rates; and the appearance of competitive instruments such as negotiable order of withdrawal (NOW) accounts at banks and other financial institutions, money market funds, and cash management accounts. A final characteristic of demand deposits is that in recent years they have been a relatively more important source of funds for smaller banks than for very large banks.[3]

NOW accounts are interest-bearing checking accounts, currently subject to Regulation Q rate maximums similar to maximums on savings deposits, which have no maturity and which must be paid by banks on demand. Although limited amounts of

[3] *1981 Annual Report* (Washington, D.C.: Federal Deposit Insurance Corporation, 1982).

TABLE 3-3
Noncapital Net Sources of Funds for All Insured Commercial Banks, Excluding All Interbank Items

End of year	Dollars (in billions)				Percentage composition			
	Demand deposits[a]	Savings deposits[a]	Time & other deposits[a]	Nondeposit liabilities[a]	Demand deposits	Savings deposits[a]	Time & other deposits[a]	Nondeposit liabilities[a]
1947	61.8		34.7	0.5	63.7		35.8	0.5
1960	94.6		53.5	1.4	63.3		35.8	0.9
1962	101.5		79.7	3.6	54.9		43.1	2.0
1964	108.3		103.6	2.5	50.5		48.3	1.2
1966	112.9		139.8	4.6	43.9		54.3	1.8
1968	131.5		175.3	8.5	41.7		55.6	2.7
1970	135.2	97.2	133.8	18.6	35.1	25.2	34.8	4.8
1972	158.4	129.2	196.3	36.4	30.5	24.8	37.7	7.0
1974	185.9	146.1	255.8	52.8	28.5	22.5	40.8	8.1
1976	225.8	190.3	293.1	67.0	29.1	24.5	37.8	8.6
1978	252.3	220.9	395.2	114.7	25.7	22.5	40.2	11.7
1980	294.8	207.1	558.7	161.5	24.1	17.0	45.7	13.2
1981[d]	282.3	201.4	594.8	181.6	22.4	16.0	47.2	14.4

[a]Net demand deposits are total demand deposits other than domestic commercial interbank and U.S. government less cash items in process of collection.
[b]Interbank deposits are excluded from both savings and time deposits.
[c]Net nondeposit liabilities use all nondeposit liabilities less federal funds sold and repos of commercial banks.
[d]As of July 1981. NOW accounts included as demand deposits.
Sources: Federal Reserve Bulletins, selected issues, and *Annual Reports* (Washington, D.C.: Federal Deposit Insurance Corporation, selected years).

NOW accounts were outstanding in the New England states in the late 1970s, they were not legalized throughout the United States until January 1, 1981. By July 1981, NOW accounts and automatic transfer accounts had reached slightly over $54 billion. Super NOW accounts became available to individuals on January 5, 1983. Future growth is likely to be rapid.

Savings deposits are interest-bearing deposits subject to fixed Regulation Q maximums. A check or other order of withdrawal cannot be written directly on a savings account, but withdrawals can be made whenever the depositor desires, and it is easy to shift funds to a demand account on which checks may be written. These accounts have no fixed maturity, and individuals keep track of their balances through passbooks or by receiving periodic statements. Savings deposits may be the lowest overall cost source of funds currently available to commercial banks; however, the low rate maximum has severely restricted the growth of these deposits. Table 3-2 shows that savings deposits constituted 13.4 percent of the total noncapital sources of funds in July 1981. Table 3-3 shows that net savings deposits fell from roughly 27 percent of the net total funds as late as 1976 to slightly above 16 percent in 1981. Unless the rate maximum is lifted or increased dramatically, savings deposits appear likely to decline as a source of funds for commercial banks.

Time deposits differ from savings deposits primarily because they have a predetermined maturity date, and withdrawals prior to that date are subject to interest penalties. By the end of 1981, total time deposits had grown to nearly 40 percent of the total sources of funds and 48.4 percent of the net fund sources (see Tables 3-2 and 3-3). In contrast, time and savings deposits combined were only 36 percent of all net deposits as late as 1960.

There are currently (early 1983) seven distinct categories of time deposits. Only the first category, time deposits under $100,000, is subject to fixed-rate maximums under Regulation Q, and this category was only $62.5 billion or slightly over 10 percent of all time deposits in July 1981. Two relatively new categories of time deposits (late 1970s vintage), money market certificates and variable-ceiling time deposits, totaled $253.8 billion or 42.6 percent of the total time deposits in July 1981. The rates on money market certificates vary with the rates on six-month Treasury bills, whereas rates on other variable-rate deposits usually vary with Treasury securities, which have maturities similar to the deposits. The fourth category, time deposits of $100,000 or more, have no rate limit and in July 1981, totaled $272.2 billion or 45.7 percent of all time deposits. A fifth category of time deposits, individual retirement and Keogh time deposits, constituted only slightly over 1 percent of all time deposits in July 1981. The lifting of rate limits and greater tax advantages which started at the beginning of 1982 should encourage very rapid growth in this type of time deposits in the early and mid-1980s. The sixth category of time deposits, 91-day savings certificates, became eligible for issuance in May 1982. They are available in small denominations and have a yield tied to the 91-day Treasury bill rate. The seventh and final category of time deposits, money market or "high-fi" accounts, become effective in December 1982, have no rate limit, no fixed maturity, and a minimum size of $2,500.

Miscellaneous other deposits, which include club accounts, all savers certificates, and Christmas and vacation savings, were $6.6 billion or 0.4 percent of the total bank sources of funds in July 1981. All savers certificates, which could be issued only after October 1, 1981, were not outstanding at the dates on Table 3-2, and could not be issued after the end of 1982.

Table 3-3 shows that less than 1 percent of the total net sources of commercial bank funds consisted of net nondeposits as late as 1960. By mid-1981, however, net nondeposit sources constituted 14.8 percent of the net sources of commercial bank funds, and the total nondeposit sources were 16.8 percent of the total bank sources of funds.

The largest nondeposit sources of funds for commercial banks are Federal (Fed) Funds purchased and securities sold under agreement to repurchase (repos). These two accounts, which are combined for reporting purposes, totaled $143.1 billion in July 1981, or 56.5 percent of nondeposit bank sources of funds and 9.5 percent of the total sources of bank funds (see Table 3-2). The majority of Fed Funds are one-day purchases of another bank's excess reserves. Security dealers, large businesses, and the Federal Reserve are also able to supply these one-day reserves, so the total Fed Funds purchased usually exceeds the amount of Fed Funds sold. There is also a limited amount of Fed Funds purchased and sold between banks maturing in periods longer than one day. Repos provide funds to banks during the period when securities are temporarily sold to another bank, a business, an individual, or other potential temporary purchaser. The temporary selling period typically ranges between 1 and 89 days, and the purchaser has title to the securities until the repo is repurchased. Repos usually have a rate slightly below the existing Fed Funds rate because they are effectively secured by the security sold

TABLE 3-4
Savings and Time Deposits and Borrowings of
Commercial Banks Subject to Rate Ceilings (in billions of dollars)

Date	Subject to Regulation Q maximum Savings	Time	Exempt from Regulation Q maximum Time deposit	Borrowings	Percentage exempt
For Weekly Reporting Banks					
12/28/65	$47.1	$42.3	$ 0.0	$ 6.2	6.5%
7/1/70	46.4	41.1	14.1	32.2	34.6
4/3/72	57.6	56.0	35.5	32.2	37.1
5/29/74	57.8	62.3	79.5	63.4	54.3
5/25/76	80.1	46.8	96.1	58.3	54.5
5/31/78	93.4	52.0	119.8	94.3	59.8
5/31/79	76.6	54.3	118.0	109.5	63.5
7/30/80	74.5	64.2[a]	134.9	129.2	65.6
9/30/82	69.6	76.5[b]	180.5	131.0	68.1

For all Insured Commercial Banks

Date	Savings	Fixed	Variable	Time deposit	Borrowings	Percentage exempt
10/25/78	220.0	162.6	13.8	185.9	118.3	43.4% (45.4%)[a]
6/30/81	202.0	62.5	253.8	278.9	176.2	46.8% (72.8%)[b]

[a]Time deposits subject to variable maximums are included.
[b]Percentages in parentheses () are for both exempt and variable maximum rate deposits.
Source: Federal Reserve Bulletins, selected issues.

whereas Fed Funds are usually unsecured.[4] In the early 1980s, some banks used small denomination, "retail" repos, paying rates above Regulation Q ceiling rates on deposits, in order to obtain funds. The total dollar amounts obtained through these retail repos were relatively small.

Other borrowed money includes a variety of other forms of borrowing, such as borrowing from the Federal Reserve and Eurodollars, which banks use as sources of funds. Many of these sources are primarily available to larger banks with international offices. At the present time (1982), commercial banks are prohibited from issuing commercial paper (large, short-term, unsecured promissory notes); however, bank holding companies can issue such paper and pass the funds through to banks they own.

A final comment about bank sources of funds in the future concerns the phasing out of Regulation Q. The Depository Institution Deregulation and Monetary Control Act, which passed in March of 1980, directed the Depository Institution Deregulation Committee to implement the orderly phaseout of Regulation Q maximums on rates banks can pay for various types of deposits by 1986. This "phasing out" may be one of the nonevents of the mid-1980s because the Depository Institution Committee appears likely to remove most ceilings in the early 1980s. Table 3-4 indicates that by September 30, 1981, slightly over 68 percent of the time and savings deposits and borrowings of

---

[4] A few banks have required other banks to pledge securities as part of fed funds transactions.

weekly reporting banks were variable rate or free of Regulation Q maximums. By comparison, at the end of 1965, only 6.5 percent of total savings and time deposits and borrowings of weekly reporting banks were not subject to Regulation Q ceilings.

Similar measures for all insured commercial banks were not available prior to 1978. The percentages not subject to Regulation Q maximums were considerably lower for all insured commercial banks, 43.4 percent in 1978 and 46.8 percent in 1981. This would seem to mean that a higher proportion of deposits in the smaller banks that do not report weekly are subject to the rate maximums under Regulation Q. On the other hand, by mid-1981 close to 73 percent of the time and savings deposits and borrowings of all insured commercial banks were either not subject to Regulation Q maximums or had variable-rate maximums that were usually close to rates on similar maturity Treasury securities. The primary funding source responsible for the relatively large proportion of variable-rate funding, particularly for smaller banks, was money market certificates, which were created in mid-1978 and which have become a very significant source of funding by 1981.

MEASURING THE COST OF BANK FUNDS

The first and perhaps the most important concern is why a bank should be interested in measuring its cost of funds. Assuming the bank is seeking to balance its return-risk tradeoff in order to maximize the value of the bank for its shareholders (discussed in Chapter 2), three reasons stand out. First, a bank will generally be seeking the lowest cost combination of sources of funds available in its market. Other things being equal, a bank will have higher returns if the cost of funds is lower without taking significantly higher risks. Second, a reasonably accurate cost of funds measure is an essential ingredient in determining the returns a bank must obtain on its earning assets. Third, the types of sources of funds a bank obtains and how these sources of funds are employed has a significant impact on the liquidity risk, interest rate risk, and capital risk of the bank. How a bank's cost of funds should be measured is examined in this section. The impact of bank funding on banking risk is examined in the following section. Methods for obtaining attractive sources of funds are then discussed in the final section.

There are several methods of measuring the cost of funds for a bank. Examples and an evaluation of the three most widely used methods—historical average cost, marginal cost of specific sources of funding, and a weighted average expected cost of all sources as a proxy for marginal cost—are presented for Community National Bank, the bank used as an example in Chapter 2. Tables 2-11, 2-12, and 2-13 contain balance sheets, income statements, and supplementary information for Community National through 1981. Table 3-5 contains projections for the bank's fund resources, amount of these attracted funds the bank can employ for 1982, and part of expected future costs of specific funds sources.

The first method, *historical average cost*, is probably still the most common method of estimating the cost of a bank's funds. The weighted average cost of funds for Community National Bank is calculated in Table 3-6. The interest cost in dollars ($14,603 for Community Bank) is either available or can be calculated by multiplying the average amount in each type of funding by the average cost of the funds during the

TABLE 3-5
Supplementary Information for Estimating Cost of
Funds for Community National Bank (in millions of dollars)

1. The bank's holdings of vault cash, deposits with the Federal Reserve and other banks, and other cash items in 1982 are expected to be:
   26 percent of noninterest-bearing demand deposits.
   20 percent of interest-bearing demand deposits.
    5 percent of all time and savings deposits.
2. The bank's investment in premises and equipment and other nonearning assets is expected to be 4 percent in 1982.
3. During 1982, the bank expects its net resources to average $200 million. The average amount and investable amount of the various fund sources are projected as follows (amounts in millions of dollars):

	Average amount	Percentage usable	Amount investable
Noninterest demand deposits	$ 60	70%	$ 42.00
Interest-bearing demand deposits	18	76	13.68
Passbook savings	12	91	10.92
Savings certificates	7	91	6.37
Money market certificates	27	91	24.57
All savers certificates	6	91	5.46
CDs $100,000 and over	32	91	29.12
Public and other time deposits	8	91	7.28
Short-term borrowing	12	96	11.52
Other liabilities	6	96	5.76
Stockholder equity	12	96	11.52
Total sources of funds	$200		$168.20

4. The bank's target rate of return on equity is 16 percent after taxes. Its marginal income tax rate is 45 percent; therefore, the pretax return is 16/1-0.45 or 29.1 percent.
5. The costs of each type of funding (percentage) are as follows:

	Interest cost 1981	Estimated interest cost 1982	Estimated net processing cost 1982
Noninterest demand deposits	0%	0%	4.6%
Interest-bearing demand deposits	5.2	5.3	2.3
Passbook savings	5.4	5.5	1.1
Savings certificates	14.4	12.0	0.2
Money market certificates	15.7	13.5	0.4
All savers certificates	12.2	10.2	0.4
CDs $100,000 and over	18.0	15.0	0.1
Public and other time deposits	13.3	12.1	0.2
Short-term borrowing	16.5	14.0	0.1
Other liabilities	7.1	7.0	0.1
Stockholders equity	29.1	29.1	0.1

period (the year 1981 in this example). The weighted average interest cost, 8.55 percent, is calculated by dividing the dollar interest cost by the total noncapital funds. The weighted average interest cost for interest-bearing funds (13.01 percent in this example) is calculated by including only interest-bearing funds in the denominator.

Such weighted average cost of funds measures may be helpful in evaluating past funds acquisition performance, but they suffer from four shortcomings. First, some

TABLE 3-6
Historical Weighted Average Cost Measures (in thousands of dollars)

1. Weighted average interest cost of funds:

Type of funds	Average amount	Interest cost	Interest amount
Noninterest demand deposits	$ 58,632	0%	$ 0
Interest-bearing demand deposits	15,107	5.2	786
Passbook savings	12,347	5.4	667
Savings certificates	6,971	14.4	1,004
Money market certificates	23,389	15.7	3,672
All savers certificates	3,181	12.2	388
CDs $100,000 and over	27,090	18.0	4,876
Public and other time deposits	7,289	13.3	969
Short-term borrowing	11,090	16.5	1,830
Other liabilities	5,795	7.1	411
	$170,891		$14,603

Weighted average interest cost: $\dfrac{\text{Interest cost}}{\text{Total noncapital funds}} = \dfrac{\$14,603}{\$170,891} = 8.55\%$

Weighted average interest cost, interest-bearing funds: $\dfrac{\text{Interest cost}}{\text{Interest-bearing funds}} = \dfrac{\$14,603}{\$112,259} = 13.01\%$

2. Earning requirements based on weighted average cost of funds:

(a) To cover interest expense: $\dfrac{\text{Interest cost}}{\text{Earning assets}} = \dfrac{\$14,603}{\$153,308} = 9.53\%$

(b) To break even: $\dfrac{\text{Interest} + \text{All other costs}}{\text{Earning assets}} = \dfrac{\$14,603 + 7,121}{\$153,308} = 14.17\%$

(c) To earn 16 percent return on capital:

Earnings to cover ROE only $= \% R \text{ on } E_{bt} \times \dfrac{\text{Equity}}{\text{Earning assets}}$

$$= 29.1\% \times \dfrac{\$10,983}{\$153,308} = 2.09\%$$

Required to cover costs and ROE $= 14.17\% + 2.09\% = 16.26\%$

Sources: Tables 2-11, 2-12, 2-13, and 3-5.

bank funds have to be employed in assets which do not earn returns, such as required reserves, correspondent balances, and premises. Since the proportion not earning returns varies with different forms of funding, adjustments need to be made in costs and the resulting returns that need to be made to cover the interest costs. Second, the cost of funds should include other expenses associated with attracting funds, such as operating and advertising expenses. Third, there are numerous questions about whether the cost of equity funds should be included in this cost of funds measure and, if so, how. Finally, historical costs can be extremely unreliable as a guide in choosing which funds to attract or as an asset pricing guide if interest rates are changing markedly over time, as they have in the early 1980s.

Adaptations are made to adjust to the first three of these shortcomings in the lower part of Table 3-6. In 2a, interest cost divided by earnings assets adjusts for funds that have to be employed in nonearning assets and shows the return (9.53 percent) the bank must earn on its earning assets in order to cover its interest expenses. The so-called break-even yield in 2b, the total of interest expenses and net other expenses (noninterest expense less noninterest income) divided by earning assets, shows how much the bank must earn (14.17 percent) in order to cover all its expenses. Finally, 2c presents one way to recognize the cost of stockholder equity. The before-tax return on equity (ROE) is multiplied by equity divided by earning assets. This earning requirement (2.09 percent) is added to the return required to cover all expenses to indicate the return required on earning assets (16.26 percent) for the bank to earn 16 percent on its equity capital. The same results could have been obtained by the following computation.

Interest expenses	$ 14,603
All other expenses (net)	7,121
Equity return $11 million $\times$ 0.291	3,201
Total	$ 24,925
$\div$ Earning assets	$153,308
Required to earn 16 percent ROE	16.26%

In spite of these adaptations, the historical average cost measures seem useful primarily in assessing a bank's past performance. For example, to help explain a bank's earning performance, a bank's actual returns on earning assets can be compared with its break-even yield and the yield required to earn a specified return on capital. If a bank wants guidance about which type of funds to seek to attract, whether or not to take on new assets, or pricing its loans, historical average costs may be very misleading. For example, when rates are rising, the historical average cost of funds already obtained is below the cost of replacing these funds, and the bank might be led into making new loans at unprofitable yields. The reverse could be true if rates fell. If predictions about fluctuating rates in the 1980s are at all accurate, it would seem that a better measure of the cost of bank funds would be essential for a bank to obtain reasonable profitability.

The second measure of the cost of bank funds, the *marginal cost of funds*, is a direct result of the deficiencies in using the historical average cost cited above. The basic idea is that the bank would use its marginal cost, the cost paid to produce one additional unit of usable funds, to determine the acceptable return on the additional assets purchased with such funds. Also, the bank would seek to attract the source of funds with the lowest cost. At first glance these concepts seem easy to implement, but figuring the full cost of a new dollar of funds is difficult—especially if it is necessary to estimate the impact of one source of funds on the cost of other sources.

The simplest approach is to determine a single source of funds a bank wants to use, compute its marginal cost, and use that cost as a basis for pricing new assets. Presumably the single source selected would be the cheapest one available to the bank. For example, let us assume Community National Bank hopes to use NOW accounts to finance its asset expansion. The interest cost of these funds is 5.3 percent, 24 percent of the attracted funds will be employed in nonearning assets, and the cost of acquiring and servicing such accounts is 2.3 percent. Usually the cost of a single marginal source is calculated as follows:

$$\text{Marginal return on funds from single source} = \frac{\text{Interest costs} + \text{Other costs}}{1 - \text{Percent in nonearning assets}}$$

$$= \frac{5.3 + 2.3}{1 - 0.24}$$

$$= 10.0\%$$

Two problems limit the usefulness of this measure. First, the cost of a single source may need to be adjusted to compensate suppliers of other sources of funds for the added risk created by using the single source. For example, if Community National's ratio of debt to equity rose because of the added NOW accounts, uninsured depositors and other creditors and shareholders might demand a higher return. Community National's cost of attracting and holding NOW accounts might be 12 percent, the 10 percent computed cost plus a two percent premium because of the higher cost of other sources. Reasonably precise measurement for such a premium seems impossible.

Second, few banks use a single source of funding over a very long period of time. Often, several sources provide significant amounts of new funding. One alternative promoted by some banks to overcome this weakness is to use the cost of the most expensive marginal sources of funds as the bank's marginal cost of funds. A second alternative is to use an average of marginal costs calculation similar to that summarized in Table 3-7 for Community National Bank. In Table 3-7 it is assumed that Community National expected to grow by $16 million in 1982, primarily through five sources of financing. The interest costs, all other costs, and percentage in nonearning assets expected in 1982 came from Table 3-5. The return required on earning assets to cover this

TABLE 3-7
Average Marginal Costs of Funding (in millions of dollars)

Type of funds	(1) Amount of increase	(2) Investable assets	(3) Investable amount	(4) Interest and all other costs	Total cost (1) × (4)
Demand deposits, interest-bearing	$ 3	76%	2.28	7.6%	$0.228
Money market certificates	4	91	3.64	13.9	0.556
All savers certificates	3	91	2.73	10.6	0.318
CDs, $100,000 and over	5	91	4.55	15.1	0.755
Supporting equity	1	95	.95	29.2	0.292
Total	$16		$14.15		$2.149

$$\text{Marginal cost} = \frac{\text{Total cost}}{\text{Total amount}} = \frac{2.149}{16.0} = 13.43\%$$

$$\text{Required return on earning assets} = \frac{\text{Total cost}}{\text{Investable funds}} = \frac{2.149}{14.15} = 15.19\%$$

Sources: Tables 2-11, 2-12, 2-13, and 3-5.

pool of funds, 15.19 percent in Table 3-7, was found by dividing the total dollar cost of the funds attracted by the amount of funds that could be invested in earning assets. While the accuracy of this measure might be improved by using the amount each category of funds was expected to rise or fall in 1982, the pooled marginal cost of financing is very sensitive to estimation (or misestimations) of sources of funding in the future.

The third and final way to estimate the cost of funds is to use the *weighted average projected cost* of all sources *as an estimation of the marginal costs.* Based on financial theory, if it is assumed that a bank has financed itself with the lowest overall cost of funds, the weighted average cost of capital should be equal to that bank's marginal weighted average projected cost of funds. Table 3-8 illustrates the calculation of the weighted average projected cost of funds for Community National Bank. The projected total dollar cost is divided by the expected noncash assets (see Table 3-5) to provide Community National with the return needed (12.85 percent) to cover its estimated marginal cost of funds. It is important to remember that if any specific source has a lower marginal cost, including premium or discount for charging risk of other funds, that source should be used. In theory, the marginal cost of each source should equal the weighted average projected cost at its lowest cost, and no form of additional funding would reduce this weighted average cost.

Which cost of funds measurement should a bank use? The answer may be any of the three measures discussed and depends on the purpose of the cost of funds figure. The historical average cost of funds is useful in assessing reasons for past performance.

TABLE 3-8
Weighted Average Projected Cost of Funds as
Estimation of Marginal Cost of Funds (in millions of dollars)

Types of funds	(1) Average amount	(2) Interest and net processing costs	(3) Total cost
Noninterest demand deposits	$ 60	4.6%	$ 2.760
Interest-bearing demand deposits	18	7.6	1.386
Passbook savings	12	6.6	.792
Savings certificates	7	12.2	.854
Money market certificates	27	13.9	3.753
All savers certificates	6	10.6	.636
CDs, $100,000 and over	32	15.1	4.832
Public and other time deposits	8	12.3	.984
Short-term borrowing	12	14.1	1.692
Other liabilities	6	7.1	.426
Stockholder equity	12	29.2	3.504
	$200		$21.619

$$\text{Weighted average projected cost of funds} = \frac{21.619}{200} = 10.81\%$$

$$\text{Required return on noncash assets to cover cost of funds} = \frac{21.619}{168.2} = 12.85\%$$

Sources: Tables 2-11, 2-12, 2-13, and 3-5.

Marginal cost of specific funds may be helpful in deciding which form of funds the bank should try to attract. Care should be exercised to measure all marginal costs. For example, a bank may believe demand deposits are cheapest because they have no explicit interest cost. However, if the acquisition of $1 million in demand deposits costs $200,000 in advertising, personnel calling, and operational cost, demand deposits may be a high-cost source of funds. Furthermore, cost adjustments for changing risks due to a change in funding sources are very difficult to measure. Finally, either the marginal cost of "pooled" funding or the weighted average projected cost of funds as an estimation of the marginal cost of funding may be acceptable as asset-pricing guides.

RISKS ASSOCIATED WITH RAISING FUNDS

The emphasis so far has been on the impact of the changing mix of bank sources of funds and how the cost of such funds affects bank profitability. Different sources of funds may also affect the risks of a bank in different ways. With a goal of achieving the highest value for the stockholder's investment, bank management must consider the risks as well as the costs of the various types of bank sources of funds. It is the purpose of this section to examine how bank sources of funds affect the primary risks of banking discussed in Chapter 2—liquidity risk, interest-rate risk, credit risk, and capital risk.

The liquidity risk associated with bank sources of funds is primarily the probability that the depositors or lenders of funds to the bank will want to withdraw their funds from the bank. The risk of such funds outflows differs markedly depending on the type of deposits and seems to have changed as the economic conditions have changed. The conventional banking wisdom of the 1940s and 1950s generally regarded demand deposits as the most vulnerable source to outflows at most banks. Savings and time deposits, dominated by passbook savings, were thought to be very stable sources of funds. Nondeposit liabilities were an insignificant source of funds for most banks (see Table 3-1). The primary liquidity pressures on a bank, therefore, came from fluctuations in demand deposits.

By the mid-1960s, the situation had changed appreciably. As interest rates rose, many bank customers managed their demand deposit balances tightly so that transaction need and compensating balances for loans were the major reasons for such deposits. The probability of large declines for all demand deposits in a bank seemed to subside. Savings deposits and time deposits grew rapidly and became more vulnerable to deposit outflows because Regulation Q put most deposits (see Table 3-4) at a competitive disadvantage with open-market instruments when interest rates rose. Therefore disintermediation of these deposits proved a liquidity problem to banks during credit tightness in 1966, 1969, and 1974. By the early 1970s, banks were willing to buy relatively more expensive deposits or nondeposit liabilities in order to escape the high liquidity risk associated with deposits subject to Regulation Q rate limits.

The gradual lifting of Regulation Q and creation of new deposit and liability forms in the late 1970s and early 1980s has again changed the liquidity risks associated with a bank's sources of funds. Corporate demand deposits remain at transaction and compensating balance levels and tend to be subject to limited liquidity risk. Consumer demand deposits, which face the competition of money market funds and interest-bearing NOW accounts of other banks and thrift institutions that can be competitively priced by balances, seem to have increasing liquidity risk. Passbook or statement savings have declined steadily in the last few years because of money market funds, NOW accounts, and Regulation Q limits considerably below open-market rates.

On the other hand, the majority of bank time deposits and other liabilities (see Table 3-4) are either not subject to Regulation Q ceilings or are subject to a variable-rate ceiling, which allows them to compete with other financial institutions and open-market instruments.[5] Since these time deposits and other liabilities have been an increasingly important source of bank funds, commercial banks appear to be likely to have lowered the liquidity risks associated *with their sources of funds*. In the 1970s bank management was more concerned with managing quantity than price, which was often fixed by regulation. In the 1980s banks may be able to get and keep the quantities they desire if they are willing and able to pay the price.

The interest-rate risk associated with bank sources of funds depends heavily on the interest sensitivity of the assets financed by these funds. For example, if six-month money market certificates, which are repriced every six months, are used for either Fed Funds (which are repriced daily) or five-year government bonds, the bank is taking an interest-rate risk. The appropriate technique is for management to compare the interest sensitivity over time of all sources of funds with the interest sensitivity over time of the assets financed by these funds. Chapter 12 on Managing the Interest Margin and Interest Sensitivity provides details of this technique. At this point, it seems worthwhile to emphasize that liquidity risk and interest-rate risk may be different for different sources of funds and to mention the broad range of interest sensitivity available among sources of funds.

Variable-rate certificates of deposit (CDs) are an example of a source of funds on which interest rates may vary with changes in market rates but which may pose little liquidity risk over the life of the CD. The same is true for most other variable-rate or nonlimit-rate time deposits, as long as the bank is willing to pay the "going" market rate. The menu of interest-sensitivity forms available among bank sources of funds is broad. Fed Funds purchased are rate sensitive on a daily basis; repos and large CDs are sensitive to rate changes in a few days to a few months; money market certificates are sensitive to rate changes each six months; longer term CDs may not be rate sensitive for several years; and capital notes may not be rate sensitive for 20 to 25 years. A bank's choice among the sources available would seem to depend on the interest cost of the source, other acquisition cost of the source, and its contribution to the liquidity and interest sensitivity balance of the bank.

A bank's sources of funds do not have a direct effect on the credit risk of the bank because the depositors or lenders of funds to the bank are taking the risk of the bank not paying them. Two indirect effects, however, are possible. A higher cost of funds may be a side effect of depositors or lenders of funds becoming worried about a bank's

---

[5] For example, money market certificates, which are priced competitively with six-month Treasury bill rates, were first offered in 1978 and had risen to approximately 15 percent of all bank noncapital sources of funds by late 1981. Individual retirement time accounts (IRAs), which seem likely to grow rapidly in the 1980s because of favorable tax legislation, are not subject to rate limits and are likely to be subject to little liquidity risk.

ability to pay its claims on time. For example, the problems of Continental Illinois Bank and Chase Manhattan Bank in 1982 raised their cost of funds appreciably. Second, if a bank has a high cost of funds, it may be encouraged to take higher credit risks in its struggle to maintain its margin.

Finally, a bank's sources of funds have a direct impact on the capital risk and leverage of a bank. A bank's equity costs much more than its deposits and borrowings because of the greater uncertainty associated with the return on equity and because the returns on equity, whether earnings or cash dividends, are not a tax-deductible expense. Thus, a bank may lower its cost of funds by increasing its leverage. As capital risk becomes more pronounced, however, these gains may be illusory. The cost of other sources of funds may rise as capital risk becomes appreciable. In addition, other bank activities, such as new branches and acquisitions, may be curtailed if regulatory authorities feel the bank's capital risk is too high. The next chapter, Financing the Bank's Capital Needs, deals in greater detail with leverage and capital risk.

STRATEGIES FOR ACQUIRING FUNDS

After a bank has decided the effects of the various types of funds on the bank's cost of funds and its risks, it must develop strategies for acquiring them. In a broad sense, this means using the marketing concept to determine what the consumer wants and then communicating to the consumer that the bank is offering the wanted product or service. In the following paragraphs, two particularly important strategies in acquiring funds are examined—product development and product attraction.

The first step in product development is to identify bank customers and their wants and needs. Once these are identified, a bank should develop and manage its products to fulfill these desires. Although there are some limitations on the product line of every bank—imposed by size, location, regulations, managerial capabilities, and so on—too narrow a conception of what products banks can provide has been the major shortcoming of most banks. Many banks have said in effect that their products are making loans and accepting deposits. In the author's opinion, banking products should be viewed as customer satisfactions, and the products of banking should include rendering (at a profit to the bank) all the financial services the customer can use. The willingness (accompanied by regulatory and legislative approval) to develop and market new financial products is one of the keys to banking success in the 1980s.

Product development strategies may be divided into two groups. First, there are those that relate to each individual product—its means of identification, product quality and features, price, and so on. Second, for its whole line of products, the bank must form strategies covering the assortment of products, the essential supporting services, hours of business, and bank location and layout. Some of the basic policy aspects of bank product development for both groups are described briefly in the following paragraphs.

Strategies that have proved useful for nonbanking firms include market segmentation and product differentiation. Market segmentation is the isolation of certain sectors of the total market and the creation of new products so uniquely designed for this sector that no immediate competition exists. This strategy may prove profitable for all banks in competition with other financial institutions. One problem with such a strategy for an individual bank is the speed with which other banks can copy most new banking products. This condition leads to the need for product differentiation. Often the purpose is to appeal to different segments of the market with an essentially standardized product. Such product differentiation is a difficult task, and effectively establishing a sense of difference often requires heavier than usual advertising and promotional expenditures.

Many banks have adopted a combination of these strategies for product development. They strive to develop new products to fill customers' wants in some segment of the market, to match their competition's new product when it appears desirable to do so, and to differentiate their products in the eyes of their customers.

Commercial banks must also develop new financial services in order to compete successfully with other financial institutions and other institutions offering financial services. Ideas for new banking products may just happen, but they will happen more often if customers' desires are studied, and sensitivity to their potential needs is cultivated among bank employees. Product ideas can come from customers, directors, employees, competing banks, other financial institutions, or trade magazines. Once the ideas are obtained, the development and selection process must start. As many as 50 to 100 new product ideas may yield only one banking product that will ultimately be marketed successfully.

Even if a bank is able to bring new banking products into the market or successfully copy the products of a competitor, it will be likely to face competition from similar products within a relatively short time. Creative pressures will force a need for product identification (which often requires at least some differentiation). The brand name, trademark, trade character, slogan, and other identification devices common to manufactured goods all have potential application to bank marketing. They may be employed for individual products or for the entire bank.

The image of a bank is related to these identification devices. A bank's image is a complex collection of attitudes and awareness on the part of customers and potential customers. All trademarks, all brand names, all contacts with bank facilities and bank personnel must combine to create a favorable image in the customer's mind. When a large part of the product is an intangible feeling of confidence, security, and trust, as it is in the case of many bank services, a favorable image is essential. We will now address the question of how an individual bank may raise specific types of funds.

Although individual banks do not have absolute control over the level of their deposits, they can nevertheless influence the amount their banks hold. Because deposits and other fund sources are so important to the profitable operation of a bank, most banks tend to compete aggressively for them. Some of the factors determining the level of deposits in a bank cannot be affected significantly by the bank. For example, monetary and fiscal policy, Regulation Q, and the level of general economic activity are exogenous factors that an individual bank must recognize but cannot control. The individual bank can control in varying degrees an intermediate group of factors—for example, the size and physical location or locations of the bank. Finally, the individual bank determines for itself such factors as its physical features and personnel, its marketing effort, the interest rates (within Regulation Q) it pays on savings and time accounts, the type of loans it is willing to make, and the level of services it offers its depositors. Following is a discussion of the major factors contributing to the attraction of the principal types of deposits.

In the case of *corporate demand deposits*, at this time banks are not permitted to pay interest on demand deposits; each bank must compete primarily on the basis of services rendered the depositor. It has long been held that the failure to charge for a service is not a payment of interest, and this concept has led to the theory of supporting or compensating balances.

As corporate depositors, particularly the larger ones, have become more sophisticated, and as alternative uses of money have become more profitable with rising interest rates, the corporate treasurer has learned to seek a specific *quid pro quo* in terms of service for every dollar of their demand deposits.

The most essential service compensated for by demand deposits is the collection and payment service in all its various forms. Every business that draws checks needs a bank account; everyone who receives checks needs a bank to collect them for him or her. The best service is rendered by the bank that can collect checks most quickly, thereby making funds available to the depositor earlier. Out of this need for faster collection has sprung a whole art of "funds mobilization" in which the Federal Reserve System has cooperated fully. These facilities include arrangements for sending large cash letters direct by air mail to Federal Reserve Banks in other districts (postage paid by the Federal Reserve) or to correspondent banks in major cities, bypassing the Reserve System entirely. Special carrier services have been established to bring checks into major cities more quickly than they can be delivered by mail. Locked-box arrangements have proliferated. Some large banks have special departments whose function is to advise the corporate treasurer on the most effective way to mobilize cash for short-term investment.

Ideally, banks should carefully calculate the costs of these services and assure themselves that the value of the related deposits compensates them for these costs as well as provides a profit margin. This is usually done by calculating a service charge representing the actual cost plus profit margin and offsetting this charge, in whole or in part, by an earnings credit. This credit is related to some money market rate representing the value of the funds in the bank. Both the service charges and the earnings credits are competitive rates, too often shaded, perhaps, in favor of the depositor.

The true net cost to the bank of the services it renders to depositors represents its cost of money for those deposits. Faced with higher costs in other markets for funds, most banks are willing to compensate the demand depositor by providing services at a charge somewhat less than net cost. Some banks waive service charges entirely, figuring that the cost of servicing those accounts is less than the interest they would have to pay on time deposits.

It is very easy, however, to become entrapped by this philosophy, and a bank can easily find itself rendering a number of services in consideration of the same demand deposit account. The aggregate cost of these services may well exceed the value of the deposit. It becomes increasingly important, therefore, to look at each account relationship as a whole, and in recent years computer programs have been developed to enable banks to measure the relative profitability of an account relationship in all its various facets. This involves coordinating in one computer printout all the services performed and their cost, the average collected balances maintained by a given customer (including other related accounts he or she may control) and their value, and credit usage, if any. Small banks do not need a computer to look at their relatively few large deposit accounts in this fashion.

Demand deposits of individuals offer a broad spectrum of opportunities. Individuals can in effect choose to receive interest on their demand deposits through NOW accounts. These accounts currently pay 5¼ percent interest and have minimum or average deposit requirement usually between $500 and $2,000. Noninterest-bearing demand deposits usually have lower or no balance requirements and often offer more services to the depositors. Service for individuals with noninterest-bearing demand deposits has proliferated in recent years. Many banks have been establishing automated tellers with which a customer with a "money card" and a secret account number can make deposits or withdraw small amounts of cash 24 hours a day, seven days a week, at scattered and convenient locations. Some banks have instituted systems whereby their customers can pay their bills by telephone. The customer states his or her account number and a personal identification number and then instructs the bank to pay designated amounts to specific payees. The customer can also designate the date on which he or she wishes the payments to be made.

The basic relationship between demand deposits and services rendered is essentially the same whether the depositor be an individual, a business corporation, or a municipality. The most successful bank will be the one that can produce the needed services at the lowest cost and thereby market its services at the lowest price and still maintain an adequate profit margin.

Of almost equal importance in attracting demand deposits, particularly business accounts, is the willingness to lend. The availability of credit is an essential need for most businesses at one time or another, a constant need for some. When funds are in short supply (as they are predicted to be in the foreseeable future), banks will give preference to those customers who maintain demand deposit accounts with them. The offer of credit accommodation is a primary factor in deposit solicitation. For this reason, banks frequently offer "solicitation" lines of credit to businesses with no present need to borrow, and by the same token businesses maintain deposit balances in anticipation of their possible future need to borrow. One outstanding example of this relationship is the so-called backup line of credit supporting a corporation's sale of commercial paper. A company actively using commercial paper to finance its current needs will obtain and advertise the availability of its unused bank lines of credit. These unused lines are typically supported by demand deposit balances of at least 10 percent of the credit available.

The willingness to lend, in short, is another vital service that banks perform for corporations or individuals who maintain or control important demand deposit balances. At times when money is extremely scarce, this relationship between deposit balances and the availability of credit seeps down even to the consumer lending field, and nondepositors will seek home mortgage loans in vain.

The *passbook or statement savings* market is primarily a market of convenience. Competing thrift institutions are permitted to pay higher interest rates than commercial banks so that, in the face of a rate disadvantage, all commercial banks can offer is greater convenience. The primary emphasis of commercial bank advertising in this field has been on "one-stop" or "full-service" banking, and the fact that commercial banks, even when they are in close competition with strong thrift institutions, still have large amounts of savings deposits is evidence of the effectiveness of this marketing technique.

It has become less effective in recent years since thrift institutions and banks are permitted to have NOW and super NOW accounts. Furthermore, the rapid growth of money market deposit accounts has cut heavily into bank passbook or statement savings deposits. The rates paid on these funds have been significantly higher than the rates banks have been permitted to pay on passbook savings.

To compete effectively in the passbook savings market (with or without an actual passbook), banks will have to go beyond mere convenience and offer fringe benefits in the form of additional services to compensate for the low permissible interest rates. A bank might offer lower or no charges on checking account facilities to savings deposit customers in some relation to the size of their savings accounts. It might offer a vacation club or special purpose accounts. Some people save for reasons; the interest earned is secondary. The reason may be general or specific, but the process should be made easy, attractive, and convenient. In spite of all efforts, passbook or statement savings of individuals in most banks will probably decline in coming years.

There are seven categories of *time deposits*. The first, *savings certificates under $100,000* with fixed maturities and rate maximums under Regulation Q, permits the payment of interest above passbook rates. However, the maximum rates have been below open-market rates, and it has been difficult for most banks to attract significant amounts of funds in these categories. These certificates are issued in a variety of forms to suit the needs and tastes of various classes of customers. They are usually sold in minimum denominations of $1,000. Interest may be paid by check on a monthly or quarterly basis or, in some cases, accumulated to maturity. For customers who cling to the passbook concept, such certificates may be issued in the form of a special passbook.

The second category, *money market certificates*, consists of six-month certificates with rates that vary with the preceding week's or month's six-month Treasury bill action. Although the interest cost on these certificates will vary over time, the money raised through such deposits will be more permanent because these certificates will always be competitive with market securities. The minimum denomination is $10,000. In order to appeal to a broader spectrum of potential customers, many banks have offered the service of combining smaller accounts or have lent their customers enough to reach the $10,000 minimum. Competition appears to be based on such special plans and promotional efforts since all banks and thrifts are offering similar yields.

A third category, *other variable-rate time deposits*, consists of time deposits other than money market certificates, which have variable rate limits. One unique subcategory is the *all savers certificates* which pays 70 percent of the rate on one-year Treasury bills sold in the preceding month. The unique characteristic of these certificates with a one-year maturity and minimum size of $500 is that up to $1,000 of the interest received per person ($2,000 on a joint return) is exempt from federal income taxes. Since the rates on these and nearly all other variable-limit deposits are the same for all banks and thrifts, competition among financial intermediaries has been based primarily on advertising and promotion. Competition with money market funds and market instruments has emphasized a competitive rate and the fact that these deposits are insured by a federal agency whereas nonintermediary forms are not.

A fourth category, *individual retirement accounts* (IRAs), offers banks a relatively new (greatly expanded in 1982) means for attracting funds. While a wage-earning individual's tax-sheltered deposit is limited to $2,000, nearly all U.S. wage earners are eligible, so the potential amounts are large. Two factors make these accounts particularly appealing. First, they are not subject to any rate maximums. Second, if attractively priced, they should represent a relatively permanent source of funds for banks. IRAs give banks the opportunity to innovate new competitive products with little regulatory constraint. Early ideas regarding interest rates have included rates fluctuating slightly above various maturity Treasury bill rates or rates set for up to one year. Advertising expenditures to try to attract these deposits have been relatively large for the more aggressive banks.

The fifth category, *91-day savings certificates*, was created to enable banks to compete more effectively with money market funds. Banks can make this type of time deposit available in relatively small denominations ($5,000 and up). The yield is pegged to the 91-day Treasury bill rate. Banks choosing to use this type of certificate should probably try to cross sell the instrument to existing customers and advertise aggressively.

The sixth category, "high-fi" accounts, was created by HR 6267, The Garn-St. Germain Financial Institutions Act of 1982. This Act mandated DIDC to create a new depository instrument "equivalent to and competitive with" money market funds. The instrument is required to have the following characteristics: (1) no minimum maturity, (2) no interest rate ceiling, (3) a minimum denomination of $2,500, (4) only three preauthorized or automatic withdrawals and three drafts permitted in any month and reserve requirements of 0 percent for individual accounts and 3 percent for corporate accounts, (5) all types of depositors eligible, and (6) insured up to $100,000 by the FSLIC or FDIC. These depository instruments were issued starting December 14, 1982.

The final category, *certificates of deposits of $100,000 and over*, is primarily for corporations and is not subject to interest rate limits. These certificates represent a fruitful source of funds, especially when market rates of interest rise above the regulatory ceilings. For the small and moderate bank, the market for large-denomination certificates will be confined to those few of its own corporate customers who from time to time may have excess cash to invest. To be effective in this market, a bank must be large enough and sufficiently well-known for its certificates to be traded in the secondary market at reasonable rates.

Although most corporate treasurers will, in theory, buy the certificates of any recognized bank at the highest rate obtainable, if rates are comparable, they are more likely to acquire the certificates issued by one of their banks of account. In times of tight money, considerable pressure may be put on treasurers by their banks to do just that. In more normal times, the major banks post their issuing rates, and, if they are seeking money, telephone the corporate treasurers with whom they have established contact. By the same token, the treasurer with funds to invest will call a number of banks and "shop the market." Actual rates are often negotiated slightly off the posted rates for large blocks of funds of especially desirable maturities.

From the standpoint of deposit attraction, it is important that the banker get to know as many treasurers and other shoppers for such funds as possible. Although the rate is always the primary factor, personal acquaintance is definitely a plus if several competitive rates are equal. Two other potentially important sources of funds are *public deposits* and *deposits of other banks*. There are several types of public deposits. Treasury tax and loan accounts are interest-bearing, demand-type accounts of the U.S. government. It is relatively easy for a bank to become a qualified depository. To keep its prorated share of these deposits for over a day or so, the bank must formally agree to pay a rate based on the going repurchase agreement rate. Qualified securities must be pledged for the uninsured part of these deposits.

Demand deposits of state and municipal governments are attracted primarily through offering services appropriate to the level of balances kept on deposit. Willingness to underwrite or purchase securities of the depositing state or municipal unit is an additional important consideration. Attracting state and municipal time deposits depends on factors similar to those affecting large denomination certificates. In some states, such deposits must go to the institution that bids the highest rate. Competition for state and municipal time deposits can be intense, and banks should be careful that the rates they bid recognize reserve requirements, pledging required, and an adequate return on capital. Repurchase agreements in which the bank agrees to rebuy securities it has sold to the political unit are an alternative way of attracting funds from these units. Many states still require pledging of securities against demand and time deposits of the state and its municipalities.

Deposits of other banks are a significant source of funds for some upstream, correspondent banks (over half of a few banks' demand deposits are from other banks). Demand balances are left by one bank in another bank because the latter offers services such as check clearance, international entry, investments advice, and loan participation. The services offered should be significant enough to attract other banks; however, the depository bank should be sure it is making a profit on the funds attracted.

Banks should also have fund attraction strategies for nondeposit sources of funds. Some forms, for example, Fed Funds and commercial paper for holding companies, clearly depend on a willingness to pay the going rate. Nonprice strategies are also important. Repurchase agreements depend on the bank having acceptable securities or other assets that can be sold subject to repurchase. A bank may be able to borrow more Fed Funds if it has good correspondent relations and a strong capital position. Eurodollar and other foreign sources may be encouraged by foreign offices and connections with foreign banks, businesses, and so forth.

In summary, the combination of all the factors discussed here will determine a bank's effectiveness in attracting sources of funds that can be profitably employed without taking too much risk. The following chapter on bank capital addresses a final source of funds which has unique characteristics related to both banking returns and risks.

4

FINANCING THE BANK'S CAPITAL NEEDS

Bank capital is not only an important service of bank funds, it also serves as a cutting edge in a bank's return-risk tradeoff decisions. Too much capital may lead to an inadequate return to a bank's owners, and too little capital may entail risks unacceptable to depositors, borrowers, and owners. The problem facing bank management and regulators is determining how much capital is too much or too little. Bank capital is also a dominant factor affecting bank growth.

In the 1980s the subject of bank capital has become a focal point in the banking industry. Capital adequacy and capital acquisition have become major concerns and topics of discussion, study, and controversy among banking personnel and regulatory authorities alike. In this chapter we will describe the principal forms of bank capital, the methods banks have used to raise capital in the past, and the likely future capital needs of the banking industry. We will then discuss the four key steps in an individual bank's capital planning process in considerable detail.

INTRODUCTION TO BANK CAPITAL

Principal Forms of Bank Capital

The three principal forms of bank capital are subordinated debt, preferred stock, and common equity. Of course, there are subclassifications within these broad categories— for example, there are several forms of subordinated debt; some debt and preferred stock can be converted into common stock, and common equity may be raised externally and generated internally. However, these subclassifications share the basic characteristics of the three principal forms.

Subordinated debt includes all forms of interest-bearing obligations that repay a fixed amount of money at some future time. The major forms of subordinated debt range from capital notes to longer term debentures. Some small capital note issues have been sold directly to bank customers. Other capital notes and some relatively small debenture issues have been sold to the issuing bank's major correspondent banks. Large debenture issues with longer maturities have been privately placed or sold through investment bankers to the public (financial institutions such as life insurance companies and pension funds have been heavy purchasers). Roughly one-eighth of the total dollar value of debentures sold in recent years has been convertible into the bank's common stock at a predetermined price. In the last few years some variable-rate debt issues have been convertible into fixed-rate debt issues. Because debt issues have contractual maturities, most regulatory authorities have rules that debt must meet to qualify as bank capital.[1] Current rules for the three federal authorities are summarized later in this chapter.

With preferred stock, the dividend and asset claims of the stockholders are fixed in amount and are subordinated to the claims of depositors and to all indebtedness of the commercial bank. Preferred stocks do not mature; however, some preferred issues have sinking funds to retire part or all of the issue, and most preferred stocks may be called at a fixed price at the option of the issuing bank. A commercial bank may issue either straight (nonconvertible) preferred stock or preferred stock that is convertible into common stock at a predetermined price at the option of the preferred stockholder. Generally, subordinated debt which qualifies as capital and preferred stock are referred to as senior capital because their claims on assets and earnings are above those of common stock.

Common equity, which is the basic form of bank capital, is the sum of the common stock, surplus, undivided profits, and equity reserve accounts. Common equity has a residual claim on income and assets behind deposits, other liabilities, indebtedness, and preferred stock. The book value of the common equity of a commercial bank can be computed by subtracting deposits, other liabilities, and senior capital from the book value of total assets. This book value figure is imperfect, because it ignores the market values of a bank's assets and liabilities. Book values are the most widely used measure of common equity and are nearly always used for capital adequacy purposes. The alternative to book value is the market value of common equity. The market value of the common equity of a commercial bank is usually estimated by multiplying the per-share market price by the number of outstanding common shares. Although this measure also has its drawbacks—some bank stocks are not traded at all or are inactively traded and, even for actively traded stock, the most recent price for a few shares determines total market value—no feasible alternative to book value has been proposed.

The common stock account consists primarily of the par or stated value of all outstanding shares of common stock. The surplus account contains funds generated both externally and internally—the accumulated premiums over par or stated value at which common stock was sold to the public (with one exception, see below) and whatever proportion of accumulated, undivided profits had been shifted to the surplus account. The primary reason for such a bookkeeping shift is that in the past the legal loan limit for all national banks and most state banks was a percentage of the combined to-

---

[1] Rules for debt to qualify as bank capital vary among different regulatory authorities.

tal of the common stock and surplus accounts. The Comptroller of the Currency now recognizes undivided profits and equity reserves as well as senior capital as part of the lending base; however, many state banks are still subject to the older legal loan limit.

The undivided profits account is the accumulated retained earnings less any amounts that have been shifted to the surplus account. Equity reserves consist of retained earnings that have been set apart for some contingency or expected event, such as the retirement of preferred stock or an anticipated court settlement. The reserve for loan losses and the reserve for security losses are technically asset valuation reserves rather than equity reserves. They are considered to be expenses (even though the reserve for security losses is not deductible for tax purposes) in the determination of earnings. The three federal regulatory authorities include most or all of these reserves in a bank's lending base[2] and consider them as capital when determining capital adequacy.

Past Record of Filling Capital Needs

A brief recapitulation of the amount of capital and forms used to raise that capital in preceding years would be helpful before turning to the future. We will discuss three pe-

TABLE 4-1
Growth in Assets, Deposits and Capital of Commercial Banks (amounts in millions of dollars)

As of end of:	Bank assets	Bank deposits	Bank capital	Common equity capital	Senior capital
1950	$ 168,932	$ 155,265	$ 11,590	$ 11,508	$ 82
1961	278,561	248,689	22,459	22,432	27
Growth (1950–1961):					
Dollar amount	$ 109,629	$ 93,424	$ 10,869	$ 10,924	$ (55)
Annual rate	4.7%	4.4%	6.3%	6.4%	a
1962	$ 297,116	$ 262,122	$ 24,094	24,039	$ 55
1973	820,690	681,621	59,248	55,131	4,117
Growth (1962–1973):					
Dollar amount	$ 523,574	$ 419,199	$ 39,216	$ 31,092	$4,062
Annual rate	9.7%	9.1%	9.2%	7.8%	b
1973	$ 820,690	$ 681,621	$ 59,248	$ 55,131	$4,117
1981	2,028,901	1,588,783	124,761	118,301	6,460
Growth (1973–1981):					
Dollar amount	$1,208,811	$ 907,162	$ 68,513	$ 63,170	$2,343
Annual rate	12.0%	11.1%	10.1%	10.0%	5.9%

aNegative annual compound rate of growth.
bLarge compound rate of growth because of smaller senior capital base.
Sources: Selected *Federal Reserve Bulletins* Washington, D.C.: Board of Governors of the Federal Reserve System, 1960–1982) and *Annual Reports of the Federal Deposit Insurance Corporation, 1960–1981* (Washington, D.C.: Federal Deposit Insurance Corporation, 1960–1982).

[2] For example, in establishing lending limits, the Comptroller allows an adjusted reserve for loan losses on bad debts, that is, the reserve less the amount of tax that would become payable if the tax-free portion of the reserve were transferred from the reserve, and the valuation for securities to be included as part of the unimpaired surplus.

riods of filling capital needs since the end of World War II—1950 through 1961, 1962 through 1973, and 1973 through 1981. During the first period, the deposits and assets of commercial banks grew slowly, and their position in relation to other financial intermediaries declined appreciably. For example, Table 4-1 shows that bank assets and deposits grew at an average annual rate of between 4 and 5 percent from 1950 through 1961. During the same period, the combined assets of nonbank financial intermediaries grew at an annual rate of roughly 12 percent. This slow growth had a positive side—it lessened the pressure for additional capital. Table 4-1 illustrates that bank capital grew considerably faster than bank assets and deposits. Although at least some of the more rapid growth in bank capital may have been caused by the shift from U.S. government securities to riskier assets, it is important to remember that the trend toward riskier assets continued through the 1960s and 1970s. The growth of bank capital did not exceed the growth in assets during most of these two decades.

The form in which bank capital was raised during the early postwar period is also interesting (Table 4-2). Outstanding senior capital (debt and preferred stock) actually declined from 1950 through 1961, primarily because none of the regulatory agencies would accept newly issued debt or preferred stock as part of a bank's capital. Long-

TABLE 4-2
Capital Accounts of Insured Commercial Banks (in millions of dollars)

As of year-end	Total capital	Long-term debt	Preferred stock	Common stock	Surplus	Undivided profits	Equity reserves
1950	11,282	20	62	3,437	5,201	2,093	469
1955	15,009	20	20	4,518	7,209	2,777	457
1960	20,659	23	15	6,170	9,916	4,021	514
1961	22,123	22	15	6,585	10,798	4,157	546
1962	23,752	21	35	6,882	11,458	4,790	567
1963	25,323	130	38	7,283	12,164	5,113	595
1964	27,438	811	41	7,886	12,893	5,113	693
1965	29,905	1,653	40	8,508	13,465	5,438	802
1966	31,693	1,730	62	8,857	13,989	6,167	880
1967	34,006	1,984	87	9,253	14,983	6,611	1,087
1968	36,628	2,110	91	9,773	16,174	7,420	1,061
1969	39,576	1,998	103	10,529	17,461	8,427	1,058
1970	42,566	2,092	107	11,138	18,073	10,146	1,011
1971	46,905	2,956	92	11,811	19,896	11,135	1,015
1972	52,653	4,093	69	12,854	21,528	13,012	1,098
1973	59,248	4,117	66	13,846	23,593	16,772	854
1974	64,836	4,259	43	14,789	25,313	19,520	912
1975	70,355	4,399	48	15,565	26,706	22,481	1,156
1976	77,372	5,123	67	16,221	28,894	25,238	1,828
1977	85,019	5,739	99	17,265	31,085	29,070	1,761
1978	92,283	5,865	114	18,158	33,203	35,943[a]	
1979	103,179	5,956	126	20,274	35,329	41,513	
1980	113,866	6,267	135	21,677	37,776	48,011	
1981	124,761	6,460	171	23,577	40,301	54,272	

[a]Undivided profits and equity reserves were combined starting in 1978.
Source: Annual Reports of the Federal Deposit Insurance Corporation, 1960–81 (Washington, D.C.: Federal Deposit Insurance Corporation, 1961–1982).

TABLE 4-3
Summary of Bank Capital Issues, 1963–1981 (amounts in thousands of dollars)

Year	Total capital raised		Common stock		Preferred stock		Nonconvertible debt		Convertible debt[a]	
	No. of issues	Amount	No. of issues	Amount	No. of issues	Amount	No. of issues	Amount	No. of issues	Amount
1963	n.a.[b]	n.a.	n.a.	n.a.	n.a.	n.a.	11	$ 223,500	1	$ 1,000
1964	n.a.	n.a.	n.a.	n.a.	n.a.	n.a.	90	634,161	5	58,862
1965	n.a.	n.a.	n.a.	n.a.	n.a.	n.a.	65	378,100	5	287,481
1966	57	$ 205,933	32	$ 41,483	1	$ 100	22	136,100	2	28,250
1967	40	297,833	24	36,438	0	—	11	229,375	5	32,020
1968	61	436,550	39	82,007	0	—	7	27,320	15	327,223
1969	48	360,939	26	68,762	1	30,446	8	60,480	13	201,251
1970	46	229,486	26	103,352	0	—	16	115,500	4	10,634
1971	91	1,699,513	26	125,533	1	1,980	51	1,154,800	13	417,200
1972	127	2,636,792	36	214,958	2	6,804	79	2,233,030	10	182,000
1973	71	1,110,940	26	87,448	0	—	39	784,750	6	238,744
1974	49	1,340,036	14	35,486	1	10,000	32	1,284,550[b]	2	10,000
1975	46	1,561,603	4	37,853	3	77,500	36	1,026,250[b]	3	420,000
1976	80	2,481,203	8	349,252	0	—	69	2,119,951	3	12,000
1977	92	2,791,757	10	176,957	4	355,000	76	2,247,800	2	12,000
1978	108	1,641,841	29	428,466	11	147,755	65	1,007,620	3	58,000
1979	61	2,451,210	21	120,081	7	53,475	28	2,140,654	5	137,000
1980	53	1,509,422	24	199,178	14	343,944	12	855,300	3	111,000
1981	59	1,425,891	36	793,291	4	36,800	9	222,500	10	337,300
1966–1981	1,089	$22,190,951	381	$2,900,545	49[c]	1,063,804[d]	560[e]	15,675,980[e]	99	2,514,622

[a]Debt convertible into common stock only (not other debt issues).
[b]Data are not available.
[c]Excludes eight floating-rate note issues totaling $1,130 million issued in 1974, and three floating-rate note issues totaling $12 million issued in 1975.
[d]Totals include 12 preferred issues totaling $216 million, which are convertible into common stock.
[e]Totals include seven debt issues totaling $34 million which had stock warrants attached.
Source: Corporate Financial Counseling Department of Irving Trust Company.

term debt and preferred stock together accounted for less than 0.2 percent of all bank capital in 1961. Moreover, the relatively rapid growth in equity capital during that period was accomplished almost entirely through retained earnings. The dollar amount of new external issues of common stocks was minimal.

In the early 1960s banks responded to the slow postwar growth in assets and deposits by (1) paying higher returns on savings and time accounts; (2) aggressively offering certificates of deposit, savings certificates, and other liability forms; and (3) requiring loan customers to keep larger demand deposit balances. The surge in asset and deposit growth was pronounced, rising to a rate of between 9 and 10 percent from 1962 through 1973. By comparison, in the same period, the assets of nonbank financial intermediaries grew at an average annual rate of slightly less than 7 percent. Among other things, this doubling in the rate of growth of bank deposits and assets meant that sources of capital other than retained earnings, usually preferable because of their low cost to the bank, had to be used.

Tables 4-2 and 4-3 demonstrate that many commercial banks responded to this choice by issuing senior securities, particularly long-term debt, to finance a high proportion of their external capital needs. This decision was encouraged by regulatory acceptance of some amounts of senior capital, by pressures to maintain returns on common stock, and by changes in the banking structure. A review of the average levels of returns, marginal tax rates, and costs for preferred stock and long-term debt reveals the leverage benefits of senior capital. Banks found they could appreciably improve return on common equity by using favorable leverage from long-term debt. As reflected in price-earnings multiples, this use of fixed-cost financing did not seem to increase appreciably the risks banks were taking.[3]

The growth of bank assets and deposits averaged between 11 and 12 percent in the period from the end of 1973 through 1981. The growth of total bank capital and common equity capital grew at a slightly lower rate than bank assets and senior capital grew at a considerably slower pace. The reasons for the slower growth included the relatively high levels of interest rate during the period, substantial debt refinancing, and increasing doubts about regulatory acceptance of debt as part of a bank's capital base.

Bank Capital Needs in the Future

The amount of capital commercial banks will need to raise in the next decade depends on three basic considerations: the rate of growth of bank assets and deposits, the capital adequacy requirements of the various bank regulatory agencies, and the availability and cost of the various forms of bank capital.

Table 4-4 presents some interesting evidence on the first consideration. For example, if for the five years from the end of 1981 through 1986 bank assets continue to grow at approximately a 12-percent rate, as they did from 1973 through 1981, and if capital remains at its 1981 level of about 6 percent of assets, commercial banks will need approximately $90 billion additional capital. This amount is nearly 1.5 times the additional bank capital raised internally and externally over the last five years (about $47 billion). Over the next 10 years, the results will be more frightening. If the growth

---

[3] All of these factors are discussed in greater detail by George H. Hempel in *Determining and Meeting a Bank's Capital Needs* (Boston: Bankers Publishing Company, 1983).

TABLE 4-4
Possible Future Growth in Assets and Capital of Commercial Banks (amounts in millions of dollars)

Growth rate (from end of year)	1981 assets	Future assets	7% Capital requirement	6% Capital requirement	1981 capital	Additional capital 7%	Additional capital 6%
From 1981 through 1986							
2%	2,028,901	2,239,907	156,793	134,394	124,761	32,032	9,633
4	2,028,901	2,469,173	172,842	148,150	124,761	48,081	23,389
6	2,028,901	2,714,670	190,027	162,880	124,761	65,266	38,119
8	2,028,901	2,980,456	208,632	178,827	124,761	83,871	54,066
10	2,028,901	3,268,560	228,799	196,114	124,761	104,038	71,353
12	2,028,901	3,574,924	250,245	214,495	124,761	125,484	89,734
14	2,028,901	3,905,634	273,394	234,338	124,761	148,633	109,577
16	2,028,901	4,260,692	298,248	255,642	124,761	173,487	130,881
From 1981 through 1991							
2%	2,028,901	2,473,230	173,126	148,394	124,761	48,365	23,633
4	2,028,901	3,002,773	210,194	180,166	124,761	85,433	55,405
6	2,028,901	3,633,762	254,363	218,026	124,761	129,602	93,265
8	2,028,901	4,380,397	306,628	262,824	124,761	181,867	138,073
10	2,028,901	5,262,969	368,408	315,778	124,761	243,647	191,017
12	2,028,901	6,301,767	441,123	378,106	124,761	316,362	253,345
14	2,028,901	7,521,136	526,480	451,268	124,761	401,719	326,507
16	2,028,901	8,949,482	626,463	536,969	124,761	501,702	412,208

of bank assets were at a 12-percent annual rate, about $253 billion of additional capital would be needed by banks. This compares with approximately $78 billion of additional bank capital in the last 10 years.

Reduction in either of two variables—the rate of asset growth or the proportion of capital required—can reduce the additional capital needed over the next 5 or 10 years. The effects of these reductions deserve further attention. Table 4-4 shows that, if the annual growth of bank assets (and corresponding growth in deposits and loans) is held to 8 percent, capital needs would fall to a more manageable level of roughly $54 billion over the next 5 years and roughly $138 billion over the next 10 years.

One must question the impact of slower growth in bank assets on our economy. In particular, what would be the effect on businesses, consumers and local governments if they received considerably less money from commercial banks during an economic period of inflation and relatively low profit? In past periods of economic recovery and boom, commercial banks have filled between 40 and 50 percent of the nation's total credit demands. Thus, weak bank capital structures could hobble an economic recovery and economic growth by preventing the banks from financing such needed business outlays as expenditures on plant expansions and inventory buildups. Slower economic growth and misallocation of credit resources may be the price paid if growth in bank assets is slower.

A lower percentage of capital required would also reduce the dollar amount of capital required in the future to more manageable amounts. Although the higher leverage multiplier would generally be appealing to banks, the cost of this alternative would be higher capital risk. Both regulators and bank management are asking themselves how much more capital ratios can decline before significant numbers of banks may be hurt by too little capital. The final column in Table 4-4 shows the amount of capital which would be required for various growth rates if the ratio of capital to assets were allowed to drop from 7 to 6 percent.

The four key ingredients an individual bank may use in deciding how much, if any, capital it needs and in what form the capital should be raised are described in the following section.

STEP 1: THE OVERALL FINANCIAL PLAN

The first of the four key ingredients in bank capital planning is the development of an overall financial plan. The amount of capital needed is clearly affected by the bank's overall financial plan, and the overall financial plan is constrained by the amount of capital the bank has raised. The financial planning process starts with a careful analysis of the bank's present position and performance. Next, the bank should predict several key variables, use these variables to develop overall financial projections, and see if the financial results of these projections are consistent with the bank's plans and policies. The sensitivity of these overall results to changes in key variables should be carefully examined. The bank should then analyze these results with emphasis on the specific question of what amounts of capital will be necessary to support the desired results.

Analyzing a Bank's Performance

A bank should know where it has been—its accomplishments and failures, strengths and weaknesses—before it projects its future course. The bank must analyze all of the primary aspects of its performance, even when the principal objective is to measure the bank's capital needs. The methods for analyzing a bank's past performance were discussed in detail in Chapter 2. The key risk-return measurements for a bank should be compared with those for peer banks or the first stage of capital planning.

Predicting Selected Key Variables in the Future

The next step in the planning process, after a complete analysis of the bank's past performance is made, is to select a few key variables for the bank and to predict the levels of these variables for targeted future periods. It is important that the predictions for these variables are not merely extrapolations of past data. They should represent plans which include reasonable policy goals and objectives as well as observation of trends from past periods.

Selecting a limited number of key variables can be a difficult task. One variable that is usually emphasized is the predicted level of deposits. When predicting the amount of deposits, a bank should consider factors affecting deposit growth that can be controlled (such as promotional efforts, services offered, rates paid on savings, etc.) and factors that cannot be controlled (such as population growth, competition, economic conditions, etc.). Deposits often must be separated by the form of deposit (demand, passbook, and time) and by type of depositor (business, individual, and public) in order to pick up the differences in factors affecting their growth. Furthermore, some banks have the ability to control their level of time deposits and other purchased obligations by changing their rates in the marketplace. Such banks may want to predict demand and passbook deposits, and then treat the level of their time deposits as a residual based primarily on their projections of profitable loan and investment opportunities (assuming that they can always purchase the funds required).

Another commonly used key variable is the predicted level of the bank's loans. Both controllable (such as the rates charged on various types of loans) and noncontrollable (such as local economic conditions and the national business cycle) variables can affect how much a bank has in its loan portfolio. Often, a bank will predict loans equal to a target percentage of deposits; however, this prediction assumes a bank can cut off loans to customers when loan demand is unusually strong or find new loan customers when demand is weak. Both of these predictions seem highly suspect, and it is preferable to predict a range of loan-to-deposit relationships depending on the national and local economic conditions during the period for which loans are predicted.

Generally, the other key variable or variables should be any factors that set limits on the progress of the bank during the prediction period. The limiting variable may be adequacy of trained personnel, target for the spread to be earned on employed assets, rate of opening new branches, or some other factor. The important criterion is that the variables will allow the bank to perform some basic activity such as increasing deposit or loan growth, in a different way than would be possible without that variable.

Once the key variables have been selected, the bank has to make estimates for what will happen to these variables during the prediction period. Selection of the prediction period is itself a difficult task. Very short term predictions, such as a month, may be subject to random fluctuations and are usually too short-term and small to have a large impact on capital needs. Longer term predictions, such as 10 years, are subject to so many changes in noncontrollable factors that taking current actions is unrealistic. The most meaningful time period for predicting the key variable is probably annually for the next three to five years. As an overall projection is developed, it may be necessary to change the predictions for one or more of the key variables or even a key variable itself. It is important to note that the availability of capital, which seems like a key variable for at least some banks, is not included as a key variable for the initial overall projection. Instead, the need for capital is established by the overall projection; then the question of the availability of capital is carefully examined.

Developing an Overall Projection from the Key Variables

The next step, once predictions have been made for the key variables, is to develop *pro forma* balance sheets and projected income statements for the prediction period. Because these statements are interrelated, they must be developed jointly. The relationships calculated in analyzing the bank's past performance can be very useful during this step. Prior experience serves as a useful guide to necessary relationships in developing an overall projection and also as a check on the reasonableness of assumptions. The management of a bank should have good reasons for projecting figures that depart significantly from prior experience. Generally the overall balance sheet predictions should include only major categories of assets and liabilities. Further detail may be essential for some other banking areas; however, for capital planning the number of categories should be kept as low as possible without materially harming the accuracy of the projection.

The first step in constructing the *pro forma* balance sheet should be to estimate a bank's major sources of funds. The deposit accounts can be predicted from forecasted growth rates for demand deposits and time and savings deposits and from the predicted dollar amount of public deposits. The other liabilities account is often a key variable in larger banks where various forms of liabilities (e.g., Fed Funds or Eurodollars) are purchased. For smaller banks, unless specific information exists, the other liabilities account is often small and may be estimated to remain constant or grow at about the same rate as deposits and capital.

In predicting the capital accounts, the planner must remember that assets will increase because of additional capital (usually from retained earnings) as well as from new deposits or increases in other liabilities. The amount of retained earnings for a period depends on the level of a bank's earnings in that period, which is partially a function of the amount of earning assets and the bank's cash dividend payout. The uncertainties and interdependence associated with these variables usually does not materially weaken the financial plan because the amount of retained earnings is a small proportion of the total additional funds in most time periods. Banks can, therefore, safely use either of two methods to initially predict the capital accounts: (1) leave total capital at the preceding year's end level (less any scheduled debt repayments) or (2) allow total capital to increase by the increase in earnings estimated from the predicted income statement less any planned cash dividends. The implications of each of these alternatives for capital planning are discussed in the section on estimating capital needs from financial projections. No changes should be made on the initial projection except for scheduled debt repayments and possibly for an estimation of retained earnings. In a later step, specific financing to meet additional capital needs will be reflected in the balance sheet.

The next step in constructing the *pro forma* balance sheet is to estimate the uses of the funds from the various deposit and other sources. The amount in cash and due from banks is estimated by multiplying the various categories of deposits times the reserve requirements for these categories for banks that are members of the Federal Reserve. The amount of cash and due from banks for nonmember state banks may be set by state law or balances required by correspondents, or both.

The loan category is often the most difficult to predict. A bank may have a target amount of loans or loan-to-deposit ratio; however, factors such as national and local economic conditions may make the target difficult to obtain. Fortunately, flexibility in security holdings can cushion the lower income if loan demand is low and provide some extra funds if loan demand is higher than predicted.

The fixed asset category changes by additions to fixed assets less depreciation on existing equipment. If the amount in this category does not change much, it can be assumed that capital expenditures are roughly equivalent to depreciation. Because non-cash expenses (such as depreciation) charged against revenues are usually relatively small for a bank, changes in the fixed asset category are usually significant only if the bank plans major physical expansion.

The other assets account is a catchall category that usually can be predicted from prior experience. Finally, the investment account is generally used as a balancing residual, that is, the difference between total (deposit and other) sources of funds and the previously discussed asset categories (cash and due from banks, loans, fixed assets, and other assets).

All of the predictions for balance sheet accounts are rough estimates, but if the predictions for the key variable are reasonable, the overall forecast will be accurate enough for thoughtful capital planning. Care must be taken at every step to keep the balance sheet in balance. The *pro forma* balance sheet for the first year provides the base for building the following year's projections and so on, until each year's projection has been completed. One additional question is whether some type of average or year-end balances should be used. In situations in which they are readily obtainable, average balances are usually preferable. If an attempt is made to calculate precise earnings on assets and interest on deposits, average figures will have to be considered. One simple alternative is to use an average of beginning and year-end figures for this purpose. A bank with significant seasonal variations, however, will have to use daily, weekly, or monthly average figures.

Sensitivity Analysis and a Range for the Projections

As the bank continues to make projections year after year, it will probably acquire increasing confidence in its projections. Still, many factors outside a bank's control affect its projections. In preparing to react to an array of possible developments, a bank must envision how sensitive its key variables are to changes beyond the bank's control and the effect of changes in these key variables on the overall forecast. For example, what would happen if a bank's deposits grew at a 20 percent compound rate annually instead of a predicted 10 percent rate? What would be the impact of a substantial drop-off in loan demand? Management should test only those key variables about which it is uncertain and which would have a significant impact. For example, substantial changes in deposit growth may be important for a bank, but changes in equipment prices may have only a very modest effect. One very useful technique is to test the key variables by changing them by the greatest amount management would think possible and then to follow the consequences through the projection.

If management believes there is a reasonable probability that some key variables may be off by a wide margin and that future events might call for different plans and decisions, it should prepare two more overall projections to bracket the range of possibilities. One projection should be pessimistic, assuming that the identified key variables are at the lower end of reasonable expectations. Capital and other plans and strategies may be appreciably different under this pessimistic outlook. The other projection should be optimistic, assuming that the identified key variables are at the upper end of reasonable expectations. Plans and strategies may vary appreciably under this alternative. It is interesting to note that this projection is likely to place greater pressure on the ability to raise external capital. In fact, capital requirements could become so great that the availability of capital becomes an important limiting variable in the overall projection.

Determining Capital Needs from Projections

The final step in the financial planning process is to determine the capital needs based on the bank's projections. The preferable way to approach this need is to determine what capital the bank believes is adequate to support its projected assets and deposits and other liabilities. The amount of capital it believes is adequate can then be compared with the bank's actual capital at the start of the year, less any capital repayments, and with its earnings less anticipated cash dividends. If the amount of capital deemed adequate exceeds the available capital, then management should consider lowering cash dividends and raising capital from external sources. If the available capital exceeds the adequate level of capital, the bank might consider raising its cash dividends. Other factors that must be considered before lowering or raising cash dividends are discussed in detail in the section on the internal generation of capital.

STEP 2: DETERMINING THE APPROPRIATE AMOUNT OF CAPITAL

The second of the four key ingredients in bank capital planning is determining how much capital is appropriate for an individual bank's financial structure. We will now examine the three primary factors affecting the appropriate amount of capital for an individual bank—the purposes of bank capital, advantages of leverage to owners, and capital adequacy as measured by regulators.

Purposes of Bank Capital

The first factor, and one of the most difficult to be considered, is determining what the purposes of bank capital are. Presumably bank capital serves useful purposes, and the level of a bank's capital is inadequate to the extent that it does not serve these purposes. The primary difficulty is that it is impossible to define the purposes of bank capital in a manner that is both (1) meaningful and (2) can be used to measure the amount of capital a bank needs.

Deciding the purposes of bank capital is somewhat simpler because of many similarities between the purposes of capital for a bank and the purposes of capital for a nonfinancial corporation. At the top of Table 4-5 is a balance sheet of a hypothetical manufacturing company. The ABC Manufacturing Company has financed roughly half of its assets with debt and half with equity capital. Equity capital assisted ABC Company by providing a substantial proportion of the funds used to finance ABC's assets; by serving as a cushion (loss absorber), which encouraged creditors to lend to the company to help finance ABC's assets; by improving confidence among creditors, lenders, and customers of the company, and so on. Now let us look at the balance sheet of a hypothetical bank, XYZ Commercial Bank. XYZ has more short-term assets and is, therefore, able to attract considerably more from short-term creditors (depositors). The relative amount of capital for XYZ is considerably lower than that for ABC; however, the primary purposes—to encourage depositors, improve confidence, finance badly needed assets—are roughly the same.

TABLE 4-5
Illustration of the Functions of Capital

ABC Manufacturing Company

Assets		Liabilities	
Cash	$ 50	Current liabilities	$ 300
Accounts receivable	300	Long-term debts	200
Inventory	200		
Plant and equipment	450	Equity capital	500
	$1,000		$1,000

XYZ Commercial Bank

Assets		Liabilities	
Cash	$ 100	Current liabilities	$ 800
Short-term loans and investments	600	Long-term liabilities	130
Long-term loans and investments	260		
Facilities and equipment	40	Equity capital	70
	$1,000		$1,000

Brenton C. Leavitt of the staff of the Board of Governors has stressed four functions of bank capital:

1   To protect the uninsured depositor in the event of insolvency and liquidation.

2   To absorb unanticipated losses with enough margin to inspire continuing confidence to enable the bank, when under stress, to continue as a going concern.

3   To acquire the physical plant and basic necessities needed to render banking services.

4   To serve as a regulatory restraint on unjustified asset expansion.[4]

A brief evaluation of each of Leavitt's four functions of bank capital provides an excellent tool for determining the basic functions or purposes of bank capital.

The idea that bank capital protects uninsured depositors in the event of insolvency and liquidation carries an element of truth but appears to overstate the case. Most weak-looking bank assets can be phased out with relatively little loss, given sufficient time, competent management, reasonable earnings, and the working of the business cycle. Even the staggering losses of the 1930s were ultimately absorbed out of earnings when banks were not forced into liquidation. This is not to say that losses were not charged to capital funds; in the short run, they were. And if too many losses are charged to capital, the bank's doors will inevitably be closed. Arguments that enough bank capital will prevent failures and, even if there is a failure, will protect uninsured

---

[4] Brenton C. Leavitt, speeches before numerous meetings of bankers and regulators.

depositors are not substantiated.[5] Often the uninsured depositor was the one who, because of fear about poor management, fraud, or lack of liquidity, withdrew his or her funds and caused the bank to fail. The remaining uninsured depositors probably did benefit if the bank did have more assets financed by capital; however, it often was several years before such depositors were paid in such workout situations.

The question of the connection between banking problems and bank capital became even more intense after several widely publicized bank failures and reorganizations in the 1970s. While some of the troubled or failing banks had below-average amounts of capital, poor management and liquidity problems seemed to be the primary causes of these problems. It is highly questionable whether higher capital alone would have kept these banks open. In his monograph, George Vojta stated:

> The consensus of scholarly research is that the level of bank capital has not been causally related to the incidence of bank failure. Historically, banking crises occurred in periods of prolonged cyclical instability. Failures resulted from a loss of public confidence in the banking system.[6]

The second function cited by Leavitt is conceptually sound and seems to draw more widespread support. A past chairman of the Federal Deposit Insurance Corporation had stated, "In my view, adequate capital is the least amount necessary for others to have confidence in your bank and its operations."[7] The primary function of bank capital according to *Management Policies for Commercial Banks* is "to keep the bank open and operating so that time and earnings can absorb losses—in other words to inspire confidence in the bank on the part of depositors and the supervisor so that it will not be forced into costly liquidation."[8] George Vojta stated that bank capital should "provide protection against unanticipated adversity leading to loss in excess of normal expectations. The capital provision against excessive loss permits the bank to continue operations in periods of difficulty until a normal level of earnings is restored."[9]

Maintaining confidence is probably the primary function of bank capital. The fact that confidence is the vital ingredient of a bank's success should be self-evident. Uninsured depositors must be confident that their money is safe, and borrowers must be confident that the bank will be in a position to give genuine consideration to their credit needs in bad times as well as good. Furthermore, under the closely supervised, private banking system of the United States, the continuing confidence of the bank supervisor is essential to a bank's continued existence. Confidence is also important to the

[5] For example, see Vincent R. Apilado and Thomas G. Gies, "Capital Adequacy and Commercial Bank Failure," *The Bankers Magazine*, Vol. 55, No. 3 (Summer 1972); Robert E. Barnett, "Anatomy of a Bank Failure," *The Magazine of Bank Administration*, Vol. 48, No. 4 (April 1972); and Paul Z. Meyer and Howard W. Pifer, "Predictions of Bank Failures," *Journal of Finance*, Vol. 27, No. 3 (September 1970).

[6] George J. Vojta, *Bank Capital Adequacy*, First National City Bank, New York (February 1973), pp. 8–9.

[7] Frank Wille, speech before ABA's Correspondent Banking Conference in 1973.

[8] Howard Crosse and George H. Hempel, *Mangement Policies for Commercial Banks* (New York: Prentice-Hall, 1980).

[9] Vojta, *Bank Capital Adequacy*.

bank's stockholders—helping to protect them from failure which generally results in complete loss of stockholders' investment and improving the bank's market price and, therefore, its ability to raise additional equity capital.

The primary concern about confidence as the primary function of bank capital is not conceptual but measurement. Any measure of how much capital is necessary for depositors, borrowers, regulators, shareholders, and other interested parties to remain confident is at best imprecise and may vary widely with economic and regulatory conditions. The bank manager who seeks to maintain capital adequate to serve this function is clearly not dealing with a precise measure.

Bank capital has other important, but probably secondary, functions. As in any business, a part of the capital is needed to supply the working tools of the enterprise. This function is immediately evident in the organization of a new bank; the first expenditure of funds supplied by the stockholders is the banking premises and the equipment needed to begin operations. The provision of such working assets is a continuing function of bank capital. One cannot expect the depositor to supply the funds for new branch buildings or drive-in facilities. One problem in measuring the adequacy of bank capital is determining the extent to which capital may be available to serve other purposes and functions of capital funds, even though it is invested in premises and equipment.

The idea that another secondary function of capital is to restrain "unjustified" expansion of bank assets is more reasonable than it may at first appear. Regulatory capital requirements may prevent a bank from growing beyond the ability of management to manage, may improve the quality of bank assets, may control the ability of banks to leverage their growth, and may lead to higher bank earnings on assets. Indeed, capital requirements have been used to prevent "unjustified" expansion in several recent bank holding company decisions. One warning is that to rely solely or even primarily on bank capital requirements to achieve all of these tasks is obviously unsound.

Other secondary functions, in addition to those listed by Leavitt include the representation of private ownership of banks and the cushion that supports a bank's normal credit and interest rate risks. All of these functions are important, nevertheless, the primary function of bank capital funds is still probably to reassure the public and the bank regulatory authorities that a bank is in a position to withstand whatever strains may be placed on it. Adequate capital provides the confidence necessary to keep a bank open so that it may be able to absorb losses out of future earnings rather than out of capital funds themselves.

The Need for Leverage to Improve the Returns to Owners

The second of the three primary factors affecting the appropriate amount of capital for an individual bank is the need for financial leverage to increase returns for the bank's owners. Tables 4-5 and 4-6 illustrate the importance of financial leverage. The ABC Manufacturing Company was 50 percent equity financed, which meant the firm had a leverage multiplier of 2.[10] A 7 percent after-tax return on assets by ABC Manufacturing Company (approximately the average return for manufacturing companies in 1979–1981) leads to a 14 percent return on equity for ABC Manufacturing.

---

[10] The concept of a leverage multiplier was discussed in detail in Chapter 2.

TABLE 4-6
Effects of Financial Leverage on Returns on Equity

	ABC Manufacturing Company[a]	XYZ Commercial Bank[a]	Typical smaller bank[b]	Typical larger bank[b]
Assets	$1,000	$1,000	—	—
Equity	$ 500	$ 70	—	—
Net earnings	$ 70	$ 9	—	—
Equity/assets	50.0%	7.0%	8.0%	5.5%
Return on assets	7.0%	0.9%	1.1%	0.7%
Leverage multiplier	2.0×	14.3×	12.5×	18.2×
Return on equity	14.0%	12.9%	13.8%	12.7%

[a]From Table 4-5.
[b]Estimated from the 1979, 1980, and 1981 *Annual Reports of the Federal Deposit Insurance Corporation*.

How can XYZ Commercial Bank, which earns only 0.9 percent on its assets (about average for banks in 1979–1981), satisfy its owners and have the ability to attract additional equity? XYZ Bank must have significantly more leverage, which means fewer assets financed by equity and a higher leverage multiplier in order to compete in the equity market with ABC Manufacturing. In Table 4-6, it is assumed that 7 percent of XYZ Bank's assets are financed by equity (above average for banks in 1979–1981). The resulting leverage multiplier of 14.3 leads to a nearly competitive return on equity of 12.9 percent.

This example indicates that in order to attract and keep owners, commercial banks must, and in the real world do, have the financial leverage resulting from low proportions of equity in relation to assets. Thus, particularly from the owner's point of view, the appropriate amount of equity capital is little enough to produce at least an adequate return on capital without taking too much capital risk. Three factors tend to keep bank owners from using excessive financial leverage to increase their bank's return on capital.

First, market constraints should keep surplus units from lending excessive amounts to banks in relation to money provided by bank owners. Some "market" advocates have gone as far as stating that the ability to attract both capital and noncapital funds should be the primary determinant of a bank's capital position. This position seems extreme because it ignores factors such as market imperfection, which may particularly affect the ability to attract funds of smaller banks and the existence of deposit insurance. Nevertheless, the market does limit the amounts of capital and noncapital funds available to most banks.

Second, banks using the suggested objective of maximizing the market price of their stock will find that overuse of financial leverage will reduce a bank's market price per share. For example, if a bank earning $2.00 per share could increase earnings per share to $2.10 by using additional leverage, the bank should increase leverage only if the market price per share increased. If, for example, the price-earnings multiple fell from 10 to 9 because of the greater risk, the bank would be wise to avoid the additional leverage because its stock price would fall from $20 to $18.90 per share.

Third, regulatory authorities force banks to keep amounts of capital that these authorities deem "adequate" to protect depositors and the banking system. At the present time, regulatory constraints are the most common factors limiting the use of financial leverage by commercial banks. Such regulatory constraints often conflict with owners' desires for more leverage and higher returns. Regulators usually seem to want more equity capital, whereas owners usually favor less equity capital.

The special characteristics of senior capital, debit and preferred stock, should be mentioned. If a debt or preferred stock issue is acceptable as capital by the appropriate regulatory authority, the issue increases the bank's capital position. However, the same debt or preferred issue also increases financial leverage and the resulting leverage multiplier of the bank. This dual advantage—both increased safety and earnings to owners—encouraged the use of senior capital by banks in the 1960s and 1970s. Factors such as high interest rates, repayment and refinancing difficulties, and regulatory concerns appear to have weakened this dual advantage substantially by the early 1980s.

The effect of bank size on the acceptable and permissible level of financial leverage is a final concern. The last two columns in Table 4-6 show the effect of financial leverage of a typical smaller bank and a typical large bank. The typical smaller bank usually has a higher return on assets but has a larger amount of equity capital. More equity capital means a lower-than-average leverage multiplier, which lowers the higher return on assets to a close-to-average return on capital. The typical larger bank usually has a lower-than-average return on assets, a lower-than-average ratio of equity capital to assets, which produces a higher leverage multiplier, and a close-to-average return on capital because of the greater leverage.

Several factors can be cited as causes for differences in capital ratios and leverage due to bank size. One is the greater management depth in most larger banks. Another is that the higher return on assets of many small banks means they have more risk and should be required to have higher capital ratios than larger banks. Some regulators have stated that smaller banks have less diversified asset portfolios than larger banks and, therefore, need a relatively larger capital base. This larger capital base will not be a major problem as long as smaller banks are able to earn an above-average return on asset. The most feasible explanation is that many larger banks use arbitrage more extensively than most smaller banks. An extreme example would be a larger bank that purchases and sells larger amounts of Fed Funds daily, often with correspondent banks, at a very low spread between bid and asked price. Or a large bank could purchase some type of deposits which it covers with similar maturity assets at a small margin. Small margins on arbitrages are usually justifiable only if little or no additional capital is needed. Such arbitrage transactions tend to build up a larger bank's asset size, reduce its return on assets, and reduce its ratio of capital to assets.

It is obvious that increased leverage has been the primary factor in improving banks' return on equity in the last couple of decades. The figures for all insured U.S. commercial banks are as follows:

	1960	1970	1980
Return on assets	0.89%	0.88%	0.80%
Leverage multiplier (assets/equity)	12.3×	14.5×	17.5×
Return on equity	11.0%	12.7%	14.1%

The figures for large money center banks, that as late as 1960 had more capital in relation to assets than the average bank, are as follows:

	1960	1970	1980
Return on assets	0.95%	0.69%	0.52%
Leverage multiplier (assets equity)	11.2×	18.2×	27.8×
Return on equity	10.7%	12.6%	14.6%

The reciprocal of the leverage ratio, the ratio of capital to assets, had fallen from 9.0 percent in 1960 to 3.6 percent in 1980. It would seem future growth in the leverage multiplier may be restricted if bankers and their regulators become concerned with rising capital risk.

Regulatory Capital Adequacy Concerns

The third primary factor asserting the appropriate amount of capital for an individual bank is the amount of capital a bank's regulators believe is adequate. Bank regulators have the responsibility of protecting depositors' funds and the safety of the banking system. Although other factors such as liquidity and interest sensitivity are as important, if not more important, in achieving such objectives, capital adequacy has been a primary concern of regulators for many years.

Federal and state laws prescribe minimum amounts of capital required for the organization of a new bank. The minimum is usually related to the population of the bank's locality. In recent years, as a matter of practical policy, supervisory authorities have usually required new banks to start with more than the legal minimum of capital.

Both federal and state laws also have minimum capital requirements for the establishment of branches (where permitted). These legal requirements have little real significance for banking today. They were enacted at a time when banks generally were much smaller. They have not been revised upward, largely because the determination of capital adequacy has become a matter of administrative judgment rather than definitive law.

With respect to member banks of the Federal Reserve System, the basis for determining capital adequacy is laid in Section 9 of the Federal Reserve Act and Regulation H of the Board of Governors. The regulation requires that the net capital and surplus of a member bank shall be adequate in relation to the character and condition of its assets and to its deposit liabilities and other corporate responsibilities. The exact nature of the relationship between capital adequacy and the character and condition of the bank is left to the judgment of the responsible regulatory authority.

Historically, the ratio of capital to deposits was widely used as a measure of capital adequacy from early in the 20th century until World War II. Early in the 20 century, a rule of thumb developed that a bank should have capital funds equal to at least 10 percent of its deposit liabilities. This rough rule was enacted in some states and received a kind of official sanction in 1914 when the Comptroller of the Currency suggested it as the minimum ratio for national banks. During World War II, bank deposits expanded rapidly as the result of bank purchases of U.S. government securities. To have maintained the 10 percent capital-to-deposit ratio in the face of ballooning deposits that were largely created by U.S. government security purchases would have seriously impeded the financing of the war.

The ratio of capital to total assets was used by the Federal Deposit Insurance Corporation (FDIC) and the Federal Reserve System in the 1940s and early 1950s. No generally accepted standard for adequately capitalized banks was developed for this ratio, although Federal Reserve System authorities suggested that an adequately capitalized bank would have capital equal to at least 8 percent of total assets, and the FDIC used the national average of the ratio for all banks as the standard.

The ratio of capital to total assets, like the ratio of capital to deposits, is unaffected by differences in risks associated with banks' differing asset structures. For example, two banks of equal asset size would require an identical amount of capital, even though one of them might have all of its assets in cash and short-term U.S. government securities and the other have 85 percent of its assets in loans. Both ratios have the virtue of simplicity and for this reason are still frequently used as a first quick test of capital adequacy.

In the early postwar years, the Comptroller's Office attempted to overcome the inability of simple ratios to recognize differences in risk on different assets by introducing a capital-to-risk assets measure. Risk assets, in the broadest sense, were defined as total assets less holdings of cash and U.S. government securities. The theory behind the capital-to-risk assets measure is that a major function of capital is to protect depositors from risk. Because holding cash carries no risk of loss, and U.S. government securities carry no credit risk, these assets do not expose depositors to risk and thus should be excluded from assets when measuring risk.

The basic capital-to-risk assets measure recognized one area of risk differential however, it obviously ignored varying degrees of risk in a bank's remaining assets. This led to the development of a capital-to-adjusted-risk asset ratio. In addition to relating capital to risk assets, this calculation includes a secondary calculation in which assets that are almost as riskless as cash and U.S. government securities, are also deducted from total assets in determining risk assets.

The Federal Reserve responded to the weaknesses in the beginning ratios by developing more comprehensive measures of capital adequacy. In 1952 the Federal Reserve of New York developed a method of measuring the minimum amount of capital an individual bank would need, given its particular asset structure. Assets were divided into six asset categories according to risk. Capital requirements of 0, 5, 12, 20, 50, and 100 percent were assigned to these categories. The sum of the capital requirements of all the categories represented the minimum capital required to be held by a bank.

In 1956 a more complex version of this formula was developed by a staff group at the Board of Governors. Labeled a Form for Analyzing Bank Capital, it was frequently referred to as the ABC formula. It combined a capital adequacy test, similar to the "New York formula," with a liquidity test, requiring more capital for less liquid banks. The results of this analysis were frequently capital requirements beyond reason, especially for "money market" banks which practiced arbitrage. The other supervisory authorities never agreed that it was a reasonable approach, and the formula has now been abandoned.

In the late 1960s and early 1970s national bank examiners moved away from any formula type of analysis. The Comptroller's Office issued the following policy statement:

> The Comptroller of the Currency will not hereafter rely on the ratios of capital to risk assets and to total deposits in assessing the adequacy of capital of national banking associations. These formulae, although of some value in assessing capital adequacy, do not take into account other factors of equal or greater importance. Henceforth, the capital position of the bank will be analyzed and appraised in relation to the character of its management and its asset and deposit position as a going institution under normal conditions, with due allowance for a reasonable margin of safety, and with due regard to the bank's capacity to furnish the broadest service to the public. These factors, which are necessarily imprecise, cannot be directly interpolated into any specific formula. The following factors will be considered by the Comptroller in assessing the adequacy of capital:
>
> (a) The quality of management;
> (b) The liquidity of assets;
> (c) The history of earnings and of the retention thereof;
> (d) The quality and character of ownership;
> (e) The burden of meeting occupancy expenses;
> (f) The potential volatility of deposit structure;
> (g) The quality of operating procedures; and
> (h) The bank's capacity to meet present and future financial needs of its trade area, considering the competition it faces.[11]

Later in the 1970s, the Comptroller's Office, the FDIC, and the Federal Reserve agreed to use trends and peer group comparisons of selected ratios to determine capital adequacy. The ratios to be considered included the following:

(a) Equity capital/Total assets
(b) Total capital/Total assets
(c) Loans/Total capital
(d) Classified assets/Total capital
(e) Fixed assets/Total Capital
(f) Net rate sensitive assets/Total assets
(g) Reserve for chargeoffs/Net chargeoffs
(h) Net chargeoffs/Loans
(i) Asset growth rate/Capital growth rate

Such comparisons have been combined with other ratios into an overall performance rating scheme called CAMEL by the regulatory bodies.

In late 1981 the three federal regulatory bodies announced new measures for evaluating capital adequacy. These measures are summarized here and appear in detail in Appendix 1. The FDIC stated that equity capital of 6.0 percent or more of total assets is

---

[11] Part 14a issued under R.S. 324 et seq., as amended; 12 U.S.C. 1 et seq.

acceptable for all sizes of FDIC member banks. Banks in strong financial shape might fall between 6.0 and 5.0 percent equity to total asset, whereas any bank below 5.0 percent would be considered undercapitalized. Equity capital consists of the total of all common stock accounts, 100 percent of equity reserves, noncallable preferred stock, and debt that must mandatorily be converted into common stock less 100 percent of doubtful loans and 50 percent of classified loans. Banks in weak financial shape were to be treated individually.

The Comptroller and Federal Reserve jointly announced a slightly different new method for measuring capital adequacy. Most banks' total capital must be a specified percentage of their total assets (generally between 6 and 7 percent) depending on the bank's size and its financial strength. Total capital consists of primary capital plus secondary capital. Primary capital is the same as the FDIC's equity capital. Secondary capital includes callable preferred, convertible (nonmandatory) debt, and subordinated debt. Debt is reduced 20 percent in value for each year between five years from maturity and its maturity date. Total secondary debt cannot be over 50 percent of primary debt. The roughly 17 largest banks and banks in low CAMEL groups or with low capital ratios are treated case by case. As time passes, the FDIC, the Comptroller's Office, and the Federal Reserve may get even closer to agreement as to what constitutes adequate capital.

In summary, three factors usually affect an individual bank's decision about the appropriate amount of capital for the bank: the purposes the bank and its regulators believe should be served by bank capital, the bank owners' desire for satisfactory returns on equity capital through financial leverage, and the regulators' opinions about how much capital is adequate to protect depositors and to provide a safe banking system.

STEP 3: THE INTERNAL GENERATION OF CAPITAL

After determining its capital needs over the next few years (both through a financial plan and determination of how much capital is appropriate), a bank must determine if all of the needed capital can be supplied through retention of earnings. If retained earnings (assuming a reasonable dividend payout) are sufficient to fill the bank's needs, they are usually the best form of bank capital to use. A general rule is that if a bank can finance all its capital needs without hurting its owners or its stock price, it should do so. Retained earnings are not a free source of capital (the cost of retained earnings includes the higher value of cash dividends received today versus those received in future years and possibly a lower stock price because of lower cash dividends), however, they are one of the least costly sources of capital for most banks and are most subject to direct management control. For those banks whose capital needs exceed their internal generation of earnings, the various forms of external capital discussed in Step 4 (following section) must be evaluated.

Sustainable Internal Growth

The three variables that combine to determine how much of a bank's growth can be sustained through the retention of earnings are (1) the amount of capital the bank and

TABLE 4-7
Examples Demonstrating Effect of Level of Required
Capital on Internally Financed Growth (figures in millions of dollars)

Example 1

1a. Start of year for bank with 8% capital to asset requirement

Assets	100	Deposits and Borrowings	92
		Capital (8%)	8

1b. End of year, same capital requirement, $1 retained earnings

Assets	112.5	Deposits and Borrowing	103.5
		Capital (8%)	9

Example 2

2a. Start of year for bank with 7% capital to asset requirement

Assets	100	Deposits and Borrowings	93
		Capital (7%)	7

2b. End of year, same capital requirement, $1 retained earnings

Assets	114.3	Deposits and Borrowings	106.3
		Capital (7%)	8

Example 3

3a. Start of year for bank with 8% capital to asset requirement

Assets	100	Deposits and Borrowings	92
		Capital (8%)	8

3b. End of year, required capital falls to 7%, $1 retained earnings

Assets	128.6	Deposits and Borrowings	119.6
		Capital (7%)	9

its regulators determine to be adequate, (2) the earnings the bank is able to generate, and (3) the proportion of these earnings that are retained in the bank.

The relationship between the proportion of capital that is deemed to be adequate and how much growth can be internally financed is illustrated in Table 4-7. Retained earnings of $1 million would finance asset growth of $12.5 million if the bank determined its present 8 percent capital-to-assets was appropriate (see Example 1 in Table 4-7). The same $1 million would support $14.3 million asset growth if its capital-to-assets was maintained at a 7 percent level (Example 2). The lower the capital requirements, the larger the amount of growth a given amount of retained earnings would finance.[12] If the capital-to-asset requirement fell from 8 to 7 percent during the year, $1 million of retained earnings would still finance $14.3 million of asset growth, but an additional $14.3 million of asset growth would be supported by the decline in the capital requirement (Example 3). An increase in the capital required would, of course, reduce the total internally financed asset growth.

The second variable, the earnings a bank is able to generate, should have a direct affect on how much growth the bank is able to finance internally. If the bank used as an example in Table 4-7 was able to earn enough to retain $1.1 million instead of $1 mil-

---

[12] The amount of growth financed with a constant capital to asset requirement will be
Retained earnings $\times$ (1/Capital to assets)

lion during the year, the growth financed internally would be proportionately (10 percent or $1.25 million for the 8 percent bank) greater.

The third variable, the percentage of a bank's earnings that is retained, has a similar direct effect on how much growth the bank is able to finance internally. Assume the bank in Table 4-7 had earned $1.5 million and paid cash dividends of $0.5 million. Reducing the dividend payout so that cash dividends would fall to $0.4 million would increase retained earnings to $1.1 million, and the growth financed internally would be proportionately greater.

Two articles have summarized the interactive effects of these three variables on the amount of asset growth that banks can support through internal generation of capital. Table 4-8 is a reproduction of a table in "Getting Capital: What Community Banks Can Do" by Simonson and Pace.[13] This particular table is for a bank maintaining a constant 7.5 percent capital-to-asset ratio. Possible after-tax return on assets appear on the vertical axis, and the dividend payout appears on the horizontal axis. The rate of asset growth (assuming a constant 7.5 percent capital-to-asset ratio) for each combination of earnings and dividend payouts appears inside these two axes. For example, if a bank earned 0.6 percent on its assets and paid out 60 percent of these earnings as cash dividends, the bank could support an asset growth rate of 3.2 percent through internal generation. If another bank earned 1.2 percent on its assets and only paid out 20 percent of its earnings, this bank could support an asset growth of 12.8 percent through internal generation. A similar table for a 6 percent capital-to-asset ratio and the formulas for constructing such tables appear in "Capacity for Asset Growth Model" by Bernon.[14]

A bank's target or planned growth can be compared with its internally supported growth resulting from its earnings, dividend payout, and capital requirements and is revealed in models such as that in Table 4-8. If the growth supportable retained earnings exceeds planned growth, the bank's capital ratios will improve or cash dividends may be increased, or both. If planned growth exceeds the growth supportable by retained earnings, external capital may be raised to support the growth or the bank may try to increase the growth supportable by internal generation. Lowering capital requirements or increasing earnings will increase internally supportable growth but may be difficult to achieve if the bank's capital position is already about as low as its regulators will allow and if the bank was already attempting to earn as much as possible within acceptable risk limits. Lowering the dividend payout (or not increasing dividends as earnings rise) is an option, but possible impacts on the bank's stock price should be weighed.

Rapidly growing commercial banks with capital needs clearly exceeding the amount of earnings that can be retained face a complex policy decision. If the bank's management believes that dividends will not significantly affect the market price of the bank's stock, the preferable policy is to pay a modest cash dividend and use typically

---

[13] Donald G. Simonson and Edgar Pace, "Getting Capital: What Community Banks Can Do," *The Bankers Magazine* (Winter 1976), pp. 89–95.

[14] David G. Bernon, "Capacity for Asset Growth Model: A Tool for Internal Bank Management and External Bank Analysis," *The Magazine for Bank Administration* (August 1978), pp. 36–39. Bernon refined the Simonson-Pace sustainable growth model in which $SG = \text{ROA}(1 - D)/(EC/TA)$ by recognizing that the retention of earnings reduced the bank's capital requirements so that $SG = \text{ROA}(1 - D)/(EC/TA)(\text{ROA})(1 - D)$.

TABLE 4-8
Sustainable Growth Rates Without External
Financing—Bank Maintains 7.5 Percent Capital-to-Assets Ratio

After-tax return on assets								
0.4	5.3	4.8	4.3	3.7	3.2	2.7	2.1	1.6
0.5	6.6	6.0	5.3	4.6	4.0	3.3	2.7	2.0
0.6	8.0	7.2	6.4	5.6	4.8	4.0	3.2	2.4
0.7	9.3	8.4	7.5	6.5	5.6	4.6	3.7	2.8
0.8	10.6	9.6	8.5	7.5	6.4	5.3	4.3	3.2
0.9	12.0	10.8	9.6	8.4	7.2	6.0	4.8	3.6
1.0	13.3	12.0	10.6	9.3	8.0	6.7	5.3	4.0
1.1	14.6	13.2	11.7	10.3	8.8	7.3	5.9	4.4
1.2	16.0	14.4	12.8	11.2	9.6	8.0	6.4	4.8
1.3	17.3	15.6	13.9	12.1	10.4	8.7	6.9	5.2
1.4	18.6	16.8	14.9	13.1	11.2	9.3	7.5	5.6
	0	10	20	30	40	50	60	70

Dividends as Percent of After-tax Earnings

Source: Donald G. Simonson and Edgar Pace, "Getting Capital: What Community Banks Can Do," *The Banker's Magazine* (Winter 1976).

low-cost retained earnings to finance as much of the expansion as possible. On the other hand, if the management believes that dividends will have an *appreciable* positive effect on the bank's stock price, the bank may gain from paying higher dividends and raising more of its needed equity capital by selling higher priced common stock.

Dividend Policy

Because dividend payout strongly affects growth supportable through retained earnings, a few comments about the appropriate criteria for a bank's dividend decision should be mentioned. The dividend policy decision of a bank should be made to maximize the value of the stockholders' return which, in turn, should benefit the bank itself. For the present investor to feel comfortable about his or her investment, a bank's dividend policy should be dependable and there should be assurances that past dividend actions by the bank will basically be continued in the future. For the potential investor, a consistent dividend policy history is an important factor in the investment decision and an aid in the investor's evaluation of the worth of the bank's stock. Probably the most important element in a bank's dividend policy is establishing a payout (dividends as a percentage of earnings) policy so that dividends will increase as earnings (hopefully) increase. The level and pattern of a bank's dividends are also key elements on which investors rely to help determine the total return that can be expected from their investments and whether or not they will invest at all in a particular bank. Also, if an investor is confident he or she understands a bank's dividend policy, that investor may place a higher value on that bank's stock.

The level of cash dividends should be set so that the bank can maintain that level over various types of business and economic conditions. Should business or economic conditions be such that earnings and profits are squeezed temporarily, cash dividends should be at a point where the bank is capable of maintaining them for a reasonable period of time until conditions improve. Dividends should not necessarily be increased immediately just because business may improve. If conditions change and the increased level of dividends cannot be sustained, then a reduction in dividends would be necessary. Cutting dividends has a negative connotation with investors and reflects a pessimistic view of the future by management. An increase in dividends is usually viewed as expected prosperity by management and, thus, investors would anticipate the persistence of the higher dividend level. A good rule to follow, therefore, is that an increase in the dividend level should lag somewhat behind actual increases in earnings in order for management to be assured it can maintain that level.

With regard to the dividend pattern, consistency is also desirable. Just as with the level of dividends, where fluctuation in the amount of the cash dividend paid is undesirable, the regularity with which this dividend is paid is also important. Skipping a cash dividend is distasteful to investors, especially those who are income-oriented. The frequency of the dividend is also of concern to many investors. The income-oriented investor will usually prefer more frequent payment of cash dividends, such as quarterly or semi-annually, as opposed to annually. Closer spaced dividend payments also help increase the investor's confidence because a definite pattern is set up more rapidly by the greater frequency of these payments.

In deciding on the level and pattern of dividends, several factors must be considered by management. These include the fulfilling of the investment objectives of the bank stock investor, the rate of return a bank can earn on its capital (as opposed to the rate that an individual could earn in an alternative situation), the earnings stability of the bank, and the bank's plans for future growth. Table 4-9 shows that the dividend payout ratio for all insured commercial banks had a slight downward trend in the 1960s and 1970s. The decline was probably caused primarily by the large capital needs to finance growth and a relatively poor market for most bank stocks. Interaction between cash dividends and bank stock prices have been questioned by some bankers.[15]

Table 4-10 shows that the average smaller bank tended to pay out less of its earn-

---

[15] Nearly every study on the subject concludes that cash dividends paid by publicly held banks tend to have a positive effect on their common stock price. For example, D. Sherman Adams (in "Are Bank Dividend Policies Too Conservative?" *Banking*, Vol. 60 (November 1967), p. 116) compiled the following statistics for a group of large banks:

Range of payout ratios	Average price-earnings ratios
Over 55%	15.0
50–55%	12.2
35–49%	11.7
Under 35%	11.3

Other studies supporting this idea include Gilbert R. Whitaker, Jr., *The Market for Bank Stocks*, Subcommittee on Domestic Finance, Committee on Banking and Currency, House of Representatives, 88th Cong. 2d sess: 1964; and James Van Horne and Raymond C. Helwig, "Patterns in Bank Dividend Policy," *Bankers Magazine*, Vol. 150 (Spring 1967), pp. 61–65. Although we cannot question the overall results of these empirical studies, we do believe that there are exceptions. For example, the stocks of rapidly growing, larger banks may actually be more appealing to institutional buyers if the dividend payout is low.

TABLE 4-9
Cash Dividend Payout Ratios for
Insured Commercial Banks, 1962–1981

Year	Percent dividend payout
1962	47%
1963	46
1964	47
1965	47
1966	47
1967	44
1968	42
1969	41
1970	42
1971	43
1972	39
1973	37
1974	39
1975	41
1976	39
1977	37
1978	35
1979	35
1980	36
1981	38

Source: Annual Reports of the Federal Deposit Insurance Corporation (Washington, D.C.: Federal Deposit Insurance Corporation, 1963–1981).

TABLE 4-10
Common Stock Dividend Payout by Size of Bank, 1981

Banks with deposits of	Percent dividend payout
Less than $5 million	28%
$5 million to $9.9 million	27
$10 million to $24.9 million	27
$25 million to $49.9 million	30
$50 million to $99.9 million	33
$100 million to $299.9 million	40
$300 million to $499.9 million	45
$500 million to $999.9 million	43
$1.0 billion to $4.9 billion	48
Over $5.0 billion	40
All banks	38

Source: Annual Report of the Federal Deposit Insurance Corporation, 1981 (Washington, D.C.: Federal Deposit Insurance Corporation, 1982).

ings in cash dividends than the average larger bank. The reasons include the more limited access to external capital of some smaller banks, the ability to reach a consensus on the tax advantages of retaining earnings among a relatively small group of owners, and the absence of any effect of dividends in market prices (since the shares are seldom traded). The lower payout of smaller banks may mean they have less to lose by reducing or omitting cash dividends.

STEP 4: EVALUATING EXTERNAL FORMS OF CAPITAL

There are numerous alternative external forms of capital for those banks whose need for capital exceeds their ability to generate such capital internally. Table 4-11 briefly

TABLE 4-11
Summary Description of Basic Types of Capital Banks May Issue

Type	Description
Capital notes	Usually smaller denomination subordinated debt at fixed rate(s) with original maturities of 10 to 15 years. Can be sold to bank customers (retail capital notes).
Capital debentures	Generally refers to larger (in denomination and total size) subordinated debt at fixed rates and with original maturity of over 15 years. A few issues have no interest payment and were sold at deep discount.
Convertible debt	Subordinated debt that is usually convertible at option of debt holder into common stock of bank at a predetermined price. Interest usually 10–20 percent below rate on straight debt; conversion price 15–25 percent above stock market prices. A few convertible issues have mandatory conversion.
Variable-rate debt	Subordinated debt on which the interest rate varies with some interest rate index.
Option-rate debt	Subordinated debt initially issued as variable-rate debt but which is convertible into fixed-rate debt at the option of the debt holding during at least some of the life of the debt.
Leasing arrangements	Financial lease, sale and leasebacks, etc., most of which are capitalized and some of which qualify as capital in a manner similar to debt capital.
Preferred stock	Stock paying fixed-rate (nondeductible for corporate income tax) dividend with claim on income and assets ahead of common stock.
Convertible preferred	Preferred stock that is convertible at the option of the preferred holder into common stock of bank at a predetermined price. Issued at lower rate and higher conversion price than straight issues. Used for some acquisitions and mergers.
Common stock	Residual but unlimited claim on income and assets of bank voting shares that elect board of directors who appoint management. Common stock may be issued; however, some new shares are sold through dividend reinvestment plans, employee stock option plans (ESOPS), and employee stock option trusts (ESOTS).

describes most of the principal forms. This section starts with the question of whether all capital should be equity capital. The use of fixed-rate subordinated debentures and preferred stock versus common stock is then evaluated. Other options for raising capital externally should be evaluated in a similar manner if they are being seriously considered.

Should All Capital Be Common Equity Capital?

When a bank finds it may need additional external capital, it must face the question of whether all of its capital should be common equity capital or senior securities (subordinated debt or preferred stock) should be used to fill some of its capital needs. All of the regulatory authorities appear to favor common equity capital over capital notes and long-term debentures. Brenton Leavitt of the Federal Reserve Board of Governor's staff summarized the disadvantages of subordinated debt from the regulator's point of view.

1 *Losses cannot be charged against debt capital in order to maintain the bank as a going concern.*

2 *Debt places the bank in a position of having to meet fixed annual charges for interest and possible redemption payments which must be met regardless of earnings.*

3 *Debt could impair future operating flexibility; restrictive covenants could limit alternatives concerning payment of dividends, mergers, and transfers of assets.*

4 *Debt already outstanding could limit the issuance of additional debt when it might be most needed.*

5 *Acceleration clauses would very likely be triggered when an institution is most vulnerable to collapse.*[16]

The Comptroller and Federal Reserve reluctantly began to accept some debt as capital in the 1960s. Rules for debt to qualify as capital included an original average maturity of over 7 years and subordination to all deposits and most other liabilities. In late 1981, the Comptroller and Federal Reserve decided the proportion of debt that qualified as capital would decline 20 percent a year during the last 5 years to prior maturity.

The Comptroller and Federal Reserve appear to have conceded that, in spite of their objections to capital notes and long-term debentures, the availability of notes and debentures adds needed flexibility to bank management. And though these regulators do not encourage the use of notes and debentures, they accept such issues (usually up to roughly a third of total capital) for two reasons. First, such debt instruments add to the basic regulatory purpose of bank capital by providing additional protection for bank depositors and others who would be adversely affected by bank failure. Second, there are some market situations in which a bank cannot sell new common equity or existing bank stockholders would be severely penalized (generally because the common stock price is significantly below book value) if regulators were to insist on an injection

---

[16] Brenton Leavitt in a talk to a BAI convention (date unknown). Some debt, he concluded, could be handled in a well-managed bank, but "it is highly desirable that it be long-term."

of new common equity funds. Even Leavitt was willing to conclude that the "risks and disadvantages of long-term debt do not appear to be insurmountable. A well-run bank in generally good condition should be able to manage the interest coverage and repayment of a reasonable amount of long-term debt."[17]

Noncallable preferred stock is now accepted as capital by three federal regulatory authorities. The restraints against using preferred stock generally come from bank management, which notes that dividends on preferred stock are not tax deductible as is the case for interest on indebtedness. As a result, financial leverage is usually much more favorable for debt issues than for preferred stock issues. Nevertheless, preferred stock should be considered for situations in which the bank cannot sell either debt or common stock at anything close to what it believes are reasonable prices.

A bank, thus, often has the power to decide if all of its capital should be common equity capital. For situations in which external capital is needed, whether all capital should be equity capital is a complex decision. In reaching this decision, a bank should emphasize three factors: (1) the availability of the various forms of external capital, (2) the need for flexibility in issuing capital in future years, and (3) the financial effects of the various forms of capital, such as leverage, immediate dilution, and earnings per share over longer periods.

The answer to the first two considerations depends in large measure on the size of the bank. Most community banks will find long-term debentures and preferred stock not available to them because such securities are only attractive to institutional investors. These institutional investors would not purchase these types of securities from banks under $100 million in total assets, and a significant market is not available for banks much under $300 million. A $2 million issue seems to be the bare minimum, and a $8 million to $10 million issue is preferred. A market for some forms of senior capital—small denomination capital notes, convertible debentures, and debt placed directly with a correspondent bank—is, however, available to many community banks.

Some community banks have been successful in selling a moderate amount of capital notes in denominations as low as $500 to depositors or friends of the bank at a rate of interest somewhat higher than they pay on long-term savings certificates but below the general market for other debt securities. Such an approach can be an attractive method of raising some additional capital. Although the buyer's investment is difficult to justify in economic terms (except perhaps that earnings are more than on savings certificates), experience has shown that buyers can sometimes be found. Even so, it is unlikely that the typical community bank can rely on its ability to sell notes whenever it chooses, and meeting maturities on notes already sold could increase the bank's need for common equity at some future date.

The option to sell convertible debentures is also available to some community banks. These debentures are typically sold locally in small denominations to the bank's friends, customers, and stockholders—the same group would also buy additional common stock in the bank. In addition, direct placement of senior debt with a correspondent bank appears to be an effective and relatively reliable channel for community banks. Bank regulatory authorities have criticized this source, however, because it simply circulates funds within the banking system and fails to add capital strength to the banking system.

[17] Ibid.

As a bank becomes larger, a separate market develops for its senior securities. There are institutional investors who would not buy much common stock of banks but would consider the bank's capital notes or debentures as an investment. A market for preferred stock of large banks has also developed among certain corporate institutional investors. Senior securities of banks compete in the marketplace with similar securities of other companies. Through security analysis, these securities are appraised as to quality and value. They suffer in relation to similar securities from other industries in periods such as 1974–1975 when confidence in the banking industry was shaken by several well-publicized failures. Nevertheless, since the market associates size with marketability, and possibly with quality, the larger the bank, the better the market for its senior securities—other things being equal.

A larger bank, therefore, generally has the option of issuing senior securities. If this is true, the bank should carefully consider the financial effects of the various forms of capital described in the following chapters. Even if senior capital is financially favorable, it is generally not wise to borrow up to the regulatory limit in order to preserve financial flexibility in the future. We, thus, see that availability of external common equity capital should be carefully evaluated by both large and small commercial banks.

The availability of new common equity capital at anything like a reasonable price varies widely among banks. Sufficient amounts of reasonably priced common stock are available to most community banks located in small and medium-sized cities and towns. In such situations, ownership of shares in a local bank is often a source of pride and of contribution to the local community. Problems such as a maintaining control, ensuring widespread ownership, and moderating the desire to be on the bank's board of directors seem more common than finding willing buyers for new stock issues.

Large money market centers and regional banks face different problems. They must compete in an impersonal national market for common equities. A bank may find its common stock selling at a low price either because the entire stock market is depressed or because the market is pessimistic about banks in general.

The availability of new common equity capital may be most limited for smaller and medium-sized banks in larger cities. These banks do not have the national markets of the larger banks or the community interest and prestige of banks located in smaller communities. Even in the best of times, such banks must work to develop a market for their stock, and there are times when such banks cannot sell common stock.

In conclusion, the available forms of capital are limited for many banks needing to raise external capital. The need for flexibility in issuing capital in future years may further restrict the use of available senior capital. Nevertheless, new equity capital may not be available at a reasonable price or senior capital may produce more favorable financial results for a bank, or both. (The financial effects of the various forms of capital are considered in the following paragraphs.) For many banks, therefore, external capital does not have to be restricted to equity capital.

Financial Effects of Senior Capital versus Equity

The two potential financial advantages of senior capital over common stock as a source of capital are illustrated in Table 4-12. First, the issuance of senior capital results in lower immediate dilution of earnings per common share unless the financing cost exceeds the amount the bank is earning on shareholders' equity. Second, in the longer

TABLE 4-12
Earnings Results Under Alternative Methods of Raising Capital

	Present capital	Additional capital financed with common stock ($30)	Additional capital financed with 12% preferred stock	Additional capital financed with 12% subordinated debentures
Earnings on Existing Assets				
Earnings on assets (1.0%)	$1,000,000	$1,010,000	$1,010,000	$1,010,000
Less interest	—	—	—	120,000
Net income before taxes	$1,000,000	$1,010,000	$1,010,000	$ 890,000
Taxes (at 25% rate)	250,000	252,500	252,500	222,500
Net income after taxes	$ 750,000	$ 757,500	$ 757,500	$ 667,500
Preferred dividends	—	—	120,000	—
Net for common stock	$ 750,000	$ 757,500	$ 637,500	$ 667,500
Number of shares	200,000	233,333	200,000	200,000
Earnings per share	$3.75	$3.25	$3.19	$3.34
Earnings on Increased Assets				
Earnings on assets (1.0%)	$1,100,000	$1,100,000	$1,100,000	$1,100,000
Less interest	—	—	—	120,000
Net income before taxes	$1,100,000	$1,100,000	$1,100,000	$ 980,000
Taxes (at 25% rate)	275,000	275,000	275,000	245,000
Net income after taxes	$ 825,000	$ 825,000	$ 825,000	$ 735,000
Preferred dividends	—	—	120,000	—
Net for Common stock	$ 825,000	$ 825,000	$ 705,000	$ 735,000
Number of shares	200,000	233,333	200,000	200,000
Earnings per share	$4.13	$3.54	$3.53	$3.68

run, senior capital usually increases the earnings per share on common stock because it usually introduces favorable financial leverage.[18]

In reference to the top part of Table 4-12, assume that the bank earns 1.0 percent before taxes on total assets and has an effective tax rate of 25 percent (roughly the average for insured commercial banks in the early 1980s). Having grown rapidly, the bank now has $100 million in assets but only $6 million in capital funds. The bank examiners strongly suggest that it should raise $1 million in additional capital. The present capitalization consists of 200,000 shares of $10 par-value stock and $4 million in surplus, undivided profits, and reserves. Assume further that the bank has three alternative methods of raising the additional capital: (1) selling 33,333 shares of common stock at $30 a share (approximately eight times earnings); (2) selling preferred stock with a 12 percent dividend rate; and (3) selling subordinated debentures with a 12 percent coupon. Immediately after any of the financing alternatives, the bank will have assets of $101 million and capital of $7 million.

[18] Financial leverage is the use of funds with fixed costs and is said to be favorable if the returns earned on these funds exceed their fixed costs.

The top part of Table 4-12 illustrates the immediate dilution of earnings per share under the three alternatives. Debt causes less dilution than common stock; however, because of the 12 percent preferred dividend rate, the dilution of earnings per share is higher for preferred stock than for common stock.

The lower part of Table 4-12 illustrates what would happen if the bank's assets increased by $10 million over time. For example, earnings per common share would be $3.54 if the additional capital had been raised by the issuance of common stock and $3.68 if the additional capital had been raised by the issuance of 12 percent debentures. This example portrays favorable financial leverage. The highest earnings per share, of course, would result if no additional capital were raised, but the bank is assumed to be seeking a more adequate capital position.

The conclusions that can be derived from Table 4-12 rest primarily on four important variables: (1) the amount the bank can earn on its total capital (or assets with a given proportion of capital) before income taxes, (2) the fixed cost of the senior capital, (3) the effective income tax rate, and (4) the proportion of total capital that is senior capital. Table 4-13 shows the effect on the earnings per common share from Table 4-12 when any one of these variables is changed after the additional capital has been raised and assets have increased by $10 million. Numerous generalizations can be made from Table 4-13. For example, a bank that earns considerably more on its capital before taxes than its interest costs and pays a high rate of income taxes will find subordinated debentures an attractive source of capital. The basic message of Table 4-13, however, is

TABLE 4-13
Effect of Changing an Important Variable on Earnings Per Common Share

Variable changes from Table 4-12 sample bank[a]	Additional capital financed with common stock	Additional capital financed with preferred stock	Additional capital financed with subordinated debentures
No change	$3.54	$3.53	$3.68
Earnings on assets rise to 1.5% before taxes	$5.31	$5.59	$5.75
Earnings on assets fall to 0.5% before taxes	$1.79	$1.46	$1.16
Cost of senior capital falls to 8%	$3.54	$3.73	$3.88
Cost of senior capital rises to 16%	$3.54	$3.33	$3.48
Tax rate is 50%	$2.36	$2.15	$2.45
Tax rate is 0%	$4.71	$4.90	$4.90
Senior capital (when used) was $2 million rather than $1 million[b]	$3.54	$3.45	$3.87

[a]The specific variable mentioned is the only one allowed to change. All other variables were left the same as in Table 4-12 (assuming additional capital was raised by one of the three methods and that assets have increased by $10 million).
[b]When senior capital was used, the equity account was reduced from $6 million to $5 million (166,667) shares. All other variables were left the same as in Table 4-12.

that each bank must consider the important variables as they apply to its particular circumstances.

Bank debt instruments, even if not currently required for capital, may also have several advantages over long-term deposits as a source of funds. First, if they meet certain requirements, debt instruments are not subject to Regulation Q rate ceilings or reserve requirements. Second, because these instruments have fixed maturities, there is not as great a need for liquidity reserves, and most of the proceeds can be invested in longer term, higher yield assets. Third, the handling and placing costs associated with debt instruments may be lower than the cost of acquiring additional time deposits. Finally, the funds acquired through debt instruments are not subject to the deposit insurance costs of the Federal Deposit Insurance Corporation. Balancing the advantages and disadvantages to determine the appropriate amount of senior capital is a difficult task. The final balance will depend on each individual bank's circumstances and managerial practices. Some broad generalizations may nevertheless prove helpful for the development of policy in this area of bank management.

Small-to-moderate-sized banks need some financial flexibility. They are therefore generally advised to meet all their capital needs with equity and to issue senior capital only when their capital needs exceed expectations or when the market for their stock is unusually poor.[19] (In the latter case, they should consider convertible capital, discussed below.) The primary source, when small or medium-sized banks do decide to issue senior capital, will probably be principal correspondent banks or the banks' existing customers.

Most larger banks should seriously consider the use of senior capital to meet part of their capital needs. The majority of larger commercial banks are subject to more than minimal income taxes and should use subordinated debentures as their source of senior capital.[20] The amount to be used will depend partially on the current and ex-

---

[19] The limited use of senior capital by small banks is shown in the following statistics for December 31, 1981, from the *Annual Report of the Federal Deposit Insurance Corporation, 1981* (Washington, D.C.: Federal Deposit Insurance Corporation, 1982).

Insured commercial banks with deposits of	Capital notes and debentures as a percentage of total assets
Less than $5 million	Less than 0.05
$5 million to $10 million	Less than 0.05
$10 million to $25 million	0.1
$25 million to $50 million	0.1
$50 million to $100 million	0.2
$100 million to $300 million	0.3
$330 million to $500 million	0.3
$500 million to $1 billion	0.5
$1 billion to $5 billion	0.6
$5 billion or more	0.5

[20] Because preferred dividends must be paid from net earnings after taxes, and interest on debt capital is normally deductible from earnings before taxes, preferred stock will only be attractive to banks that have a low effective income tax rate or that pay no income taxes. The earnings-per-share figures in Table 4-13 show that preferred stock produces the same after-tax earnings as similar-cost debt in the no-tax situation. Preferred stock might be attractive in such a situation because of its lower priority and generally smaller charges (because repayment or sinking funds are not usually required). And in low-tax situations, interest payments on debt capital may not be deductible from earnings before taxes if the Internal Revenue Service can associate tax-exempt income with the proceeds of the debt issue.

pected cost of such debentures in relation to the bank's pretax return on its entire capital base. A bank should use debt within reasonable limits as long as its earnings on total capital exceed the current cost of debt by approximately 50 percent or more. Bank managers should limit indebtedness to between one-half and two-thirds of the maximum amount acceptable to regulatory authorities in order to assure themselves of some financial flexibility. The limit should be broad and flexible because of the economies of issuing debt in large blocks.

Convertible Senior Capital: A Special Case

The reasons for issuing senior capital that is convertible into common stock are quite different. In essence, the sale of such convertible capital usually represents a deferred sale of common stock, typically at a price between 10 and 25 percent above current market value. The dilution effect of convertible capital is less immediate and smaller than that of a new issue of common stock. In 1982, several banks issued debt which had to be converted into common stock by the end of a certain period of time. Regulatory authorities prefer this form, but the bank and bondholder lose flexibility.

Convertible debentures have been used much more often than convertible preferred stock.[21] Such debentures usually have lower interest costs than those of straight debentures because of the potential value of the conversion privilege. This lower cost further reduces the immediate dilution in earnings per share (see Table 4-13 for examples). In addition, when converted into equity these debentures will tend to restore a bank's borrowing reserve. On the other hand, convertible debentures usually carry higher underwriting fees to protect the underwriters against possible fluctuations in the market price of the bank's common stock prior to the issuance of the debentures. Another possible disadvantage of convertible debentures is that if the bank does poorly, it will still have to pay the interest charges because the holders (who have the option of deciding when and whether to exercise the conversion privilege) probably will continue to hold the debentures in the debt form.

Because of these considerations, bank policy should encourage the issuance of convertible debentures, particularly when management believes the common stock to be underpriced and when it wants the additional capital to be permanent rather than temporary.

External Common Stock Issues

Common stock has to be issued when a new bank is formed and may be the appropriate form of raising external capital to finance growth. When a new bank is organized, its capital stock is usually sold to a small group of interested investors. Additional stock may later be offered to this group and their friends; however, if the bank grows rapidly and needs larger amounts of additional common stock, it may have to offer its stock to the public.[22] The pricing of a bank's initial public offering is extremely diffi-

---

[21] Convertible preferred stock is appropriate primarily in unusual situations, such as when the bank has a very low tax rate or when it is financing acquisitions. It has been used more frequently by bank holding companies than by banks.

[22] Common shareholders usually benefit from public ownership and trading, which tend to facilitate transfers, add the dimension of marketability, and help establish tax costs for estate planning.

cult. Generally, the bank's book value, earning power, and dividends are compared with actively traded stocks of similar-sized banks for the determination of a reasonable stock price. It is not generally advisable for the issuing bank to try to squeeze the last dollar out of such an offering. The presence of a group of pleased initial shareholders who are satisfied because of appreciation in the market price of their stock will encourage higher common stock prices in future years. It is also generally advisable for the initial public offering to be priced in the popular range for new issues. A stock split may be used to adjust the price of previously issued shares if their value is not between $10 and $30 per share.

Once the stock is reasonably actively traded, the offering price of new issues will be determined primarily by the market price of outstanding shares. In addition to improving operating efficiency, the bank may take several steps to improve its market price. First, it should foster an effective dividend policy (discussed earlier). Second, it should try to publicize the bank and its activities as much as possible (for example, in the news media and to financial analysts' meetings). It is imperative that the senior management and director always be honest and realistic in presenting information about the bank. The investment community is very slow in forgetting unjustifiably optimistic predictions. The directors and senior management should also use stock splits[23] to keep the market price of the stock in an attractive price range. Most financial analysts seem to favor between $20 and $60.

Finally, bankers, should consider various alternative procedures, such as preemption (offering new shares to existing shareholders on a *pro rata* basis), public offerings, and private placements, for external issues of common stock. Most banks are not forced to make preemptive offerings; national banks and most state banks are no longer subject to laws requiring preemptive rights, and corporate articles requiring preemption can be amended. Flexible bank management should evaluate the probable costs and benefits of all available alternative procedures.[24]

SUMMARY AND CONCLUSIONS

Bank capital is much more than a source of bank funds. Relatively lower bank equity capital increases returns to owners but at the same time increases risk for the banks' depositors and the banking system. Considerable controversy still exists over the restrictions that should govern the recognition of subordinated debt as bank capital. There is little controversy over conclusions that capital needs of the banking system will grow

---

[23] Stock dividends can also be used for this purpose. Stock dividends tend to be smaller than splits, and they force the bank to capitalize a portion of its undivided profits. Smaller stock dividends provide shareholders with a lower cost opportunity to sell a small portion of their holdings but are more expensive to effect than stock splits.

[24] In an article on preemptive rights in banking, Paul Jessup ("Why Preemptive Rights in Banking?" *Bankers Magazine*, Vol. 153 [Summer 1970], pp. 85–90) concludes, "In the innovative and competitive environment of modern banking, use of preemption—as one possible financing procedure—is not rejected. What must be rejected are traditional provisions requiring preemption, and unexamined decisions to use preemption, without analysis of alternative financing procedures that may better serve the interests of a bank and its shareholders."

rapidly in the next decade and that many individual banks' activities will be curtailed or changed in some way because of a lack of "adequate" capital. Such conclusions have caused the emergence of capital planning as one of the key bank mangement tools in the coming decade.

Four primary steps were identified for the capital planning process. The first of these steps is to forecast a bank's anticipated course of development. Such a forecast is based on certain key variables from which projected financial statements and control ratios for the next year, as well as three to five years into the future, can be forecast. Multiple sets of estimates should be formulated using varying assumptions for the key variables.

The second step is derived from the first and involves forecasting how much capital the bank must have in its financial structure within the context of its anticipated development. The bank must ask what functions capital serves for the bank. It should then determine the effects of varying degrees of financial leverage on shareholder returns. Finally, management must determine how much capital adequacy tend to set the minimum tolerable level of capital, but those measurements tend to be gray rather than black or white.

In the third step, the bank has to decide how much of the needed capital will probably be generated internally. Three factors—required capital relationships, earnings, and dividend payouts—affect the amount of growth a bank can finance through retained earnings. A bank's dividend policy (the earnings it pays as cash dividends) may affect not only the earnings retained but also the bank's market price, which in turn affects its cost of equity capital. Retained earnings have a cost related to dividends and possible stock appreciation given up by shareholders; however, the flexibility and reliability of retained earnings tend to make such funding the largest source of capital for most banks.

Fourth and finally, if internally generated capital is inadequate to finance the bank's anticipated capital needs, the bank must choose among available external sources. Three interrelated factors generally are considered in making this choice: the cost and availability of the various sources, the need for future capital flexibility, and the immediate and longer term financial effects of the various sources.

APPENDIX   Capital Guidelines of Federal Bank Regulatory Agencies

INTRODUCTION

Late in 1982, the three federal bank regulatory agencies adopted guidelines for assessing the adequacy of bank capital. After a year of trying to establish a uniform policy on bank capital, the Federal Deposit Insurance Corporation (FDIC) rejected the guidelines announced by the Comptroller of the Currency and the Board of Governors of the Federal Reserve System and opted for a more conservative stance.

There are two noteworthy differences between the capital guidelines of the FDIC and the other two agencies. First, the corporation does not include limited-life instruments in its definition of bank capital. Second, the corporation has adopted uniform capital standards that apply to all nonmember insured banks regardless of size or holding company affiliation.

DEFINITION OF BANK CAPITAL

Bank capital is divided into two components, *primary* and *secondary*, for purposes of defining bank capital for supervisory determinants regarding capital adequacy. The primary components are characterized by their permanence and include the following:

1   Common and perpetual preferred stock,
2   Surplus,
3   Undivided profits,
4   Contingency and other capital reserves,
5   Mandatory convertible instruments,
6   Loan loss reserve.

The secondary components include the following:

1   Limited-life preferred stock,
2   Subordinated debt.

These financial instruments possess certain features of capital, but they lack permanence because they have maturity or redemption dates.

The *total capital* of a bank includes the primary and secondary components of bank capital with the following restrictions:

1   Limited-life preferred stock or subordinated debt issues must have an original final maturity of at least 10 years and an original weighted average maturity of at least 7 years to be counted as capital in determining capital adequacy.

2   The upper limit on the amount of secondary components that can be counted as capital is 50 percent of the amount of primary capital.

3   Secondary components with maturity or redemption dates of five years or more are counted fully. Below five years, the qualifying balance of secondary capital instruments approaching maturity or redemption is reduced by 20 percentage points per year. Thus, the qualifying balances are as follows:
    (a) One hundred percent of the amount of secondary capital instruments maturing or due for payment in five or more years,
    (b) Eighty percent between four and five years,
    (c) Sixty percent between three and four years,
    (d) Forty percent between two and three years,
    (e) Twenty percent between one and two years,
    (f) Maturities of less than one year are not counted as capital at all.

CAPITAL GUIDELINES OF THE COMPTROLLER OF THE CURRENCY AND THE BOARD OF GOVERNORS OF THE FEDERAL RESERVE SYSTEM

The guidelines divide national banks, state member banks, and bank holding companies into three categories: (1) multinational organizations, which, at present, consist of 17 institutions with assets of more than $15 billion; (2) regional organizations with assets of $1 billion or more; and (3) community organizations with assets of less than $1 billion. Capital requirements for the multinationals will continue to be set individually. The minimum level of primary capital to total assets is 5 percent for regional organizations and 6 percent for community organizations. Generally, these institutions are expected to operate above the minimum levels.

The regional and community organizations are split into three zones based on their ratios of total capital to total assets. The regulatory agencies will vary their treatment of an institution's capital adequacy according to the zone into which it falls.

1 Regionals with ratios of total capital to total asset above 6.5 percent and community organizations with ratios above 7 percent fall into zone 1. For these institutions, the agencies will presume adequate capital if the primary capital ratio is also acceptable.

2 Regionals with a ratio of 5.5 to 6.5 percent and community organizations with a 6 to 7 percent measure fall into zone 2. In these cases, the agencies will presume that the institutions may be undercapitalized and will engage in extensive contact and discussion with the managements and require the submission of comprehensive capital plans acceptable to the agency concerned.

3 If an institution's total-capital-to-total-assets ratio is below the minimum for zone 2, it will fall into zone 3. In this case, the agencies will presume that the organization is undercapitalized and will press management to augment capital. These institutions will be under continuous supervision.

CAPITAL GUIDELINES OF THE FEDERAL DEPOSIT INSURANCE CORPORATION

The capital composite to be used in assessing the capital adequacy of insured nonmember banks will be adjusted equity capital (the primary components of bank capital less assets classified as loss and one half of assets classified as doubtful) expressed as a percentage of adjusted total assets (total assets minus assets classified as loss and one half of assets classified as doubtful).

The FDIC will *not* consider the secondary components of bank capital in evaluating capital adequacy, since they lack permanence, are not available to absorb losses in a going concern, and impose mandatory servicing requirements. The FDIC neither encourages nor discourages banks from issuing these obligations for funding or other purposes; its view is that these instruments are not a substitute for equity capital.

The FDIC has established a "threshold" level for adjusted equity capital for all insured nonmember banks at 6 percent of adjusted total assets. When the adjusted equity capital ratio falls below this level, the FDIC will contact bank management and require the submission of a comprehensive capital plan acceptable to the FDIC and the state banking department.

The FDIC has set the minimum acceptable level of adjusted equity capital at 5 percent of adjusted total assets for any insured nonmember bank. When the ratio falls below this level, the FDIC will insist on a specific program for remedying the equity capital deficiency promptly. To bring about increases in capital, the FDIC will utilize its authority to withhold approval of applications of various types and, in cooperation with the state banking departments, to initiate administrative actions.

To provide protection against unforeseen adversity, the FDIC encourages even the highest quality institutions to maintain equity capital above the threshold and minimum levels. For institutions that are exposed to greater degrees of risk, higher equity capital levels must be maintained.

CASE 4
Premier National Bank *

The Premier National Bank was a $2.5 billion organization operating 68 offices in a major industrial state. The bank had stressed a broad range of commercial and consumer services and had achieved reasonably strong profitability and controlled growth and, at the same time, increased its reliance on noninterest sources of income.

In 1979, Premier recorded the highest level of operating earnings in its history and reached a record return on average equity capital. The bank advertised aggressively for consumer deposits throughout the year and it recorded a net increase of $225 million on its "Super-T" six-month money market certificates and $72.6 million in its "Checking/Savings" automatic funds transfer program. These programs helped PNB post a 7.4 percent increase in regular savings balances when most banks reported only modest growth in savings.

The bank's preliminary 1980 financial plan forecast a growth rate in average total assets of 11 percent, a growth in average gross loans of 12

percent, and an increase in average total deposits of 16 percent. The anticipated deposit growth included $80 million in average demand deposit balances and $100 million in the Super-T account. Management planned to reduce the average outstanding balances in other borrowings by $10 million and to reduce reliance on average federal funds purchased to a range of $40 million to $50 million. The preliminary budget for 1980 was targeted to a net income of $33 million, a return on average equity of 16.0 percent, and a cash dividend payout ratio of 35 percent. Management hoped that short-term interest rates would peak by midyear and that the prime lending rate would be at 9.50 percent by year-end, although it was recognized that interest rate forecasting had become increasingly difficult recently.

Helen Fowler, executive vice-president at Premier, had become increasingly concerned in early 1980 at the growing volatility in money and capital markets due in part to extremely high rates of inflation coupled with a high degree of economic and political uncertainty. Interest rates had moved sharply higher recently and very careful financial planning and operational control were therefore required to avoid further ad-

---

* This case is adapted from a case originally written by Harry Blythe and David Cole, both of Ohio State University, and is used with their permission.

verse pressure on profit margins. Fowler realized that the extreme volatility of interest rates and money market conditions would necessitate close monitoring of the "spread" between earning assets and the bank's cost of funds from all sources. Any significant mismatch between the amount of interest-sensitive assets and liabilities could put the bank in a highly exposed position in relation to profitability.

Although a preliminary profit and operating plan for 1980 had been prepared, Fowler believed that a more fundamental examination was required of the bank's overall competitive position and an assessment of Premier's strengths and weaknesses. In addition, Fowler was especially anxious to do a study of Premier Bank's weighted average and marginal cost of funds for 1979 with estimates for 1980. She had hoped to use these cost-of-funds data to better manage the planning process in order to appreciate the profit opportunities and risks presently facing Premier Bank.

EXHIBIT 1

Premier National Bank—Balance Sheet As of December 31 (dollars in thousands)

	1978		1979	
	Amount	Percentage	Amount	Percentage
Assets				
Cash and Due from Banks	260,843	11.87	256,118	10.15
Investment Securities:				
U.S. Treasuries	65,072	2.96	88,393	3.50
Federal agencies	34,817	1.58	50,412	2.00
State and local government	354,950	16.16	422,680	16.75
Other	8,084	0.37	8,910	0.35
Total	462,923	21.07	570,395	22.60
Federal Funds Sold	66,775	3.04	44,782	1.77
Interest-Bearing Bank Balances	32,500	1.48	0	0.00
Loans:				
Real estate	304,606	13.86	340,210	13.49
To financial institutions	3,700	0.17	4,900	0.19
To purchase and carry securities	5,900	0.27	5,100	0.20
Farm	11,600	0.53	13,700	0.54
Commercial and industrial	526,571	23.96	612,360	24.26
To individuals	508,698	23.15	607,514	24.08
Other loans	9,300	0.42	10,600	0.42
Total gross loans	1,370,375	62.36	1,594,384	63.18
Less:				
Reserve for loan losses	14,650	0.67	17,059	0.68
Unearned loan interest	76,679	3.48	91,226	3.61
Total net loans	1,279,046	58.21	1,486,099	58.89
Direct-Lease Financing	14,897	0.68	34,749	1.38
Acceptances	1,099	0.05	1,410	0.06
Bank Premises, Net	47,936	2.18	56,168	2.23
Other Assets	31,381	1.42	73,999	2.92
Total assets	2,197,400	100.00	2,523,720	100.00

EXHIBIT 1 (continued)

	1978		1979	
	Amount	*Percentage*	*Amount*	*Percentage*
Liabilities and Equity				
Demand Deposits	695,469	31.65	731,034	28.97
Savings Deposits	452,532	20.59	470,245	18.63
Time Deposits, $100,000 and Over	230,947	10.51	407,679	16.15
Other Time Deposits	477,000	21.71	512,000	20.29
Total deposits	1,855,948	84.46	2,120,958	84.04
Federal Funds Purchased and Repurchase Agreements	99,072	4.51	136,138	5.39
Other Borrowings	49,293	2.24	50,967	2.02
Acceptances	1,099	0.05	1,410	0.06
Other Liabilities	27,865	1.27	30,249	1.20
Subordinated Debt	0	0.00	0	0.00
Total liabilities	2,033,277	92.53	2,339,722	92.71
Equity Capital	164,123	7.47	183,998	7.29
Total liabilities and equity	2,197,400	100.00	2,523,720	100.00

EXHIBIT 2
Premier National Bank—Average Balance Sheet (Average Daily Balances) (dollars in millions)

	1978		1979	
	Amount	*Percentage*	*Amount*	*Percentage*
Assets				
Cash and Due from Banks	205.1	10.24	233.4	10.07
Investment Securities:				
U.S. Treasuries	71.3	3.56	77.3	3.33
Federal agencies	26.3	1.31	40.4	1.74
State and local government	353.7	17.66	390.9	16.86
Other	7.1	0.35	8.3	0.36
Total investments	458.4	22.88	516.9	22.29
Federal Funds Sold	32.9	1.64	38.4	1.66
Interest-Bearing Bank Balances	3.8	0.19	9.6	0.41
Loans:				
Real estate	319.5	15.95	349.1	15.06
To financial institutions	2.8	0.14	4.3	0.19
To purchase and carry securities	6.3	0.31	5.3	0.23
Farm	10.7	0.53	12.3	0.53
Commercial and industrial	479.5	23.94	599.0	25.83
To individuals	402.1	20.07	438.7	18.92
Other loans	8.6	0.43	10.1	0.44
Total gross loans	1,229.5	61.38	1,418.8	61.20

EXHIBIT 2 (continued)

	1978		1979	
	Amount	Percentage	Amount	Percentage
Less:				
Reserve for loan losses	13.1	0.65	15.5	0.67
Total net loans	1,216.4	60.73	1,403.3	60.53
Direct-Lease Financing	9.8	0.49	23.4	1.01
Acceptances	0.9	0.04	1.2	0.05
Bank Premises, Net	45.8	2.29	51.8	2.23
Other Assets	30.0	1.50	40.5	1.75
Total assets	2,003.1	100.00	2,318.5	100.00
Liabilities and Equity				
Demand Deposits	607.8	30.34	623.1	26.88
Savings Deposits	439.2	21.93	471.8	20.35
Time Deposits, $100,000 and Over	244.6	12.21	361.9	15.61
Other Time Deposits	403.2	20.13	493.4	21.28
Total deposits	1,694.8	84.61	1,950.2	84.12
Federal Funds Purchased and				
Repurchase Agreements	82.3	4.11	112.9	4.87
Other Borrowings	43.3	2.16	50.1	2.16
Acceptances	0.9	0.04	1.2	0.05
Other Liabilities	25.3	1.26	28.1	1.21
Subordinated Debt	0.0	0.00	0.0	0.00
Total liabilities	1,846.6	92.19	2,142.5	92.41
Equity Capital	156.5	7.81	176.0	7.59
Total liabilities and equity	2,003.1	100.00	2,318.5	100.00

EXHIBIT 3
Premier National Bank—Income Statement For Years Ended December 31 (dollars in thousands)

	1978		1979	
	Amount	Percentage	Amount	Percentage
Income				
Interest Income				
Loans:				
Commercial and industrial	49,485	27.03	76,159	31.96
Real estate	28,556	15.60	32,792	13.76
Consumer	43,976	24.02	52,755	22.14
Credit card	14,959	8.17	15,351	6.44
Total	136,976	74.81	177,057	74.29
Investment Securities:				
Treasuries and federal				
agencies	7,516	4.10	11,138	4.67

EXHIBIT 3 (continued)

	1978		1979	
	Amount	*Percentage*	*Amount*	*Percentage*
State and local governments (FTE)	17,498	9.56	21,285	8.93
Total	25,014	13.66	32,423	13.60
Money Market Instruments:				
Federal funds sold	2,773	1.51	4,221	1.77
Interest-bearing CDs	341	0.19	1,033	0.43
Total	3,114	1.70	5,254	2.20
Total interest income	165,104	90.17	214,734	90.10
Total Interest Income (FTE)	181,300		232,881	
Lease Financing Income	1,623	0.89	3,857	1.62
Income from Fiduciary Activities	2,625	1.43	3,097	1.30
Service Charges on Deposits	6,972	3.81	8,048	3.38
Other Income	6,784	3.70	8,581	3.60
Total other income	18,004	9.83	23,583	9.90
Total Income	183,108	100.00	238,317	100.00
Total Income (FTE)	199,304		256,464	
Expenses				
Salaries and Related Costs	30,809	16.83	36,962	15.51
Net Occupancy Expense	2,365	1.29	2,821	1.18
Depreciation	3,922	2.14	4,772	2.00
Taxes, Other Than Income Taxes	4,388	2.40	4,134	1.73
Other Operating Expenses	23,809	13.00	29,047	12.19
Total operating expenses	65,293	35.66	77,736	32.62
Interest Expenses:				
Savings deposits	20,781	11.35	22,964	9.64
Time deposits	45,957	25.10	76,663	32.17
Total deposits	66,738	36.45	99,627	41.81
Federal funds purchased	5,878	3.21	12,360	5.19
Other borrowings	4,232	2.31	4,264	1.79
Total interest expense	76,848	41.97	116,251	48.78
Provision for Loan Losses	7,313	3.99	8,274	3.47
Income Before Federal Income Taxes and Loss on Sale of Securities	33,654	18.38	36,056	15.13
Federal Income Taxes:				
Currently payable	9,507	5.19	5,158	2.16
Deferred	(2,214)	(1.21)	441	0.19
Total	7,293	3.98	5,599	2.35
Income Before Loss on Sale of Securities	26,361	14.40	30,457	12.78
Net Loss on Sale of Securities	656	0.36	401	0.17
Net Income	25,705	14.04	30,056	12.61
Cash Dividends Paid	8,569		10,333	

EXHIBIT 4
Premier National Bank—Income Statement As Percentage of Average Total Assets

	1978	1979
Income		
Interest Income		
Loans:		
Commercial and industrial	2.47	3.28
Real estate	1.43	1.41
Consumer	2.20	2.28
Credit card	0.75	0.66
Total	6.84	7.63
Investment securities:		
Treasuries and federal agencies	0.38	0.48
State and local governments (FTE)	1.67	1.69
Total	2.05	2.17
Money market instruments:		
Federal funds sold	0.14	0.18
Interest-bearing CDs	0.02	0.04
Total	0.16	0.22
Total interest income (FTE)	9.05	10.02
Lease Financing Income	0.08	0.17
Income from Fiduciary Activities	0.13	0.13
Service Charges on Deposits	0.35	0.35
Other Income	0.34	0.37
Total other income	0.90	1.02
Total Income (FTE)	9.95	11.04
Expenses		
Salaries and Related Costs	1.54	1.59
Net Occupancy Expense	0.12	0.12
Depreciation	0.20	0.21
Taxes, Other than Income Taxes	0.22	0.18
Other Operating Expenses	1.19	1.25
Total Operating Expenses	3.27	3.35
Interest Expenses:		
Savings deposits	1.04	0.99
Time deposits	2.29	3.31
Total deposits	3.33	4.30
Federal funds purchased	0.29	0.53
Other borrowings	0.21	0.18
Total interest expense	3.83	5.01
Provision for Loan Losses	0.37	0.36
Income Before Federal Income Taxes and Loss on Sale of Securities	2.48	2.32

EXHIBIT 4 (continued)

	1978	1979
Federal Income Taxes:		
Currently payable	0.47	0.22
Deferred	(0.11)	0.02
Tax equivalent adjustment	0.80	0.77
Total	1.16	1.01
Income Before Loss on Sale of Securities	1.32	1.31
Net Loss on Sale of Securities	0.03	0.02
Net Income	1.29	1.29

EXHIBIT 5
Premier National Bank—Additional Information (dollars in thousands)

	1978	1979
1. Investment Securities		
(End-of-period information):		
(a) Maturities		
One year or less	21.28%	17.76%
One to five years	37.86	38.31
Five to ten years	22.05	18.07
Over 10 years	18.81	25.86
Total	100.00%	100.00%
Market Value/Book Value		
U.S. Treasuries	97.43%	95.60%
Federal agencies	100.53	97.20
State and local government	96.80	94.56
Other securities	101.43	99.89
(c) Pledged Investment Securities	$286,100	$321,827
Percentage of total investment securities	61.80%	56.42%
(d) Interest Yield (based on daily averages)		
Taxable Securities	7.18%	8.84%
Tax Exempt (FTE)	9.47%	10.03%
Total (FTE)	8.95%	9.74%
2. Loan Losses and Loan Reserves:		
(a) Past-Due Loans as Percentage in Category (end of period):		
Real estate	0.98%	0.88%
Commercial	0.91	1.47
Consumer	1.77	1.96
Total	1.23%	1.51%

EXHIBIT 5 (continued)

	1978	1979
(b) Nonperforming Assets:		
Loans on nonaccrual	$ 3,346	$ 3,481
Renegotiated loans	374	364
Real estate owned	1,099	1,407
Total	$ 4,819	$ 5,252
Percentage of loans outstanding	0.35%	0.33%
(c) Provision for Loan Losses to Average Total Loans	0.59%	0.58%
(d) Gross Loan Losses/Average Total Loans	0.69%	0.85%
(e) Net Loan Losses/Average Total Loans	0.37%	0.46%
(f) Five-Year Average: Net Loan Losses/Average Total Loans	0.55%	0.53%
(g) Recoveries/Gross Loan Loss in Prior Period	53.90%	65.88%
(h) Ending Allowance/Net Loan Losses	3.21×	2.68×
(i) Earnings Coverage of Net Loan Losses	8.96×	6.84×

3. Annual Growth Rates:

	1978	1979
(a) Equity Capital	12.11%	12.11%
(b) Total Assets	13.11%	14.85%
(c) Gross Loans	19.66%	16.35%
(d) Total Deposits	13.50%	14.28%

4. Asset Yields:

	1978	1979
(a) Total Loans	11.14%	12.48%
(b) Investment Securities (FTE)	8.95%	9.74%
(c) Interest-Bearing Bank Balances	8.97%	10.76%
(d) Federal Funds Sold	8.43%	10.99%
(e) Average Earning Assets	10.63%	11.89%

5. Liability Costs:

	1978	1979
(a) Deposits		
Savings	4.73%	4.87%
Time	7.09%	8.96%
Total interest-bearing deposits	6.14%	7.51%
(b) Borrowings		
Federal funds purchased	7.14%	10.95%
Other	9.77%	8.51%
Total borrowings	8.05%	10.20%
(c) All Interest-Bearing Funds	6.34%	7.80%

EXHIBIT 5 (continued)

	1978	1979
6. Other Information:		
(a) Deposit Service Charges/ Average Demand Deposits	1.15%	1.29%
(b) Personnel Expenses per Full- Time-Equivalent Employee	$ 11,335	$ 12,333
(c) Full-Time-Equivalent Employee per $1 million of Average Assets	1.36	1.29
(d) Maturity and Rate Sensitivity of Business Loans as of Year-End		
Rate-sensitive loans/Total loans	69.16%	63.69%
Fixed-rate loans/Total loans	30.84%	36.31%
Fixed-rate loans over five years to maturity/Total business loans	21.81%	21.39%
(e) Rate-Sensitivity Analysis as of Year-End:		
Interest-rate sensitive assets/ Total assets	24.16%	21.60%
Interest-rate-sensitive liabilities/ Total assets	19.93%	29.64%
Gap/Total assets	4.23%	(8.04)%

EXHIBIT 6
NBSS Peer Group Data—Insured Commercial Banks with Assets
Between $1 and $5 BILLION (Percentage of Average Total Assets)

	1978	1979
Assets		
Cash and Due from Banks	12.57	12.50
Investment Securities:		
U.S. Treasuries and federal agency	9.55	8.80
State and local government	9.33	9.42
Other	0.70	0.61
Total investment securities	19.58	18.85
Trading Account Securities	0.45	0.44
Interest-Bearing Bank Balances	3.71	3.54
Federal Funds Sold	4.43	4.33
Loans:		
Real estate loans	14.54	15.32
To financial institutions	3.30	3.02
To purchase and carry securities	1.15	0.97
Farm	0.73	0.71
Commercial	18.07	18.26

EXHIBIT 6 (continued)

	1978	1979
Individual	12.64	13.27
Other loans	4.19	3.93
Total gross loans	54.62	55.47
Less: Reserve for loan losses	0.40	0.61
Total net loans	54.22	54.86
Direct-Lease Financing	0.63	0.77
Acceptances	0.78	1.11
Bank Premises and Equipment	1.64	1.59
Other Assets	1.99	2.03
Total assets	100.00	100.00
Liabilities and Equity		
Demand Deposits	30.51	28.31
Savings Deposits	17.37	14.99
Time Deposits, $100,000 and		
Over	16.22	16.65
Other Time Deposits	15.15	17.20
Total deposits	79.25	77.15
Federal Funds Purchased and		
Repos	10.12	10.80
Other Borrowings	1.03	2.13
Acceptances	0.78	1.12
Other Liabilities	1.90	2.13
Subordinated Debt	0.72	0.67
Equity Capital	6.20	6.00
Total liabilities and equity	100.00	100.00

EXHIBIT 7
NBSS Peer Group Data—Insured Commercial Banks with Assets
Between $1 and $5 BILLION (Percentage of Average Total Assets)

	1978	1979
Income		
Interest Income:		
Loans	5.72	6.80
Securities (FTE)	1.78	1.91
Federal funds sold	0.37	0.49
Interest-bearing bank		
Balances	0.29	0.39
Total interest income (FTE)	8.16	9.59
Noninterest Income	0.86	0.89
Total gross income (FTE)	9.02	10.48

EXHIBIT 7 (continued)

	1978	1979
Expenses		
Interest Expense	4.13	5.49
Provision for Loan Losses	0.31	0.31
Operating Expenses:		
Personnel costs	1.55	1.59
Occupancy costs	0.49	0.48
Other operating costs	1.00	1.02
Total operating costs	3.04	3.09
Total expenses	7.48	8.89
Profit Before Taxes	1.54	1.59
Applicable Income[a]		
Taxes (FTE)	0.74	0.75
Profit After Taxes	0.80	0.84
Security Gains (Losses), Net	(0.01)	(0.03)
Net Profit	0.79	0.81

[a]The FTE income tax adjustment, as a percentage of average total assets, was 0.50 percent in 1978 and 0.56 percent in 1979.

EXHIBIT 8
NBSS Peer Group Data—Insured Commercial Banks with Assets
Between $1 and $5 billion (Various Balance Sheet and Income Statement Ratios)

	1978	1979
1. **Investment Securities** (End-of-period information):		
(a) *Maturities*		
One year or less	21.58%	19.41%
One to five years	36.52	35.86
Five to 10 years	19.90	20.78
Over 10 years	22.00	23.95
Total	100.00%	100.00%
(b) *Market Value/Book Value*		
Taxable securities	96.11%	94.42%
Tax-exempt securities	94.84	92.53
(c) *Pledged Investment Securities/Total Investment Securities*	45.91%	43.24%
(d) *Interest Yield (based on average balances)*		
U.S. treasuries and federal agencies	7.19%	8.24%
Tax Exempt securities (FTE)	10.30%	11.11%
Total (FTE)	8.73%	9.82%

EXHIBIT 8 (continued)

	1978	1979
2. Loan Losses and Loan Reserves:		
(a) *Past-Due Loans as Percentage of Loans in Category (end of period):*		
Real·estate	5.06%	4.54%
Commercial	3.27	3.92
Consumer	2.99	3.20
All other	3.74	3.93
Total	3.60%	3.74%
(b) *Provision for Loan Losses/Average Total Loans*	0.54%	0.53%
(c) *Gross Loan Losses/Average Total Loans*	0.54%	0.55%
(d) *Net Loan Losses/Average Total Loans*	0.41%	0.40%
(e) *Five-Year Average: Net Loan Losses/ Average Total Loans*	0.54%	0.51%
(f) *Recoveries/Gross Loan Loss in Prior Period*	39.49%	42.67%
(g) *Ending Allowance/Net Loan Losses*	6.62×	4.98×
(h) *Earnings Coverage of Net Loan Losses*	14.16×	10.67×
3. Profitability Ratios:		
(a) *Profit Margin (FTE)*	8.76%	7.73%
(b) *Asset Utilization (FTE)*	9.02%	10.48%
(c) *Return on Average Assets*	0.79%	0.81%
(d) *Equity Multiplier*	16.13×	16.67×
(e) *Return on Average Equity*	12.74%	13.50%
(f) *Cash Dividend Payout Ratio*	41.01%	43.77%
4. Leverage Analysis (End of period):		
(a) *Equity Capital/Total Assets*	5.94%	5.90%
(b) *Total Capital/Total Assets*	6.60%	6.51%
(c) *Net Loans/Equity Capital*	9.37×	9.48×
(d) *Deposits, Federal Funds Purchased, and Borrowings/Total Capital*	14.14×	14.25×
5. Annual Growth Rates:		
(a) *Equity Capital*	11.85%	11.68%
(b) *Total Assets*	14.09%	11.26%
(c) *Gross Loans*	15.89%	12.33%
(d) *Total Deposits*	11.33%	9.76%
6. Asset Yields:		
(a) *Total Loans*	10.27%	12.03%
(b) *Investment Securities (FTE)*	8.73%	9.82%

EXHIBIT 8 (continued)

	1978	1979
(c) *Interest-Bearing Bank Balances*	7.89%	10.91%
(d) *Federal Funds Sold*	8.43%	11.37%
(e) *Average Earning Assets*	9.71%	11.41%
7. Liability Costs:		
(a) *Deposits*		
Domestic CDs—$100,000+	7.50%	10.37%
All interest-bearing deposits	6.33%	8.04%
(b) *Borrowings*		
Federal Funds purchased	7.96%	10.82%
Other borrowings	6.22%	7.13%
Total borrowings	7.68%	10.15%
(c) *Subordinated Debt*	6.98%	7.38%
(d) *All Interest-Bearing Funds*	6.58%	8.53%
8. Other Information		
(a) *Deposits Service Charges/Average Demand Deposits*	0.68%	0.77%
(b) *Personnel Expense per Full-Time-Equivalent Employee*	$14,310	$15,590
(c) *Full-Time-Equivalent Employee per $1 Million of Assets*	1.12	1.06
(d) *Market Rate Assets/Total Assets (year end)*	39.25%	38.41%
(e) *Market Rate Liabilities/Total Assets*	33.75%	38.67%
(f) *Gap/Total Assets*	5.50%	(0.26)%

CASE 5
Second National Bank

The Second National Bank of Albuquerque was incorporated in New Mexico in 1921, and enjoyed rapid growth through 1930, at which time it was the largest bank in New Mexico. Although Second National's growth was temporarily halted by the Depression of the 1930s, the bank resumed its expansion in the 1940s and grew steadily through 1978. Although Second National's postwar growth was steady, the postwar growth of many other Southwestern banks proved to be much more rapid, and by 1978 Second National had become the sixth largest bank

in New Mexico, with total assets of $135 million and net operating earnings of $1.7 million.

In mid-1974, after having refused a merger offer from a rapidly expanding Sante Fe holding company, the board of directors of Second National decided to accelerate sharply the bank's expansion program. To direct the proposed expansion program, the board hired a new president, John Jackson.

In order to assist in planning for the rapid expansion at Second National, Jackson established a long-range planning group in August

1974. To head this group, he selected Georgia Watkins. Watkins had graduated from the Southern Methodist University's School of Business in 1969, and had joined the corporate planning group of Aerodyne, Inc., a large Texas aerospace firm. In 1971, Watkins left Aerodyne and joined the Second National Bank. By 1974, she had been promoted to cashier, and she received the title of vice-president concurrently with her assignment to organize the long-range planning group.

During the first year or so of its existence, the long-range planning group was primarily occupied with the location and construction of a new drive-in facility and with plans to become a bank holding company (New Mexico does not permit branching). When the facility was completed, however, the holding company's plans were at least temporarily shelved because the Federal Reserve had indicated that, in order to be approved, the holding company would need more equity capital and because the bank was not convinced that the extra costs of the holding company were justified, particularly in light of the premiums that had to be paid to acquire banks. In 1977 and 1978, the long-range planning group had emphasized methods for attracting deposits and improving its planning techniques. In mid-1978, it had become evident to the long-range planning group that Second should plan to have a new bank building by 1980 or 1981. Current space was overutilized and a new building was important to their planned expansion. By early 1979, however, the rapid expansion of Second National had caused other areas of concern for Watkins.

In particular, the growth of the bank's capital account had not kept pace with the bank's asset and deposit expansion, as shown in Exhibit 1. This weakening of Second National's capital position could be traced to several factors. First, as shown in Exhibit 2, Second National's profits in the mid-1970s had not proven as favorable as that of other banks in New Mexico. Until 1976, this lower level of profitability had resulted primarily from the nature of Second National's loan portfolio, which was dominated by large loans to well-known customers at levels near the prime rate. The shift to higher yielding loans had only become evident in 1978's net income. Second, the new facility had increased costs appreciably in 1976 and 1977, and had probably increased the need for capital. Third, dividend payout had averaged 30 to 40 percent of net income in recent years and there was widespread sentiment among the bank's stockholders that cash dividends should be increased again in 1979. Finally, Second National had not issued new common stock because its board of directors felt the price of its stock was depressed from the $15 to $20 range (after splits and dividends) where at which the stock had sold during the late-1960s. "We're a much better bank but the market can't recognize it," stated one board member. Other forms of capital, such as preferred stock, capital notes, or convertible debentures, had not been seriously considered because "we're just a small bank."

By early 1979, Jackson had become increasingly concerned over the adequacy of Second National Bank's capital. Although he did not feel that the reduced capital position had become critical as of December 1978, he knew that the national bank examiners would closely scrutinize the bank's situation during the next regular examination. Accordingly, he directed Watkins to study Second National's capital position and make specific recommendations concerning the following problem areas:

1 Does Second National Bank need additional capital in 1979? If so, how much is needed?

2 If additional capital is needed, what is the best way to obtain it?

3 If Second National must go to the market in the near future for additional capital, are current market conditions favorable to a new issue or should the issue be delayed?

Because capital adequacy has remained a controversial topic, and since standards of capital adequacy have changed considerably over the past three decades, Watkins began her study by reviewing the arguments concerning the importance of adequate capitalization for commercial banks. She also studied the various techniques that had been used to measure the adequacy of a bank's capital account.

THE IMPORTANCE OF ADEQUATE CAPITALIZATION OF COMMERCIAL BANKS

Watkins believed that in most industrial firms the primary function of capital is to finance the firm's assets, such as its buildings, machinery, and inventories; the secondary function of capital is to provide protection to the firm's short- and long-term creditors. In commercial banks, however, the primary function of capital is to absorb losses that may occur; the financing of the bank's tangible assets becomes a secondary function. Because additional capital does not necessarily lead to an increase in the earnings assets of a commercial bank, but may simply increase the protection of depositors, Watkins felt that the capital adequacy issue in banking necessarily requires a compromise between two differing sets of objectives and points of view: external regulatory agencies whose policies are designed to protect depositors, and management whose fundamental objectives are aimed at maximizing stockholders' return on investment consistent with prudent bank operations. In effect, management's attempts to maximize stockholders' returns on investment may be constrained by the capital adequacy tests of the regulatory agencies.

Although there is no law requiring a commercial bank to increase its capital investment, Watkins was aware of several methods by which the regulatory agencies could persuade a bank to take such action. If bank management did not respond to a suggestion that the capital position might be somewhat weak, the regulatory agency could conduct special examinations, publish a report of the bank's condition, or search for some violation of banking law to use as a lever to ensure a strengthened capital position. In addition, the Comptroller of the Currency could publish a report of the condition of a bank which did not comply with his or her recommendations within 120 days, withhold permission to establish branches in states that permit branch banking, and remove officers and directors from office for unsafe and unsound banking practices after having warned them about such practices and required their discontinuance, although this latter power had never been used. Finally, the Federal Deposit Insurance Corporation could deny permission to merge, to reduce, or retire capital stock, to establish a new branch, or to change the location of the main office. Watkins did not believe that there was any possibility that Second National's situation would warrant any such drastic measures. Nonetheless, any actions of this nature could undermine public confidence in the bank. Because Jackson and the bank's board of directors felt that public confidence was the single most important determinant of a bank's ability to operate successfully, Watkins realized it was essential that the regulatory agencies be satisfied concerning Second National's capital position. She therefore reviewed the measures of capital adequacy employed by various regulatory agencies to evaluate the bank's present and projected position.

CAPITAL ADEQUACY STANDARDS

Watkins soon found that it was far easier to discover the capital adequacy standards that had been abandoned by the regulatory agencies than to pinpoint a minimum standard that would be currently acceptable. Until the late 1930s, the Comptroller of the Currency assumed that the most serious risk in banking was the possibility of a rapid reduction in deposits. The Comptroller thus felt that capital adequacy measures should relate capital to deposits. He stated that "a commercial bank whose capital and surplus amount to less than one-tenth of its deposits, is, except possibly under very exceptional conditions, doing business on too small a capital and upon too narrow a margin for safety, and does not furnish its creditors the protection to which they are entitled against unexpected losses and contingencies which are liable to, and do, so frequently arise."[1]

[1] Annual Report of the Comptroller of the Currency, Washington, D.C., Vol. 1, 1919, p. 21.

Although this 1-to-10 capital/deposits ratio was widely accepted by the regulatory agencies, the standard was seriously eroded by events of the late 1930s. The Depression caused overwhelming changes in the structure of commercial bank assets and liabilities, with the result that many banks fell below the 1-to-10 standard. At the same time, the logical basis for the test was challenged on the grounds that the ratio measured neither the quality nor the quantity of the assets in which the deposits were invested. In short, regulatory agencies began to feel that capital should bear no necessary relationship to deposits, but that it should stand in fixed proportion to a bank's assets, since the potential risk lay in the employment of depositor funds rather than in the deposits themselves. Thus, by 1939, the Federal Deposit Insurance Corporation had begun to urge the use of the capital-to-total-assets ratio as the appropriate test of bank capital adequacy.

During the Second World War, when banks greatly expanded their assets because of pressure from the Treasury to hold massive amounts of U.S. government securities, the capital-to-total-assets ratio was largely ignored by the regulatory authorities. Between 1940 and 1945, the amount of U.S. government securities held by commercial banks rose from $18 billion, or approximately 42 percent of total bank assets in 1940, to $85 billion, or 73 percent of total commercial bank assets in 1945. This asset expansion led to a notable reduction in the ratio of capital to total assets for all U.S. commercial banks from 15 percent in 1940, to under 7 percent in 1945. As banks emerged from the war with inflated holdings of U.S. securities, which were virtually riskless from a credit standpoint, both the pragmatic and the theoretical shortcomings of the capital-to-total-assets test became apparent. As one authority states, "Although the function of capital is to provide for losses that may occur in the assets of a bank, all assets do not possess the same risk. For example, some municipal securities are inherently more risky than others due to the strength of the economy that supports the issue, the taxing power of the issuing authority, and

possibly the management ability of the public officials. Loans differ in risk because of management efficiency, the borrower's financial strength, his ability to generate income, the vitality of the borrower's economic area, and for many other reasons. If all assets possessed the same degree of risk, the capital to assets ratio might be valuable in judging the capital adequacy of a bank, but this is obviously not the case."[2]

With the demise of the capital/total assets test, regulatory authorities began to concentrate on a capital/risk assets measure of capital adequacy. Several definitions of risk assets have been used in determining this ratio. Risk assets have been defined as all assets less cash and U.S. government securities, as all assets less cash and U.S. government securities due in five years or less, or in the more comprehensive manner illustrated in Exhibit 3. Typically, banks have been considered sufficiently capitalized if capital is more than 8 percent of risk assets. Although these ratios all separate "risky" and "riskless" assets, it is apparent that the "risk assets" include assets with widely differing exposures to risk. For example, an AAA municipal bond is not as risky as a seven-year term loan to a small business, although both are classified as "risk assets" in the above ratios. Thus, in 1952, several banking groups urged the use of a modified risk asset measure.

In 1954, the American Bankers Association issued a statement of principles regarding capital adequacy which carefully avoided the use of a mechanical yardstick, but stated that "it is far more important and essential to evaluate the specific elements of weakness and strength to determine what burden the capital funds of the bank might be expected to bear."[3] As one interested party put it, "The ratio of capital to deposits has fallen into disuse on the grounds that the function of capital is to absorb losses which are likely

---

[2] E. W. Reed, *Commercial Bank Management* (New York: Harper & Row, 1963, p. 526.

[3] "The Adequacy of a Bank's Capital Funds" (New York, American Bankers Association, Oct. 1954).

to arise not from the liability side of the balance sheet but from the asset side. It must be recognized, however, that a sudden deposit drain which forces liquidation of assets could produce losses that capital must be prepared to absorb; hence, the composition and volatility of deposits does have a bearing on the needs for bank capital."[4] In the later 1970s the Comptroller's Office, supported by the other regulatory agencies, began to examine the relative trend of a selected group of ratios for a bank. Ratios such as assets to total capital, assets to equity capital, loans to capital, and loan losses to loans are compared with similar ratios for peer group banks over time. In other words, the regulatory authorities now seem to believe that a capital adequacy standard should include consideration of a bank's assets, its liabilities, the interaction between assets and liabilities, and selected income and expense items. This opinion is reflected in the capital adequacy statements of the Comptroller's Office, as shown in Exhibit 4.

Although Watkins felt that the regulatory authorities' current approaches to capital adequacy were theoretically sound, she found that the lack of a definite, easily computed standard complicated the decision as to whether Second National Bank was adequately capitalized. In the course of previous "unofficial" conversations with a national bank examiner, however, Watkins had learned that the examiner still used the basic capital/risk assets and capital/asset ratios as informal measures of minimum acceptable capitalization. Only if a bank's capital position fell outside the acceptable ranges for these ratios would the subjective factors proposed by the Comptroller of the Currency come under close scrutiny by the examiner. On the basis of this information, Watkins decided to use the capital/risk assets and capital/assets ratios as basic tests of Second National's capital adequacy. Exhibit 5 shows the recent trend of the conventional capital ratios for all insured commercial banks in the United States. Exhibit 6 compares Second Na-

[4] *National Banking Review*, Sept. 1963, p. 6.

tional's capital adequacy with the capital adequacy of the other competitor banks in the Southwest.

From the analysis of the data she had gathered thus far, Watkins realized that Second National was somewhat undercapitalized as of early 1979. She felt, however, that the projected future growth of the bank should somehow be considered in making the decision concerning how much additional capital Second National needed in 1979. She, therefore, made some tentative projections summarizing the possible future growth of Second National. These projections are shown in Exhibit 7. With this information in hand, Watkins set out to estimate specifically how much capital, if any, Second National Bank should raise in the near-term future.

CHOOSING AMONG THE BASIC METHODS OF RAISING BANK CAPITAL

Since Watkins was interested in developing a long-run capital structure plan as well as in solving the bank's capital adequacy problem, she decided to begin her analysis by summarizing the general advantages and disadvantages that would result from the three basic methods of obtaining additional capital. She then thought that current conditions in the money and capital markets might dictate the appropriate solution to the bank's short-run problem.

Retained Earnings

Second National Bank's retained earnings could be increased in two ways. The most obvious method would be to increase the bank's profitability. As shown in Exhibit 2, the bank's profits had been below average in the mid-1970s. Profits were higher in 1978 because the bank had made loans at attractive yields. Watkins' profit forecast was for little increase in profits in 1979 but for an appreciable increase in 1980, if loan demand increased as she predicted. Even with this increase in earnings, the bank's capital ratios would be even lower in 1980. Thus, although increased profitability might help to fill Second

National's capital needs in the long run, Watkins did not believe that earnings could be increased rapidly enough to supply the additional capital needed by the bank in the near future.

The second possible method of increasing the amount of earnings retained would be to decrease the dividend payout. For several years, Second National Bank had maintained a policy of paying dividends between 30 and 40 percent of earnings. Watkins was aware of several stock valuation formulas currently in use which valued dividends more highly than earnings, and thus she knew that a major reduction in dividend payout might cause the bank's stock price to fall. She believed that cash dividends could be partially replaced by stock dividends without causing a deterioration of the attractiveness of the bank's stock to the average investor. She knew, however, that some of the bank's current stockholders had been trying to put pressure on Jackson and other members of Second's board of directors to increase cash dividends because of the 1978 increase in earnings. These shareholders seemed to feel that the bank's stock price would increase if cash dividends were increased.

Watkins had recently suggested to Jackson, Second National's president, that the bank begin to issue an annual stock dividend, but Jackson had opposed this idea for several reasons. Although a stock dividend might forestall a dividend increase, he argued, it could not offset a cash dividend decrease. Thus he felt strongly that the Second National Bank was committed to paying a dividend of *at least* $0.50 per share in 1979, and this commitment would negate any beneficial short-term capital effects of a stock dividend program. Second, Jackson argued that a reduction in the bank's dividend payout below 30 percent would not by itself ensure an adequate supply of capital to the bank during the present period of expansion. He noted that even if the bank had maintained a dividend payout rate of only 20 percent since 1974, instead of the 30 + percent actual average payout rate maintained since 1974, the bank's 1978 capital/total assets and capital/risk assets ratios would still be below

average and the bank would still need additional capital. Finally, Jackson expressed some concern over the basic rationale behind stock dividends. Small stock dividends were relatively costly, and he questioned whether they might serve only to decrease the bank's real value to its shareholders, especially since Second National had no evidence that shareholders would value additional stock certificates.

Faced with these objections, Watkins decided that increased earnings retention would not solve Second National's short-term capital adequacy problem, although she still believed that greater earnings combined with a stock dividend program should be strong factors in the bank's long-run capital adequacy plan. She, therefore, turned to the consideration of external capital sources as possible solutions to the bank's short-term problem.

Additional External Equity

One external method for raising additional capital was to issue additional common or preferred stock. A common stock issue had several advantages when compared with a long-term debt issue. One advantage, in Watkins' opinion, was that a common issue would enable Second National to issue senior securities at a later date without the risks associated with adding debt on existing debt. It was her opinion that the investing public was apt to resist the future pyramiding of more debt in banks that had previously issued senior securities. She also believed that the future flexibility gained by issuing common stock in 1979 might prove quite valuable to Second National in the next few years. A further advantage in issuing common was that the proceeds from the sale of new equity would increase the bank's legal loan limit of 10 percent of capital and surplus, whereas the Federal Reserve would not include proceeds from the sale of senior debt securities in computing the basis for the legal loan limit. A final argument for a common stock issue was that the obligatory interest and sinking fund payments associated with debt would constitute a greater risk to Second National in the event of a severe reduction in the bank's earning power, although in view of the bank's past earnings record, Watkins thought that this argument was more academic than real.

There were, however, potential disadvantages of issuing common stock in 1979. Watkins was particularly disturbed by the possible dilution in earnings per share which would result from an issue of common. As an example, she calculated that if Second National Bank issued an additional 200,000 shares of common stock in early 1978, the 1978 earnings per share would drop from $1.86 to $1.45 and the bank would have been accused of having no earnings growth again. Of course, that was hypothetical, but Watkins feared the dilution would be nearly as much if new shares were issued in 1979.

A related disadvantage of issuing common stock in 1979 resulted because Second National Bank's common stock price had been depressed due to several conditions. First, the bank had publicized its desire to become a holding company, then was unable to explain its failure to achieve this result. Second, because earnings had not grown in 1976 and 1977, the bank had become known to local investors as a slow-growth institution. Third, the general market for bank stocks was very poor in 1978 because of widely publicized banking problems in recent years. Thus, Watkins thought that the postponement of an equity issue might lead to less dilution to earnings per share in the long run.

If the bank decided to sell common stock, there was the additional question of whether the issue should be offered to new or to existing stockholders. National banking laws require that external issues of equity by existing national banks be privileged subscriptions (rights issues) unless the rights are specifically waived by holders of two thirds of the existing shares. Watkins believed that there might be several advantages to a rights offering of additional common stock in late 1979. First, she believed most of the approximately 1,000 current holders of the bank's

common stock would be willing to purchase a new offering of common stock. Second, with a rights offering Watkins believed the bank's management would be less concerned about the fact that book value might exceed the offering price and about the immediate dilution in earnings per share. Third, although she believed the market price of the bank's stock was still way below what it should be, she felt the bank might be able to sell common stock for $16 to $17 per share in late 1979 ($13 to $14 had been the range in early 1979).

Jackson, on the other hand, seemed to favor asking the current shareholders to forgo their preemptive rights. He noted that nearly all of the bank's current shareholders were from New Mexico and many of them were customers of the bank. Jackson believed Second National could use a common stock issue to new shareholders to attract these shareholders as bank customers. Since the stock was already widely held, Jackson did not think control was an important consideration.

Having reviewed the advantages and disadvantages of issuing common stock in 1979, Watkins turned to the consideration of preferred stock—a second possible means of raising additional equity. She soon dismissed this alternative because, in her opinion, preferred stock was basically inferior to common stock and long-term debt. The only advantages of preferred stock over debt, in Watkin's view, were that (1) preferred stock could be considered in computing the basis for the bank's legal loan limit and (2) the fixed dividends on preferred stock could be passed without declaring insolvency in the event the bank's earnings declined. These advantages did not appear of particular importance to Second National, however, the fact that preferred dividends would be paid from after-tax profits did seem important. Watkins calculated, as a rough estimate given 1979 market conditions, that the dividends on preferred stock would cost the bank roughly 10 percent per year in after-tax profits.

Long-Term Debt

Watkins realized that the history of banks' use of senior debt securities to raise capital had been a short one. Prior to 1933, commercial banks were capitalized only with capital stock and retained earnings, since they normally did not possess the authority to issue debt capital or preferred stock. Prompted by a dramatic rise in bank failures from an average of 600 per year in the 1920s to 2,200 in 1931, the federal government had established the Reconstruction Finance Corporation (RFC) early in 1932, in order to support the nation's banks. Although the RFC made extensive use of its power to make loans ($950 million in 1932) to banks that could "fully and adequately" secure them, the further deterioration of the economy in 1932 and early 1933 caused a continuation of the high failure rate of commercial banks. Thus, on March 9, 1933, Congress introduced and passed the Emergency Banking Act, which authorized the RFC both to purchase the preferred stock of banks and to make loans against bank preferred stock subject to approval by the Comptroller of the Currency. In a later amendment, the RFC was granted power to purchase both capital notes and debentures subordinated to deposits.

Although the RFC purchases of bank senior securities continued through 1943, the stigma attached to the distress nature of the use of senior securities by banks in the 1930s caused most bankers to attempt to eliminate these issues as fast as possible. Furthermore, after the financial crisis had moderated, the Comptroller and nearly all state banking authorities would approve the issue of senior securities only when common stock could not be sold. Thus, with the exception of a few state-regulated banks, the presence of senior issues in the capital structure became regarded as a sign of a bank's weakness with the result that very little long-term debt financing was done through the early 1960s.

In 1961, the Commission on Money and Credit, concerned over the decreasing adequacy of the capitalization of financial institutions, urged in its report to the President that "the authorization [of banks] to issue debentures subordinated to the claims of the depositors and to issue preferred stock" should be explored.[5] In September 1962, following a survey of national bank managements, the Advisory Committee on Banking, a committee of bankers appointed by the Comptroller of the Currency, recommended to the Comptroller that (1) the use of preferred stock and debentures should no longer be regarded as an emergency measure but should be recognized as a normal method of obtaining capital funds, and that (2) flexibility should be afforded by permitting the use, where appropriate, of features such as convertibility and subordination.[6]

In December 1962, national banking regulations were changed by the Comptroller to permit the use of convertible or nonconvertible subordinated capital debentures after specific approval by the Comptroller of the amount, terms, and conditions of the issue and the consent of the holders of two thirds of the common shares.[7] The amount of indebtedness of national banks is limited, under the terms of the National Banking Act, to 100 percent of capital stock plus 50 percent of unimpaired surplus. Many state banking authorities followed suit in liberalizing their own policy with respect to debt. In a later decision, the Comptroller ruled that capital notes and debentures could be included in the base for determining a national bank's lending limit.[8] However, shortly thereafter the Federal Reserve Board issued a regulation for member banks which disagreed with the Comptroller's interpre-

[5] *Report of the Commission on Money and Credit* (Englewood Cliffs, N.J.: Prentice-Hall, 1961), p. 1974.

[6] *National Banks and the Future* (Washington, D.C.: U.S. Treasury Department, Comptroller of the Currency, Sept. 17, 1962), pp. 81–83.

[7] See Exhibit 8 for the statement of the Comptroller of the Currency regarding the issue of capital debentures by national banks.

[8] *Code of Federal Regulations*, Title 12, Chap. 1, p. 65.

tation of the law by stating that capital notes or debentures do not constitute "capital" for purposes of compliance with the various provisions of the Federal Reserve Act which limit the size of various assets (including a loan to a single customer) to a stated proportion (currently 10 percent) of capital and surplus.[9]

Despite the combined opposition of the chairman of the Federal Reserve board and the chair of the House Committee on Banking and Currency to the concept of debt capital for commercial banks, a large number of banks seized the opportunity to improve their capital position in the 1960s and 1970s through the use of long-term debt. Exhibit 9 shows that the total amount of long-term debt issues of commercial banks far exceed the amount of common and preferred stock that has been issued.

In studying the literature concerning capital notes and in discussing this alternative with other members of the financial community, Watkins discovered several general advantages and disadvantages to issuing a straight (nonconvertible) capital note. The primary advantage of capital notes stemmed from the leverage provided to the common stockholder through the use of tax-deductible, interest-bearing securities. While Watkins knew that leverage could operate in both directions, she felt sure that it would prove favorable in Second National's case. Her rough estimate, based on the assumption of a 12 percent margin (net operating earnings as a percentage of total revenue) was that a straight capital note issue at 10 percent would increase earnings per share slightly.

Watkins also foresaw several disadvantages of a straight capital note issue. First, there was the slight risk of default on the interest payments should the economic climate deteriorate markedly. A second and more important consideration, in Watkins' opinion, was that the use of capital notes in 1979 might limit Second National's flexibility in the future, since investors might

resist future pyramiding of debt. A further reduction in flexibility might result from the sinking fund payments normally associated with capital notes or from the terminal repayment provision of the notes, or both. And, while particular sinking fund provisions could alter the timing of the cash flows needed to repay the borrowing, the fact remained that the debt had to be repaid at some point. Thus, Watkins thought that the increase in future capital needs caused by borrowing to cover present capital needs might substantially increase Second National's risk position and decrease its future flexibility. Finally, three members of Second National's senior management were opposed to the use of debt by commercial banks simply because it ran against banking tradition; but Watkins felt that recent capital debenture issues by several competitors provided *prima facie* evidence that "tradition" had changed.

One possible method of circumventing the reduction in future flexibility resulting from a straight capital note issue was to make the capital notes convertible into common stock at some date in the future. If the notes were then converted before Second National again needed external capital, the bank would have the option of issuing debt at that time without piling debt on debt. Furthermore, the conversion of the capital notes would reduce or eliminate the interest and sinking fund payments associated with the notes, and thus would eliminate the risk associated with these fixed payments. Watkins calculated that if the bank issued capital notes convertible at $18, the notes would become convertible by early 1983, if her earnings forecast proved correct and the bank's price/earnings ratio did not change.

A convertible capital note issue offered Second National two advantages in addition to increased flexibility. First, the interest rate on convertibles was less than the likely rate that would apply to a straight capital note issue; consequently, earnings per share and profitability ratios were likely to be higher under a convertible as opposed to a straight note issue. Watkins believed that the difference in the interest rate

[9] *Code of Federal Regulations*, Title 12, Sect. II, pp. 216–217.

would be 1 to 2 percentage points lower. The second advantage in using convertible capital notes was that, since the conversion ratio would normally be 15 to 25 percent above the current market price of the common stock, the potential dilution in earnings per share—both in fully diluted earnings per share and if the issue were converted—would be considerably lower than if common stock were issued.

There were, however, some serious disadvantages to a convertible issue. Most important was the fact that the decision to exercise the convertible option rests with the investor, who may decide not to exercise the option. Assuming a 30 percent payout ratio, a future price/earnings ratio equal to the past five-year historical average, and a 10 percent rate of growth for Second National Bank, Watkins computed that the dividend yield on the future market price of common shares would never exceed the assumed stated yield of 9 percent on the convertible notes. If these assumptions proved correct, the "crossover point" at which the holder of the note would begin to consider voluntary conversion would not be reached, and the notes might never be voluntarily converted. In this event, the bank would not obtain the future flexibility promised by the convertible issue. Of course, conversion might be forced by the judicious use of a call schedule if the future market price were sufficiently above the conversion price, but Watkins believed that a call schedule might arouse the suspicions of investors with respect to the probable life of the issue and would necessitate a substantial increase in the interest rate offered, thereby sacrificing some of the interest advantage in using convertibles as described previously.

Another disadvantage of convertible notes was that the prospect of conversion might "overhang the market" for the common and restrain the rise in the market price of the bank's stock. This could mean that the convertibles might never convert and the bank would, in essence, have semipermanent senior capital in its capital structure. Finally, Watkins felt that the "overhang" of possible conversions might limit the bank's bargaining position on acquisition possibilities if Second National became a holding company.

After restudying Exhibits 1 through 9, Watkins began to make specific recommendations concerning the three problem areas (see beginning of this case). She was careful to explain why she reached her decisions.

EXHIBIT 1

Second National Bank of Albuquerque—Statement of Condition (dollars in thousands)

	Dec. 31, 1978	Dec. 31, 1977	Dec. 31, 1976	Dec. 31, 1975	Dec. 31, 1974	Dec. 31, 1973
Assets						
Cash and Due from Banks	$ 12,120	$ 10,785	$ 9,592	$ 8,642	$ 9,346	$ 6,119
Investment Securities:						
U.S. Treasury	1,832	2,815	3,032	2,984	2,802	5,994
Other securities	19,642	21,156	14,847	9,954	9,473	11,199
Total securities	$ 21,474	$ 23,971	$ 17,879	$ 12,938	$12,275	$17,193
Loans:						
Commercial and real estate	41,774	33,004	31,709	27,875	27,210	28,374
Installment and credit card	52,558	47,075	39,711	37,603	31,792	26,962
Total loans	$ 94,332	$ 80,079	$ 71,420	$ 65,478	$59,002	$55,336
Other Assets	7,801	9,615	12,432	10,275	7,705	6,794
Total assets	$135,727	$124,450	$111,323	$ 97,333	$88,328	$85,442
Liabilities and Capital						
Deposits:						
Demand	$ 46,266	$ 44,938	$ 40,938	$ 37,418	$34,831	$31,901
Time and Savings	72,353	63,363	56,154	45,767	36,538	37,761
Total deposits	$118,619	$108,301	$ 97,092	$ 83,185	$71,368	$69,662
Other Liabilities	8,514	8,271	6,935	7,486	10,944	10,111
Capital Accounts:						
Capital stock	3,000	3,000	2,929	2,719	2,499	2,499
Surplus	3,000	3,000	2,929	2,719	2,621	2,405
Undivided profits	3,007	2,191	1,755	1,541	1,213	1,065
Total capital	$ 9,007	$ 8,191	$ 7,613	$ 6,979	$ 6,333	$ 5,970
Less: Treasury stock	313	313	317	317	317	301
Net capital	$ 8,694	$ 7,878	$ 7,296	$ 6,662	$ 6,016	$ 5,669
Total liabilities and capital	$135,727	$124,450	$111,323	$ 97,333	$88,328	$85,442

EXHIBIT 2

Second National Bank of Albuquerque—Historical Summary of Operations (dollars in thousands)

	Dec. 31, 1978	Dec. 31, 1977	Dec. 31, 1976	Dec. 31, 1975	Dec. 31, 1974	Dec. 31, 1973
Operating Income	$15,894	$13,068	$12,186	$11,181	$11,279	$10,544
Operating Expenses	14,192	11,693	10,842	9,840	10,395	9,714
Income Before Taxes and						
Security Gains (Loses)	$ 1,702	$ 1,375	$ 1,344	$ 1,341	$ 884	$ 830
Applicable Income Taxes	594	472	481	477	309	289
Security Gains (Losses)	8	26	12	0	6	9
Net Income	$ 1,116	$ 877	$ 875	$ 864	$ 569	$ 532
Per Share[a] Data:						
Book value/share	$ 14.49	$ 13.13	$ 12.43	$ 11.69	$ 12.03	$ 11.34
Net income/share	1.86	1.47	1.49	1.51	1.14	1.07
Dividends/share	0.50	0.50	0.40	0.36	0.33	0.33
Market price (range)	9-15	10-16	12-17	9-15	13-16	10-14

[a]Adjusted to reflect stock splits and stock dividends (600,000 shares outstanding at December 31, 1978).

EXHIBIT 3
Second National Bank of Albuquerque—Sample
Computation Form for Ratios of Capital to Risk Assets and Deposits[a]

Capital, as used in the computations below, consists of total capital accounts plus valuation reserves, less assets classified loss and 50 percent of assets classified doubtful.

Risk Asset Ratio

Total Assets	$_____	
Add:		
Total reserve for bad debts and		
unallocated charge-offs and valuation		
reserves on loans	_____	
Unallocated charge-offs and valuation		
reserves on securities	_____	$_____
Deduct:		
Total estimated losses	$_____	
50 percent of assets classified doubtful	_____	
Cash due from banks	_____	
U.S. government obligations, direct and guaranteed	_____	
Federal corporation obligations	_____	
Commodity Credit Corporation loans	_____	
New Housing Authority bonds	_____	
Loans or portions of loans	_____	
Secured by obligations of U.S. government and		
federal corporations	_____	
Insured under Title I of the National Housing Act	_____	
Insured under Titles II and VI of the National		
Housing Act	_____	
Guaranteed under the Servicemen's Readjustment Act	_____	
Guaranteed by the Small Business Administration	_____	
Secured by hypothecated deposits	_____	
Secured by dealers' reserves required by agreement	_____	
Loans made under Exceptions 10, 11, and 12 of Section		
5200, Revised Statutes	_____	
Federal Reserve Bank stock	_____	
Income collected, not earned	_____	_____
Risk Assets		$_____

The Ratio of Capital to Risk Assets is: 1 to _____
The Ratio of Capital to Total Deposits is: 1 to _____

[a]Included in Howard Crosse and George H. Hempel, *Management Policies for Commercial Banks,* 3d ed. (Englewood Cliffs, N.J.: Prentice-Hall, 1979).

EXHIBIT 4

Second National Bank of Albuquerque—Stated Capital Adequacy Policy of the Comptroller of the Currency

National bank examiners are guided by the following statement of policy:

The Comptroller of the Currency will not hereafter rely on the ratios of capital to risk assets and to total deposits in assessing the adequacy of capital of national banking associations. These formulae, although of some value in assessing capital adequacy, do not take into account other factors of equal or greater importance. Henceforth, the capital position of the bank will be analyzed and appraised in relation to the character of its management and its asset and deposit position as a going institution under normal conditions, with due allowance for a reasonable margin of safety, and with due regard to the bank's capacity to furnish the broadest service to the public. These factors, which are necessarily imprecise, cannot be directly interpolated into any specific formula. The following factors will be considered by the Comptroller in assessing the adequacy of capital:

(a) The quality of management;
(b) The liquidity of assets;
(c) The history of earnings and of the retention thereof;
(d) The quality and character of ownership;
(e) The burden of meeting occupancy expenses;
(f) The potential volatility of deposit structure;
(g) The quality of operating procedures; and
(h) The bank's capacity to meet present and future financial needs of its trade area, considering the competition it faces.

Source: Comptroller's Manual for National Banks, Section 14.1, (Washington, D.C.: Comptroller of the Currency).

EXHIBIT 5

Second National Bank of Albuquerque—Conventional Capital Ratios for Insured Commercial Banks

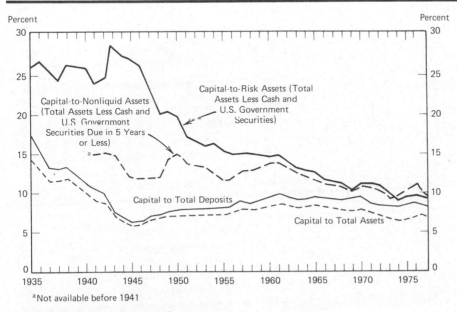

[a] Not available before 1941

Source: Federal Deposit Insurance Coporation.

EXHIBIT 6
Second National Bank of Albuquerque—Capital as a Percentage of Risk Assets in Major
Southwestern Banks (1973-1978) (Risk assets = Total assets − Cash and U.S. Governments)

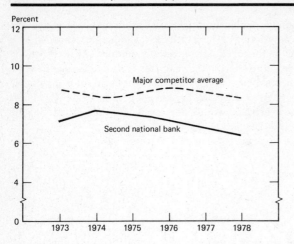

EXHIBIT 7
Second National Bank of Albuquerque—Planning Objectives for Years Ending 1979 and 1980

	1979	1980
Estimated Growth in Demand Deposits	8%	8%
Estimated Growth in Time and Savings Deposits	14%	16%
Target Loan-to-Deposit Ratio	75%	80%
Target Operating Income (in thousands)	$16,350	$17,800
Target Operating Expenses (in thousands)	$14,600	$15,750

Projected Income Statements and Balance Sheets, for Year-End 1979 and 1980[a]

1979

Operating Income	$16,350
Operating Expenses	14,600
Taxes	600
Net Income	1,150
Dividends (0.50 × 578,300)	290
To Undivided Profits	$ 860

Assets		*Liabilities*	
Cash	$ 14,000	Demand Deposits	$ 50,000
Governments	3,000	Time and Savings Deposits	82,000
Other Securities	25,900	Other Liabilities	8,000
Loans	99,000	Capital and Surplus	6,000
Other Assets	8,000	Undivided Profits	3,900
	$149,900		$149,900

EXHIBIT 7 (continued)

	1979	1980

1980

Operating Income	$17,800
Operating Expenses	15,750
Taxes	750
Net Income	1,300
Dividends (0.50 × 578,300)	290
To Undivided Profits	$ 1,010

Assets		*Liabilities*	
Cash	$ 16,000	Demand Deposits	$ 54,000
Governments	3,000	Time and Savings Deposits	95,700
Other Securities	22,800	Other Liabilities	10,000
Loans	119,800	Capital and Surplus	6,000
Other Assets	9,000	Undivided Profits	4,900
	$170,600		$170,600

[a]Assuming no new capital issued and dividends of $0.50 per share, on shares outstanding, not including treasury stock.

EXHIBIT 8
Second National Bank of Albuquerque—Stated Policy of the Comptroller
of the Currency Regarding the Issue of Capital Debentures by National Banks

14.5 Capital Debentures

(a) It is the policy of the Comptroller of the Currency to permit the issuance of convertible or nonconvertible capital debentures by national banking associations in accordance with normal business considerations.

(b) Subject to the provisions of 12 U.S.C. 82, the bank may, with the approval of stockholders owning two-thirds of the stock of the bank, entitled to vote, or without such approval if authorized by its Articles of Association, issue convertible or non-convertible capital debentures in such amounts and under such terms and conditions as shall be approved by the Comptroller: *Provided, however,* that the principal amount of capital debentures outstanding at any time, when added to all other outstanding indebtedness of the bank, except those forms of indebtedness exempt from the provisions of 12 U.S.C. 82, shall not exceed an amount equal to 100 percent of the bank's unimpaired paid-in capital stock plus 50 percent of the amount of its unimpaired surplus fund.

Source: Code of Federal Regulations, Title 12, Chap. 1 (Washington, D.C.: Office of the Federal Register, National Archives and Record Service), p. 20.

EXHIBIT 9

Second National Bank of Albuquerque—Summary of Bank Capital Issues, 1967–1978 (dollar figures in thousands)

Year	Total capital raised		Common stock		Preferred stock		Nonconvertible debt		Convertible debt	
	No. of issues	Amount	No. of issues	Amount	No. of issues	Amount	No. of issues	Amount	No. of issues	Amount
1967	57	$ 205,933	32	$ 41,483	1	$ 100	22	$ 136,100	2	$ 28,250
1968	40	297,833	24	36,438	0	—	11	229,375	5	32,020
1969	61	436,550	39	82,007	0	—	7	27,320	15	327,223
1970	48	360,939	26	68,762	1	30,446	8	60,480	13	201,251
1971	46	229,486	26	103,352	0	—	16	115,500	4	10,634
1972	91	1,699,513	26	125,533	1	1,980	51	1,154,800	13	417,200
1973	127	2,636,792	36	214,958	2	6,804	79	2,233,030	10	182,000
1974	71	1,110,940a	26	87,448	0	—	39	784,750a	6	238,744
1975	46	1,359,986b	14	35,486	1	10,000	29	1,304,500b	2	10,000
1976	51	1,567,603	4	37,853	3	77,500	41	1,032,250	3	420,000
1977	80	2,486,077	8	353,126	0	0	70	2,125,957	2	7,000
1978	89	2,766,757	11	176,957	4	355,000	72	2,222,800	2	12,000
1967–1978	809	15,158,409	272	1,363,403	14	481,830	445	11,426,862c	77	1,886,322

aExcludes seven floating-rate note issues totaling 1,130,000.
bExcludes three floating-rate note issues totalling $12,200.
cTotals include five debt issues totaling 18,000, that had stock warrants attached.
Source: Corporate Financial Counseling Department of Irving Trust Company.

CASE 6
Wells Fargo Bank*

At 3:00 p.m. on August 31, 1981, Frank Newman, executive vice president and chief financial officer of Wells Fargo & Company, had just received a phone call from Donald Moore of Morgan Stanley & Co. Mr. Moore, a vice president within the Financial Institutions Business Unit of this investment banking firm, was responsible for keeping Wells Fargo, an important client of the firm, informed of market opportunities, as well as initiating financing ideas and executing any transactions which might develop.

Their telephone conversation centered on an innovative financing idea called a "stock-for-debt" swap. In light of his bank's current financial position, the overall outlook for 1981 earnings and the market for bank stocks, Mr. Newman wondered how Wells Fargo would benefit from such a transaction. In 1980 Morgan Stanley had completed a somewhat similar transaction for Wells Fargo, a cash repurchase of sinking fund bonds. As a pure cash transaction, the previous exchange was not completely analogous to the stock-for-debt swap being proposed.

COMPANY DESCRIPTION

Wells Fargo & Company is a bank holding company whose principal asset is Wells Fargo Bank, the 11th largest bank in the U.S. and the 3rd largest west of the Mississippi on the basis of deposits. As of December 31, 1980, the Bank had total assets of $21.8 billion and total net loans of $14.9 billion.

---

* This case was written by Donald Moore and Mike Pepe of Morgan Stanley & Co., with assistance from George G. C. Parker, senior lecturer in management at the Stanford Graduate School of Business, and Bowen H. McCoy, managing director for Morgan Stanley & Co. Financial support for this project was provided in part by the Program in Finance of the Graduate School of Business, Stanford University. Copyright © 1981 by the Board of Trustees of the Leland Stanford Junior University. Used by permission.

Wells Fargo is primarily a domestically oriented bank, with U.S. activities accounting for 85 percent of consolidated earnings. Retail banking activities are conducted through 383 branch offices throughout California and constitute the most significant portion of the company's business, accounting for almost 70 percent of the loan portfolio and 48 percent of consolidated earnings in 1980. Consumer banking services include savings programs, checking accounts, credit card services, home mortgage loans, and installment loans.

FINANCIAL PERFORMANCE

1974-1979

During the period 1974–1979, Wells Fargo was one of the best performing banks in the country. Consistent growth was achieved in both the size of the bank's operations, as measured by its asset base, and in net income from operations (before security transactions). Assets grew by approximately 11 percent per annum, while net income increased at an impressive rate of over 22 percent per annum during the six-year period. The increase in the bank's earnings could be attributed largely to a substantial improvement in profitability, with return on assets increasing from 0.41 percent to 0.64 percent and return on equity increasing from 10.36 percent to 15.62 percent during the six-year period. Exhibit 1 illustrates this performance.

1980

Despite a 14.5 percent increase in assets in 1980, the bank's earnings declined to 1.2 percent, as return on assets decreased from 0.68 percent to 0.55 percent and return on equity decreased from 16.48 percent to 13.98 percent.

Earnings suffered in 1980 principally because of a decline in loan volume coupled with a narrower spread between the yield on earning assets and the rates paid on interest-sensitive liabilities. A drop in real estate lending activity resulted in a significant decline in real estate loan origination fees, an important source of income to Wells Fargo. Moreover, the bank's cost of funds increased from 7.35 percent in 1979 to 9.10 percent in 1980 due to a shift in the mix of the bank's liabilities. Relatively low-cost consumer deposits, such as savings, declined as a proportion of total funding sources while more costly deposits and borrowings, such a six-month Treasury certificates, commercial paper, and federal funds, increased. Since a portion of the bank's consumer installment and single-family mortgage portfolios were funded on a short-term basis with interest-sensitive liabilities, the company's net interest spread—the difference between the average yield on earning assets (on a tax equivalent basis and including loan fees) and the average cost of funding assets—decreased from 4.47 percent in 1979 to 3.89 percent in 1980. Exhibit 2 tracks the increases in Wells Fargo's cost of funds from 1974 to 1980.

1981

These trends continued during the first six months of 1981, as average earning assets increased 13 percent, while the interest spread narrowed from 3.92 percent in the first six months of 1980 to 3.81 percent in the first six months of 1981. Contributing to the decline in spread was a continuing shift in the composition of consumer deposits to higher paying, interest-sensitive instruments, which are more expensive than traditional sources of bank funds. The bank's sizable portfolio of residential mortgages also adversely affected the results because it included a number of long-term mortgages with low, fixed rates of interest which were funded with interest-sensitive liabilities.

Income in the first quarter rose $5.6 million or 10 percent over the comparable period in 1980, including an $8.8 million gain on the sale of equity securities from a 49 percent-owned un-

consolidated small business investment company.

Common Stock Performance

In 1976 and 1977, Wells Fargo's common stock was trading at or close to book value. In April 1977, Wells Fargo sold 2 million shares of common stock at $27 ⅛ per share when book value per share was $27. The net proceeds of $52 million served to strengthen Wells Fargo's capital base; by the end of 1977, average equity, as a percent of average assets, an important measure of leverage for a bank holding company, had increased to 4.35 percent. However, this ratio declined steadily (see Exhibit I) to a low of 3.86 percent for the first six months of 1981.

Wells Fargo's leverage had increased, as assets had grown faster than equity. In addition, the company was aware of the regulatory agencies' concern over the banking industry's declining capital ratios. Wells Fargo believed full utilization of its leverage capacity would impair its flexibility, thereby restricting the company's ability to take advantage of business opportunities that were expected with deregulation. In order to remedy this situation, the company had filed for $35 million of preferred stock in April of 1981, but the fixed-income market subsequently declined and the cost of borrowing to Wells Fargo became unattractive. The issuance of common shares was also unattractive—with the stock trading at $26 ¼ compared to a book value of over $41 per share. Nevertheless, a common stock offering would augment the company's capital base and strengthen its equity position.

Environment for Fixed-Income Securities

The U.S. capital markets during 1980 and through the first six months of 1981 were characterized by both absolute increases in interest rates and extreme volatility. During the 12-month period ending June 1981, for example, yields on U.S. Treasury notes with six-year maturities increased from 11.00 percent to 14.25 percent. The deterioration in the corporate bond market was even more pronounced with yields on intermediate term (3–10 years) corporate issues rising to 100 to 150 basis points above Treasury securities with comparable maturities. Interest rates increased in the short-term money markets as well, with the prime rate reaching historic highs and exceeding 20 percent through much of early 1981.

The volatility in interest rates in the various capital market sectors was also significant. Long-term government bond yields reached a high of 13.5 percent and a low of 9.4 percent, a range which was twice that experienced in 1979, and four times that occurring in 1978. During the first six months of 1981, long-term treasury yields continued to fluctuate between the 12.5 and 13.5 percent range.

DISCOUNT BOND REPURCHASES AND EXCHANGES

Advance Repurchase of Sinking Fund Bonds

This market environment provided a unique opportunity in 1980 for Wells Fargo to repurchase a portion of its sinking fund bond issues in advance of mandatory sinking fund requirements. The depressed corporate bond market enabled the bank to repurchase the outstanding debt securities at a significant discount, since they were trading at approximately 74 percent of their original face value. The advance repurchase at a discount could serve to reduce the cost of meeting Wells Fargo's sinking fund requirements in future periods if the bond market improved and the price of the bonds approached their original face value. It could also act as a defense against a sinking fund "corner," whereby an institutional investor "hoards" an issue in an attempt to force the bank to purchase the bonds to satisfy the mandatory sinking fund requirement at prices substantially higher than market.

In evaluating the cash repurchase transaction in 1980, the Company looked at a variety of factors. One analysis compared the present value of cash flows associated with two alternatives: (1) leaving the bonds outstanding and repurchas-

ing them on each of the mandatory sinking fund dates or (2) repurchasing the bonds in advance by borrowing the cash at current market rates. In general, a net cash flow advantage is produced because the replacement borrowings have higher interest payments and a lower principal payment, which serves to reduce the company's after-tax cash payments.

Another analysis compared the immediate gain from repurchase with the future earnings benefit from the low-rate long-term debt. One advantage of the immediate gain is that it would augment the company's capital position and support future asset growth that would otherwise not be possible due to leverage constraints. The analysis of one of the issues involved in the transaction, the 8.60 percent sinking fund debentures due 2002, is summarized in Exhibit 4.

Moreover, repurchasing its debt securities was attractive to Wells Fargo management in that the profit from these transactions would partially offset the decrease in net interest income occurring in 1980. Specifically, by repurchasing $40 million principal amount of the bank's debentures and capital notes, $12 million of gains were realized during the year, accounting for 10 percent of net income.

Bankruptcy Act of 1980

A favorable tax treatment was critical to the economic advantage associated with the advance repurchase. According to the 1980 tax law, an issuer who repurchased bonds at a discount could reduce the tax base of its assets by the difference between the tax basis of the bonds (their principal amount) and their repurchase price. Income taxes on the profits arising from the transaction, therefore, would be deferred over the depreciable life of the assets, usually five to seven years. The largest asset of Wells Fargo & Company (a bank holding company) is the stock of the bank (a nondepreciable asset) and, pursuant to the tax laws, the company was able to write down its tax basis in the stock of the bank, thereby deferring taxes on the transaction indefinitely.

However, the Bankruptcy Act of 1980 (effective January 1, 1981) contained provisions eliminating the most favorable elective tax options associated with this transaction. The new rule stated that only depreciable assets could be written down, therefore enabling an issuer to defer taxes for only five to seven years. Purchasing discount bonds with cash lost some of its attractiveness in that Wells Fargo could only defer for five to seven years taxes payable on the difference between the face value of the bonds (the original sales price) and the discount repurchase price.

Stock-for-Debt Swap

During their telephone conversation, Mr. Moore and Mr. Newman discussed the way in which a stock-for-debt recapitalization could be structured. Morgan Stanley could buy Wells Fargo's outstanding debt securities from institutional investors for Morgan Stanley's own account and, if agreement were reached between Wells Fargo and Morgan Stanley, the investment banker could then exchange its holdings of Wells Fargo debt securities for newly issued Wells Fargo stock with an equivalent market value. Morgan Stanley could then resell the shares of Wells Fargo stock to equity investors.

Mr. Newman believed that the exchange would be beneficial to Wells Fargo for several reasons. Wells Fargo would increase its equity base by the sum of the gains achieved on the debt retirement and the value of the shares issued in the exchange. As a result, a stock-for-debt recapitalization could have a favorable impact on Wells Fargo's leverage ratios. It would permit the company to retire discount debt at a time when bond prices were at record lows without incidence of "forgiveness of indebtedness" taxation. As noted above, on a cash purchase of an outstanding debt instrument bought at a discount, there was a tax liability on the gain which could only be deferred five to seven years. In a stock-for-debt recapitalization, however, there was no tax liability. Wells Fargo would record a gain equivalent to the difference between the principal

amount of the bonds retired and the value of the bonds tendered in the exchange.

The Mechanics of the Transaction

Effecting a stock-for-debt exchange was a somewhat complicated transaction which involved a number of areas of expertise within an investment bank. A specialized group of fixed-income salespersons and traders determined the amount of outstanding bonds which could be purchased at various prices and devised a strategy for purchasing the bonds in negotiated transactions with institutional investors. Because tax law required that exchanges could only take place between principals, Morgan Stanley would acquire the bonds for its own account. When Morgan Stanley had acquired sufficient bonds to effect an exchange, and if an agreement could be reached between Morgan Stanley and Wells Fargo on an appropriate exchange ratio, then the contemplated exchange could take place. Wells Fargo would have to file a Registration Statement with the Securities and Exchange Commission covering the new shares to be issued. Subsequent to the filing, Morgan Stanley would commence its marketing effort to develop interest in the shares which it would receive as principal. Later, the SEC would declare the Registration Statement effective and Morgan Stanley and Wells Fargo would attempt to reach agreement as to an appropriate exchange ratio. For example, if a price of $11.9 million were agreed upon, Morgan Stanley would deliver $17 million principal amount of debt (market value of $11.9 million) in exchange for an equivalent amount of Wells Fargo common stock. The number of shares of common stock would be based upon a negotiated market price including an underwriter's spread of 4 percent. Thereafter, Morgan would attempt to reoffer the stock to institutional investors.

FRANK NEWMAN'S DECISION

Wells Fargo & Company's second quarter of 1981 earnings were down 11 percent from the second quarter of 1980 principally because interest rates paid for federal funds and negotiable certificates of deposit during the quarter were the highest in U.S. banking history. To give greater flexibility in a fluctuating interest-rate environment, the bank's long-range plan called for a continued shift in the emphasis of its loan portfolio to interest-sensitive loans in the real estate, commercial, corporate, and international areas.

Without the stock-for-debt swap, the controller's department of the bank estimated operating earnings per share to be $5.30.

It was unclear to Mr. Newman whether earnings per share from the swap would be considered operating or nonoperating earnings on the income statements.

Mr. Newman believed that current market conditions provided an economically attractive opportunity to augment the bank's equity position and liability mix through the stock-for-debt transaction. During their telephone conversation, Mr. Moore told the Wells Fargo executive vice-president that he was confident that Morgan Stanley could purchase up to $17 million aggregate principal amount of the bank's 8.60 percent debentures due in 2002 at an average cost of $640 per $1000 debenture. However, before Mr. Newman recommended the recapitalization to the board of directors, he had to consider the following:

- The economic benefits of the transaction. Estimated cash flows associated with the repurchase of the 8.60 percent sinking fund debentures due 2002 is provided in Exhibit 5.
- The impact on earnings per share this year and in the future.
- The contribution the recapitalization would make to the company's equity position and leverage.
- The perception of the financial community and the impact on Wells Fargo's common stock.
- The reaction of the bank's regulators.

The before-tax cost of new borrowing for Wells Fargo was thought by Newman to be approximately equal to the yield to maturity on a before-tax basis, of the existing notes outstanding.

As he thought about these issues, Mr. Newman glanced at a document sent to him by Morgan Stanley that provided a hypothetical analysis of the stock-for-debt transaction (see Appendix). He also knew that several Wall Street firms were estimating earnings of $5.50 per share in 1981 and $6.25 for 1982. Wells Fargo's common stock on the New York Stock Exchange closed at $27.75 per share, down $.125 from the prior day's close.

EXHIBIT 1

Wells Fargo & Company—Financial Performance, 1974–1981 (June) (dollars in millions)

	1974	1975	1976	1977	1978	1979	1980	Latest 12 months ended 6/30/81
Average Equity	$ 444.0	$ 477.0	$ 517.0	$ 613.0	$ 706.0	$ 790.0	$ 871.0	$ 938.0
Average Assets	11,799.0	11,740.0	12,352.0	14,097.0	16,650.0	19,269.0	22,055.0	24,274.0
Net Income	46.0	55.4	62.3	85.4	110.1	123.4	121.9	127.4
Return on Average Assets	0.41%	0.47%	0.50%	0.61%	0.66%	0.64%	0.55%	0.52%
Return on Average Equity	10.98	11.48	12.04	14.09	16.41	16.48	13.98	13.98
Average Equity/Average Assets	3.76	4.06	4.19	4.35	4.24	4.10	3.95	3.86
Earnings per Share	$ 2.46	$ 2.74	$ 3.10	$ 3.99	$ 5.16	$ 5.75	$ 5.32	$ 5.42
Number of Shares Outstanding	—	—	—	—	—	—	—	23,505,535

EXHIBIT 2

Wells Fargo & Company Cost of Funds, 1974–1980

	1974	1975	1976	1977	1978	1979	1980	Latest 12 months ended 6/30/81
Cost of All Funds[a]	6.87%	5.20%	4.56%	4.53%	5.52%	7.35%	9.10%	9.69%
Cost of Interest-Bearing Liabilities[b]	8.20	6.35	5.65	5.67	6.83	8.90	10.84	11.23
Net Interest Spread[c]	1.68	2.65	2.87	3.02	3.19	2.93	2.15	1.80

[a]Defined as interest expense divided by average earning assets.
[b]Defined as interest expense divided by interest-bearing liabilities.
[c]Defined as earning asset yield less cost of interest-bearing funds.

EXHIBIT 3
Wells Fargo & Company—Market Information

	1974	1975	1976	1977	1978	1979	1980	6/30 1981
Common Stock Prices								
High	$27.125	$20.500	$27.000	$28.875	$33.250	$33.375	$29.000	$36.125
Low	9.500	12.875	15.625	24.125	24.000	25.375	21.625	30.625
Close as of 12/31	13.000	15.500	27.000	26.875	27.125	26.875	28.500	33.000
Price change in relation to S&Ps 400[a] (%)	—	90.4	133.0	151.0	148.8	130.6	108.5	121.7
Price/Earnings Ratio	5.3	5.7	8.7	6.7	5.3	4.7	5.4	6.1[b]
Market Value/Book Value	0.57	0.63	1.01	0.91	0.82	0.73	0.71	0.80
Selected Per-Share Statistics								
Earnings Per Share	$ 2.46	$ 2.74	$ 3.10	$ 3.99	$ 5.16	$ 5.75	$ 5.32	$ 5.42[b]
Book Value Per Share	22.95	24.74	26.79	29.46	32.94	36.58	39.93	41.46
Dividend Per Share	0.96	0.96	0.99	1.12	1.40	1.72	1.92	0.96
Dividend Yield	7.40%	6.20%	3.70%	4.20%	5.20%	6.40%	6.70%	5.8%

[a]Based on close; 1974 = 100.
[b]Latest 12 months.

EXHIBIT 4

Wells Fargo & Company—Analysis of Partial Prepurchase of 8.60 percent Sinking Fund Debentures Due 4/1/2002 and Cash Flow Analysis for a Prepurchase of $5,500,000[a]

Semiannual period	Old issue			Total savings	Net savings
	Balance outstanding	After-tax interest	Sinking fund payment		
0	$5,500,000	$ 0	$ 0	$ 0	$(4,070,000)
1	5,500,000	127,710	0	127,710	127,710
2	5,500,000	127,710	0	127,710	127,710
3	5,500,000	127,710	0	127,710	127,710
4	5,500,000	127,710	0	127,710	127,710
5	5,500,000	127,710	0	127,710	127,710
6	5,500,000	127,710	0	127,710	127,710
7	5,500,000	127,710	0	127,710	127,710
8	5,500,000	127,710	0	127,710	127,710
9	5,500,000	127,710	0	127,710	127,710
10	5,500,000	127,710	0	127,710	127,710
11	5,500,000	127,710	0	127,710	127,710
12	5,500,000	127,710	0	127,710	127,710
13	5,500,000	127,710	3,000,000	3,127,710	3,127,710
14	2,500,000	58,050	0	58,050	58,050
15	0	58,050	2,500,000	2,558,050	2,558,050
Total		$1,733,760	$5,500,000	$7,233,760	$3,163,760

[a]Net present value discounted at 7.56 percent (after tax) = $575,633. Internal rate of return (after tax) = 10.17 percent. Sinking fund bonds at a price of 74 or $4,070,000.

EXHIBIT 5

Wells Fargo & Company—Analysis of Partial Prepurchase of 8.60 percent Sinking Fund Debentures Due 4/1/2002 and Cash Flow Analysis for a Prepurchase of $17,000,000[a]

Semiannual period	Old issue			Total savings	Net savings
	Balance outstanding	After-tax interest	Sinking fund payment		
0	$17,000,000	$ 0	$	$ 0	$10,880,000
1	17,000,000	394,740	0	394,740	394,740
2	17,000,000	394,740	0	394,740	394,740
3	17,000,000	394,740	0	394,740	394,740
4	17,000,000	394,740	0	394,740	394,740
5	17,000,000	394,740	0	394,740	394,740
6	17,000,000	394,740	0	394,740	394,740
7	17,000,000	394,740	0	394,740	394,740
8	17,000,000	394,740	0	394,740	394,740
9	17,000,000	394,740	0	394,740	394,740
10	17,000,000	394,740	0	394,740	394,740
11	17,000,000	394,740	0	394,740	394,740
12	17,000,000	394,740	0	394,740	394,740
13	16,500,000	394,740	500,000	894,740	894,740
14	16,500,000	383,130	0	383,130	383,130
15	13,500,000	383,130	3,000,000	3,383,130	3,383,130
16	13,500,000	313,470	0	313,470	313,470
17	10,500,000	313,470	3,000,000	3,313,470	3,313,470
18	10,500,000	243,810	0	243,810	243,810
19	7,500,000	243,810	3,000,000	3,243,810	3,243,810
20	7,500,000	174,150	0	174,150	174,150
21	4,500,000	174,150	3,000,000	3,174,150	3,174,150
22	4,500,000	104,490	0	104,490	104,490
23	1,500,000	104,490	3,000,000	3,104,490	3,104,490
24	1,500,000	34,830	0	34,830	34,830
25	0	34,830	1,500,000	1,534,830	1,534,830
Total		$7,639,380	$17,000,000	$24,639,380	$13,759,380

[a]Sinking fund bonds at a price of 64 or $10,880,000.

CASE 6 APPENDIX

Stock-for-Debt Recapitalization—An Illustrative Example

ABC Corporation is considering a stock-for-debt recapitalization. Among its outstanding debt obligations are the following:

1 $75 million 8.40 percent debentures due 1987.

2 $100 million 7 ⅜ percent debentures due 1992.

Morgan Stanley is aware that an insurance company which owns $20 million of the 8.40 percent debentures needs to take a loss for tax purposes and is willing to sell its debentures for a price of 74 ¾ (14.84 percent yield) which, with costs and fees, implies a cost to ABC of $75. Further, Morgan Stanley believes it can accumulate $25 million principal amount of the 7 ⅜ percent debentures at an average cost, including fees, of $67. ABC currently has 16 million shares outstanding on which it currently pays an annual dividend of $1.60. ABC stock closed yesterday at $40.

THE EXCHANGE

The total market value of securities which can be accumulated for exchange is $31,750,000.

$$\$20 \text{ million} \times 0.75 = \underline{15.00}$$
$$\$25 \text{ million} \times 0.67 = \underline{16.75}$$
$$\$31.75$$

Based on yesterday's closing price and a discount to Morgan Stanley of 5 percent, ABC would issue 835,526 new shares (5.2 percent increase in shares outstanding) in exchange for the debt obligations as follows:

$$\frac{31,750,000}{40-(0.05 \times 40)} = 835,526$$

ACCOUNTING EFFECTS

ABC's capitalization prior to the exchange is as follows:

August 31, 1981 (in thousands)	
8.40% debentures due 1981	$ 75,000
7⅜% debentures due 1992	100,000
Stockholders' equity	650,061
Total	$825,061
Book value per share	$40.63

On the exchange, ABC would report a gain of $13.25 million (principal amount of debt retired less its market value).

In the 12 months ended August 31, ABC had earned $6.02 per share ($96.3 million in aggregate). Pro forma for the exchange, per share earnings rise to $6.62 per share (10 percent increase).

	Actual	Pro Forma
	(in thousands except per share amounts)	
Earnings Before Interest and Taxes	$226,008	$226,008
Interest Expense	47,675	44,151[a]
Pretax Earnings	$178,333	$181,857
Other Income	—	13,250
Taxes[b]	82,033	83,654
Net Income Before Extraordinary Items	$ 96,300	$111,453
Shares Outstanding	16,000,000	16,835,526
EPS	$6.02	6.62

[a]47,675 less coupon interest on $20 million at 8.40 percent—1.68 million; $25 million at 7⅜ percent—1.84 million.
[b]at 46 percent.

In future years, the exchange will have a dilutive effect on earnings per share as the increase in shares outstanding will not be fully offset by higher net income (which results from reduced interest expense). Looking at the 12 months ended August 31, on a pro forma basis, but this time excluding the impact of the gain exchange, one would find EPS of $5.83, a 3.1 percent decrease.

The exchange does have favorable impacts on ABC's capitalization. Long-term debt is reduced by the principal amount of debt retired or $45 million. Stockholders' equity is increased by the market value of stock issued ($31.75 million) plus the gain recognized ($13.25 million) or $45 million in total.

	Pro Forma August 31, 1981
8.40% Debentures due 1981	$ 55,000
7⅜% Debentures due 1991	75,000
Stockholders' Equity	695,061
Total	$825,061
Book Value per Share	$41.29

TAX EFFECTS

There would be no tax liability associated with the gain, as there is no discharge of indebtedness in a stock-for-debt recapitalization. This rule is based on case law and on Rev. Rul. 59-222. The Bankruptcy Tax Act of 1980 amended the Code provisions on the discharge of debt and more or less confirmed 59-222. However, one new section (108(e) (8) IRC) essentially states that 59-222 and the case law behind it do not apply to any case in which nothing more than "nominal" or "token" shares are issued. This should not present a problem in the recapitalization explained above. Care must be taken, however, to ensure that the transaction is structured so that the Internal Revenue Service does not claim that the exchange is a two-step transaction for ABC—that is, the purchase of debt obligations for cash and then issuance of stock for cash.

CASH FLOW AND ECONOMIC EFFECTS

The cash flow effects of the exchange are very straightforward. There is no cash flow associated with the exchange itself. In subsequent years, cash outflow will be reduced by the after tax interest saved ([(20 × 0.084) + (25 × 0.07375)] × 0.54) or $1.9 million and ultimately by the principal amount of the debt retired ($45 million). Cash outflow will be increased by the dividend requirements on the new shares. Initially, this will be $1.32 million.

CASE 7
First Bank & Trust Company

CAPITAL ADEQUACY: A NEW APPROACH TO AN OLD PROBLEM

Brenda Barnes had been employed for five years by the Federal Deposit Insurance Corporation (FDIC) in Washington, D.C. She recently had been transferred to the San Francisco office of the FDIC to serve as a special assistant to the regional director. Shortly after beginning her new assignment, Barnes was asked by the regional director to assist in responding to a request from Washington for regional office opinion on a possible new approach to the problem of capital adequacy for banks.

Specifically, officials at the FDIC and other regulatory agencies in Washington had become increasingly interested in exploring new or alternative ways to recognize and, perhaps, relieve the growing pressures on bank capital throughout the United States.

The FDIC had, a short time ago, received the text of a speech discussing a new view of bank capital by a Texas banker, Glen Lemon, chairman of the board, First Bank and Trust Company, Booker, Texas. The ideas Lemon proposed appeared interesting to some who had read his remarks, and it was decided to circulate this speech informally to obtain some reaction. The regional office in San Francisco was asked, among others, to submit written reactions to Lemon's remarks (see below) and to submit an evaluation of the concepts and the actions recommended.

In asking Barnes to undertake this assignment, the regional director sent her a memorandum, in which she made these additional observations:

Background Information

A few months ago, the FDIC, in cooperation with other regulatory agencies, developed new capital standards for commercial banking institutions. We have adjusted our acceptable and threshold levels of capital adequacy to 6 percent and 5 percent levels, respectively, for small and regional institutions and less capital for multibillion dollar banks. Simultaneously, we have promulgated some clear-cut objectives to include greater uniformity and consistency in the supervision of the nation's banks and their capital/asset ratios. As we consider the continued long-term decline in capital ratios, however, we feel it is imperative to consider further alternative solutions to the problem of bank capital.

One of the alternatives we are considering is the possibility of allowing commercial banks to insure to some extent a capital deficiency. Since the insurance industry provides protection to the banking industry in many ways, we wonder if it would be possible to provide protection in the capital area at considerably less cost to the banking industry than the alternative of investing capital in a cash form.

As an example, assume the 6 percent capital ratio for a particular commercial bank amounts to $4 million. Would it be appropriate for the FDIC to allow $3 million to come from normal "dollars" capital and the remaining $1 million to be covered through insurance protection?

Assumptions

1 It would be necessary to assume that there is an insurance facility acceptable to the FDIC which could provide coverage for insuring capital deficiencies for commercial banks.

2 It should also be assumed that the coverage could be provided at a cost of less than 5 percent per year and that the insurance premium would represent a tax-deductible expense to the bank.

3 Recent statistics suggest that the annual failure rate for commercial banks has historically been less than $\frac{1}{10}$ of 1 percent per year.

4 Insured capital coverage might be compared to a life insurance policy purchased on an individual. No payment is made on pure life insurance until death. Once the death certificate is submitted, payment is automatic. In the case of a bank failure, the injection of insured capital would be comparable.

5 In the event that capital deficiency insurance coverage is terminated, or if the insurance carrier were not willing to renew coverage, a 90-day notice would be required by the FDIC. This same type of "notice" is presently utilized in Form 24 Fidelity Bond Insurance coverage.

6 The insurance carrier would find it necessary to hold the FDIC completely free from any liability in providing capital deficiency insurance coverage to a particular commercial bank.

The Need for Capital

The FDIC has recognized that adequate capital represents the backbone of any commercial banking institution. Capital provides, through the operation of an informed free market system, a mechanism to maintain discipline against unreasonable growth. Capital also provides a buffer when operating losses exceed income.

The FDIC has a tremendous responsibility for maintaining the stability of the commercial banking system. Adequate capital significantly reduces the FDIC's "exposure" in insuring depositors. The provision of FDIC coverage for depositors has probably provided more stabilization to the commercial banking industry than any other financial influence. FDIC coverage has given a measure of security to the American public which is absolutely necessary. . . . It has allowed depositors guaranteed protection on their bank deposits.

Some argue capital ratios are unfair and should not be based on any "peer group" or aggregate average data, but should be analyzed according to the individual needs of a particular bank. The FDIC fully recognizes that capital/risk asset ratios in commercial banks may vary greatly. The loan quality, the bank's liquidity, the gain or loss reflected in its securities portfolio, the quality of bank management, the profitability of the bank . . . all these factors and more have a direct bearing on the particular capital needs and requirements of an individual banking institution. Much of this variability has been taken into consideration in the new guidelines for acceptable and threshold capital requirements issued recently by the FDIC.

The following questions will need to be considered in analyzing the possibility of allowing banks to purchase capital deficiency insurance:

1 Should capital insurance be administered similarly to life insurance: that is, when an insured person becomes deceased (i.e., when the bank is officially closed by regulatory authorities), should the policy pay off, and the insurance carrier have no further interest in the failed institution (just as the life insurance carrier has no further claim against the estate of the deceased)?

2 Should the capital insurance carrier provide insurance that would be similar to subordinated debentures, and would pay off only in the event that all "dollars" capital were first exhausted?

3 Should the capital insurance carrier have any claims against recoveries made by the FDIC during periods of liquidation of a failed bank?

4 How should premiums be computed for capital deficiency insurance? Is it feasible to give a more favorable premium to a bank that earns a "1" or "2" on the FDIC CAMEL[1] rating concept? Should banks which are designated a "3" rating pay a higher premium and should banks in the "4" or "5" category be ineligible to purchase the coverage?

5 If capital deficiency insurance is approved, and capital protection actually takes two different forms ("dollars" capital and insurance coverage for capital deficiencies) what effect will this have an various state requirements for legal lending limits (based on capital) and also on the amount of funds that can be invested in fixed assets and the amount of public funds a bank may accept for deposit?

6 Even though our assumptions plainly state that a commercial insurance carrier acceptable to the FDIC is available to provide the coverage, is this an insurance coverage which the FDIC itself should consider underwriting?

7 In the event that a bank which is near failure is assumed or merged into another bank or another bank holding company, what effect would capital deficiency insurance have on the merger? Should capital deficiency coverage be assigned under these circumstances?

---

[1] See definition and discussion of CAMEL concept in Lemon's remarks.

EXHIBIT
Capital Adequacy Alternatives*

Capital adequacy . . . it has been discussed a thousand times. It is almost always analyzed

* This exhibit has been prepared by Glen E. Lemon, Chairman of the board and chief executive officer, First Bank & Trust Co., Booker, Texas.

when regulators convene. It is normally called to the attention of management when bank examiners make their final remarks. And bankers discuss it nearly always when they assemble for a seminar, meeting, or convention.

Every banker, regulator, and bank examiner who has been in the profession for more than 10 years can remember when the rule of thumb was "10 percent capital." Yes, those of us who have had a few years' experience can remember when it was necessary to have $1 of capital for every $10 of deposits.

In the last 20 years, as deposit growth has increased at a very rapid pace, this ratio has slowly declined; first to an 11 to 1 level, then during the 1970s to the 12 to 1 level. Some of the largest banks in the country experienced even more rapid deposit growth, and in some cases the deposits-to-capital ratio rose to a 20 to 1 level. If we look at historical evidence, the concept that an individual bank, or the banking industry, can be made secure from failure by sufficiently high capital ratios is not supported. This can be substantiated by such recent major failures as the Franklin National Bank in New York and the First National Bank of San Diego.

The level of capital perceived as adequate has changed from time to time, and must continue to do so as banking adjusts to alterations in global capital markets and economic conditions. The essential point is that adequacy of capital is, and should remain, a management decision, with oversight from regulators. As Justin T. Watson, then first deputy comptroller of the currency, commented in 1975: "There is no amount of capital that will salvage a bank which is grossly mismanaged. Conversely, a strong, well-managed bank can operate on a very thin capital base . . ." Establishing a capital ratio requirement high enough to protect the country's most poorly managed banks is not likely to benefit the banking industry, its customers, or the general economy.

No one in the banking industry can deny that the FDIC has proved invaluable in stabilizing the banking industry. It has provided a measure of security to the American public which is absolutely necessary—it has allowed depositors guaranteed protection on their deposits.

With heavily regulated banks and less-regulated businesses vying for capital in the same market, investors have responded by placing their funds with industries other than banking, because earnings in nonbank institutions have generally been higher. It has, therefore, become increasingly difficult to raise new capital in most commercial banks.

The commercial banking industry has been competing for investor's funds with a very wide range of institutions—financial and nonfinancial. Nonbank and nonregulated financial enterprises operate in American financial markets with a distinct advantage over commercial banks. These nonbank institutions do not have to cope with many of the onerous restrictions imposed on the banking industry. Regulatory restrictions do present, in my opinion, a serious barrier to banking in its quest for external funding and new capital.

Capital levels have, therefore, been steadily declining, and prior to recent regulatory revisions (February 1982), many of the country's largest banks had less than a 4 percent capital-to-assets ratio. The medium range of banks ($150 million to $1 billion in deposits) had capital-to-asset levels averaging below 7 percent, while most small banks ($150 million and below) maintained capital ratios barely reaching the 8 percent to 8½ percent range.

In a formal examination of bank capital adequacy undertaken by Citibank in 1981, Walter Wriston, chairman, commented that the most fundamental finding of the study was that "the stability of a banking institution and of the entire banking system, does not depend on abiding 'reserves' of capital so much as day-to-day 'access' to funding markets. Therefore, proved competence in liquidity management is a greater assurance of viability than any arbitrary or traditional capital ratio requirement."

Fortunately, we have recently witnessed some revisions in regulatory capital guidelines. The FDIC, the Comptroller of the Currency, and the Federal Reserve Bank have all adjusted their acceptable and threshold levels of capital adequacy to a 6 percent capital-to-assets level. At the same time, these agencies have promulgated

CAPITAL ADEQUACY ALTERNATIVES (continued)

some clear-cut objectives which they hope to achieve through these new capital guidelines. One of these objectives is to achieve greater uniformity and consistency in the supervision of various capital measures in the nation's banks.

But what is the real function and purpose for bank capital? It has but one purpose . . . the protection of depositors' funds. Capital will also have a bearing on a bank's loan limit, and in some states it may determine the amount a bank can invest in fixed assets. In other instances, capital will control the amount of public funds a bank may accept for deposit, and the amount of dues a bank may pay to various banking associations. Capital provides, through the operation of an informed free market system, a mechanism to maintain discipline against unreasonable growth. But in reality, the only real purpose for capital is to protect depositors against loss.

A banker projecting costs today for new capital over the next several years would probably assume a level in excess of 14 percent. In many instances, the cost of capital could run as high as 20 percent, depending on the methods used to measure cost. And always, the question remains: How much capital is needed? Based on present trends, capital ratios will probably continue to decline. Given very high capital cost, is there an alternative to invested capital?

Sufficient "dollars capital" must always be maintained to absorb losses from operations and declining asset values. But why is it necessary to require an additional amount of dollars capital over and above that which will cover operating losses in a going concern? Would it be possible to design an insurance program to cover deficiencies in capital beyond that level?

Presumably, that portion of capital in excess of potential operating losses would be needed only in the event of bank failure. It should be possible, therefore, to cover this potential lack of dollars capital through those who specialize in risk management: the insurance industry. Let's look at the possibility of such coverage being provided by the commercial insurance industry.

Historical data suggest the annual failure rate for commercial banks is less than $\frac{1}{10}$ of 1 percent for all institutions. Since the inception of the FDIC in the early 1930s, there have been approximately 580 banks which have failed, or an average of about 12 banks per year. With such a favorable record and with banking practices continually improving, why wouldn't the insurance industry be a potential candidate to underwrite bank capital deficiencies? With prudent underwriting, the risk should run substantially less than the present $\frac{1}{10}$ of 1 percent rate.

If the insurance industry could insure a bank's capital deficiency of, for example, $100,000, (at a cost far less, probably, in the $4,000 to $5,000 premium range annually), wouldn't the depositor's funds be just as well protected if the $100,000 was made available through an insurance company in the event of bank failure? The insurance premium payment would be a deductible expense, and it would represent the total cost to the bank in contrast to the current alternative which requires the investment of new capital, which, if a debt instrument is used, would require payment of interest and retirement of principal while requiring the retention of still additional earnings to support future growth.

It must be assumed, of course, that the insurance industry could provide a policy acceptable to the bank's directors and stockholders, and more important, to the bank's regulators. These state and government agencies, however, have already approved the Form 24 Bankers Blanket Bond, which provides a similar service to depositors.

The insurance industry is already tremendously knowledgeable regarding the underwriting of the banking industry as a result of writing the Form 24 Blanket Bond. In order to do this, insurance companies look thoroughly at each area of a bank's operations, management, and its general administrative capacity. The only area of the bank not normally considered for Form 24 underwriting is the area of credit. A credit examination by the insurance carrier would, however, require little additional effort.

CAPITAL ADEQUACY ALTERNATIVES (continued)

In this regard, the FDIC has recently initiated the AELMO[1] concept of classification to replace the older CAMEL[2] approach for commercial banks. Banks are rated Zone I through Zone III. The three zones were established for regional and community organizations in regard to the total capital to assets ratio. Zone I calls for regional banks to maintain a capital ratio above 6.5 percent, and community banks to maintain a ratio above 7 percent. Zone II has a range of 5.5–6.5 percent for regional banks and 6–7 percent for community banks. Regional banks operating below 5.5 percent, and community banks with less than 6 percent, are classified in Zone III. The very best banks carry Zone I ratings, while those that need considerable capitalization and regulatory attention carry Zone III ratings.

For insurance purposes, a bank earning a Zone I rating would probably not require further underwriting from an insurance carrier. A bank carrying a Zone II rating might automatically be assessed a 10 percent surcharge on its annual premium, and banks receiving a Zone III rating might require a representative of the insurance industry to visit the bank and determine the problems associated with that particular institution. In some instances, coverage might be denied because of internal problems.

In the event that capital insurance coverage were terminated, or the insurance carrier were not willing to renew coverage, a 90 day notice would be forwarded to the respective regulator. This same type of "notice" is presently utilized for Form 24 coverage.

As of February 1982, if a community bank's capital ratio drops below the new 6 percent floor, the regulators' response is essentially as it has been in the past, that is, the FDIC, in cooperation with state banking departments, requires the bank to submit an acceptable "comprehensive

_____
[1] AELMO is an acronym signifying assets, earnings, liquidity, management, and other activities exposing a bank to risk.

[2] CAMEL is an acronym signifying capital, assets, management, earnings, liquidity.

capital plan." Should the bank's ratio fall even lower, say below 5 percent, the FDIC insists on a "specific program" to remedy the situation promptly.

The insurance industry would certainly find it necessary to hold regulators compeletely harmless in their analysis and classification of various banks, if the insurance carrier expected to utilize regulators' classification information in their underwriting experience.

A problem bank might have to pay additional premium in order to acquire coverage, and in some instances such a bank might not be able to purchase the coverage at any price. In these situations a bank's stockholders would be faced with the same alternative they have now, namely, injecting more dollars capital. The amount of required new capital would, of course, depend on the requirements set forth by regulatory authorities in each case.

If insured capital could be purchased at a fee of less than 5 percent annually, tax deductible, its availability would be a great incentive for improving bank management. Bank officers would have a considerable incentive to maintain "a clean bank" so that capital insurance coverage could be purchased. Naturally, invested dollars capital would have a higher cost, and presumably most would want their bank management to make certain that the institution would remain eligible to purchase insurance capital coverage.

We certainly would not expect regulators to agree to a significant portion of a bank's capital being provided through insurance protection. Regulators could clearly point to examples which have necessitated the availability of dollars capital to absorb unusual operating losses which have exceeded a bank's annual earnings.

Under this proposal, dollars capital would be present in varying amounts to provide the "cushion" for any abnormal operating losses. The balance of any capital requirements comfortably beyond this point could then be provided by insurance, as determined by the appropriate regulatory agency. In reality, the amount

CAPITAL ADEQUACY ALTERNATIVES (continued)

of capital required should be determined by the perceived risk level for a particular bank.

In this regard, bankers have sometimes objected to the CAMEL concept, that it places capital up front, implying first consideration. Today a more appropriate order might be just the opposite—LEMAC (liquidity, earnings, management, assets, and capital).

In its most recent new policy statement on bank capital, the FDIC included a revised rating concept, AELMO. If these areas were judged satisfactory, the bank would be considered financially sound and well managed, and, under revised capital adequacy guidelines, would be required to maintain a capital-to-assets ratio of 6 percent.

It seems clear that most commercial banks would welcome the opportunity to purchase insured capital as opposed to investing added dollars capital, or to purchasing debentures or issuing preferred stock. Financial statements would, of course, be required to reflect clearly, through footnote disclosure, that level of capital covered by insurance. Obviously, close cooperation between regulators, the banking industry, and the insurance industry would be necessary to initiate an insured capital plan. An agreement by the insurance industry to provide capital funds (in the event of bank failure) would be totally binding and payment would be made without contest. The insurance carrier of insured capital would pay the proceeds at the time bank failure was reported and would maintain no further interest in the bank as to distribution of any proceeds to depositors and/or stockholders.

With a proper approach to insured capital, the insurance industry should identify this opportunity as a profitable service. From the standpoint of regulators, the continuing decline in capital ratios should cease. For stockholders, the purchase of insured capital probably would result in improved earnings.

An alternative to providing bank-insured capital from private sources would be to provide the service through the Federal Deposit Insurance Corporation itself. Several advantages would result:

1   Additional insurance coverages for the banking industry, properly underwritten by the FDIC, would yield additional income to the agency (FDIC) which provides the insurance backbone for the entire commercial banking system.

2   The FDIC is the master comptroller (auditor) for insured commercial banks. Their genuine interest in protecting depositors' funds, and in maintaining adequate capital ratios should provide bank depositors with the greatest protection, at the least possible cost, for the banks purchasing coverage.

3   If the FDIC were providing the coverage for insured capital, there would be no potential conflict with a private insurance carrier resulting from the failure to pay a claim.

4   Present insurance rates for FDIC coverage are based on actual loss ratios, which are probably available to the banking industry at costs far less than they would be through outside insurance carriers. If this type of underwriting could be available for insured capital, the FDIC should have the best price available to the banking system.

5   For those depositors who concern themselves with capital ratios, insured capital through the FDIC may be more significant than through private insurance carriers.

I recognize that this proposal for insuring capital deficiencies is unfamiliar and that the subject itself is complex. I believe, however, that the concept merits consideration. As Justice Holmes once noted, "Every thought with a claim to truth must be tested by its ability to gain acceptance in the marketplace."

III

MEETING THE BANK'S LIQUIDITY AND SECURITIES NEEDS

5

MEASURING AND PROVIDING RESERVES AND LIQUIDITY

The subject of the next two sections of this book is how the funds the bank is able to attract are employed. This chapter covers decisions involving the bank's reserve (or money) position and its liquidity position. The following chapter covers management of the bank's security portfolio. The section following these chapters discusses various aspects of managing bank loan portfolios. Since the employment of bank funds is strongly related to, and often occurs simultaneously with, their attraction, the final section of the book emphasizes techniques and policies related to tying together asset and liability management.

Management's discretion regarding the employment of funds varies considerably—the minimum amount of cash and deposits with Federal Reserve Banks is set by regulatory decision, but the amount to be held in short-term U.S. Treasury securities is a matter of management choice. This chapter covers how a bank measures its reserve needs and what assets the bank can use to meet these needs. It then turns to measuring the various types of liquidity needs and evaluating the methods of meeting these needs.

DETERMINING A BANK'S RESERVE NEEDS

A bank's reserve needs are generally set by regulatory requirements and the types of funds attracted by the bank. National banks, which have to be members of the Federal Reserve, and state banks that have chosen to be members of the Federal Reserve must meet reserve requirements, which are the percentages of the types of funds attracted

TABLE 5-1
Reserve Requirements for Commercial Banks That are Members of the Federal Reserve

March 1, 1982

1. *Reserve Requirements for Transaction Accounts* (demand deposits, NOW accounts, share draft accounts, savings accounts that allow automatic or electronic transfer, accounts that allow over three telephone or preauthorized payments each month).

Transaction Balances	Reserves Required
$26 million or less[a]	3%
Over $26 million	3% of first $26 million plus 12% of rest

2. *Reserves Required for Other Savings and Time Deposits*

Description of Deposits	Reserves Required
Personal savings deposits (nontransferable)	0%
Nonpersonal savings deposits	3%
Personal time deposits (nontransferable)	0%
Nonpersonal time deposits (original maturity <del><4 years</del> 1½ yrs	3%
Nonpersonal time deposits (original maturity <del>>4 years</del> 1½ yrs	0%

3. *Ineligible Acceptances and Obligations by Affiliates*

Description	Required Reserves
Maturity in less than 14 days	Treated as addition to transaction accounts (3% through 12%)
Personal—14 days to 4 years	0%
Nonpersonal—14 days to 4 years	3%

4. *Reserves Required for Eurocurrency Liabilities* (net borrowing from related foreign offices, gross borrowings from unrelated foreign depository institutions, loans to U.S. residents made by overseas branches of domestic depository institutions, and sales of assets by U.S. depository institutions to their overseas offices).

3% of dollar amount of Eurocurrency liabilities

[a]Up from $25 million or less in 1981.

times the amount of funds attracted in the particular category as set forth in Regulation D of the Federal Reserve. The reserve requirements for state banks that are not members of the Federal Reserve (nonmember banks) used to be set by the regulatory authority in each state. The Depository Institution Deregulation and Monetary Control Act of 1980 included provisions for equalization of reserve requirement for nonmember banks by September 1988.[1] The level of reserves required for member banks as of March 1, 1982, is shown in Table 5-1.[2]

Table 5-2 shows Form 2900, which a member bank can use to tell its Federal Re-

---

[1] For most nonmember banks, reserve requirements are phased in over an eight-year period, beginning with one eighth in November 1980 and increasing by one eighth in September of each year after 1980. It is expected that by 1988 the reserves required for nonmember banks will exceed reserve requirements in all states and govern all banks.

[2] Regulation D itself, with detailed descriptions and answers to typical questions, appears in *The Federal Reserve Reserve Requirements* (Washington, D.C.: Federal Reserve Board of Governors, 1981).

serve Bank the member bank's transaction accounts, other deposits, and vault cash for a week from a Thursday through the following Wednesday. Deposits are recorded as of the end of each business day. Therefore, a bank that is open Monday through Friday will record the same amount for deposits on Friday, Saturday, and Sunday of a statement week. If a bank is also open on Saturday, its Saturday and Sunday will be the same. Deposits and vault cash are recorded on a seven-day basis with the total for the week appearing in column 8 regardless of the days the bank conducts business. The figures filled in Form 2900 on Table 5-2 are rounded figures for a sample moderate-size bank not located in a financial center.

Table 5-3 illustrates the calculation of the member bank's reserve needs for the week starting the second Thursday after the Wednesday covered by the bank's deposits and vault cash report in Form 2900. The sample bank's deposits and vault cash figures in Table 5-2 and the reserve requirements in Table 5-1 are used in Table 5-3. Demand balances due from depository institutions in the United States and cash items in process of collection are subtracted from total transaction deposits to find the transaction amounts subject to reserves. The first $26 million of transaction accounts subject to reserves are multiplied by the 3 percent requirement with the remaining transaction accounts subject to 12 percent reserves. The amount of reserves on transaction accounts are added to reserves on savings and time deposits and other obligations subject to reserves (at 3 percent rate in 1982). Vault cash is subtracted from this total amount of reserves to determine the reserves to be maintained at the Federal Reserve directly or on a pass-through basis during the reserve week ending two weeks later.

Figure 5-1 illustrates the timing for the sample bank when reserve needs measured from March 4 to 10, 1982 (see Table 5-3) must be met during the March 18 to 24, 1982, period. The need for the following week (March 11 to 17) would be filled in the week ending two weeks later (March 25 to 31), and so on. In addition, the Federal Reserve allows member banks to carry a reserve excess or deficiency of up to 2 percent of its reserve requirements into the following week. Thus, a bank can miss its reserve requirements by up to 2 percent on either side and be allowed to carry this position to meet or increase its new reserve requirement in the next week. An excess or deficiency cannot be carried over to the second week following the week in which the excess or deficiency occurs.

The process of measuring reserve requirements for state nonmember banks varies widely among the regulatory authorities in different states. Reserve requirement percentages, reserve period length, reserve period timing, and carryover provisions differ from state to state. Nevertheless, the basic idea—multiplying deposits in a previous period by reserve requirements to determine the reserve needs for a period—holds in most states. Furthermore, the Depository Institution Deregulatory and Monetary Control Act of 1980 will standardize the determination of reserves for member and nonmember banks by 1988.

MEETING REQUIRED RESERVES AND MANAGING THE MONEY POSITION

There are four basic asset accounts in what most banks label as their "money" position. Each of these accounts is briefly described:

TABLE 5-2
Report of Transaction Accounts, Other Deposits and Vault Cash (Federal Reserve Form 2900)

Items	Column 1 Thursday Mils. Thous.	Column 2 Friday Mils. Thous.	Column 3 Saturday Mils. Thous.
Transaction Accounts			
Demand Deposits			
1. Due to depository institutions			
(a) Banks	12,230	12,250	12,250
(b) Other depository institutions	9,991	9,894	9,894
2. U.S. government	15,200	15,205	15,205
3. Other demand	8,150	8,150	8,150
Other Transaction Accounts			
4. ATS accounts	9,600	9,614	9,614
5. Telephone and preauthorized Transfers	5,210	5,391	5,391
6. NOW accounts/share drafts	18,205	18,205	18,205
7. Total (must equal sum of Items 1 through 6 above)			
Deductions from Transaction Accounts			
8. Demand Balances Due from Depository Institutions in the United States	4,190	4,192	4,192
9. Cash Items in Process of Collection	6,231	6,235	6,235
Other Savings and Time Deposits			
Other Savings Deposits			
10. Personal	7,250	7,210	7,210
11. Nonpersonal	9,630	9,622	9,622
12. Total (must equal sum of Items 10 and 11)			
Time Deposits			
13. Personal (regardless of maturity)	5,555	5,495	5,495
14. Nonpersonal			
(a) Original maturity of less than 4 years	3,110	3,110	3,110
(b) Original maturity of 4 years or more	3,900	3,901	3,901
15. Total (must equal sum of Items 13 and 14)			
16. All Time Deposits in Denomination of $100,000 or more (included in Items 13 and 14)	1,614	1,841	1,841
17. *Vault Cash*	1,613	1,613	1,613

Items	Column 1 Thursday Mils. Thous.	Column 2 Friday Mils. Thous.	Column 3 Saturday Mils. Thous.
Schedule A: Other Reservable Obligations by Remaining Maturity			
Ineligible Acceptances and Obligations by Affiliates			
1. Maturing in less than 14 days			
2. Maturing in 14 days or more but less than 4 years			
(a) Personal			
(b) Nonpersonal			

TABLE 5-2 (continued)

		Report all balances as of the close of business each day to the nearest thousand dollars			
Column 4	Column 5	Column 6	Column 7	Column 8	Column 9
Sunday	Monday	Tuesday	Wednesday	Total	Daily Average
Mils. Thous.	Mils. Thous.	Mils. Thous.	Mils. Thous.	Mils. Thous.	Mils. Thous.
12,250	12,269	12,248	12,250	85,747	12,250
9,894	9,897	9,899	9,912	69,381	9,912
15,205	15,310	15,310	15,260	106,695	15,242
8,150	8,162	8,164	8,164	57,090	8,156
9,614	9,620	9,620	9,611	67,293	9,613
5,391	5,312	5,310	5,370	37,315	5,331
18,205	18,214	18,241	18,241	127,516	18,217
				551,037	78,720
4,192	4,194	4,191	4,191	29,342	4,192
6,235	6,230	6,230	6,230	43,626	6,232
7,210	7,210	7,241	7,241	50,572	7,225
9,622	9,625	9,627	9,627	67,375	9,625
					16,850
5,495	5,499	5,499	5,499	38,537	5,505
3,110	3,116	3,116	3,111	21,783	3,112
3,901	3,916	3,916	3,916	27,351	3,907
					12,524
1,841	1,843	1,843	1,843	12,666	1,809
1,613	1,617	1,617	1,619	11,305	1,615

		Report all balances as of the close of business each day to the nearest thousand dollars			
Column 4	Column 5	Column 6	Column 7	Column 8	Column 9
Sunday	Monday	Tuesday	Wednesday	Total	Daily Average
Mils. Thous.	Mils. Thous.	Mils. Thous.	Mils. Thous.	Mils. Thous.	Mils. Thous.

TABLE 5-3
Calculation of Required Reserves[a] (for March 4–10, 1982)

	Amount (dollars in thousands)	Required reserves (%)	Reserves (dollars in thousands)
Transaction Accounts			
Total Transaction Accounts	78,720		
Less Deductions	10,424		
Subject to Reserves	68,296		
Initial Amount	26,000	3	780
Remaining Amount	42,296	12	5,076
Other Reservable Transaction Obligations	0	12	—
Total Transaction Reserves			5,856
Savings and Time Deposits			
Personal Savings	7,225	0	—
Nonpersonal Savings	9,625	3	289
Personal Time	5,505	0	—
Nonpersonal Time<4 years	3,112	3	93
Personal Time>4 years	3,907	0	—
Other Reservable Obligations	0	3	—
Eurocurrency Transactions	0	3	—
			382
Total Reservable Deposits and Obligations			6,238
Vault Cash			1,615
Daily Average Balance—To be maintained at Federal Reserve directly or on pass through basis (before consideration of carry-over)			4,623

[a]Based on data in Tables 5-1 and 5-2.

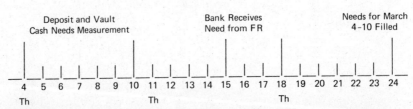

FIGURE 5-1 Timing Sequence of Measuring and Filling Reserve Needs (for March, 1982)

1   *Currency and coin* (or vault cash) consists of money that the bank holds to meet its daily transaction needs. When a bank has more vault cash than it needs, it deposits the excess in the Federal Reserve or a correspondent bank; the reverse (getting cash from the Fed or a correspondent) is true when the bank has less vault cash than it needs.

2   *Due from the Federal Reserve* represents the deposits of the bank with its Federal Reserve District Bank. This account is the basic reserve account of banks that are members of the Federal Reserve. The net of most checks and electronic fund transfers are ultimately taken from or added to this account. Other ways to increase this account include the purchase of Fed Funds, borrowing from the Federal Reserve, depository currency and coins, and the redemption of maturing Treasury securities. Methods for decreasing Federal Reserve accounts include letting purchased Fed Funds mature, selling Fed Funds, repaying borrowing from the Federal Reserve, withdrawing coin and currency, and directly purchasing Treasury securities.

3   *Due from other commercial banks* consists of all deposits the bank has in other commercial banks. In most states, nonmember banks are currently permitted to count balances due from other banks to meet required reserves. These nonmember banks use their correspondent banks to clear checks (often through their Federal Reserve account), conduct Fed Fund transactions, and provide other services as compensation for such balances. Legislation passed in 1980 forces nonmember banks in step-by-step fashion over the following eight years to hold reserves directly (or indirectly through pass-through accounts) in the Federal Reserve. Member banks also hold balances with other banks, but these reserves do not qualify to meet reserve requirements. Services such as loan participations, international transactions, and investment advice are required to compensate banks for balances left in correspondents.

4   *Cash items in process of collection* represent checks deposited in Federal Reserve banks or correspondent banks for which credit has not yet been received. The size of these cash items depends on the volume of checks and the time it takes to clear the checks.

As discussed earlier, the primary objective for a bank should be to maximize the value of the owner's investment in the bank. Since the assets represented by the bank's money position are generally nonearning assets, the objective for these assets should be to minimize the amount invested in such assets without taking excessive risk. The techniques and factors used to achieve this objective can be divided into three groups: cash items in process of collection, nonreserve correspondent balances, and required reserves.

In managing cash items in process of collection, banks should generally strive to process and collect cash items as rapidly as possible. This may involve working evenings to process checks earlier, using electronic fund transfer effectively, flying checks by courier to key collection cities, and so forth. The primary analytical technique is to ascertain that the marginal benefits—return on asset changed from nonearning to earning assets—exceed the marginal costs of speeding up the collection process.

Demand deposit balances of correspondent banks that cannot be used to meet reserve requirements should be justified by careful evaluation of the service-cost relationship. Larger correspondent banks are usually active in the collection of checks for their "downstream" correspondent banks. In return for deposit balances, many correspondent banks perform services such as giving investment advice, holding securities in safekeeping, arranging for the purchase and sale of securities, trading Federal Funds, arranging international financial transactions, participating in loans too large for smaller banks, and selling participations in loans to banks with surplus funds. The services should be provided at a lower cost than the recipient bank can perform them, yet contribute to the profits of the correspondent bank. The cost of the correspondent balances should be the returns given up because the deposits are nonearning assets, and such costs should not exceed the benefits from the services received.

The final category, required reserves, should be treated as the required dues to be in the business of banking. These dues are required to conduct business, but dues above the required amount earn no return or returns significantly below what the bank can earn on other earning assets. The philosophy in managing the required reserve portion of a bank's money position is usually to just meet the bank's required reserves with acceptable assets—vault cash, deposits at the Federal Reserve, deposits at correspondent banks for non-Federal Reserve members in many states, and specified securities in a few states.[3]

It is important to remember that required reserves allow the bank to be a bank and are useful in controlling the money supply through monetary policy. Required reserves are not liquid assets, which can be used to meet loan demands or deposit outflows. Indeed, vault cash and deposits at the Federal Reserve which are required as reserves would seem to be about as nonliquid as bank premises. Interaction between reserves and liquidity are strong—the reserve position of a bank serves as the clearing account for liquidity needs, such as new loans and deposit outflows, and the liquidity position is a buffer for the money position—however, both needs must be met separately.

In managing the money position, a bank must meet its reserve requirements within the time constraints discussed in the preceding section. Random demands for loans and fluctuations in supplies of funds may force it either to buy funds at a higher than optimal price because it needs funds quickly or to employ funds at lower than optimal returns because it has excess reserves to invest immediately. The leeway provided by knowing reserve requirements in advance does not greatly simplify the problem because the balances themselves are subject to change each day. Having determined the bank's requirement at opening time, it is the money-position manager's task to keep track of all-important transactions that affect the reserve balance during the day and to take steps to counteract any adverse effects.

The principles of managing the money position are virtually the same in large and small banks, it is the number rather than the nature of the transactions that greatly complicates the task for larger banks in money centers. For the latter, especially for banks serving the New York City money and securities markets, the management of reserve positions is not only a daily but an hourly or virtually continuous task. The ra-

---

[3] By 1988, only vault cash, deposits at the Federal Reserve, and pass-through accounts to the Federal Reserve will be allowed to meet reserve requirements.

pidity with which funds flow through the money market banks reflects the payment for most of the nation's security transactions as well as the financing of brokers and dealers. It results from the high degree to which national corporations have consolidated their balances in the money centers as well as how fully they keep them invested. And, finally, the balancing adjustments of all of the country banks and the settlement of the Federal Funds markets are made on the books of banks in the money centers.

The basic problems involved in managing a money position can be more readily seen in the analysis of procedures that are adequate for the moderate-sized bank not located in a financial center used in Tables 5-1, 5-2, and 5-3. Table 5-4 presents a sample worksheet that such a bank might use to manage its money position. On the Monday before the new reserve week starts (March 15 based on March 4–10 accounts in this example), the Federal Reserve lets the member bank know the amount of average reserves it must carry with the Federal Reserve directly or on a pass-through basis (for the period March 18–24 in this example).

Any surplus or deficit position from the previous week is placed at the head of columns 3 and 8 on the worksheet in Table 5-4. These amounts are included only in the excess or deficiency figures because they do not, of course, affect the actual amounts of deposits on record. If a surplus or deficit position is reached for the week, these starting figures are subtracted out or added to the final balance of the week so that they will not be carried over into the next week.

A glance at the final column of the worksheet will tell the person responsible for

TABLE 5-4
Worksheet for Computing Reserve Position

Reserve balances for		Required balances with Federal Reserve Bank	Potential balances with Federal Reserve Bank	Potential excess or deficiency	Federal Funds actions		Other adjustments affecting reserve position[b]	Closing balances with Federal Reserve Bank	Actual excess or deficiency
					Federal Funds purchased	Federal Funds sold			
Day	Date	(1)	(2)	(3) +30[a]	(4)	(5)	(6)	(7)	(8) +30[a]
Thur.	March 18	4,623	4,692	+69				4,692	+69
Fri.	March 19	4,623	4,603	−20				4,603	−20
Cumulative		9,246	9,295	+79				9,295	+79
Sat.	March 20	4,623	4,603	−20				4,603	−20
Sun.	March 21	4,623	4,603	−20				4,603	−20
Cumulative		18,492	18,501	+39				18,501	+39
Mon.	March 22	4,623	3,980	−643	200			4,180	−443
Cumulative		23,115	22,481	−604	200			22,681	−404
Tues.	March 23	4,623	4,722	+99	400			5,122	+499
Cumulative		27,738	27,203	−505	600			27,803	+95
Wed.	March 24	4,623	4,483	−140				4,483	−140
Cumulative		32,361	31,686	−645	600	—	—	32,286	−45[c]
Average		4,623	4,527	−92	86	—	—	4,612	—

[a]Allowable excess or deficiency in reserve balances brought forward.
[b]Such as borrowing from the Federal Reserve and payments for and receipts from direct transactions on Treasury securities.
[c]Allowable excess or deficiency in reserve balances to be carried forward.

TABLE 5-5
Estimated Money Position Calculations—Tuesday, March 23 (dollar amounts in thousands)

	Current	Cumulative
Accumulated actual excess or deficiency		(−)404
Required reserves tonight	4,623	
Reserve balances collected (our books)	4,180	
Potential reserve position	−443	
Known transactions affecting reserves today		
Credits:		
Yesterday's immediate cash letter	2,181	
Deferred items available today	885	
Security sales available today	737	
Currency and coin in transit	100	
Credit in local clearings	—	
Other	—	
Total credits	3.903	
Debits:		
Remittances charged today	3,206	
Securities purchased charged today	—	
Notes due today	—	
Tax and loan call	100	
Currency and coin orders	—	
Debits in local clearings	55	
Other	—	
Total debits	3,361	
Net credits minus debits	(+)542	
Potential excess or deficit tonight	(+)99	(−)305
Adjusted today		
Credits:		
Transfers from bank account	—	
Borrowing from Federal Reserve	—	
Federal funds bought	400	
Securities sold for "cash"	—	
Total credits	400	
Debits:		
Transfers from reserve account	—	
Federal funds sold	—	
Total debits	—	
Net adjustments	(+)400	
Adjusted excess of deficiency	499	(+) 95

the bank's money position just where it stands at the opening of business each day.[4] This person then needs to calculate the effects of the debits and credits that he or she believes will be posted to the reserve account during each day. He or she is then in a position to project the current and cumulative average balance as of the close of business the same day. On the basis of this projection, a decision can be made regarding what actions, if any, will be necessary to keep this position in reasonable balance. Table 5-5 provides a suggested form for making these calculations. For small banks with only moderate deposit fluctuations, not much more is needed. For larger banks seeking to keep excess reserves to the barest minimum, a closer scrutiny of daily transactions will be necessary.

The bulk of the credits and debits affecting the reserve accounts of a bank not located in the money centers are usually evident in the clearing figures each morning (checks presented to it and checks forwarded by it for collection) or are the result of transactions, such as securities purchases and sales, that it has itself originated. In sharp contrast is the situation of banks that operate in the money centers or that carry substantial amounts of due-to-bank balances. During the course of each day, the latter are subject to immediate and unpredictable demands in the form of interbank transfers and other payments arranged in Federal Funds by their depositors.

Nevertheless, even for a small community bank, the unpredictable can loom large in the management of its reserve position. The volatility of large deposit accounts can cause management of the money position to go awry as the result of unexpectedly large withdrawals or even large deposits that cannot be put to use. Alert money managers will therefore attempt to keep a close watch over the larger depositors and will take notice of the transactions that may affect the reserve position not only on a particular day but later in the reserve-computation period as well. Large deposits and withdrawals can be scanned daily for clues to future deposit swings, and an attempt can be made to get advance notice of future transactions from the financial officers of important corporate customers. At the same time, a calendar of maturing certificates of deposit and securities and large loan repayments should be maintained and taken into consideration in the daily adjustments of the reserve position. The money-position manager should also receive a brief daily memorandum of the sources of funds available to him or her and a list of correspondent balances and liquidity instruments. Most large banks require that branch managers and department heads report large transactions to the "money desk" as soon as they become known.

In addition to gathering data, the money market manager seeks to match reserve requirements with actual reserve positions. At the start of the statement week, a bank should forecast its expected reserve position for each day in the coming week. The manager of the reserve position must then plan out the bank's activity during the week

---

[4] Since the Federal Reserve is open only five days a week, no transactions are recorded over the weekend, and hence the reserve balance that the bank achieves Friday afternoon will also be its deposit balance for Saturday and Sunday. When holidays occur on Mondays or Fridays, the position is carried a day longer. For example, if a holiday falls on a Monday, the Federal Reserve being closed, the bank's reserve position as of Friday will apply not only to Saturday and Sunday but also to Monday. Hence, locking into a surplus reserve position over a holiday weekend is one method of meeting reserve requirements for that week.

on the basis of the mean forecast of reserve positions and the possible deviations from the mean forecast that might be experienced.

If the projected deposit balances at the Federal Reserve are as shown in Table 5-4, it is likely that the hypothetical bank under review will need to buy Fed Funds (or borrow from the Federal Reserve) sometime during the week in order to meet its reserve requirements. However, if the possible deviations from these expected levels are small, the reserve manager may want to wait until the end of the week, observe how the reserve position is actually developing throughout the week, and then (since the reserve deficiency is not expected to be large) enter the market and buy funds if necessary. Since the distribution of possible outcomes is small and the expected deficit is also small, the manager can wait until more information is available before making a move.

On the other hand, if there is a great deal of uncertainty about the upcoming week, the reserve manager may want to go into the Fed Funds market early in the week and establish a cushion of reserves so as to avoid the need to go to the market at the last minute for a sizable amount. In this case the bank will sell Fed Funds toward the end of the week if reserve positions have worked out to be much easier than forecasted. The bank will act defensively in this time period, sacrificing returns to be able to satisfy legal reserve requirements.

ESTIMATING A BANK'S LIQUIDITY NEEDS

A bank's liquidity needs consist of immediate obligations, such as deposit withdrawals or legitimate loan demands, the bank must meet in order to be recognized as a going financial intermediary.

Table 5-6 illustrates the changing liquidity needs for a sample bank with reserve requirements of 12 percent on transaction accounts and 3 percent on time and savings deposits. During a period of low liquidity needs (see 2 in Table 5-6), the bank's deposits would be likely to grow while its loan demand might decline or at least grow less rapidly than the increase in deposits. On the other hand, rapid loan growth accompanied by slow growth or declines in deposits led to the period of high-liquidity needs illustrated in Table 5-6. In this example, a small amount of the $40,000 liquidity needed was provided by lower required reserves of $1,500 with the majority supplied by increasing borrowings by $10,000 and selling $28,500 of securities.

Clearly one of the important tasks of bank management is measuring and meeting a bank's liquidity needs. Long-run profitability may be hurt if a bank has too much in low-earning liquidity sources in relation to its needs for such liquidity. On the other hand, too little liquidity may lead to severe financial problems and even failure for a bank.

Daily (hourly in the case of money center banks) liquidity needs are usually met by appropriate management of the money position. There remain, however, short-term, cyclical, and trend needs for liquidity which the well-managed bank will try to estimate as accurately as possible. The best guides available to most banks are their past experience and knowledge of events likely to affect liquidity needs. After we discuss how to measure these liquidity needs, we will investigate the appropriate sources for filling these liquidity needs.

TABLE 5-6
Liquidity Needs for Sample Bank

1. Starting Position

Assets		Liabilities and Capital	
Reserves	17,100	Transaction accounts	100,000
Securities	75,000	Savings and time deposits	170,000
Loans	200,000	Borrowings	10,000
Other assets	7,900	Capital	20,000
	$300,000		$300,000

2. Period of Low Liquidity Need

Assets		Liabilities and Capital	
Reserves	18,000	Transaction accounts	105,000
Securities	84,100	Savings and time deposits	180,000
Loans	200,000	Borrowings	5,000
Other assets	7,900	Capital	20,000
	$310,000		$310,000

3. Period of High Liquidity Need

Assets		Liabilities and Capital	
Reserves[a]	15,600	Transaction accounts	90,000
Securities[a]	46,500	Savings and time deposits	160,000
Loans	220,000	Borrowings[a]	20,000
Other assets	7,900	Capital	20,000
	$290,000		$290,000

[a]A $20,000 decline in deposits and $20,000 increase in loans financed by additional borrowings of $10,000, lower required reserves of $1,500, and sale of $28,500 of securities.

Short-term liquidity needs of a bank may arise from several causes. For example, seasonal factors often affect deposit flows and loan demand. Since loans are generally to deposit customers, seasonal increases in loans tend to occur at the time when deposits are at seasonal lows, and visa versa. For example, a bank in a farming community might find high liquidity needs from its loan demand rising and deposits falling in spring when the need to plant and fertilize crops was high. After the crops were sold in the fall, loans would tend to fall and deposits increase. Banks that are heavily dependent on one or a few types of customers may find seasonal liquidity needs particularly important. Most seasonal fluctuations can be predicted reasonably accurately on the basis of past experience.

The holders of sizable deposit balances and the customers who borrow in substantial amounts also may influence the short-term liquidity needs of an individual bank to a degree that is directly related to their size. The short-term needs of important customers for funds strongly affect the short-term liquidity needs of the bank. Some customer's needs are highly predictable, such as the school district that has $5 million in certificates of deposits which will be used to pay for a new school building as the certificates mature. The short-term needs of other customers may be very difficult to predict, such as the loan needs of a volatile business which may use its $10 million line of credit (borrowing authority) to finance inventory. Much of the estimation of this type of short-term liquidity need will revolve around a knowledge of the needs and intentions of large customers.

As an example, Fifth National Bank is used in a simplified illustration in Tables 5-7 and 5-8 of how a bank may measure its short-term liquidity needs. The balance sheet for Fifth Bank for the end of 1983 appears at the top of Table 5-7. Assume that Fifth National has (1) classified loans as volatile (large customers subject to rapid loan increases or decreases) and other (primarily subject to seasonal fluctuations); (2) classi-

TABLE 5-7
Measuring Liquidity Needs of Fifth National Bank

Balance Sheet at End of Year December 31, 1983 (in thousands of dollars)

Assets		Liabilities and Capital	
Reserves	$ 17,100	Transaction accounts	$100,000
Securities	75,000	Vulnerable time deposits	20,000
Loans (volatile)	20,000	Other savings and time deposits	150,000
Loans (other)	180,000	Borrowings	10,000
Other assets	7,900	Capital	20,000
	$300,000		$300,000

Monthly Loan and Deposit Fluctuations (from Table 5-8)

End of Month	Total Loans	Total Deposits	Estimated Liquidity Needs[a]
January	192,800	273,000	+10,200
February	193,200	278,000	+14,800
March	205,000	269,000	−6,000
April	223,000	263,000	−30,000
May	212,000	262,000	−20,000
June	198,400	264,000	−4,400
July	191,200	271,000	+9,800
August	199,800	273,000	+3,200
September	210,600	273,000	−7,600
October	214,200	273,000	−11,200
November	210,600	272,000	−8,600
December	210,000	277,000	−3,000

Balance Sheet, Time of Highest Liquidity Need April 30, 1984 (in thousands of dollars)

Assets		Liabilities and Capital	
Reserves	$ 16,350	Transaction accounts	94,000
Securities	45,750	Vulnerable time deposits	15,000
Loans (volatile)	25,000	Other savings and time deposits	154,000
Loans (other)	198,000	Borrowings	10,000
Other assets	7,900	Capital	20,000
	$293,000		$293,000

[a]Total loans and deposits for month minus total at start of year without adjustment for required reserves. Minus (−) means liquidity is needed, and plus (+) means added liquidity from the end of the year.

TABLE 5-8
Seasonal Indexes and Calculation of Monthly Loans and Deposits for Fifth National Bank

End of month	Loans (volatile), in thousands of dollars	Loans (other) Index	Loans (other) Thousands of dollars	Transaction accounts Index	Transaction accounts Thousands of dollars	Vulnerable time deposits (Thousands of dollars)	Other time and savings deposits
January	20,000	96	172,800	102	102,000	20,000	151,000
February	25,000	94	169,200	106	106,000	20,000	152,000
March	25,000	100	180,000	101	101,000	15,000	153,000
April	25,000	110	198,000	94	94,000	15,000	154,000
May	25,000	104	187,200	92	92,000	15,000	155,000
June	22,000	98	176,400	98	98,000	10,000	156,000
July	22,000	94	169,200	104	104,000	10,000	157,000
August	27,000	96	172,800	105	105,000	10,000	158,000
September	27,000	102	183,600	104	104,000	10,000	159,000
October	27,000	104	187,200	98	98,000	15,000	160,000
November	27,000	102	183,600	96	96,000	15,000	161,000
December	30,000	100	180,000	100	100,000	15,000	162,000

fied savings and time deposits as vulnerable (subject to large withdrawals or increases) and other (estimated to grow $1 million each month in 1984); (3) required reserves of 12 percent on all transaction accounts and 3 percent on all time and savings deposits. Monthly patterns for volatile loans and vulnerable deposits have been estimated by bank management. The seasonal indexes for transaction accounts and other loans, which appear in Table 5-8, were estimated from Fifth Bank's seasonal deposit fluctuations over the past several years.

The appropriate seasonal relative (index for month/index for December) was multiplied by the December transaction accounts and other loans to estimate the dollar amounts in these categories. The various categories of loans and deposits in Table 5-8 are added and used in Table 5-7 to project the bank's estimated liquidity needs from December 31, 1983, to the end of each month in 1984. An estimated balance sheet for the month of highest liquidity needs appears at the bottom of Table 5-7. It is assumed that the liquidity needs from the $23 million increase in loans and $7 million decrease in deposits were financed by a $750,000 drop in required reserves and sale of $29,250,000 of securities (methods of filling liquidity needs are discussed in detail in the final section of this chapter).

While the example in Tables 5-7 and 5-8 is a simplified situation, the sample bank serves to illustrate the basic methods for estimating the short-term liquidity needs of a bank. Loans and deposits need to be categorized according to their seasonal or other short-term potential fluctuations. There may be as many as 20 to 30 categories of loans and deposits and many banks use weekly rather than monthly data. Canned computer programs to estimate short-term liquidity needs are available, and many banks have found micro-computers are helpful in estimating liquidity needs.

Cyclical liquidity needs of a bank are much more difficult to estimate. Such cyclical needs often are out of the control of any individual bank. Economic recession or boom and interest rate movements, particularly when banks may be constrained from changing their own rates because of regulation, can cause significant liquidity pressures. Furthermore, the timing of such cyclical pressures can be very difficult to predict. A bank that provides for all potential cyclical liquidity needs would probably end up holding primarily low-earning liquid assets at the cost of significantly lower profitability. The lower risk of high liquidity would probably not offset the negative impact of these lower returns.

The impact of cyclical liquidity needs can be illustrated by looking back at Fifth National Bank in Table 5-7. If it is assumed that a cyclical boom leads to a 25 percent or $50 million increase in loans, Fifth National will have to sell most of its securities and borrow heavily at times when interest rates are high and security prices are low. Similar liquidity pressures might occur because of deposit outflows if interest rates rose and the bank was unable to compete with market rates because of Regulation Q rate ceilings. If both events occurred simultaneously, as in the credit crunches in the 1970s, Fifth National Bank and, indeed, most banks in the United States would face severe liquidity pressures.

As mentioned earlier, cyclical liquidity pressures are usually extremely difficult to predict. Some helpful indications about the magnitude of cyclical liquidity needs may come from the following methods.

First, cyclical vulnerability to loans may be partially estimated for many banks by looking at the proportion of lines of credit currently used versus the highest use of lines in a previous cyclical boom. For example, if 40 percent of a bank's lines of credit is currently used and if 62 percent was the highest past usage of such lines, the bank might estimate an increase of 22 percent of its total lines as the cyclical liquidity needs from such lines. Second, correlation patterns between deposit flows and selected indicators, such as the level of rates, changes in rates, and rate ceilings, may provide guidelines for deposit inflows and outflows because of cyclical pressures. Third, there are statistical programs (in computer software packages) that can remove seasonal and trend effects from time series of various loan and deposit accounts. The residuals should give a rough estimation of the type of cyclical liquidity pressures these accounts were subject to in the past. Thus, if large CDs had fallen 10 to 15 percent in past credit crunches, the bank might try to make sure it had the ability to meet liquidity needs for 15 percent of current large CDs.

Trend liquidity needs are required by banks for liquidity demands that can be predicted over a longer time span. These longer term liquidity needs are generally related to the secular trends of the community or markets that a bank serves. In rapidly expanding areas, loan demand grows faster than deposits accumulate. One function of longer term liquidity is to provide funds for loan expansion.

In stable communities, on the other hand, deposits may show a steady rise while loan demand remains virtually unchanged. In such cases, the longer view of liquidity requirements may enable the bank to keep more fully invested than it otherwise would. In either case, to gauge the bank's needs for longer term liquidity, bank management must attempt some long-range economic forecasting on the basis of which it can reasonably estimate loan and deposit levels for both the next year and perhaps five years ahead.

Figure 5-2 graphically illustrates a methodology that a bank might use to plan its trend on longer term liquidity needs. The bank starts by classifying every account on its balance sheet as to whether it is liquid (convertible into usable funds within less than 90 days with little, if any, loss if the asset is sold) or nonliquid. The accounts listed to the left of the liquidity and nonliquidity columns in Figure 5-2 are representative of the types of assets that would fall into each category. Next, the sources of funds, liabilities and capital, are divided into two categories—volatile (subject to withdrawal because of seasonal, rate, or other pressures) and stable. The accounts listed to the right of the volatile and stable columns are representative of the types of liabilities and capital that would fall into each category. The difference between liquid assets and volatile sources is termed the liquidity gap. The gap is positive if liquid assets exceed volatile sources and negative if the reverse is the case.

The broken lines used in Figure 5-2 represent expected fund flows during the next period which are added to the balance sheet totals. The primary increase in assets is usually growth in loans, while deposit growth represents the primary source of funds for the bank depicted in Figure 5-2. If predicted loan growth exceeds predicted deposit growth, the bank has a liquidity need that may be covered by reducing a positive liquidity gap or by purchasing funds (methods for meeting liquidity needs are discussed in the following section). On the other hand, if predicted deposit growth exceeds predicted loan growth, the bank can improve its liquidity position or seek to employ the excess liquidity in higher return assets.

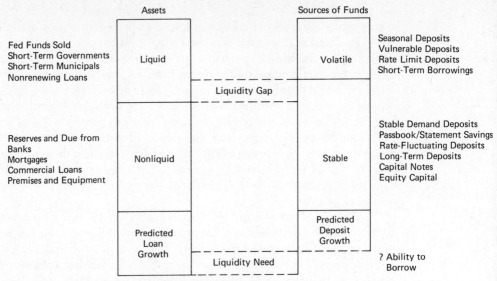

FIGURE 5-2   Illustration of Trend Liquidity Planning for a Bank

Figure 5-3 illustrates a method for combining the short-term and trend liquidity pressures into a unified model for measuring liquidity needs. Again, Fifth National Bank is used as the example, but the bank's growth in 1983 and predicted growth as well as its past and predicted seasonal pattern are the basis for charting liquidity needs. While the charts in Figure 5-3 are simplified to serve as illustrations, micro-computers can be used for more elaborate calculations and to trace more detailed charts.

The volatility of Fifth National Bank's deposits are shown in the chart of deposits as of months' end at the top of Figure 5-3. (For most banks with over $100 million in assets, this chart should be the summation of several charts for specific categories of deposits and should cover successive reserve-computation periods.) A trend line drawn through or near the low points should indicate the trend of stable deposits. The amount of deposits above this baseline represents the bank's seasonal liquidity needs because of volatile deposits subject to withdrawal. More complex charts or calculations would recognize liquidity needs for volatile deposits and would be the total of such deposits less the percentage of required reserves held against them, because as deposits decline the release of reserves provides a small part of the requisite liquidity.

The middle chart in Figure 5-3 depicts the liquidity needs from rising and fluctuating loan demands. Part of this demand may be seasonal and can be depicted in a chart of month-end totals. (As with deposits, larger banks will have charts or calculations for several types of loans and will use successive reserve-computation periods.) A trend line, drawn through or near the high points, represents the ceiling trend to which loans may be expected to rise periodically or seasonally. The amount by which loans are below the ceiling at any given time represents the liquidity needs of the bank to meet seasonal demands for loans.

The lower chart in Figure 5-3 traces the combined seasonal and trend liquidity needs for Fifth National Bank. Trend liquidity is calculated by subtracting the changes

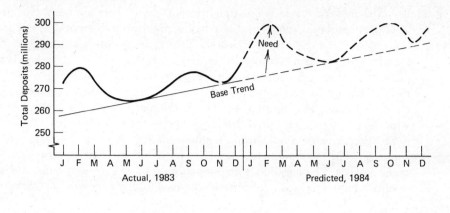

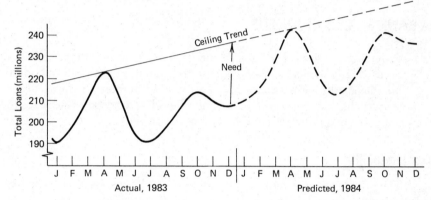

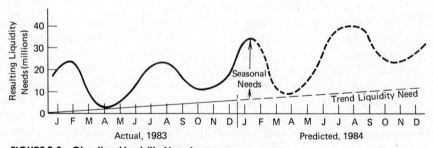

FIGURE 5-3 Charting Liquidity Needs

in the deposit trend line from the changes in the loan trend. If loan growth exceeds deposit growth, there will be a liquidity need; if the reverse is true, there will be a liquidity excess. For example, if the trend line of deposits rose from $250 million to $270 million and the loan trend line from $220 million to $250 million in the same period, there would be a trend liquidity need of $10 million. Total seasonal liquidity needs would be the total of deposit deviations from the base trend and loan deviations from the ceiling trend. These seasonal liquidity needs would be added to the trend liquidity previously calculated to trace the bank's total need for liquidity.

This method is relatively straightforward, but there are numerous practical problems. First, isolating which part of past fluctuations in loans and deposits are seasonal, cyclical, and trend is difficult. Second, forecasting future seasonal patterns and trends based on the past is hazardous at best. Seasonal patterns may change. The trend in deposits may change because of regulatory or competitive actions the bank cannot control. Trends in loans may change because of such actions, economic conditions, or changes in bank lending policies. Third, the method ignores cyclical liquidity needs, which are often the least predictable and can be the most harmful if not at least partially recognized. Most banks using methods similar to those illustrated in the charts in Figure 5-3 add some additional liquidity needs for forecasting error and unpredictable cyclical needs. The question is how much. In spite of such problems, the method seems to offer a bank significant information on its liquidity needs.

FILLING A BANK'S LIQUIDITY NEEDS

Providing for a bank's liquidity needs if often more complex than estimating such needs. Many banks have available some estimates of the bank's liquidity needs but do not have adequate policies and procedures for meeting these needs. A variety of sources that can be used to fill a bank's liquidity needs are described, then methods for matching liquidity needs and sources are discussed.

Sources of Liquidity

The primary sources of liquidity fall into two basic categories. The first category consists of assets in which funds are temporarily invested with the assurance that they either will mature and be paid when liquidity is needed or will be readily salable, without material loss, in advance of maturity. The second category includes the various methods by which banks can borrow or otherwise obtain funds. Large certificates of deposit are an example of a classification conflict between deposits, which presumably are used to measure liquidity needs, and funds borrowed to provide liquidity. A general rule of thumb for smaller and medium-sized banks in such conflicts could be to classify deposits that can be readily purchased or sold in an ongoing market as sources of liquidity and to include all other deposits in measuring liquidity needs. Such a rule of thumb for some very large banks might be misleading because a significant proportion of their deposits comes from such marketable sources. These sources are permanent as long as the bank can afford to pay the going market rate.

Most of the primary sources of liquidity are briefly described in Table 5-9. The rule of thumb is that assets must be high-credit quality and either short maturity or very marketable with little chance of loss. The amount of liquid assets may be limited by the willingness of the bank to hold such assets, which generally earn less than loans or less liquid securities. The use of borrowings or other increases in liabilities to fund liquidity needs is typically limited in one or more ways. Large, money center banks and bank holding companies that use purchased liabilities extensively as a source of funds are primarily limited by how much the money market and its participants think can be used by such banks. Regional banks may have limited access to some markets and will probably have lower limits on their total usage of purchased liabilities. Smaller banks'

TABLE 5-9
Potential Sources of Bank Liquidity

Liquidity Source	*Description*
Asset Stores of Liquidity	
Cash and due from	A bank's money position is a source of liquidity only if (1) there are excess reserves, (2) there are extra balances in correspondent accounts or checks not credited, or (3) deposits drop, freeing decline times 1 - reserve requirement.
Fed Funds sold	Excess reserves of a bank usually sold to another bank to provide earning asset to selling bank. Most mature daily, but can be easily renewed; "term funds" are also short maturity with good market. Unsecured.
Short-term U.S. government	Treasury bills and notes or bonds close to maturity are widely used sources of liquidity because they are short-term and tend to be bought and sold in active markets. Thought to have no risk of nonpayment.
Commercial paper, bankers' acceptances, and negotiable CDs	Obligations of private borrowers that are bought and sold through money market dealers. Generally on a discounted basis and most issues have a fairly active secondary market. Still high quality, i.e., risk of nonpayment very low.
Other marketable securities	Short-term government agency and state and local obligations which have slightly higher yield than governments, and yield and secondary markets similar to commercial paper, CDs, etc. Must be high quality (range available) if used for liquidity.
Securities purchased under agreement to resell (repos)	Temporary purchase of government or other securities in which seller has agreed to repurchase securities at fixed price and set time in the future. Difference between sale and purchase price is return received by holder.
Other liquid assets	Other credit-worthy securities, loans, or assets if their maturity conforms with the bank's liquidity needs and if the bank will have no compunction about reducing the size of such assets if necessary.
Purchased Forms of Liquidity	
Borrowing from Federal Reserve (discounts or advances)	Credit extended on a short-term basis by a Federal Reserve Bank to a bank or other depository institution. Rate is set by Fed and called discount rate with penalty rates for frequent or unusually heavy users. Security (securities or acceptable loans) required for either discounts or advances.
Fed Funds purchased	Purchase of another bank's excess reserves on daily or short-term basis. Other side of Fed funds sold. Purchased through correspondent or informal phone market at existing "fed funds" rate. Banks that are continual users often subject to informal limit by sellers. Unsecured.
Securities sold under agreement to repurchase	Temporary sale of government or other securities in which bank has received funds from purchaser and agreed to rebuy securities at predetermined price. In effect, short-term (often daily) secured borrowing from purchaser.

TABLE 5-9 (continued)

Liquidity Source	Description
Large certificates of deposits	Certificates of deposits in minimum amounts of $100,000 which can be issued to corporate treasurers with excess cash. Larger issues may be marketable. Bank must bid at least going market rate. Since unsecured and insurance limited to $100,000, corporate treasurers check soundness of bank.
Public deposits	Treasury tax and loan accounts may be retained if bank is willing to pay market rate and has pledgeable securities. Many state and local time deposits go to the bank bidding the highest rate.
Eurodollar and other foreign sources	Eurodollars are deposits in U.S. banks held outside the United States with maturities from overnight to a year. Active secondary market with overseas branch essential to continual involvement. Rates set in international market. Other foreign sources also used by very large banks.
Other liability forms	Other liability sources of liquidity include capital notes, ineligible acceptances, commercial paper sold through holding companies, etc. Key element is bank can raise funds through form if pays going market rate.

access to some markets is closed and they may find that their usage of borrowed funds is limited to how much their correspondent banks and the Federal Reserve are willing to lend them. These types of limits indicate that banks should have considerable unused borrowing capacity if they plan to borrow to fund liquidity needs.

Providing for Liquidity Needs

Providing for a bank's liquidity needs if often more complex than estimating such requirements. Many banks have available reasonable estimates of the bank's liquidity needs but do not have adequate policies and procedures for providing for these needs. Such banks are not sure which among the various assets or liabilities, such as those listed in Table 5-9, they should use to fill their liquidity needs. The wide variety of potential and actual choices used in providing for liquidity needs is often a bewildering menu of potential solutions. The choice among the variety of sources of liquidity should depend on several factors which are discussed in the following paragraphs: (1) purpose of liquidity needed, (2) access to liability markets, (3) management philosophy, (4) costs and characteristics of the various liquidity sources, and (5) interest rate forecasts.

The reason that liquidity is needed can affect the source of liquidity used to fill that need. Seasonal liquidity needs tend to be reasonably repetitive in extent, duration, and timing. Forecast of seasonal needs can usually be based on past experience, and most banks should be reasonably confident in such forecasts. There would, therefore, seem to be only moderate risk associated with the use of purchased forms of liquidity to cover seasonal liquidity needs. There should be a high probability that subsequent cash inflows will provide the funds to repay these purchased forms. The Federal Reserve seems to recognize this in its lending policies by having less stringent requirements for discounts and advances which are clearly for seasonal purposes. The potential gain from using purchased forms to meet seasonal liquidity needs is that the loan and investment portfolios can be structured on the basis of fund availability as seasonal highs. Since loans and investments usually earn higher returns than liquid assets, earnings should be higher from using purchased funds than from building up liquid assets during periods of low seasonal needs.

On the other hand, the use of purchased forms to meet cyclical needs seems less appropriate. Cyclical needs are much more difficult to predict, and when and if borrowings can be repaid may be a serious concern. The contribution of purchased forms in providing liquidity needs during cyclical boom may be limited and is likely to be very costly. Loan demands tend to run high in such periods, and liability sources (1) tend to become expensive, (2) may be limited by the ceiling on interest rates that banks can pay on deposits, and (3) may be restricted to only larger and better quality banks. For all but very large banks with good access to broad money market sources, holding liquid assets in slow periods to meet rising loan demands in boom times seems preferable to the use of purchased funds. By holding an adequate amount of liquid assets—an approach that may involve some loss of current income during the early stage of a cyclical expansion—most banks will avoid higher costs and possibly far greater capital losses (from the sale of depreciated bonds) during the later stages of expansion. Put in more precise terms, the essence of liquidity management is to equate the probable earlier loss of income with the subsequent higher fund cost and possible capital losses.

Meeting longer term liquidity needs can be more complex. Loan growth exceeds deposit growth for most banks with longer term liquidity needs. Such net growth can be financed by selling liquid assets or purchasing funds. The problem is that the supply of saleable liquid assets and the amount of borrowing permissible are limited in size. Thus, a bank that sells all of its liquid assets cannot use this source to finance a continuing excess of loans in relation to deposits. A bank that aims for rapid growth is likely to have some finite limit on how much of its sources of funds can be purchased funds. This limit will vary widely depending on bank size and entry into various financial markets, but there is some limit. The message would seem to be that a bank must finally limit its longer term liquidity needs. Either more permanent deposit sources must be found or bank loans must be limited in some meaningful way.

A final point related to longer term liquidity is that any bank should limit its use of purchased forms of liquidity enough to have a borrowing reserve if future unpredicted liquidity needs occur. This may mean that a smaller bank will seldom use purchased funds, keeping its limited ability to borrow as a liquidity or borrowing reserve. A large bank that believes it can purchase additional funds of up to 50 percent of its core deposits may restrict this source to 30 percent in order to have a borrowing reserve for future unpredicted liquidity needs.

The preceding paragraphs on the purposes of needed liquidity have alluded to differences in access to liability markets, the second primary determinant of the sources of liquidity that banks use to fill their liquidity needs. Many small banks are limited to borrowing from the Federal Reserve or purchasing Federal Funds through a larger correspondent. Most of this group of banks want to avoid borrowing from the Federal Reserve unless the borrowing is classified as seasonal. Furthermore, the use of Federal Funds is often limited to between 50 and 100 percent of the borrowing bank's capital base. The result of such limited access to sources of purchased liquidity forms is that most banks in this category use the sale of assets as their primary source of liquidity. The small borrowing reserve that exists is not used but left available for unpredicted liquidity needs.

The opposite extreme is large banks and bank holding companies located in money center cities. Assuming they are reasonably managed, such banks and holding companies usually have access to a variety of purchased forms in both domestic and international financial markets. Large bank holding companies have access to a few liability forms (for example, commercial paper) not available to banks. Furthermore, the total combined size of all purchased forms available to such banks and holding companies tends to be much larger in relation to total assets and capital than for smaller banks. Large banks and holding companies, therefore, usually have the ability to choose between liquid assets that may be sold and purchased forms of liquidity. The other determinants of filling liquidity should have a strong impact on this choice.

Many banks fall between these two extremes. Purchased sources include not only borrowing from the Federal Reserve and purchasing Fed Funds but also such forms as large certificates of deposit (not subject to rate limits) and public funds put up for bid. Such medium-sized banks generally lack access to the commercial paper market and most international markets and have relative borrowing limits between those of the small and large banks. While there is considerable variation in the sources used to provide for liquidity needs, a typical pattern seems to be to use purchased forms for seasonal needs and liquid asset sales to meet other liquidity needs.

The philosophy of a bank's management, the third primary determinant of the sources of liquidity that banks use to fill their liquidity needs, consists of a set of implicit or explicit liquidity guidelines laid down by top management. The primary liquidity guideline is the extent to which the bank is willing to rely on sources of funds that might disappear in difficult times. A bank that makes little or no use of purchased sources of funding liquidity needs, that is, one that relies exclusively on its liquid assets, reflects a conservative management philosophy. Presumably, such a bank would encounter little difficulty in meeting its liquidity needs even in troubled times. At the other end of the spectrum is the bank that seeks out purchased funds from any available source, as long as the total cost of such funds is less than the net rate of return the bank is earning by investing them. Such a bank generally relies heavily on outside sources of funds and reflects an aggressive management philosophy. Most banks in the United States fall somewhere between these two extremes; however, management philosophy has a profound effect on the methods individual banks use to provide for their liquidity needs.

The fourth primary determinant of the sources of liquidity a bank should use is the cost and characteristics of the various liquidity sources. Usually the source of liquidity chosen by a bank will be the lowest cost source that achieves the given liquidity need. This lowest cost principle is subject to the overall constraints imposed by access to financial markets and by the bank's management philosophy. In the case of assets the bank is considering selling to provide for liquidity needs, the "cost" is the income given up during the life of the assets adjusted for any gain or loss, tax effects, brokerage fees, and so on. When considering purchased forms, the cost includes not only interest cost but also reserve requirements, processing costs, insurance fees, and other factors. (Measurement of such costs was discussed in Chapter 4.)

Managing Liquidity

In addition to directly comparing costs, banks should look at differences in costs for different time periods. For example, a bank facing a seasonal increase in loans may finance these loans with either large CDs or repurchase agreements. One fundamental difference between the two instruments is that repurchase agreements are commonly renewed on a daily basis with different customers. Moreover, because they involve the literal sale and repurchase of securities, repos require a great deal of paperwork. Thus the total costs of repurchase agreements are largely variable, rising steadily as a function of the length of time for which the funds are needed. Issuing CDs, in contrast, involves the bank in high fixed costs (including insurance premiums and nonearning reserves), but no variable costs; once the CDs are issued, no further expenses are incurred. Thus, other considerations aside, the bank should tend to finance a loan expansion of a few days' duration with repurchase agreements and a loan expansion of several weeks' duration with CDs.

The bank's opinions on the future course of interest rates also affect the choice among alternatives for meeting liquidity needs. Using the previous CDs versus repos example, if interest rates were expected to rise in the future, the cost of CDs would become lower than that of repos at a shorter maturity. Because the repos would have to be rolled over at higher and higher rates, total costs would rise at an increasing rate. Under such circumstances, the bank would prefer to "lock in" the current low CD rate for all but its most temporary needs. That is, only if the bank needed the funds for only a very short time period would it prefer to use repurchase agreements. Alternatively, if interest rates are expected to fall in the future, the total costs of bank borrowing through repurchase agreements would rise at a decreasing rate of increase. In this case, the bank would prefer to avoid a comparatively long-term commitment at the currently high CD rate and instead would prefer to stay in repos to take advantage of the expected lower rates in the future. Thus, in periods when the bank expects interest rates to rise, the tendency is to raise funds through longer term adjustment instruments. In periods when rates are expected to fall, the tendency is to utilize very short-term sources of funds, such as Federal Funds and repurchase agreements.

The shape of the yield curve (maturities versus yields for securities with similar credit risks) for both liquid assets and potential borrowed sources may also affect the choice among the various sources of liquidity.[5] For example, if the yield curve for Treasury bills has a positive slope (which is the normal situation), the yield of a longer term bill for the period held (remember that one year is the maximum maturity) will usually be higher than the yield to maturity for a bill with a maturity that matches the holding period.

---

[5] Advocates of the "pure expectations" explanation for yield curves do not believe banks can gain from "playing the yield curve." In essence they believe a longer rate (any 180-day bills) is the average of today's 91-day bill rate and the 91-day bill rate expected in three months.

As example should help clarify this concept. Suppose a bank feels that it will need $100,000 to meet seasonal loan demands in approximately three months. Should the bank purchase 91-day bills yielding 13 percent or 182-day bills yielding 14 percent? Using the yield formula for the estimated holding period,[6] the bank would find that the yield over 91 days for the 182-day bill will be 15 percent if interest rates remain constant. Further, the bank should find that unless the rate on 91-day bills rises about 15 percent,[7] the bank will be better off buying the 182-day bills. Thus, unless the bank believes that the rates on 91-day bills will increase from 13 to above 15 percent in the next three months, the 182-day bills would be the preferable financial instrument. The same type of yield curve considerations and calculations can be used to assist in decisions about different maturity CDs or other purchased sources.

Possible liquidity needs arising from cyclical or secular increases in loan demands might be satisfied by holding longer term liquidity instruments. The major forms of assets acceptable for this purpose are U.S. government securities, federal agency securities, and higher quality, marketable state and local securities.[8] Under most circumstances, these securities will have maturities of one to three years at the time they are bought. Short-term securities are appropriate if the bank believes there is a high probability that rates will rise over the next year or so. The potential price fluctuations for securities maturing in much over three years disqualifies such securities for even longer term liquidity needs.

Changing Regulatory Opinions on Liquidity

As late as the 1970s, the primary regulatory authorities tended to look at static balance sheet measures of liquidity. Typically, the amount of unpledged, short-term securities were compared with some proxy for liquidity needs, such as total deposits. If this ratio met some preconceived target, the bank was deemed to be liquid. The static and arbitrary nature of this type of liquidity measure coupled with the rapidly changing nature of banking weakened the usefulness of regulatory evaluations of liquidity.

The emerging approach used by the three federal regulatory authorities seems much more reasonable. The examiner asks bank management for the bank's information on its liquidity needs and its ability to meet those needs. If the examiner believes

[6] The formula for determining the yield for the holding period (Y_h) is

$$Y_h = Y_o + \frac{T_r(Y_o - Y_m)}{T_h}$$

where Y_o is the original yield, Y_m is the market yield when sold, T_r is the remaining time to maturity, and T_h is the time held (in units consistent with T_r).

[7] The break-even market yield (Y_b) is determined by

$$Y_b = Y_o + \frac{T_h(Y_o - Y_c)}{T_r}$$

where Y_c is the market yield for a security maturing at the end of the holding period and the other symbols are the same as those in Note 6 above.

[8] The marketability of state and local bonds varies widely. For example, see George H. Hempel, *Postwar Quality of State and Local Debt* (New York: NBER, 1977), and "Liquidity and Muni Bonds," *Monthly Review* (Federal Reserve Bank of San Francisco, Jan. 1968), pp. 10–12.

the bank's system for assessing liquidity provides appropriate information and the bank's liquidity is adequate, the bank meets the regulatory requirements. If the bank's method for measuring liquidity is weak, the examiner compares his or her calculation of the bank's short-term liquidity needs with that bank's ability to meet such needs. Liquidity needs include estimated credit demands, probable volatility of deposits, and borrowed funds that must be repaid. Sources of meeting these needs include securities maturing in less than a year, other securities with market values exceeding book value, and other assets that appear to be readily sellable with little loss. The examiner is satisfied if sources exceed needs. If needs exceed sources, the examiner will consider the bank's ability to sell securities under agreement to repurchaser (repos) and the bank's ability to borrow, for example, Fed Funds, before making the final regulatory liquidity decision.

SUMMARY

This chapter has covered the measurement of and provision for a bank's reserve position and its liquidity needs. It described the correct way to measure a bank's reserve requirements. Methods for meeting these requirements so that a bank's actual reserves equal its required reserves were then disclosed. We presented several alternative methods for measuring a bank's seasonal, cyclical, and trend liquidity needs. All the methods emphasized fund flows rather than static balances as the appropriate measure of needs. We then evaluated alternative asset and liability sources for filling these liquidity needs. The matching of liquidity sources with appropriate needs was stressed. Current regulatory measures of liquidity seem to be close to the method for measuring and providing liquidity described in this chapter. The following chapter examines in considerable detail the entire securities portfolio, including securities that provide liquidity.

6

MANAGING THE SECURITY PORTFOLIO

A bank's security portfolio consists primarily of impersonal financial assets which pay the bank a fixed return until the assets (usually a debt instrument) mature. The common pattern that many banks follow consists of four sequential steps to employ the funds they are able to attract. First, they must meet the legal reserve requirement. Second, adequate provision is made for the bank's liquidity needs. Some of this liquidity need may be met through borrowing, but the majority of the liquidity needs of most banks (including money center and large regional banks) are met through having cash flows or liquid assets available to meet such needs. Third, the bank meets the loan demand in its market area, which may range from a small community to the world. Loans, which generally tend to be made on a personal contact basis, usually have higher yields than securities and are an important aid in attracting deposits. Fourth, and finally, any remaining funds are invested in the bank's security portfolio.

This common pattern of treating securities as the residual use of funds inevitably leads to timing problems in their purchase and sale. In recessions and periods of slow economic growth, when loan demands and interest rates tend to be lower, banks usually have relatively large amounts of funds to invest in securities. In the ensuing boom period, when loan demands and interest rates tend to be high, the bank is usually unable to purchase securities and may be forced to sell previously purchased securities at losses in order to finance loan growth. In this chapter we examine strategies for mitigating the problems resulting from investing funds in securities at the wrong times.

The economic conditions in the late 1970s and early 1980s—double-digit inflation, high loan demands, rapidly rising and fluctuating interest rates—led to a different kind of concern about the management of a bank's security portfolio. Most bank managers concentrated their efforts on making loans and acquiring funds to finance these loans. "Good" management of the security portfolio has come to mean purchasing only very short-term securities. Many "high" earnings-performance banks in this period had large loan portfolios and small security portfolios. Such performances have led at least some banks to downplay the importance of managing the security portfolio.

Such sentiment seems unjustified if one looks at the functions of a bank's security portfolio in the current and future environment. First, a bank's security portfolio is often its primary source of liquidity. Even large banks with access to many markets for purchased funds still look at the security portfolio as a source of liquidity. Thus, the security portfolio is important in reducing liquidity risk (a function of the interrelationship between liquidity needs and liquidity sources). Second, and equally important, a bank's security portfolio is an important contribution to bank earnings. In 1981, for example, 26.4 percent of the total revenue of all banks in the United States came from these banks' securities portfolios.[1] Because of the much lower cost of acquiring and managing securities compared with acquiring and managing loans,[2] it appears that the security portfolio's proportionate contribution to banks' net income is even higher than its contribution to total revenues. Other important contributions of the security portfolio include providing acceptable collateral for public deposits, borrowing from the Federal Reserve, and so on; providing a vehicle for repurchase agreements; dressing up the balance sheet appearance for customers and regulators; and *most important*, allowing impersonal flexibility, which can be used in managing a bank's overall maturity and interest-sensitivity position. Such important functions indicate that managing the security portfolio still deserves considerable attention.

This chapter is divided into two sections. The first section covers the types of securities banks usually purchase and the methods of measuring returns and risks on such securities. The second section covers the five steps a bank's management should follow in actively managing its security portfolio.

MEASURING RETURNS AND RISKS ON SECURITIES IN BANK PORTFOLIOS

Banks are generally restricted to buying debt instruments in their security portfolio. The returns and risks associated with debt instruments have been widely discussed; however, the appropriate data are in some cases quite difficult to obtain. Returns are usually treated as if they were relatively certain when the instruments were acquired. This assumption may not be appropriate for debt instruments that may have to be sold before maturity. Risk is generally even more complex to measure. Some of the complexities in measuring returns and risks on individual debt securities are considered below.

Debt securities generally promise to pay a fixed cash flow (coupon) for a specified number of periods and a payment of principal at a maturity date.[3] There are three po-

---

[1] *Annual Report of the FDIC 1981*, (Washington, D.C.: U.S. Government Printing Office, 1982).

[2] See *Functional Cost Analysis: National Average Reports*, various years. Published annually by the Federal Reserve Board of Governors.

[3] Other forms of debt instruments, such as paying variable coupon rates, paying variable amounts at maturity, and paying no coupon payment during the life of the instrument, exist but are a very small proportion of debt instruments at this time.

tential return measures: coupon rate, current yield, and yield to maturity. The coupon rate is simply the annual coupon divided by the principal payment at maturity, that is,

$$R = \frac{C}{B} \tag{1}$$

where R is the coupon rate, C is the annual interest payment, and B is the principal payment at maturity. Since the market price of the bond is usually not the same as its principal payment at maturity, B, the coupon rate is seldom very meaningful. The current yield, Y, is the annual coupon divided by the current market price, M, or

$$Y = \frac{C}{M} \tag{2}$$

This measure ignores the fact that the principal repaid at maturity is usually different from the current market price. The current yield is the rate quoted for listed bonds in financial papers such as the *Wall Street Journal* and may be helpful in determining if bond purchases using borrowed funds are able to cover borrowing costs.

The yield to maturity is by far the most meaningful and useful bond return measure. The yield to maturity on any maturity debt instrument is the rate of discount (internal rate of return) that equates the discounted value of interest and principal flows to the investor with the current market price of the security. If the interest payments are assumed to occur at the end of the period, then the yield on a debt instrument can be determined by solving the following equation for r,

$$M = \frac{C_1}{1+r} + \frac{C_2}{(1+r)^2} + \frac{C_3}{(1+r)^3} + \ldots + \frac{C_n + B_m}{(1+r)^n} \tag{3}$$

where M is the current market price of the instrument, C_i is the amount of annual interest payments to the investor in year i, B_m is the principal payment at maturity, and r is the rate of discount or yield. The rate of discount, r, is readily available by using bond yield tables or special calculators.

There are several potential weaknesses in this common method for measuring the return on debt securities. First, there may be differences in income tax rates applied to interest (for example, interest payments on state and local debts are exempt from federal income taxes) or differences between purchase price and sale or maturity price. Second, if there is any risk of nonpayment of interest or principal, the rate of discount will be the maximum return and not the expected return. Third, there is an implicit assumption that as cash flows are received they can be reinvested at the rate of discount. Finally, the return calculated from equation 3 is a yield to maturity and may differ from the holding period yield if the debt security is sold prior to maturity.[4]

There are four potential sources of risk for debt securities.

---

[4] These potential weaknesses are discussed in greater detail in Sidney Homer and Martin L. Leibowitz, *Inside the Yield Book* (Englewood Cliffs, N.J.: Prentice-Hall, 1972).

1   There is the risk that the investor will be forced to sell a particular security that does not have broad marketability prior to maturity. Price concessions required in order to sell the security may decrease the security's return appreciably. This risk is called marketability risk.

2   A second source of risk comes from changes in the general level of interest rates. Changes in the market value of outstanding securities are inversely related to the change in interest rates. For most bonds, the magnitude of such changes will increase with the maturity of the debt instrument. This rate of increase declines as the maturity of the security decreases.[5] This risk is called interest rate risk.

3   A third risk is the possibility of nonpayment of interest or principal, or both. The possibility of nonpayment, often labeled the credit risk, is a relevant consideration for most debt securities except those that are obligations of the federal government.

4   Finally, there is a purchasing power risk associated with all debt instruments. If dollars received as interest or principal payments will purchase less than the dollars used to purchase the debt instruments, the investor suffers a loss of purchasing power. The investor attempts to overcome this risk by requiring a higher return or by having dollar liabilities that are paid in lower purchasing power dollars, or both. To the extent that interest rate and price level changes are positively correlated, it is difficult to separate interest rate and purchasing power risk. That is, nominal (market) interest rates normally adjust to changes in the expected rate of inflation.

The formula for converting nominal rates of return, R_n, to real rates, R_r is

$$R_r = \frac{1+R_n}{1+q} - 1 \tag{4}$$

where q denotes the actual rate of change in the general price level over the holding period. Equation 4 is commonly expressed as

$$R_r \approx R_n - q \tag{4a}$$

Table 6-1 summarizes the debt instruments that have been and will likely continue to be purchased by commercial banks. The short-term instruments were discussed in Chapter 5, Measuring and Providing Reserves and Liquidity. The long-term debt instruments are described in the following section. Bank security purchases usually fall into the first three categories briefly described here.

U.S. Treasury Securities

The lack of credit risk on U.S. Treasury securities and the highly efficient market for such securities explain the importance of Treasury securities to the commercial banking

---

[5] See Jess Yawitz, George Hempel, and Bill Marshall, "Average Maturity as a Risk Proxy in Investment Decisions," *Journal of Finance*, 30:2 (May 1975), for a discussion of the relationship between maturity and price changes on debt instruments.

TABLE 6-1
Securities Purchased by Commercial Banks

Security	Issuer	Brief description
Short-term		
Treasury bills	Federal government	Highly marketable debt with no credit risk; often sold on discount basis
Agency notes	Government agencies	Obligation of federal agencies; very high quality and nearly as marketable as federal debt
State and local notes	State and local governments	Short-term tax or bond anticipation obligations of state and local governments; interest is tax exempt
Commercial paper	Business or finance companies	High-quality business promissory notes; sold on discount basis
Negotiable certificates of deposit	Commercial banks and other financial institutions	Large-size interest-bearing deposits which can be traded before maturity
Long-term		
Treasury notes and bonds	Federal government	Longer term interest-bearing notes and bonds which are obligations of the federal government
Agency bonds	Government agencies	Longer term interest-bearing bonds of federal agencies
General obligations	State and local governments	Bonds backed by full faith, credit, and taxing power of issuing unit; interest is tax exempt
Revenue bonds	State and local governments	Bonds backed by revenues from specific project or tax source; interest is tax exempt
Corporate bonds	Business	Interest-bearing long-term business debt with varying degrees of quality and marketability
Mortgage-backed bonds	Consumers (packaged)	Interest-bearing long-term debt backed by grouping of mortgages and guarantee of government agency.

system. Income from all Treasury securities is subject to federal income taxes but is exempt from state and local income taxes. Marketable Treasury securities may be used as security for deposits of public monies and for loans from Federal Reserve banks.

There are three basic types of marketable Treasury securities: bills, notes, and bonds. The characteristics of Treasury bills were discussed in Chapter 5. The primary difference between notes and bonds is in their maturity. Treasury notes are issued with a maturity of not less than 1 year and not more than 10 years. These notes are available in minimum denominations of $10,000 in either registered or bearer form. Interest is paid on the registered notes semiannually and on the bearer notes when the appropriate coupon is surrendered. Treasury bonds can be issued with any maturity, but their maturities have generally been in excess of 10 years at date of issuance. Bonds are available in either registered or bearer form and pay interest semiannually. Treasury bonds cover a wide range of maturities; maturity selections by buyers are based on portfolio requirements and the willingness to assume interest rate risk.

Agency Obligations

The amount of outstanding securities that are not a direct obligation of the Treasury but that, in one way or another, involve federal sponsorship or guaranty has increased rapidly in recent years. Yields on securities of federal agencies are generally somewhat higher than the yield on Treasury securities of similar maturity. Although agency securities are not the direct obligations of the federal government, they are regarded in the investment community as being of a credit quality nearly equal to that of Treasury securities. It is generally felt that the U.S. government would not allow a default on any of these bonds. Agency issues are therefore treated as noncredit-risk assets and usually may be carried separately from risk assets in a bank's statement of condition. Although all agency securities are subject to federal income taxes, most agency securities are exempt from state and local income taxes. In addition, agency securities may be used as collateral to secure the fiduciary, trust, and public funds of the U.S. government and many state and local governments. Some agency issues have slight marketability risk. The interest rate risk on agency securities is similar to that on Treasury securities.

State and Local Government Bonds

The increasing demand of state and local governments for funds has resulted in a rapidly growing market for state and local securities. The interest payments on this type of indebtedness are exempt from federal income taxes and generally from income taxes imposed within the state of issue.

Intermediate and longer term authority bonds are issued by local housing agencies to build and administer low-rent housing projects. Although the bonds are issued under the auspices of local housing agencies, the Housing Act of 1949 provided that the full faith and credit of the United States is pledged to the payment of all amounts agreed to be paid by the local agencies.

A bond is called a general obligation if all the property in a community can be assessed and taxed at a level that will produce the revenues necessary to pay the debt. The primary tangible tax base is real estate on which the taxing authorities possess a lien equivalent to a first mortgage. Sales taxes, income taxes, and governmental subsidies are also important state and local revenue sources. The pledge of full faith and credit by a state or local unit usually includes a promise to levy taxes at whatever level debt service payments require.

Revenue bonds are payable solely from the earnings of a designated public project or undertaking. This type of bond includes all obligations not payable from or guaranteed by the general taxing power of the state or local government. The revenue supporting these bonds may come from (1) specifically dedicated taxes, such as those on cigarettes, gasoline, and beer; (2) tolls for roads, bridges, airports, or marine port facilities; (3) revenues from publicly owned utilities; or (4) rent payments on buildings or office space. Some banks have become heavy purchasers of industrial revenue bonds or pollution control bonds, which are secured by revenues promised to the issuing unit by large corporations.

Because housing authority bonds are guaranteed by the federal government, they are virtually free of credit risk. The credit risks inherent in other types of state and local debt are related to the ability and willingness of the governmental unit either to pay its obligations or to revise its capitalization. With general obligation bonds, the ability to pay is mainly contingent on the economic background of a community, the diversity of industry, the stability of employment, and so on. The ability to pay revenue bonds can generally be ascertained by comparing operating income with debt service requirements.[6] This ability to pay could be changed by recapitalization, the issuance of additional debt with a credit position and a claim on taxing power or earnings equal to or superior to the existing bonds. Issues of revenue bonds usually specify the extent to which additional debt may be undertaken. There is usually no such protection for general obligation bonds.

Marketability risk varies widely among state and local issues and may be quite high for smaller issues. Interest rate risk is primarily a function of maturity, as is true of Treasury and agency securities. Two other characteristics of state and local debt are particularly pertinent for commercial banks. First, nearly all general obligations have serial maturities. A bank could, therefore, buy one issue with maturities in several years. Second, banks own nearly half of the outstanding state and local debt. This strong ownership position tends to widen price fluctuations in periods when many banks are buying or selling these securities.

Corporate Bonds

The corporate bond is an obligation (usually long term) of a private corporation. Although a municipal body may generally be assumed to have a continuing existence, a private corporation is subject to the vicissitudes of a market economy. The credit risk assumed by purchasers of corporate bonds is therefore a quite serious consideration; the failure of the enterprise may result in permanent and total loss. Marketability risk and interest-rate risk are similar to state and local issues.

Banks generally do not purchase corporate bonds because there have been only brief interludes in recent history when the tax-equivalent yield on state and local bonds did not exceed the yield on corporate bonds of equal quality. The market for corporate bonds is primarily composed of institutions subject to minimal or no federal income taxation.

Other Bank Portfolio Instruments

Two mortgage-related instruments that made their initial appearance in the late 1970s are Government National Mortgage Association (GNMA) fully modified mortgage-

---

[6] For a more complete analysis of the credit risks of general obligation and revenue bonds, see George H. Hempel, *Measuring Municipal Bond Quality* (Ann Arbor: University of Michigan Press, 1967); George H. Hempel, *Postwar Quality of State and Local Debt* (New York: National Bureau of Economic Research, 1971); and George H. Hempel, *Understanding the Market for State and Local Debt* (Washington, D.C.: ACIR, 1976).

backed pass-through securities and the Federal Home Loan Mortgage Corporation (FHLMC) mortgage participation certificates. The cash flow to pay debt service on both securities comes from the selected groups of mortgages backing the security. The GNMA pass-throughs represent a share in a pool of Federal Housing Authority (FHA) or Veterans' Administration (VA) mortgages. GNMA guarantees the timely payment of principal and interest on these securities, and this guarantee is backed by the full faith and credit of the U.S. government. The participation certificates represent undivided interests in specified residential conventional mortgages underwritten and owned or partly owned by FHLMC. These securities are not guaranteed by the U.S. government, but the FHLMC itself does guarantee debt service payments. Early prepayment by mortgagers has typically caused the average maturity of these instruments to be less than the 12-year basis used for determining initial yield quotations.

In addition to the government-sponsored agencies, private institutions have issued mortgage pass-through certificates. These are participations in a pool of trusteed mortgages that may be either conventional or FHA or VA. They are not guaranteed by the issuing institution. They are typically issued through major underwriters for broad public distribution.

Another potential security is the mortgage guaranteed or insured by the federal government. FHA-insured and VA-guaranteed mortgages may be purchased by commercial banks from several federal agencies as well as other banks or nonbank financial intermediaries. The government-sponsored Federal National Mortgage Association and Government National Mortgage Association have contributed to the development of a national secondary mortgage market; purchasing and making purchase commitments where and when investment funds are in short supply and selling when and where investment funds are available. Even with the efforts of these agencies, however, the liquidity of guaranteed or insured mortgages may be limited in periods of restrictive monetary conditions.

STEPS IN MANAGING A BANK'S SECURITY PORTFOLIO

Management of the security portfolio will differ among commercial banks because of differences in size, location, condition, loan demand, and managerial capabilities. There are, however, five basic steps that should lead to sound and flexible management of a bank's security portfolio.

Step 1: Establishing General Criteria and Objectives

Policies for managing the security portfolio (often the investment portfolio) generally should be in writing. Policy statements in written form are highly desirable, if for no other reason than that memories may be short. Written policies provide continuity of approach over time, as well as concrete bases for appraising investment portfolio performance. It cannot be emphasized too often that portfolio policies become clear only when the people concerned in their formulation and execution have agreed on their exact wording. All policies, of course, should be reviewed periodically in the light of changing circumstances.

The first section of the written portfolio policies should be a clear statement of the objectives of the security portfolio. In the broadest sense, these are the same for all banks: to obtain income, to maintain high quality in the portfolio, to keep the bank's funds fully employed, to provide an adequate supply of securities for pledging, and to reduce tax liability to a practical minimum. Some adaptation to individual circumstances may be necessary, and it is generally useful to state the bank's portfolio objectives carefully to provide continuing and mutual understanding of these objectives.

Step 2: Forecasting the External Environment

It is obviously difficult to forecast key elements of the external environment, such as growth of the economy, interest rates, inflation, and unemployment. Weaknesses in many past forecasts indicate that forecasting is still more of an art than a science. Nevertheless, forecasting of at least general trends in key economic indicators is an important step in management of the security portfolio. In nearly every security decision, there is an implicit forecast of the external environment. For example, the decision between buying long-term or short-term bonds generally contains an implicit forecast for interest rates and the future inflation rate. It is preferable to make security management decisions consistent with an explicit forecast, rather than make security decisions that contain an implicit forecast which may or may not be consistent with what the security portfolio manager believes will happen.

Some of the authors' predictions (as of mid-1982) for the future external environment—slow real growth, fluctuating interest rates, continuing inflation—were contained in Chapter 1. Whether these predictions are correct or not is not the major concern, the point is that our security management decisions at that time would be consistent with these predictions. Furthermore, because of the uncertainty of any economic predictions, decisions should be made with adequate safeguards to protect the bank in the case of incorrect predictions. The key point in this second step is that the bank should make its best forecast of the external environment.

Step 3: Inventorying Security Management Needs of a Bank

After the broad objectives have been established and the external environment forecast, bank management must formulate its bank's specific portfolio policies suited to the characteristics and conditions of the individual bank. There is a logical sequence of stages that management can take to inventory the security management needs of its bank.

Identifying the Portfolio. The "investment account" usually refers to all holdings of securities by a bank. It is common practice for bank management to provide directors and owners with only a list of the bank's security holdings, showing book values, market prices, and the range of maturities. The list is generally subdivided into U.S. government securities, state and municipal securities, and other securities. Few attempts are made, however, to distinguish the liquidity position from the investment portfolio, that is, to identify those securities held specifically for liquidity purpose and those held for long-term investment.

Length of maturity alone will not be the distinguishing feature because, under certain circumstances (in the anticipation of rising rates, for example), a portion of the investment portfolio could well be held temporarily in short-term issues. The real distinction is the purpose for which the securities are held. Liquidity assets are to meet estimates of potential deposit withdrawals and increased demands for loans. The investment portfolio, by contrast, represents the investment of surplus funds for income. The first stage, therefore, in inventorying portfolio needs is to consider the two sets of assets separately.

Evaluating Pledging Requirements. The second stage is to evaluate the pledging requirements necessitated by the bank's public deposits. Some banks have only limited amounts of public deposits, whereas others aggressively seek them.[7] The types of securities acceptable for pledging vary greatly with the type of public deposit. For example, Treasury securities are the only collateral acceptable for securing some public deposits. Other public deposits can be secured by Treasury securities, agency securities, or state and local securities of the same state or municipality depositing the funds. Clearly, bank managements must know their specific pledging requirements in inventorying their portfolio policy needs.

Assessing the Risk Position. The third stage in inventorying a bank's security management needs is to determine the appropriate proportion for risk assets in the investment portfolio. This decision will depend primarily on three considerations. The first is the amount of risk the bank has already assumed in its loan portfolio and other assets. If a bank has aggressively filled loan demands and is in an area where the demand is reasonably strong, it may be wise to limit risk exposure in the investment portfolio. The extent of this limitation depends on the second and third considerations.

The second consideration is the bank's capital position in relation to the assets it already holds. Bank management should determine whether it has capital in excess of the amount it should hold against its present and anticipated loans and other risk assets. If an excess exists, portfolio policy should encourage increasing the proportion of fully taxable obligations or tax-exempt securities to improve the bank's net income after taxes. If capital funds are inadequate to support additional risks, two alternatives exist. If management believes the cost of raising new capital exceeds the benefits from a higher risk portfolio, the bank should take little risk in its investment portfolio. If management believes the after-tax benefits from a higher risk portfolio exceed the cost of raising new capital, serious thought should be given to raising additional capital.

The third consideration is a realistic evaluation of the amount of expertise available and effort applied to the investment portfolio area. Many small and medium-sized banks either do not have the necessary managerial investment expertise or they apply what expertise they do have to banking functions other than investments. Some lack of managerial expertise and effort may be overcome through the use of large correspondents, however, it is generally advisable for banks in this position to limit the risks they take with their security portfolio. If such a bank does not take much risk with its other assets and has excess capital, it should compare the costs of providing the necessary ex-

---

[7] Banks that hold substantial amounts of unpledged tax-exempt state and municipal securities can particularly benefit from actively soliciting state and municipal deposits. Eligible tax-exempt securities can serve as the required collateral for such deposits. Because the interest payments on these deposits are a tax reducing expense, the tax-equivalent differential can be a source of considerable profit.

pertise with the additional after-tax returns which competently administered policies could generate. The bank will be better off providing the necessary expertise if the incremental returns exceed the additional costs.

Determining the Tax Position.   The fourth logical stage in inventorying portfolio needs is to estimate as nearly as possible the bank's net taxable income and to calculate the amount of additional tax-exempt income, if any, that the bank could profitably use. Since tax-exempt income is usually obtained at some sacrifice of gross revenue, it is obviously poor planning to have tax-exempt income exceed current operating earnings. In fact, even if a bank had complete flexibility—that is, a portfolio large enough to provide all the tax-exempt income it could use—it would not ordinarily plan to eliminate all taxable income. Enough of a margin of taxable income should be left to provide for maximum legal tax-free transfers to the reserve for bad debt and to absorb actual losses should they develop. In the latter connection, it is important to consider the losses that the bank may wish to take in shifting maturities within the portfolio, a process that will be discussed in greater detail later.

The tax considerations for small banks with incomes of less than $100,000 will be vastly different from those affecting large banks because of the disparity in their effective tax rates. Factors other than taxes usually determine the investment policies of small banks. For the large banks, tax considerations may outweigh all others in the determination of portfolio policy. There are other ways of legally reducing or avoiding taxes, such as leasing, timing losses, and accelerating depreciation, available to larger banks. Shielding income with tax-exempt securities should be compared with such alternatives. The objective, in any case, should be to reduce taxes as much as the law permits without compromising the bank's obligation to make sound local loans and its ability to support risk assets with adequate capital funds.

What this will mean as a practical matter to individual banks will vary widely. Banks have a choice of a broad menu of lending and investing opportunities. Management must know its own costs to determine the true net income from alternative uses of funds and relate the anticipated net income to its own particular tax situation. Table 6-2 illustrates this concept by presenting calculations for a hypothetical bank considering the investment of $100,000, either in an expansion of its wholesale consumer loans or in state and local bonds. Management does not view the loans as a demand for credit that the bank is obliged to meet; the loans are from a dealer in a neighboring community now being served by a major finance company. The decision is, therefore, based solely on relative profitability.

The table reflects the average experience of a number of banks, and the results would vary for each of the banks included in the group. The basic objective of the table is to illustrate the method of calculation, not to demonstrate the advantage of either alternative. Nevertheless, it does show the importance of a bank determining its tax position and suggests strongly that gross yields can sometimes be deceptive. Bank managers faced with such decisions have a right to insist that top management supply them with the tax information necessary to make similar calculations.

Coordinating Investment and Liquidity Planning.   The fifth stage in inventorying portfolio needs is to decide whether the bank's investment strategy should be coordi-

TABLE 6-2
Comparison of Net Profits After Taxes from an
Investment in Consumer Loans and in State and Local Bonds

	If $100,000 is invested in			
	Consumer loans		Municipal bonds	
Net current operating earnings				
before investment	$191,000		$191,000	
(Tax-exempt income included)	(52,000)		(52,000)	
Proceeds of $100,000 investment				
Gross yield	18,000		10,000	
Less direct expenses[a]	3,150		210	
Less cost of funds[a]	9,000		9,000	
Net yield	5,850		790	
Less overhead allocation[a]	1,450		140	
Net operating income	4,400	4,400		650
Accumulated net current operating				
earnings		195,400		191,650
Total tax-exempt income	52,000		62,000	
Total taxable income	$143,460		$129,650	
Taxes		46,530		40,489
Net income after taxes		$148,870		$151,261

[a]Roughly estimated from the average functional income and expense analysis in *Functional Cost Analysis: National Average Reports* by the Federal Reserve.

nated with its liquidity position. Some banks, in effect, plan to provide funds to the investment portfolio in exchange for high-quality securities close enough to maturity to qualify as liquidity assets. This strategy is followed principally by banks that establish a policy of structured maturities. Other banks never plan for the liquidity portfolio to draw from the investment portfolios.

Estimating the Need for Diversification.   The sixth and final stage in the inventorying sequence is an estimation of the need for diversification. The bank should determine the industrial and geographical distribution of its loans and its state and local securities acquired for collateral or community relations. Investment additions in areas of heavy concentration might be limited: advantages gained by diversification should be weighed against the possible loss of expertise of evaluation that bank management may have in areas of concentration.

Step 4: Formulate Policies and Strategies for Managing the Security Portfolio

Next, the bank should formulate policies and strategies for managing the security portfolio that are consistent with the bank's written objectives, its economic forecast, and its inventoried needs. Constructive policies and strategies will vary greatly among banks, and each bank should be sure to allow adequate flexibility for management discretion as conditions change. Specific policies and strategies for several key areas of security management are discussed, and then the idea of integrating security portfolio management with total asset and liability management is introduced.

Size of the Security Portfolio.   The size of the portfolio will be determined by (1) the amount of available funds not required for the provision of liquidity and to meet the legitimate loan demands of the community, (2) the amount of securities required for pledging, and (3) the relative profitability of investing in securities. The first is the residual of the bank's liquidity calculations, as discussed in Chapter 5, and the demand for loanable funds and the bank's lending policies. The second will vary with the laws of the state in which the bank is located and with the aggressiveness with which the bank seeks public deposits.[8] The third will depend on the profitability on securities in comparison with other competing forms of employing bank funds.

The concept of identifying part of the portfolio as a "core portfolio" is a useful strategy. After providing for all the liquidity needs from the portfolio, a bank may want to identify some or all of the remaining portfolio as a "core," which management will not use to meet liquidity needs. The bank can be more aggressive with regard to type of security, maturity, and other strategies, knowing it will not be forced to sell the portfolio at an inopportune time.

The federal government and most states require that nearly all categories of public deposits be secured by specified securities.[9] The type of securities that are acceptable for pledging varies greatly with the type of public deposit. Bank managements must know their specific pledging requirements to determine their portfolio needs.

The needed computations for comparing returns of securities with other earning assets appear in Table 6-2. Banks should make sure the assets being compared have similar credit quality and maturity.

Investment Media and Quality Levels.   The essence of establishing flexible portfolio policies and strategies pertaining to security media and quality levels is matching the type and quality of security portfolio instruments with the portfolio needs of the bank. Both the needs and the related policies should be reviewed periodically.

The first portfolio need affecting investment media is the level of the bank's pledging requirements. The bank must have acceptable Treasury securities or state and local securities, or both, to meet these requirements. In cases in which more than one type of security can be used to meet the pledging requirements, the choice will depend on the bank's risk and tax positions. In practically all banks, policymakers should insist that the pledged securities be the eligible securities that the bank is least likely to want to sell. Substitution for pledged securities, though possible, can be a time-consuming process.

Risk position will have a strong impact on the policies affecting the investment media and quality levels of the bank. Banks taking considerable lending risks (in relation to their capital position) and banks lacking managerial expertise or effort should limit their purchases to Treasury securities, agency obligations, AAA or AA rated state and local securities or corporate bonds, and federally insured or guaranteed mortgages. Such a policy (in conjunction with reasonable maturity policies) should restrict the risk

---

[8] Some banks actively solicit state and municipal deposits on which interest payments are a tax-reducing expense. The deposits are then invested in tax-exempt securities that are used to secure the deposits. The differential, on a fully tax equivalent basis, can be a source of considerable profit. This technique is discussed more fully later.

[9] For a detailed study of security for public deposits, see George H. Hempel, *The Impact of Increased Insurance of Public Deposits* (Washington, D.C.: ACIR, 1977).

in the investment portfolio and can be implemented with limited managerial expertise and effort. Many small banks, in particular, should adopt this type of policy because of their limited senior managerial resources.

On the other hand, banks that have the necessary managerial talent and time and are in a position to take additional risks in their investment portfolio should usually be less restrictive in their quality limits. Such banks should be able to purchase lower quality bonds, which usually have higher yields. Before prudent policy allows the purchase of state and local securities or corporate bonds rated below Aa, the board of directors and senior management should make sure that talent and time are available for the required credit analysis by the bank staff. The following written policy statement by a medium-sized Midwestern bank reflects less restrictive quality limits:

> *The quality requirements of the municipal bond portfolio is a medium portfolio rating of A. A reasonable investment in lower-rated or non-rated securities and in revenue bonds is allowed within this requirement. A credit review is required for all bonds rated A or below or not rated.*

The tax position of the bank is an essential element in determining whether bank policy should encourage concentration in state and local securities with tax-exempt interest payments or in other investment instruments which pay taxable interest. If the yields on state and local obligations continue to range from 20 to 30 percent lower than the yields on other obligations of comparable quality, bank policy may want to emphasize state and local obligations as long as the bank's marginal income is taxed at the 46 percent rate. Care should be taken so that the marketability of the portfolio is not unduly limited. When marginal income is not taxed or is taxed at only the 15, 18, or 30 percent rate, bank policy should usually emphasize taxable securities.

Any desired coordination with the liquidity position will also have an effect on policies determining the investment media and quality levels. If the bank expects to periodically receive a certain volume of securities close enough to maturity to qualify as liquidity assets, bank policy should require that sufficient high-quality, marketable securities will be available to meet such needs.

Finally, if the bank feels that the gains from diversification outweigh the loss of expertise of evaluation that bank management has in areas of concentration, policies should be formulated indicating the portfolio requirements for industrial or geographic diversification.

Maturity Policies and Strategies.   Maturities may present two types of policy problems: the establishment of a maximum maturity limit, if considered sound policy, and the scheduling of maturities within the portfolio. The latter is closely related to the bank's appraisal of the economic climate. Arranging and rearranging portfolio maturities also bring the portfolio manager into the area of taking profits and losses with its own special tax connotations. These aspects of the maturity problem are all interrelated but can perhaps be understood more readily if they are examined separately.

There are two risk-related reasons that some banks limit the maximum acceptable maturities in their portfolio. First, the quality of state or local securities and corporate bonds may vary over time. A bank that lacks sufficient managerial expertise or time to evaluate the probability of deterioration in the quality of some securities in its portfolio can reduce its exposure to this risk by setting some fairly short-term limits on the maturities of such securities. The second reason pertains to interest rate movements. If interest rates rise, the price of longer term bonds deteriorates much more than the price of short-term bonds. Instead of being able to purchase bonds at higher yield or fill expanding loan demands at profitable rates, the holders of long-term bonds have securities with large capital losses.

Commercial bank experience with longer term bonds generally has been very unfavorable in the 1970s and early 1980s because of the rising trend of interest rates. Many banks still find themselves with substantial depreciation on holdings of such bonds acquired 5 to 10 years ago. Especially if a bank is purchasing securities with the expectation of holding them to maturity, one could readily counsel, "Never buy a yield that you are not willing to live with." In light of the uncertainties of a rapidly changing world, such advice might well limit portfolio commitments to no longer than three years. Even that is a long time to look ahead.

On the other hand, one should not lose sight of the full sweep of history and the long periods in the past during which the secular trend of interest rates was downward. Should the policymakers be convinced that this particular phase of history was in the process of repeating itself, there would be ample justification for extending maturities beyond 15 or 20 years. And to a certain extent, current tax laws soften the effect of realized losses on investments.

Clearly, one should not be doctrinaire. If the bank lacks managerial expertise or effort in the investment portfolio area or if management expects interest rates to rise and loan demand to continue as strong as it did in the 1970s and early 1980s, it probably should set a fairly short maximum maturity (between three and seven years) for the bulk of portfolio investments. On the other hand, if the bank has the managerial competence *and* is willing to accept some security losses and recognize the higher risks and returns generally associated with longer term bonds, no maximum maturity limit seems necessary. Over the long run, the higher risks associated with these bonds should result in larger profits.

Scheduling maturities within the investment portfolio is undoubtedly the most difficult and exacting task of portfolio management. Other policies can be established, periodically reviewed, and occasionally adapted to new circumstances. Maturity policy, in contrast, requires constant review and decision making as funds become available for investment or as opportunities to improve the income position present themselves. There are three major philosophies for scheduling maturities: cyclical maturity determination, spaced or staggered maturities, and a "barbell" maturity structure.

From the previous discussion, it would appear that the ideal course of action in portfolio management would be to hold short-term securities when interest rates are likely to rise and to lengthen maturities when rates are expected to decline. This strategy is tantamount to shortening maturities when business conditions (and the demand for credit) are expected to improve and lengthening maturities when the first signs of a recession appear. There are several problems in the application of this theoretical ideal. First, even in cyclical periods such as the 1960s, bank portfolio managers found themselves under heavy pressure to produce profits (and thereby encouraged to buy longer term securities) when interest rates were low. When interest rates were high (and expected to decline), banks tended to have only limited amounts to invest in any maturity. Second, business cycles do not always act as the textbooks say they should. For example, the 1970s might be described as 10 years of stagflation and fluctuating, rising interest rates with only limited vestiges of traditional seasonal movements. Third, portfolio management can be seen to be closely integrated with economic forecasting, which is considered by some to be a dubious art at best.

Because of the manifest uncertainties involved in such an ideal approach, banks have frequently been counseled to solve the problem of maturity distribution by spacing maturities more or less evenly within the maximum range, if any, previously established. In this way, the bank will assure itself of at least average yields, or a little better. It will not be gambling on changes in the level of rates or the state of the economy. As long as the yield curve is rising, the reinvestment of maturing assets at the longest end of the maturity schedule will assure the bank of maximum income on a portfolio of which the average maturity will be relatively short. Figure 6-1 illustrates a staggered portfolio in which maturing bonds are invested in bonds that mature in 10 years.

Banks using the barbell maturity structure tend to strengthen their liquidity position by investing a part of their investment portfolio in short-term liquid securities. The remainder of the typical barbell portfolio usually consists of high-yield, very long term bonds. Figure 6-2 illustrates a barbell portfolio. Advocates of this maturity philosophy reason that the greater liquidity and the higher returns more than compensate for any additional risks associated with it. Barbell portfolios tend to be trading portfolios, and it is typical for the long-term proportion of the portfolio to be largest when interest rates are high and for the short-term portion of the portfolio to grow when rates are low. Managerial expertise is clearly a prerequisite for the barbell maturity structure.

For bank managements that lack the managerial competence in the investment area, or that do not wish to take the trouble to frame a more flexible portfolio policy, average results obtained through regularly spaced maturities are undoubtedly better than what might result from a purely haphazard or intuitive approach to the problem. Spaced maturities are probably an acceptable solution for the very small bank. The barbell structure or other flexible approaches are generally preferable for bank man-

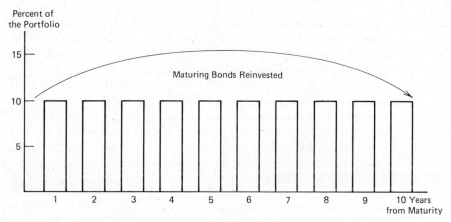

FIGURE 6-1   10-Year Staggered Maturity Portfolio Distribution of Bonds by Maturity

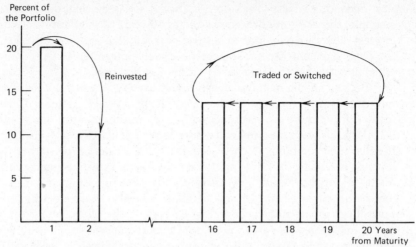

FIGURE 6-2   **30 Percent Short-Term Barbell Portfolio Distribution of Bonds by Maturity**

agements that have the necessary competence and are willing to exercise judgment.[10] It certainly does not make sense for such managers to invest the proceeds of maturing securities in the longest term bonds permitted by the bank's policy at a time when the economy is obviously in a slack condition, when banks hold excess reserves, and when money rates are abnormally low.

Not even the most competent investment managers, of course, will be able to call every turn, nor do they need to. Alert and informed managers can take advantage of events that have already occurred. They do not need to gamble on the future.

Interest Rate Effects on Security Policies and Strategies.   Figure 6-3 illustrates how interest rates for securities of similar quality and maturity have varied over time. Income from securities is determined by the level of rates existing in the market at the time of purchase. Market levels also affect risk because prices are most likely to decline when they are abnormally high. Conversely, when securities are acquired at relatively low prices (high returns), the chances of market depreciation should be smaller. The problem is identifying when rates are low or high. For example, in late 1979 some banks believed returns were high (prices low); however, inflationary pressures soon forced rates still higher (prices lower) in 1980 and 1981.

The rates in the market at any given time reflect, in the first instance, the current equilibrium between the forces of supply and demand. The supply-and-demand conditions also mirror the market's expectations of changes in interest rates. Short-maturity obligations reflect almost entirely the current and short-term prospective strength of the supply and demand for funds; however, longer term rates are substantially colored by market guesses about probable future conditions. Among these, the rate of inflation has recently loomed large.

[10] For a comparison of the simulated performance of spaced and barbell maturity policies from 1950 through 1970 and under four hypothetical interest rate conditions for the following decade, see George H. Hempel and Stephen R. Kretschmen, "Comparative Performance of Portfolio Maturity Policies of Commercial Banks," *Mississippi Valley Journal of Business and Economics*, 9 (Fall 1973): 55–75.

Many bond market analysts separate longer term rates of return into two segments. The first segment is a projection of what the "real" rate of return (excluding inflation) historically has been on bond investments. The second segment is a risk factor representing the expected rate of inflation. For example, historically the real return on high-grade corporate securities has been about 4 percent; if inflation is expected to average 8 percent annually, investors will demand a 12 percent rate of return unless they believe the rate of inflation will decline or speed up.

Short-term securities and marketable paper are part of the floating supply of money and near-money substitutes, although the supply of longer term market instruments is more closely related to the flow of savings into investment channels. Therefore, while the level of rates may move up and down, the relationships among rates for different maturities are also constantly shifting as changes take place in the supply of money and the flow of savings.

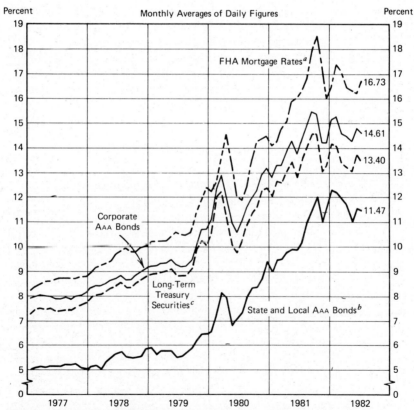

aFHA 30-year mortgages. Dashed lines indicate data not available.
bMonthly averages of Thursday figures.
cAverage of yields on coupon issues due or callable in 10 years or more, excluding issues with federal estate tax privileges. Yields are computed by this bank.
Latest data plotted: July
Prepared by Federal Reserve Bank of St. Louis.

FIGURE 6-3   Long-Term Interest Rates

The maturity pattern of rates (often called the term structure of interest rates) in the market at any given time can be graphically portrayed by plotting the yields of outstanding securities of equal credit standing for different maturities. The yields on Treasury obligations are usually plotted, and the resultant yield curve presents a visual image of investor preferences and expectations.[11] The shape of the yield curve is closely related to the state of the economy, to expectation for inflation, and to the countercyclical operations of monetary and fiscal policy. When business activity is high, the demand for money is strong, and the Federal Reserve System is likely to restrict the creation of new credit. The growing demand and shrinking supply of money are generally reflected in the sharp advance of short-term interest rates. Longer term rates, reflecting expectations of a return to more normal market conditions over a period of time, do not ordinarily increase as rapidly or as far. When short-term rates are rising, the shape of the yield curve tends to become flat, with short-term rates equaling the long-term rates. If short rates rise above the long, as they have on occasion, the curve is said to be descending. Prior to 1979, a descending yield curve was thought to be unusual, but the double-digit inflation in much of 1979, 1980, and 1981 caused such havoc in the financial markets (tight monetary policy, confused inflationary expectations, etc.) that descending yield curves were the rule rather than the exception in that period.

When business conditions are slack and inflationary expectations relatively low, the demand for money tends to decline. At this time, the Federal Reserve typically attempts to increase the availability of credit through open market purchases of securities, channeling funds directly into the commercial banking system. An overabundance of funds sharply depresses short-term rates; the decline in longer rates lags behind. In periods of business recession and low inflation, therefore, the yield curve is usually ascending or sloping upward.

The St. Louis Federal Reserve has made the following explanations of yield curves:

> There are two widely held theories that are often combined for the interpretation of yield curves. The liquidity-preference theory holds that the risks of holding long-term maturities are greater than those of holding short-term maturities and that the community of bondholders prefers to avoid risk; therefore, the yield curve normally will be positively sloped, with long-term rates higher than short-term rates. The expectations theory holds that long-term rates are an average of a series of expected short-term rates; the yield curve normally will be flat, because the holder of a long-term security will earn, on the average over a specified time, the same amount as a holder of a series of short-term securities. Over the course of a business cycle, a shift may occur in the level of the entire yield curve as well as in the relation between long- and short-term rates. At cyclical troughs, both liquidity and expectational factors act to produce a positively sloped yield curve, indicating that short-term rates are expected to increase faster than long-term rates in the future. At cyclical peaks, liquidity factors act to produce a positively sloped yield curve, and expectational factors act to produce a negatively sloped yield curve. The slope of the curve in this instance will depend on the relative strength of the two forces.[12]

---

[11] A Treasury yield curve is published monthly in the *Treasury Bulletin*. Yield curves for several earlier time periods are contained in Figure 6-4.

[12] *Weekly Bulletin*, Federal Reserve Bank of St. Louis.

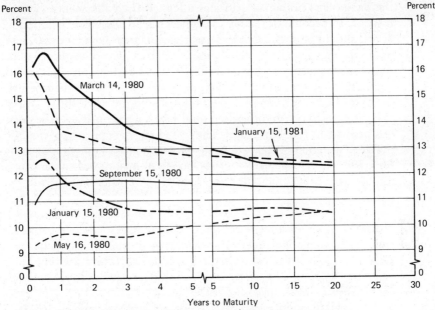

FIGURE 6-4 Yields on Various Maturities of U.S. Government Securities
Source: Prepared by Federal Reserve Bank of St. Louis. Released: February 13, 1981.

These explanations are appropriate but fall short of recognizing the strong influence double-digit inflation may have on the factors affecting the yield curve. Figure 6-4 shows the yield curve for Treasury securities on January 15, 1980; March 14, 1980; May 16, 1980; September 15, 1980; and January 15, 1981. The solid curves illustrate dramatically how much the level of interest rates can shift in a relatively short period. In early 1980, the combination of double-digit inflation, high demands for borrowing, and tight monetary policy led to very high levels of interest rates and a downward sloping yield curve. The brief but steep recession in spring of 1980 led to much lower credit demands and considerable easing in monetary policy. By May 1980, all yields had fallen sharply and the yield curve had a more normal upward slope. Renewed concern about credit demands and inflation caused a rise in yields by early 1981, and the yield curve was sharply downward sloping by January 1981.

Changes in the level of interest rates are a vital concern of portfolio management. They are of special significance in relation to maturity, which was discussed previously, and trading and switching strategies, to be discussed later. It would naturally seem desirable for banks to acquire securities when prices are low and rates high and to sell when the opposite conditions prevail. However, it is usually when rates are high that banks have the least funds available and are experiencing the heaviest demand for loans. When banks have a surplus of funds, rates tend to be low.

When the yield curve is sharply ascending, the temptation is strong for commercial banks to confuse their liquidity positions with their portfolios and to lengthen maturities in search of higher return. In the process, they may commit themselves to too low a rate for too long a time. A subsequent rise in rates will cause these purchases to decline in market value; when the banks need the funds for lending, they are faced with the prospect of selling securities at a loss. If the banks cannot afford to absorb these losses, they become "locked in" to unnecessarily low yields.

It should be noted that this error of judgment is not a mistake in portfolio policy but in the management of the liquidity position. The poor record of some banks in this regard during periods of high credit demands and double-digit inflation in 1979–1981 emphasizes the thesis that the liquidity position should be kept clearly separated from the portfolio in the minds of bank policymakers and investment officers.

As pointed out in the section on the size of the portfolio, the portfolio is a more or less permanent revolving fund. The size of the core portfolio should change only with the slow accretion of stable deposits or with fundamental modifications of the demand for credit. Its management consists largely of making adjustments to changing interest rate levels in ways that will increase after-tax profits without substantially increasing risk.

Trading and Switching Policies and Strategies.   Many banks buy securities and hold them in the bank's portfolio until they mature. This is not the way to maximize returns consistent with reasonable levels of risk. There are times to buy and times to sell (and buy something else), and even smaller banks can take advantage of the broad movements in the securities markets.

A valid distinction can be made between trading and switching. *Trading* is a day-to-day operation that requires easy access to the markets and an expertise not available to many banks. *Switching* involves the mobility of a portfolio in relation to changes in economic conditions and related changes in rate levels. A bank that is alert to switching activities will be in the market far less than a bank that has the capacity to trade actively, but its purchases and sales can, nonetheless, add appreciably to its income over time.

Current accounting rules applicable to banks make a distinction between trading profits and losses and portfolio profits and losses. A trading bank will establish a trading account, and the profits and losses resulting from its trades will be shown as a part of its operating earnings. To operate a trading account a bank must take depreciation as well as actual earnings into its operating results. It must "mark to market"—treat depreciation as an actual loss, with respect to those securities that it has designated as its trading account. Gains and losses on portfolio transactions, on the other hand, are shown "below the line"—not as operating earnings but as unusual transactions. Thus, banks report operating earnings that include trading account results and then their net profits, taking portfolio gains and losses into consideration.

Many securities clearly held for liquidity should probably be treated for accounting purposes as a trading account, whether they are actively traded or not. For the most part, they will be of short maturity and their value as liquidity instruments will be their market value. Those banks that are able to trade their liquidity portfolios because of their own knowledge or because of access to expert advice will probably add appreciably to their income over a period of time.

Intelligent security policies should provide the opportunity to use switching strategies that lead to increased returns. These increases are beneficial to the bank's stockholders, whether they are reported as earnings above the line or as the result of security transactions below the line. Switching of maturities and the taking of profits and losses to best advantage is a technical aspect of security management, however, the general principle discussed here can serve as a beginning guide for rational policies and strategies.

In cyclical periods of high loan demand, high interest rates, and monetary restraint or in trend periods of high inflation and rising interest rates, most bonds in a bank's security portfolio will show market depreciation. This will be the time to take tax losses and possibly to extend maturities in anticipation of lower interest rates and higher security prices. The amount and extent of maturity extensions depends on management's confidence that the cyclical boom or inflationary-interest rate spiral is ending. As the manager becomes confident in such periods, security portfolio policy should flexibly encourage three actions: investing any funds available to the investment portfolio at the longer end of the portfolio; "refunding in advance" by selling short-term issues and reinvesting the proceeds of such sales in longer term bonds; and switching from a security of a given maturity into one of comparable maturity to improve yields and long-term profit.

The first and second actions achieve the major portfolio objective of lengthening maturities when losses are taken so that the portfolio may benefit from the expected easing of rates in a later period. The advantages of higher income and greater potential for gain in market price are evident. The third action is more limited in objective but may contribute considerably to the long-run profitability of banks using a barbell type of portfolio policy. For example, assume that a bank owns some 10-year bonds which it bought at par a few years earlier and which are currently selling at 80. If the bank sells $1 million worth of them for $800,000, the $200,000 loss after taxes costs $100,000. By reinvesting the $800,000 in similar bonds, the bank will have a built-in future appreciation of $200,000 which after taxes will net it roughly $100,000 at maturity. This is not a break-even proposition, however, because the bank has close to $100,000 more in cash than it would have had if it had not taken the loss. This $100,000 is invested now at the high yields and provides higher yields over the 20 years as well as the possibility of even greater appreciation.

One may wonder why all the banks do not sell most of their holdings at a loss in periods of high interest rates. The foremost consideration is how much reduction in reported net income the owners of the bank are willing to accept. Current accounting rules require that attention be focused on net income after securities gains and losses rather than on net operating earnings. Explaining to shareholders that reductions in profits are advantageous is not easy. Also, there is the limitation of taxable income. Losses are valuable only to the extent that they save taxes. Finally, losses may reduce (or limit the increase in) bank capital, thereby encouraging supervisory authorities to ask for more capital to replace that sold off.

When the economy is clearly in a recession stage and interest rates are relatively low, at least some bonds will be selling at above-average prices. Portfolio holdings, if acquired at comparatively low prices during a previous period of high interest rates, will show market appreciation. This is the time when banks generally should keep their new investments short. They can largely offset the sacrificed income by taking profits in the longer bonds.

Taking profits always seems more desirable than absorbing losses, but it can be dangerous merely to take profits and reinvest in comparable (or longer) maturities. To do so is to leave the bank even more vulnerable than before to declines in prices that are bound to come, since these declines will affect booked profits rather than unbooked appreciation. The general rule, therefore, should be do not take profits without shortening maturities. The conviction that the economy is close to the bottom of a recessionary period, which should lead a bank to take profits, should also convince it to shorten maturities in anticipation of a later rise in rates.

Profits (after taxes), taken in times of low money rates, should not be looked on as permanent additions to the bank's capital funds. They should be carried as reserves against future security losses, where they will be available to absorb the losses when the next turn in interest-rate levels provides new profit possibilities.

Tax consideration should not be overlooked. The distinction between short- and long-term capital gains is not relevant for banks because all capital gains are taxed as ordinary income and all capital losses used to reduce ordinary income. Most banks are willing to take losses (reducing taxable income) on any type of security; however, they often prefer to avoid taking gains on state and local securities. The reason is that such gains are subject to federal income tax whereas the interest on such bonds is exempt from federal income taxes. This tax characteristic also discourages many banks from buying securities selling considerably below their maturity value, that is, selling at a substantial discount. A portion of this discount must be included as taxable income each year these discounted state and local bonds are held. A substantial part of the yield to maturity may, therefore, be taxable.

Table 6-3 illustrates the effect of two security switches. In example 1, $100,000 of 8 percent A-1 rated Baytown bonds with seven years remaining to maturity are sold for $90,000, which is approximately a 10 percent yield to maturity basis. Denton 10 percent, A-1 rated bonds with a seven year maturity are purchased. A hypothetical investment of the proceeds from the Baytown sale, $90,000 plus the estimated lower taxes of $4,600, the bank's 46 percent marginal tax rate times the $10,000 of lower income, are invested in the Denton issue. The earnings effect is that the bank takes a $5,400 after-tax loss in the current year and will gain higher after-tax income of $1,460 each year for the next seven years. The $5,400 loss is recovered in roughly three years and nine months and there is an implied return (the discount rate equating the loss with semiannual payments of $730 for 14 periods) of slightly above 19 percent. Whether the bank would make such a switch depends on the bank's condition (strong or weak capital, acceptable to have earnings lowered by the loss) and rules of thumb the bank may have developed, such as recovery of loss within half of the remaining life of the bond.

In the second example, $1 million of a 14 percent Treasury note is sold at a gain and the after-tax proceeds are invested in a similar maturity Treasury note. Assuming the bank is in a 46 percent marginal income tax bracket, the bank will have only $1,054,000 of the $1,100,000 proceeds to reinvest in lower yielding bonds. The results are a $54,000 after-tax profit this year but $20,898 in lower taxable income each year for the next five years. In nearly every switch in which banks realize a gain, this gain is at the cost of lower income in future years. Taking gains makes sense in a few situations, such as when the bank wants to smooth income or increase capital; however, the usual rule is not to take gains unless the proceeds are used to shorten maturities.

Such a rule opens Pandora's box. Portfolio switches that involve changing credit quality or changing the maturity of the security portfolio need to be evaluated under broader criteria than those discussed here. Even the basic analysis without quality or maturity changes is more complex because potential taxable gains or losses at maturity also have to be considered. Nevertheless, the measures presented in Table 6-3 present

TABLE 6-3
Measuring the Effect of Security Switches

Example 1: Municipal Bond Switch at Loss

Sell	*Book value*	*Sale price*	*Coupon income*	*Yield to maturity*
$100,000 7-year Baytown (A-1)	$100,000	$90,000	$ 8,000	10%
Purchase				
$100,000 7-year Denton (A-1)	$100,000		$10,000	10%
Hypothetical[a]	94,600[a]		9,460[a]	10%

Earning Effect: Bank will take $5,400 after-tax loss (10,000 times 1 minus marginal tax rate of 46%) now for $1,460 increase in tax-exempt income each year for seven years—an after-tax return of slightly over 19 percent.

Example 2: Treasury Note Switch at Gain

Sell	*Book value*	*Sale price*	*Coupon income*	*Yield to maturity*
$1 million 5-year Treasury notes	$1,000,000	$1,100,000	$140,000	11.3%
Purchase				
$1 million 5-year Treasury notes	$1,000,000		113,000	11.3%
Hypothetical[a]	$1,054,000[a]		119,102[a]	11.3%

Earning Effect: Bank will take $54,000 after-tax gain this year ($100,000 times 1 minus marginal tax rate of 46%) but will have $20,898 lower taxable income each year for the next five years.

[a]Hypothetical amount so that purchase equals proceeds of sale plus lowered taxes or minus higher taxes.

the basic elements for an analysis of switching opportunities. Many banks now have computer or micro-computer programs that they can use to evaluate a large number of potential switches.

Securities as an Asset/Liability Balancing Factor. The preceding discussion of policies and strategies affecting the management of security portfolios has ignored one of the most important functions of the portfolio and several useful techniques. This important function is for the security portfolio to serve as a balancing factor for a bank's overall asset/liability structure. The maturity structure, interest sensitivity, overall credit risk, and liquidity needs that result from the type of funds attracted and type of loans made can be at least partially balanced by a bank's security portfolio. Funds attracted and loans made are strongly affected by factors beyond a bank's control, such as competitors' actions and the bank's location. Securities represent nonpersonal assets which, when flexibly managed, can be used to assist the bank in achieving such objectives as a balanced asset/liability maturity structure, the desired interest-sensitivity position, an overall credit risk target, and liquidity sources matching liquidity needs. Thus, managing the security portfolio should be seen in the context of overall asset/liability management rather than as a separate piece. Uses of the security portfolio in overall asset/liability management are discussed in Chapters 12 and 13 of this book.

TABLE 6-4
Duration of a 12 Percent Coupon Seven-year Bond Priced at Par

(1) Year	(2) Cash flow	(3) Present value of $1 at 12%	(4) Present value of flow	(5) Present value of price	(6) Duration (1) × (5)
1	$ 120	0.8929	$ 107.12	0.1071	0.10771
2	120	0.7972	95.66	0.0957	0.1914
3	120	0.7118	85.42	0.0854	0.2562
4	120	0.6355	76.26	0.0763	0.3052
5	120	0.5674	68.09	0.0681	0.3405
6	120	0.5066	60.79	0.0608	0.3648
7	1,120	0.4523	506.58	0.5066	3.5462
Sum			1,000.00	1.0000	5.1072
Price			1,000.00		
Duration					5.11 years

Two useful measures, heretofore ignored, are duration and immunization. The duration of debt securities explicitly considers the timing of the return of principal and interest payments. Cash flows are weighted by the length of time until they are received. Table 6-4 illustrates how the duration of a seven-year, 12 percent coupon bond could be calculated. It is assumed interest is paid annually and that after seven years this bond will pay off $1,120. Notice that the 5.11 years' duration of this bond is less than its term to maturity of seven years. The duration of a bond can never exceed its term to maturity and will be less than the terms to maturity except for no-coupon bonds.

Although some of the claims about the usefulness of duration appear to be overstated,[13] duration would seem to improve management's knowledge about the bank's securities and, more important, its overall asset/liability portfolio. Duration is a better indicator of the interest sensitivity of any asset or liability than the asset or liability's maturity alone. Duration indicates a reinvestment rate risk and relative price volatility better than maturity alone. Some argue that duration is a more appropriate horizontal axis for constructing a yield curve than maturity. Finally, duration figures for various types of assets, or liabilities are more additive in a meaningful way than maturities.[14]

Immunization recognizes two basic parts of the interest risk of an individual security or portfolio of securities. One part is the risk of decline in market value if rates rise. Of course, the market value increases if rates fall. The second part is the risk that cash flows will be reinvested at lower rates if interest rates fall; however, cash flows will be reinvested at higher rates if rates rise. Therefore, a rise in rates hurts a security's market value but allows reinvestment at higher rates, whereas a fall in rates hurts because reinvestment is at a lower rate although the market value of a security rises. Immunization

[13] One of the assumptions with traditional duration measures is parallel movements in the yield curve (see Yawitz, Hempel, and Marshall, *Journal of Finance*). This assumption can be particularly damaging for short-duration securities because of large changes in the shape of the yield curve in this maturity range. Ian Cooper suggested a potential adjustment to partially overcome this defect in "Asset Values, Interest Rate Changes, and Duration," *Journal of Financial and Quantitative Analysis* (Dec. 1977), pp. 701–53.

[14] Many of these points are described more fully by Richard McEnally in "Durations as a Practical Tool for Bond Management," *Journal of Portfolio Management* (Summer 1977), pp. 53–57.

results from the offsetting nature of these two risks when rates move in either direction. A security portfolio would be completely immunized from interest rate movements if the market value risk was exactly offset by the reinvestment.[15]

The concepts of duration and immunization can be applied to bank assets other than securities, such as loans, and to bank liabilities. It is more useful to match the duration of most bank assets with that of most bank liabilities than to measure the duration of a single security or even a portfolio of securities. Likewise, immunization of the bank's total portfolio of assets and liabilities from interest rate movements seems to deserve more attention than immunization of the security portfolio alone. These concepts are, therefore, discussed again in Chapters 12 and 13 on integrative asset/liability management.

Step 5: Delegate Authority But Maintain Control

The arrangements for the delegation of authority while maintaining control are an essential part of security portfolio policy. The board of directors has the ultimate responsibility and should share responsibilities for the policy determination role with members of senior management. The portfolio manager should be in charge of day-to-day management and may recommend major courses of action or policy change to the board and senior management.

A bank's investment policy should delegate specific authority to designated officers to purchase or sell securities up to certain amounts, just as a bank's loan policy should permit the bank's lending officer to commit the bank for stated amounts. Opportunities for profitable switching or trading that may be evident to the investment officer, or called to his or her attention by a correspondent bank, a dealer, or an investment advisory service, do not last long in the market. If decisions must be referred to an investment committee, or even to a chief executive officer who may be away from the bank at the moment, profitable opportunities will be irretrievably lost. A sound policy, therefore, will set trading limits, based on the size of the bank and investment officer's knowledge and experience, within which he or she should have full discretion. It is relatively simple to compare the results of trading, say every six months, with what would have resulted had no purchases or sales been made. Such a comparison should be a clear indication of the investment officer's acumen.

SUMMARY

Security portfolio management should recognize differences in size, location, condition, and managerial capabilities among banks. There are, however, five basic steps that should lead to sound and flexible security policies and strategies. Security portfolio policies should be in writing and start with a statement of the objectives of the security portfolio. After the objectives have been established, the bank should make its forecast for the economy and interest rates. Next, the bank should inventory its own investment needs by identifying the portfolio, estimating pledging requirements, assessing the risk position, determining the tax position, coordinating with the liquidity

[15] For further information on immunization see Lawrence Fisher and Roman L. Weil, "Coping with the Risk of Interest-Rate Fluctuations: Returns to Bondholders from Naive and Optimal Strategies," *Journal of Business* (Oct. 1971), pp. 408–31.

planning, and estimating the need for diversification. After inventorying its needs, the bank should establish policies and strategies affecting the size, risk, maturity, and marketability of the investment portfolio that are consistent with these needs. Finally, bank policies should delegate authority for action commensurate with responsibility and reward outstanding performance. All of these steps should be coordinated with overall asset/liability management, as discussed in Chapters 12 and 13. One of the most important contributions of the security portfolio is that it permits impersonal flexibility in balancing a bank's overall maturity and interest-sensitivity position.

CASE 8
Missouri National Bank

The Missouri National Bank, a large unit bank located in Kansas City, Missouri, had total resources in July 1981 of over $1 billion (see Exhibit 1). As with other banks that are members of the Federal Reserve, Missouri National's reserve needs for weeks ending each Wednesday must be filled in the week ending two weeks later. The bank knows how much it will be required to keep on deposit at the Federal Reserve (figured by multiplying the average balance in the appropriate deposit classification by the percentage required then subtracting vault cash) by Monday for the week starting the following Wednesday. In addition, 2 percent leeway on deposits at the Federal Reserve on either side can be carried forward for one week. Numerous noncontrollable (e.g., net checking transactions) and controllable (e.g., Federal Funds transactions) transactions affect a bank's balances at its Federal Reserve. The reserve requirements in July 1981 were the following:

Deposit classification	Required percent
Transaction Balances up to $25 thousand	3
Transaction Balances Over $25 thousand	12
Personal Savings and Time Deposits (nontransferable)	0
Nonpersonal Savings and Time Deposits	0
Most Ineligible Acceptances, Eurocurrency, Liabilities, etc.	3

Exhibit 4 contains a summary of the Missouri National's accumulated cash reserve position for a portion of the reserve week ending July 15, 1981.

The Missouri National's overall cash position[1] reflected a great number of individual investment, loan, and liquidity decisions made by the bank's officers throughout the year. As a basis for planning, a staff economist forecast the level of deposits and expected loan demand on a continuous basis for periods of three months, six months, and one year. Once these sources and applications of funds had been estimated, and the bank had made its forecasts of interest rates for the coming months, the bank could then determine its target asset and liability composition and make asset and liability management decisions to move toward that position.

Early in 1981, the bank's senior officers concluded that interest rates would probably fall over the next 12 months. In anticipation of these lower interest rates, it was decided that the bank should remain as fully invested as possible in order to benefit from higher interest income and from the capital appreciation in the bond portfolio that would result as interest rates began to fall. This strategy looked good when rates fell in the first three months of 1981; however, the rapid increase in credit demands and interest

---

[1] A commercial bank's "cash position" is defined as the sum of cash in vault and deposits due from correspondent banks and from the Federal Reserve Bank.

rates in spring and early summer (see Exhibit 2) had forced Missouri National to compete aggressively for certificates of deposit in order to obtain the funds they needed from April through mid-July 1981.

After the bank's deposit, loan, liability, and investment objectives had been estimated and short-run policies established, it was the responsibility of Arthur Patton, a vice-president, to manage the daily cash position in order to adjust for short-run cash fluctuations and to ensure that the bank maintained the required minimum balances with the Federal Reserve Bank. It was Patton's objective to minimize the cost of meeting the bank's reserve requirements at the Fed and to invest any temporarily excess funds as profitably as possible.

The month of July was usually the Missouri National Bank's peak period for accumulating excess funds. The high point in deposits generally occurred during the weekend closest to the middle of the month, after which they declined (see Exhibit 3). In 1981, the weekend closest to the middle of July was Saturday the 11th and Sunday the 12th.

On Friday, July 10, Patton sold $7.9 million in Federal Funds, thereby deliberately creating a cumulative deficit reserve position of approximately $48 million (see Exhibit 4) for the week.[2] Patton assumed that a $30 million to $35 million reserve surplus would occur on Monday, thereby

canceling the effect of Friday's sale of Federal Funds. A large part of this reserve surplus was expected to come from immediate credit at the Federal Reserve on one-day items. These items consisted of checks drawn on other banks, which Missouri National forwarded to the Kansas City Clearing House and to its correspondent banks. When these checks were cleared, the cash became usable funds on deposit in Missouri's Federal Reserve account. Patton further assumed that the bank would experience its typical small reserve drain on Tuesday,[3] hence with a moderate purchase of Federal Funds, the average reserve balances for the week would closely approximate the legal requirements.

By mid-morning on Monday, July 13, Patton realized that his assumptions were not proving correct. The bank opened on Monday with a cumulative reserve deficit of $47.8 million for the reserve week ending Wednesday, July 15. The large immediate credits to the bank's account at the Federal Reserve had not materialized. A number of factors were responsible:

1   Incoming deposits over the weekend were smaller than expected.

2   A larger than normal deficit was incurred at the Kansas City Clearing House.

3   A large correspondent bank withdrew funds one day earlier than was considered normal.

4   Several important depositors made larger than normal withdrawals.

5   An adverse arithmetical error of $3 million was made in the general books department.

On Monday the bank experienced a further reserve deficit which Patton thought would approximate $9.0 million for the day. As a result of

---

[2] Federal Fund sales on Friday are for three days; thus selling $7.9 million for three days is the equivalent of selling $23.7 million for one day. Federal Funds are additional reserves that a commercial bank may either loan to or borrow from other banks in order to adjust its reserve position to the required level. These loans are generally made on a 24-hour basis but can also be made for longer periods. The cost is determined by the forces of supply and demand for such funds within the commercial banking system.

[3] The Missouri National's proof and transit department worked each Friday and Sunday night to process the heavy volume of "banking-by-mail" transactions. As a result, incoming items arriving over the weekend were cleared more promptly than by other banks in the area, and Missouri National generally experienced a peak in usable funds on Monday. This peak typically declined on Tuesday and Wednesday as other banks completed the processing of weekend mail.

these developments, the bank's cash reserve position required immediate attention. Since the normal Tuesday clearing deficit generally averaged approximately $15 million, Patton realized that by the close of business on Tuesday, the bank could have a cumulative reserve deficit of as high as $80 million. A deficit of this size would be difficult to overcome through normal adjustments such as borrowing Federal Funds or selling short-term Treasury securities.

On Monday afternoon, Patton decided that some action should be taken before the close of business that day in order to offset at least a substantial portion of the over $56 million cumulative deficit existing at that time (see Exhibit 4). There were several alternatives from which Patton could choose in order to adjust the bank's reserve position.

	Income lost	Added expense
1. Purchase of Federal Funds		17–18%
2. Borrowing from the Federal Reserve		14%
3. Borrowing by means of repurchase agreements		16.5–17.5%
4. Other means of borrowing (including CDs)		18–19%
5. Sale of short-term securities	11–12%	
6. Cancellation of $20 million brokerage participation with New York correspondent	16%	
7. Selling part of the investment portfolio	?	

DISCUSSION OF ALTERNATIVES

Purchase of Federal Funds

This was the device most commonly used by Missouri National to adjust deficit balances at the Federal Reserve Bank. It was Missouri National's policy, however, to limit Federal Funds purchases to no more than $15 million. As a mat-

ter of policy, the bank did not want to be either an excessive seller or buyer of Federal Funds. Patton considered the use of Federal Funds as a "fine adjustment" in the bank's reserve position. Since short-term adjustments in cash reserves usually ranged from $5 million to $10 million, Federal Funds provided the bank with a convenient means of either profitably employing excess reserves or offsetting small reserve deficits. The bank's limited use of Federal Funds sometimes made it necessary either to extend reserve adjustments over a longer period or to make adjustments of a more permanent nature.

Borrowing from the Federal Reserve

The accumulated reserve deficit could be made up through borrowing from the Federal Reserve Bank. The Missouri National Bank, however, looked on the use of such borrowing as a privilege. Missouri National had found it necessary to borrow heavily at the Federal Reserve during the month of June in order to meet substantial fund requirements as the bank's customers withdrew deposits in order to make their quarterly income tax payments. Patton preferred, therefore, to avoid using the "discount window" for as long thereafter as possible.

Borrowing by Means of Repurchase Agreements

Provident National could sell a part of its government or agency portfolio and agree to repurchase it at some future date at a predetermined price or yield. The cost of this form of secured borrowing tended to be lower than unsecured forms. There were two potential problems: (1) nearly $44 million of U.S. government and agency securities as well as $52 million of state and municipal securities were pledged to cover governmental deposits, and (2) the maturities of repos were generally daily although they could be as long as several months. In Patton's opinion, use of this form might cause the bank to shift permanently to liabilities other than deposits as a source of funds.

Other Means of Borrowing

Patton also felt that Missouri National might obtain the needed funds by bidding for CDs from ¼ to ½ percent above the existing certificates of deposit rate. He was concerned about the difficulties some regional banks had experienced in obtaining CDs and with the potential maturity of the CDs for which he would bid. Other forms of borrowing, such as the Eurodollar market, ineligible acceptances, and so on, were generally not available to Missouri National Bank.

Sale of Short-term Securities

If the adjustment of the cash position required funds for more than a few days, short-term securities could be sold to provide the necessary funds. Patton was reluctant, however, to sell any securities to meet the present reserve deficit unless absolutely necessary because of the bank's current policy of remaining as fully invested as possible. He regarded the losses on the securities he would have to sell as worrisome and knew that a majority of the current short-term securities were pledged as collateral for public deposit. Patton hoped to be able to retain until maturity most of his $46 million of short-term securities (see Exhibit 5).

Brokerage Collateral Loans or Other Loans Callable on Demand

These loans were usually arranged through the Missouri National's correspondent banks in New York. When Missouri National negotiated a brokerage collateral loan, it indicated the length of time it wished to employ its funds. Although such loans were callable on demand, the bank normally would not recall the funds until the agreed time had expired.

Selling a Portion of the Investment Portfolio

On June 30, 1981, the Missouri National's investment portfolio (securities with maturities of over one year) was approximately $145 million (see Exhibit 5). Over half of the securities were pledged as collateral for public deposits, and most of these securities could only be sold at very substantial losses. "It may be bad for the bank to take losses at this time," mused Patton.

He also realized he must try to make some assessments of Missouri National's liquidity needs for July 1981, especially related to the data in Exhibits 3 and 4. Because of recent discussions among the bank's senior officers, he wondered how the regulatory authorities (the Controller of the Currency) would view Missouri National's liquidity position. The bank's liquidity situation had been a subject of some spirited debate among the bank's senior management, with opinions divided as to whether overall liquidity was too high or too low.

Patton also was unsure whether he should talk further with senior management regarding the bank's short-term deposit, loan, and investment objectives before he decided on specific actions in managing the reserve position. Patton was not really convinced now that he should have sold the $7.9 million of Federal Funds on Friday, July 10, thus deliberately creating a reserve deficit.

By Monday afternoon, July 13, the cumulative reserve deficit for the week remained at approximately $50 million. Patton had still not decided, however, which of the several alternatives he should choose to reduce or eliminate the deficit. He knew, however, that he must evaluate the alternatives available, given the above considerations, and take action before the close of business on Monday afternoon. He wanted to be certain there were not any other alternatives available to him that he had not yet studied.

EXHIBIT 1
Missouri National Bank—Statement of Condition, June 30, 1980–1981 (dollar figures in thousands)

	June 30, 1980	June 30, 1981
Resources		
Cash and due from banks	$ 80,931	$ 92,882
U.S. government and agency securities	74,113	75,320
State, county, and municipal bonds	111,887	110,731
Federal Reserve Bank stock	764	1,140
Loans and discounts	664,000	760,478
Accrued interest receivable	1,492	1,579
Customers' liability under letters of credit and acceptances	10,681	10,351
Bank premises, furniture, and fixtures	1,851	2,518
Other resources	224	816
Total resources	$945,943	$1,055,815
Liabilities		
Transaction deposits	$322,201	$ 361,862
Savings deposits	175,090	182,103
Time deposits	344,000	402,560
Other liabilities	43,285	46,625
Capital notes	11,000	10,500
Capital stock	9,104	9,104
Surplus	26,361	27,044
Undivided profits	14,902	16,017
Total liabilities and capital	$945,943	$1,055,815

EXHIBIT 2
Missouri National Bank—Interest Rates in 1981

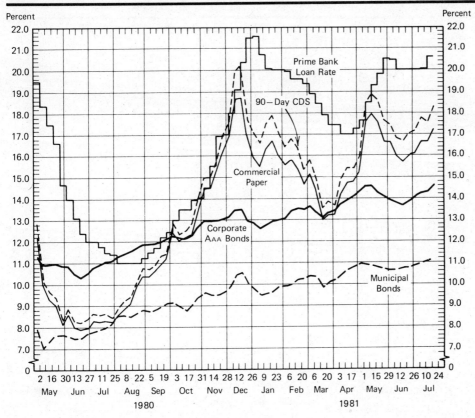

EXHIBIT 3

Missouri National Bank—Total Transaction and Saving/Time Deposits for
the Month of July 1978–1980 and July 1–10, 1981 (dollar figures in millions)

Day of Month	1978	1979	1980	1981
1	—	—	837	940
2	—	687	851	947
3	595	692	840	952
4	—	—	—	—
5	606	699	—	—
6	617	717	—	956
7	640	—	850	960
8	—	—	861	972
9	—	716	862	971
10	622	728	873	976
11	627	732	870	—
12	621	713	—	—
13	615	710	—	
14	618	—	877	
15	—	—	861	
16	—	724	852	
17	628	697	864	
18	609	690	850	
19	611	681	—	
20	607	695	—	
21	601	—	846	
22	—	—	853	
23	—	683	827	
24	582	691	837	
25	595	686	835	
26	597	678	—	
27	597	691	—	
28	593	—	826	
29	—	—	832	
30	—	682	834	
31	591	685	829	

EXHIBIT 4

Missouri National Bank—Worksheet for Computing Reserve Position

Day	Date	Beginning balances with Federal Reserve[a]	Noncontrollable factors affecting reserves	Controllable factors affecting reserve position	Potential balances	Reserve adjustments Fed Fund or FR borrowing	Closing balances with Federal Reserve	Required balances with Federal Reserve	Reserve excess (+) or deficiency (−)
Thurs.	July 9	50.6	−13.0	−5.0c	32.6	− 7.6	25.0	48.6	− 0.8b
Fri.	July 10	32.6	+16.1	—	48.7	− 7.9	40.8	48.6	−23.6
	Cumulative	83.2	+ 3.1	−5.0	81.3	−15.5	65.8	97.2	− 7.8
Sat.	July 11	48.7	—	—	48.7	− 7.9	40.8	48.6	−32.2
	Cumulative	131.9	+ 3.1	−5.0	130.0	−23.4	106.6	145.8	− 7.8
Sun.	July 12	48.7	—	—	48.7	− 7.9	40.8	48.6	−40.0
	Cumulative	180.6	+ 3.1	−5.0	178.7	−31.3	147.4	194.4	− 7.8
Mon.	July 13	48.7	− 9.0	—	39.7	0d	39.7	48.6	−47.8
	Cumulative	229.3	− 5.9	−5.0	218.4	−31.3d	187.1	243.0	− 8.9
Tues.	July 14	39.7f	−15.0e	—	24.7f	—	24.7f	48.6	−56.7f
	Cumulative							291.6	−23.9f
Wed.	July 15							48.6	−80.6f
	Cumulative							340.2	
	Average							48.6	

a After reversal of overnight Fed Funds or FR borrowing.
b Deficit from preceding week.
c Purchase of U.S. Government Security.
d Fed funds sold were not sold again on Monday.
e Estimated commercial factors expected on Tuesday.
f Predicted if there were no adjustments.

EXHIBIT 5
Missouri National Bank—Maturity Distribution of Securities at Book Value, June 30, 1981 (dollar figures in thousands)

Maturity (years)	U.S. government obligations	Federal agency obligations	State and municipal obligations	Total
1	$17,740	$17,900	$ 10,660	$ 46,300
2	5,460	17,300	9,904	32,664
3	4,000	4,400	7,790	16,190
4	0	0	6,970	6,970
5	0	4,170	6,220	10,390
6	3,740	0	6,870	10,610
7	0	0	6,120	6,120
8	0	0	6,378	6,378
9	0	0	5,210	5,210
10	0	0	5,784	5,784
11–15	0	3,830	17,870	21,700
15–20	0	0	16,921	16,921
Over 20	0	0	5,710	5,710
Total	$30,940	$47,600	$112,407	$190,947

CASE 9
Mountain National Bank

"Look at these figures, Tina. Zeb Roberts up at Mountain National Bank in Maryville has been in to us for over $9 million in Federal Funds almost every day now for three weeks. I know our present limit on Federal Funds loans to Mountain is $10 million, but the market is awfully tight right now and we do have other customers to service. Besides, with the lack of rain up in the Valley last year and with the Fed tightening up on the money markets, Roberts could be pretty illiquid about now and our Federal Funds loans to him could be risky. How about running our standard analysis on Mountain National within the next couple of days, and showing me the results."

Sanford Arthur was an officer in the Investment Department at First National Bank of Commerce, a large East coast bank with head offices in Richmond, Virginia. In January 1980, First National maintained active correspondent relationships with approximately 300 banks throughout the United States, each of which carried a deposit account with First National. Although these individual correspondent deposits varied greatly in both size and volatility, the sum of correspondent demand deposit balances at First National averaged from $600 million to $800 million, about 10 percent of their total deposits. After deducting the normal 12 percent legal reserve that First National must maintain against demand deposits, the remaining balances, when invested, added considerably to First National's gross income.

First National gained several additional benefits from its various correspondent banks. When a correspondent bank's commercial customer was expanding into the Virginia market, the correspondent would often refer the customer to First National for Virginia banking services. Furthermore, when a correspondent's customer desired a loan larger than that bank's legal lending limit (normally 10 percent of capital), the correspondent would frequently invite First National to participate with the "overline." Although the monetary value to First National of these business referrals and loan participations was hard to appraise, the bank's officers believed they were very important to First National's long-run growth and profitability.

In return for the correspondent deposit balances and the other courtesies mentioned, First National performed a number of important services for its smaller correspondents. Sanford Arthur, Tina Barton, and several assistants in First National's Investment Division were intimately involved in several of these services. For example, many smaller banks occasionally found that they needed additional reserves at the Federal Reserve Bank in order to meet their legal reserve requirement or, conversely, that they had excess reserves. In such cases, these banks desired to buy the excess reserves of another bank for a short period, normally for a day or a few days at a time. Small banks were effectively precluded, however, from dealing in the Federal Funds market because they did not maintain the required market contacts to deal directly and because their desired transactions were often less than the $1 million minimum transaction required in the established Federal Funds market. Accordingly, First National Bank would purchase or sell Federal Funds in multiples of $100,000 for its small correspondents. Recently, First National had been able to circumvent the red tape and paperwork of a true Federal Funds transaction by convincing regulatory authorities to allow First to buy or sell Federal Funds for its correspondent's deposit account at First.

Regardless of the particular transaction, however, the fact remained that when First National arranged for the purchase of Federal Funds by one of its small correspondent banks, First National was essentially making a large, unsecured, short-term loan to that correspondent. Should the correspondent bank fail, First National stood to lose an amount up to the entire amount of Federal Funds loaned. Thus, in order to ensure the safety of First National's correspondent Federal Funds transactions, Arthur or an-

other member of his group would investigate the investment policy and basic soundness of any correspondent bank that desired to deal in Federal Funds with First National. After an initial review, an upper limit was established with respect to the amount of Federal Funds First National would loan to that bank. This limit was reviewed periodically or on any occasion when a member of the Correspondent Investment Group felt an additional review was necessary. It was a special review of this type concerning the Mountain Valley National Bank in Virginia which Arthur had asked Tina Barton to prepare.

Arthur's group also provided investment services for approximately 100 smaller correspondent banks whose officers had neither the time nor, in some cases, the experience to manage effectively their bank's investment portfolios. In some cases, members of the Correspondent Investment Group actually worked on a day-to-day basis with the officers of correspondent banks in developing their investment strategies and executing daily transactions. The officers of approximately 200 other small correspondent banks managed their own investment portfolios but requested special or periodic reviews of their investment policy by Arthur's group. Such reviews were conducted annually, or when requested.

First National also provided their small correspondent banks several services in addition to the Federal Funds and investment services already mentioned. First National's size and its consequent large legal lending limit made its overline loan participations extremely valuable to small correspondent banks in dealing with their large customers. First National could also reduce the "float" of a correspondent by clearing checks drawn on other Eastern banks that had been deposited in that correspondent bank. As these checks were cleared, their value would be credited to the correspondent's deposit balance at First National, and the funds then immediately available.

An additional service First National offered to its correspondents was the physical custody of the correspondent's bond portfolio and the performance of associated clerical work involved in clipping and processing the bond coupons and crediting interest income on the portfolio to the correspondent's deposit balance. This service not only saved a correspondent bank clerical costs but also reduced its insurance premiums, since the dollar amount of assets stored in the correspondent's vault was reduced considerably. Finally, First National provided its correspondents with many small services, such as buying and selling foreign exchange for them and entertaining their officers when they visited the Richmond area.

On April 1, 1980, Barton began to gather data for her study on the Federal Funds borrowing limit of Mountain National Bank. The Mountain National Bank, located in Maryville, Virginia, was a unit bank with total resources in March 1980 of $130 million. Mountain Bank had 9 officers and employed 27 other people (including 4 on a part-time basis). The president of Mountain National was Zebediah Roberts, who had controlled the bank since its founding in 1967.

Maryville, Virginia, was a small town with an estimated 1980 population of 23,700, and was located in Appalachian Valley, approximately 150 miles northwest of Richmond. Maryville was in the northwest corner of a fertile valley farming region, and the town's economy was primarily based on the financing, supplies, and shipping facilities needed by farmers; a booming tourist business due to the town's beautiful surroundings; and an automobile tire plant that had opened in the mid-1970s. The town had grown rapidly in the 1970s, but there was some question now whether this growth would continue. There were five banks in Maryville. One (Mountain National) was a unit bank; the other four were branches of a larger bank or part of a bank holding company.

On April 1, 1980, Barton's department had gathered some material for a routine annual review of Mountain National's asset/liability management performance. From this material Barton knew she could obtain much relevant information about Mountain National's basic financial soundness. She also realized, however, that because bank examiners had access to this material, any major deficiencies might be minimized in some of this information and then discussed informally with correspondent bank managers.

Barton thought her analysis of Mountain National should attempt to answer several questions:

1   What is the past and expected future profitability of the bank?

2   How would an examiner evaluate the bank's asset and liability management?

3   Will the bank's liquidity and interest-sensitivity position allow it to prosper in the 1980s? Why?

4   What asset and liability management policy changes might be suggested to Mountain National in 1980?

5   Should First National continue to sell Federal Funds to Mountain National? If so, should a revised limit be set? If so, at what amount?

As she began her analysis, Tina Barton was well aware of the exceptionally unsettling events that had occurred in the money markets during the past few months. In October 1979, the Federal Reserve Board had declared it would henceforth manage unborrowed reserves and the money supply and allow interest rates to fluctuate as the free market dictated. This would surely mean a much greater fluctuation of interest rates, thought Barton. Also, the Depository Institution Deregulation and Monetary Control Act was passed in late March 1980. Barton was concerned about the effects of nationwide NOW accounts and the gradual lifting of Regulation Q on banks such as Mountain National. All available evidence suggested much greater volatility of interest rates and a higher level of uncertainty in the capital markets, but it was not yet clear what practical effects would arise from these new Federal Reserve Board policies.

In any event, Barton realized that financial and economic conditions in the 1980s would almost surely prove more volatile and risky for all bankers, large and small. Certainly, the prevailing attitudes within her bank and among her banking associates elsewhere reflected caution and concern due to extremely high interest rates and the unusually high economic uncertainty that prevailed at this time throughout the country.

EXHIBIT 1
Mountain National Bank—Statements of Condition, Year-End 1973–1979

	Actual						
	1973	1974	1975	1976	1977	1978	1979
Assets							
Cash and Due from Banks	2,968	2,082	7,242	4,318	9,054	10,382	11,846
Investments	2,584	5,425	11,976	19,194	22,990	27,358	26,782
Federal Funds Sold	2,800	4,200	3,200	5,800	8,200	6,600	0
Loans	12,116	17,706	22,474	34,606	53,506	67,030	84,253
Fixed Assets	402	864	2,322	2,468	2,366	2,892	3,217
Other Assets	236	297	398	494	746	1,418	1,664
Total Assets	21,106	30,574	47,612	66,880	96,862	115,680	127,762
Liabilities and Capital							
Demand Deposits	7,282	12,454	19,012	27,382	40,000	44,716	46,281
Savings Deposits	1,578	1,994	4,800	8,896	17,724	17,154	15,782
Other Time Deposits	6,826	10,178	17,144	19,994	27,958	39,256	43,966
Total Deposits	15,686	24,626	40,956	56,272	85,682	101,126	106,029
Federal Funds Purchased	0	0	488	3,524	2,016	3,568	9,493
Other Liabilities	100	360	258	574	1,824	2,284	2,676
Shareholder Equity	5,320	5,588	5,910	6,510	7,340	8,702	9,564
Total Liability and Capital	21,106	30,574	47,612	66,880	96,862	115,680	127,762

EXHIBIT 2
Mountain National Bank

	Actual						
	1973	1974	1975	1976	1977	1978	1979
Return on Shareholder Equity (%)	1.3	4.9	6.0	9.2	11.3	15.1	12.0
Return on Assets (%)	0.33	0.90	0.74	0.90	0.86	1.13	0.90
Shares Outstanding (in thousands)	350	350	350	350	385	446	446
Total Commercial Lines ($)	13,463	10,729	16,647	28,835	44,588	55,860	67,389
Total Used Lines ($)	4,039	5,901	7,491	11,534	17,835	22,344	29,651
Percentage Utilization (%)	30	55	45	40	40	40	44
Loans/Capital (×)	2.3×	3.2×	3.8×	5.3×	7.3×	7.7×	8.8×
Capital/Assets (%)	25.2	18.3	12.4	9.7	7.6	7.5	7.5

EXHIBIT 3
Mountain National Bank—Sensitive Sources and Use of Funds

	1973	1974	1975	1976	1977	1978	1979
Sources							
Sensitive—Interest Bearing	3,426	5,178	9,132	14,018	28,674	41,524	52,159
Nonsensitive—Interest Bearing	4,978	6,994	13,300	18,396	19,024	18,454	17,082
Nonsensitive—Noninterest Bearing	12,702	18,402	25,180	34,466	49,164	55,702	58,521
Total	21,106	30,574	47,612	66,880	96,862	115,680	127,762
Uses							
Sensitive—Interest Bearing	8,039	8,601	16,191	26,334	36,035	42,444	42,651
Nonsensitive—Interest Bearing	9,461	18,731	21,459	33,266	48,661	58,544	68,384
Nonsensitive—Noninterest Bearing	3,606	3,242	9,962	7,280	12,166	14,692	16,727
Total	21,106	30,574	47,612	66,880	96,862	115,680	127,762

EXHIBIT 4
Mountain National Bank—Factors Affecting Liquidity

Potential Funds Shortfall	Level	Volatility coefficient	Potential funds shortfall
Demand Deposits	46,281	0.03	1,388
Savings	15,782	0.06	947
Consumer Time	23,866	0.08	1,909
Money Market CDs	8,100	0.12	972
Public Time	12,000	0.08	960
Total Potential Shortfall			6,176

Potential Funds Demand	Outstanding lines	Current utilization	Funds required for peak	New funds
Loans	67,389	29,651	37,064	7,413
		44%	55%	

Policy Secondary Reserve

Potential Shortfall	6,176
Potential Demand	7,413
Policy Reserves	13,589

Source of Reserves

Liquid Bonds/Investments	14,782
Less: Seasonal Funds	4,500
Net Liquid Assets	10,282
Liquid Assets versus Policy Reserves	(3,307)

CASE 10
Greenville National Bank*

Precisely at 9:00 A.M. on July 2, 1979, the regular biweekly meeting of the Investment Committee of Greenville National Bank met in the board room of that bank. Those attending were Bill Stone, the president of Greenville National Bank; Richard Bowyer, the 64-year-old senior vice-president in charge of investments of Greenville Bank; Wilma Sullivan, the 28-year-old assistant vice-president, who worked under Bowyer and hoped to replace him when he retired; Linda Smith, a member of a medium-sized investment firm in Dallas, which handled many of Greenville Bank's investment orders; and Tom Phillips, a vice-president of the Second Bank of Dallas—Greenville's primary correspondent.

DISCUSSION OF ECONOMIC AND MONETARY CONDITIONS

The meeting got underway as usual with a discussion of economic and monetary conditions by Bowyer. Most of the discussion centered on the effects of rapid economic growth and inflation in the past several months. Bowyer reviewed the events over the past six months and pointed out that while monetary policy had become tighter, demand for bank loans had remained high and neither monetary policy nor fiscal policy had been successful in slowing inflation. He seemed optimistic about the continuation of economic growth after a slowdown and at least stabilization in the rate of inflation. "Monetary policy is achieving its objectives and if the growth of government spending is controlled we can have a short recession and a controlled rate of inflation, then a reasonably fast resumption of real economic growth," stated Bowyer.

Smith agreed with Bowyer's analysis of the past but disagreed with his predictions. She noted that the federal government's deficit was

---

* This case was prepared by Dr. George H. Hempel, professor of finance, Southern Methodist University.

large and might grow larger if revenues did not grow as rapidly as the government forecast. Recent rapid growth in the money supply indicated further tightening of monetary policy by the Federal Reserve. "Investors believe that the Federal Reserve will overreact to inflation and keep the economy from growing. Tight monetary policy will severely damage consumer demand for housing and durables and business demand for plants and equipment, but will not be effective against the type of inflation we now have," stated Smith. Smith, supported by Stone, believed that no growth and high inflation would persist in the second half of 1979 and a full-fledged recession might occur in late 1979. She believed the improvements during the first and second quarters of 1979 were temporary and cited the fact that most leading economic indicators were declining again. Stone cited overextension of consumer credit, particularly for housing, as a possible cause of a serious economic decline starting in late 1979.

Sullivan seemed to side with Bowyer, stating that she felt slower inflation and a return to reasonable economic growth in 1980 was the likely pattern. She felt that the Federal Reserve would be forced to ease monetary policy but that the lack of faith in government leadership was an important negative consideration. Phillips, wisely, refused to take sides in the disagreement about the future course of the economy. He said that the analysis of the past was accurate and Greenville National Bank's economic and monetary forecast should affect its investment decisions.

DISCUSSION OF CURRENT CONDITIONS IN MONEY AND CAPITAL

Stone then asked Smith to discuss current conditions in the money and capital markets. Smith stated that most sectors of the money and capital markets had slumped in the last two weeks, following a two- or three-week struggle to show slight gains. The average rate on Federal Funds had risen to nearly 10½ percent over the last week (from 10 percent a month ago and 7½ percent a year ago). The rates on 91- and 182-day Treasury bills had been in the 9.9 to 10 percent range for the last week (increasing from 6.4 to 6.5 percent a year ago). Exhibits 1 and 2, which Smith distributed to the Investment Committee, showed that other short-term rates had followed a similar pattern. Long-term rates had also performed similarly, but rate changes had been less dramatic and results for different types of securities had been more mixed. For example, interest rates on intermediate- and long-term governments and government agency bonds had risen 100 to 130 basis points from May 1978 to May 1979, possibly because of the increased supply due to a large Treasury deficit and heavy demand by corporate and consumer borrowers. Long-term municipal yields, on the other hand, had risen only 40 to 50 basis points during the same period. A return of investor confidence, heavy demand by the new tax-exempt bond mutual funds, and renewed heavy demand for municipal bonds by individuals had caused the slower deterioration in this market. There was concern, however, that prices might fall rapidly because tax exempts were being used to finance housing in some areas and surging loan demand was reducing bank demand for municipals.

Smith stated that she felt the short-term outlook for interest rates was from mixed to weak. In the case of municipal bonds, the Blue List, containing dealer supplies on hand, increased to $937 million from $824 million. Last week's new offerings of municipals was a rather high $1,165 million and sold slowly. Last week's Acceptance Ratio was 64 percent, a decline from 77 percent the preceding week. On the other hand, the 30-day Visible Supply had fallen some in recent weeks but still stood at a high $2,950 million as of late June.

The short-term outlook for all maturities of government and agency securities seemed worse, according to Smith. While she felt that the Treasury's borrowing needs were somewhat overstated, she was pessimistic about an oversupply of securities beginning to be felt. "In May, the Treasury sold both 10-year notes and 30-year bonds, FNMA and several private corporations also announced large new issues, and municipalities are borrowing at record pace. How long can the market absorb this with the savings at 5 percent of disposable personal income as people use more of their income to purchase goods and services?" Smith asked. Smith was also pessimistic about the longer term prospects of all fixed-return securities in the money and capital markets.

Phillips seemed to agree with Smith. He showed the group a series of interest rate predictions (see Exhibit 3) a professor had given in a recent speech. The professor predicted the largest proportional increase in rates would occur in the municipal market because of a decline in bank demand for municipal bonds because of an increase in bank loans. Phillips believed that continued inflation would force the Federal Reserve to tighten monetary policy in the coming months. In addition, he felt that there would be continual shortage of capital intensified by heavy federal borrowing into the 1980s, leading to the continuation of the upward trend in interest rates.

Stone was even more pessimistic about future interest rates than Phillips. Stone stated that he had heard Bill Miller had just made a speech that as long as a high rate of inflation persisted interest rates would rise. Stone forecasted increased supplies of government, corporate, and possibly municipal securities accompanied by continued low rates of total saving. He felt that possible legislation permitting a state or local government to issue taxable municipal bonds would compound the problem in the long-term taxable market. Fed Funds at or above 11 percent, prime at 13 percent and 10-year governments at or above 10 percent were Bowyer's predictions for interest rates by year-end.

Bowyer disagreed with Stone's pessimism about interest rates increasing. He felt all interest rates would remain stable or increase only moderately over the next few months (see Exhibit 3). Short-term rates should benefit from the Fed's promise to Congress to keep interest rates more stable if the Congress would lower the budget deficit. Longer term rates should benefit from lower demands for funds by business borrowers because of a recession in late 1979. Bowyer also stated that he believed rates would decline in late 1979. He felt the situation in the last half of 1979 and early 1980 would be similar to that in late 1974 and 1975, when rates declined rather rapidly.

PRESENT POSITION OF GREENVILLE NATIONAL BANK

As was usual after the review of economic and monetary conditions and the money and capital markets, Stone offered his opinions on the present general asset and liability conditions of Greenville Bank which pertained to investment decisions. He used Exhibits 4 through 8 to support his ideas. Stone was deeply concerned about the bank's ability to attract enough deposits to meet its soaring loan demand. He stated that the bank's board of directors had told him to maintain a loan-to-deposit ratio of roughly 60 percent. In the first six months of 1979, however, the loan-to-deposit ratio had grown above this level, in spite of the fact that the first half of each year was usually seasonally slow for loan growth. Stone forecasted that, in spite of higher rates and more restrictive lending practices, the bank's loan portfolio probably would grow by roughly $5 million in the second half of 1979.

The major reason for Stone's concern about rapidly increasing loan demand was his belief that deposit growth had slowed appreciably in the last few months and that deposits would continue to be difficult to attract. "Most of our deposit growth in the first five months of 1979 came from paying high rates on certificates of deposit growth in the first six months of 1979 tively in that market with the Dallas banks," he stated. "Demand deposit growth will probably continue to be slow because of restrictive Federal

Reserve monetary policies. At best we will probably increase total deposits between $2 million and $3 million in the last half of 1979," Stone predicted.

Stone also covered two other areas of concern. First, he was concerned about the bank's liquidity position. He noted the sale of some short-term Treasury bills and the shift from a net selling to a net buying position in Fed Funds. Second, he was concerned with the lack of growth in Greenville Bank's profits. He pointed out that although interest rates were higher, deposits had grown, the proportion of assets in loans was higher, and the bank was in a cost-efficiency program, net income for Greenville Bank was lower in the first six months of 1979 than in 1978. In this regard, he had three questions for the investments area of the bank:

"Why were we selling Federal Funds when the rate was below 7 percent early last year and now buying them when the rate is above 10 percent?

"Why did we take losses on our investments in the first six months of 1979 as opposed to the gains we took in early 1978 which I liked?

"Why don't we tie down some of these high rates in our investment portfolio?"

REVIEW OF RECENT ASSET AND LIABILITY MANAGEMENT DECISIONS

"Now, Mr. Stone, you know you asked us to take capital gains and lengthen the maturity of our securities to increase net income in early 1978," stated Bowyer. (Bowyer thought to himself that memories of the past were short.) In addition to some smaller transactions to round out some agency and municipal holdings, Bowyer said that the bank had two primary security transactions in spring 1979. First, he sold some $250,000 of Treasury bills at a loss of $1,820. Bowyer stated that he had bought the bills with original maturities of a year at a 7¾ percent basis at a time when 91-day bills were yielding 7 percent. "I thought I was smart getting the higher yield, but I was forced to sell to provide an 8¼ percent yield for the remaining days." He felt forced to sell them at a loss to help meet the bank's rising loan demand and because the Fed Fund rate had stayed above 10 percent this spring. He mentioned that his idea of "trading on the yield curve" was based on the assumptions of relatively constant rates and a rising yield curve. "The yield curve has been inverse in recent months as opposed to the rising yield curves in much of 1978," stated Bowyer. Recent yield curves, including the inverse yield curve in 1974, are depicted in Exhibit 9.

Second, early in the year when everybody was optimistic that rates were going to remain stable or fall slightly, Bowyer said that he had sold $100,000 FNMA 6¼ percent debentures due in 1984 at a loss of $10,000 in order to purchase $100,000 of the FNMA 9.20 percent debentures due in 1986 at par. Bowyer stated that Smith had strongly encouraged this transaction by citing advantages such as higher yield and greater potential for capital gain because of the longer maturity (now is the time to lengthen maturities, Smith had said); however, Smith had not mentioned the undesirable aspects of taking a capital loss, lower price appreciation of premium bonds, or the possibility of greater price depreciation (as had occurred over the last two or three months) for the longer maturity issue.

Bowyer seemed excited about the possibility of raising funds through "liability management." "We can meet liquidity needs through selling assets or purchasing liabilities," stated Bowyer. He then reviewed the available liability sources and their estimated costs. First, the bank could borrow at the Fed's discount window at a recently increased cost of 9½ percent (Stone appeared to lose his breath at the mention of something the bank had never done); purchase Fed Funds at a rate of 10¼ percent; try to use repurchase agreements on unpledged government securities at a cost of 9¾ percent; or try to attract additional certificates of deposit. While the bank's size limited access to larger CDs, Bowyer believed the recently authorized six-month certificates could prove useful. In just a little over a year the bank

had obtained nearly $1 million with the new six-month certificates (unfortunately, over 80 percent of this came from money already in lower cost certificates at our bank, thought Bowyer).

STATISTICAL STUDY TO IMPROVE LIQUIDITY POSITION

Bowyer then stated that he had asked Sullivan to prepare a statistical study to assist in planning the bank's liquidity needs. Sullivan said she had studied the seasonal pattern of loans and demand deposits and the trend of loans, demand deposits, and time deposits for the last 10 years. She had done nothing to adjust for cyclical movements over that period. The monthly seasonal pattern for loans and demand deposits is shown in Exhibit 10. Sullivan found that loans had been growing at a 12 percent compound annual rate while demand deposits had been growing at 5 percent, and time and savings deposits at a 6 percent compound annual rate over the 10-year period. Sullivan warned that the growth of time and savings deposits did not have a regular pattern and had been influenced by certificates of deposit in the last four or five years. "The difference between loan growth and deposit growth (less required reserves) was financed by a reduction in our investment portfolio," stated Sullivan.

Sullivan also warned of several types of deposit accounts that might warrant special attention. "We have roughly $1 million of highly vulnerable (to withdrawal) demand deposits and nearly $5 million of public time deposits. We have to hold 110 percent of eligible securities against these public deposits. Furthermore, while we can probably keep most of these monies by paying the going rate, we will lose $1 million in Denton school funds over the next year as they complete their building," Sullivan said. "My calculations, which ignore cyclical pressures, show loans rising to $27.7 million, demand deposits falling to $16.1 million, and time deposits rising to $20.6 million by mid-September. This does not include the probable drop of $1 million in public funds. However, some of these pressures will be lowered by early next year when the seasonal demand for loans declines and demand deposits have a seasonal inflow," she said. Stone muttered something about the worthlessness of statistical studies and the meeting continued.

PROPOSED INVESTMENT DECISIONS

Bowyer then pointed out that in view of the bank's position and Smith's and Phillips' forecasts, any future investment activities should be limited to the sale of securities to supply funds to meet increases in loan demand and to effect swaps that would either be profitable or shorten the portfolio. He stated that he had asked Sullivan to prepare a list of government or agency securities that could be liquidated in the event the portfolio was called on to provide funds for loans. He also had asked Sullivan to call Smith about possible portfolio swaps.

Sullivan presented the following list of securities that could be sold (in order of preference) for the approval of the investment committee:

1 $400 M Treasury bills
2 $600 M Treasury bonds of 1990
3 $200 M Treasury bonds of 1984
4 $300 M Treasury notes of 1987
5 $200 M Fed Land Banks of 1981

"After selling these securities, we should purchase Fed Funds," Sullivan stated. Sullivan's reasoning was that the Treasury bills were the most liquid assets and the Treasury bonds of 1990 were providing low yields because they were "Flower" bonds.[1]

Stone, Greenville Bank's president, seemed upset with these recommendations. "If we sell the Treasury bills, we will lose the rest of our liquid bonds," he said. He stated that the sale of the Treasury bonds of 1990 would destroy the bank's net income for 1978 and that neither the stockholders nor the examiners would be happy with

[1] So called, because these bonds may be used, at par, to pay federal estate and inheritance taxes due on the death of the owner of such bonds.

such a large loss. "My first choices for sale would be the Florida Board of Education bonds and the FNMA debentures maturing in 1979," Stone declared.

Phillips was opposed to the sale of the Florida Board of Education bonds. His primary reason was that it would weaken the spaced maturity municipal portfolio he had advised the bank to establish several years ago. Although he did not have any advice on the Treasury bills or long-term bonds, he did feel the bank would be wise to sell the Treasury bonds of 1984 and notes of 1987 and purchase 90-day bills. The loss from selling these securities would be relatively small and the bank would improve its yield position. "Furthermore, price fluctuations in intermediate maturity bonds can be quite wide," Phillips stated.

Sullivan then proposed a swap which Smith had suggested. Sell $200,000 of Greenville Independent School District 4½s of 1989 at 91 and purchase Chicago Public Building Commission's 5½ percent revenue bonds maturing in 1989 with the proceeds. She pointed out that there was a potential buyer for the Greenville bonds at a good price and a distressed seller was willing to sell the Chicago bonds at 95½. "The bank will increase its tax-exempt income by $2,000 per year and will better diversify its portfolio without lengthening maturity or decreasing quality," Sullivan said.

While not necessarily disagreeing with this exchange, Phillips had two additional strategies he felt the bank should consider. Phillips proposed that the bank should sell a substantial proportion of its U.S. government and agency portfolio and use the proceeds to repay the bank's current Fed Funds borrowing and to invest the remainder in Fed Funds. He pointed out that the Fed Funds rate would probably consistently exceed 10 percent while the yield to maturity on government and agency securities was under 10 percent. "Greenville Bank can earn nearly enough to recover losses on most government and agency issues," stated Phillips. Phillips' second proposal (if the first proposal was not accepted) was to use repurchase agreements on most of the government and agency securities instead of Fed Funds. He pointed out that since repos were, in essence, a secured form of borrowing, the bank could probably sell some of its securities under repurchase agreement at a cost of approximately 9¾ percent, rather than the 10¼ percent rate of Fed Funds. Stone gasped and remarked that such liability management techniques were only appropriate for large city banks.

At this point the meeting became disorderly. The use of liability management by a small bank was questioned. The quality of revenue bonds was questioned. The advisability of taking tax losses was debated. There was considerable argu-

ment over whether buying a municipal issue the bank knew well was better than buying a far away issue which would better diversify the bank's municipal portfolio. There was also considerable disagreement about whether the bank's policy of spaced maturities was serving the bank's investment objectives. Smith pointed out that many larger banks felt they got more liquidity and more income from using a "barbell" investment strategy, which emphasized very short term and very long term securities. As the meeting was adjourned, everyone agreed to carefully review the appropriate asset and liability management for Greenville National Bank.

EXHIBIT 1
Selected Interest Rates (Averages of Daily Rates Ended Friday)

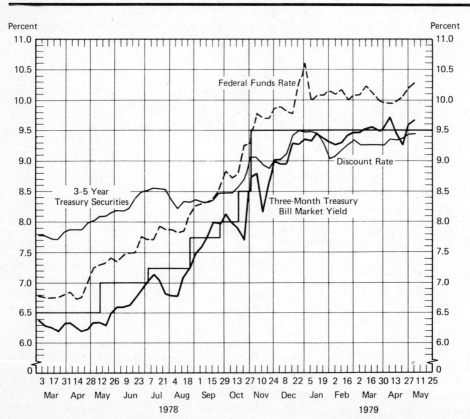

EXHIBIT 2
Yields on Selected Securities (Averages of Daily Rates Ended Friday)

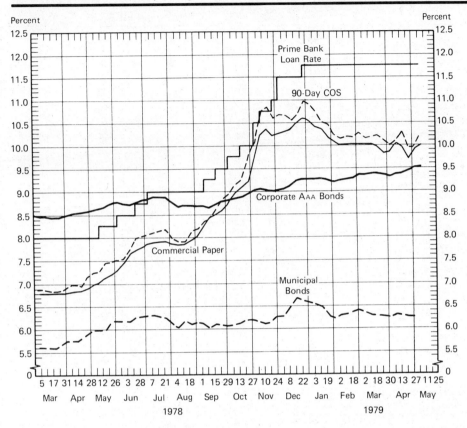

EXHIBIT 3
Selected Interest Rates

	December 1976	December 1977	February 1979	July 1979	February 1980
Fed Funds	4.7	5.5	10.2	11.5	8.0
Prime rate	6.2	7.5	11.7	12.5	9.0
Commercial paper	4.7	6.4	9.6	10.5	7.5
3-Month Treasuries	4.4	6.0	9.6	10.3	7.0
1-Year Treasuries	4.6	6.5	10.2	10.6	7.9
5-Year governments	6.0	7.0	9.1	9.6	8.6
Municipals (BB)	5.9	5.9	6.3	6.9	6.7
Corporates (AA)	8.4	8.8	9.6	10.2	9.4

EXHIBIT 4
Greenville National Bank—Balance Sheets (figures in thousands of dollars)

	12/31/78	6/30/79
Assets		
Cash and balances	$ 4,844	$ 5,148
Federal funds sold	200	0
U.S. Treasury securities	2,530	2,302
Government agency securities	2,032	2,086
State and local obligations	5,838	5,878
Other securities	344	344
Trading account securities	0	0
Loans and discounts	21,744	25,152
Fixed assets (net)	666	622
Other assets	50	86
Total assets	$38,248	$41,618
Liabilities, Reserves, and Capital		
Demand deposits	17,030	17,312
Time and savings deposits	17,854	20,270
Federal fund purchased	0	600
Other indebtedness or liabilities	466	436
Reserves for loan losses	72	82
Other reserves	0	0
Common stock-par	670	670
Surplus	956	956
Undivided profits	1,200	1,292
Total liabilities, reserves and capital	$38,248	$41,618

EXHIBIT 5
Greenville National Bank—Income Statements

	Year ended 12/31/78	Six months 6/30/79
Operating Income		
Interest and fees on loans	$1,581,290	$ 895,224
Income from fed funds and repos	50,194	2,934
Interest on investments		
U.S. Treasury securities	112,394	59,051
Government agency securities	112,674	57,076
State and local obligations	237,180	123,880
Other securities	20,518	10,844
Trust department income	20,724	10,268
Service charges on deposit accounts	105,416	55,074
Other service charges, fees, commissions, etc.	30,404	14,879
Other operating income	116,552	58,130
Total operating income	$2,387,346	$1,287,360

EXHIBIT 5 (continued)

	Year ended 12/31/78	Six months 6/30/79
Operating Expenses		
Salaries and wages (including benefits)	$ 538,966	$ 281,464
Interest on deposits	900,528	502,293
Expense of fed funds and repos	80	10,027
Interest on other borrowed funds	0	0
Occupancy expenses	153,884	78,608
Other operating expenses	292,692	136,605
Provision for loan losses	72,168	54,168
Total operating expenses	$1,958,318	$1,063,165
Income before taxes and security gains or losses	$ 429,028	$ 224,195
Applicable income taxes	82,555	40,547
Income before security gains or losses	$ 346,473	$ 183,648
Net security gains or losses (net of taxes)	13,880	(5,985)
Extraordinary charges or credits	0	0
Net income	$ 360,353	$ 177,663
Cash dividends	173,440	86,720
To undivided profits and other reserves	$ 186,913	$ 90,943

EXHIBIT 6
Greenville National Bank—List of Treasury and Agency Securities Owned[a]

Amount (in thousands)	Name—maturity	Stated value	Market value	Gain or loss
400	Treasury bills (various)	—	$ 398	$− 2,000
300	6⅜ Treasury bonds 2/15/82	Par	92.16	− 22,500
400	3¼ Treasury bonds 6/15/83–1978	90.16	83.16	− 32,000
200	6⅜ Treasury bonds 8/15/84	Par	89.16	− 21,000
200	6⅛ Treasury bonds 11/15/86	Par	85.5	− 29,000
300	7⅞ Treasury notes 11/15/87	Par	90.16	− 28,500
600	3½ Treasury bonds 2/15/90	90	80.00	− 60,000
	Totals	$2,302 M	$2,107 M	$−195,000
400	6.40 FNMA debentures 9/20/79	$ 96.16	$ 99.00	$+ 10,000
300	6.70 Fed land banks 4/10/81	Par	95.00	− 15,000
400	7.20 Fed Land Banks 1/10/83	Par	93.00	− 28,000
400	6¼ FNMA debentures 6/11/84	Par	87.00	− 52,000
200	7.60 Fed Home Loan Bank 8/10/87	Par	89.00	− 22,000
400	7.05 FNMA debentures 6/10/92	Par	83.00	− 68,000
	Totals	$2,086 M	$1,911 M	$−175,000

[a]Market price figures (expressed in 32ds) as of June 1, 1979. The list has been condensed to avoid making it too long. Each item represents 5 to 10 separate issues rather than 1, but maturities and returns are similar to those in the bank's portfolio.

EXHIBIT 7
Greenville National Bank—List of State and Local Obligations Owned[a]

Amount (in thousands)	Name	Coupon	Maturity	Stated value (in thousands)	Market value (in thousands)	Gain or loss
475	Florida Board of Education	7½	5/1/80	100.00	102.60	$+ 12,350
600	Lufkin, Tex., G.O.	4½	5/1/81	100.00	98.80	− 7,200
250	Irving, Tex., G.O.	3.80	12/1/82	100.00	96.80	− 8,000
700	Texarkana G.O.	3⅜	7/1/83	100.00	93.50	− 45,500
600	Dallas G.O.	5.35	4/1/84	100.00	103.00	− 18,000
350	Baytown G.O.	4.10	5/1/86	100.00	91.00	− 31,500
700	State of Texas	3.50	6/1/88	100.00	85.00	−105,000
600	Greenville I.S.D.	4½	3/1/89	100.00	91.00	− 54,000
750	Terrebonne Parish	4.00	6/10/90	97.25	84.25	− 97,500
375	Denton G.O.	4.85	2/1/92	100.00	90.00	− 37,500
500	Albany Co., N.T.	6.25	6/1/93	100.00	96.00	− 20,000
Totals				$5,878.00	$5,502.00	$− 375,850

[a]Market price figures (shown in decimals) as of July 1, 1979. This list shows undue concentration in a few names to avoid making it too long. Consider that each of the items represents 5 to 10 separate issues rather than 1, but of a similar quality rate and maturity so that the condition is not changed as to overall market value.

EXHIBIT 8
Greenville National Bank—Approximate Yields to Maturity

Name	Ratings	Approximate yield to maturity
6⅜ Treasury bonds 1982		9.3%
3¼ Treasury bonds 1983/1978		9.1
6⅜ Treasury bonds 1984		8.9
6⅛ Treasury bonds 1986		8.8
7⅝ Treasury notes 1987		9.1
3½ Treasury bonds 1990		6.1
6.40 FNMA debentures 1979		9.7
6.70 Fed Land Banks 1981		9.6
7.20 Fed Land Banks 1983		9.4
6¼ FNMA debentures 1984		9.4
7.60 Fed Home Loan Board 1987		9.4
7.05 FNMA debentures 1982		9.3
Florida Board of Education	Aa	4.9
Lufkin	Baa	5.4
Irving	Aa	5.0
Texarkana	A	5.2
Dallas	Aaa	4.8
Baytown	A-1	5.5

EXHIBIT 8 (continued)

Name	Ratings	Approximate yield to maturity
State of Texas	Aaa	5.4
Greenville I.S.D.	A-1	5.7
Terrebonne Parish, La.	A-1	6.0
Greenville	A-1	5.9
Albany Co., N.Y.	Baa	6.6

EXHIBIT 9
Yields on U.S. Government Securities

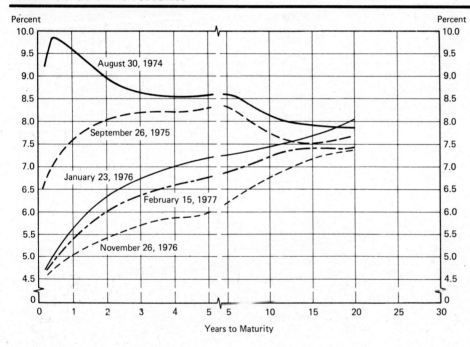

EXHIBIT 10
Greenville National Bank—Monthly Seasonal Index for Loans and Demand Deposits

Month	Loans	Demand Deposits	Month	Loans	Demand Deposits
January	93	105	July	101	98
February	92	110	August	102	97
March	90	112	September	110	93
April	93	103	October	108	92
May	100	100	November	103	94
June	100	100	December	108	96

EXHIBIT 11
Greenville National Bank—Review of Recent and Proposed Security Transactions

Sold	Issue	Original cost	Market	Gain or loss	Coupon income	Yield to maturity
$100M	FNMA 6.25 debentures of 1984	$100,000	$ 90,000	−10,000	$ 6,250	8.7%

Bought	Issue	Original cost			Coupon income	Yield to maturity
$100M	FNMA 9.20 debentures of 1986	$100,000			$ 9,200	9.2%
95M[a]	FNMA 9.20 debentures of 1986	95,000			8,740	9.2%
	(after-tax loss of $5,000)		(additional taxable income of $2,490 per year)			

Sell	Issue	Original cost	Market	Gain or loss	Coupon income	Yield to maturity
$200M	Greenville ISF (A-1)	$200,000	$182,000	−$18,000	$ 9,000	5.7%

Buy	Issue	Current market			Coupon income	Yield to maturity
$200	Chicago Bldg. Revs (A-1)	$191,000			$11,000	6.1%
	(after-tax loss of $9,000)		(additional tax-exempt income of $2,000 per year)			

[a]Hypothetical amount to equalize investment.

IV

MANAGING THE LOAN PORTFOLIO

7

ORGANIZING THE BANK'S LENDING EFFORT

To many bankers, the major business of banking is lending. In truth, national financial data seem to confirm this view. For example, U.S. bank loans outstanding now exceed $1 trillion. In 1980, loans accounted for about 55 percent of U.S. banks' total assets, and interest and fees on loans accounted for 68 percent of banks' total operating income. Historically, the major path to professional advancement and high salaries as a bank employee was through the lending function, although at present other major paths to progress increasingly are opening as bank operations, funds management, trust, and other activities become more complex.

Bank loans finance diverse groups in the economy. Manufacturers, distributors, service firms, farmers, builders, home buyers, commercial real estate developers, consumers, and others all depend on bank credit. The ways in which banks allocate their loanable dollars can strongly influence the economic development of the community and nation. Every bank bears a degree of risk in its granting of credit and, without exception, every bank experiences some loan losses. Whatever the degree of risk taken, loan losses can be minimized through highly professional organization and management of the lending function.

This section of the book reviews the principles of controlling the bank's lending activity. This chapter explains the need for and formulation of a *loan policy* to steer the bank toward the desired makeup of its loan portfolio. The chapter also covers technical aspects of *loan administration*, basically the legal and pecuniary protection of the loan portfolio. Finally, it explains the indirect controls on the loan portfolio that result from the examination of the bank by the various bank supervisory agencies. The following chapter presents the process of analyzing the borrower's credit worthiness.

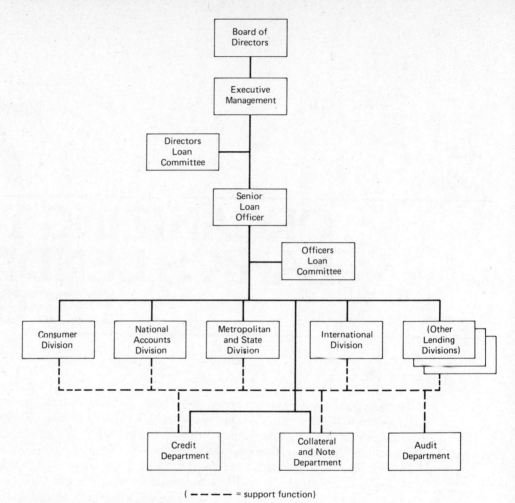

(— — — — = support function)

FIGURE 7-1   The Lending Organization

LOAN ORGANIZATION STRUCTURE

The organizational structure of the lending function varies with the banks' size and type of business. An officer of a small bank may perform all of the detailed work associated with making a loan, including the credit investigation and analysis, negotiation, customer contact, periodic review of the loan file, and, at times, collection. In larger banks individual loan officers specialize in consulting and negotiating with customers and there is greater departmentalization of support functions such as credit analysis, loan review, and loan collection.

Figure 7-1 shows a representative loan organization for a medium to large bank.

Loan Divisions

The several types of loan divisions shown in Figure 7-1 perform the basic mission of generating loan business and supporting customers. In larger banks the divisions usually are organized along both geographic and industry lines. Large banks develop lending expertise in specialized businesses such as energy, mining, public utilities, or commercial real estate. Separate loan divisions are necessary to service the special needs of these industries. At the same time, national and regional loan divisions which cut across different industries are needed to serve geographically dispersed customers.

Credit Department

The primary mission of the credit department is to evaluate the credit worthiness and debt payment capacity of present loan customers and of new loan applicants. This evaluation process is covered in detail in the next chapter. Because of the technical nature of its credit evaluation function, the credit department is an excellent place to train future loan officers. Trainees are exposed to a variety of good and not so good loan cases on which they assist loan officers in making credit decisions.

The credit department may also be responsible for loan review, although in larger banks this function is likely to be handled by the audit department. Credit departments are sometimes responsible for collections of past-due loans. This function usually would be handled by a specialist within the department.

Collateral and Note Department

A crucial and complex loan function is the perfection of the bank's security interest in collateral offered in support of a loan. The legal complications and paperwork generated in this function often justify separation from other activities in a unit such as a collateral and note department. This department also performs the discount function: the monitoring and crediting of payments received on outstanding notes.

Loan Committees

All banks need effective committees for the review of major loan proposals and of loan delinquencies. Two committees are needed: a directors' loan committee and an officers' loan committee. Loans above certain minimum sizes must be submitted to the officers' committee, consisting of the bank's most experienced loan officers. The officers' committee meets frequently. In large banks it may meet daily and only once a week in small banks.

The officers' loan committee serves as a check on, and not a substitution for, the individual officer's judgment. The committee's duties are to:

1   Review major new loans.
2   Review major loan renewals and ascertain reasons for renewal.
3   Review delinquent loans to determine cause.
4   Ensure compliance with stated bank policy.
5   Ensure full documentation of loans.
6   Ensure consistency in treatment of loan applications.

The directors' loan committee reviews major loans approved by the officers' committee. It is usually composed of the bank's president, the senior loan officer, and two or more board members. The committee makes final judgment on the officers' loan committee decisions, giving closer scrutiny to the largest credits. It is especially concerned with conformity to policy matters. The directors' committee also reviews past-due loans and problem credits.

LOAN POLICY FORMULATION

The composition and quality of a bank's loans should be a reflection of its loan policy. The latter should serve to give guidance and focus to the bank's lending activities. To ensure that such direction is clear and communicated to all concerned, the loan policy should be in written form. Indeed, the Comptroller of the Currency puts great emphasis on a formal *written* loan policy being handed down from the board of directors to management. From the Comptroller's viewpoint, a written loan policy should serve to obtain three results:

1   Produce sound and collectible loans.

2   Provide profitable investment of bank funds.

3   Encourage extensions of credit that meet the legitimate needs of the bank's market.

Loan policies may change over time. For example, immediately after World War II, most banks considered consumer lending inappropriate.[1] However, as demand for consumer durable goods and housing increased, the resulting attractive interest rate spreads on consumer and mortgage finance encouraged banks to shift loan funds to these markets. In the past decade or so, many large banks have adopted policies to aggressively seek international loans. In addition, loan policies vary over the credit cycle. In periods of tight money, banks often have to restrict their loan growth. On the other hand, when funds are plentiful, and local borrowers relax their demand for credit, banks may seek to lend outside of their *normal market* areas. Clearly, the loan policy should be adaptable to changes in cyclical and secular circumstances. In fact, it is crucial that loan policies be updated to reflect current circumstances and to maintain their relevance as a control tool.

Loan Policy Outline

A representative outline for a written loan policy is shown in Table 7-1. The outline is divided into three parts. The first part contains general policy statements that specify in broad terms the mission of the bank's loan department and the desired qualities of the loan portfolio. The second part of the outline describes technical principles and procedures to be followed in structuring and administering the loan portfolio. The third part introduces detailed procedures and parameters that apply to each of the various types of loans made by the bank. In the following sections, the general policy statements included in the first part are discussed specifically and then several of the technical procedures indicated in the second part are discussed.

---

[1] The postwar evolution of bank lending policies is reviewed in Douglas A. Hayes, *Bank Lending Policies: Domestic and International* (Ann Arbor: Division of Research Graduate School of Business Administration, University of Michigan, 1977).

TABLE 7-1
Outline for a Written Loan Policy

I. General Policy Statements	III. Parameters and Procedures by Type of Loan
A. Objectives	A. Real Estate Mortgage Loans[a]
B. Strategies	1. Loan description
1. Loan mix	2. Purpose of loan proceeds
2. Liquidity and maturity structure	3. Preferred maturities
3. Size of portfolio	4. Pricing: rates, fees, balances
C. Trade Area	5. Minimum and maximum amounts
D. Credit Standards	6. Insurance requirements
1. Types of loans	7. Perfection of collateral
2. Secured vs. unsecured guidelines	8. Channels of approval for policy
3. Collateral	B. Interim Construction Financing
4. Terms	C. Accounts Receivable Loans
E. Loan Authorities and Approval	D. Inventory Loans
	E. Term Loans
II. Principles and Procedures	F. Securities Purchase Loans
A. Insurance Protection	G. Agricultural Loans
B. Documentation Standards and Security Interest	H. Small Business Loans
C. Problem Loan Collections and Chargeoffs	I. Consumer Loans
D. Legal Constraints and Compliance	J. Purchased Loans
E. Loan Pricing	
F. Financial Information Required from Borrowers	
G. Ethics and Conflicts of Interest	
H. Loan Review	

[a]The discussion following A, numbered 1 to 8, also pertains to each loan category that follows (Sections B to J).

Loan Objectives and Strategies

The objectives section sets forth the bank's external and internal missions. Included are statements about its perceived business role in its trade area, perceived market niche, profitability, maintenance of public confidence, and degree of competitiveness and aggressiveness. It might quantify loan growth and earnings objectives, including the desired size of the loan portfolio in relation to total deposits or total assets.

A meaningful loan policy will express strategies in concrete terms. The desired loan mix should be quantified: for example, working capital commercial loans, 40 percent; consumer loans, 30 percent; real estate loans, 15 percent; term commercial loans, 15 percent. Also, loans to be deemphasized often merit mention. The bank's liquidity strategy should be indicated because it acts as a constraint on lending activity and because liquidity is partly determined by the maturity structure of the loan portfolio.

Trade Area

A primary and secondary trade area should be designated to instruct loan officers on the bank's geographic priorities. Banks understand their own trade areas best and are apt to misjudge the quality of loans originating outside of the area. Loan officers will be less alert to the economic deterioration of communities outside of their trade areas.

Banks should (1) define the area to be serviced routinely by each of its offices; (2) set limits on loan participation with other bank customers outside the area; and (3) process any other loans as an exception to policy.

Trade area definitions must comply with the Community Reinvestment Act of 1977. This act is discussed in Chapter 10.

The extent of a trade area obviously depends on the size and special characteristics of banks. The trade area for large, money center banks is not limited geographically but is truly national and international in scope. Also, geographic limits mean less to many regional banks with lending expertise in narrow fields such as oil and gas, meat packing, electronics, or public utilities or for regional banks that have major relationships with corporations with national and international locations.

Credit Standards

The written loan policy states the types of loans the bank considers desirable. Desirable loans routinely include the primary lending function to grant short-term loans to business customers in the trade area to the extent resources and opportunities permit. For such working-capital type loans, a minimum out-of-the-bank period, say 30 or 60 days each year, should be specified. Nonworking capital short-term loans should indicate a specific source of repayment.

Other, less conventional loans are normally discussed in the policy statement. Cautions should appear about lending to new businesses that are not well capitalized or backed by a strong private guarantor or by federal guarantors such as the Small Business Administration or Farm Home Administration.

The types of loans to be avoided should be mentioned. Loans to acquire a business or to buy out stockholders in the borrower's present business might be prohibited. The funds from such capital loans effectively replace part of a firm's equity with debt. The borrower normally expects to repay the loan from earnings on the business which may drain the business of needed equity funds. Also, in new acquisition borrowing, the borrower is usually less familiar with the business than the former owner, so that future profits may slip below their historic level. Policy might limit such loans to cases in which the borrower's other resources are ample or exowners guarantee the loan.

So-called bridge loans are often cited as contrary to bank loan policy. Such loans "bridge" a firm's needs until it can raise additional equity funds. The bank's exposure is especially great when repayment depends on a small firm's ability to sell stock under uncertain future market conditions. Speculative loans also are frequently proscribed by policy unless the borrower can qualify independently on the basis of his or her normal business performance. If a borrower has depleted working capital funds through speculative activity, loans to replenish the working capital normally would not be permitted.

Loan policy should indicate both desirable and unacceptable types of collateral. It should further indicate circumstances in which unsecured lending is prohibited. The quality and liquidity of collateral must be verified and maximum loan-to-collateral-value ratios should be applied before a secured loan is approved. Responsibilities and procedures for appraisals should be specified, including the time intervals between reappraisals.

Loan Authorities and Approvals

The loan policy should establish lending limits for all loan officers and for combinations of officers and loan committees. Limits for individuals will normally be predicated on their prior experience and length of service as lenders. Secured loans will carry higher limits than unsecured loans for comparable purposes, and seasonal working capital loans might carry higher limits than term loans. Individual officer's lending authorities for any one borrower are determined by totaling all of the borrower's existing loans, credit lines, and credit requests under consideration. Joint authorities might be used to approve larger loans than the officers involved would be permitted to approve individually, although in such cases it should be made clear that each officer is responsible for monitoring the performance of the loan. Division (e.g., commercial, real estate, dealer) or branch heads should be held responsible for loans made by their subordinate officers. Individual officer limits also depend on the bank's capital base and its ultimate legal loan limit. For example, a vice-president in a bank with $50 million in assets may have a loan limit of $25,000 while an officer of identical rank in a $5 billion bank may have a $200,000 limit.

PRINCIPLES AND PROCEDURES

Part II of the loan policy outline in Table 7-1 deals with several procedural areas to be covered. It sets forth policy in relation to the technical requirements involved in the loan function.

Insurance Protection

Most borrowers are exposed to risks that threaten their ability to repay their bank loans. Death or disability might strike the borrower or one of the borrower's indispensable employees. A catastrophic fire or flood may interrupt the borrower's business or destroy the loan collateral.

The loan policy should indicate the types of borrowers who must be insured. The policy must designate the bank as loss payee, or, when the cash value of a life insurance policy is offered as protection, it must be properly assigned to the bank. An increasingly common form of protection is the credit life policy written by the bank. Credit life is simply term life insurance written on consumer loan customers. It pays off outstanding balances due the bank in the event of the customer's death.

A somewhat different form of protection is obtained through *reinsurance*. If the borrower defaults, reinsurance pays out and the insurance company pursues collection on its own behalf on the bank's defaulted note. Reinsurance premiums are rather costly and policy should indicate what classes of borrowers, if any, should be under reinsurance programs.

Documentation Standards

Loan policy should prescribe uniform credit files and documentation procedure. Such requirements are routine for most medium-sized and larger banks, however, too often documentation procedures in many small banks are determined by the preferences of individual loan officers. An effective and efficient documentation system will promote uniformity and almost certainly will result in lower loan losses, especially when coupled with a good loan review program (discussed in the next section).

A uniform loan documentation checklist should be required for each credit file. The listed documents should include the following:

1 Credit application.
2   Borrower financial statements.
3 Credit reports.
4 Evidence of perfection of security interest.
5 Borrower's life or casuality insurance policies (showing bank as loss payee).
6 Corporate borrowing resolution.
7 Partnership agreement.
8 Continuing guarantee.
9 Financial statements on guarantor.
10 Correspondence.

Other data and documents pertaining to the credit should also be included. Item 4 pertains to documents that establish the bank's legal claim to collateral in the event of default. This subject produces must of the concern banks have over documentation and it is discussed in detail in Chapter 9.

The *corporate borrowing resolution* or the *partnership agreement* indicates those employees of the borrowing firm who are authorized to commit the borrower to an indebtedness. Loan officers must confirm that the name of the person who signs a loan agreement appears on the appropriate borrowing authorization instrument. The loan officer should obtain a certified copy of the instrument for the credit file.

In cases in which a corporate borrower's loan is backed by a guarantor, such as a *suretyship*, the credit file should contain the signed personal guarantee document, called a *continuing guarantee*. A continuing guarantee is often required of a firm's majority stockholders to ensure that the loan is protected against the possibility of corporate insolvency. Without a guarantee, stockholders might permit their insolvent corporation to simply abandon its debt obligations.

CONTROLLING LOAN LOSSES

The Loan Review Function

Banks find that invariably a small portion of their loans become delinquent and eventually must be written off. This basic risk of the lending function is not entirely bad; banks would be remiss in not bearing such risk in the course of underwriting a variety of business enterprises and consumer needs. Nevertheless, well-managed banks should do all they can to minimize loan losses.

The loan review process is a crucial tool in reducing losses and in monitoring loan quality. Loan review consists of a periodic audit of the ongoing performance of some or all of the active loans in a bank's loan portfolio. Other than its basic objective of reducing loan losses, some intermediate objectives of loan review are as follows:

1 To detect actual or potential problem loans as early as possible.

2 To enforce uniform documentation.

3 To insure that loan policy is followed.

4 To inform management and the board about the overall condition of the loan portfolio.

The procedures for loan review should be set forth in the loan policy. In general, all of the materials needed for loan review should be in the credit files set up for each loan made. The process typically requires the arduous task of manually handling a great many files, although recently many banks have begun to store credit file data in computer memory.

The scope of a bank's loan review operation is partly a matter of bank size. Some large banks establish a separate loan review staff directly under executive management to ensure its independence from loan personnel. There is a compelling logic to this approach because the chief executive officer is ultimately accountable for loan quality and can act directly to remedy deficiencies. Medium-sized banks tend to make the review operation an additional duty of the credit department or assign it to their audit department. The smallest banks often do not have a loan review program or they depend on loan officers to conduct the loan review as their time permits. Loan officers should not review their own loans; human nature prevents people, including loan officers, from being objective when reviewing their own work.

Whatever means are used to conduct loan review, the following points should be covered:

1 Financial condition and repayment ability of borrower.

2 Completeness of documentation.

3 Consistency with loan policy.

4 Perfection of security interest on collateral.

5 Legal and regulatory compliance.

6 Apparent profitability.

Most banks are unable to review regularly every loan on their books. Some banks review all loans in excess of a certain cutoff value, and review only a random sample of loans below the cut off. The frequency of review of individual loans is determined by the size and quality of the loan; large, poor-quality loans are reviewed most frequently. Many banks have a loan grading system which establishes the quality and, therefore, the frequency of review of each loan. Table 7-2 shows an example of such a system.

TABLE 7-2
A Loan Grading System[a]

Loan rating	Review schedule	General description	Specific circumstances
A	360 days	Top Grade	1. Unsecured loans to very substantial companies with unquestionable financial strength 2. Loans adequately secured by cash surrender value, government bonds, CDs, or savings accounts 3. Loans well secured by listed stock
B	180 days	Good	1. Loans where the risk is reasonable but the overall situation is less desirable than grade A 2. Loans adequately secured by listed stock 3. Loans generously secured by receivables, inventory, and other readily marketable collateral
C	90 days	Marginal	1. Loans that require more-than-average service and attention to collateral and financial information or counseling 2. Loans for which collateral values are less than standard 3. Loans that are not conforming to the repayment schedule but are not seriously past due. Creditworthiness or collateral values are in evidence
D	30 days (minimum)	Workout Doubtful Loss	1. All loans classified by bank examiners 2. Unusually high credit risks that require constant supervision

[a]Margaret A. Hoffman and Gerald C. Fischer, *Credit Department Management* (Philadelphia: Robert Morris Associates, 1980).

Correcting Problem Loans

The loan policy should require diligence on the part of all loan personnel to detect and attempt to correct problem loans. Although loan review personnel are important in the early detection of problem loans, individual loan officers frequently have special ongoing knowledge to contribute. Loan officers attempt to maintain good rapport with their borrowers. If the borrowers' business deteriorates, the loan officer frequently will find this rapport deteriorates as well. Any unexplained change in the borrower's attitude toward the loan officer or the bank may be a clue to borrower financial difficulties. Unexpected declines in deposit balances or occurrences of overdrafts are signs of such difficulties.

Other clues include abnormal delays by the borrower in submitting periodic financial statements as required in the loan agreement. Delays might indicate a reluctance to submit unfavorable financial results to the bank. In the event of such delays, the loan officer should immediately inquire about reasons for the delays. Payment delinquencies also must be followed up quickly because they frequently indicate the borrower is undergoing a financial crisis. Periods of economic recession bring on rashes of problem loans and loan losses. Table 7-3 indicates net loan losses as a percentage of total loans outstanding for U.S. banks during 1971–1980. Note the higher loss ratios for years immediately following recession years. Such periods require greater than normal surveillance of marginal borrowers. Poor economic conditions produce declines in sales and profit margins. Falling sales may generate unexpected increases in inventory, and falling profits prompt attempts to cut overhead. These changes can be readily observed from the customer's interim statements and may foretell a coming delinquency.

When a problem loan is detected, the responsible loan officer should take immediate corrective action to prevent further deterioration and to minimize potential loss. The preferred solution to a problem loan is to negotiate a plan of action with the borrower to try to extract both the bank and borrower from possible loss. The plan of action is actually a revised loan agreement. It should set forth a new repayment schedule, provide covenants limiting the customer's activities, establish requirements for the customer to report operating and financial activities for the bank to monitor, and specify the extent of the bank's authority to participate in management decisions.

Problems with secured loans may arise when the collateral is inadequate. The market value of certain types of collateral, such as securities, may fall below the loan value. Also, the loan may have been inadequately secured at the outset, because of either improper documentation or an excessive loan-to-value ratio. An obvious solution would be to obtain additional collateral in the form of marketable securities, cash value of life insurance, receivables, inventory, or even real estate equity.

A problem loan might be remedied through the addition of guarantees or endorsements. Of course, the extent of the improvement in the bank's position is directly related to the financial strength of the guarantors.

Loan officers must be especially alert to detect fraud. Possible types of fraud include false financial statements, false documents, securities, and titles for collateral. In the event of bankruptcy, proof that fraud was used in obtaining a loan may be basis for gaining legal access to a borrower's resources ahead of other creditors.

TABLE 7-3
Net Loan Loss Ratios for Insured U.S. Commercial Banks

Year	Net loan losses (in millions)	Net loan losses, percentage of equity capital
1971	$1,087	2.57
1972	887	1.92
1973	1,159	2.27
1974[a]	1,957	3.46
1975[a]	3,243	5.25
1976	3,503	5.10
1977	2,797	3.69
1978	2,497	2.97
1979	2,564	2.77
1980[a]	3,599	3.51

[a]Designates recession years.

Borrower's Financial Statements

Loans should always be supported by concrete financial data. The data may consist of a small consumer borrower's personal financial statement or a multinational corporate borrower's unqualified audited financial statements studied by professional analysts, CPAs, and attorneys. The loan policy should establish certain guidelines for such data. Normally, common dated balance sheets and income statements for at least the immediate past three years are required of commercial borrowers.

For small banks that deal regularly with small businesses, the professionalism of borrower financial statements can be expected to vary a great deal. Small businesses often present statements prepared by an owner who has no formal training in accounting. Statements prepared by professional accountants may be derived solely from the company's accounts without audit. Even professionally audited statements may contain broad disclaimers as to the integrity of certain information presented. When financial data are insufficient, the loan officer should ask the customer for clarification. For example, it is frequently necessary to clarify how receivables, inventory, or equipment are valued and whether or not they have been pledged for other purposes. Also, the delinquency of trade payables or the maturity of other debt may need clarification. Written clarifications of such issues should be a part of the credit file.

Personal financial statements should be required of all comakers, guarantors, or endorsers. Details of real estate owned, stocks and bonds, mortgages, loans, and other debt maturities should be included so that personal net worth is clearly indicated.

Interest Rate Policy

Interest rates charged on loans potentially depend on one or more of several considerations such as the following:

1　The bank's cost of funds (sometimes including cost of equity funds).

2　The riskiness of the borrower.

3　Compensating balances and fees.

4　Interest rates charged by competitors.

5　Usury ceilings.

6　Other banking relationships with the borrower.

Chapter 9 deals with many of these considerations in its discussion of the pricing and profitability of commercial loans. General guidelines should be included as part of loan policy principles and procedures. For example, the bank's own prime loan rate—that interest rate quoted to the bank's most creditworthy borrowers—should be explained. Most small or medium-sized banks' prime rate is based on a national prime rate but is modified according to their customer base and market competitive situation. Bank pricing policy for single-pay, balloon maturity loans ("bullet" loans) versus fully amortized loans might be indicated. Also, lawful exceptions to established usury ceilings are sometimes detailed for the benefit of loan officers.

Unethical Conduct and Conflicts of Interest

The success of any bank depends partly on its customers' confidence that the bank's employees will not exploit their unique positions of trust for unethical gain. Bankers deal more directly and routinely with money than perhaps any other professional group. The exchange of money is the very basis and not just the outcome of customer interaction. Bankers also deal with highly sensitive and confidential information related to their customers. As a result, the potential for conflicts of interest is unusually serious.

Loan policy statements frequently list improper activities or relationships that loan officers should avoid. Such a list should include acceptance of gifts of value or loans from customers or loan applicants, investment in a customer's business or other uses of privileged information for personal gain, and improper use of credit information on a customer. On this latter point, the Robert Morris Associates Code of Ethics for the Exchange of Credit Information is used by many banks to govern the exchange of credit information. The code prescribes controls on the creditors' sharing between themselves their credit experiences with customers without unduly violating the customers' right to privacy.

Conflicts of interest may also arise between the commercial loan division and the trust department when the loan division has inside data on a firm whose securities are held by the trust department. Policy should prohibit the trust department's access to such files.

LEGAL AND REGULATORY CONTROLS ON LENDING

Historically, commercial banking has been one of the most regulated industries in the United States. There are several rationales for such tight control. First, banking risks must be minimal because banks are so pivotal in our system of monetary exchange. In the public mind, the safety of the nation's monetary system and its currency is dependent on the safety of its banks. Second, commercial banks are instruments of national monetary policy. Tight control over banks ensures an elastic currency by enforcing desired and more predictable behavior by banks. Third, memories of past banking panics and failures make special precautions politically appealing. Intertwined in these rationales is the perceived need to uphold the concept of deposit insurance by preventing drains on deposit insurance resources. Finally, incentives and controls are sometimes placed on banks' power to create credit in order to allocate credit toward socially desirable ends.

Although not all of these rationalizations directly address the bank lending function, they do result in prominent regulation of the loan portfolio from which most of the risk in banking is derived.

Legal Provisions

Constraints on lending activity are reflected in enacted legislation and interpretive decisions of supervisory agencies. Regulations that deal with limited types of loans (consumer, commercial, real estate) are discussed in Chapters 9, 10, and 11. This section summarizes the general laws and regulations applicable to national banks. Most state regulations closely parallel federal regulations.

Loans to single borrowers are limited to prevent the concentration of a bank's assets in one risky customer. In the case of national banks, the 1982 Depository Institutions Act established the limit on loans to single borrowers at 15 percent of the bank's capital and surplus plus an additional 10 percent for loans fully secured by readily marketable collateral. Still higher limits are possible for loans secured by specific types of collateral. For the purpose of defining capital, eligible notes and debentures have been included since the early 1960s. There are several exceptions to these limits, including drafts or bills of exchange used to finance domestic and international trade. Also, goods secured by shipping documents are exempt and those secured by warehouse receipts are partially exempt.

The Financial Institutions Regulatory Act of 1978 tightly restricts loans to executive officers, directors, and principal shareholders. Loans to bank examiners are illegal.

Regulation U sets margin restrictions on credit granted to acquire or carry securities and is intended to prevent speculation in securities markets. The regulation does not apply to loans secured by stocks, assuming that loan proceeds are not to be used to acquire stocks.

National banks are limited in the size of their real estate loan portfolio to the larger of either capital and surplus, or 70 percent of time and savings deposits. Loans on real estate are confined to improved farm, business, and residential properties.

Many states have usury laws that establish ceilings on interest rates charged consumers and small businesses by state banks. National banks are permitted to charge up to 1 percentage point above the Federal Reserve discount rate. A federal preemption of state usury ceilings was effective in the late 1970s and early 1980s, permitting banks to earn market rates of interest on previously restricted loans.

Supervisory Examination of Loan Quality

In-bank examination by federal or state regulatory authorities has as its primary goals the evaluation of the following:

1 The bank's liquidity and solvency.
2 The bank's compliance with banking laws and regulations.
3 The quality and liquidity of the bank's assets.
4 The sufficiency of internal controls and safeguards.
5 The adequacy of capital.
6 The soundness of management's policies.

The evaluation of each of these factors directly or indirectly involves the quality of the loan portfolio. Indeed, since it typically contains the majority of bank assets, the loan portfolio probably occupies more examiner time than all of the other examination procedures combined. Considering that several thousand person-hours might be spent on a single examination of a $1 billion bank, depending on the extent of the bank's problems, it is clear that the loan portfolio receives considerable examiner attention. The examiner's summary evaluation regarding the condition of the bank and the soundness of its management is colored heavily by the examiner's assessment of the bank's loans.

Loan examination, in its broadest aspects, requires an evaluation of a bank's lending policy and the administration of the whole loan portfolio. Problems in the loan portfolio of many banks often stem from inexperienced and poorly paid managers at the top. Loan problems also arise because of inadequate internal loan review systems in which loan officers, management, and directors are not alerted to deteriorating loans in need of followup and correction. Other problems occur because of failure to ascertain how loan proceeds are to be used, failure to establish clear loan repayment programs, failure to obtain sufficient credit information, and too much dependence on collateral.

Ultimately, however, the examiner's evaluation of the loan portfolio comes down to appraisal of individual loans. Some of the appraisal process is quite mundane and includes detailed steps such as proving each note to the general ledger, verifying the accuracy of collateral described in the note, recording loan details on the examiner's line card, and verifying that loan proceeds have actually been disbursed in the manner intended in the note.

Other aspects of the appraisal process are less mundane and require the examiner to have substantial experience and to exercise judgment, perceptiveness, and analytical ability in evaluating the risk of a loan. Primarily, the measurement of loan risk must be based on the willingness and ability of the borrower to perform as agreed in the loan negotiation. Consideration is given to the character, capacity, financial responsibility, and record of the borrower. Tests are made to determine if the borrower's actual and potential earnings or liquid assets will cover interest payments and enable the loan principal to be repaid on the agreed schedule.

Some loans or groups of related loans, individually representing no more than normal credit risks, may be scheduled because they represent a concentration of credit supported by one borrower within several entities or by one potentially vulnerable industry. Loans that lack technical or legal documentary support are also scheduled. Scheduled loans are *adversely classified* if they present more immediate risk of nonpayment. Adversely classified loans are more finely divided as to their risk among three categories:

1 *Substandard* loans are inadequately protected by the net worth and paying capacity of the borrower, or the pledged collateral. The bank will likely sustain some loss if deficiencies are not corrected.

2 *Doubtful* loans have all the weaknesses of substandard loans but have deteriorated such that they have a high probability of substantial loss.

3 *Loss* loans are considered uncollectible and of little or no value as a bank asset.

The examiner relates loans classified as doubtful and loss to the bank's capital adequacy; specifically, the book value of capital is reduced by the uncollectible portions of these classifications. For example, suppose a half-billion-dollar bank with $40 million in capital and reserves was found to have the following adversely classified loans:

Doubtful loans	= $4,000,000
Loss loans	= $8,000,000

These values would be applied to debit capital as follows:

Capital and reserves	$40,000,000
Less: Loss	8,000,000
50% of doubtful	2,000,000
Adjusted capital and reserves	$30,000,000

In the examiner's view, the bank's adjusted capital-to-assets ratio would be 6 percent, not the 8 percent ratio, implied by the bank's regular balance sheet. Such an approach gives a truer picture of the amount of capital protection afforded to depositors and other bank creditors after accounting for probably uncollectible loans.

There is good evidence that examiners are rather successful in evaluating and classifying problem loans. Of the loans they examine, they manage to classify most of those that are subsequently charged off (although not all of the loans they classify are charged off). In a long-term study of the classification of loans by examiners in a sample of 12 banks, it was found that of the charged off loans that had been previously examined, 87 percent were adversely classified. Examiners also appear to be successful in assigning loans to the substandard, doubtful, and loss classification categories according to their relative risks of default. In the aforementioned 12-bank sample, higher charge-off rates occurred for the lowest classification categories; 10 percent of substandard, 58 percent of doubtful, and 95 percent of loss classifications were eventually charged off.[2]

SUMMARY

Effective organization and control of the lending function is vital to the profitability and solvency of every bank. The lending function is perhaps the most diverse and complex activity in banking. Also, for most banks, it is the function involving risk to management, depositors, and stockholders.

The key tool for control and for communicating the bank's lending goals and strategies is the written loan policy. Formal loan policy is handed down from the board of directors to the loan officers for implementation; that is, loan officers' lending authority is derived from the directors. Bank directors are ultimately responsible for the quality and condition of the loan portfolio, and, as in all matters pertaining to the bank, they must answer to stockholders and bank regulatory authorities for deficiencies. Reg-

[2] Kenneth Spong and Thomas Hoenig, "Bank Examination Classifications and Loan Risk," *Economic Review*, Federal Reserve Bank of Kansas City, June 1979, pp. 15–25.

ulators expect the directors to conduct a regular internal examination of the loan portfolio in order to assess the quality and documentation of the loans, to review specific large credits, to ensure that proper loan approval and other policies are being followed, and to generally evaluate the performance of loan officers.

Inherent in loan policy is the directors' attitude toward risk taking. Taking risks is a natural part of lending to consumers, businesses, farmers, and others, and, inevitably, losses will occur. The bank can do much to minimize loan losses in relation to the risks it does take, however, through a loan policy that mandates complete and uniform loan information and documentation, prompt action on delinquencies, secondary protection in the form of insurance on borrowers, and adequate collateral, profitable pricing, and, most important, loan review.

Small banks have had a tendency to rely on the bank examiner to perform their loan review or credit examination function. Although examiners appear to be quite proficient in classifying problem loans, regulatory examinations were becoming less frequent in the early 1980s in relation to earlier periods. Examination personnel had not increased at the same pace as bank assets or new regulations and compliance requirements. It appears that, in the future, banks of all sizes will need to provide for a professional and uniform internal loan review function. This function should be independent of the loan divisions and the loan approval channels.

In the next chapter, we discuss credit analysis, a loan function that is perhaps the most basic of all in minimizing loan losses. Through credit analysis, the bank attempts to determine the ability of a borrower to repay legitimate extensions of credit. By refusing credit to a potential borrower who, on analysis, cannot demonstrate sufficient financial strength, the bank hopes to improve on its chances to avoid unnecessary losses in its loan portfolio.

8

LENDING PRINCIPLES AND THE BUSINESS BORROWER

In its fullest meaning, credit analysis is the process of assessing the risk of lending to a business or individual. The so-called credit risk must be evaluated against the benefits the bank expects to derive from making the loan. The direct benefits are simply the interest and fees earned on the loan and, possibly, the deposit balances required as a condition of the loan. Indirect benefits consist of the initiation or maintenance of a relationship with the borrower that may provide the bank with increased deposits and with demand for a variety of bank services. In Chapters 9, 10, and 11, we will discuss the ways in which banks structure the loans they make in order to provide benefits commensurate with loan risks.

Credit risk assessment has both qualitative and quantitative dimensions; the qualitative dimensions of risk are generally the more difficult to assess. The steps in qualitative risk assessment are primarily gathering information on the borrower's record of financial responsibility, determining his or her true purpose for wanting to borrow funds, identifying the risks confronting the borrower's business under future industry and economic conditions, and estimating the degree of commitment the borrower will have regarding repayment. The quantitative dimension of credit risk assessment consists of the analysis of historical financial data and the projection of future financial results to evaluate the borrower's capacity for timely repayment of the loan and, indeed, the borrower's ability to financially survive possible industry and economic reverses.

The first section of this chapter introduces the four fundamental lines of inquiry in credit analysis. The second section discusses the resources and procedures used in credit investigation. The remainder of the chapter is devoted to financial statement analysis. Section three deals with the techniques of financial analysis, especially aspects of working capital analysis and financial forecasting. An appendix is included for readers who wish to review the basics of financial ratio analysis.

FOUR BASIC CREDIT FACTORS

The essence of all credit analysis can be captured in four basic credit factors or lines of inquiry:

1   The borrower's character.
2   The use of loan funds.
3   The primary source of loan repayment.
4   Secondary sources of repayment.

Character

Most bankers agree that the paramount factor in a successful loan is the honesty and goodwill of the borrower. Dishonest borrowers do not feel morally committed to repay their debts. A determined and skilled dishonest borrower usually can get a loan through misrepresentation. Because loan officers must spread their time over many loan relationships, they do not have time to uncover elaborate schemes to defraud the bank.

The bank must protect itself from dishonest borrowers by thoroughly investigating the credit background of the borrower. The borrower's previous credit relationships can be evaluated from records of the local credit bureau suppliers, past banking relationships, and customers. If the borrower has built a record of prompt payment of interest and principal, it is likely that future loans will be similarly serviced. If the borrower has been routinely late in paying past debts, the reasons should be determined. If previous creditors have experienced losses, the loan officer should almost automatically reject the credit.

Use of Loan Funds

On the surface, the borrower's need and proposed use for funds usually seems perfectly clear. In many commercial loans, such is frequently not the case. More often than not, determining the true need and use for funds requires good analytical skills in accounting and business finance.

Ostensibly, most business loans are made for working capital purposes—usually additions to current assets. However, the specific purpose for the loan may be substantially different. The loan proceeds may provide emergency funds to meet the firm's payroll, they may be used to pay aggrieved suppliers' overdue accounts, they may replace working capital that was depleted to purchase fixed assets, or they may replace funds depleted through operating losses. Also, the analyst should determine whether working capital needs are seasonal or permanent. Frequently, short-term loans are made to finance working capital needs that initially appear seasonal but subsequently prove to be permanent needs arising from general sales growth. As a result, short-term loans often become de facto term loans.

Assets financed by term commercial loans in fact should meet the legitimate needs of the borrower's business. An asset purchased in the hope of profiting from its resale is speculative. Banks ordinarily do not lend for such a purchase because it does not contribute to the economic needs of the business.

Primary Source of Repayment

The analyst's accounting and finance skills are crucial in determining the ability of the borrower to repay a loan from cash flow. For seasonal working capital loans, cash flows are generated by means of the orderly liquidation of the seasonal buildup in inventories and receivables. In term loans, cash flows are generated from earnings and noncash expenses (depreciation, depletion, etc.) charged against earnings. The analyst must ascertain the timing and sufficiency of these cash flows and evaluate the risk that cash flows will fall short.

Sources of repayment other than cash flow should be viewed with caution. The borrower may plan on a future injection of investor capital to repay the loan. Unfortunately, if the firm fails to produce attractive profits, future investment in the firm by outsiders is usually withheld. The customer may be depending on borrowing from another institution to repay the bank. Unless a formal commitment exists from another institution, this source suffers from the same limitation as a planned equity injection. An exception is the interim construction loan in which another, long-term lender has formally committed itself to provide "takeout" funds. The future sale of a fixed asset is not a reliable source of loan repayment. The borrower is either unwilling or unable to sell the asset at the time of the loan, and a future, possibly forced, sale of the asset to repay the loan is highly speculative.

Secondary Source of Repayment

In general, cash flow from business operations is the most dependable source of loan repayment. However, if sufficient cash flows fail to materialize, the bank can prevent a loss if it has secured a secondary source of repayment.

Collateral should always be viewed as a secondary and not a primary source of repayment. Banks hope to avoid foreclosing on collateral because foreclosure entails much time and expense. Collateral value should cover, in addition to the loan amount and interest due, the legal costs of foreclosure and interest during foreclosure proceedings. Collateral is the preferred secondary source of repayment.

Other secondary sources are guarantors and comakers. Collection from guarantors and comakers often requires expensive litigation and results in considerable ill will between the bank, borrower, and guarantor.

CREDIT INVESTIGATION

The purpose of credit investigation is to acquire enough information to determine the loan applicant's willingness and capacity to service the proposed loan. The investigation attempts to develop an understanding of the nature of the borrower in terms of the four basic credit factors just discussed: the borrower's character, the true purpose of the loan, and the primary and secondary sources of repayment. There are three fundamental sources of information: the customer, internal bank sources, and external sources available through institutions outside the bank.

Customer Interview

Ordinarily, the loan customer will provide the most important information needed in credit investigation. The prospective borrower should be expected to indicate the type and amount of loan requested, designate the proposed source and plan of repayment, identify the collateral or guarantors, name other previous and current creditors, list primary customers and trade suppliers, identify the firm's accountant, indicate the principal officers and shareholders, and give personal and business histories. The borrower also should provide documents needed in establishing the lending relationship, including such items as the latest three or more years of business financial statements, personal financial statements, borrowing authorities, evidence of insurance, and continuing guarantees.

Internal Sources of Information

If the loan customer has existing relationships with the bank, a great deal of information is available internally to the bank about the customer's willingness and capacity to service the proposed loan. The investigator should study credit files on any current or previous borrowings, examine checking account activity, and review other deposits previously or currently held. These sources will indicate the degree of the bank's satisfaction with past payment performance, and they may reveal tendencies for overdrawing deposit accounts. Also, these sources will identify primary customers, suppliers, and other creditors with whom the borrower has had financial transactions.

External Sources of Information

There are several service agencies that provide credit reporting on businesses and business principals.

Business Information Report, published by Dun and Bradstreet, summarizes the financial history and current payment status of businesses. This basic credit report provides a composite credit rating, describes the promptness of trade payments by the subject firm, and indicates the highest credit carried during the most recent year. Other details include balance sheet, sales and profit records, insurance coverage, lease obligations, biographical information on principals, the firm's history, and its recent business trends.

Credit Interchange Service of the National Association of Credit Management (NACM) is a national subscription service that provides information on a firm's current trade payment habits. The NACM sponsors local associations of trade suppliers and financial institutions, which share their credit listings and records on their payment experiences with businesses in their market areas.

Credit Bureaus are local, regional, and national organizations that produce pay-

TABLE 8-1
General Spread Form

GENERAL SPREAD FORM

NAME						
AUDITED STATEMENT						
STATEMENT DATE						
CASH						
MARKETABLE SECURITIES						
NOTES RECEIVABLE						
ACCOUNTS RECEIVABLE						
INVENTORY						
ALLOW. FOR DOUBT. ACCT.						
TOTAL CURRENT ASSETS						
FIXED ASSETS – NET						
NON-MARKETABLE SECURITIES						
NON-CURRENT RECEIVABLES						
PREPAID AND DEFERRED EXPENSES						
INTANGIBLES						
TOTAL NON-CURRENT ASSETS						
TOTAL ASSETS						
CURRENT MTY. OF TERM DEBT						
NOTES PAYABLE						
ACCOUNTS PAYABLE						
ACCRUED EXPENSE & MISC.						
INCOME TAX LIABILITY						
TOTAL CURRENT LIABILITIES						
SUBORDINATED DEBT						
TOTAL LIABILITIES						
MINORITY INTEREST						
DEFERRED INCOME / RESERVES						
TREASURY STOCK						
PREFERRED STOCK OUTSTANDING						
COMMON STOCK OUTSTANDING						
CAPITAL SURPLUS						
RETAINED EARNINGS (DEFICIT)						
NET WORTH						
TANGIBLE NET WORTH						
WORKING CAPITAL						
EXCESS CUR. ASSETS OVER TOT.LIAB.						
CURRENT RATIO						
CASH, MKT.SEC.& A/R TO CURR.LIAB.						
A/R COLLECTION PERIOD—DAYS						
NET SALES TO INVENTORY						
COST OF SALES TO INVENTORY						
INVENTORY TO WORKING CAPITAL						
SR. DEBT TO (TANG. N.W.& SUB. DEBT)						
NET PROFIT (LOSS) TO AVG. NET WORTH						

TABLE 8-2
Income Statement Analysis

NAME												
PERIOD COVERED (MONTHS)												
STATEMENT DATE												
NET SALES												
COST OF SALES												
GROSS PROFIT												
SELLING EXPENSES												
GENERAL & ADMINISTRATIVE EXP.												
TOTAL OPERATING EXPENSES												
OPERATING PROFIT												
OTHER INCOME (EXPENSE) — NET												
NET PROFIT (LOSS) BEFORE TAXES												
INCOME TAXES												
NET PROFIT (LOSS) AFTER TAXES												
ADDITIONAL DATA												
DIVIDENDS — PREFERRED STOCK												
DIVIDENDS—COM.STOCK or WITHDRAW												
OFFICER REMUNERATION												
INTEREST EXPENSE												
OTHER CHANGES IN WORTH												
CONTINGENT LIABILITIES												
LEASE OBLIGATIONS												
ANALYSIS OF CHANGES IN WORTH OR SURPLUS												
AT BEGINNING OF PERIOD												
ADD NET PROFIT												
DEDUCT DIVIDENDS OR WITHDRAW.												
WORTH OR SURPLUS REPORTED												
ANALYSIS OF WORKING CAPITAL												
AT BEGINNING OF PERIOD												
ADD: NET PROFIT												
NON-CASH CHARGES												
MISCELLANEOUS												
TOTAL ADDITIONS												
DEDUCT:												
DIVIDENDS/WITHDRAWALS												
PLANT EXPENDITURES												
MISCELLANEOUS												
TOTAL DEDUCTIONS												
NET CHANGE (+ OR −)												
AT END OF PERIOD												
W/C AS ABOVE												
INVENTORY												
EXCESS OF W/C OVER INVENTORY												
ANALYST INITIALS												

ment and employment information on individuals. Although this information source is generally used in connection with a consumer loan request, it may be used to obtain the payment history of principals in a business. Banks and other financial institutions are legitimate credit references and should be consulted. In the exchange of commercial credit information, bank officers are expected to govern themselves according to principles such as those set forth in the Robert Morris Associates Code of Ethics for the Exchange of Credit Information. The code describes ethical standards for confidentiality and accuracy in making and replying to credit inquiries.

A variety of commercial publications provide descriptive written and statistical information. These include Moody's, *Polk's City Directories*, Standard and Poors, *Thomas Register*, and other special purpose directories. Articles on individual firms or industries are published in many trade publications and may be found through the *Business Periodical Index* at any library. Official public information sources include filings of titles and mortgages, registration of corporation status, and business licenses.

Spread Sheets and Statement Spreading

Bankers generally use so-called spread sheets for recording a credit applicant's financial information (see Tables 8-1 and 8-2). Spread sheets permit the analyst to organize financial data in a consistent manner. This frequently requires that certain data submitted by the applicant be reclassified to match the bank's purposes. For example, an item included as a current asset in the applicant's statement might be reclassified as noncurrent on the spread sheet if the credit analyst has doubts about its liquidity. An example of such an item might be a note due from one of the business's officers or principals.

The spread sheet is arranged to allow easy comparison of current and historical trends and is readily updated as the columns are completed from left to right.

Columns are provided for common size ratios for each balance sheet and income statement account. Space is provided for several key financial ratios and for analysis of changes in net worth and working capital. Supplementary forms are often used to enter a time series of other key ratios.

Credit Analysis Rationale: A Case Example

The calculation of financial ratios provides the basis of most technical, quantitative credit analysis. For the uninitiated reader, Appendix 8A contains a review of some commonly used financial ratios. This section demonstrates, through a simple case example, the kind of analytical reasoning used in credit evaluation. Tables 8-3, 8-4, and 8-5 present, respectively, balance sheets, income statements, and key financial ratios for three years' for a small television and appliance retailer. In addition, each table includes the most recent comparable data on a local competitor and on the sample of TV and appliance retailers from Robert Morris Associates' (RMA) *Statement Studies*.

Even a cursory look at the common size balance sheets and income statements reveals a great deal about the character of the loan applicant's business. Table 8-3 shows that the firm's accounts receivable make up only 14 percent of its assets in 1983 compared with 19 percent for its local competitor and 21 percent for the RMA firms. From this comparative data, the firm appears to have good control of its credit sales. By the

TABLE 8-3
TV and Appliance Retailer—Comparative Balance Sheet (dollars in thousands)

	12/31/81	Percentage of total assets	12/31/82	Percentage of total assets	12/31/83	Percentage of total assets	Local competitor 1983	RMA
Assets								
Cash	$ 11	6%	$ 12	5%	$ 16	6%	5%	11%
Accounts receivable	22	13	48	21	41	14	19	21
Inventory	122	69	147	65	203	72	66	46
Total current assets	155	88	207	91	260	92	90	78
Net fixed assets	21	12	21	9	24	8	10	22
Total assets	$176	100	$228	100	$284	100	100	100
Liability and Equity								
Accounts payable	$ 16	9%	$ 10	4%	$ 4	1%	2%	12%
Flooring finance	112	64	127	56	149	53	63	34
Total current liabilities	128	73	137	60	153	54	65	46
Long-term debt	23	13	57	25	90	33	8	10
Total equity	25	14	34	15	37	13	27	44
Total liabilities and equity	$176	100	$228	100	$284	100	100	100

TABLE 8-4
TV and Appliance Retailer—Comparative Statement of Income (dollars in thousands)

	1981	Percentage of total income	1982	Percentage of total income	1983	Percentage of total income	Local competitor 1983	RMA
Income	713.4	100.0%	866.2	100.0%	911.7	100.0%	100.0%	100.0%
Less: Cost of sales	592.2	83.0	706.2	81.5	745.1	81.7	70.5	71.3
Gross profit	121.2	17.0	160.0	18.5	166.6	18.3	29.5	28.7
Operating Expenses								
Wages and salaries	46.4	6.5	60.1	6.9	54.7	6.0	17.7	
Sales expense	19.6	2.7	24.3	2.8	39.7	4.4	4.2	25.2
Other operating expense	30.0	4.2	41.6	4.8	42.1	4.6	4.1	
Operating profit	25.2	3.5	34.0	3.9	30.1	3.3	3.5	3.5
All Other Expenses	15.9	2.2	21.3	2.5	22.9	2.5	0.5	0.7
Profit before taxes	9.3	1.3	12.7	1.5	7.2	0.8	3.0	2.8
Income taxes	2.4	0.3	3.9	0.5	4.4	0.5	0.4	—
Net income	6.9	1.0	8.8	1.0	2.8	0.3	2.6	2.8

TABLE 8-5
TV and Appliance Retailer—Financial Ratio Analysis

	1981	1982	1983	Local competitor	RMA
Liquidity					
Current	1.2	1.5	1.7	1.4	1.7
Quick	0.3	0.4	0.4	0.4	0.7
Leverage					
Debt to total assets	0.86	0.85	0.87	0.72	0.54
Interest coverage	1.7	2.0	1.2	2.6	3.5
Fixed charge coverage	1.4	1.5	1.1	2.3	N/A
Activity					
Inventory turnover	5.4×	5.2×	4.3×	4.9×	5.7×
Average collection period (days)	14	15	18	20	27
Fixed assets turnover	34×	41×	39×	30×	13×
Cash-to-cash cycle (days)	87	90	109	101	98
Profitability					
Profit margin on sales	1.0%	1.0%	0.3%	2.6%	2.8%
Return on (average) total assets	4.6%	4.6%	1.1%	7.4%	6.8%
Return on (average) net worth	32.6%	29.8%	7.9%	26.2%	17.5%

same type of reasoning, the firm appears to be overinvested in inventory, which represents 72 percent of its assets versus 66 percent for the local competitor and 46 percent for RMA firms. This suggests that the firm stocks slow moving items or a more complicated product mix or both. On the other hand, in relation to others, the firm has less invested in fixed assets.

The firm's funds come predominantly from floor plan and long-term debt. Both categories of debt far exceed in importance the same sources for RMA firms, although the local competitor firm relies even more heavily on floor plan debt. The applicant's accounts payable appear to be relatively small for this line of business and suggest little conflict with trade creditors. The firm's equity base is dramatically smaller than those of other firms, offering much less protection to its creditors.

Table 8-4 shows the firm's 1983 cost of sales in relation to total income was 81.7 percent, compared with a cost of sales in the 70 percent range for other firms. In this retail business, an unusually high cost of sales suggests the likelihood of underpricing, that is, the use of price cutting as a sales tool. Operating expenses, consisting of the sum of wages and salaries, sales expense, and other operating expense, totaled only 15 percent of income in 1983, compared with 26 percent for the local competitor and 25 percent for RMA firms. This indicates an exceptionally low-cost operation capable of supporting somewhat lower product prices. Unfortunately, all other (nonoperating) expenses nearly wiped out the firm's remaining revenues, so that the net income compared unfavorably with those of other firms.

It is obvious that the common size balance sheet and income statement highlight some key differences among firms in a similar line of business. However, common size ratios occasionally are misleading. If one asset account is grossly large, other asset accounts appear relatively small in ratio terms. For example, it is possible for a firm's total assets to be so inflated by gross overinvestment in, say, fixed assets that all other asset proportions, such as the inventory common ratio, are dwarfed and falsely appear insufficient. Thus, liquidity, leverage, activity, and profitability ratios are necessary to complete a clear analytical picture.

Table 8-5 shows that the firm's current ratio of 1.7 is in line with that of the Robert Morris firms and exceeds that of the local competitor. However, the firm's quick ratio of 0.4 is well below the Robert Morris quick ratio. Together, the current and quick ratios indicate that the firm's balance sheet liquidity depends predominantly on inventory. If inventory is obsolete or otherwise not readily marketable, the firm would have great difficulty meeting its short-term obligations. It should be noted that there is no provision for the current portion of long-term debt, a current liability. If a portion of long-term debt is to be repaid currently, the firm's liquidity would be further squeezed.

The firm's 1983 debt ratio of 0.87 indicates that, in relation to its peers, it offers a very small equity cushion for its creditors. Only 13 percent of its funds come from its owners whereas 28 percent of its local competitor's funds and 46 percent of RMA firm funds come from owners. The 1983 interest coverage ratio of 1.2 and the fixed charge ratio of 1.1 are far short of the comparative ratios. This indicates insufficient earnings or excessive interest payments or a combination of these two factors.

Inventory turnover of 4.3 in 1983 for the firm compares unfavorably with 4.9 for the local competitor and 5.7 for RMA firms, again suggesting excessive investment in inventory. A similarly unfavorable comparison exists for the firm's 109 days cash-to-cash cycle versus 101 days and 98 days, respectively, for its competitor and the RMA firms. This factor, when considered along with the firm's favorable average collection period of 18 days, is further indicative of an abnormally large inventory; specifically, the short average collection period demonstrates that receivables are not the cause of the long cash-to-cash cycle and implies that the cause is too much inventory. The firm's fixed asset turnover of 39 compared with 30 and 13 for its peers indicates that relatively little is invested in illiquid buildings and equipment.

Table 8-5 shows that the firm's profitability lags far behind that of its peers. Its return on sales of 1.0, 1.0, and 0.3 percent for the last three years compares with its competitor's 2.6 percent and the RMA firms' 2.8 percent. As determined from its common size income statement, this poor performance is due to the extreme underpricing of its merchandise. A similarly unfavorable return on assets, bottoming out at 1.1 percent in 1983, further reflects poor earnings and may indicate excessive investment in assets, particularly inventory. Despite poor earnings performance, the firm's return on net worth figures for 1981 and 1982 are biased upward, in relation to those of its peers, because of the small amount of equity in the firm (the denominator in the return on net worth ratio). If the firm operates at a loss in the future, its return on net worth would be dramatically biased negatively by the small amount of equity.

Financial analysis alone is not always sufficient to determine the credit worthiness of a firm. As a loan applicant, the firm would have to provide additional information such as the purpose of the loan and how the loan would affect the financial statements and ratios. However, the previous evidence indicates that the historical earnings, liquidity, inventory management, pricing, and equity support of the firm are all deficient. In the case of the TV and appliance retailer, financial analysis creates substantial doubts about the advisability of extending credit to the firm.

WORKING CAPITAL ANALYSIS AND FINANCIAL PROJECTIONS

Concept of Net Working Capital

Historically, the major role of banks in commercial lending has been to finance nonpermanent additions to working capital, defined simply as all current assets. Such additions enable a business to increase its cash balances and inventory in anticipation of seasonal bulges in sales and to temporarily extend larger amounts of credit to its customers as an aftereffect of such sales. Working capital loans are said to be self-liquidating because repayment occurs with an orderly reduction in inventories as sales rise, followed by reductions in receivables after collections are made on credit sales. The repayment of these traditional commercial loans is largely independent of long-term profitability and long-term cash flows.

The measure known as *net* working capital, defined as current assets minus current liabilities, indicates the amount of a firm's working capital that is financed by long-term or so-called *permanent* sources of funds.[1] This relationship is illustrated in Figure 8-1. The assets and the liabilities/net worth sides of the balance sheet are represented by two bars. Each bar is divided into short-term and long-term items. Net working capital is a good indicator of a firm's liquidity because it identifies the part of a firm's most liquid assets that is supported by reliable (long-term) funds, that is, it is the amount of current assets that is not subject to claims by holders of current liabilities. As such, it indicates the ability of a firm to meet its short-term debt obligations. Everything else being equal, a loan officer would be more confident in a borrower with a large net working capital position than one with little net working capital.

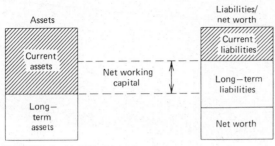

FIGURE 8-1 Net Working Capital

[1] In practice, net working capital is often incorrectly called, simply, working capital.

Sources and Uses of Funds Analysis

In evaluating a working capital loan proposal, it is not enough simply to determine a borrower's net working capital position for one historic point in time. The loan officer should attempt to understand the dynamics in the borrower's balance sheet as seasonal activity ebbs and flows. Historical comparisons of the firm's balance sheet in a base period with its balance sheet during peak business activity will demonstrate how working capital is provided and used in operation. Table 8-6 shows comparative January 1983 and June 1983 balance sheets for a wholesaler of garden supplies whose sales and funds requirements usually peak in June. The differences between January 1983 and June 1983 in each account are recorded at the right as either a source or a use of funds. Decreases in assets and increases in liabilities constitute sources of funds, whereas increases in assets and decreases in liabilities are uses of funds.

In the case of Garden Wholesalers, the net working capital hardly improved at all from January to June 1983. A total of $535,000 was used for a net increase in current assets ($550,000 in uses and $15,000 in sources) of which $525,000, or nearly all of it, was financed by increases in current liabilities. Nearly three fourths of the increased current liabilities was provided by bank funds in the form of $385,000 in notes payable and a little over one fourth was provided by trade credit in the form of $140,000 new accounts payable to suppliers. Garden Wholesalers' cash flows from depreciation (as-

TABLE 8-6
Comparative Balance Sheets—Sources and Uses
of Funds for Garden Wholesalers (dollars in thousands)

	January 1983	June 1983	January to June Sources	Uses
Assets				
Cash	30	15	15	—
Accounts receivable	150	450	—	300
Inventory	300	550	—	250
Current assets	480	1015	15	550
Net fixed assets	180	175	5	—
Total assets	660	1190		
Liabilities and Net Worth				
Accounts payable	60	200	140	—
Notes payable	0	385	385	—
Current liabilities	60	585	525	0
Long-term debt	200	190	—	10
Common stock	50	50	—	—
Retained earnings	350	365	15	—
Total liabilities and net worth	660	1190		
Total sources and uses			560	560

sumed to be $5,000) and retained earnings were rather insignificant sources of funds for financing additions to working capital.

Financial Projections

The sources and uses of funds analysis can also be used to make simple financial projections. Suppose that in the following January, Garden Wholesalers' bank attempts to determine the firm's need for funds for the peak of the coming season. The loan officer should review all of the factors affecting sales and funds flows, including economic conditions, industry and local market conditions, the impact of potential regulation, and the characteristics of the firm's operation. From these factors it can be determined that by June 1984 receivables will increase by $425,000, inventories by $350,000, and accounts payable by $230,000. Also, a $100,000 addition to fixed assets, $5,000 in depreciation, and $20,000 in retained earnings will occur. Finally, an estimate of change in cash balances and a partial repayment of long-term debt are included. Table 8-7

TABLE 8-7
Financial Projection—New Funds Requirements for Garden Wholesale (dollars in thousands)

	January 31, 1984	June 30, 1984 (projected) Sources	June 30, 1984 (projected) Uses	January to June 1984, sources and uses (projected)
Assets				
Cash	30	—	—	30
Accounts receivable	175	—	425	600
Inventory	350	—	350	700
Current assets	555	0	775	1330
Net fixed assets	170	5	100	265
Total assets	725			1595
Liabilities and Net Worth				
Accounts payable	70	230	—	300
Notes payable	45	? 575	45	575
Current liabilities	115	230 100		875
Long-term debt	180	?	10	270
Common stock	50	—	—	50
Retained earnings	380	20	—	400
Total liabilities and net worth	725	255	930	1595

930
−255
675
New funds needed to balance

| **Net Working Capital** | 440 | | | 455 |

shows that, starting with the end of January 1984 balance sheet, the forecasted uses exceed the forecasted sources, indicating a need for new external funds of $675,000 (including refinancing of January's notes payable). The sources of the new funds are assumed to be a $575,000 bank loan and a $100,000 addition to long-term debt; the latter is considered to be the source of financing of the addition to fixed assets. Net working capital will increase nominally from $440,000 to $445,000.

A more detailed projection is probably warranted in the form of a cash budget. Preparation of a cash budget requires projecting specific cash inflows and cash disbursements on a monthly or even more frequent basis. The cash budget more closely identifies the amounts and timing of specific draws against a credit line extended by a bank or, alternatively, it identifies periods of excess cash where short-term money market investments can be considered.

Table 8-8 shows a monthly cash budget for Garden Wholesalers' for the same period covered in the balance sheet projection of Table 8-7. The cash budget is divided into three parts: cash inflows, cash disbursements, and a cash and loan summary. It projects monthly additions to and subtractions from the firm's balances and reflects bank borrowings to replenish cash balances. Note that the June cash balance and bank loan agree with their respective accounts on the pro forma June 1984 balance sheet in Table 8-7. In addition, the cash budget directly reflects transactions indicated in the sources and uses analysis in Table 8-7 such as the long-term debt repayment, issuance of new bonds, and payments on the addition to fixed assets. Still other cash budget entries are more directly related to the pro forma income statement, and the sum of every month's profit or loss is ultimately reflected in pro forma additions to retained earnings of $20,000, shown in Table 8-7.

TABLE 8-8
Cash Budget for 1984—Garden Wholesalers (dollars in thousands)

	February	March	April	May	June
Cash Inflows					
Collections	100	75	265	369	476
Issue bonds	—	100	—	—	—
Cash Disbursements					
Accounts payable	70	110	150	200	220
Operating expenses	20	20	20	20	20
Wages	100	130	180	250	300
Taxes paid	—	—	23	—	22
Repayment on long-term debt	—	—	—	10	—
Additions to fixed assets	—	50	—	—	50
Cash and Loan Summary					
Net inflow (outflow)	(90)	(135)	(58)	(111)	(136)
Beginning cash	30	30	20	22	26
Loan increase (repayment)	90	125	60	115	140
Accumulated loan	135	260	320	435	575
Ending cash	30	20	22	26	30

The pro forma income statement is not shown, but most of its ingredients are implicit in the sources and uses balance sheet projections and the monthly cash budget. Sales for January 31 to June 30, 1984, are not shown in the previous example, although they generally lead the cash collections shown in Table 8-8 by a more or less regular time period. The firm's cost of goods sold can be derived from the beginning inventory level plus additions to inventory minus ending inventory. Additions to inventory usually can be derived from purchases plus employee wages. Operating expenses and taxes constitute other expense items. The aggregate of sales, cost of goods sold, and other expense items provide the information needed to develop a pro forma income statement that is consistent with the pro forma balance sheet and cash budget.

Long-Term Financial Requirements

The principle of sources and uses of funds analysis to obtain balance sheet projections is as valid for long-term as it is for short-term estimates of funds requirements. For long-term purposes, however, the emphasis is on overall financial needs and not simply on the financing of temporary additions to working capital. The approach is to project the balance sheet for some future period—say, three to five years from the present. The differences between the future and present accounts indicate how funds will be used (invested) in the interim and determine how much external financing will be required. The future balance sheet is established using at least two kinds of data. First, discrete planning data are usually given, such as a planned dollar amount to be invested in new equipment or plant expansion. The second kind of data are derived by relating certain balance sheet accounts to key planning variables. For example, receivables and inventories may be a percentage of the sales anticipated in the future period. The ratios used to relate an account to sales may be derived from the firm's experience or may be equal to known norms in the firm's industry, such as those given in the Robert Morris *Statement Studies*.

To illustrate, in Table 8-9 we have constructed a balance sheet for three years hence for a manufacturer for June 1986, taking the actual June 1983 balance sheet as a base. The following guidelines are applied:

1 Sales will be $4.8 million during each of the next three years.

2 Minimum cash should be $50,000.

3 Receivables should be sales for 60 days (2 months).

4 Inventories will turn over three times. Inventories are valued at the cost of goods, which will be 80 percent of sales.

5 Additions to fixed assets will total $500,000. Depreciation will be $50,000 per year.

6 Accounts payable will be equal to one fourth of inventories.

7 Existing long-term debt will be retired at a rate of $100,000 per year.

8 After tax profits will total 5 percent of sales each year. Forty percent of profits will be paid out in dividends.

9 Net working capital must be at least $1.2 million.

TABLE 8-9
Three-Year Balance Sheet Projection for a Manufacturing Firm (dollars in thousands)

	June 1983	June 1986	Sources	Uses
Assets				
Cash	70	50	20	—
Accounts receivable	700	800	—	100
Inventory	850	1280	—	430
Current assets	1620	2130		
Fixed assets				
Gross	1800	2300	—	500
Accumulated depreciation	(300)	(450)	150	—
Net fixed assets	1500	1850		
Total assets	3120	3980		
Liabilities and Net Worth				
Accounts payable	250	320	70	—
Notes payable	300	610	310	—
Current liabilities	550	930		
Long-term debt (old)	1300	1000	—	300
Long-term debt (new)	—	348	348	—
Total long-term debt	1300	1348		
Common stock	200	200	—	—
Retained earnings	1070	1502	432	—
Total liabilities and net worth	3120	3980		
Total sources and uses			1330	1330

Each June 1986 balance sheet account is derived either explicitly or implicitly from the guidelines. The explicit derivations are as follows:

1 Cash = $50,000 as specified

2 Accounts receivable = $\dfrac{2 \text{ months}}{12 \text{ months/year}} \times \$4.8 \text{ million sales}$

= $800,000

3 Inventory = 0.80 × $4.8 million sales/3 × turnover

= $1.28 million

4 Net fixed assets = $1.5 million (June 1983) + $500,000 additions
− $50,000 depreciation × 3 years

= $1.85 million

5 Accounts payable = $1.28 million inventory × ¼

= $320,000

6   Notes payable =   \$2.13 million current assets − \$320,000 payables − \$1.2 million required net working capital

           =   <u>\$610,000</u>

7   Total long-term debt =   plug figure to balance the balance sheet after deducting \$100,000 × 3-years of old debt retirement

8   Retained earnings =   \$1.07 million (June 1983)
                      + 0.05 aftertax profit × \$4.8 million sales
                      × 3 years × 0.6 retention rate

           =   <u>\$1.502 million</u>

The sources and uses data in Table 8-9 reveal a lot about the financial dynamics of the firm over the coming three-year period. One debatable issue is the allocation of new debt between bank loans (notes payable) and new long-term debt. If the additions to working capital are considered permanent, the firm's banker might consider financing part or all of it through term lending in the future, or the banker might urge that other long-term sources be tapped such as the bond market.

SUMMARY

Well-managed banks carefully assess the risk they incur in lending to a business borrower. They investigate the borrower's credit background, ascertain the reason for borrowing, and usually identify a source of repayment that is related to the successful business operations of the borrower.

Credit analysis requires the cooperation of the borrower and of informants both inside and outside the bank. Subjective judgment must be used in evaluating a borrower's trustworthiness and, therefore, his or her moral commitment to repay the loan as agreed on.

The borrower's *ability* to repay is mostly a matter of financial analysis. Historical financial analysis is two-dimensional. Time series analysis is used to spot evolving financial strengths and weaknesses with the perspective of the passage of time. Cross-sectional analysis permits the analyst to determine how effectively the borrower has performed in relation to other firms with like market opportunities and risks.

Fund flow analysis demonstrates the dynamic fund needs of the firm. Its use in financial projections provides a comprehensive view of the future and gives the analyst a reality check against the borrower's request.

Chapter 9 discusses commercial loan negotiation and reviews the considerations that determine the terms and structure of the loan.

Appendix 8A   Financial Ratio Analysis

The more technical part of credit analysis and its use in making loan decisions has to do with concrete methods of analysis of financial statements. These methods of analysis generally rely on financial ratios calculated from various combinations of balance sheet and income statements accounts. Financial ratios may relate balance sheet accounts to each other, relate income statement accounts to each other, or cross-relate balance sheet and income statement accounts. Financial ratios are usually separated into categories based on the intended purpose or characteristics of the firm. The following are five frequently used classifications:

1   Common size ratios.
2   Profitability ratios.
3   Liquidity (short-term solvency) ratios.
4   Financial leverage (long-term solvency) ratios.
5   Activity or turnover ratios.

Short-term lenders are concerned foremost with liquidity ratios and, to a lesser extent, with activity ratios. Long-term lenders are mainly interested in profitability and financial leverage ratios.

Common size ratios are perhaps the simplest form of financial ratios. They express each balance sheet account as a percentage of total assets and each income statement account as a percentage of total revenue to create *common size statements*. The purpose of common size statements is to reduce firms of different size to a common basis and reveal underlying differences in their allocation of assets, sources of funds, and expenses.

Profitability ratios give the relationship of a firm's profitability in relation to some investment base or to net sales. They attempt to measure the overall operational efficiency of the firm's management. The following three ratios are most commonly used, although many others can be constructed.

$$\text{Return on equity} = \frac{\text{Net income available to common stock}}{\text{Common stock equity}}$$

This ratio is a summary measure of how effectively common stockholders' funds have been employed, including the effectiveness of the use of financial leverage. The numerator is aftertax income less any preferred dividends. The denominator is the average of balance sheet equity over the period of income and is usually derived by averaging the equity of the beginning and ending of the period.

$$\text{Return on assets} = \frac{\text{Net income after tax}}{\text{Average total assets}}$$

This measure indicates the efficiency with which management employed the total capital resources available to it. It is a better measure of operating performance than return on equity because the latter is affected by the degree of financial leverage. The denominator can be formed by averaging the beginning and ending values of total assets.

$$\text{Profit margin} = \frac{\text{Net income after tax}}{\text{Net sales}}$$

This ratio measures the profit per dollar of net sales. Its complement $(1-\text{profit margin})$ indicates the expense incurred to generate \$1 of revenue and reveals the effectiveness of cost controls or of pricing policies.

Liquidity ratios indicate the firm's capacity for meeting its short-term liabilities as they become due. Two ratios are usually evaluated.

$$\text{Current ratio} = \frac{\text{Current assets}}{\text{Current liabilities}}$$

This ratio indicates the extent to which the claims of short-term creditors are covered by assets that can be readily converted into cash without loss. High values of the current ratios suggest a high margin of safety for short-term creditors. However, the ratio does not consider the quality of receivables and inventories.

$$\text{Quick (acid text) ratio} = \frac{\text{Current assets} - \text{inventories}}{\text{Current liabilities}}$$

Concern over the quality or liquidity of inventories is purged in the quick ratio. Only the "quick assets" of cash, marketable securities, and receivables are included. For many industries in which inventory values may be suspect, the quick ratio is a more reliable measure of liquidity than the current ratio.

Because of their role as short-term lenders, banks have sought more reliable measures of liquidity than the static data reflected in the current and quick ratios. One such measure is the *cash flow interval ratio*, which relates quick assets to the firm's daily operating expenditures and other known cash disbursements. It indicates the days of net funds expenditures covered by quick assets. The cash budget, discussed in the text of this chapter, can be used in its daily form to derive daily cash disbursements.

Financial leverage ratios indicate (1) the degree to which creditors, rather than owners, are financing a firm and (2) the firm's ability to meet long-term interest and principle payments on debt. From a lender's viewpoint, the amount of equity represents a cushion against operating losses or against a decline in the value of the firm's assets. As a result, lenders prefer to hold financial leverage within safe limits. On the other hand, the use of debt permits owners to control a firm with less personal investment. Assuming that borrowed funds can be invested to earn a rate of return greater than their cost, owner's are motivated to increase financial leverage. Three ratios are commonly used to analyze the degree of financial leverage.

$$\text{Debt ratio} = \frac{\text{Total debt}}{\text{Total assets}}$$

The debt ratio represents the portion of assets being financed by creditors. It is a measure of the financial risk of the firm. Generally, the more debt in the firm's financial structure, the more volatile its earnings and the greater the risk to owners and creditors.

$$\text{Interest coverage ratio} = \frac{\text{Pretax income plus interest}}{\text{Interest expenses}}$$

This ratio indicates the margin of safety that earnings provide creditors in relation to interest charges. A more liberal measure that is sometimes of value includes depreciation in the numerator to reflect the coverage provided by total cash flow.

$$\text{Fixed charged coverage ratio} = \frac{\text{Pretax income plus interest plus lease payments}}{\text{Interest plus lease expenses}}$$

This measure simply extends the interest coverage ratio to account for contractual commitments under leasing agreements. Here again, depreciation may be added to the numerator to obtain the coverage of fixed charges by cash flow and not just income. In both types of coverage ratios, the cyclical volatility of earnings must be analyzed to determine the appropriate coverage multiple.

Activity ratios indicate the intensity of use of various assets in achieving a given sales level. In effect, they test for the operating efficiency of specific groups of assets. We will next discuss four of the more widely used activity ratios.

$$\text{Average collection period} = \frac{\text{Accounts receivable}}{\text{Sales per day}}$$

$$= \frac{\text{Accounts receivable}}{\text{Net sales (annual)}/365 \text{ days}}$$

When compared with the credit policy and terms granted by the firm, this ratio measures the quality of credit extended and the effectiveness of collections. It indicates, on average, the time the firm must wait to collect after making a sale. Another important analysis of accounts receivable is the receivables' aging schedule, which classifies the proportions of receivables according to the period of time they have been outstanding, such as 1 to 30 days, 31 to 60 days, and over 60 days. The average collection period and the aging schedule together indicate the degree of liquidity of receivables. Relatively short collection periods combined with an aging schedule with very few overdue accounts suggest liquid and high-quality receivables.

$$\text{Inventory turnover ratio} = \frac{\text{Cost of sales (annual)}}{\text{Average inventory}}$$

This ratio indicates the effectiveness of management's inventory controls. It measures the number of times per year that the firm rolls over its entire investment in inventory. If the turnover of inventory is too high, it may indicate a less-than-optimal inventory level, which could result in stockouts and lost sales. A too-low turnover may indicate poor purchasing, production, and handling controls or obsolete merchandise. The cost of sales is used in the numerator since inventory is usually valued at cost.

$$\text{Fixed asset turnover} = \frac{\text{Net sales}}{\text{Average net fixed assets}}$$

Fixed asset utilization is measured by the rate at which the product value flows

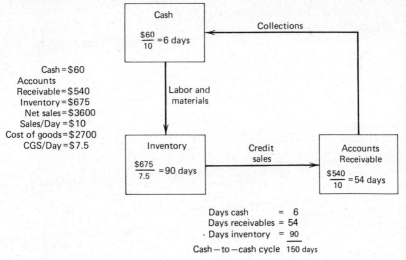

FIGURE 8A-1 Cash-to-Cash Cycle

through the firm's plant and equipment. Low rates of flow or turnover indicate below-capacity operations; a high rate of flow may reflect inadequate investment in plant and equipment. Differences in depreciation policies distort this ratio so that appropriate adjustments must be considered.

$$\text{Cash to cash cycle} = \frac{\text{Average cash}}{\text{Net sales per day}} + \text{Average collection period}$$

$$+ \frac{\text{Average inventory}}{\text{Cost of sales per day}}$$

This ratio measures the turnover rate of working capital. As shown in Figure 8A-1, it represents the time required for a single dollar to move through the working capital cycle. Conceptually, funds are invested first in operating cash balances, then converted to inventories by means of purchases of labor and material, then transformed into receivables as inventory is sold on credit, and finally returned to cash as receivables are collected.

SOURCES OF COMPARATIVE FINANCIAL DATA

Unfortunately, financial ratios cannot be analyzed easily in isolation because there are no reliable *absolute* standards for their values. Rather, financial ratios are analyzed in two basic comparative modes: cross sectional and time series. Cross-sectional analysis is concerned with comparing the firm's ratios with peer firms in its industry for a common period or point in time. This section mainly discusses cross-sectional analysis and the use of comparative financial data of similar firms.

TABLE 8A-1 Industry Statistics for Retailers–Family Clothing

RETAILERS - FAMILY CLOTHING
SIC# 5651

Current Data						Comparative Historical Data				
62(6/30-9/30/81)		**114(10/1/81-3/31/82)**				6/30/77-3/31/78	6/30/78-3/31/79	6/30/79-3/31/80	6/30/80-3/31/81	6/30/81-3/31/82
0-1MM	1-10MM	10-50MM	50-100MM	ALL	ASSET SIZE	ALL	ALL	ALL	ALL	ALL
110	57	6	3	176	NUMBER OF STATEMENTS	164	158	156	185	176
%	%	%	%	%	**ASSETS**	%	%	%	%	%
8.1	9.4			8.4	Cash & Equivalents	8.5	8.5	8.6	8.9	8.4
13.2	15.6			14.4	Accts. & Notes Rec. - Trade(net)	15.2	14.5	14.4	14.0	14.4
54.8	49.4			52.2	Inventory	52.1	53.9	51.6	51.9	52.2
1.5	1.3			1.4	All Other Current	1.7	1.1	1.6	1.1	1.4
77.6	75.7			76.4	Total Current	77.5	78.0	76.2	75.9	76.4
16.8	17.6			17.6	Fixed Assets (net)	17.3	17.4	18.2	17.3	17.6
.8	1.1			.8	Intangibles (net)	.4	.4	.7	1.0	.8
4.8	5.6			5.2	All Other Non-Current	4.8	4.2	5.0	5.8	5.2
100.0	100.0			100.0	Total	100.0	100.0	100.0	100.0	100.0
					LIABILITIES					
10.4	11.3			10.6	Notes Payable-Short Term	9.9	10.5	9.9	9.5	10.6
3.9	2.4			3.4	Cur. Mat.-L/T/D	2.8	3.3	4.0	3.0	3.4
16.6	17.0			16.6	Accts. & Notes Payable - Trade	16.1	17.1	15.2	16.2	16.6
5.2	6.2			5.5	Accrued Expenses	4.9	5.6	5.5	6.1	5.5
3.5	3.1			3.4	All Other Current	3.0	3.7	3.6	3.4	3.4
39.6	40.1			39.5	Total Current	36.8	40.3	38.1	38.4	39.5
14.0	12.3			14.3	Long Term Debt	16.4	15.4	16.7	15.2	14.3
2.4	2.1			2.4	All Other Non-Current	.8	2.2	1.3	2.2	2.4
44.0	45.5			43.8	Net Worth	46.1	42.1	43.9	44.2	43.8
100.0	100.0			100.0	Total Liabilities & Net Worth	100.0	100.0	100.0	100.0	100.0
					INCOME DATA					
100.0	100.0			100.0	Net Sales	100.0	100.0	100.0	100.0	100.0
61.8	58.9			60.7	Cost Of Sales	61.3	61.2	59.7	60.7	60.7
38.2	41.1			39.3	Gross Profit	38.7	38.8	40.3	39.3	39.3
33.1	38.0			34.7	Operating Expenses	34.7	35.5	37.1	35.2	34.7
5.1	3.1			4.6	Operating Profit	4.0	3.4	3.3	4.1	4.6
1.8	.5			1.4	All Other Expenses (net)	.5	-.9	.3	.9	1.4
3.3	2.6			3.1	Profit Before Taxes	3.4	4.3	2.9	3.2	3.1
					RATIOS					
3.2 / 2.0 / 1.5	2.4 / 1.9 / 1.5			3.0 / 2.0 / 1.5	Current	3.3 / 2.2 / 1.6	3.0 / 2.0 / 1.5	3.0 / 2.1 / 1.5	2.9 / 2.0 / 1.5	3.0 / 2.0 / 1.5
(109) 1.0 / .4 / .2	1.2 / .6 / .2		(175) 1.1 / .5 / .2		Quick	(163) 1.2 / .6 / .2	1.1 / .6 / .2	1.1 / .6 / .2	(184) 1.1 / .6 / .2	(175) 1.1 / .5 / .2
1 398.6 / 10 36.2 / 40 9.1	1 692.2 / 23 15.7 / 47 7.8			1 329.9 / 12 29.7 / 45 8.1	Sales/Receivables	1 390.7 / 13 27.5 / 48 7.6	2 228.1 / 16 23.3 / 46 7.9	2 199.3 / 15 24.3 / 43 8.4	2 225.4 / 12 30.1 / 42 8.6	1 329.9 / 12 29.7 / 45 8.1
107 3.4 / 146 2.5 / 228 1.6	101 3.6 / 135 2.7 / 174 2.1			107 3.4 / 135 2.7 / 203 1.8	Cost of Sales/Inventory	101 3.4 / 140 2.6 / 192 1.9	101 3.6 / 140 2.6 / 192 1.9	101 3.6 / 135 2.7 / 192 1.9	101 3.6 / 130 2.8 / 192 1.9	107 3.4 / 135 2.7 / 203 1.8
3.4 / 5.7 / 10.6	4.3 / 5.7 / 9.4			3.6 / 5.6 / 9.5	Sales/Working Capital	3.7 / 4.9 / 9.4	3.9 / 5.8 / 10.4	3.8 / 5.4 / 9.3	4.3 / 6.1 / 10.5	3.6 / 5.6 / 9.5
(97) 5.4 / 2.5 / 1.2	(44) 4.3 / 2.0 / 1.0		(149) 5.2 / 2.4 / 1.2		EBIT/Interest	(132) 8.3 / 3.5 / 1.7	8.7 / 3.7 / 1.4	(127) 8.7 / 3.7 / 1.4 ... (126) 6.5 / 2.7 / 1.3	(149) 5.8 / 2.5 / 1.2	(149) 5.2 / 2.4 / 1.2
(40) 3.8 / 1.8 / .8	(30) 6.3 / 2.0 / .4		(77) 4.7 / 2.0 / .6		Cash Flow/Cur. Mat. L/T/D	(69) 5.8 / 2.2 / .9	(66) 8.8 / 3.3 / 1.2	(72) 3.8 / 1.9 / .8	(79) 4.3 / 2.1 / .8	(77) 4.7 / 2.0 / .6
.1 / .3 / .7	.2 / .4 / .7			.2 / .4 / .7	Fixed/Worth	.2 / .3 / .6	.2 / .4 / .6	.1 / .4 / .6	.2 / .4 / .8	.2 / .4 / .7
.6 / 1.3 / 2.7	.7 / 1.4 / 2.2			.7 / 1.4 / 2.6	Debt/Worth	.6 / 1.1 / 2.4	.7 / 1.4 / 2.7	.6 / 1.2 / 2.4	.7 / 1.2 / 2.5	.7 / 1.4 / 2.6
(106) 32.7 / 14.7 / 1.9	22.8 / 8.8 / 1.0		(172) 30.3 / 13.7 / 1.9		% Profit Before Taxes/Tangible Net Worth	(161) 30.4 / 14.2 / 5.6	(154) 30.7 / 14.8 / 3.8	(151) 28.9 / 14.1 / 3.7	(181) 30.2 / 16.0 / 3.2	(172) 30.3 / 13.7 / 1.9
13.1 / 5.6 / 1.0	9.4 / 4.9 / .3			12.1 / 5.3 / .9	% Profit Before Taxes/Total Assets	13.8 / 6.2 / 1.9	13.0 / 6.2 / 1.5	13.1 / 6.2 / 1.1	13.6 / 6.4 / 1.2	12.1 / 5.3 / .9
46.1 / 19.9 / 11.0	27.5 / 15.5 / 8.7			35.0 / 17.8 / 9.2	Sales/Net Fixed Assets	33.7 / 16.6 / 8.7	31.1 / 16.6 / 9.1	30.3 / 15.7 / 8.4	37.6 / 16.4 / 9.6	35.0 / 17.8 / 9.2
2.8 / 2.1 / 1.6	2.6 / 2.1 / 1.8			2.7 / 2.1 / 1.7	Sales/Total Assets	2.6 / 2.1 / 1.7	2.9 / 2.2 / 1.7	2.7 / 2.1 / 1.8	2.8 / 2.2 / 1.8	2.7 / 2.1 / 1.7
(98) .7 / 1.2 / 1.7	(52) .8 / 1.4 / 1.7		(159) .8 / 1.3 / 1.8		% Depr., Dep., Amort./Sales	(148) .7 / 1.1 / 1.8	(144) .8 / 1.2 / 1.7	(143) .8 / 1.3 / 1.7	(169) .8 / 1.2 / 1.8	(159) .8 / 1.3 / 1.8
(76) 2.2 / 3.9 / 6.5	(35) 2.6 / 3.8 / 5.4		(115) 2.3 / 3.9 / 6.2		% Lease & Rental Exp/Sales	(114) 2.4 / 3.8 / 5.2	(103) 2.3 / 3.3 / 4.7	(116) 2.3 / 3.4 / 5.5	(125) 2.1 / 3.1 / 4.8	(115) 2.3 / 3.9 / 6.2
(59) 3.3 / 7.1 / 11.0	(21) 1.9 / 3.2 / 6.7		(80) 2.7 / 6.1 / 10.3		% Officers' Comp/Sales	(75) 2.8 / 4.6 / 7.5	(81) 2.9 / 4.5 / 6.8	(76) 3.3 / 5.0 / 7.9	(83) 2.9 / 5.8 / 9.2	(80) 2.7 / 6.1 / 10.3
102364M	313974M	201550M	485254M	1103142M	Net Sales ($)	533356M	688600M	654166M	1280864M	1103142M
45060M	139757M	104543M	252708M	542068M	Total Assets ($)	252776M	333144M	308714M	534308M	542068M

M = $thousand   MM = $million
See Pages 1 through 12 for Explanation of Ratios and Data

Time series analysis is concerned with the historical trend of the firm's ratios, that is, it measures the firm against itself at different points in time. Time series analysis can detect trends that may indicate looming problems before they occur. For example, the analyst may find that a firm experiencing rapid sales growth has a steadily falling profit margin because of a rising trend in its cost of goods sold. Without a time series perspective, the euphoria of rapid growth might conceal the dangerous deterioration in profit margin.

Several sources of comparative financial ratios are used by analysts in both time series and cross-sectional analysis:

Statement Studies, published annually by the Robert Morris Associates, is the most familiar such source to bankers. Table 8A-1 shows a standard summary page from this publication consisting of financial ratios for a sample of family clothing retailers. A common size balance sheet and income statement and a series of liquidity, leverage, activity, and profitability ratios are presented for several hundred types of businesses. The ratios are derived from a sample of over 40,000 sets of statements submitted by bank loan officers throughout the nation. The ratios are reported by firm size so that a small firm can be compared with other small firms in its industry and a large firm can be compared with large firms. The most recent three years of time series data is given for the entire sample of firms in each line of business. In addition, three stratified values are reported for each ratio: upper quartile, median, and lower quartile. This distributional data for ratios gives the analyst a better sense of how extreme the difference between a loan applicant's ratios and those of its peers is.

Dun and Bradstreet publishes *Key Business Ratios in 125 Lines* of Business. This publication reports 14 ratios and, like the *Annual Statement Studies*, gives the interquartile ranges. It does not, however, provide the ratios by firm size categories, nor does it report recent historical or time series date.

The *Almanac of Business and Industrial Financial Ratios* published by Prentice-Hall reports financial ratios for 170 lines of business and industries. The sample of firm data is taken from Internal Revenue Service corporate tax filings and is quite accurate and complete. However, the data are available only with a two-to-three-year lag.

RATIO INTERRELATIONSHIPS: THE DUPONT SYSTEM

Crucial information about the financial condition of a firm is revealed in several financial ratios and not just one. A combination or a *system* of financial ratios can reveal a great deal about the sources of a firm's profit performance. No single ratio can explain more than one facet of the firm's performance.

The duPont system of analysis breaks the summary profitability ratio return on equity into its constituent leverage, profit margin, activity, and common size ratios. This system enables the analyst simultaneously to view the key relationships governing a business enterprise. Return on equity (ROE) may be defined as follows:

$$\text{ROE} = \frac{\text{Total assets}}{\text{Equity}} \times \frac{\text{Net income after taxes}}{\text{Total assets}}$$

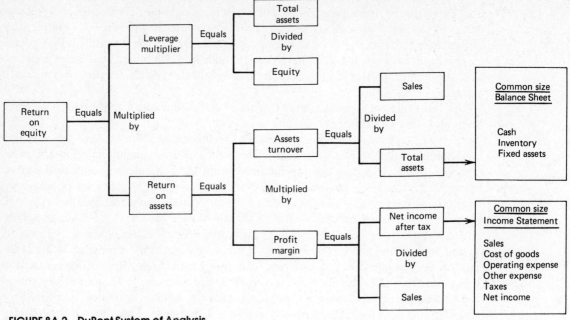

FIGURE 8A-2   DuPont System of Analysis

ROE is simply a multiple of Total assets/Equity—dollars of all sources of debt plus equity for every dollar of equity in the firm—and return on assets (ROA). ROA can be defined as follows:

$$ROA = \frac{Sales}{Total\ assets} \times \frac{Net\ income\ after\ taxes}{Sales}$$

The term (Sales/Total assets) is the activity ratio called total assets turnover, and the term (Net income after taxes/Sales) is the profitability ratio called profit margin.

Total assets can be further broken into the assets side of the common size balance sheet, and the net income after taxes can be shown as the residual from the common size income statement. Figure 8A-2 graphically presents the complete system.

9

COMMERCIAL LENDING CONSIDERATIONS

The hallmark of the commercial bank's lending skills is the business loan. Banks have proven to be remarkably versatile in their ability to tailor loans to businesses under varied conditions for a great variety of purposes. Nearly every type of business borrows bank funds at one time or another. Even large public utilities, with their relatively free access to open-market, long-term funds, routinely borrow "bridge" funds from banks to span the periodic public issue of their securities.

Businesses borrow to finance the following:

1 Seasonal working capital.

2 Long-term working capital.

3 New fixed assets.

4 Replacement of fixed assets.

5 Changes in payment patterns.

6 Unexpected one-time expenses.

7 Replacement of funds lost due to unprofitable operations.

There are a host of other purposes for borrowing. Each loan purpose creates a need for a more or less unique loan arrangement. Although diverse, loans can be lumped by type according to their maturity, security, and other special features. Our discussion in this chapter covers short-term loans, term loans, security considerations, loan pricing, and types of restrictions or covenants used in loan agreements.

SHORT-TERM LOANS

Well over half of all bank commercial loans are made on short term, that is, for periods of less than one year. Of these, about half are made on an unsecured basis to seasonal businesses and to borrowers with short-lived and project-oriented needs for funds. Secured short-term borrowers typically are less strong financially or are untested businesses without an earnings record.

Seasonal Open Lines of Credit

The most common type of short-term loan is the working capital line of credit extended to financially strong borrowers who have seasonal swings in their operations. Retailers and seasonal manufacturing firms are regular users of such credit. Through the line-of-credit commitment, a bank indicates its intention to honor borrowings up to the amount of the line. The amount is established on the basis of the customer's pro forma peak funding requirement, and it assures the borrower of the availability of funds to finance bulges in working capital as sales expand and contract. The customer "takes down" only parts of the line as the need arises so that redundant borrowings are unnecessary. Loan interest is charged on only the amount actually borrowed, and the loan may be repaid as reflows of cash to the firm occur when seasonal sales decline.

In quite a few instances, line-of-credit borrowing is unsecured. As a condition of the line, however, the agreement requires that the customer be out of debt to the bank for some period of time during the year. This required "rest period" is usually 30 to 90 consecutive days and is intended to provide confirmation that the customer's funding need is not permanent. If the need appears to be permanent, the bank may seek to collateralize and otherwise restructure the loan.

The seasonal line of credit is most often structured so as not to be legally enforceable. Normally, the total of banks' open line commitments exceed their practical capacity to instantaneously honor them all.[1] This is a reasonable posture for banks to take because it is extremely improbable that all line-of-credit customers would try to take down a large part of their line all at the same time. Therefore, banks can hedge against such an occurrence and preserve flexibility by structuring their line commitments informally so that they are not legally binding. Usually a letter evidencing the commitment is used to specify the terms, the amounts, and the commitment expiration date. To avoid legal enforceability on informal commitments, banks normally do not take collateral or invoke commitment fees.

On the other hand, despite their lack of legal standing, informal line commitments are faithfully honored by banks. Even an infrequent failure to honor its lines would risk a bank's reputation and standing with its present and potential customers. Of course, if the borrower's soundness deteriorates, lines of credit are subject to reduction or even cancellation. Formal line-of-credit commitments fully obligate the bank to advance funds as established in a formal loan agreement, unless the borrower fails to fulfill the terms and conditions set forth.

Other Short-Term Loans

Other types of short-term loans have more of a *project*, as opposed to a seasonal, character. Project-type borrowers tend to have regular and large needs for short-term

---

[1] For example, in May 1980, a period of very high loan demand, large U.S. banks reported only $137 billion of loans made under commitments out of total commercial and industrial loan commitments of $425 billion. "Changes in Bank Lending Practices: 1979–1980," *Federal Reserve Bulletin* (Sept. 1980), pp. 671–86.

funds. For example, money center and regional banks make large loans to investment bankers to support their underwriting and placement of securities issues. Investment bankers must borrow to temporarily finance new issues before they are able to sell them to investors. Large banks also lend short-term funds to securities dealers who must finance margin accounts of their clients. Also, securities dealers borrow to finance inventories they must carry in order to make markets for the securities they handle. The securities are used as collateral for the loans in these cases.

Interim construction and real estate loans are normally short-term loans to builders and land developers for the purpose of acquiring and improving real estate. Such loans are secured by the subject real estate and are conditional on a commitment of long-term funds by a permanent lender. These "takeout" funds enable the borrower to repay the commercial bank loan at the completion of the project. Interim construction lending is the norm for construction of single- and multifamily housing, office buildings, shopping centers, warehouses, motels, and restaurants and for land development.

Banks are major lenders to business and consumer finance companies under line-of-credit arrangements. Finance companies are an anomaly in that they permanently rely on short-term borrowings. They satisfy the rest period requirement for line-of-credit borrowing by rotating from one bank to another, paying off one bank's loan with loan proceeds from other banks. Large finance companies have shifted significantly to commercial paper in recent years and are gradually reducing their reliance on bank loans.

TERM LOANS

Term loans are defined as loans (other than consumer and real estate loans) with maturities of over one year. Typically, they are amortized by installment payments derived from a firm's operating cash flows, primarily earnings. Loan proceeds are generally used for permanent increases in working capital and for fixed asset purchases. In reality, term loans provide intermediate term credit; maturities are usually limited to 10 years and are mostly in the 2-to-5-year range.

Revolving Credit Loans

A type of loan related to the term loan is the *revolving credit* loan. In essence, the revolving credit is the term loan equivalent of a line-of-credit loan in that it is a commitment to lend up to a maximum credit during a longer term, usually not more than five years. Unlike the line-of-credit commitment, a revolving credit commitment gives the borrower assurances of the availability of funds over unforeseen periods of tight money in future years.

Term loans and their revolving credit variation have become an increasingly important part of bank loan portfolios. For large banks, such loans now amount to one half of their commercial and industrial loans. Data for banks with assets in excess of $1 billion suggest that the growth in the term loan portion of their commercial and industrial loan portfolios accounted for all of the growth in those portfolios over the three-year period from September 1978 to September 1981. During this period, term commercial and industrial loans grew by $33 billion in large banks while their total commercial and industrial loans grew by $31 billion.[2] This growth was particularly remarkable given that the period was one of increasingly tight money when banks' concern over their own liquidity would be expected to induce them to shorten their outstanding loans.

In part, banks have promoted the growth in term loans as part of their aggressive search for higher yielding assets. The intermediate-term maturities offered by banks seem to fill a "maturity gap" in markets for capital funds. From a banker's perspective, however, it is somewhat difficult to explain this growth in bank term loans. Contrary to the traditional seasonal bank loan, term loans expose the bank to default risk over long periods. The banker must invest considerable faith in the borrowing management's ability to produce regular earnings into a dimly visible future.

The more probable explanation for the growth in bank term loans is their attractiveness to businesses. In many ways, they are a superior substitute for bond financing. Unlike bond financing, raising relatively small amounts of term bank funds is as viable as raising larger amounts. Prepayment penalties, sinking funds, and onerous refunding stipulations often are avoided. Also, a lengthy registration period and costly legal fees are not required. Finally, more flexible refinancing and later restructuring of the loan agreement to fit the firm's developments is feasible.

TAKING A SECURITY INTEREST

In the secured loan, the borrower grants the bank the right to sell the collateral assets and apply the proceeds to the loan if the borrower cannot repay the funds as agreed. A majority of bank loans to businesses are made on this basis. Although half or more of all short-term loans are not secured, most long-term loans are secured. In fact, the loan policies of many small and medium-sized banks generally forbid most unsecured term loans. Large banks, in dealing with large prime borrowers, are more liberal in granting unsecured loans because such borrowers tend to have stronger equity support in their capital structures, more stable cash flows, and more certain investment opportunities.

Banks follow precise procedures to establish and document their claim to the proceeds of collateral assets in the event the borrower defaults. Different procedures and documents are required for real, as opposed to personal, property. Also, there is a difference in the procedures for securing personal property, depending on whether the property remains in the possession of the bank or the borrower. These distinctions are illustrated in Figure 9-1 in a schematic diagram of the methods and documents for gaining an enforceable security interest.

Real Property

When real estate (land and improvements, including structures) collateral is offered, the bank must record the associated mortgage with a public agency such as the county clerk. This recording or filing protects the bank against subsequent claims by third parties. A *title search* is required to establish the existence of defects in the title in the form

[2] *Federal Reserve Bulletins*, Nov. 1978 and Nov. 1981.

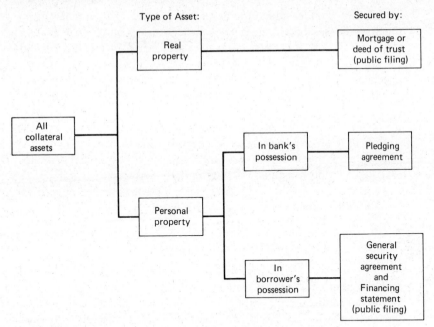

FIGURE 9-1   Methods and Documents for Taking Security Interest

of other possible claims on the real estate. A major concern is the status of taxes and assessments on the real estate. These items are senior to all other claims; ideally the borrower should be current on them. Title companies sell *title insurance* to protect the bank against loss due to defects that were not disclosed by the title search.

In addition to matters of title, there are other routine considerations in real-estate-secured lending. A professionally prepared *appraisal* is necessary to document the real estate's value at the present market or in case of possible liquidation. A *certified survey* is required to ascertain the secured property's physical location and dimensions and to ensure that improvements are properly located on the borrower's (and not infringing on someone else's) property. Evidence of *insurance* on the property is needed, including the designation of the bank as payee in the event of loss.

Personal Property in the Bank's Possession

A security interest in the property of the borrower is *perfected* when the bank or its agent actually take physical possession of it. The borrower completes a *pledge agreement*, which authorizes the bank to hold the collateral and to derive cash from it in the event of default. Because the asset is already in the bank's possession, it is not necessary to publicly file a pledge agreement.

There are several considerations in dealing with the more common types of collateral secured under pledge agreements. When negotiable securities are held as loan collateral, the borrower must execute a *stock power assignment*. The stock power simply authorizes the bank to sell the stock on default of the loan. Stock loans are subject to

Regulation U under which the Federal Reserve Board controls the *margin financing* of stock purchases. The bank must report the purpose of stock loans and observe additional restrictions if the purpose is to purchase margin stock.

Loans secured by the cash value or face value of a life insurance policy require a special pledge agreement to assign the policy to the bank. To be valid, the bank's security interest in the policy must be formally acknowledged by the issuing insurance company.

Banks commonly take a security interest in a savings account or certificate of deposit belonging to an owner or stockholder of a borrowing firm. If the borrower's deposit is in another financial institution, that institution must formally acknowledge the assignment. This third-party notice actually perfects the lending bank's claim. For borrower's deposits within the lending bank, a pledge agreement is important to block the possible withdrawal of the funds by the borrower.

Personal Property in the Customer's Possession

The bank perfects its security interest in collateral property held by the borrower with a public filing of a *general security agreement*. The general security agreement simply grants the bank a security interest. It is generally accompanied by a *financing statement* that describes the collateral and gives the legal names and addresses of the borrower and the bank. The financing statement officially "places the world on notice" of the collateral position granted to and taken by the bank. To survive beyond their normal five-year expiration term, financing statements must be renewed by the filing of a *continuation statement*.

Guarantees

As noted in Chapter 7, *guarantees* of loans to small corporations are often required of major stockholders to prevent the firm from avoiding indebtedness under the shield of limited corporate liability. In general, loans are not made on the strength of a guarantee; loans should be based on the business source of repayment. The bank's position may be strengthened somewhat if the proposed guarantor signs as a *comaker* instead. This may prevent litigation that could arise in loans with guarantors when the guarantors contest a possible later restructuring of the loan.

Accounts Receivable Financing

Accounts receivable financing is a form of collateralized lending with a particularly intimate link between the loan and its collateral. The bank lends money against an agreed on percentage (in the range of 50 to 90 percent) of accounts receivable assigned to it. The borrowing firm usually continues its regular credit and collection functions and its customers are not notified of the assignment of their debt to the bank. Collections are automatically paid down on the loan and new loan funds are granted as new receivables are generated.

This type of financing has advantages for both the bank and borrower. It gives the bank access to the readily convertible collateral of weaker customers who otherwise might not provide a viable loan market. Credit is well controlled in that receivables financing permits borrowing only as the borrower generates sales. It also provides for automatic repayment of the loan as collections come in.

Accounts receivable financing gives relatively weak borrowers access to credit they otherwise might not obtain. The credit is "evergreen" in that no rest period is required. The amount of credit is more or less tailored to the rolling needs of the borrower, particularly because financing reacts to expanding sales, thus supporting the necessary buildup of inventories. However, the cost of accounts receivable financing is higher than a borrower qualified for unsecured lending might pay.

Banks proceed cautiously because of the unusual reliance on the collateral in receivables financing. The collateral needs to be examined carefully and continually to ensure performance and to eliminate ineligible receivables from the borrowing base.

Factoring

Accounts receivable financing is often confused with factoring. In factoring, a bank or a commercial factor actually purchases selected accounts receivables from its customer at a percentage of their face value. In a strict sense, then, factoring is not a form of collateralized lending but an outright purchase of the customer's assets. The bank notifies the customer's debtors to remit all payments directly to the bank and not to the customer. Generally, the customer is required to maintain a cash reserve against losses due to buyers' claims against the customer firm.

Table 9-1 summarizes the differences between accounts receivable financing and factoring.

Inventory Financing

For our purposes, inventory financing can be defined as any loan that is secured by inventory and scheduled to be repaid from the sale of that inventory. Like accounts receivable financing, it is a highly specialized lending service to business; it is often combined with accounts receivable financing. Lending against inventory is a high-risk venture because such financing is usually extended to businesses that are financially weak. Also, the lender frequently encounters problems relating to the valuation and marketability of inventory as well as difficulties in physical control of the inventory.

TABLE 9-1
Accounts Receivable Financing Versus Factoring

	Accounts receivable financing	Factoring
Credit function performed by	Borrower	Bank
Collection function performed by	Borrower	Bank
Proceeds allowed via	Loan	Purchase
Cash reserve required	No	Yes
Account ownership	Borrower	Bank
Debtor notification	No	Yes
Cost	Lower	Higher

There are several forms of inventory lending. All of the borrower's inventories can be used as security on a loan under the *floating lien*. However, the seller is not constrained from selling inventories so that the bank cannot control specific inventory items. The floating lien may be used to provide continuing security on receivables created when the inventory is sold.

Trust receipt financing, also known as *floor planning finance*, is vitally important in many retail businesses and involves transitory legal ownership of inventory by the bank. Typically, the borrower is provided funds with which to pay for goods received from suppliers. The borrower holds the goods in trust for the bank by issuing the bank a trust receipt. As sales occur, the borrower transmits the proceeds to the bank. Also, contracts from the borrower's credit sales are frequently sold to the bank so that, in effect, the bank provides continuous financing.

Trust receipts can only be issued on specifically identifiable goods. The goods must lend themselves to easy verification when the bank runs its audit of the customer's inventory. Trust receipts are most convenient when used to finance new and used automobile dealers, other durable consumer goods retailers, and machinery dealers.

Warehousing financing facilitates inventory lending by providing controls on the disposition of the inventories. Two different warehousing arrangements are used: the public warehouse and the field warehouse. The public warehouse is owned and operated remote from the borrower's site by an independent third party in the storage business. The field warehouse is controlled by an independent third-party operator on the borrower's site and is more suitable when the goods handled are too bulky to relocate or when goods are moved in and out with great frequency.

In both public and field warehouse arrangements, the independent third party receives and stores the inventories and provides the bank with warehouse receipts. The bank then creates a deposit for the borrower for 50 to 80 percent of the value of the receipted goods. As the borrower's customers submit orders for the goods, the bank releases goods to make the sales, and the proceeds of the sale are remitted directly to the bank to repay the loans. The costs of warehouse financing are quite high and become prohibitive for smaller operations. Banks undertake a major risk in warehouse financing because of the difficulty of verifying the quality of goods on which they acquire warehouse receipts. Also, fraud has played a prominent part in warehouse finance. The great salad oil scandal of the early 1960s, in which banks advanced many millions of dollars against warehouse receipts for which no goods existed, stands as testimony to the inherent risk.

LOAN COVENANTS

In making any business loan, there is the risk that the loan's purpose will go awry or that the borrower's financial condition will deteriorate to an extent that repayment of the loan is jeopardized. The possibility for errant loans and borrower deterioration increases with the length of time a loan is outstanding. To protect themselves against these risks, banks write restrictive covenants into loan agreements. Term loans are usually the main objects of often extensive loan covenants, although standard "boiler plate" covenants are typically a part of all loan agreements.

Affirmative versus Negative Covenants

There are two types of covenants in most term loan agreements: *affirmative* and *negative*. Affirmative covenants set out the borrower's obligation to regularly submit financial statements, to maintain adequate insurance, to periodically certify compliance with provisions of the loan agreement, and to pay principal and interest as scheduled as well as other requirements for reporting on company activities. Negative covenants range from requiring the borrower to maintain reasonable financial health to outright restraints or prohibitions on the borrower's activities. Because negative covenants might restrict or impose costs on the borrower, they are the subject of often intense negotiations.

There may be a great many negative covenants in a term loan agreement or just a few. The banker must determine in each case the types of covenants to include and how they should be quantified.[3]

Objective of Covenants

In framing the loan agreement covenants, the banker must first decide what he or she wants to control and achieve. Covenants may be classified by their objectives as follows:

1   Cash flow control.
2   Trigger call or restructuring of the loan.
3   Balance sheet control.

The most common objective is cash flow control, that is, assurance that the cash flow from the borrower's operations will be available to service the loan interest and principal. For term loans, the most important dimension of cash flows is profits. The banker reviews the firm's business plan and the way in which the proceeds of the loan will be used. If the firm's plans are considered too risky, the banker might use loan covenants to force a modification such as reducing the amount that the firm will invest in a high-risk venture or even prohibiting the firm from entering a new, high-risk market or product line.

However, it is not enough that a borrower's future profits seem assured. The banker may insist on covenants preventing dividend payments, excessive capital investments, or repayment of debt owed other lenders in order to ensure that future cash flows will repay the bank's loan.

The trigger type of loan covenant establishes critical financial thresholds, which, when violated, trigger the bank's right to some form of protective recourse. For example, if the borrower fails to maintain some minimal profitability or a minimal net working capital level, the bank might gain the right to call the entire loan. This call would protect the bank against deterioration in the value of the firm's working capital; if the firm cannot repay the loan on call, the bank's recourse lies in the firm's assets. Alterna-

---

[3] A description of how restrictive covenants are set is given in Jasper H. Arnold, III, and John H. Crockett, "Analysis of Restrictive Covenants of Bank Term Loan Agreements," unpublished manuscript, First City National Bank of Houston, 1981.

tively, a call on the loan opens the way for the bank to increase the loan interest rate, increase collateral, or write stricter covenants.

Balance sheet control loan covenants are aimed at restricting future actions by the firm that will weaken the balance sheet, often as a reaction to changes in the firm's business situation. Covenants may be used to limit further indebtedness or depletion of current assets in order to maintain an acceptable debt-to-equity ratio, current ratio, or other balance sheet standards.

PRICING CONCEPTS

The profitability of banks depends on how the prices they charge for loans and myriad services compare with their costs of funds and operations. As the major source of revenue, loan prices have a crucial role in bank profitability. Indeed, because loans represent the central activity of banking and are the basis of most banks' relationships with their major customers, loan pricing tends to be the focal point of both revenues and costs.

For pricing purposes, we can divide customers into three basic types:

1   Prime customers.
2   Perceived value customers.
3   Relationship customers.

The various aspects of loan pricing apply differently to each of these customer types.

Prime Customers

Large banks have customers who are eligible to borrow either at the national prime rate of interest or, recently, at just above the open market rate of interest. The prime rate is the base short-term loan rate that large banks ostensibly charge their largest and most credit-worthy customers. The prime is a so-called administered rate, which the large banks adjust, more or less in concert, according to changes in open market rates of interest. For less than prime quality borrowers, banks offer loans at interest rates that are scaled up from the prime rate base.

When money market rates of interest fluctuated dramatically in recent years, banks' loan pricing systems became largely based on floating rates. When market rates rise, the cost of many sources of bank funds rise as well, and if bank loans are all at fixed rates, bank profitability becomes squeezed. Recognizing this effect of rate fluctuations, banks have made a major shift to floating rate provisions in business loans. This pricing tactic ties the loan rate to a base rate that responds to the movement of market rates in general, predominantly the prime rate.

The first large-scale introduction of floating rate loans dates from the early 1970s. At that time large banks offered floating rates that were guaranteed not to exceed an average or absolute "cap."[4] This ceiling rate policy had the effect of partly protecting

[4] An interesting discussion of these developments appears in Randall C. Merris, "Business Loans at Large Commercial Banks: Policies and Practices," *Economic Perspectives* (Nov./Dec. 1979), pp. 15–23, Federal Reserve Bank of Chicago.

the bank against rising market rates and also giving the customer a guarantee against unlimited increases in rate. However, market rates unexpectedly rose to record heights in 1973 and 1974, leaving rates on many outstanding loans at cap rates well below market. As a result, banks have generally rejected the cap rate tactic during more recent periods of rising rates. Banks surveyed by the Federal Reserve system during 1979–1981 made over half of their loans on an open-ended floating rate basis.

Also, during the period 1979–1981 banks made a significant number of loans under their stated prime rates.[5] This occurred for several reasons. First, banks were competing with low rates in the commercial paper market. Second, when market rates fell, banks resisted lowering their prime rates because they would have lost revenue on floating rate loans already on their books. Thus, new "prime" loans were made at rates below their announced prime rates. Floating rates based on the London Interbank Offering Rate (LIBOR) have become especially prominent. LIBOR is a widely quoted rate on short-term European money market credits. For some time it has influenced the overseas lending rates of large U.S. banks, particularly when the spread between the national prime and LIBOR rates favors the latter. Also, U.S. bank access to overseas sources of funds has recently made LIBOR an increasingly popular base rate among borrowers of regional and even smaller banks.

When banks are "loaned up" because of intense loan demand, they are able to maintain or raise the level of their loan rates. When loan demand slackens, banks may reduce their rates to attract more business borrowers. Slack loan demand is usually accompanied by falling market rates of interest on other nonbank sources of funds. To keep customers who have alternative sources of funds, banks are further compelled to lower their lending rates.

Prime borrowers, those customers who are granted loans at or below banks' lowest rate, are usually highly credit worthy and have ready access to other institutional and open-market sources of funds and, therefore, are able to borrow where the lowest interest rate is offered. The individual bank knows that it probably will not be able to make a loan to a prime customer if it attempts to charge a rate higher than its lowest rate.

Unlike weaker and more local borrowers, national prime borrowers tend not to tie their borrowing needs to their needs for other bank services, that is, they seek only a rather limited relationship in most of their banking dealings. As a result, banks are less able to bundle the pricing of loans and services together for prime customers. Instead, banks must price prime loans to be competitive with market sources of funds available to prime borrowers. The lack of interplay between lending and other services offered by banks makes loan pricing for prime borrowers uniquely straightforward.

Perceived Value Customers

Another method for pricing loans, or for that matter any other bank service, is based on the value of the funds or services to the customer. The reasoning is that the bank can probably expect to attract customers if the price of bank loans or services does not exceed their applied value when used by the same customers. This appears to be based on

---

[5] Warren T. Trepeta, "Changes in Bank Lending Practices," *Federal Reserve Bulletin* (Sept. 1981), pp. 671–86.

sound economic reasoning; from the customers' viewpoint, services whose marginal costs are below the marginal (perceived) benefits provided are worth the cost. Thus, according to this approach, the bank's pricing should be derived from knowledge of the value that customers perceive in borrowed funds or services. Obviously, no two customers perceive value exactly alike and any given price might exceed the value perceived by some customers but not the value perceived by other customers. In essence, using this approach, the bank's task is to estimate the elasticities of a demand curve for its customers and to price its funds or services where the price-quantity combination maximizes net revenue. Theoretically, in this context, the prime borrowers discussed earlier have infinitely elastic demand for funds because none will borrow at rates above market rates and all will try to borrow at rates below the market. That is because prime borrowers have alternative sources of funds and services; competition for their business is intense.

One of two basic circumstances under which perceived value pricing works is when the customer lacks these alternative sources. If, for example, a single bank is the only feasible source of loan funds for a local customer, that customer should be willing to borrow at any rate up to the value it places on the use of the funds (although the bank might refuse such a loan if it considers a high rate to be detrimental to the borrower's financial health). Of course, if the rate exceeds the customer's perceived value, a rational customer will not borrow at all.

The other circumstance under which perceived value pricing works is when customers view a loan or other bank service as a part of a total banking relationship. A bank may price a loan or service above the customer's alternative sources of supply for the loan or service (and below the value perceived by the customer) if the customer uses a wide array of bank services. For example, even though a bank may charge the highest price in town for wire transfers of funds, its business customers probably will not switch their wire transfer activity to another institution if they want to continue using the bank's other services. They probably will continue to use the bank's wire transfer services. In this case, the most important thing is that the wire transfer cost does not exceed its perceived value.

Relationship Customer

Loan pricing for the majority of borrowers, those that can be classified between prime and weak marginal borrowers, is conditioned by a strong customer relationship. A strong relationship exists when the customer uses a broad range of banking services and borrows regularly and is a good source of future loan demand. To such a borrower, loan rates are usually established nominally at a spread above the prime rate. However, the focus of concern is the yield on the total activities, including loans, associated with the relationship.

LOAN PRICING FRAMEWORK

Customer Profitability Analysis

As already noted, banks traditionally have priced loans as well as deposits and other services according to prices prevailing in the market; for example, interest rates set on commercial loans usually bear some relationship to the prime rate. This pricing method is implicitly assumed to compensate the bank for the cost of a wide variety of "free" services the bank offers which are not explicitly priced. However, with increased competition for good customers, and the desire to treat them equitably, banks have developed pricing techniques that recognize in detail all of the many facets of a single customer relationship. They now tend to explicitly price computerized payroll, funds wire transfers, lockbox, and other services provided in addition to interest rate pricing on loans. According to this approach, loans should be priced so that the profitability of a bank's *total relationship* with a borrower meets its profitability standard. This method of analyzing bank pricing is called *customer profitability analysis*.

To restate the concept, customer profitability analysis provides a conceptual framework that induces loan officers to consider the whole customer relationship when pricing a loan. The method simply compares the revenues and costs of a customer relationship. For a profitable account, the comparison must show

$$\text{Revenues} > \text{Costs}$$

These two quantities must be carefully identified. They are discussed in the following sections and then combined in a summary customer profitability analysis statement.

Revenues

Table 9-2 lists the sources of revenue stemming from all aspects of the bank's relationship with the hypothetical ABC Corporation. All explicit service charges, as well as loan interest, are included. The service charges are not incorporated in the loan interest rate but are priced independently on the basis of the customer's actual activity. In this

TABLE 9-2
Revenue Derived from ABC Corporation

Loan Interest		
Commercial loan, $1,200,000 average at 14%		$168,000
Commitment Fee Income		
Unused line, $2,300,000 at 0.5%		11,500
Loan Service		
(a) Accounts maintenance	48	
(b) Legal fees	400	
(c) Officer time	2000	
Subtotal		2,448
General Bank Services		
(a) Unencoded items, 120,000 at 0.02	2400	
(b) Wire transfer, 280 at $2	560	
(c) Loan handling expense, $1,200,000 at 0.5%	6000	
Subtotal		8,960
Total Revenue Derived		$190,908

way, the customer does not pay for more or less of the bank's services than it uses and high service users are not subsidized by low service users.

Costs

The costs associated with the ABC Corporation loan are listed in Table 9-3. There are two basic types of costs: the cost of bank funds and the cost of other services provided. The amount of bank funds required to support the loan is divided between general (nonequity) funds and equity capital. The cost of all of the bank's funds must be recovered by earning assets. Therefore, an appropriate amount of general funds and equity capital must be prorated to the ABC loan. Banks use different methods of assigning and charging for funds used to support a loan. Following is an example of the one method of prorating general and equity funds to a customer's loan.

$$\text{General funds used} = \frac{\text{Bank general funds}}{\text{Bank earning assets}} \times \text{Loan amount}$$

$$\text{Equity funds used} = \frac{\text{Total equity capital}}{\text{Bank earning assets}} \times \text{Loan amount}$$

Note that the funds required are $1,410,000 of general funds plus $120,000 of equity funds for a total of $1,530,000, which exceeds the $1,200,000 amount loaned. The

TABLE 9-3
Costs Assigned to ABC Corporation

Cost of Funds		
(a) Charge for general funds, $1,410,000 at 9.60%		$135,360
(b) Charge for equity capital funds, $120,000 at 30.00%		36,000
Cost of Services		
(a) Unencoded items, 120,000 at 0.01	1200	
(b) Paid checks, 30,000 at 0.10	3000	
(c) Wire transfers, 280 at $1.50	420	
(d) Loan handling charge $1,200,000 at 0.5%	6000	
Subtotal		10,620
Deposit Analysis		
(a) Actual cost of deposits		
1. Demand account, $125,000 at 3.5%[a]	4375	
2. CD, $50,000 at 10.1%[b]	5050	
(b) Expected cost of funds, $175,000 at 11.2%[c]	(19600)	
		(10,175)
Total Net Cost		$171,805

[a]Cost of servicing.
[b]Interest expense plus cost of servicing.
[c]Composite of cost of general funds and cost of equity capital.

excess occurs because reserve requirements and float on deposit sources of funds require the bank to tie up funds in cash items that consequently cannot be used for lending. Because it is based on earning assets and not on total assets, the method of proration given above automatically provides the excess funds to cover reserve and float requirements.

Other methods of assigning funds to loans may be equally or more valid. Some banks, in recognition of the role of equity in absorbing risk, assign equity funds to earning assets on the basis of risk. In this case, high-risk loans would be assigned a greater share of equity than low-risk loans and so on. In the present example, we use the simple equal proration described by the above equations.

The cost rate for general funds is the sum of the weighted cost of nonequity source of funds. If the purpose of the analysis is to review past profitability, then the weighted *average* cost of funds based on past interest and other funds expense is appropriate. However, for pricing purposes the weighted *marginal* cost of funds, representing the cost of a composite of new funds at the bank's present funds mix, is appropriate. In Table 9-3, the weighted marginal cost of general funds is 9.60 percent.

The cost of the prorated amount of equity capital is based on the pretax rate of return required by stockholders; in Table 9-3, this rate is assumed to be 30 percent. All cost rates and costs of services provided are expressed in pretax terms.

To extend the procedure to a full customer profitability analysis, the value to the bank of ABC's $175,000 deposits must be evaluated. This involves a comparison of the *expected* cost of deposits provided by ABC in relation to the *actual* cost of its deposits, where the expected cost is based simply on the bank's average overall cost of funds (including equity funds). The difference between expected and actual costs indicates the value to the bank. In Table 9-3, the actual cost is less than expected, yielding a positive value (a "negative cost") to the bank.

Indeed, the total relationship with ABC appears to have excess value to the bank. Revenues exceed costs even when costs include the desired return on equity funds. Comparing the total revenues in Table 9-2, and the total costs, in Table 9-3, yields the following:

$$\text{Revenues} - \text{Costs}$$
$$= \$190,908 - 171,805$$
$$= \$19,103$$

Before declaring the $19,103 excess value, however, the bank must assess the relative riskiness of its loan to ABC. If the loan risk is more than the average risk of the bank's earning assets, the bank must determine whether or not $19,103 is an adequate compensation for this additional risk. If it is not, a higher loan interest rate should be considered.

Cost Accounting Systems

It should be clear that customer profitability analysis assumes the bank has a good understanding of its costs. Actually, many banks are latecomers in developing and accepting cost accounting techniques. Banks have historically applied a major part of their staffs and their creative efforts to procuring low-cost deposits and freely servicing depositors. The slow-to-die tradition of not charging to recover the costs of a great many deposit-related services retarded the development of accounting systems to determine banks' costs for those services.

However, most large banks now do have rather sophisticated cost accounting systems in place. Other banks participate in the Federal Reserve System's Functional Cost Analysis program or use the data generated by this program as a reference point for cost-dependent decision making. The Functional Cost Analysis program collects uniform cost and income data from a group of participating Fed member banks. The data are structured to indicate the profitability and cost characteristics of various functional activities in banks.

NONINTEREST ASPECTS OF LOAN PRICING

Direct Factors

In our previous discussion, we neglected pricing aspects on loans other than the explicit interest rate charged. Foremost among these are compensating balance requirements and commitment fees. Both of these factors *directly* affect loan yield.

Compensating Balances

Compensating balance requirements obligate the borrower to hold demand deposits or low interest time deposits as part of a loan agreement. Also, balance requirements are sometimes set on loan commitments. The balance requirement on loans usually requires that balances must average an agreed on percentage of the loan amount. The use of an average and not a minimum requirement permits the borrower to draw balances down to well below the average requirement when loan funds are applied to their intended purpose, and then to raise the average balance as funds accummulate to well above the average requirement pending repayment of the loan.

Average balance requirements range from 10 to 20 percent, with 15 percent perhaps being most common. At times balance requirements are applied to both the loan and the total commitment; for example, "10 and 10" indicates balances of 10 percent on the loan and 10 percent on the total commitment. This actually results in a 20 percent requirement on the loan and 10 percent on the unused commitment.

One rationale for compensating balance requirements is that they ensure that borrowers will remain as customers on both sides of the balance sheet, that is, as both borrowers and providers of funds. Banks obviously do not want their borrowers to redeposit loan proceeds at another institution. Another rationale is that compensating balances permit banks to pay implicit interest that they are prohibited from paying explicitly under Regulation Q. The implicit interest arises from the fact that banks can change lower loan rates because borrowers' balances have considerable value to them. Also, it is argued that the compensating balance requirement simply adds discipline to the borrower's management of working balances, much of which the borrower would maintain on deposit in any case. Finally, compensating balances reflect a traditional belief in deposit taking as the central function of banks. At the extreme, this belief states that loans are made in order to ensure the availability of deposits in the present and the future.

The cost of compensating balance requirements to the borrower can be directly reflected in the cost of a loan. If a borrower needs $80,000 but must retain an average compensating balance of 20 percent, the borrower must obtain a $100,000 loan. If the loan rate is 16 percent or a cost to the borrower of $16,000 in interest charges annually, the effective rate on the $80,000 portion of the loan usuable by the borrower is then 20 percent. Of course, these factors apply only if the borrower would otherwise maintain a zero deposit balance, a most unlikely event. The actual amount of redundant borrowing is the amount by which the required average balance exceeds the amount that the borrower would otherwise maintain.

Compensating balances are criticized as being an inefficient pricing mechanism because, although they raise the effective borrowing cost, banks must hold idle reserves against the additional deposits and therefore cannot fully invest them in earning assets. These rationales strike some borrowers and bankers as questionable. In some instances among banks that have moved toward unbundled and explicit pricing, balance requirements have been replaced by fees or higher loan rates. Banks that substitute fees or higher rates for balances reflect their belief in lending, rather than deposit taking, as the bank's central function; they do not hold the traditional belief that lending is primarily a tool for obtaining deposits. Their concerns are, first, to generate good loans and, second, as skillful liabilities managers, to obtain deposits or purchased sources of money to fund the loans.

Nevertheless, in periods of tight money and high interest rates, compensating balances tend to become more attractive to banks than fees. During such times the balances ought to provide the bank with a higher yield because interest rates increase on bank earning assets whereas the cost to the bank for handling compensating balances is relatively unaffected. However, borrowers, in recent years, have learned to minimize demand deposits as interest rate levels rose, and more than ever before they are inclined to resist restrictive balance requirements.

Commitment Fees

Formal loan commitments arise mostly for revolving credits and, to a lesser extent, for term loans and short-term credits. They set forth a bank's firm obligation to provide a specified amount of credit in the future at a specified price or pricing formula. Unlike the informal loan commitment on seasonal short-term credit, the formal commitment also frequently sets forth the fee to the borrower for making future credit available. In essence, the commitment fee is the price for a call on future credit.

Commitment fees on revolving credits are more prevalent because of the delay and relative unpredictability of the takedown by the customer. For the usual commitment period of two to five years, fees on the unused portion average about 0.5 percent. The percentage typically increases to as much as 0.75 percent during periods of tight money and may fall below 0.5 percent in periods of slack loan demand.

In theory, commitment fees are related to the cost to the bank of maintaining liquidity or borrowing capacity to meet a future call on credit. This cost can be explained in the following ways. If the bank is compelled to hold assets in short-term government securities in order to provide commitment credit on call, it forgoes returns on higher yielding but less liquid assets. In the more likely case of the bank maintaining borrowing capacity to meet a future call on credit, the bank forgoes current borrowing and investing in earning assets to ensure its ability to borrow in the future.

Noninterest Aspects of Loan Pricing: Indirect Factors

In addition, there are several *indirect* noninterest factors involved in loan pricing. These include collateral requirements, loan maturity limits, and loan covenants. In our discussion so far regarding loan pricing we have ignored the effect of these factors or assumed that they remain constant for every loan. In fact, these indirect factors are important variables in any loan negotiation. If the terms involving collateral, maturity, and loan covenants become more restrictive, the risk to the bank is reduced and the effective cost to the customer increases. Highly restrictive terms ought to ease other, more direct, pricing elements. Specifically, shortened loan maturities, increased amounts of collateral, and more restrictive loan covenants should result in a lowering of some or all of the direct pricing elements of loan rates, commitment fees, and compensating balance requirements.

In addition, the indirect noninterest pricing factors are frequently used as a means of rationing loan funds, particularly during periods of tight money when banks struggle to find sufficient funds. To qualify for a larger loan at the going rate of interest, certain borrowers are required to put up more collateral and accept shorter loan maturities and stricter covenants. Borrowers subjected to these forms of credit rationing are generally those with few if any alternative sources of funds and tend to be perceived value customers. If indirect or direct pricing factors are too restrictive, that is, too costly, perceived value customers become rationed out of the loan market altogether.

SUMMARY

Most banks actively seek to make business loans. In the past, banks offered only short-term, self-liquidating credit. Such loans were usually for temporary additions to working capital that would soon be sold off to generate cash for repayment of the loans. This type of loan included a requirement that borrowers pay off their loans sometime during the year. Borrowers often refinanced their loans at other banks to meet this "clean-up" rule and then later returned to the bank of origin to renew the loan. Bankers call such loans "evergreen." Evergreen loans engaged banks in term lending despite their intentions to grant short-term loans. From such beginnings, many banks have shifted aggressively to longer term credits to finance plant and equipment. This shift has produced dramatic changes in bank lending principles by tying loans to borrowers' long-term profitability as a primary source of repayment and routinely tying them to collateral as a secondary source of repayment. Large banks in particular provide revolving credits, revolving credit commitments, and term loans structured to meet intermediate term financing needs of businesses.

A crucial dimension of term credits is the negotiation of covenants. Restrictive or negative covenants can be classified into three categories according to their objectives.

Cash flow covenants have as their objective the protection of cash flows for loan repayment. They can be used to restrict the borrower's actions that introduce unacceptable risks to earnings or to restrict uses of cash flow other than loan repayment. Trigger covenants protect the bank from the borrower's financial deterioration by establishing minimum financial standards that, when violated, authorize the bank to call or restructure the loan. Balance sheet covenants protect the loan by restraining the borrower from taking actions that would unduly weaken the balance sheet and jeopardize the value of collateral assets.

For most borrowers, loan interest rates are typically set on a prime-plus basis to account for the risk associated with the credit. However, banks are increasingly dealing with loan pricing in the context of a total customer relationship. Customer profitability analysis explicitly prices and tracks the cost of individual (unbundled) services rendered in addition to the usual loan and deposit aspect of the relationship.

Compensating balances and commitment fees directly affect loan yield and the cost to the customer of borrowing. Some argue that compensating balance requirements are an anachronism left over from an era when the main focus of banking was deposit taking. Although balance requirements are being replaced by fees in some banks, they will undoubtedly persist in some banks into the future.

10

CONSUMER CREDIT

The individual consumer has always been an important factor in the business of banking. For a long time, retail customer deposits have been the *source* of over half of commercial banks funds and it is estimated that in 1985 retail deposits will total roughly two thirds of bank funds.[1] However, the history of significant consumer *use* of bank funds is considerably shorter; that is, consumers are a relatively recent factor in banks' loan portfolios.

The primary consumer use of bank funds is installment credit. This type of credit did not really come into its own until after World War II. During earlier years, the use of installment credit tended to be frowned upon and installment borrowers were thought to violate societal rules of moral and prudent behavior. Following World War II, installment lending was quickly legitimized by millions of consumers who were eager to obtain new automobiles, household appliances, and other durable goods that had not been available during the war. As a result, the level of installment lending in the United States rose from an insignificant $2.5 billion in 1945 to $29 billion in 1955. By 1981, outstanding installment credit from all categories of lenders stood at $330 billion, including $145 billion held by commercial banks. Mortgage debt on nonfarm property has undergone similar development with the postwar housing boom, growing from $45 billion in 1950 to $1,424 billion in 1981.

The growth of consumer lending reflects the steady postwar rise of income and employment and the increased job security of scores of millions of middle-class workers. The consumer's growing and secure future income is the key in the extension of consumer credit because buying on time means acquiring automobiles or other goods with tomorrow's income. In part, the growth of consumer lending also reflects the aggressive marketing by banks and other financial institutions in competing for the consumer loan market. Newer forms of credit such as credit cards, overdraft facilities, and longer loan maturities have made credit more attractive and more available to con-

[1] International Business Machines, Inc., "The Business of Retail Banking" (1979).

sumers. In addition, growth in consumer lending is based on ever-broadening penetration and distribution of credit to more and more households. The percentage of households having home mortgages and installment debt appears to rise continuously. This wider ownership of householder debt occurs in all age categories and not just younger families, although the latter are likely to be the most heavily in debt.

Nevertheless, consumers have been surprisingly consistent in the amount of debt they have been willing to assume over the years. Data show that the ratio of consumer installment credit outstanding to the amount of consumer-held liquid assets (meaning assets that are readily convertible into cash) has stayed around the 20 percent level for the past two decades. The ratio falls moderately during recessionary years and rises slightly during years of economic expansion.

COMMERCIAL BANK CONSUMER CREDIT

Table 10-1 gives a breakdown of consumer credit outstanding at banks in 1971 and 1981. In 1981, the total consumer-related credit of $347 billion held by banks represented 35 percent of the $990 billion worth of all types of credit in U.S. banks' loan portfolios. During the period of 1971–1981, commercial banks accounted for half of net installment lending to consumers. Further discussion here is limited to nonmortgage consumer credit; mortgage credit will be discussed in Chapter 11.

Credit Card and Debit Card Lending

Of the approximately $175 billion nonmortgage loans, credit and debit card overdraft loans (included in revolving installment credit in Table 10-1) seem to promise the highest rate of growth in the future. Credit card and debit card lending is based on preauthorized lines of credit that can be taken down as the consumer takes cash advances or makes purchases from any of the more than 1.5 million merchants who accept such cards. This easy access to credit through plastic cards will be helped dramatically by the rapid deployment of electronic banking devices. These devices include automatic

TABLE 10-1
Consumer Credit Held by Commercial Banks, 1971 and 1981 (billions of dollars)

	1971	1981
Installment	$ 51.2	$144.6
Automobile		
Indirect	12.9	34.4
Direct	7.9	24.2
Revolving	7.4	31.1
Mobile home	4.4	10.3
Other	18.6	44.5
Noninstallment	14.0	30.8
Mortgage (1–4 family residence)	52.0	171.6
Total	$117.2	$347.0

teller machines (ATMs), at which bank customers conduct direct deposit and cash withdrawal transactions, and point-of-sale (POS) machines at merchant locations, which credit the merchant's account and either debit the cardholder's checking account or trigger an overline debit in payment for goods or services. As indicated in a later section of this chapter, card-type lending was hampered during the past decade or so by state usury laws, which restrict the interest rates charged for this high-risk credit, and by laws that prohibit card banks from charging the consumer an annual fee for card services.

Automobile Lending

After several decades of rapid growth, automobile debt grew sluggishly in the early 1980s because of slow automobile sales and uncertainties concerning the future direction of the industry. Nevertheless, in 1981 outstanding direct and indirect automobile loans from banks amounted to nearly $100 billion and comprised more than one third of all nonmortgage bank consumer credit. In addition, a significant portion of other installment loans, noted in Table 10-1, were made to finance the purchase of automobiles. These less obvious automobile loans were secured by the borrowers' savings or time deposits or some form of collateral other than the automobile purchased.

Both direct and indirect automobile loans usually have a maximum maturity of 48 months. Direct automobile loans are simply loans made to the consumer for the purchase of an automobile where the automobile secures the loan through a chattel mortgage. Indirect automobile loans are loans acquired from automobile dealers. In this latter instance, the consumer applies for a loan to the dealer who conveys essential information regarding the consumer's credit worthiness to the bank. Typically, banks attempt to aid the auto dealers in executing their transactions by indicating acceptance or rejection of such credit requests as quickly as possible. Banks acquire indirect loans from automobile dealers in "packages." In the dealer relations of many banks, it is understood that the individual loans in a package will vary in quality; that is, dealers are normally permitted some buyers of marginal credit worthiness for the size of loan or collateral value involved. As a result, delinquencies and losses on indirect automobile loans might be twice as high as on direct loans. In addition, banks pay automobile dealers a rebate on loans the dealers provide. Finally, in the interest of maintaining and promoting its dealer relations, banks frequently offer floor plan financing to dealers at favorable rates as well as financing support for dealers' automobile leasing programs. However, the attractiveness of the relationship changes over the business cycle, and during periods of high loan demand many banks play down these support factors.

As indicated earlier, the growth of automobile debt in the early 1980s mirrored the depressed condition of the automotive market. Consumers clung to the family car for a longer period of time and were pressed by rising expenses elsewhere in their family budgets, resulting in a reduced percentage of their income that they allocated to automobiles. Economists at one major bank estimated that the percentage of consumer income allotted to car purchases fell to about 5 percent in the early 1980s compared with 6.7 percent in the late 1970s.

Mobile Home Financing

Mobile home financing is not unlike the financing of automobiles. Most of mobile home financing is indirect, that is, arranged through dealers. Bank relationships with mobile home dealers often include financing their inventory.

Mobile home financing grew rapidly in the 1960s and 1970s with the explosive growth of the industry. The continuing high cost of conventional housing indicates that mobile homes and mobile home finance will probably continue to grow. Many borrowers on mobile homes do not have solid credit histories, and default and delinquency rates on mobile home loans are relatively high. Compared with conventional home mortgages, mobile home loans have shorter maturities, normally 7 to 12 years, and higher interest rates.

INTEREST CHARGE CONSIDERATIONS

Add-On Rates

For automobile loans and most other types of consumer installment loans, interest charges are quoted in terms of an "add-on" rate. The add-on rate is the rate applied to the original loan principal and is charged over the life of the loan despite the amortization of principal by means of installment payments. For example, suppose an add-on rate of 8 percent is charged on a $1,200, one-year loan to be repaid in monthly installments. The interest amount of $96 (8 percent of $1,200) is added up front on the amount borrowed, and monthly payments are determined by dividing principal plus interest or $1,296 by 12 (the number of payments). Although interest charges of $96 are assessed, the *average* outstanding loan balance during the year will be only $600. The resulting effective annual rate will be nearly 16 percent or double the add-on rate quoted.

When more than one payment is made over the life of the loan, the add-on rate will always result in an effective rate that exceeds the nominal rate. This is because the borrower does not have full use of the amount borrowed for the whole time period. Also, the effective rate is higher the more frequent the installment payments are made. Installment loan rates must also be quoted in annual percentage rates (APRs), and the total dollar finance charge must be disclosed in accordance with truth-in-lending legislation and Regulation Z, discussed later in this chapter.

Bank Discount Rate

Another method for calculating loan interest is based, simply, on the amount to be repaid. The amount loaned is equal to the amount to be repaid minus the interest amount. Suppose $1,200 is borrowed at 15 percent and repaid after one year. The interest amount would be 15 percent of $1,200 or $180. In the simple interest method, the $180 interest amount would be for use of $1,200 over the entire year. In the bank discount method, however, the $180 would be deducted from the $1,200, leaving $1,020 to be used for the year. The effective interest rate in this case would be 17.647 percent ($180 divided by $1,020), or considerably more than 15 percent. The bank discount method is sometimes used for single-payment consumer loans and for small business loans. Once again, Regulation Z requires the bank to disclose the true annual percentage rate.

State Usury Ceilings

As with credit card and other revolving loans, installment loan interest rates normally are subject to state usury limits. The usury ceilings usually specify limits on add-on as well as true annual rates; lenders obviously cannot avoid legal interest limits by quoting add-on rates. In 1983, a federal preemption of state usury laws was under consideration. If such federal legislation is passed, lenders would be able to price consumer loans to make them competitive with prevailing market interest rates. However, the proposed legislation would undoubtedly permit an individual state to override the federal preemption by reestablishing its own structure of usury ceilings.

Floating Rate Consumer Loans

In the early 1980s, several major banks and bankers' associations were studying the feasibility of floating interest rates for installment loans.[2] It was argued that variable rates on these loans would help to offset the variable costs of bank funds in an era of volatile market rates of interest. Floating rate loans are readily accepted by large corporate and government borrowers. However, consumer acceptance of floating rate loans still has not been tested. It may be that consumers will have to adapt to floating rates to compete for loan funds in the future.

Prepayment Penalties

Another matter of importance in consumer loan charges concerns the assessment of charges on installment loans that are paid off before maturity. A method must be used to refund unearned income to the customer when a loan is prepaid. However, the bank is entitled to collect more than the interest that would be prorated to the length of time the loan is outstanding because of the high average loan balance during the early part of the loan period and because the bank incurs origination costs which it intended to recover over the full life of the loan.

The usual approach to determining the customer's rebate is the Rule of 78s method. The method varies the rebate amount according to the time at which prepayment occurs and is based on the sum of the installment period numbers. The finance charge in any month when prepayment occurs will be a proportion of the sum-of-the-months digits over the maturity of the loan. For 12-month loan, the sum of the digits is:

$$1+2+3 \ldots +12=78$$

---

[2] Geoff Brouillette, "Clausen Calls for Floating Rates on Consumer Loans," *American Banker* (March 24, 1981), pp. 1, 16.

In this case, the bank's total finance charge in the first month will be 12 times the amount charged in the 12th month; $^{12}/_{78}$ of the total finance charge is earned in the first month, $^{11}/_{78}$ in the second month, and so forth to $^{1}/_{78}$ in the 12th month. If the customer repays the loan in the second month, the bank keeps $^{23}/_{78}$ (12 plus 11 divided by 78) of the total finance charge. The method is appealing to bankers because it is relatively simple to compute.

The Rule of 78s is sometimes criticized as being too ad hoc and unfair to the borrower. In fact, the accurate method of computing loan prepayment charges is to calculate the earned finance charge on the actual (declining) balances before prepayment occurred (the actuarial method). Bankers find the actuarial method to be too time-consuming. In most cases, the Rule of 78s method does approximate the actuarial method reasonably well. The rule is not a good approximating tool if the annual percentage rate is very high or the loan maturity is unusually long, or both.

CREDIT ANALYSIS IN CONSUMER LENDING

Banks' consumer lending activities involve the handling of a large volume of customers. Each consumer borrower represents a small amount of loan business, and banks need to process a great many of them in order to generate a substantial dollar volume of consumer loan business. With such large numbers of borrowers, it is vital that bank managements exercise effective control over the consumer credit-granting process. Figure 10-1 shows four distinct control points in processing consumer loan requests. These control points are discussed in the following section.

Credit Information

As in commercial lending, the most valuable credit information available in consumer lending is supplied by the loan applicant. A bank asks consumer borrowers to provide this information on the bank's own standardized credit application forms. The form generally requires data on employment, income, living arrangements, marital status, assets owned, and outstanding debts.

Equal Credit Opportunity. Under the Equal Credit Opportunity Act (ECOA) and Regulation B, under which the ECOA is implemented, borrowers have the right to withhold information that is irrelevant to the loan transaction. Because of the complexities of Regulation B, it is not always clear to bankers what information they are not

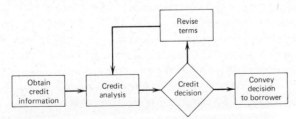

FIGURE 10-1 Processing Consumer Loan Requests

permitted to require of the consumer borrower. To avoid requesting proscribed information, most banks model their loan application form after a standard form published by the Federal Reserve Board that conforms with Regulation B.

In general, the information that is not required is that which might be used to illegally discriminate against the applicant. Information concerning the borrower's marital status generally must not be required if the borrower applies for individual credit as opposed to joint credit. An exception is permitted for secured loans because, in the event of default, the bank's access to the collateral might be affected by the borrower's marital status. This is particularly important in community property states where assets owned by a married person may also be owned by the person's spouse. In cases in which the bank can legally inquire about marital status, it cannot inquire whether or not the applicant is divorced. Such information might be used unfairly in judging the applicant's general stability.

The bank may not require an applicant (usually a separated or divorced woman) to provide information on alimony, child support, or separate maintenance *income* unless the applicant wishes to offer the information in support of her (or his) credit worthiness. The bank may, however, require disclosure of the liability to *pay* alimony, child support, and separate maintenance since such payments clearly could impair the applicant's ability to repay the loan.

A bank may not discriminate against women loan applicants because of their potential to bear children. A bank may, however, inquire about present dependents, including their ages and expenses. Regulation B prohibits inquiries about an applicant's race, color, religion, or national origin. The bank may not refuse credit to aliens because they are not citizens, although it may inquire about immigration status to determine credit worthiness.

It might seem that Regulation B interferes with a bank's natural desire to know as much as it can about a loan applicant in order to be comfortable about its evaluation of credit worthiness. However, Regulation B probably does not prevent inquiries that are clearly germane to the evaluations. The regulation does attempt to block the use of extraneous information that might reinforce unreasoned and often subconscious biases that lenders sometimes develop. On the other hand, some bankers believe that they should avoid requiring too much information so that loan applicants will not feel that their privacy is being invaded. In this regard, requiring too much information may inhibit the bank's efforts to market its consumer lending service.

Credit Reporting Agencies.

An important secondary source of credit information is credit reporting agencies. These agencies gather extensive data on consumers' credit histories, including a listing of outstanding debts and the promptness of payment. Credit agencies compile this data from information supplied by creditors. Regulation B governs the way in which creditors maintain their customer's credit records and how they report the records to credit agencies or other inquirers. The intent of the regulation is to enable married women to build a credit record when credit is extended jointly to married couples. This Regulation B provision corrects a common practice of creditors that omit a spouse (usually the wife) from the credit history on accounts for which the spouse was jointly liable. On the other hand, Regulation B prohibits creditors from associating a person with a spouse's bad credit history if he or she was not responsible for the debts of the spouse.

Consumer Credit Analysis

Bank management must have an efficient credit analysis system to evaluate the large number of consumer loan applications it receives. There are two basic types of errors that can be made in evaluating loan applications, and these should be balanced to minimize overall losses. The first type of error is the obvious one of granting a loan to a borrower who ultimately does not pay satisfactorily. The bank risks the direct loss of income and, potentially, the loss of its funds when it lends to such customers. To prevent these losses, the bank can tighten its lending standards, but it does so at the risk of eliminating good borrowers. The elimination of good borrowers is the second type of error in evaluating applications: the bank may deny loans to applicants who would have paid exactly as agreed. Of course, this type of error can be offset by liberalizing the granting of credit, which increases the probability of including unsatisfactory borrowers. In the simplest terms, the bank's loan application evaluation system should achieve an acceptable tradeoff of losses due to default and losses due to the rejection of borrowers who would have paid satisfactorily.

Credit Evaluation Systems

There are two pure types of credit evaluation systems; judgmental and empirical. In reality many banks use elements of both systems.

Judgmental Credit Analysis. The judgmental system of consumer credit analysis relies on the consumer loan officer's experience and insight when appraising a borrower's ability and willingness to repay. This evaluation is similar to the evaluation of a business loan at perhaps a lower level of sophistication. As in commercial lending, the consumer loan officer also must assess the applicant's character, primary source of repayment, and any secondary or collateral sources of repayment.

In the judgmental method of credit analysis, character can be evaluated from the applicant's credit history and from the degree of dependability demonstrated through length and consistency of employment, length and type of residency, apparent sincerity, and other factors. The loan officer must be as objective as possible and, under the ECOA, must not apply subjective values or personal biases. In using judgmental systems, the ECOA prohibits taking into direct account the applicant's age, although the lender may consider age as a factor in the applicant's future income because age usually is a determinant of time to retirement and life expectancy. Prospective retirement and life expectancy are germane when setting loan maturity.

The applicant's income is almost always the primary source of the repayment of consumer loans. Income, of course, must be adequate in relation to the borrower's debts and other financial obligations. The loan officer must also evaluate secondary sources of repayment and establish the present and probable future value of collateral offered.

Empirical Credit Analysis.   Empirical consumer credit analysis, also known as credit scoring, assigns point values to various applicant characteristics. The points are added to award the applicant a numerical score, which is then compared with a predetermined accept-reject score. Credit is automatically granted to applicants whose scores equal or exceed the accept-reject score, and credit is denied those whose scores are below this. An example of one bank's credit scoring system is shown in Table 10-2. Note that each applicant characteristic used in a scoring system is weighted so that one characteristic, for example, "time with present employer," may have more influence than another, such as "own or rent principal residence." Under the ECOA, such systems cannot use race, color, religion, national origin, or immigration status.

Unlike judgmental systems, empirical systems of analysis can consider age, but only as a postive factor. In congressional testimony on the ECOA, it was determined that most creditors find credit worthiness increased with age and to prohibit the use of age in credit scoring systems would reduce the points usually awarded to older applicants. However, for credit scoring systems using age, the ECOA requires "a demonstrably and statistically sound empirically derived credit system." There should be no age penalty for elderly applicants. When using age as an attribute of the applicant, Regulation B requires that credit scoring systems:

1   Be based on data from an appropriate sample of creditor's applicants.
2   Separate credit-worthy from noncredit-worthy applicants "at a statistically significant rate."
3   Be periodically reevaluated as to their ability to predict good versus bad loans.

The appeal of a credit scoring system is that its allegedly pure objectivity clearly precludes discriminatory evaluation of credit applications. However, this system requires highly sophisticated statistical tools, which makes it expensive to derive and to revalidate periodically. The derivation is based on multivariate statistical methods of either multiple regression or a technique known as multiple discriminant analysis (MDA). The latter technique is an especially good solution to the credit scoring problem and its conceptual base is explained in the following discussion.

The objective of credit scoring is to predict whether a borrower is a "good" (credit worthy) or "bad" (not credit worthy) risk, based on certain characteristics such as time with present employer, income, bank accounts held, time in present residence, and so forth. MDA determines the importance of each characteristic and how the characteristics can be combined to distinguish "bad" from "good."

The actual statistical concept of MDA can be illustrated in a diagram. Figure 10-2 shows a three-dimensional diagram of a simple credit scoring system with only two applicant characteristics—time with present employer on the Y axis and income on the X axis. In reality, credit scoring systems use as many as 10 to 15 characteristics, but they cannot be plotted like the system in Figure 10-2 because each characteristic requires its own dimension; that is, 10 characteristics would require 10 dimensions to plot! The profiles of both bad and good past borrowers are plotted in two dimensions in Figure 10-2, with circles designating bad and xs designating good. The boundaries of each group are drawn to enclose a specified proportion of related points, such as 98 percent. Notice that the boundary enclosing 98 percent of one group also encloses a small pro-

TABLE 10-2
Sample Credit Scoring System—Characteristics and Weights

	Points			Points
1. Own or Rent Principal Residence			(e) Loan only	10
			(f) None given	10
(a) Owns/buying	40		(g) No answer	10
(b) Rents	8			
(c) No answer	8	6.	Major Credit Card/Dept.	
(d) Other	25			
			(a) Major CC(s) and department store(s)	40
2. Time at Present Address			(b) Major CC(s) only	40
(a) Under 6 months	12		(c) Department store(s) only	30
(b) 6 months–2 years	15		(d) None	10
(c) 2 years–6½ years	22			
(d) over 6½ years	35	7.	Finance Company Reference	
(e) No answer	12		(a) One	15
			(b) Two or more	10
3. Time with Present Employer			(c) None	35
(a) Under 1½ years	12		(d) No answer	10
(b) 1½–3 years	15			
(c) 3 years–5½ years	25	8.	Income	
(d) over 5½ years	48		(a) $0–10,000	5
(e) Retired	48		(b) $10,000–15,000	15
(f) Unemployed with alimony/ child support/public assistance	25		(c) $15,000–30,000	30
			(d) Over $30,000	50
(g) Homemaker	25			
(h) Unemployed—no public assistance	12	9.	Monthly Payments	
(i) No answer	12		(a) $0–100	35
			(b) $100–300	25
4. Applicant's Age			(c) Over $300	10
(a) Under 45 years	4		(d) No payments	45
(b) 45 years or older	20		(e) No answer	10
(c) No answer	4			
		10.	Derogatory Ratings	
5. Banking Reference			(a) No investigation	0
(a) checking and savings	60		(b) No record	0
(b) Checking	40		(c) Two or more derogatory	−20
(c) Savings	40		(d) One derogatory	0
(d) Loan and checking and/or savings	30		(e) All positive ratings	15

portion of the other group. Now, we draw a straight line through the points at which the group boundaries intersect and project the line to the Z axis. This is the line, condensed into a "Z score," which best separates the bads from the goods. Also, the bad and good group points, themselves, are projected onto the Z axis where they form frequency distributions of their Z scores. These distributions overlap, indicating the existence of a few bad borrowers among the good borrowers' group (type 1 error) and a few good borrowers among the bad borrower group (type 2 error). The cutoff Z score

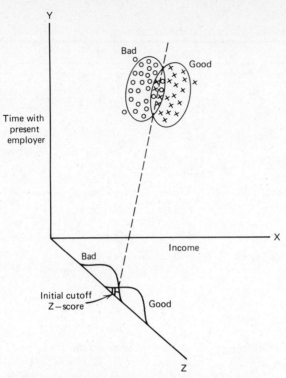

FIGURE 10-2   Illustration of a Credit Scoring System
Source: Adapted from Paul E. Green and Donald S. Tull, **Research for Marketing Decisions**, Englewood Cliffs, Prentice-Hall, 1970.

can be adjusted toward the origin in Figure 10-2 to liberalize credit granting. This adjustment would reduce the elimination of good borrowers but would also increase the acceptance of bad borrowers. Adjusting further away from the origin would reduce the acceptance of bad borrowers and also eliminate more good borrowers.

The credit scoring system illustrated in Figure 10-2 combines the two characteristic profiles of good and bad borrowers into simple numbers. The line projected to the Z axis that best discriminates between good and bad borrowers, implicitly assigns unique weights to each of the two characteristics.

Statistically derived credit scoring systems have two technical flaws that are commonly cited. First, the borrower data used are historical and might be obsolete in detecting current predictors of credit worthiness. Second, the data consist of only those loan applications that were accepted and omit applications that were rejected. There can never be an actual record of the credit worthiness of rejected applications.

Judgmental Versus Empirical Systems.   In comparing the effectiveness of judgment and credit scoring systems for evaluating consumer loan applications, it is important to consider their ability to predict the credit worthiness of an applicant. If credit worthiness can usually be predicted, the bank is protected against abnormal losses on its loans and is assured of a dependable flow of payments of interest and principal. However, there are other factors to consider in this comparison. Perhaps equally important is management's control over the process of granting credit. Control factors such as consistency and objectivity are important to the bank's reputation and to its obligation to comply with laws and regulations.

Both systems are capable of using the same applicant characteristics. However, credit scoring assigns weights to each characteristic and reflects a hierarchy of their significance. In other words, credit scoring consistently weighs each characteristic according to its statistical importance in relation to other characteristics. Judgmental systems are subject to variation of the hierarchy of significance and, in addition, may consider certain intangible factors that cannot be quantified. Credit scoring considers only characteristics that historically have been associated with credit worthiness whereas judgmental systems might use other factors, some of which might be contrary to regulations.

A feature of credit scoring systems is that they consider the multitude of credit worthiness characteristics *simultaneously*. Judgmental systems cannot consider simultaneously all relevant information because of the processing limitations of the human brain. Loan officers probably weigh the information they do use differently from one applicant to the next.

The volume of credit granted and the amount of loan losses are difficult to control under judgmental credit evaluation. Control requires an explicit consumer loan policy which describes credit standards. Policy statements that refer to the many possible relevant characteristics of consumers are difficult to convey and difficult to monitor. As a result, policy tends to be carried out in a nonuniform fashion from one loan analyst to the next. Credit scoring, on the other hand, removes all issues of policy interpretation.

Judgmental methods of evaluation are better able to take into account present and future changes in economic conditions. An experienced analyst should be able to quickly incorporate significant changes in the environment in predicting a loan applicant's future credit worthiness. Credit scoring systems usually are less effective when major environmental changes are occurring. At such times, they suffer from the fact that they are based on customer data from an unrepresentative period in the past.

In practice, many banks use a combination of judgmental and credit scoring systems. Credit scoring readily isolates the clearly noncredit worthy and the clearly credit worthy applicants. The applicants that fall in between in the gray zone are then subjected to further information inquiries and to judgmental evaluation. For example, all applicants scoring below X are rejected, all scoring Y (higher than X) and above are granted credit, and all scoring between X and Y are evaluated further.

Reporting the Credit Decision

The final step in the consumer lending process is notifying the borrower of the decision. Of course, an affirmative decision by the bank is simply conveyed along with actual credit to the customer's deposit account or other means granting the customer access to funds.

If the loan application is unsuccessful, the bank is required under the Fair Credit Reporting Act of 1971 to report the denial of credit to the applicant. The bank either must provide the applicant with the reasons for the denial or advise the applicant of his or her right to a statement of the principal reason or reasons for the adverse action. If the denial is based wholly or partly on information from a credit bureau, the bank must provide the name and address of the credit bureau. The bank does not have to reveal anything the credit bureau's report contains.

The purpose of the Fair Credit Reporting Act is to enable consumers to trace the reasons for the denial of credit so that they can refute or challenge the accuracy of unfavorable information. The consumer is given the right to full disclosure of the contents of his or her credit bureau file.

BANKS AND CREDIT CARD FINANCE

Lending associated with bank credit cards has had the fastest growth rate of all the areas of consumer lending in recent years. Bank credit cards first became popular over 20 years ago. At that time, individual banks issued their own cards and recruited local merchants who agreed to accept the cards from customers. Participating merchants daily presented the bank with vouchers signed by their card-using customers. The merchants' bank accounts then received immediate credit, less the bank's discount. The arrangement provided benefits to all three parties. The bank collected fees derived from discounting merchants' sales vouchers and charged interest on cardholder balances that were carried beyond the grace or free period of 25 days or so. Cardholders enjoyed unquestioned credit from participating merchants, avoided the burden of carrying cash for large purchases, and did not have the hassle of uncertain acceptability of written checks. Merchants passed credit risk to the bank, were spared the need to support their own credit departments, and received immediate cash for credit sales. Merchants also expanded their sales appeal to a growing pool of cardholders.

However, the local bank credit card plan had serious drawbacks. The card's usefulness was restricted to the circle of participating merchants in the card bank's market area. Also, bank card plans proliferated among competing banks, forcing merchants to either choose one plan to the exclusion of others or to operate with perhaps several parallel systems. These drawbacks were overcome in the late 1960s when two national credit card plans emerged to replace the local bank cards. These two plans—Visa and MasterCard—distribute their cards through a network of regional *issuing banks* which, in turn, enlist smaller *agent banks* that further distribute the cards. Issuing banks retain control of the approval of new card applicants, including the establishment of credit limits assigned to each applicant. The issuing banks (not their agent banks) extend revolving credit to cardholders who do not wish to pay their monthly statement in full within the due date. In addition, issuing banks collect merchant fees and incur the costs associated with operating the card system.

An important and complex feature of the national bank card systems is the nationwide computer credit record maintained on card users. Merchants can call into their card issuing bank for credit verification on card users. The issuing bank accesses the national file through computer lines to determine whether the proposed purchase would put the card user over his or her credit limit and whether the card has been reported lost or stolen. The national character of this credit interchange system permits immediate verification of card users from distant issuing banks. The verification process is normally conducted by an operator at the merchant's issuing bank although direct telephone lines connecting the merchant with the interchange computer are increasingly in use.

By 1982, the Visa and MasterCard plans combined had 120 million bank credit cards outstanding. The appeal of Visa and MasterCard to consumers is their worldwide acceptance. Cardholders can purchase an almost unlimited array of goods and services from merchants all over the United States and in many foreign countries. Increasingly, even large retail chains with their own card systems are accepting the two major bank cards in order to remain competitive. The Visa and MasterCard credit cards are not only a convenient form of consumer credit, they are also a convenient form of payment. In this latter role, national bank cards are virtually as acceptable and effective as currency.

The pricing and other features of the two bank credit card programs are similar. Merchant discount fees generally range from 2 to 6 percent with high-volume merchants paying lower percentages. It is doubtful, however, that banks' revenue from merchant discounts exceeds the cost of providing immediate cash against merchant sales, absorbing credit risk, and performing monthly billing services.

The laws in many states prohibit banks from charging consumers annual fees for the use of their cards. Charges to consumers on revolving or unpaid balances are also frequently limited by statute. Before 1981, a maximum charge of 1½ percent per month or 18 percent per year was enforced in many states. Since then, a number of states have authorized statutory limits of 1¾ percent or 21 percent per year. Table 10-3 shows usury rates that applied to finance charges on credit card revolving credit in 1981. In many jurisdictions banks are prohibited from levying a finance charge on card users who make full payment on their card purchases within 25 days of billing. Thus, card users who make purchases early in the monthly billing cycle actually have use of the bank's funds for almost two months. This free period does not apply to card users who make only partial payments on their outstandings; in cases of partial payment, retrospective finance charges are applied to the whole balance.

The statutory limits on fees and finance charges and the legally required free period were not matters of grave concern to banks until market rates of interest rose dramatically in 1973–1974 and the early 1980s. During high-interest periods, restrictions apparently produce substantial losses on bank card programs. This point is demonstrated in Table 10-4, which reports the aggregate net profitability of all Visa member bank programs for 1980. The table shows that income and expense from merchants resulted in only a $15 million profit, which was quite modest for the volume of activity. On the other hand, substantial losses occurred from servicing cardholders. The loss on nonrevolving cardholders, who themselves make virtually no income contribution, totaled $234 million. The revolving cardholder also produced a net loss. In the high interest rate environment of 1980, this loss was due largely to Visa member banks' high cost of funds and these banks' inability to levy adequate finance charges under existing usury laws. In low interest rate periods, fund costs might total half as much while finance charges would be similar to those of 1980.

Another concern over statutory restrictions is that they cause inequities of charges to customers. Studies by the Credit Research Center at Purdue University indicate that consumers with higher levels of education and those with greater income tend to pay

TABLE 10-3
State Usury Limits on Credit Card Finance Charges (1981)

State	Monthly rate	Annual percentage rate
Washington	1% on full balance	12%
Connecticut, Pennsylvania	1.25% on full balance	15
Minnesota	1.333% on full balance	16
Washington, D.C. Massachusetts, Texas	1.5% through $500	18
	1% over $500	12
Maryland, New Jersey	1.5% through $700	18
	1% over $700	12
West Virginia	1.5% through $750	18
	1% over $750	12
California, Missouri	1.5% through $1,000	18
	1% over $1,000	12
Kansas	1.5% through $1,000	18
	1.2% over $1,000	14.4
Mississippi	1.5% through $800	18
	1% over $800	12
Iowa, Vermont	1.5% through $500	18
	1.25% over $500	15
Wisconsin	1.5% through $1,000	18
	1.25% over $1,000	15
New Mexico	1.5% through $500	18
	1.35% over $500	16.2
Michigan	1.7% on full balance	20.4
Nebraska	1.75% through $499.99	21
	1.5% over $499.99	18
Idaho, Wyoming	1.75% on full balance	21
South Carolina	1.8% through $500	21.6
	1.5% over $500	18
Arizona, Delaware, Illinois, Kentucky, Montana, Nevada, New Hampshire, New York, Oregon, Utah	1.8% on full balance	21.6
All other states	1.5% on full balance	18

the lowest annual percentage rates (APR) for credit card services. Highly educated and high-income consumers are most likely to not revolve their credit card balances and they therefore avoid payment of finance charges. They use their bank card for its payment convenience and not as a means of gaining access to credit. As a result, banks must rely on income from their revolving card users to subsidize the free services given to nonrevolving users.

In sum, banks in many states are forced to give away credit card services to consumers who are most able to pay for them. In the future it is likely that banks will be

TABLE 10-4
VISA Issuing Bank Programs—Profitability in 1980 (millions of dollars)[a]

	Merchant	Nonrevolving (paid in full)	Revolving	Total
Income				
Finance charges			$1877	$1877
Discount	$555			555
Per account fees		$ 24	45	69
Service charges			45	45
Fee and rental	7			7
Interchange fees		271		271
Other		11	20	31
Total	$562	$306	$1988	$2855
Expenses				
Operating costs	545	254	396	1195
Fraud and credit chargeoffs	2	152	237	391
Cost of funds		134	1471	1605
Total	$547	$540	$2104	$3191
Net	$ 15	$(234)	$(116)	$(336)

[a]Adapted from Philip S. Hayman, "The Need for Equitable Pricing of Card Services," *Journal of Retail Banking* (March 1981).

permitted universally to charge annual user fees or per-transaction fees. Another possibility is that banks will levy finance charges from the date of purchase. The effect of these changes is not clear. In general, such changes would probably reduce credit card use by consumers who do not presently pay for card services. In addition, nonpaying consumers might switch to the use of debit cards, which electronically debit the consumer's deposit account at the time of purchase and credit the merchant's account. Both types of cards—the credit card and the debit card—serve as a means of payment as readily as cash. However, debit cards have several efficiencies that credit cards do not possess. With debit cards, card users forgo check writing, card-issuing banks need not prepare monthly billings and, in the simplest debit card system, credit risk is eliminated. If enough consumers substitute debit cards for credit cards, ultimately banks' credit card lending might be reduced. It is likely, however, that banks will offer to tie debit cards to personal lines of credit in the form of overdraft protection. With this arrangement, if the consumer's debit card–based purchases exceed the funds in the consumer's bank account, a prearranged line of credit will be triggered. The size of the credit line for overdraft protection for a given consumer presumably will be identical to the credit limit on a credit card issued to the same consumer. In either case, the bank will be exposed to the same risk of default. The total effect on the volume of consumer credit extended by banks remains to be seen.

It is also uncertain whether the two national credit card associations will dominate future debit card plans. Despite their success in gaining the worldwide acceptance of merchants, these associations are only accepted reluctantly by their issuing banks. These banks would prefer to preserve more of their own identity instead of subordinating it to the MasterCard or Visa names. They also voice reluctance over sharing with their local bank competitors the electronic transaction networks that will undoubtedly be the heart of future debit card plans.

CONSUMER LOAN LOSSES AND THE BANKRUPTCY CODE

With the impressive growth of consumer lending since World War II, banks experienced rather sharp increases in loan losses. Loans to consumers usually are burdened with the highest loss rates of all types of loans. Table 10-5 shows losses on major types of loans as a percentage of loan values outstanding. The data are taken from the 1979 Functional Cost Analysis published by the Federal Reserve system.

Banks make a determined effort to try to recover principal and interest from seriously delinquent borrowers. And most consumers conscientiously work to stay current in repaying their loans. However, consumers who are under severe financial pressure can deter the collection efforts of banks and other creditors by filing for bankruptcy under the Federal Bankruptcy Code. The code permits consumers to eliminate part of their indebtedness without being rendered destitute; that is, consumers are permitted to retain certain assets that will help them to achieve financial rehabilitation.

Bankruptcy Reform Act of 1978

Until recently, bankruptcy procedures in the United States were governed by bankruptcy laws written in 1898. In 1978, the Congress passed the Bankruptcy Reform Act, which modernized and consolidated into one consistent code the many amendments and court rulings since 1898. A stated objective of the Bankruptcy Reform Act was to "better protect the American consumer and the unfortunate debtor." This objective was provided for in the new code by setting forth a generous list of debtor assets that are exempt from the claims of creditors. This provision is intended to make it more feasible for financially distressed debtors to voluntarily repay their debts over time.

Two parts of the Bankruptcy Code provide relief for debtors while protecting certain of their assets. The first part, under Chapter 7 of the code, provides for liquidation

TABLE 10-5
Loan Loss Rates (Banks over $200 Million Deposits)

Loan type	Losses—percentage of loans outstanding
Installment	0.548
Credit card	1.966[a]
Commercial, agricultural, construction, lease loans	0.294
Real estate mortgage	0.131

[a]Includes net credit losses plus net fraud losses.
Source: Functional Cost Analysis, 1979 Average Banks (60 to 80 banks participating), (Washington, D.C.: Board of Governors of the Federal Reserve System).

of the debtor's assets to service debts. The second part providing debtor relief, under Chapter 13, sets forth procedures for repayment planning based on the debtor's future earnings (the "wage earner plan").

Chapter 7.　Chapter 7 provides for the conversion of the debtor's assets to cash and the pro rata distribution of the cash proceeds to creditors. The cash distribution results in a formal discharge of the debts. Certain debts, including taxes, alimony, child support, embezzlement, or debts incurred through misrepresentation cannot be discharged. In relation to the previous outdated code, the new code significantly liberalizes the list of protected debtor's assets that are exempted from liquidation. These exempted subsistence-related assets include a portion of home equity, a motor vehicle, and limited amounts of jewelry, household goods, and tools of trade. One banker has determined that a husband and wife jointly can actually exempt up to $40,000 in assets.[3] Moreover, debtors may choose between federal and state exemption provisions, selecting the most favorable. The liberal exemption of household goods in California, for example, is quite favorable to debtors in comparison with the federal provisions.

Chapter 13.　Chapter 13 provides for debtors to retain all of their assets while repaying their debts out of future earnings on the basis of a schedule approved by the court. Initially, the repayment schedule is distributed to all creditors who file a proof of claim with the courts. Secured creditors vote on the debtor's repayment plan. Unsecured creditors may not vote but the value they receive under Chapter 13 must not be less than they would receive under a Chapter 7 liquidation, as estimated by the court. Unfortunately, the liberal asset exemptions of Chapter 7 usually result in no distribution at all to unsecured creditors. As a result, the repayment plans submitted to the creditors and the court under Chapter 13 often provide little or no payments to unsecured creditors. This loophole is highly controversial and appears to deny these creditors a fair remedy.

Once the debtor has paid off the creditors according to the plan, the court formally grants a discharge. The new code liberalizes the old code's wage-earner plan concept by extending it to self-employed persons and by permitting unrestricted joint filings of married couples. Under another section of Chapter 11, many of the concepts discussed above that protect consumers are extended to businesses.

Creditors are prohibited or "stayed" from taking direct action against a debtor who has filed for bankruptcy or against his or her property. For example, if a borrower has filed for bankruptcy, a bank cannot use a setoff against its borrower's account, nor can the bank foreclose on a mortgage or repossess an automobile it financed for the debtor.

Criticism of the New Bankruptcy Code

Bankers contend that the new Bankruptcy Code so liberalizes bankruptcy procedures that it actually encourages debtors to use the bankruptcy court to abandon their debts. In the opinion of one banker, "Congress may have inadvertently created a law by

---

[3] Paul J. Pfeilsticker, "Soaring Personal Bankruptcies: The Realities of the New Act," *Journal of Retail Banking* (Sept. 1980), pp. 7–15.

TABLE 10-6
Personal Bankruptcy Filings

Year	Number of filings
Before new code	
1975[a]	266,000
1979	228,000
After new code	
1981[a]	460,000

[a]Recession years.
Source: Division of Bankruptcy of the Administrative Office of the United States Courts.

which most people in the United States could lawfully walk out on their debts while keeping all of their property."[4] In fact, the rise of personal bankruptcy filings nationally following the effective date of the new code on October 1, 1979, seems to support this contention, although recessionary conditions after 1979 have also contributed to this rise.

Table 10-6 shows the considerable increase in filings in the recent recession year 1981 (after the new code) over earlier recession year 1975. Moreover, one estimate suggests that in a recent single year, over $2 billion in consumer debts were discharged through bankruptcy proceedings.[5] Bankers point out that the costs of writing off bad consumer debts must be passed along to other consumers. Otherwise, it is argued, banks could not afford to continue with their consumer lending programs. However, another lesson is also implied in the profusion of bankruptcies. That lesson is that bankers must realistically evaluate a consumer's ability to pay and they must avoid making easy credit available to marginal borrowers.

CONSUMER REGULATION AND COMPLIANCE

During a decade beginning in the late 1960s, the U.S. Congress passed a comprehensive regulatory legislation package to protect consumers in their dealings with financial institutions. Table 10-7 shows a listing and description of the most significant regulations included in this package. As described previously in this chapter, Regulation B (Equal Credit Opportunity) and the Fair Credit Reporting Act are vital considerations in the process of credit investigation and analysis. Regulation Z (Truth in Lending) has had such a significant impact on bank compliance efforts that it warrants separate discussion in a later section. Several regulations deal primarily with housing and mortgage matters and are relevant to the discussion on real estate lending in Chapter 11.

Banks have developed intricate systems of internal controls to be sure that they

[4] Frank Sennott, "Bankruptcy Abuse Jeopardizes Consumer Credit Privileges," *American Banker* (March 24, 1981), pp. 13, 14, 17.

[5] Michael G. Noah, "Bankruptcy: One Bank's Response," *Journal of Retail Banking* (Sept. 1981), pp. 15–22.

TABLE 10-7
Regulations and Laws Pertaining to Consumer Lending

Regulation AA (Consumer Inquiries and Complaints)

Sets forth procedures for investigating and processing complaints by a consumer in relation to the denial of credit. (Applies to state member banks.)

Regulation B (Equal Credit Opportunity)

Prohibits discrimination against a credit applicant on the basis of race, sex, color, marital status, religion, age, receipt of public assistance, and national origin in any credit transaction.

Regulation BB (Community Reinvestment)

Forbids the arbitrary consideration of geographic factors or redlining in granting credit within the financial institution's local community. Redlining consists of blanket refusal to grant credit within circumscribed (redlined) neighborhoods deemed by the bank to be in physical and economic decline.

Regulation C (Home Mortgage Disclosure)

Details reporting requirements of geographical data on mortgages to enable regulators to detect redlining practices.

Regulation E (Electronic Funds Transfer)

Limits consumer liability for unauthorized use of lost credit or debit cards. Controls issuance of cards and specifies information to be supplied consumer in using electronic transfer devices.

Regulation Z (Truth in Lending)

Requires that consumers be given meaningful and consistent information on the cost of credit. Certain nonprice information must also be disclosed.

Fair Housing Act

Prohibits discrimination in housing and housing credit on the basis of race, color, religion, national origin, or sex. The FHA preceded passage of the Equal Credit Opportunity Act, which defined several additional bases of discrimination. The FHA prohibits redlining housing credit.

Fair Credit Reporting Act

Grants consumers access to their credit bureau records, and entitles them to check the source of information and its accuracy. Denials of credit by banks on the basis of credit bureau information must be reported to consumers.

Real Estate Settlement Procedures Act

Requires detailed statement of settlement costs on real estate transactions and reporting of borrowers' rights in the granting of mortgage credit.

comply with these regulations. These controls ensure that documentation required by the new regulations is produced and they set up mechanisms to monitor actual functional compliance.

Most banks employ a compliance officer who is responsible to senior management for seeing that the bank's compliance program is effective. Large banks may have several persons responsible for the compliance function. Small banks usually assign the compliance function as an additional duty for an officer who carries conventional banking responsibilities as well. Compliance programs create a lot of expense for banks. However, noncompliance is potentially much more expensive because it can lead to severe pecuniary penalties and even prison sentences for managers who knowingly fail to observe consumer regulations.

A bank's policies and procedures in relation to regulatory compliance are generally set forth in a compliance manual. This manual contains the banks' policy statement on compliance, detailed procedures including instructions to employees on completing loan and consumer disclosure forms, and instructions on the filing and retention of documents proving compliance. The compliance manual serves two basic purposes. First, its existence satisfies examiners who wish to see the bank's policies and procedures made explicit. Second, and probably more important, it serves as a control tool to uniformly instruct and inform bank personnel.

Truth in Lending

Originally passed by the Congress in 1968, the Truth in Lending Act and the associated Regulation Z enforced by the Federal Reserve system represent a major compliance burden on banks. The Truth in Lending Act, as with much of consumer protection legislation, was prompted by what the Congress considered to be abuses by creditors. The Congress believed that banks and other lenders were not giving consumers enough information about credit. It thought that the terminology used by lenders varied too widely, causing confusion and poor borrowing decisions by consumers. The Truth in Lending Act was designed to standardize the methods of disclosing loan terms of creditors, so that consumers could effectively shop for the best deal on a loan among alternative lenders. The act emphasized disclosure of key credit information in straightforward terms by focusing on "the finance charge" and "the annual percentage rate" (APR).

The finance charge simply expresses the total dollar amount of the cost of credit. This total includes not only interest costs but also ancillary charges such as points[6] or credit insurance premiums. In addition to the finance charge sum, the lender must disclose prepayment penalties, charges in the event that the borrower defaults, and any security interest taken on collateral.

The second crucial provision specifies standard rules for determining the APR. The APR is the simple annual rate computed by the actuarial method. For example, the lender cannot represent the add-on rate used in installment contracts as the APR. Unlike the add-on rate, the APR must be computed in such a way that any declining loan balance outstanding is recognized. In the case of credit card or other revolving-type credit, the APR is the monthly percentage finance charge multiplied by 12. For example, if an open-end credit plan charges 1.75 percent per month on the unpaid balance, the APR would be 21 percent.

In general, lenders must "clearly and conspicuously" disclose all material terms of the loan and must do so before the credit is extended. The act further regulates credit

---

[6] One point represents 1 percent of the total loan amount charged "on the front end" as a loan origination fee. For example, 3 points on a $10,000 loan equals $300.

advertising. Most important, the lender cannot advertise one feature of its credit offer without stating other details such as means of determining the finance charge and the actual APR.

Truth in Lending contains provisions for certain civil penalties to force compliance. Initially, an automatic $100 minimum civil penalty was imposed for violations.

As passed in 1968, the Truth in Lending Act was so exacting in its requirements that consumers were actually confused with the technical details of statements of disclosure of loan terms. Out of frustration, many consumers failed to read the disclosure statements, making the technical details self-defeating. Furthermore, compliance by lenders was quite difficult under the disclosure requirements and ambiguities of the act coupled with the Federal Reserve system's literal interpretations. Compliance was made even more difficult by the highly technical findings in over 15,000 civil lawsuits filed in federal courts under Truth in Lending through 1980.

Finally, in 1980, the Congress passed the Truth in Lending Simplification and Reform Act. This act reduced some of the original disclosure requirements, exempted agricultural credit from the act, and provided standard disclosure forms that ensured compliance if used by lenders.

SUMMARY

The granting of all types of credit to consumers by banks has grown dramatically in the past 30 or more years. This type of credit now makes up over one third of the average bank's loan portfolio. Installment credit is mostly used for the purchase of household durables and automobiles. Revolving credit, especially that associated with credit or debit cards, is increasingly used to purchase a wide variety of personal goods and services. Card-type transactions are valued by consumers for their convenience as a virtual cash substitute as well as a source of credit.

The mix of consumer credit appears to be changing rather rapidly. Credit extended by means of credit cards and, increasingly, debit cards is expanding at a fast rate. The future growth of this form of consumer debt seems assured as electronic devices that utilize them proliferate. On the other hand, automobile lending most likely will gradually shrink as a proportion of total bank consumer lending due to future slow growth or even a decline in automobile sales.

Installment lending is characterized by low amounts per loan and high volume in terms of numbers of loans. Banks have to organize efficiently to receive, analyze, and evaluate loan applications and to advise consumers of their decisions. Formal credit scoring systems are an appropriate approach to efficient processing at banks with a particularly high flow rate of installment loan applications. For large banks, the benefits of a credit scoring system probably outweigh the costs of maintaining and updating the system through the sophisticated statistical techniques on which such systems are based. No credit scoring system can be entirely devoid of judgment, however; applications that fall in the gray area need further individual attention. Small banks probably cannot justify a statistically verified scoring system tailored to their clientele. Probably small banks will always need to depend primarily on judgment.

Consumer lending is further complicated by a host of federal consumer protection regulations that require careful compliance. Part of any major consumer lending program in a bank must be a system for monitoring and documenting the bank's adherence to consumer regulations. Regulation B (Equal Credit Opportunity) and Regulation Z (Truth in Lending) particularly demand the bank's comprehension and careful implementation. Recognition of the complexity of such regulations is growing, and, as a result, the Congress is regularly promoting legislation to simplify them.

11

SPECIAL MARKETS FOR BANK LOANS

Chapters 8 and 9 covered in a general way the major facets of making loans. Chapter 8 presented the general principles associated with credit investigation and analysis of business borrowers. Four factors are basic in evaluating the likelihood that a loan will be repaid promptly and in full. First, the character and credit history of the borrower must be determined. Second, the specific use of the loan funds and its appropriateness should be ascertained. Third, a source of repayment normally related to the borrower's primary activity must be evaluated. And, finally, a secondary (collateral) source of repayment should be identified. Chapter 9 discussed the general considerations involved in structuring a loan. These considerations included term to maturity, securing collateral and realizing on it, pricing, commitments, and covenants.

Though covered in general terms, most of these facets apply to a cross section of loans made to a special customer group or made routinely for a narrow purpose.

The present chapter reviews selected narrow purpose types of loans in light of the principles and considerations covered in Chapters 8 and 9. The specific types of loans we will review include the following:

1 International.

2 Agricultural.

3 Real estate.

4 Government guaranteed.

5 Lease financing.

6 Oil and gas.

INTERNATIONAL LENDING ACTIVITY

Commercial banks truly are at the heart of the international financial system. They facilitate world trade and support the international expansion of multinational corporations by financing an array of international transactions. Their major role in short-term finance is to guarantee customers' international trade obligations, discount international paper, and make international payments. Larger U.S. banks, those with over a half billion dollars in total assets, usually engage directly in these aspects of international banking. Smaller banks can offer these international loan-related services through correspondent banks.

U.S. banks' role in longer term international finance consists of direct lending to foreign entities, including banks and nonbanks. All U.S. money center banks, as well as many large regional banks, do a significant amount of this type of lending.

Short-Term Finance

International trade credit and the documents associated with it are more complicated than their domestic equivalents. This is because international trade cuts across two bodies of laws and regulations and because the buyers and sellers (importers and exporters) are less accessible to each other. These complications often require that banks help to intermediate import-export transactions.

Simple Trade Account.   In the simplest form of international trade, the *open account* basis, banks actually have only a simple transactions role. In the open account basis, the importer and exporter are well-known to each other and probably have established a successful working relationship. The importer orders goods and promptly pays for them when the goods and title thereto are received.

Almost as simple is the *foreign collection* basis, in which a bank is used to transmit collected funds. Before shipment, the importer places funds with his or her bank so that the exporter is assured that payment will be made with collected funds. In this instance, the bank is merely an agent and not a lender.

Bank Drafts.   Financial instruments such as *bank drafts* and *letters of credit* reduce some of the uncertainties of international transactions. A *sight draft* is usually prepared by the exporter and addressed to the importer ordering the importer to pay on receipt of the goods. When signed and "accepted" by the importer and formally acknowledged by the importer's bank, the exporter can use the draft as collateral to borrow funds from his or her own bank, creating, in effect, an international form of accounts receivable financing. Acceptance by the importer or the importer's bank makes the draft an irrevocable instrument of payment.

An alternative form of draft is the *time draft*, which allows a specified period of time after the goods are delivered before payment is due. For example, payment terms might be 30, 60, or 90 day's sight. A time draft that has been accepted by the importer's bank is called a *banker's acceptance*. When the bank accepts the draft, the bank guarantees that it will pay the draft on maturity; that is, it effectively replaces the importer's credit with its own credit. As a rule, the exporter as well as the investment markets put greater stock in the bank's credit worthiness than the importer's credit worthiness.

The exporter may attempt to sell the banker's acceptance to an investor at a discount that is consistent with the market rate on banker's acceptances at the time. Alternatively, the bank might effectively extend credit by buying the acceptance from the exporter at the appropriate discount. The bank might then choose to sell it in the banker's acceptance market and later, at maturity, pay off the investor at par as the payment from the importer comes due.

Letters of Credit. The sight or time draft transactions described above usually involve *letters of credit*. The letter of credit (L/C) is typically issued by an importer's bank, that is, the *issuing bank*. The issuing bank's L/C signifies that the bank agrees to pay the importer's obligation to an exporter resulting from a sales agreement, contingent on receiving documentation proving that shipment was made. In return for the L/C, the importer warrants that he or she will pay the bank the sales amount and any fees.

The letter of credit is crucial to exporters when a foreign customer is not well-known or if the customer's credit is suspect for any reason. The L/C substitutes the issuing bank's credit and reputation for that of the importer.

The issuing bank sends the L/C covering the amount of the sale to the exporter's bank (called the *paying bank*) in the exporter's country. The paying bank, in turn, sends the L/C to the exporter. When shipment is made, the exporter presents its sight or time draft along with proof-of-shipment documents to its (paying) bank. The ex-

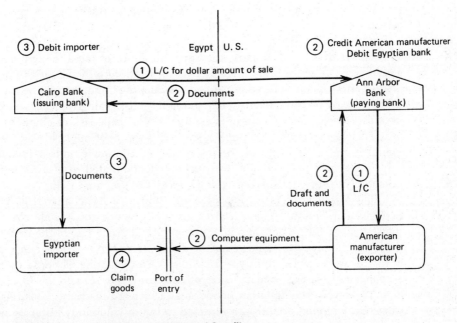

FIGURE 11-1 Typical Path of Letters of Credit

porter's bank then pays the seller, debits the account of the importer's bank, and sends the documents on to the importer's bank. Upon receipt of the documents, the importer's bank debits the importer's account and conveys the documents, representing title to the goods, to the importer.

Figure 11-1, based on an agreement by an American computer manufacturer (exporter) to sell computer equipment to an Egyptian buyer (importer), illustrates the transactions just described. In Step 1, the buyer's bank in Cairo issues its L/C to the computer manufacturer's bank in Ann Arbor, which sends it to the manufacturer. In Step 2, the manufacturer in Ann Arbor ships the computer equipment to Cairo and presents the sight draft and shipping documents to its bank. The bank in Ann Arbor credits the manufacturer's account for the amount of the sale, debits the Egyptian's issuing bank's account, and sends the documents to the issuing bank. In Step 3, the Egyptian bank receives the documents and debits the dollar equivalent amount from the buyer's account and presents the documents to the buyer. Finally, in Step 4, with the shipping documents and effective title in hand, the buyer claims the computer equipment.

Letters of credit may be confirmed or unconfirmed and revocable or irrevocable. Confirmed irrevocable L/Cs bear the guarantee of payment by both the issuing and confirming (paying) banks. An unconfirmed irrevocable L/C bears the guarantee of the issuing bank only, and a revocable L/C does not carry either bank's guarantee.

Insuring Against Foreign Exchange Risk

An ever-present dimension of international trade, particularly with credit sales, is the risk of changing currency values. International transactions are invariably denominated in the currency of either (1) the exporter's nation, (2) the importer's nation, or (3) a third nation. In the case of the computer sale, if payment terms are 90 days and the sale is in terms of U.S. dollars, the Egyptian importer faces foreign exchange risk because the value of the dollar may increase in relation to the Egyptian pound during the credit period. Then, when payment comes due, the importer may be forced to pay out more pounds for any fixed dollar amount. If the sale is denominated in Egyptian pounds, the U.S. manufacturer is exposed to the same risk of changing currency values. This currency risk compounds the credit risk that might already be born by the manufacturer when it extends 90-day credit to the importer unless it requires an irrevocable confirmed L/C. Finally, transactions denominated in a third nation's currency potentially exposes both exporter and importer to exchange risk.

Banks assist traders in covering or insuring against exchange risks by putting them in the *forward market*. The forward market offers contracts to sell or buy a foreign currency at some future date at a guaranteed rate of exchange. In the case just described, the Egyptian importer could *cover* the dollar transaction 90 days hence by contracting in the forward market to buy or sell dollars. For example, suppose the current (spot) exchange rate for U.S. dollars to Egyptian pounds is $1.23 and the 90-day forward rate is $1.12; that is, the Egyptian pound is at a forward discount. This relationship indicates that Egyptian pounds are expected to fall in value in relation to the U.S. dollar, which would result in an increase in the Egyptian pound price of the computer equipment. As protection against this increase in price, the importer would *sell* Egyptian pounds against dollars for delivery in 90 days. The amount of forward Egyptian pounds sold would be the approximate amount of the computer equipment sales agreement.

The details of hedging against foreign exchange risk are beyond our coverage of the topic here. Suffice to say, however, that such hedging will permit a firm to lock in the cost of fluctuations in currency values at an amount equal to the forward discount. In this case, regardless of whether the Egyptian pound appreciates or even depreciates more than implied by the forward rate, the net cost of foreign exchange exposure will correspond to the discount on the forward Egyptian pound in relation to the present or spot rate.

Longer Term Finance

Foreign lending by the domestic and foreign offices of U.S. banks totaled over $650 billion at the end of 1981. U.S. banks accounted for about half of all international bank loans outstanding worldwide. The extraordinary penetration of foreign loan markets is, of course, stimulated by profit opportunities. The impact on the earnings of the largest money center banks is extremely important. International earnings frequently account for over half of the total annual earnings of the largest dozen or so banks. For Citicorp in New York City, international earnings provided over 80 percent of the bank's earnings in several recent years.

Foreign lending by banks takes place through both their domestic offices and their foreign branches. Before 1960, most foreign credits were extended by U.S. banks to foreigners and to U.S. companies that were investing in their own foreign operations; in many ways, U.S. banks were a unique source of capital in a capital-short world.

Eurodollar Markets. In the 1960s and 1970s, international financial markets blossomed and flourished. They were fed by the flow of U.S. dollars abroad by means of balance-of-payments deficits and United States-imposed controls in the 1960s on the use of dollars to finance foreign operations. The combination of these two factors led to the development of the Eurodollar market. This market mobilized dollar balances held in foreign countries for the financing of foreign business. U.S. banks quickly established branches throughout the world in order to participate in Eurodollar-based lending.

Lending to Developing Countries. During the 1970s, U.S. banks rapidly expanded their lending to the developing countries of the world. They were especially active in recycling dollars that flowed to oil-exporting nations after the extreme increases in world oil prices that occurred in 1973–1974 and 1979–1980. With these increases, the OPEC nations rapidly built up their deposits with U.S. banks. Conversely, the developing countries of Africa, Asia, and Latin America borrowed huge sums from U.S. banks to cover their balance-of-payments pressures due to the increased cost of oil and rising imports.

Long-term international loans take several forms. Private-sector firms in industrial nations borrow long term under guarantees by their respective governments. Governments and private borrowers in less developed countries (LDCs) borrow large blocks of funds from syndicates of international banks. Much of the latter types of loans are not guaranteed and might represent unusual risk to banks.

Banks with large international credits limit their concentrations of loans in any one country according to the perceived "country risk." Country risk generally refers to economic and political conditions existing in a country. In any case, a loan to the foreign nation's government or its agencies is generally safer than a loan to a private-sector borrower. Even loans to governments may be unsafe, however, because of what is called "sovereign risk." When foreign governments experience economic or political pressures, there is a risk that they will divert resources to the correction of their domestic problems at the expense of servicing their debts to external lenders. There have been several instances in which less developed nations have requested the rescheduling of bank loans at considerable sacrifice in interest income to the banks involved. At the extreme, governments might simply repudiate their debts; that is, they might no longer recognize their obligations to external creditors.

Clearly, the credit analysis process for international lending is a big, sometimes global, task. Banks with major foreign loans must understand the foreign country's history, forecast its future economic performance and monitor its internal political and structural changes. In addition, because of nations' world economic interdependence, banks must be cognizant of how their client nations are affected by changes in the world economy.

Country risk among large banks that have been so active in recycling OPEC dollars back to poor, nonoil exporting countries, probably cannot be increased much further. Still, the developing countries will continue to run deficits in their current accounts. Where will their future borrowings to cover their deficits be found?

Several promising financial innovations have been introduced that involve large U.S. and foreign commercial banks but that do not increase the country risk of these banks. For example, recent issues of intermediate-term notes on behalf of developing countries are being underwritten by U.S. banks for sale in Euromarkets. Small banks and other institutional investors purchase the notes and unburden the large banks of further country risk. In addition, some developing countries borrow in the U.S. commercial paper market and partially back their issues of paper with bank lines of credit. Also, some experts believe big banks will sell packages of their LDC loans to smaller institutions, thus further distributing the country risk. In any case, it is hoped that large banks will be able to develop new financial instruments to continue to meet the needs of LDCs for funds without proportional increases in their country risk.

AGRICULTURAL LENDING

For about one-third of all commercial banks, farm loans are very significant, exceeding 25 percent of their loan portfolios.[1] These rural area banks hold more than half of all commercial bank farm loans. However, farm-related lending only comprises about 5 percent of the loans made by the banking industry as a whole.

[1] E. O. Melichar, "Some Current Aspects of Agricultural Finance and Banking in the United States," *American Journal of Agricultural Economics*, 59 (1977), pp. 967–92.

Although farm loans are not a major factor in the banking industry, banks *are* a major part of the market for farm credit. In 1980, banks held nearly $40 billion in farm debt, which constituted 25 percent of the market for farm credit.[2] Of this debt, over $30 billion or three fourths was nonreal estate debt; bank's market share of farm real estate debt was comparatively minor. Nonreal estate farm debt finances the crop cycle in which funds needed for the planting season are not repaid until the crop is harvested and marketed. Farmers sometimes delay the sale of crops by storing them in the hope of getting a better price later on. This frequently results in further demand for loan funds to carry the unsold crops and to finance ongoing operations. Farm capital equipment is another source of loan demand. Increasingly sophisticated and expensive farm mechanization has added considerably to farm term loans.

Farm Credit Evaluation

Loan officers in agricultural area banks must have experience with farm problems and must develop the ability to judge the risks of adverse commodity prices, crop failure, and poor financial planning by the farmer.

In judging the farmer's ability to service bank debt, it is important to consider the farmer's financial leverage.[3] One measure of financial leverage is the debt-to-assets ratio, which shows what proportion of the farm's assets are subject to the claims of debt holders rather than the claims of the owners. Even though debt has increased rapidly for farms in general since the mid-1960s, the debt-to-assets ratio has remained rather constant, indicating that equity has kept pace. In reality, increases in equity have mostly come from the price appreciation of farmland, and it is against this collateral that banks have based much of their extension of farm credit. An apparently strong loan-to-assets ratio suggests that a farm is solvent, however, it does not reveal the cash flow problems that a farmer often faces.

A second and more meaningful measure of financial leverage in the short run is the interest-to-return-on-assets ratio. This measure, a reciprocal coverage ratio, gives a more dynamic view of the farmer's ability to service debt from current income. For the farm industry, this ratio has risen dramatically over the past decade, and especially in the early 1980s period of high interest rates. This trend signifies the increased share of return on farm assets that is going to creditors for interest payments. Unfortunately, the interest-to-return ratio is unstable because the farmer's return on assets is relatively volatile due to the uncertainties of weather and crop prices. As the ratio increases generally, the lender's cushion against such uncertainties is seriously eroded.

Farm Loan Competition

Table 11-1 shows the amount and share of nonreal estate farm debt held by various lenders, including commercial banks. The major nonbank financial institution lenders

---

[2] Peter J. Barry, "Prospective Trends in Farm Credit and Fund Availability: Implications for Agricultural Banking," *Future Sources of Loanable Funds for Agricultural Banks* (Kansas City: Federal Reserve Bank of Kansas City, 1980).

[3] The following discussion is based on Barry, *Future Sources of Loanable Funds*, pp. 17–21.

TABLE 11-1
Nonreal-Estate Farm Debt Held, 1980 (millions of dollars)

	Amount	Percent
Commercial banks	$31,034	41.3
Production credit associations	18,323	24.4
Farmers Home Administration	8,892	11.9
Commodity Credit Corporation	4,500	6.0
Other financial institutions	666	0.9
Individuals and others	11,720	15.6

are described in this section. Individuals and others are nonfinancial institution lenders whose extensions of farm credit stem from their primary, nonfinancial business. Most of this credit arises from trade receivables.

The *Production Credit Associations* are a major part of the federally supervised cooperative Farm Credit System (FCS). This system consists of three cooperative lending groups:

1 Twelve federal land banks and 492 local federal land bank associations which finance farm real estate.

2 Thirteen banks for cooperatives, which lend to farmers' supporting operations such as marketing, supply, and business service cooperatives.

3 Twelve federal intermediate credit banks (FICBs) and 424 local production credit associations (PCAs).

The cooperative Farm Credit System's role in nonreal estate farm lending is performed by the 424 PCAs. The PCAs are borrower-owned cooperatives that lend short- and intermediate-term funds to farmers for crop and livestock operations. The PCAs are funded by the federal intermediate credit banks, which, in turn, raise their funds through bond issues in the national financial markets.

The *Farmers Home Administration* (FmHA) is a federal government agency that engages in direct lending to farmers and guarantees farm loans originated by commercial banks. Also, FmHA was recently authorized under the Emergency Agricultural Credit Act of 1978 (amended 1980) to lend funds to farmers who are temporarily unable to acquire funds from their normal lenders at reasonable loan rates. As with the federal intermediate credit banks, the FmHA raises its funds in the national capital markets.

The *Commodity Credit Corporation* (CCC) is a federal government agency that is involved in a unique aspect of farm lending. The CCC is an instrument of the government's price support and farm income policies and provides price support loans and crop storage loans. This form of lending was more substantial in the 1940s and 1950s than it has been recently.

The future share of farm credit supplied by commercial banks probably depends on the economic conditions to be faced by farmers, including the interest rate environment, food and commodity prices, inflation, and export demand. Government agencies and government-supervised (borrower-owned) cooperatives are important buffers against periods of poor farm income and cash flow as well as high interest rates. In periods of farm prosperity, government involvement is less important. At such times, loans to farmers are low in risk and therefore are attractive to commercial banks. If the farming industry enjoys economic well-being, commercial banks will probably increase their share of the market for farm credit.

REAL ESTATE LENDING

Except for savings and loan associations, commercial banks lend more funds for the purchase, development, and construction of real estate properties than any other type of lender. At the end of 1981, banks accounted for $282 billion in mortgage lending, exclusive of mortgages held by bank trust departments. The bank holdings of mortgage debt represented 18.5 percent of the total of $1,525 billion in total mortgage debt outstanding by all types of lenders.

The $282 billion in mortgage debt held by banks in 1981 accounted for almost 30 percent of total bank loans outstanding of about $1 trillion. However, the significance of mortgages in bank loan portfolios differed with the size of the bank. For large banks, with assets of over $750 million, mortgages represented about 25 percent of loans whereas they represented almost one third of smaller banks' loans. For some individual smaller banks, particularly those in developing suburban locations, mortgages often constituted well over half of their loan portfolios.

Legal Restrictions

National banks must conform to the requirements of 12 U.S. Code 371 governing real estate loans. This section of the Code considers a loan to be a real estate loan if it is secured either by a lien (mortgage, deed of trust, or other) or by a leasehold agreement on the subject real estate and if its original maturity is at least 60 months. The code requires the following:

1 A loan on unimproved real estate must not exceed 66.67 percent of the property's appraised value.

2 A loan on real estate improved by a building must not exceed 90 percent of the property's appraised value.

3 Real estate loans generally should be fully amortized within 30 years.

4 Total real estate loans must not exceed the bank's capital plus unimpaired surplus or the bank's time and savings deposits, whichever is greater.

5 Total second mortgages plus the amount unpaid on all prior liens must not exceed 20 percent of the bank's capital plus unimpaired surplus.

The loan-to-value restrictions set forth in the code do not apply to government-insured or -guaranteed mortgages or to privately insured mortgages.

TABLE 11-2
Commercial Bank Mortgage Debt Outstanding

Type of property	Amount (billions of dollars)	Percent
1-to-4-family	172	61
Multifamily	13	5
Commercial	88	31
Farm	9	3
Total	282	100

Residential Mortgages

As shown in Table 11-2, mortgages are classified by type of properties. Residential properties, consisting of one-to-four-family and multifamily properties, account for two thirds of bank mortgage loans. Mortgages on single-family residences make up most of these loans. Many banks appear to avoid permanent mortgage lending on large apartments, preferring to leave such loans to life insurance companies or pension funds. Banks view apartments as high risk and as requiring an imprudently large concentration of funds. To the extent that banks do make apartment mortgages, they tend to be of relatively short maturity and at low loan-to-value ratios.

Government-Backed Mortgages

Most residential mortgages held by banks are "conventional" loans, meaning that they are not insured or guaranteed by a government agency. However, a significant proportion are not conventional and are supported by government agencies. The Federal Housing Administration (FHA) insures, and the Veterans Administration (VA) guarantees, payment of principal and interest on certain qualifying residential mortgages originated by banks and other private lenders. FHA or VA backing is available on loans that meet certain standards, set periodically by the agencies involved, including the following:

1   Maximum loan-to-value ratio.
2   Interest rate restriction.
3   Maximum loan size.
4   Minimum down payment.

Also, residences that are subject to FHA- or VA-backed mortgages must meet certain construction and design standards. These features reduce the risk of the subject mortgages, make them more attractive to lending institutions, and thereby increase the flow of mortgage funds. These same features also make it possible for lenders to accumulate a bundle of guaranteed or insured standardized mortgages for sale either to larger institutional investors, the Federal National Mortgage Association (FNMA or "Fannie Mae"), or the public by means of the Government National Mortgage Association (GNMA or "Ginnie Mae"). The ability to package standardized loans helps banks to overcome the lack of marketability of small-denomination single loans whose characteristics would otherwise be highly dissimilar.

Secondary Markets.   The ability to sell their mortgages helps banks and savings and loan associations to avoid the problem of liquidity associated with borrowing from short-term depositors and lending long term. Fannie Mae, a privately financed and managed association, developed the first resale market for mortgages. Although Fannie Mae was initially authorized to purchase and sell only FHA mortgages, it has become active in purchasing VA and, beginning in the 1970s, conventional loans. Actually, Fannie Mae does not create a pure secondary market because it deals only in mortgages on which forward purchase commitments have been made. Banks and other institutions bid for Fannie Mae purchase commitments of a certain amount and the commitment price is established at auction. Successful bidders acquire a commitment from Fannie Mae that assures them of a resale market for a bundle of loans to be made anytime up to the expiration date of the commitment.

Ginnie Mae is a government agency, established in 1968, under the Department of Housing and Urban Development. Ginnie Mae shares with Fannie Mae the objective of making mortgages more liquid. Ginnie Mae developed the mortgage-backed "pass-through" security on which it guarantees the payment of principal and interest. To create a pass-through security issue, Ginnie Mae acquires pools of FHA and VA mortgages from banks and other lenders and uses the pools to back its securities. Payments to Ginnie Mae securities holders are passed through from payments made on the underlying pool of mortgages. Ginnie Mae's guarantee makes its securities attractive to investors who would not otherwise invest in the mortgage market. All of this increases the flow of money ultimately available to mortgage lenders.

The Federal Home Loan Mortgage Corporation (FHLMC or "Freddie Mac"), created in 1970, accomplishes for conventional mortgages what Ginnie Mae accomplished for FHA and VA mortgages. Like Ginnie Mae, Freddie Mac sells participations in mortgage pools and guarantees payment of interest and principal. But unlike Ginnie Mae, Freddie Mac deals in conventional mortgages and has truly advanced the marketability of these nongovernment-supported loans. Freddie Mac does, however, require private insurance on most mortgages in which it deals.

In addition to the three national mortgage associations described, there exists a significant interinstitutional market. Banks, savings and loan associations, and mutual savings banks are able to sell bundles of mortgages to larger banks, insurance companies, and other institutional investors.

Credit Standards.   In the early 1980s era of virulent interest rates and soaring costs of interest-sensitive funds, banks mostly sought only to originate, and not hold, new mortgages. As a result, the marketability of mortgages has become so important to banks that their mortgage loan standards increasingly call for conformance to the standards of the secondary market. The standards of the national mortgage associations and institutional investors described above profoundly influence the approach banks take to mortgage lending.

Table 11-3 lists the primary credit standards observed by Freddie Mac, Fannie Mae, and the private mortgage insurance companies in the early 1980s. The standards

TABLE 11-3
Primary Credit Standards for Mortgage Resale Organizations (One-to-four-Unit Residential Properties)

Standard	FHLMC	FNMA	Private Mortgage Insurance Co.
Maximum Loan Amounts	1 unit, $98,500 2 units, $126,000 3 units, $152,000 4 units, $189,000	1 unit, $110,000 2 units, $136,800 3 units, $164,100 4 units, $205,300	No maximums
Loan-to-Value Ratio			
(a) Owner-occupied	90–95%	95%	95%
(b) Nonowner occupied	Not acceptable	75–80%	90%
(c) Refinance of owner's present home	80–90%	Same as a and b	90%
Downpayment Minimum	5% cash or other equity	Not addressed	5% cash or land equity
Alternative Mortgage Instrument (AMI) Policy	Accepts AMIs with (a) Adjustment caps (b) Adjustment of maximum 2% per year No negative amortization	Accepts full variety of AMIs, including negative amortization	Acceptability determined by adjustment rate index, frequency of adjustment, and potential increase in payments
Maximum Buyer's-Housing-Expense-to-Gross-Income Ratio[a] (expense is principal, interest, taxes, homeowners association dues)	25–28%	25%	25–30%
Maximum Monthly Debt-Payment-to-Income Ratio[a]	33–36%	33–36%	33–38%

[a]Requirements for mortgage insurance.
Source: Bank Administration Institute, circa 1982.

listed in Table 11-3 should not be viewed in absolute terms; a particularly favorable ratio may offset an unfavorable ratio. For example, lenders might accept a housing-expense-to-owner's-income ratio that significantly exceeds 25 percent if the loan-to-value ratio is well below the maximum listed. This specific relationship is common in areas such as California where housing values inflated much faster than home buyer incomes. If a home buyer's previous home has appreciated in price dramatically, he or she will probably be able to produce considerable equity for the purchase of the next home. In this case, a favorable loan-to-value ratio of 70 or 60 percent would offset an abnormal housing-expense-to-income ratio of 40 percent or more.

Alternative Mortgage Instruments. The standards listed in Table 11-3 are generally based on the traditional fixed-interest rate and fixed monthly payment mortgage. In reality, the fixed-rate mortgage is giving way to a group of alternative mortgage instruments (AMIs). Because of high interest rates in recent years, banks and other depository institutions were earning less on their old, low-rate mortgages than they were paying for their funds. This "negative carry" severely impacted on the earnings of all thrift institutions and many banks. Most AMIs permit mortgage yields to adjust periodically and to stay ahead of the cost of bank funds when interest rates rise. Several types of AMIs appear to be gaining favor.

The *adjustable-rate mortgage* (ARM) has an interest rate that can be adjusted to changes in a reference index, which is generally tied to open-market interest rates. The Comptroller of the Currency permits national banks to issue ARMs and to adjust their rates by an amount up to 1 percent every six months. A disadvantage of the ARM is that home buyers' payments might rise so much that they go beyond the buyers' capacity to pay. However, to avoid an increase in his or her monthly payment, the home buyer is allowed instead to add the increased interest to principal and thus to stretch out the loan beyond the original maturity date.

Another type of AMI is the *graduated-payment adjustable mortgage loan.* It is designed for young, first-time home buyers who cannot afford high mortgage payments initially but whose incomes are expected to rise. An adjustable interest rate feature allows for below-market rates initially and above-market rates several years into the life of the mortgage. This mechanism causes the mortgage principal to increase in the early years to compensate the lender for the below-market yield. This build-up of principal, known as negative amortization, might add to the loan's risk by automatically increasing the loan-to-value ratio.

Still another alternative is the *renegotiable-rate mortgage* (RRM), which provides for a periodic rollover of the loan every three to five years. The RRM is guaranteed to be renewed, with the interest rate reestablished at each renewal. A problem is that the mortgagor is exposed to possibly major increases in the monthly payment at rollover time, and as a result, the lender is again exposed to default risk.

It is unclear which of the AMIs, if any, will be the dominant form of mortgage lending in the future, although the renegotiated rate mortgage seems to be favored by many lenders. Although AMIs have been accepted in resale markets, they have been purchased only at a discount from prices paid on comparable fixed-rate loans. Probably, as the mortgage market gains experience with the level of mortgagor defaults on alternative mortgages and as the future financial environment clarifies, lenders will settle their preferences among the various types of mortgage instruments.

Nonresidential Mortgages

As indicated in Table 11-3, most nonresidential bank mortgages are made on commercial properties, consisting primarily of shopping centers, business and professional (e.g., medical or dental) office buildings, warehouses, hotels and motels, restaurants, and other commercial structures. Many such mortgages are direct extensions of banks' regular relationship with commercial customers; for example, mortgage financing of a warehouse for a manufacturer who is a regular working capital loan customer.

In comparison with residential lending, most commercial mortgage financing by banks has shorter maturities (10 to 15 years) and smaller loan-to-value ratios (60 to 70 percent). Unlike residential mortgages, commercial mortgages have been based on variable-interest rates for quite a few years; typical rates float above the prime rate.

Construction Lending

Many commercial properties are permanently financed by nonbank lenders, especially life insurance companies and, to a lesser extent, private pension funds. Nevertheless, banks do a substantial volume of interim lending to finance the construction stage of these properties as well as residential projects. Construction financing is a relatively high-risk activity. It often involves a large loan commitment over a period of time long enough to cover the planning, building, and final acceptance by owners or permanent lenders. Construction time is subject to many contingencies, including poor weather, materials shortages, and labor stoppages; on large projects construction time might amount to several years. In addition, faulty construction and underestimation of costs are commonplace. Finally, building contractors tend to be very modestly capitalized in relation to the value of their construction projects and are, therefore, less cushioned against insolvency.

Construction lending can be classified into two types: those loans for which a permanent "takeout" commitment exists and those loans without a takeout. In situations with a takeout commitment, a long-term lender such as a life insurance company agrees to advance permanent funding on completion and acceptance of the construction. Interim construction loans usually require regular supervision, including site inspections, commitment takedowns against construction progress, and assurance that subcontractor liens and other claimants are satisfied. Long-term takeout lenders usually are not equipped to offer these services.

Banks must treat a construction loan that is not backed by a takeout commitment as they would treat a high-risk working capital loan. In a sense, the process of converting construction materials into a finished product is similar to a typical manufacturing process. However, a collateral position is frequently awkward. Contractors must usually post a performance bond, and the project collateral is normally subject to the claim of the bond underwriter.

Because of the risks, construction loans are priced above most bank commercial loans. Commitment fees are 1 to 1.5 percent (instead of the 0.5 percent typical on commercial loans), and loan interest rates float at about 2 percent over the prime rate.

GUARANTEED SMALL BUSINESS LENDING

Small businesses represent an enormous potential for bank lending, particularly for small banks. There are an estimated 14 million small business firms operating in the United States and most of these firms must shop for borrowed funds at one time or another.

Unfortunately, because small firms are riskier borrowers than large, well-established firms, they have few alternative sources of credit. Historically, banks have loaned predominantly to the low-risk minority of small business firms. Business finance companies traditionally have loaned to select higher risk firms at substantially higher interest rates than those on bank loans. However, with the establishment of the Small Business Administration (SBA) in 1953, another credit alternative became available in the form of guaranteed loans.

SBA Loan Guarantee Program

The SBA offers a loan guarantee program in which a participating bank can obtain a guarantee on 90 percent of the principal of a qualified small business loan. Currently, the SBA extends its 90 percent guarantee to a principal value of up to $500,000. However, until recently, many banks believed that participation in the SBA loan guarantee program was too inefficient to make it worth their effort. SBA guarantees were restricted to a narrow range of loan purposes. In addition, the SBA tightly tied the interest rates on guaranteed loans to a base rate it determined in relation to its own borrowing rate and other factors. Also, SBA application procedures and lengthy loan approval times further deterred bank participation. Recently, however, SBA pricing and procedure rules have been greatly loosened and simplified. Interest rates on floating rate loans can now be set up to $2\frac{1}{4}$ to $2\frac{3}{4}$ percent (depending on maturity) over the prime rate. Moreover, the approval process has been speeded up partly through simplification and partly because the SBA now certifies participating banks to conduct the SBA's credit evaluation. This latter step eliminates the delays of sending the application forms to the SBA, waiting for the SBA to conduct its own evaluation, and waiting for the SBA to advise the bank of its approval or denial. These factors and the increased liquidity due to the development of a secondary market, make SBA-guaranteed loans increasingly viable and profitable.

The present application procedure for SBA-guaranteed loans requires the borrower to complete several forms, including a detailed cash flow analysis. Although they appear quite technical, the requirements are no more stringent than a conscientious bank loan officer would ask of a borrower in applying for a conventional loan. The SBA typically is able to respond with its decision to guarantee or not in a week or 10 days.

Secondary Market

The SBA-guaranteed portions of loans are readily marketable. Qualified institutional investors are often eager to bid on the guaranteed portions at prices that provide them yields close to those of government-issued securities. Banks retain the nonguaranteed portion of the loans and continue to service them. The economics of this transaction often are quite favorable to the originating bank.

To illustrate this, suppose the bank makes a $500,000 SBA 90 percent guaranteed loan and sells the guaranteed portion of $450,000. Furthermore, suppose the loan is priced at a fixed rate of 2 percent over a prime of 15 percent at a time when short-term U.S. Treasury bills are yielding $13\frac{1}{2}$ percent. Investors might thereby bid for the 90 percent guaranteed portion at a price that yields 14 percent. At that yield to investors, the bank would collect a guaranteed spread of 3 percent (17 percent minus 14 percent) on the entire guaranteed portion of the loan just for servicing the loan. In addition, of

TABLE 11-4
Yield on $500,000 SBA-
Guaranteed Loan Sold in Secondary Market

Income

$450,000 at   3 percent $= \$13,500$

50,000 at 17 percent $=$ $\underline{8,500}$

Total $= \$22,000$

Bank funds invested $= \$50,000$

Gross yield to bank $= \dfrac{22,000}{50,000} = 44$ percent

course, the bank will continue to earn 17 percent on the nonguaranteed 10 percent of the loan that it still owns. As shown in Table 11-4, this arrangement yields a 44 percent overall return on bank funds invested in the loan.

Although the loan terms appear extremely favorable to the bank, the rates and servicing spreads shown are achievable. In addition, compensating balance requirements might be included in the final loan agreement. The inclusion of compensating balances as an offset to the net amount of bank funds invested would inflate the yield to the bank even more.

The extraordinary yields possible with making and selling SBA-guaranteed loans readily illustrate the distortion that results from market intervention. In the present case, public policy implemented through the SBA calls for diverting funds to high-risk small firms from other uses of funds. The high yields indicated provide a powerful incentive for banks to allocate funds to SBA-guaranteed loans to small business.

LEASE FINANCING

Lease financing by banks is a unique means of funding a firm's need for capital equipment without actually lending to that firm. Just as with a term loan, leases typically give the lessee firm use of an asset over most of the asset's life including the right to purchase the asset at the expiration of the lease term. The distinction between a term loan to purchase equipment and a lease covering the same equipment is formalized in the Federal Reserve's Regulation Y, which restricts leasing by bank holding companies to situations in which the lease is "the functional equivalent of an extension of credit." Types of assets that are commonly leased include the following:

- Computers
- Production machinery
- Transportation equipment
- Pollution control equipment
- Medical equipment
- Material handling machinery
- Oil drilling equipment

Financial Versus Operating Leases

The principle of leasing recognizes that it is the *use* of an asset that gives it value and not ownership of the asset. In a lease agreement, the lessor owns equipment that it makes available for the lessee's use in return for rental fees and possibly other benefits. There are two basic types of leases—financial and operating—and banks can only offer financial leases.

In a financial lease, the lessor expects to recover the entire acquisition cost of the leased asset plus profit. The lessor's proceeds include the rental fees, salvage value, and, either directly or indirectly, tax benefits due to investment tax credits and tax deferrals from accelerated depreciation. Financial leases are not cancellable by either party and they are usually "net" leases, meaning that the lessee is responsible for maintenance, insurance, and applicable taxes. To qualify as a financial lease (and not a sale) under the rules of the Internal Revenue Service (IRS), the lease should include (1) an option for the lessee to buy the asset usually at fair market value, (2) a lease term not exceeding 30 years, and (3) rental payments that provide a "reasonable" rate of return to the lessor. Qualification as a financial lease and not a sale, according to the IRS, is necessary to enable the lessee to deduct as expense the full amount of rental payments.

On the other hand, operating leases are cancellable and do not bind the lessee for a long period. Their term is significantly shorter than the asset's economic life. Also, unlike with the financial lease, the lessor is responsible for maintenance, insurance, and applicable taxes.

For many years, banks could not hold an equity position in real earning property. Finally, in 1963, the Comptroller of the Currency authorized national banks to own and lease real property and, subsequently, the Federal Reserve extended the same privilege to bank holding companies. Bank acquisitions of real earning assets must occur in response to a customer's request to enter into a financial lease agreement. Banks are specifically forbidden to acquire real assets *in anticipation* of unidentified customer leasing needs.

Forms of Bank Participation in Lease Finance

The value of direct lease financing by banks in 1980 totaled $11.6 billion. This activity took place in two basic forms: straight leases and leveraged leases.

Straight Leasing. The most straightforward form of leasing is the direct lease in which the bank provides 100 percent financing. The customer firm develops specifications for an asset needed in its operations. The customer then determines the manufacturer or dealer that is best able to supply the asset and makes arrangements for a purchase. Then the bank acquires the asset, which is delivered to the customer; simultaneously, the bank completes an agreement to lease the asset to the customer.

Most often, this type of leasing negotiation evolves out of a total banking relationship with an established customer. However, some leasing deals are developed by brokers who bring together a client needing to lease equipment and a bank willing to participate. A broker relationship might be especially good for a bank that does not have loan officers experienced with leasing.

Banks also get involved in a modified form of lease financing through leasing companies. In this approach, the bank does not take an ownership position in the asset. The leasing company acquires the asset using bank loan funds and then leases the asset to a client. The lessor pledges the asset against its loan through a security agreement and also pledges the lease revenues.

Leveraged Leasing. A somewhat more sophisticated form of leasing in which banks may engage is *leveraged leasing.* Typically, a bank holding company affiliate acts as the lessor and sets up an ownership trust, which acquires an asset to be leased. The holding company provides only a small part of the funds for purchase of the asset and the trust borrows the remaining funds from an institutional lender such as an insurance company. The holding company funds represent the equity investment and must be at least 20 percent of the cost of the asset. From another point of view, the purchase is leveraged with up to 80 percent borrowed funds.

The institutions providing the debt funds to the trust do not have recourse to the holding company bank (lessor). They look to the ability of the lessee to make rental payments and to the collateral value of the asset. To the bank holding company (BHC), the profitability of leveraged leasing is heavily affected by the tax benefits of owning the asset. The principal tax benefits are the investment tax credit and tax deductibility of accelerated depreciation and interest on borrowed funds. In relation to the amount of equity dollars invested, these benefits are multiplied by leveraging with debt. Generally, the tax benefits of ownership are more significant to the BHC than to the lessee and the benefits are passed through to the lessee in the form of lower lease rental payments. For example, a public hospital (nontaxable) lessee would benefit from leveraged leased medical equipment because of tax advantages that inure to the lessor and that are passed on through reduced costs of leasing. On the other hand, if the lessee is able to take full advantage of the tax benefits, there may be little financial advantage in leveraged leasing.

OIL AND GAS LENDING

A highly specialized form of lending that has increased dramatically in recent years is oil and gas lending. Opportunities in oil and gas production for large and small energy businesses alike were very lucrative through 1981 because of the extraordinary increase in world petroleum prices beginning in 1973 and the subsequent decontrol of domestic oil and gas prices in the United States. Although there are many technical variables that must be accounted for, successful oil and gas loans require the loan officer to apply general lending principles, combined with good judgment.

There are about 40 large commercial banks that are especially active in energy lending. These banks provide working capital and development and production loans to large energy companies as well as to small independent producers. The huge multinational energy corporations need funds to support their activities in exploration, development, refining, transportation, marketing, research, and, for more diversified companies, certain nonenergy enterprises. These large firms obtain services from a number of large banks in support of their diverse activities. Many additional banks in energy-producing areas of the country are involved in lending to the independent pro-

TABLE 11-5
Net Cash Flow Forecast Oil and Gas Proved Reserves

Period ending	Oil production, MBBL[a]	Gas production, MMCF[b]	Value after tax (in millions of dollars)	Net operating expenses (in millions of dollars)	Capital investment (in millions of dollars)	Net revenue (in millions of dollars)	Cumulative present value of net income at 10% (in millions of dollars)
6/30/84	0.575	21.804	56.179	4.410	0.000	51.769	50.081
6/30/85	0.872	23.653	81.790	10.672	0.000	71.118	108.824
6/30/86	3.761	13.377	184.451	12.913	10.600	160.938	229.688
6/30/87	2.361	10.699	134.278	14.205	0.000	120.073	311.698
6/30/88	1.632	8.678	105.515	15.480	0.000	90.035	367.610
6/30/89	0.913	5.917	66.632	15.480	0.000	51.152	396.460
6/30/90	0.717	4.961	55.569	15.480	0.000	40.089	417.026
6/30/91	0.575	4.197	47.409	15.480	0.000	31.929	431.937
6/30/92	0.328	2.658	32.567	15.480	0.000	17.087	439.182
6/30/93	0.278	2.313	29.500	15.480	0.000	14.020	444.594
Subtotal	12.012	98.257	793.890	135.080	10.600	648.210	444.594
Remaining	0.184	4.378	12.859	8.277		4.582	
Total of 16 years	12.196	102.635	806.749	143.357	10.600	652.792	

Present value profile:
At 12%, present value is $420.073
At 18%, present value is $324.426
At 24%, present value is $239.324
At 30%, present value is $182.688

[a]MBBL = millions of barrels.
[b]MMCF = billions of cubic feet.

ducers. The independents represent a large and usually profitable segment of energy lending. Our discussion will focus on the independents because they best illustrate the part of bank lending business that is most directly associated with energy development and production.

Mechanics of Oil and Gas Loans

Oil and gas production loans are usually for the purpose of acquiring mineral rights and developing proved reserves. Proved oil and gas reserves are reserves that are expected to be recovered with the new wells being financed or with existing wells whose recompletion (i.e., further development) is being financed.

Information on the quantity and productibility of the reserves come from geological and engineering data. The data provide a reasonable certainty that given amounts of oil and gas can be recovered economically under existing prices for oil and gas products and costs of operation. Because of the highly technical and crucial nature of this information, many larger banks have their own petroleum engineering staffs to aid in the interpretation of this data as well as the preparation of cash flow analyses. A standard cash flow analysis is presented in Table 11-5.

The individual loan is normally amortized through regular payments out of gross or net revenues that flow from the development and recovery of the proved reserves. The loan officer must ascertain whether this projected cash flow is sufficient to service and repay the loan over a time period that is suitable to the bank.

One issue is whether the projected cash flow for servicing the loan should come from a percentage of gross revenues or from net revenues. Net revenues are those revenues remaining after operating expenses are subtracted. This issue is a source of potential conflict between the lender and the borrower. The loan officer usually prefers to have the right to some of the gross revenues so that the borrower and not the bank has to worry about actual expenses exceeding projected expenses.

Most oil and gas loans take the form of revolving "borrowing-base" loans. The bank extends a flexible commitment which is based on progressive estimates of the oil and gas reserves, that is, the borrowing base. The loan agreement provides for periodic reviews to reestimate the oil and gas reserves as recovery progresses and the commitment is adjusted according to the findings of the reviews. If the review indicates that the new estimate of the reserves, that is, the new borrowing base, will not support the outstanding loan, the borrower is required either to reduce the loan to the level of the borrowing base, to pledge additional producing properties, or to begin making payments out of the revenues from properties already pledged.

SUMMARY

Our discussion of several special or narrow-purpose loan markets centered on the uniqueness of each. For example, international letter of credit services involve a unique type of commitment financing conditioned on individual trade transactions. Moreover, when a time letter of credit is used, the bank's commitment may be made negotiable and sold as a banker's acceptance. Oil and gas lending is unique in its tie to a highly technical determination of the value of proven reserves to be developed and produced. Real estate loans, SBA-guaranteed loans, and agricultural loans are all strongly influenced by the unique role played by government or quasi-government agencies in markets for these loans. Direct-lease financing actually does not entail a loan per se, but rather creates a rental agreement.

However, most of the general loan principles and considerations presented earlier in Chapters 8 and 9 are readily applicable to each of these loan markets. First, the borrower's character and ability to pay is always a central issue. In each lending category we have discussed, an unscrupulous and determined borrower can defraud the bank out of loan funds.

Second, the primary source of repayment must be carefully evaluated as it is the basis of any loan. For example, a mortgagee must demonstrate that his monthly income is an adequate multiple of the proposed monthly mortgage payment. Also, an importer using international time letter-of-credit services must be able to promptly resell imported goods to cover any credit received. SBA-guaranteed borrowers must offer a source of loan repayment derived from business operations. Farm borrowers must be expected to generate funds for loan repayment out of crop or livestock production. Oil and gas producers must offer technical data on their reserves to generate a cash flow schedule that is capable of servicing development loans.

Finally, secondary sources of repayment in the form of collateral are important in almost all loan markets. For example, the appraised value of a home is the secondary source of repayment in the event of default on a home mortgage. In lease agreements, the equipment being leased is already the bank's asset and can be liquidated for value should the lessee fail to meet rental payments. Farmers put up their equipment or real estate as secondary sources of loan recovery should they fail to produce salable agricultural commodities.

It is clear that different markets for bank loans have unique and sometimes technical factors that differentiate them and require loan officers with narrow expertise. However, general lending factors such as those discussed in this chapter are common to all loan situations and are the basis for most loan decisions.

CASE 11
Century Cable Company, Inc.

BACKGROUND

Century Cable Company, Inc., a manufacturer of battery cables, was founded in 1969 in Denver, Colorado, as a partnership by John H. Loren and Alexander M. Parsons. Loren and Parsons each made an initial investment of $15,000 and they shared equally in the company's management. The company was incorporated in 1977. At this time Loren assumed the presidency and Parsons became vice-president. This title designation was, however, more a matter of formal necessity than a definition of rank in the organization. Loren became primarily involved in sales, while Parsons took charge of production.

Century Cable, Inc., sold its battery cables and related products throughout much of the United States. Over 90 percent of sales were made through distributors. The production process involved some fabrication as well as assembly. The company employed 23 persons.

During the first three years, Century sustained operating losses, but beginning in the early 1970s the company became profitable and its performance showed modest but steady improvement throughout the later 1970s. This was especially true since the two principal officers received reasonably generous salaries and perquisities, totaling nearly $65,000 per year for each of them.

Late in 1978, Alex Parsons was compelled to move to California for family reasons and he offered to sell his company interest to Loren for $55,000. A short-term bank loan was negotiated for that purpose and in December 1978, Century, Inc., acquired all of Parsons' stock, treating the transaction as a treasury stock acquisition. At about the same time, John Loren hired a new production manager, Jane R. Scott.

MANAGEMENT

John H. Loren, age 43, held a master's degree in electrical engineering from the University of Col-

orado and was employed by a large national battery manufacturing corporation before founding Century, Inc., in 1969. He had proven himself as a capable manager.

Jane R. Scott, age 32, became the company's production manager in late 1978. She had received a B.B.A. degree from Colorado State University in 1968 and was assistant manager for production in a large manufacturing firm in Boulder, Colorado, before coming to Century, Inc. John Loren was satisfied that Scott could fill the management gap created by Parsons' departure.

BANK RELATIONSHIP

Since its founding 10 years ago, Century Cable, Inc., had been a customer of the First Colorado State Bank in Denver. During 1978, the company had negotiated an $80,000 credit with First Colorado State, which was fully utilized by the end of the year. The firm had been very gradually increasing its bank borrowing for the past several years. The credit was secured by accounts receivable and inventory under a loan agreement. The most recent loan agreement was intended to restrain operations and expansion so that the company could devote its efforts to strengthening its financial position, which was not viewed by Henry Brookings, the Loan Officer, as being sufficiently strong. Borrowings were limited to $80,000 or 80 percent of acceptable receivables and inventory, whichever was lower. Although Brookings increased the credit line from $50,000 in 1978 to help finance the company's purchase of Parsons' stock, he had some misgivings about this action.

Century, Inc., had made steady progress during recent years, but the bank had become somewhat concerned with recent information that accounts receivable collections had slowed. Delinquency percentages, which for some time had been quite modest, were beginning to increase. Credit reports and credit inquiries directed to the bank also began to suggest that the company had begun "stretching" its accounts payable.

Accordingly, Brookings decided to call on Loren to review the company's current situation. During the visit it quickly became apparent that Century was experiencing serious cash flow problems. Nonetheless, Loren thought these problems could be resolved because the difficulties resulted primarily from some slowness in collecting accounts receivable. Loren did not seem unduly concerned.

About three weeks after Brookings's visit, Loren came to the bank with news that a large number of battery cables that had been recently produced were defective. After several months of use, the plastic cable head was cracking and coming loose from the battery terminal. Distributors were, of course, reluctant to pay for inventory purchases until this situation had been corrected. Loren estimated that it would require at least $25,000 to replace defective goods and to correct the production problem. He indicated to Brookings that the product failure was the direct result of a defect in material supplied by a major chemical company. The chemical company had solicited Century's business for some time before obtaining a contract to sell this product to Century, beginning in 1978. The contract appeared to contain a warranty covering quality and pro-

duction specifications which Loren believed would apply to the cracking problem Century had encountered. He planned to pursue the matter, taking whatever legal steps might be necessary to recover losses from the supplier.

During the meeting with Brookings, Loren also reported that demand for the company's products remained good and that the firm had a backlog of orders totaling nearly $125,000, a record high. The company was, however, utilizing all of its $80,000 line of credit as of April 1979, and cash flow pressures continued. Though he remained optimistic that these current operating problems could be resolved promptly, Loren pressed Brookings to consider an increase in the firm's secured line of credit up to perhaps $100,000 to $110,000. Loren said that, as of March 31, 1979, inventory and accounts receivable totaled nearly $150,000, hence on an 80 percent advance basis, Loren felt the higher credit level could be properly secured.

Brookings promised Loren to review Century's total situation and to give a response to Loren within the next few days. After Loren left the bank, Brookings summarized the recent data and he underlined several questions that required resolution, including how much and what kind of money Century needed, what options were open to the bank, and his own assessment of Century's management.

EXHIBIT 1
GENERAL SPREAD FORM—Century Cable Company, Inc. (figures in thousands)

GENERAL SPREAD FORM

NAME Century Cable Company, Inc.	(000 Omitted)				
AUDITED STATEMENT	Audit	Audit	Audit	Audit	Audit
STATEMENT DATE	12-31-74	12-31-75	12-31-76	12-31-77	12-31-78
CASH	3	4	8	9	10
MARKETABLE SECURITIES					
NOTES RECEIVABLE					
ACCOUNTS RECEIVABLE	45	48	47	49	66
INVENTORY	46	50	57	55	68
ALLOW. FOR DOUBT. ACCT.					
TOTAL CURRENT ASSETS	94	102	112	113	144
FIXED ASSETS – NET	30	37	35	42	43
NON-MARKETABLE SECURITIES					
NON-CURRENT RECEIVABLES					
PREPAID AND DEFERRED EXPENSES	2	2	2	2	2
INTANGIBLES					
TOTAL NON-CURRENT ASSETS	32	39	37	44	45
TOTAL ASSETS	126	141	149	157	189
CURRENT MTY. OF TERM DEBT	1	4	4	4	4
NOTES PAYABLE	33	33	30	13	50
ACCOUNTS PAYABLE	33	34	34	35	49
ACCRUED EXPENSE & MISC.	9	10	11	12	14
INCOME TAX LIABILITY					
TOTAL CURRENT LIABILITIES	76	81	79	64	117
Term Debt	8	12	8	4	7
SUBORDINATED DEBT					
TOTAL LIABILITIES	84	93	87	68	124
MINORITY INTEREST					
DEFERRED INCOME / RESERVES					
TREASURY STOCK					(55)
PREFERRED STOCK OUTSTANDING					
COMMON STOCK OUTSTANDING	30	30	30	30	30
CAPITAL SURPLUS					
RETAINED EARNINGS (DEFICIT)	12	18	32	59	90
NET WORTH	42	48	62	89	65
TANGIBLE NET WORTH					
WORKING CAPITAL	18	21	33	49	27
EXCESS CUR. ASSETS OVER TOT.LIAB.	10	9	25	45	20
CURRENT RATIO	1.24	1.26	1.42	1.77	1.23
CASH, MKT.SEC.& A/R TO CURR.LIAB.	.63	.64	.70	.91	.65
A/R COLLECTION PERIOD–DAYS	40 days	41 days	38 days	35 days	41 days
NET SALES TO INVENTORY	8.8	8.5	7.8	9.2	8.5
COST OF SALES TO INVENTORY					
INVENTORY TO WORKING CAPITAL	2.6	2.4	1.7	1.1	2.5
SR. DEBT TO (TANG. N.W.& SUB. DEBT)	2.00	1.93	1.40	.76	1.91
NET PROFIT (LOSS) TO AVG. NET WORTH	.26	.13	.25	.36	.40

EXHIBIT 1 (continued)

NAME Century Cable Company									(000 Omitted)			
PERIOD COVERED (MONTHS)	12 mos.		12 mos.		12 mos.		12 mos.		12 mos.			
STATEMENT DATE	12-31-74		12-31-75		12-31-76		12-31-77		12-31-78			
NET SALES	406	%	425	%	442	%	508	%	580	%		
COST OF SALES							407		477			
GROSS PROFIT	68	17	69	16	85	19	101	20	103	18		
SELLING EXPENSES												
GENERAL & ADMINISTRATIVE EXP.												
TOTAL OPERATING EXPENSES												
OPERATING PROFIT												
OTHER INCOME (EXPENSE) – NET												
NET PROFIT (LOSS) BEFORE TAXES												
INCOME TAXES												
NET PROFIT (LOSS) AFTER TAXES	10	2.0	6	1.5	14	3.2	27	5.3	31	5.3		
ADDITIONAL DATA												
DIVIDENDS – PREFERRED STOCK												
DIVIDENDS–COM.STOCK or WITHDRAW												
OFFICER REMUNERATION												
INTEREST EXPENSE												
OTHER CHANGES IN WORTH												
CONTINGENT LIABILITIES												
LEASE OBLIGATIONS												
ANALYSIS OF CHANGES IN WORTH OR SURPLUS												
AT BEGINNING OF PERIOD			42		48		62		89			
ADD NET PROFIT	10		6		14		27		31			
DEDUCT DIVIDENDS OR WITHDRAW.												
Purchase Treas. Stock									(55)			
WORTH OR SURPLUS REPORTED	42		48		62		89		65			
ANALYSIS OF WORKING CAPITAL												
AT BEGINNING OF PERIOD			18		21		33		49			
ADD: NET PROFIT	10		6		14		27		31			
NON-CASH CHARGES	4		6		6		7		7			
Incr. – Term Debt			4						3			
MISCELLANEOUS												
TOTAL ADDITIONS			16		20		34		41			
DEDUCT:												
DIVIDENDS/WITHDRAWALS												
PLANT EXPENDITURES			13		4		14		8			
Purchase Treas. Stock									55			
Decr. Term Debt					4		4					
MISCELLANEOUS												
TOTAL DEDUCTIONS			13		8		18		63			
NET CHANGE (+ OR –)			+3		+12		+16		-22			
AT END OF PERIOD	18		21		33		49		27			
W/C AS ABOVE	18		21		33		49		27			
INVENTORY	46		50		57		55		68			
EXCESS OF W/C OVER INVENTORY	(28)		(29)		(24)		(6)		(41)			
ANALYST INITIALS	JEB		JEB		JEB		JEB		JEB			

CASE 12
Fireworks, Inc.

BACKGROUND

Fireworks, Inc., a wholesaler of all types of fireworks to dealers throughout the United States, was started on a modest scale in 1947 by James T. Wilson. Within a few years, Wilson accumulated a sizable net worth and expanded into other enterprises to the extent that he was unable to devote full time to the fireworks business. In 1965 he sold 50 percent of the business to the present owner, Frances O. Bass. Bass took over active management of the fireworks business at that time. Although Wilson devoted virtually no time to the business, he continued to draw up to $80,000 per annum from the firm in salary and bonuses.

In October 1978, Wilson agreed to sell his 50 percent equity in Fireworks to the company for $162,488, with the understanding that he would continue personally to guarantee bank loans. At the time of this agreement, Fireworks, Inc., was indebted to Wilson for $180,000. This amount represented an accumulation of salaries, bonuses, and working capital advances. The company's note to Wilson, which totaled $342,488, was secured by all the corporation's stock that was owned by Bass. Subsequent to this transaction, Wilson died in May 1979, thereby ending his agreement to guarantee bank loans.

Inventory for Fireworks, Inc., came from two sources: about 50 percent from two suppliers in the United States and the remainder imported from Japan and Taiwan. Fireworks was obliged to pay cash for purchases from domestic suppliers. The company posted bank letters of credit for overseas purchases to guarantee payment on receipt of merchandise. No prompt payment discounts were offered by domestic or foreign suppliers.

There were two selling periods in the company's totally seasonal pattern of operation: July 4 (65 percent) and Christmas (35 percent). Inventory build-up began in September for Christmas and continued through May for 4th of July business. Selling terms offered were 30 days net after July 4 or Christmas. Receivables were, in fact, largely collected within 30 days after December 25 and July 4, but bank debt was normally not liquidated following the Christmas sales because of early spring inventory shipments from Taiwan and Japan. Bank loans in past years had been paid in full about the middle of July each year, and the company was able to stay out of the bank until the middle of November.

Fireworks, Inc., leased one office building and eight sheet iron warehouses on 20 acres just outside the city limits. Buildings were scattered to reduce the fire hazard. One major fire had taken place 15 years ago when the business was housed in a wooden building; there had been no fires or explosions since that time.

Fireworks, Inc., employed 12 persons, all but 2 of whom handled clerical, workhouse, crating, and shipping responsibilities.

MANAGEMENT

The company's owner, Frances O. Bass, was 60 years of age. Before assuming the management of Fireworks, Inc., 14 years ago, she had served as an assistant manager in a construction engineering firm.

Bass's chief assistant, Teressa W. Clark, was 38 years old. She had a B.B.A. degree from a nearby state university and had been associated with the company for seven years. Clark handled the company's accounting and assisted Bass in general company operations.

FINANCIAL INFORMATION

Fireworks, Inc.'s, debt to James Wilson totaling $342,488 was now payable to his estate in the amount of $72,488 due October 15, 1978, and

$45,000 on October 15 in each of the following six years, through 1983. This repayment schedule had been agreed to by Wilson and Bass based on a forecast of earnings and cash flow projections related to the company's prior operating experience. Interest on the principal was set at 8 percent. The agreement between Fireworks, Inc., and Wilson stipulated that Wilson (or his estate) could declare the full obligation due and payable if:

1 The company defaulted on one installment.

2 There were a change in management without the noteholder's approval.

3 Bass should die or become unable to function effectively as company administrator.

The provision relating to the death of Bass could, however, be waived provided life insurance totaling $250,000 was provided on Bass's life, with proceeds of the policy assigned to the noteholder. Because of the expense involved, Bass had not elected to purchase the insurance coverage.

Bank borrowing had increased over the years, and all loans had been supported solely by Wilson's personal guaranty. Aside from the fire insurance protection, there had been no additional company collateral to support bank loans. Bass had no independent resources beyond a limited amount of personal assets. As noted earlier, Fireworks, Inc., carried no bank debt for about 120 days each year. The company's compensating balances had proven satisfactory to the bank. For about five months each year these had averaged about $200,000, and about $50,000 for the remaining seven months.

The company's financial statements are summarized in Exhibits 1 to 3. These statements had been prepared by Fireworks' local accounting firm, Hastings and Hawkins, which enjoyed a good reputation in the community. The statements carried an unqualified opinion by the accountants that the balance sheet and income statement fairly represented the company's financial condition according to generally accepted accounting principles.

Net worth, or capital accounts, could not be reconciled accurately, however, from these statements since for several years prior to fiscal 1978 the company had elected to be taxed as a small business corporation. Under this arrangement, profits were allocated as in a partnership, and income taxes were paid on an individual basis. During 1977, however, the status was changed to the usual corporate tax entity.

BANK RELATIONSHIP

Fireworks, Inc., had been a customer of the National Bank of Commerce for the past 11 years. Bass had begun discussions with the loan officer, Oscar Harrison, asking for a commitment to carry the firm through the July 1980, season. She requested the same credit arrangements as in the previous year—$250,000 in direct loans and up to $100,000 for letter-of-credit accommodations to finance imported purchases. In the past the bank had seldom been called on to make loans to pay drafts drawn against letters of credit, but this necessarily had to be considered as part of the company's total requirement.

In her discussion with Harrison, Bass stated that Fireworks' excellent earnings history and Bass's management record should permit the bank to deal with the firm on an unsecured basis. Moreover, the company's success was well-known in the community, and two other local banks had previously inquired about establishing a relationship with Fireworks.

After discussion with the executor of the Wilson estate, Harrison learned investments had proven highly speculative. Except for sufficient good quality common stocks to pay estate taxes, there were no other readily marketable assets of substantial value. The heirs to the Wilson estate were two sons and a daughter, who ranged in age from 35 to 42 years. None of the heirs had any resources of consequence except those they expected to receive from their father's estate. Harrison also believed that the three heirs had a reputation for careless spending.

Harrison was reviewing Bass's loan request

and it was agreed the two would meet again within a few days to finalize any decisions of Fireworks' credit arrangements. In view of Wilson's death, however, Harrison felt somewhat more concerned about the new annual credit agreement. Harrison believed he should study the Fireworks proposal more carefully than in past years, and he decided to include additional analysis of the situation in his presentation to the bank's loan review committee.

EXHIBIT 1
Fireworks, Inc.—Balance Sheet

	For the years ended June 30			
	1979	1978	1977	1976
Assets				
Cash on hand and in banks	$176,042	$ 69,803	$180,302	$151,125
Trade receivables—net	271,914	281,465	195,130	184,944
Advances to employees	843	685	455	300
Advances to officers	26,378	25	19,535	0
Merchandise inventory	182,904	142,175	135,675	107,971
Prepaid expenses	7,399	8,777	7,715	8,258
Total current assets	665,480	502,930	538,812	452,598
Fixed assets—net	22,282	23,686	20,563	18,657
Other assets	11,697	8,524	31,481	25,112
Total assets	699,459	535,140	590,856	496,367
Liabilities				
Bank loans	0	0	0	0
Accounts payable	16,196	5,386	1,513	1,499
Current notes—Wilson	72,488	734	5,520	1,864
Loans from officers[a]	35,000	74,180	45,000	0
Bonuses, salaries—officers[a]	95,549	52,490	47,398	40,194
Accrued liabilities	14,869	19,478	14,990	8,012
Federal income tax payable	76,035	0	0	0
Total current liabilities	310,137	152,268	114,421	51,569
Long-term notes—Wilson	270,000	192,204	204,300	191,412
Total liabilities	580,137	344,472	318,721	242,981
Capital stock	2,000	2,000	2,000	2,000
Surplus	279,810	188,668	270,135	251,386
Treasury stock	(162,488)	0	0	0
Net worth	119,322	190,668	272,135	253,386
Total net worth and liabilities	$699,459	$535,140	$590,856	$496,367
Current ratio	2.15:1	3.30:1	4.71:1	8.78:1
Debt-to-worth ratio	4.86:1	1.81:1	1.17:1	.96:1

[a]In 1979 these amounts were owed to Bass only. In prior years they were owed to Bass and Wilson equally.

EXHIBIT 2
Fireworks, Inc.—Profit and Loss Statement in Dollars and Percentages

	For the years ended June 30			
	1979	1978	1977	1976
Dollar Amount Comparison				
Sales—net	$1,645,364	$1,492,044	$1,258,815	$1,090,000
Cost of sales	1,228,763	1,124,725	959,355	833,430
Gross Profit	416,601	367,319	299,460	256,570
Operating expenses	229,397	187,510	172,773	167,262
Net operating profit	187,204	179,809	126,687	89,308
Nonoperating income or (expense)—net	(20,026)	(2,056)	(18,300)	3,977
Net income before federal income taxes	167,178	177,753	108,387	93,285
Provision for federal income taxes	76,035	0	0	0
Net income	$ 91,143	$ 177,753	$ 108,387	$ 93,285
Percent of Sales Comparison				
Sales—net	100.00%	100.00%	100.00%	100.00%
Cost of sales	74.68	75.38	76.21	76.46
Gross profit	25.32	24.62	23.79	23.54
Operating expenses	13.94	12.57	13.73	15.35
Net operating profit	11.38	12.05	10.06	8.19
Nonoperating income or (expense)—net	(1.22)	(0.14)	(1.45)	(0.36)
Net income before federal income taxes	10.16	11.91	8.61	8.56
Provision for federal income taxes	4.62	0	0	0
Net income	5.54%	11.91%	8.61%	8.56%

EXHIBIT 3
Fireworks, Inc.—Interim Statements (in thousands of dollars)

Date: 1/30/79	
Current assets	1,016
Current liabilities	666
Working capital	350
Total liabilities	921
Net worth—less intangibles	167

EXHIBIT 3 (continued)

Cash	50
Accounts receivable—customers (net)	250
Inventory	716
Total current assets	1,016
Real estate and buildings (net)	22
Notes or accounts receivable—off. emp., etc.	28
Other assets	12
Prepaid charges	10
Total assets	1,088
Notes payable—bank	300
Accounts payable	50
Federal income taxes and other taxes	50
Miscellaneous accruals	50
Due officers, partners, etc. (current)	216
Total current liabilities	666
Dfd. debt—officers	255
Total liabilites	921
Capital stock	2
Surplus	327
Subordinated debt (Treasury stock)	(162)
Net worth	167
Total	1,088

CASE 13
Southland Drug Corporation

BACKGROUND

Southland Drug Corporation, a Texas corporation, was located in Southland, Texas, a trade center of 400,000 people. It was incorporated in the early 1970s as a successor to a partnership owned by the two principal stockholders, Judith Anderson and Thomas Logie, who currently served as chair and president, respectively. The partnership had owned two pharmacies, and four stores had been added by fiscal year 1978. All six stores were located in the company's home town.

Late in 1978 the company acquired a seventh pharmacy in a growing suburban commu-

nity located 200 miles from Southland. The acquisition was the first in a plan to buy stores in healthy, growing towns from proprietors who had reached or were approaching retirement age. The $160,000 cash purchase price for the recently purchased pharmacy was financed from Southland Drug's cash together with additional short-term borrowing of $130,000 from the firm's bank, Southland Commerce Bank and Trust. The purchase price was approximately one and a half times book value. Anderson and Logie hoped to acquire additional stores in the same general area of the recent acquisition, primarily in small communities and suburban centers.

All stores except the pharmacy that housed

the headquarters were in leased space. Management intended to lease future store locations rather than purchase real estate.

Southland Drug was planning to open two new pharmacies in key new suburban areas in its hometown as quickly as locations could be identified and financing arranged. The company's goal was to add three or four stores per year, some through start-up and others through acquisition.

The company had standardized its stores to contain approximately 2,400 square feet of floor space. Inventories per store ranged from $50,000 to $100,000, depending on sales volume. About 70 percent of sales were prescription drugs, with the balance including items such as vitamins, first-aid materials, and nonprescription drugs. There were no food or beverage departments.

Each unit had a pharmacist/manager who was paid a salary of $1,800 per month, plus 1 percent of gross sales for a top potential income of $30,000 per year. A second pharmacist was paid $1,800 per month and a smaller percentage of gross sales. Stores grossing $600,000 annually and up required a third pharmacist. Additional personnel were employed as needed; such personnel included pharmacy students and trainee graduates. Three years ago the company established a profit-sharing plan covering most employees. Contributions to the plan amounted to $14,000 in the last fiscal year.

All sales were cash, except to doctors, who were billed monthly. Accounts receivables at year-end 1978 totaled only $38,000. Record keeping had been simplified by keeping customer purchases by social security number only, in order to assist customers in collecting medical insurance and medicare payments.

Training of store personnel was outstanding. The company had its choice of graduate pharmacists from nearby schools, thus creating a reservoir of potential managers for new locations.

The home office of Southland Drug Corporation was adjacent to one the original stores. Headquarters included corporate offices together with attached warehouse facilities. Some inventories were carried here, which were then redistributed among the stores. Most merchandise, however, was shipped from wholesale suppliers directly to each unit.

MANAGEMENT

Judith Anderson, Southland's chair, was 52 years old in 1978. She was a graduate pharmacist whose education included a few business courses. Anderson had spent all her working life in the drugstore business. She had acquired her first store in 1961. Anderson was also responsible for Southland's financial management. Anderson's salary was $40,000 per annum.

Thomas Logie, president, was 47 years old. He also was a graduate pharmacist with a similar background to that of Anderson. Logie was responsible for operations and earned $35,000 per year.

Anderson and Logie were the company's two principal stockholders, together owning 82 percent of the outstanding common stock. The remaining 18 percent was owned by employees and personal friends of the two principals. There were a total of 10 stockholders.

Harold Carter, age 35, served as the company's vice-president and treasurer. He held an undergraduate degree in finance from a large state university. Carter was employed by an accounting firm for two years before joining Southland seven years earlier. His salary was $26,000 per year.

The company's corporate attorney was a partner in a respected law firm.

COMPETITION

Southland was the largest chain of "pure" drugstores in Southland, but two much larger drugstore chains with pharmacy departments had more outlets, and there were a number of individually owned pharmacies in the city. With the addition of two more units in nearby suburban areas, management believed that it would have covered the city adequately for the foreseeable future and that further expansion would be concentrated in other locations.

BANKING RELATIONSHIP

Southland Drug Corporation had been a customer at Southland Commerce Bank and Trust for over 10 years. It had maintained attractive balances and had handled credit and checking transactions in a satisfactory manner. The company and its officers were considered desirable customers and they had been solicited from time to time by other banks in Southland. One of the banks that had been active in trying to obtain the account, the First National Bank in Southland, was approximately 50 percent larger than Southland Commerce and had recently obtained a personal account with the company's president, Thomas Logie. The chair, Anderson, and the vice-president and treasurer, Carter, continued to maintain their personal accounts with Southland Commerce Bank and Trust.

FINANCIAL INFORMATION

The company's long-term debt consisted of a 12-year $134,000 mortgage note, carrying an annual rate of 8 percent borrowed in 1976 from a local savings and loan association. This loan was secured by the home office and pharmacy building; payments were $1,450.49 per month. The company also had a 10-year $75,184 note with the same savings association. This loan was also at 8 percent interest and was secured by the fixed assets and inventory of a subsidiary. This note was also obtained in 1976 and was payable in monthly installments of $912.19.

Long-term leases currently totaled $57,600 per year, with lengths varying up to 15 years. Annual provision for depreciation and amortization charged to expenses amounted to $31,078 in 1977 and $37,016 in 1978.

An additional $60,000 on a short-term note had been borrowed from the Southland Commerce Bank and Trust in August 1978 to help finance a store purchase. Recent personal financial statements from the Southland Drug Corporation principals indicated that their personal net worth was centered in their ownership of Southland Drug common stock and their homes. Anderson and Logie had no liabilities except their home mortgages and nominal current bills; their personal insurance programs appeared adequate; and they recently had completed estate plans.

In the stockholders' opinion, Southland Drug had enjoyed good growth and profitability. Anderson and Logie believed the corporation should have the opportunity to expand steadily by adding about two stores per year as start-ups and acquiring two locations per year from owners who wished to sell in anticipation of retirement. They estimated that each store location would require about $160,000 ($50,000 for fixtures and leasehold improvements and $110,000 for inventory and working capital). Normally, a new store start-up required 6 to 12 months after opening to reach the financial break-even point.

Financial data for 1977 and 1978 are summarized in Exhibits 1 and 2. Projected balance sheet and income statements for the three fiscal years 1979 through 1981 (Exhibits 3–7) suggest that Southland would need slightly over $2 million in additional financing to proceed with the anticipated expansion. This would amount to approximately $780,000 in 1979, $660,000 in 1980, and $595,000 in 1981. In these projections Southland indicated as one possible approach borrowing the $780,000 in August 1979, $660,000 in August 1980, and $595,000 in August 1981, all as 10-year term loans at 8 percent annual interest.

At the end of the three-year planning period, the management hoped the firm would be in a financial posture that would allow growth at an accelerating rate. Southland Drug Corporation's long-term goal was to become a publicly owned company, using common stock in part to finance further growth.

Anderson planned to ask the bank to review the feasibility of these plans and, if they appeared reasonable, to help the company formulate a finance plan that would provide the $2 million capital required.

In preparation for this analysis, the bank's credit department had prepared pertinent ratios (Exhibit 8) and had examined Robert Morris Associates (RMA) averages for drug retailers (Exhibit 9) to aid in evaluating Southland's financial condition, performance, and projections.

EXHIBIT 1
Southland Drug Corporation—Balance Sheet, Year-End 1977–1978

	August 31 1978	August 31 1977
Assets		
Cash	$ 152,784	$ 58,062
Certificate of deposit and accrued interest	—	88,944
Trade accounts receivable	38,442	21,678
Recoverable federal income taxes	—	20,104
Inventories—at lower of cost (first-in, first-out method) or market	748,344	690,444
Notes receivable—current portion	8,160	—
Prepaid expenses	4,864	4,968
Total current assets	$ 952,594	$ 884,200
Other Assets		
Notes receivable, less portion classified as current asset, and other assets	$ 5,448	$ —
Goodwill and organization expense—at cost, less amortization	11,160	—
Total other assets	$ 16,608	$ —
Property Plant and Equipment (On the basis of cost)		
Land	$ 68,600	$ 74,600
Buildings	131,026	131,026
Furniture, fixtures, and equipment	221,180	171,498
Automobiles	45,256	40,196
Leasehold improvements	14,374	12,864
Allowances for depreciation and amortization (deduction)	(172,252)	(150,450)
Total property, plant and equipment	$ 308,184	$ 279,734
Total assets	$1,277,386	$1,163,933
Liabilities and stockholders' equity		
Notes payable to bank	$ 60,000	$ —
Trade accounts payable	163,186	179,488
Accrued expenses	42,848	39,710
Federal income taxes	36,044	—
Other accounts payable	—	—
Current portion of long-term debt	13,053	18,052
Total current liabilites	$ 315,131	$ 237,250
Long-term Debt	$ 184,089	$ 197,131
Minority Interest in Subsidiary	$ 10,400	$ —

Stockholder's Equity

Common stock, no par value:

EXHIBIT 1 (continued)

	August 31 1978	August 31 1977
Authorized 600,000 shares		
Issued and outstanding 200,000 shares	400,000	400,000
Additional paid-in capital	219,000	219,000
Retained earnings	148,766	110,552
Total stockholders' equity	$ 767,766	$ 729,552
Total liabilities and stockholders equity	$1,277,386	$1,163,933

Income Statement[a]

	6 mos. ended 2/28/79 without audit	Year ended August 31	
		1978	1977
Net sales	$2,143,780	$3,443,360	$3,020,164
Cost of sales	1,419,744	2,275,274	1,997,074
Total	$ 724,036	$1,168,086	$1,023,090
Selling, administrative, and	675,974	1,132,914	1,018,674
general expenses	48,062	35,172	4,416
Other income (discounts on	51,070	83,614	73,950
purchases)	99,132	118,786	78,366
Other deduction—interest	7,240	20,098	16,223
Income before income taxes and minority interest	91,892	98,688	62.143
Federal Income Taxes	32,896	39,074	19,828
Income before minority interest	58,996	60,614	42,315
Minority interest in net loss of consolidated subsidiary		1,600	—
Net income		62,214	42,315
Retained earnings at beginning of year		110,552	68,237
		172,766	110,552
Cash dividend on common stock		24,000	—
Retained earnings at end of year		148,766	110,552

[a]Provision for depreciation and amortization charged to expenses amounted to $31,078 in 1977, and $37,016 in 1978, for six months ended February 28, 1979, $11,667.

EXHIBIT 2

General Spread Form—Southland Drug Corporation

NAME	Southland Drug Corporation							
AUDITED STATEMENT								
STATEMENT DATE	1978	1977						
Cash	152 784	58 062						
Marketable Securities	0	88 944						
Notes Receivable—Net	8 160	0						
Accounts Receivable—Net	38 442	21 678						
Inventory	748 344	690 444						
Cash Value of Life Insurance—Net	0	0						
Recoverable Fed Inc Taxes	0	20 104						
TOTAL CURRENT ASSETS	947 730	879 232						
Total Fixed Assets	480 436	430 184						
Accumulated Depreciation	172 252	150 450						
Fixed Assets—Net	308 184	279 734						
Non-Marketable Securities	0	0						
Non-Current Receivables	5 448	0						
Prepaid and Deferred Expense	4 864	4 967						
Goodwill	11 160							
TOTAL NON-CURRENT ASSETS	329 656	284 701						
TOTAL ASSETS	1,277 386	1,163 933						
Notes Payable	60 000	0						
Accounts Payable	163 186	179 488						
Accrued Expense	42 848	39 710						
Income Tax Liability	36 044	0						
Current Port.of Long-Term Debt	13 053	12 052						
TOTAL CURRENT LIABILITIES	315 131	237 250						
Long Term Debt	184 078	197 131						
TOTAL LIABILITIES	499 209	434 381						
Minor. Int in Subsidiary	10 400	0						
Deferred Income								
Subordinated Debt								
Preferred Stock Outstanding								
Common Stock Outstanding	400 000	400 000						
Capital Surplus	219 000	219 000						
Retained Earnings or Deficit	148 766	110 552						
TOTAL CAPITAL FUNDS	767 766	729 552						
TOTAL LIABILITIES & CAPITAL FUNDS	1,277 375	1,163 933						
Working Capital	637 463	646 950						
Excess Current Assets Over Total Liabilities	453 385	449 819						
Current Ratio	3.02	3.72						
Cash, Mkt. Sec. and Receivables to Curr. Liab.	.64	.81						
Accounts Receivable Collection Period	4.01	2.58						
Net Sales to Inventory	4.60	4.37						
Cost of Sales to Inventory	3.04	2.89						
Inventory to Working Capital	1.17	1.06						
Total Debt to Capital Funds	.65	.59						

EXHIBIT 2 (continued)

	1978		1977								
Period Covered (Months)											
Statement Date	1978		1977								
Net Sales	3,443	360	3,020	164							
Cost of Sales	2,275	274	1,997	074							
Gross Profit	1,168	086	1,023	090							
Selling Expenses											
General and Administrative Expenses											
Total Operating Expenses	1,132	914	1,018	674							
Operating Profit	35	172	4	416							
Other Income or Expense — Net	63	516	57	727							
Net Profit or Loss Before Taxes	98	688	62	143							
Income Taxes	39	074	19	828							
Net Profit or Loss After Taxes	60	614	42	315							
Dividends — Preferred Stock											
Dividends — Common Stock or Withdrawals	24	000									
Minority Interest	1,600										
Net Change in Retained Earnings	38	214	42	315							
Retained Earnings — Beginning of Period	110	552	68	237							
Retained Earnings — End of Period	148	766	110	552							
Net Profit or Loss	62	214	42	315							
Depreciation	18	508	15	539							
Total Cash Production	80	722	57	854							
Officer Remuneration											
Gross Profit to Net Sales	.33		.33								
Operating Profit to Net Sales	.01		.001								
Net Profit or Loss to Net Sales	.01		.02								
Net Profit or Loss to Average Net Worth	.08		.05								
Analyst Initials											

EXHIBIT 3
Southland Drug Corporation—Basic Assumptions Used in 1979–1981 Projections

1. Number of stores: FYE 1979—11; FYE 1980—15; FYE 1981—19.
2. Sales: $5,600,000 in FYE 1979; FYE 1980 and 1981, based on a $600,000 average store opened prior to the start of the fiscal year and a $300,000 average per store for those stores opened or acquired during the fiscal year (see Exhibit 5).
3. Operating profit (profit before interest, depreciation, amortization, and taxes) plus other income (which represents discounts on purchases): 4.3 percent of sales.

EXHIBIT 3 (continued)

4. Gross fixed assets: $50,000 per store for each new store and $25,000 per store for each acquired store.
5. Depreciation: Average 7 years.
6. Inventories: $100,000 per store plus inventory in their warehouse of about $26,000 per store in FYE 1979 and $36,000 per store in FYE 1980 and FYE 1981.
7. Intangibles: six acquired stores with an average goodwill of $52,000 per store amortized over 40 years.
8. Accounts payable: Based on relation to projected cost of goods sold and to projected level of inventories.

EXHIBIT 4
Southland Drug Corporation—Balance Sheet (dollars in thousands)

| | Period ending August 31 | | | |
| | Actual | | Projected | |
	1978	1979	1980	1981
Cash	$ 152.0	$ 227.6	$ 302.7	$ 317.3
Surplus funds	0.0	0.0	0.0	0.0
Accounts receivable	38.0	56.0	78.0	100.0
Inventory	748.0	1,370.0	2,000.0	2,600.0
Prepaid expenses	6.0	11.2	15.6	20.0
Other current assets	8.0	11.2	15.6	20.0
Current assets	952.0	1,676.0	2,411.9	3,057.3
Gross fixed assets	479.1	644.0	794.0	944.0
Accumulated depreciation	172.0	230.0	308.0	406.0
Net fixed assets	307.1	414.0	486.0	538.0
Investments	0.0	0.0	0.0	0.0
Intangibles	12.0	126.0	210.0	300.0
Notes receivable	6.0	6.0	6.0	6.0
Total assets	1,277.1	2,222.0	3,113.9	3,901.3
Notes payable	60.0	0.0	0.0	0.0
Accounts payable—trade	164.0	344.0	526.0	706.0
Income taxes payable	36.0	0.0	0.0	0.0
Current maturing long-term debt	13.0	40.2	115.5	165.6
Accrued expenses	42.1	72.7	101.4	130.0
Current liabilities	315.1	456.9	742.9	1,001.6
Senior long-term debt	184.0	0169.9	154.6	1380
Deficit funds	0.0	753.9	1,314.5	1,761.0
Total liabilities	499.1	1,380.7	2,212.0	2,900.6
Minority interest	10.0	12.0	14.0	16.0
Total net worth	768.0	829.3	887.9	984.7
Total liabilities and equity	1,277.1	2,222.0	3,113.9	3,901.3
Net working capital	636.9	1,219.1	1,669.0	2,05!
Tangible net worth	756.0	703.3	677.9	684.7

EXHIBIT 5
Southland Drug Corporation—Income Statement (dollars in thousands)

| | Period ending August 31 | | | |
| | Actual | | Projected | |
	1978	1979	1980	1981
Net sales	$3,440.0	$5,600.0	$7,800.0	$10,200.0
Cost of goods sold	2,236.0	3,640.0	5,070.0	6,630.0
Gross profit	1,204.0	1,960.0	2,730.0	3,500.0
Sell, general and administrative expenses	1,132.0	1,853.6	2,581.8	3,376.2
Total operating expenses	1,132.0	1,853.6	2,581.8	3,310.0
Operating profit	72.0	106.4	148.2	193.8
Depreciation	37.0	58.0	78.0	98.0
Amortization	0.0	0.0	0.0	0.0
Interest expense[a]	19.0	48.4	128.5	159.0
Other expense	0.0	0.0	0.0	0.0
Other income	76.0	134.4	187.2	244.8
Pretax profit	100.0	134.4	128.9	181.6
Income taxes	38.0	47.1	44.3	58.8
Net profit	62.0	87.3	84.6	122.8
Minority interest	2.0	2.0	2.0	2.0
Earnings after minority interest	60.0	85.3	82.6	120.8
EPS after preferred dividend	0.150	0.1	0.21	0.30
Common dividend per share	0.060	0.060	0.060	0.060

[a]Includes interest on "deficit funds" at 8 percent.

EXHIBIT 6
Southland Drug Corporation—Sources and Uses of Funds Statement (dollars in thousands)

| | Period Ending August | | |
	1979	1980	1981
Sources			
Net profit	$ 87.3	$ 84.6	$ 122.8
Depreciation	58.0	78.0	98.0
New senior long-term debt	780.0	660.8	595.6
Increase in current liabilities	141.8	286.0	258.7
Total	1,067.1	1,109.4	1,075.0
Uses			
Capital expenditures	$ 164.9	$ 150.0	$ 150.0
Payment senior long-term debt	40.2	115.5	165.6
Preferred dividends	0.0	0.0	0.0
Common dividends	24.0	24.0	24.0
Increase: other assets	114.0	84.0	90.0
Increase: working capital	582.4	449.9	386.7
Total	$1,067.1	$1,109.4	$1,075.0

EXHIBIT 7
Southland Drug Corporation—Key Assumptions

| | Period Ending August 31 | | | |
| | Actual | | Projected | |
	1978	1979	1980	1981
Key Assumptions				
Sales growth rate		0.626	0.393	0.307
Cost of goods/sales	0.650	0.650	0.650	0.650
Selling, general and administrative/Salaries	0.329	0.331	0.331	0.331
Taxes/Pretax profit	0.380	0.350	0.343	0.323
Common dividends/Earnings − Preferred dividends	0.400	0.281	0.290	0.198
Cash/Sales	0.044	0.040	0.038	0.031
Receivables/Sales	0.011	0.010	0.010	0.010
Inventory/Sales	0.217	0.245	0.256	0.254
Accounts payable/Sales	0.048	0.061	0.067	0.069
Depreciation/Previous gr. plant	0.085	0.117	0.121	0.123
Sales/Net plant	11.201	13.527	16.049	18.959
Interest Rates				
Senior long-term debt		0.080	0.080	0.080
Subordinate long-term debt		0.000	0.000	0.000
Short-term debt		0.080	0.000	0.000
Deficit funds		0.080	0.080	0.080
Surplus funds		0.000	0.000	0.000

EXHIBIT 8
Southland Drug Corporation—Key Financial Ratios

| | Period ending August 31 | | | |
| | Actual | | Projected | |
	1978	1979	1980	1981
Liquidity Tests				
Current ratio	3.02	3.67	3.25	3.05
Acid	0.65	0.67	0.55	0.46
Cash ratio	0.48	0.50	0.41	0.32
Current debt to inventory	0.42	0.33	0.37	0.39
Working capital	636.90	1,219.10	1,669.00	2,055.70
Efficiency Tests				
Sales to working capital	5.40	4.59	4.67	4.96
Receivable turnover	90.52	100.00	100.00	102.00
Collection period	4.03	3.65	3.65	3.57
Inventory to working capital	1.17	1.12	1.19	1.26
Inventory turnover	4.59	4.09	3.90	3.92
Asset turnover	2.69	2.52	2.50	2.61
Gross Margin as a percentage of sales	0.02	0.02	0.02	0.02

EXHIBIT 8 (continued)

	Period ending August 31			
	Actual		Projected	
	1978	1979	1980	1981
Profitability Tests				
Earnings margin after taxes	0.02	0.02	0.01	0.01
Earnings margin before taxes	0.03	0.02	0.02	0.02
Return on assets after taxes	0.05	0.04	0.03	0.03
Return on assets before taxes	0.08	0.06	0.04	0.05
Return on working capital	0.10	0.07	0.05	0.06
Return on common stockholders' equity	0.15	0.22	0.21	0.30
Return on owners equity	0.08	0.11	0.10	0.12
Sales to tangible net worth	4.55	7.96	11.5	14.89
Leverage Tests				
Current debt to tangible net worth	0.42	0.65	1.09	1.46
Total debt to tangible net worth	0.66	1.96	3.26	4.23
Fixed assets to tangible net worth	0.40	0.59	0.72	0.79
Total debt to working capital	0.78	1.13	1.32	1.41
Times interest earned	3.26	1.80	0.65	0.77
Debt ratio	0.39	0.62	0.71	0.74
Long-term debt ratio	0.14	0.42	0.43	0.49
Market Tests				
Earnings per share	0.15	0.22	0.21	0.31
Dividend payout ratio	0.39	0.27	0.28	0.20

EXHIBIT 9
Industry Comparative Data

INTRODUCTION

Robert Morris Associates, the national association of bank loan and credit officers, is proud to publish this 56th edition of the *Annual Statement Studies*. This publication is made possible through the voluntary cooperation of RMA's member banks, and because it is a product of the commercial banking community, it is directed primarily at commercial bankers. However, the *Statement Studies* has become an indispensable tool for businessmen, financial managers, and others who seek to make sound lending and business decisions.

The *Statement Studies* contains composite financial data on 305 lines of business engaged in manufacturing, wholesaling, retailing, services, and contracting. Financial statement data on each industry are shown in common size form and are accompanied by widely used ratios.

In this edition, the method used to compute the common size balance sheet and income statement has been modified to reflect more clearly the financial position of a typical company within an industry group. By giving equal weight to each of the statements that make up a sample population, larger company statements no longer have a disproportionate effect on the data.

Using the new method of calculation, a common size statement is computed for each individual statement in an

EXHIBIT 9 (continued)

industry group. All the figures are then added and averaged. The method used previously was simply to average all of the statements in an industry group. Although the new method does not have a radical effect, it does refine the statement data. Since the ratios have always been calculated individually, the new calculation method will have no effect on them.

PARTS I, II, and III

Each page of Parts I through III of the *Statement Studies* contains a common-size balance sheet and income statement for two different lines of business. The statements are grouped into four asset size or contract revenue size columns and are then combined into an "All Sizes" column. Only firms with total assets under $50 million are used, except in the contractor section which is based on revenues with no upper limit.

The industry information shown at the top left and right of each page includes the name of the industry, its Standard Industrial Classification (SIC) number, the sample size and dates of the statements used, the asset size categories, and the number of statements in each category. Although abbreviated, the information remains understandable. For instance, 16 (6/30–9/30/77) means that 16 statements with fiscal dates falling between June 30 and September 30, 1977, make up part of the sample population. The number of statements with fiscal dates falling between October 1, 1977, and March 31, 1978, are shown in the same manner.

When there are less than ten financial statements for a particular size category, the composite data are not shown in that category because such a small sample is usually not representative and could be misleading. However, *all* of the data for an industry are shown in the "All Sizes" column. The number of statements for each size or revenue category is shown in bold print at the top of each page.

At the bottom of each page, the total sales or revenues and total assets for all of the financial statements in each size category are shown. These data are provided to allow recasting of the common size statements into dollar amounts. To do this, the total amount at the bottom of the page should be divided by the number of statements in the size category and the result multiplied by the percentages in the common size statement for that category.

Balance sheets and income statements are common-size with every item shown as a percentage and with total assets and sales, or revenues, respectively, equaling 100%. In some cases, the figures appearing after the decimal point do not balance perfectly with totals shown because the figures were rounded off by the computer during the computation process. Credits and losses are indicated by a minus sign beside the value.

PART IV

This section includes only statements on contractors. Since there is more than one accounting method used by contractors, we have chosen, for uniformity, to present only those statements using an accrual method of accounting on a percentage-of-completion basis. In this section, size categories are determined by contract revenues instead of total assets with no upper limit placed on revenue size. The format of the contractor page is different from that appearing elsewhere in the book, and additional operating data follow the main data pages.

PART V

Comparative ratios on consumer finance companies are provided in this section to assist in the analysis of that industry. These ratios were prepared by The Bank of New York and The First National Bank of Chicago. RMA is grateful to these banks for their contribution.

This final section of the book entitled, "Sources of Composite Financial Data," can serve as a valuable reference tool for those seeking more specialized financial information on specific industries.

EXHIBIT 9 (continued)

RMA thanks the Statement Studies Chapter Chairmen, analysts, and the many other people who have made this publication possible, not the least of which were the representatives of our member banks who submitted over 52,000 financial statements this year.

The Credit Division of RMA will be happy to answer any inquiries concerning this publication.

James M. Nelson
Chairman-National
Statement Studies Committee

Jerome L. Roderick
Director-Credit Division

Susan M. Kelsay, Editor
Assistant Director-Credit Division

September 1978

DRUGS   RETAILERS

SIC# 5912

105(6/30-9/30/77)		90(10/1/77-3/31/78)			
0-250M 103	250M-1MM 58	1-10MM 24	10-50MM 10	ALL 195	ASSET SIZE NUMBER OF STATEMENTS
%	%	%	%	%	**ASSETS**
7.2	7.3	8.0	7.0	7.3	Cash & Equivalents
13.3	16.7	8.5	15.8	13.8	Accts. & Notes Rec. - Trade(net)
56.3	47.8	57.2	52.0	53.7	Inventory
1.1	1.2	1.2	.4	1.1	All Other Current
77.9	73.1	74.9	75.2	76.0	Total Current
15.0	15.4	17.4	18.4	15.6	Fixed Assets (net)
2.7	1.4	.7	.4	1.9	Intangibles (net)
4.4	10.1	7.1	6.0	6.5	All Other Non-Current
100.0	100.0	100.0	100.0	100.0	Total
					LIABILITIES
9.7	7.2	6.8	3.0	8.3	Notes Payable-Short Term
4.2	4.3	2.4	1.2	3.9	Cur. Mat.-L/T/D
23.1	21.5	19.1	24.8	22.2	Accts. & Notes Payable - Trade
4.3	5.1	6.8	7.2	5.0	Accrued Expenses
3.8	2.9	4.8	2.6	3.6	All Other Current
45.1	40.9	40.0	38.8	42.9	Total Current
17.8	15.5	17.4	11.6	16.7	Long Term Debt
1.5	2.5	2.6	.7	1.9	All Other Non-Current
35.6	41.0	40.1	48.9	38.4	Net Worth
100.0	100.0	100.0	100.0	100.0	Total Liabilities & Net Worth
					INCOME DATA
100.0	100.0	100.0	100.0	100.0	Net Sales
65.9	65.0	70.4	73.3	66.6	Cost Of Sales
34.1	35.0	29.6	26.7	33.4	Gross Profit
31.1	32.0	26.4	23.3	30.4	Operating Expenses
3.0	2.9	3.2	3.4	3.0	Operating Profit
.6	.3	.6	.2	.5	All Other Expenses (net)
2.4	2.6	2.6	3.2	2.5	Profit Before Taxes
					RATIOS
2.8	2.5	2.6	2.2	2.5	
1.9	2.0	2.1	1.9	2.0	Current
1.4	1.5	1.7	1.7	1.5	
.8	.9	.6	1.2	.8	
(101) .5	.5	.4	.2 (193)	.5	Quick
.2	.3	.3	.2	.2	
5 73.5	9 39.2	2 152.0	2 146.1	5 70.3	
11 33.1	20 18.4	5 81.0	6 65.2	12 29.4	Sales/Receivables
21 17.3	32 11.3	12 31.1	43 8.4	24 15.0	
73 5.0	78 4.7	78 4.7	63 5.8	73 5.0	
91 4.0	99 3.7	89 4.1	74 4.9	91 4.0	Cost of Sales/Inventory
118 3.1	130 2.8	118 3.1	104 3.5	118 3.1	
6.2	5.8	6.6	4.8	6.2	
9.4	8.0	9.2	9.1	9.0	Sales/Working Capital
17.6	13.4	11.7	13.1	13.7	
7.0	8.1	7.9		7.9	
(73) 3.0	(48) 3.1	(20) 5.3	(148)	3.3	EBIT/Interest
1.1	1.7	2.4		1.5	
2.0	4.1	6.7		3.2	
(26) .6	(19) 1.3	(13) 2.1	(64)	1.4	Cash Flow/Cur. Mat. L/T/D
.3	.6	1.2		.5	
.1	.2	.2	.1	.1	
.4	.3	.3	.5	.3	Fixed/Worth
1.2	.8	.9	.6	.9	
.8	.9	.8	.5	.8	
1.9	1.5	1.4	1.1	1.5	Debt/Worth
5.4	2.8	3.1	1.7	3.7	
58.2	30.5	38.6	37.8	42.5	% Profit Before Taxes/Tangible
(92) 25.4	(57) 15.6	19.1	18.3 (183)	20.0	Net Worth
8.5	3.3	11.3	9.7	6.8	

EXHIBIT 9 (continued)

	16.0		10.7		12.7	14.9		14.6	% Profit Before Taxes/Total
	6.9		5.8		8.3	9.9		6.8	Assets
	1.1		1.2		4.4	4.6		1.4	
	64.8		49.7		47.0	48.3		57.6	
	36.0		24.6		22.8	18.0		26.6	Sales/Net Fixed Assets
	16.6		13.0		17.5	10.0		15.5	
	4.1		3.2		3.9	3.8		3.8	
	3.5		2.7		3.4	3.1		3.2	Sales/Total Assets
	2.6		2.1		2.5	2.4		2.3	
	.6		.6		.5	.4		.6	
(93)	.9	(52)	.9	(21)	.8	.7	(176)	.9	% Depr., Dep., Amort./Sales
	1.3		1.1		1.1	1.2		1.2	
	1.7		1.6		1.6			1.7	
(90)	2.5	(44)	2.8	(17)	2.4		(157)	2.6	% Lease & Rental Exp/Sales
	3.7		3.6		3.5			3.6	
	4.5		2.3					2.9	
(65)	7.4	(40)	4.3				(114)	5.5	% Officers' Comp/Sales
	10.3		7.2					9.0	
	44599M		77592M		206422M	902506M		1231119M	Net Sales ($)
	13384M		27875M		67162M	306410M		414831M	Total Assets ($)

©Robert Morris Associates 1978   M = $thousand   MM = $million

CASE 14
Interstate Wholesale Grocers, Inc.

BACKGROUND

Interstate Wholesale Grocers, Inc., a wholesaler of groceries to hotels, restaurants, hospitals, clubs, airlines, railroads, and schools, was founded in 1961 as a sole proprietorship by Thomas M. Randall. Randall was assisted in the business by his wife, Mary, and in later years by his sons George and Anthony Randall. George and Anthony assumed an active role in Interstate Wholesale Grocers during their college years and after graduation from college; however, Anthony left the business after only a short time to pursue other career interests. The company was incorporated in 1963. In 1975 George, then 31, was made responsible for the sales division.

Early in 1977, Thomas Randall died after a long illness. He had owned approximately two thirds of Interstate's common stock. Randall left a $76,000 life insurance policy payable to the company, and that sum was recorded as an additional capital contribution to Interstate. George Randall then purchased his father's common stock—at book value—by a personal note payable to his father's estate in five equal annual installments plus 8 percent interest. The note had a

face value of $197,600. Neither Mrs. Randall nor Anthony Randall had any desire to involve themselves in Interstate's business affairs, and they voiced no objection to this arrangement. George Randall had no personal resources except his common stock in the company and a substantial equity in his home.

Interstate Wholesale Grocers, Inc., sold to some 3,000 accounts located in Texas, Oklahoma, and Louisiana. Accounts were serviced by fifteen 2-ton trucks operating from a modern warehouse centrally located in the territory served. Sales were made on terms of 15 percent payment in cash on delivery, with the balance due in 30 days. The firm employed approximately 30 persons, 6 of whom were sales representatives receiving salary plus commission. Sales showed moderate seasonality, with peak sales occurring in the fall; the summer months were relatively slack.

FINANCIAL INFORMATION

At the time of incorporation in 1963, Interstate Wholesale Grocers, Inc., had a total capitalization of $87,500. Earnings fluctuated considerably, including a few loss years, but sales grew steadily. By 1976, $116,113 in net earnings were retained in the business; the company steadily improved its gross profit margin, but operating expenses also increased steadily. The net profit margin growth slowly declined, and there had not been much growth in total dollar profit up to 1976.

In 1977, the company sold its old warehouse and purchased a new facility with almost twice the storage capacity of the older facility. A portion of the purchase price was added to the earlier mortgage on fixed assets, while the remainder of the financing came from the new capital contribution, retained earnings, and some other liabilities. With this additional plant capacity, the company was able to increase its sales, related inventory, and accounts receivable, facilitated in part by its bank line of credit. In August 1978, the company purchased 100,000 square feet of land, approximately 2.3 acres, adjacent to its present location; this was the only available land on which the company could conveniently expand in the future. The purchase price of $75,000 was financed by adding $47,000 to the existing mortgage loan (long-term debt) with the balance temporarily absorbed into the bank's line of credit. Self-prepared financial statements are given in Exhibits 1 and 2.

BANK RELATIONSHIP

In 1975, Interstate Wholesale Grocers, Inc., moved its account of 23 years at the Farmers and Merchants State Bank to the Second National Bank. Second National had granted the company a $75,000 line of credit for each of the past 5 years, and this line had been actively used. Several overline extensions had been granted with a high credit ranging to $100,000. The credit had been totally repaid only twice during the past 4 years.

When the company moved into its new quarters, George Randall requested that the firm's credit line be increased to $175,000 to help finance the expected increase in inventory and accounts receivable. This increase was granted, and since early 1978 borrowings had ranged from a high of $200,000 to a low of $90,000, with no annual clean-up effected.

Joyce Parker, vice-president of Second National Bank, contacted George Randall to discuss the bank's concern over the company's inability to reduce seasonally its line of credit. Randall indicated that the line could probably be reduced to $75,000 during the slack period in the summer. He gave no encouragement, however, as to possible further reductions and an annual "clean-up."

Interstate Wholesale Grocers, Inc.'s, line of credit was personally guaranteed by George Randall. In addition, moderately adequate compensating balances had been maintained by the company and by Randall's own accounts to further support the credit line.

Parker was trying to evaluate the Interstate Account from the Second National Bank's point of view. She wondered whether the bank should urge any restructuring of the season credits or "let matters ride" for the time being. She did not want to discourage George Randall's efforts to improve the sales and profits of Interstate, but Parker was somewhat concerned over the general direction of Interstate's finances, especially in light of the recent substantial fixed asset expansion.

EXHIBIT 1
Interstate Wholesale Grocers, Inc.—General Spread Form (figures in thousands)

NAME INTERSTATE WHOLESALE GROCERS, INC.				(In 000's)			
AUDITED STATEMENT	Self	Self	Self	Self			
STATEMENT DATE	6-30-76	6-30-77	6-30-78	6-30-79			
CASH	29	26	13	19			
MARKETABLE SECURITIES							
NOTES RECEIVABLE							
ACCOUNTS RECEIVABLE	102	106	142	161			
INVENTORY	201	287	270	408			
ALLOW. FOR DOUBT. ACCT.							
TOTAL CURRENT ASSETS	332	419	425	588			
FIXED ASSETS – NET	148	405	427	410			
NON-MARKETABLE SECURITIES			1	1			
NON-CURRENT RECEIVABLES			1	3			
PREPAID AND DEFERRED EXPENSES	14	15	18	12			
CUI	1	1	2	3			
LAND				75			
INTANGIBLES							
TOTAL NON-CURRENT ASSETS	163	421	449	504			
TOTAL ASSETS	495	840	874	1,092			
CURRENT MTY. OF TERM DEBT	20	26	45	73			
NOTES PAYABLE			90	90			
ACCOUNTS PAYABLE	77	110	95	196			
ACCRUED EXPENSE & MISC.	15	36	28	61			
Notes Payable - Officers	45	85	9	9			
INCOME TAX LIABILITY	6	14	10	21			
TOTAL CURRENT LIABILITIES	163	271	277	450			
Mortgage	87	238	246	265			
Term-Due Officers	42	24	15	6			
SUBORDINATED DEBT							
TOTAL LIABILITIES	292	533	538	721			
MINORITY INTEREST							
DEFERRED INCOME / RESERVES							
TREASURY STOCK							
PREFERRED STOCK OUTSTANDING							
COMMON STOCK OUTSTANDING	87	87	87	87			
CAPITAL SURPLUS		76	74	72			
RETAINED EARNINGS (DEFICIT)	116	144	175	212			
NET WORTH	203	307	336	371			
TANGIBLE NET WORTH	203	307	336	371			
WORKING CAPITAL	169	148	148	138			
EXCESS CUR. ASSETS OVER TOT.LIAB.	40	(114)	(113)	(133)			
CURRENT RATIO	2.0	1.5	1.5	1.3			
CASH, MKT.SEC.& A/R TO CURR.LIAB.	.8	.5	.6	.4			
A/R COLLECTION PERIOD—DAYS	18	17	21	20			
NET SALES TO INVENTORY	10.0	7.6	9.0	7.1			
COST OF SALES TO INVENTORY	8.3	6.2	7.3	5.7			
INVENTORY TO WORKING CAPITAL	1.2	1.9	1.8	3.0			
SR.DEBT TO (TANG. N.W.& SUB. DEBT)	1.4	1.7	1.6	1.9			
NET PROFIT (LOSS) TO AVG. NET WORTH	.08	.12	.10	.12			

EXHIBIT 2

Interstate Wholesale Grocers, Inc.—General Spread Form (figures in thousands)

NAME INTERSTATE WHOLESALE GROCERS, INC.							(In 000's)		
PERIOD COVERED (MONTHS)	12		12		12		12		
STATEMENT DATE	6-30-76		6-30-77		6-30-78		6-30-79		
NET SALES	2,018	%	2,195	%	2,433	%	2,904	%	
COST OF SALES	1,667	83	1,793	82	1,965	81	2,335	80	
GROSS PROFIT	351	17	402	18	468	19	569	20	
SELLING EXPENSES									
GENERAL & ADMINISTRATIVE EXP.									
TOTAL OPERATING EXPENSES	327	16	344	16	417	17	463	16	
OPERATING PROFIT	24	1	58	3	51	2	106	4	
OTHER INCOME (EXPENSE) – NET	(2)		(13)	(1)	(10)		(43)	(2)	
NET PROFIT (LOSS) BEFORE TAXES	22	1	45	2	41	2	63	2	
INCOME TAXES	6		15	1	10	1	21	1	
NET PROFIT (LOSS) AFTER TAXES	16	1	30	1	31	1	42	1	
ADDITIONAL DATA									
DIVIDENDS – PREFERRED STOCK									
DIVIDENDS–COM.STOCK or WITHDRAW									
OFFICER REMUNERATION									
INTEREST EXPENSE									
OTHER CHANGES IN WORTH			+74		(2)		(7)		
CONTINGENT LIABILITIES									
LEASE OBLIGATIONS									
ANALYSIS OF CHANGES IN WORTH OR SURPLUS									
AT BEGINNING OF PERIOD			203		307		336		
ADD NET PROFIT			30		31		42		
DEDUCT DIVIDENDS OR WITHDRAW.									
Capital Surplus			76		(2)		(2)		
Officer's Life Ins. Prem.			(2)		(2)		(5)		
Rounding – Unexplained					+2				
WORTH OR SURPLUS REPORTED			307		336		371		
ANALYSIS OF WORKING CAPITAL									
AT BEGINNING OF PERIOD			169		148		148		
ADD: NET PROFIT	16		30		31		42		
NON-CASH CHARGES	15		15		17		21		
Incr. in Worth			74						
Incr.-Def'd Liabilities			133				10		
MISCELLANEOUS									
TOTAL ADDITIONS			252		48		73		
DEDUCT:									
DIVIDENDS/WITHDRAWALS									
PLANT EXPENDITURES			272		39		4		
Decr. in Worth					2		7		
Incr. Def'd Assets			1		6		72		
Decr. Def'd Liabilities					1				
MISCELLANEOUS									
TOTAL DEDUCTIONS			273		48		83		
NET CHANGE (+ OR –)			(21)		0		(10)		
AT END OF PERIOD			148		148		138		
W/C AS ABOVE	169		148		148		138		
INVENTORY	201		287		270		408		
EXCESS OF W/C OVER INVENTORY	(32)		(139)		(122)		(270)		
ANALYST INITIALS	JEB		JEB		JEB		JEB		

CASE 15
First Intermediate National Bank

GEOGRAPHIC LOCATION AND HISTORY

The First Intermediate National Bank (FINB), with total deposits of $25 million, was located in what was, until three years ago, an agricultural community 10 miles distant from a large city in New Mexico. Since its establishment in the late 1940s, the bank had experienced a slow but healthy growth, catering to the banking needs of townspeople and farmers, most of whom were personally well-known to all the bank staff.

ECONOMIC CHANGES

In 1974, a major oil company decided to relocate a large section of its executive and administrative staff to new offices just outside the town's boundaries. In the same year, construction began on a large residential development aimed at middle-class homeowners. Since that time, FINB had realized exceptional growth both in deposits and loans, especially consumer lending, which by 1978 totaled $6.5 million outstanding. All evidence pointed to continued demand for still higher consumer credit.

STAFFING

With the exception of the president and executive vice-president (who was also the senior credit officer), the bank's lending staff consists of a total of five officers. Two of these five loan officers serviced primarily commercial, real estate, and agricultural loans. The remaining three officers handled all consumer-related requests.

The two commercial loan officers had been trained by the senior credit officer. One of the consumer loan officers had been with the bank since it opened and training of the two other consumer lenders had been more or less left up to her. The consumer loan officer received excellent support from both loan operations and the credit

section, thus relieving them of nearly all clerical functions.

PORTFOLIO CONDITION

Two months ago a profitability study submitted to the president and board of directors indicated that, although growth was continuing in the consumer loan portfolio, profitability declined due to delinquency losses and low rates. It was recognized that the demographic profile of the bank's customer base had changed dramatically. Accordingly, a knowledgeable and experienced consumer loan manager was employed to reverse the declining profitability trend.

After performing an audit of the portfolio and an evaluation of the staff, the consumer loan manager identified the following problem areas:

1 Little or no written documentation could be found on consumer borrowers other than some incomplete applications accompanied only by credit bureau reports.

2 In cases in which borrower information was obtained, no basis for loan decisions was evident either for approvals or rejections.

3 Average losses on auto repossessions had been greater than national or state averages.

4 Five percent of the losses over the past year on automobiles were directly attributable to physical damage losses of the collateral, and no insurance coverage was evident at the time of repossession.

5 Thirty-day and other delinquent accounts were being contacted by either mail-out notices or letters sent out by the individual loan officers at month-end.

6 Many single-maturity loans had been renewed without reduction and files contained no liquidation agreements.

7 Extensions on installment payments appeared excessive.

8 Many errors on forms and incorrect collateral documents were noted.

9 There appeared to be no consistency to consumer loan rates and terms.

10 Loan officers were unaware of any lending or overdraft limitations.

11 Several "balloon" contracts had been noted together with other unattractive loans.

12 There was evidently confusion between loan officers, loan operations, and the credit section relating to loan officer responsibilities.

13 Loan officers appeared to base loan decisions primarily on intuitive reasons rather than on an analysis of facts, sound credit principles, acquisition costs, and potential exposure.

RECOMMENDATIONS

The consumer loan manager recommended that an extensive staff training program be implemented and a written credit policy be adopted.

Both recommendations were approved. After a consumer credit policy was submitted, however, the senior credit officer indicated reluctance to approve some facets of it. His reluctance was based on feelings that the policy might be overrestrictive, demoralizing to personnel, create additional expense and paper work, and act as a deterrent to the acquisition of loans.

Accordingly a meeting was scheduled by the senior credit officer to discuss the proposed policy with all concerned. A copy of the draft policy is included as Exhibit 1.

EXHIBIT 1
First Intermediate National Bank Consumer Credit Policies—A Draft Proposal, June 2, 1979

General Statement and Purpose

It is the intent of the consumer lending section, in accordance with total bank objectives, to increase growth and earnings while contributing to the development of the community through the employment of funds invested in a profitable and liquid consumer loan portfolio.

To achieve these objectives certain standards, authorizations, responsibilities, and guidelines must be set forth in order to provide affected personnel with direction, development, and control.

It is recognized that all conditions as well as objectives and goals are subject to change. As a result, this policy will be reviewed quarterly or at any time deemed necessary by the senior credit officer or the consumer loan manager.

Organization Chart

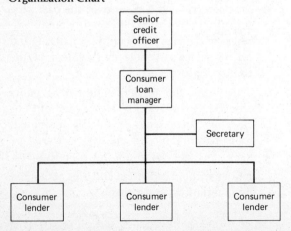

EXHIBIT 1 (continued)

I. *Lending Guidelines*

A. *Service Area*
The service area of First Intermediate National Bank shall be considered within a 15 mile radius of the bank's location.

B. *Loan Eligibility*
Loan requests will only be entertained for bank depositors. However, the opening of a new deposit account at the time of application may constitute eligibility.

C. *Minimum Loans*
Single maturity—$500.00.
Installment—$300.00.

Single Maturity—Minimum 10 percent simple; term maximum 12 months with reduction each 90 days.

Secured New Auto—Minimum 6.5 percent add-on; term maximum 42 months.
New Auto—Minimum 6 percent add-on; term 36 months.
Used Auto (one year old)—Minimum 6.5 percent add-on; term maximum 30 months.
Used Auto(two years old)—Minimum 7 percent add-on; term maximum 24 months.
Used Auto (three years old)—Minimum 7.5 percent add-on; term maximum 18 months.

Any financing on autos older than three years pledged as collateral should be considered as a personal loan not to exceed a term of 12 months at the maximum rate of 8 percent add-on.

New cars primarily used for business purposes will be limited to a maximum term of 30 months and 6.5 percent add-on rate.

Home improvement loans (insured program):
Maximum $15,000—Maturity 120 months; rate 7.5 percent add-on.
Less than $2,500—Maximum maturity 60 months; rate 7.0 percent add-on.

All home improvement loans exceeding a $5,000 net advance or 60-month term must have the manager's joint approval with the loan officer.

Secured Savings:
Minimum installment rates for time saving on deposit pledged as collateral—5.5 percent not to exceed 36 months maturity.

Minimum single maturity—1½ percent over prime on loans exceeding $1,000 with a floor of 1½ percent of deposit interest; maximum 10 percent simple on a 365-day base computation.

Boat Loans:
New boats—6.5 percent minimum; maturity 36 months.
Used boats (one year model)—7 percent minimum maturity 30 months.
All others—8 percent not to exceed 24 months.

Appliances, Furniture, etc.:
All such requests fall into the personal loan category. Except for special considerations, these applications should be treated as unsecured credits not to exceed 12 months at a minimum rate of 8 percent add-on.

D. *Downpayments*
All new auto requests for 42-month financing will require a minimum downpayment of 20 percent of the selling price. All other new car loan requests should have a minimum of 12 to 15 percent of the selling price. Used car financing should not exceed NADA loan value.

Boat loans—required minimum downpayment is 15 percent of the selling price. Home improvement loans—subject to mortgage equity and borrower credit worthiness.

EXHIBIT 1 (continued)

    E.   *Unattractive Credits*

        1.   Single-Maturity Auto Loans—As a matter of policy, no auto loans will be approved without the written authorization of the manager or the senior credit officer.

        2.   "Balloon" Notes—Requests of this type should be discouraged and will not be approved without the written authorization of the manager or the senior credit officer.

        3.   Consolidation Loans—Unless 100 percent collateralized, this type of loan will not be approved without the written authorization of the manager or the senior credit officer.

        4.   Speculative Ventures—Loans to finance commodity issues, "get rich quick" real estate, and so on will not be approved.

        5.   Commercial Requests—All commercial requests will be referred to the commercial loan officers.

    F.   *Special Requests*
Consumer-related loan requests such as mobile home, recreational vehicle, and cosigner or guarantor should be referred to the manager.

    G.   *Applicant Requirements and Qualifications*

        1.   Effective with this policy, all new borrowers will have a file established consisting of an application, credit investigation, and any other information allowable by law pertaining to the borrower. New applicants will be required to complete a written application form. Loan requests on existing or former borrowers having an in-file credit investigation older than one year must be revised through the credit bureau and third-party sources if necessary. Credit applications older than two years will require new applications.

        2.   Stability—Applicant must have six-month occupational stability in present employment unless previous employment was in a similar or related field. Applicant must show previous concurrent employment and residence of three years.

        3.   Minimum Income—No limitations are placed on income; however, lenders will be requested to compute total monthly net income and monthly expenditures.

        4.   Credit Worthiness—Since this is a subjective decision, it must be left to the loan officer's discretion.

    H.   *Installment Extensions*
No more than one extension per 12 months of contract will be granted without the manager's written joint agreement with the loan officer.

    I.   *Overdrafts*
No overdrafts will be approved for borrowers having delinquent payments without the written authorization of the manager.

    J.   *Single-Maturity Repayment Agreements*
Lenders will require repayment agreements satisfactory to the bank and the borrower. Such agreements will be documented and retained in the borrower's file. Deviations from such agreements should be discouraged.

    K.   *Financial Statements*
All applications for unsecured loans of $2,500 or more must be accompanied by a financial statement in the applicant's credit file.

  II. *Authorizations*

    A.   *Lending*

        Loan Manager:
        Secured—$15,000.

EXHIBIT 1 (continued)

Unsecured—$7,500.
No restrictions of terms.

Loan Officers:
Secured installment—$7,500; maximum term 36 months.
Unsecured installment—$2,500; maximum term 24 months.
Single-maturity secured—$7,500; maximum term 12 months.
Single-maturity unsecured—$2,500; maximum term 12 months.
Home improvement—$5,000; maximum term 60 months.

These authorizations pertain to the net aggregate advanced for each individual borrower.

The loan manager may join a loan officer to the sum of both loan limits.

B. *Overdrafts Limits*
All authorized loan officers will have overdraft limits up to the same amount as unsecured single-maturity lending limits.

C. *Repossessions*
Only the loan manager or the senior credit officer may authorize repossessions.

D. *Chargeoff's*
Only the loan manager will determine the uncollectibility of a loan and make chargeoff recommendations to the senior credit officer.

III. *Loan Officer Responsibilities*

A. *Applicant Information*
Loan officers will be responsible for ensuring that factual information is obtained through applicant interview, credit bureau reports, and third-party reporting sources relating to a loan request and that applications and up-dates conform to this policy.

B. *Analysis*
Loan officers will be responsible for confirming collateral insurance through an agent prior to making a loan decision where such coverage is required on pledged collateral. Additionally, the approving loan officer will be responsible for follow-up efforts in the event of cancellations, expirations, or terminations of such insurance.

C. *Repossessions*
Only the loan manager or the senior credit officer may authorize repossessions.

D. *Documentation*
Special emphasis is placed on each loan officer's responsibility for documenting all information and retaining such information on file pertaining to the borrower.

E. *Loan Closing*
Although clerical personnel will complete all legal documents, loan officers are responsible for proper forms, accuracy, and legality prior to closing. Loan officers will ensure during the closing that the borrower is aware of the contractural agreements and that legal disclosure is made.

F. *Collections*
Loan officers will be responsible for collection follow-up, skip-tracing, and so on. Letter contact will be discouraged and personal phone contact will be required. Delinquent nonseasoned accounts (less than six months) will be contacted on the 15th day from the due date.

EXHIBIT 1 (continued)

    G.   *Regulatory Compliance*
Although a separate consumer regulation compliance policy will be implemented, all loan officers will be charged with the responsibility for working knowledge of and complying fully with all federal and state regulations governing the lending function.

IV.   *Delinquency and Loan Loss Measures*

Loan officers will be required to maintain a delinquency 30-days-and-over percentage not to exceed 1.5 percent of their total monthly outstanding loans. Losses should not exceed 0.25 percent of individual outstanding loans at year-end.

V.   *Loan Review*

    A.   *Loans and Pending Applications*
All new loans and pending applications will be reviewed on a daily basis by the loan manager and loan officers during the morning loan meetings from 7:45 to 8:30.

    B.   *Delinquency and Collateral Insurance*
Delinquency and collateral insurance follow-up will be reviewed by the loan manager with each loan officer on a weekly basis.

    C.   *Chargeoff*
Potential chargeoffs will be reviewed by the loan manager and individual loan officer on the third week of each month for month-end chargeoff recommendations. Additionally, chargeoff loan applications will be used for training purposes.

    D.   *Rejected Applications*
Rejected applications will be reviewed weekly for regulatory compliance, documentation, and loan judgment quality. Exceptions will be utilized for training purposes.

    E.   *Installment Extensions*
The loan manager will review daily all the loan extensions granted.

VI.   *Training*

In-bank training will consist of the following:
    1.   Morning loan meeting.
    2.   Weekly training meeting.

American Institute of Banking courses will be encouraged, and loan officers meeting the necessary requirements will be scheduled for formal outside schooling at the bank's expense.

VII.   *Evaluation*

All lenders will be evaluated on an annual basis and counseling will be conducted during a quarterly review. Primary considerations in the evaluation of performance will consist of the following:
    1.   Loan volume.
    2.   Delinquency.
    3.   Losses.
    4.   Credit life insurance penetration.
    5.   Average portfolio effective rate.
    6.   Credit policy and regulatory compliance.
    7.   Justified customer complaints.
    8.   New business.

EXHIBIT 1 (continued)

Conclusion

The purpose of this policy is to provide direction and development for lending personnel while exercising control to attain bank objectives. It should not, however, be utilized by loan officers as a crutch to lay blame, discourage profitable loan acquisition, deter customer service, or detract from the bank's image. Moreover, the quoting of policy to customers may detract from the credibility and authority of the loan officer.

 It is recommended that no policy can encompass all the situations and conditions related to every loan request. Flexibility must be exercised for a policy to work effectively. As a result, individual judgment and discretion is encouraged within reasonable and justifiable limits.

CASE 16
Pueblo National Bank

Wilma Harwood, an experienced banker, had just received an offer to join the Pueblo National Bank in Albuquerque as a senior vice-president. Since she currently held a very satisfactory position in a nearby competing bank, she had not yet decided whether she should accept this new opportunity and leave her current employment.

 The proposed position represented a promotion and commensurately higher title, a much broader level of responsibility, and a salary increase of about 25 percent above her present compensation level. In spite of these obvious attractions, Harwood wanted to study Pueblo National's situation closely, since she was very happy at her current bank, even though she concluded that promotions and broader opportunity might come a little more slowly due to the age distribution of the officer staff.

 As a new senior vice-president at Pueblo National, Harwood would be responsible for the bank's commercial loan portfolio, which totaled nearly $335 million. She would also serve as a member of the bank's executive committee, which was responsible for asset/liability management decisions; and, finally, Harwood would be chair of the officer loan committee. Harwood realized she must study the bank very carefully before making this important career decision, since a "mistake" could prove costly from a career development point of view.

Pueblo National Bank was a $1.7 billion institution operating three branches in the Albuquerque metropolitan area. The bank historically had stressed commercial loans to medium-sized manufacturing and retailing firms. Beginning in 1973, however, senior management decided that increased emphasis should be given to consumer loans and deposits. To improve its ability to expand in consumer finance, the bank employed Janice Fisher, a vice-president with a large retail-oriented bank, to become Pueblo's senior vice-president and head of the consumer division.

 During the first three years of Fisher's tenure at Pueblo National, she succeeded in raising loans to individuals from 20 to 28 percent of the gross loan portfolio and in increasing construction and permanent financing of residential structures from 18 to 27 percent of the gross loan portfolio.

 Despite loan portfolio growth and increased attention to consumer lending and deposit markets, the bank's profitability did not improve very much in 1974 and 1975. For example, from 1970 to 1973, Pueblo National earned an average return on assets of 0.50 percent, about 25 basis points below the return on assets in similar-sized American banks. In 1974 and 1975, Pueblo National's average return on total assets reached only 0.58 percent. Similar-sized banks earned a comparable return of 0.74 percent. Relative profitability for Pueblo National continued in the same manner through 1978.

In late 1978, an officer resignation opened the position now being considered by Wilma Harwood. The departing officer was offered the presidency of a $250 million bank, and he decided to accept that opportunity. The president of Pueblo National promptly began seeking a replacement, which led him after a short search to Harwood.

After meeting with Pueblo National's president and several other senior officers, Harwood promised to reach a decision on the employment offer within the next few days. Harwood had studied the bank's annual report, and she had gathered additional information, which is included in Exhibits 1–7.

Harwood did have a number of questions based on impressions from her personal interviews and from the financial data at her disposal. Her primary areas of concern were the following:

1   What were the real causes of relatively low profitability? Specifically, Harwood wanted to examine the bank's margin or spread, its asset utilization, return on assets, equity multiplier (from leverage), and return on equity. She was particularly concerned how these matters might affect the future loan portfolio.

2   What were the particular risks associated with Pueblo National Bank? Specifically, Harwood knew she must examine overall credit stategies and risks related to liquidity, interest rate fluctuations, and the bank's capital position. She needed to relate these areas to the potential for the commercial loan portfolio since that would be her principal opportunity for career growth and development.

3   How had the bank been funding its earning assets? What was the cost of funding these assets? How did these costs affect the loan portfolio?

4   What was the performance of the loan portfolio itself? What additional information would she need to assess the loan portfolio and to develop her ideas about needed changes and improvements?

5   What was her opinion about the bank's loan portfolio?

Harwood's final concern, of course, was whether she should accept the position offered her and, if so, under what conditions. As she began her more detailed review of the financial data, she realized that she was not dissatisfied in her current position and that any career change should be motivated only by clear professional and personal advantage.

EXHIBIT 1

Pueblo National Bank—Statement of Financial Condition As of Year-End (in thousands of dollars)

	1976	1977	1978
Assets			
Cash and due from banks	$ 120,759	$ 190,606	$ 284,322
Interest-bearing bank balances	86,641	35,000	22,379
Investment securities:			
U.S. Treasuries and agencies	284,010	115,950	221,856
Municipal securities	148,408	143,835	174,139
Other securities	49,029	37,914	39,677
Total investment securities	481,447	297,699	435,672
Trading account securities	0	1,305	7,927
Federal funds sold	42,300	47,163	36,500

EXHIBIT 1 (continued)

	1976	1977	1978
Loans:			
Real estate loans	159,836	196,352	227,186
Loans to financial institutions	10,469	21,997	28,230
Commercial and industrial loans	223,307	315,304	334,217
Loans to individuals	161,984	200,204	243,206
Other loans	15,634	27,511	24,551
Total loans, gross	571,230	761,368	857,390
Less:			
Unearned income	16,621	21,799	27,311
Allowance for loan losses	5,204	7,170	8,220
Total loans, net	549,405	732,399	821,859
Direct-lease financing	8,187	7,216	8,784
Bank premises and equipment, net	45,673	56,144	58,898
Acceptances	1,653	1,079	2,184
Other assets	15,285	10,832	17,501
Total assets	$1,351,350	$1,379,443	$1,696,026
Liabilities			
Demand deposits:			
Individuals, partnerships, and corporations	$ 323,191	$ 390,774	$ 402,959
Public	73,971	76,166	70,152
Banks, domestic	8,600	11,634	15,095
Foreign institutions	211	684	345
Other	12,083	13,791	15,737
Total demand deposits	418,056	493,049	504,288
Time and savings deposits:			
Individuals, partnerships, and corporations	557,796	614,176	726,498
Public	126,489	68,499	98,935
Banks, domestic	500	500	500
Total time and savings deposits	684,785	683,175	825,933
Total deposits	1,102,841	1,176,224	1,330,221
Federal funds purchased	121,160	66,084	85,182
Securities repurchases	0	0	93,376
Other borrowings	877	1,383	1,213
Acceptances	1,653	1,080	2,184
Other liabilities	22,103	28,105	72,354
Total liabilities	1,248,634	1,272,876	1,584,530
Capital			
Common stock and surplus	75,000	75,000	75,000
Undivided profits	27,716	31,567	36,496
Total capital	102,716	106,567	111,496
Total liabilities and capital	$1,351,350	$1,379,443	$1,696,026

EXHIBIT 2

Pueblo National Bank—Statement of Financial Condition Based on Average Balances (in thousands of dollars)

	1976	1977	1978
Assets			
Cash and due from banks	$ 112,308	$ 159,466	$ 239,344
Interest-bearing bank balances	107,961	45,667	24,494
Investment securities:			
U.S. Treasuries and agencies	241,102	209,515	158,690
Municipal securities	168,526	137,966	164,392
Other securities	47,438	41,157	37,823
Total investment securities	457,066	388,638	360,905
Trading account securities	0	804	10,735
Federal funds sold	19,688	29,730	25,855
Loans:			
Real estate loans	147,436	176,252	209,985
Loans to financial institutions	11,585	20,401	26,298
Commercial and industrial loans	220,717	271,033	321,833
Loans to individuals	154,048	180,533	217,041
Other loans	12,678	20,669	26,620
Total loans, gross	546,464	668,888	801,777
Less:			
Unearned income	15,755	19,380	23,558
Allowance for loan losses	3,256	5,884	7,723
Total loans, net	527,453	643,624	770,496
Direct-lease financing	8,493	8,035	8,316
Bank premises and equipment, net	39,762	49,551	57,606
Acceptances	1,673	1,339	1,361
Other assets	12,381	12,355	12,750
Total assets, average	$1,286,785	$1,339,209	$1,511,962
Liabilities			
Demand deposits	$ 391,697	$ 428,381	$ 460,090
Savings deposits	299,950	343,137	346,390
Time deposits, $100,000 and over	240,371	193,650	306,626
Time deposits, under $100,000	111,436	127,894	133,506
Total time and savings deposits	651,757	664,681	786,522
Total deposits	1,043,454	1,093,062	1,246,613
Federal funds purchased and repurchases	118,513	116,010	114,606
Other borrowed money	1,287	1,205	1,210
Acceptances	1,673	1,339	1,361
Other liabilities	23,033	22,733	39,160
Total liabilities	1,187,960	1,234,349	1,402,950
Capital			
Equity capital	98,825	104,860	109,012
Total liabilities and capital	$1,286,785	$1,339,209	$1,511,962
Average earning assets	$1,120,661	$1,116,499	$1,200,800

EXHIBIT 3
Pueblo National Bank—Income Statement for Year Ended December 31 (in thousands of dollars)

	1976	1977	1978
Interest Income:			
Interest and fees on loans	$48,897	$60,106	$ 76,124
U.S. Treasuries and agencies	16,682	13,875	10,439
Municipal securities (FTE)	16,114	13,215	16,911
Other securities	3,376	2,737	2,624
Total investment interest	36,172	29,827	29,974
Interest on due from banks	4,543	1,137	1,898
Federal funds sold and resales	658	1,044	2,487
Direct-lease financing	605	380	529
Trading account securities	0	234	131
Total interest income (FTE)	$90,875	$92,728	$111,143
Interest Expense:			
Time certificates, $100,000 and more	$12,476	$ 9,436	$ 23,456
Other deposits	22,286	25,724	26,570
Federal funds purchased and repos.	9,476	8,056	9,488
Borrowed money	104	88	299
Total interest expense	44,342	43,304	59,813
Net interest margin (FTE)	$46,533	$49,424	$ 51,330
Other Income:			
Trust department	$ 2,394	$ 2,562	$ 2,926
Deposit service charges	2,360	2,308	4,054
Other service charges	5,168	5,057	3,830
Other	248	249	315
Total other income	10,170	10,176	11,125
Noninterest Expenses:			
Personnel expenses	18,566	18,305	20,140
Gross premises expense	5,611	7,862	6,050
Less: rental income	368	1,303	2,228
Net premises expense	5,243	6,559	3,822
Furniture and equipment expense	2,882	1,931	2,619
Other operating expenses	10,289	15,645	17,810
Total operating expenses	36,980	42,440	44,391
Provision for Loan Losses	4,100	3,715	2,377
Pretax Net Operating Income (FTE)	15,623	13,445	15,687
Applicable income taxes	(199)	(622)	(802)
Municipal security tax benefit	7,996	6,595	8,443
Total	7,797	5,973	7,641
After-Tax Net Operating Income	$ 7,826	$ 7,472	$ 8,046
Net Security Gains (Losses)	(45)	(699)	(467)
Net Income	$ 7,781	$ 6,773	$ 7,579
Cash Dividends Declared	$ 3,000	$ 2,400	$ 2,650

EXHIBIT 4
Pueblo National Bank—Other Information (dollars in thousands)

	1976	1977	1978
Earning Assets			
Year-end	$1,167,980	$1,120,782	$1,333,121
Average	1,120,661	1,116,499	1,200,800
Investment Portfolio			
Maturity distribution of investment Securities, end of year:			
One year or less	10.55%	1.30%	23.98%
One to five years	44.24	33.24	21.43
Five to 10 years	14.89	15.67	12.65
Over 10 years	30.32	49.79	41.94
Total	100.00%	100.00%	100.00%
Investment securities Appreciation (depreciation), end of year	($10,163)	($15,967)	($30,328)
Taxable securities, market to book value, end of year	100.37%	95.44%	94.89%
Nontaxable securities, market to book value, end of year	92.32%	93.63%	90.12%
Loan Portfolio			
Standby letters of credit to average assets	0.85%	0.90%	1.05%
Past due loan analysis (end of year):			
Total	$21,622	$29,825	$38,583
As percentage of loans in category:			
Real estate	n.a.	7.56%	6.73%
Commercial and industrial	n.a.	2.56	4.12
Individuals	n.a.	2.80	3.46
Other	n.a.	2.65	2.10
Total	n.a.	3.92%	4.50%
Income earned not collected:			
(1) Amount	n.a.	n.a.	$12,029
(2) As percentage of loans	n.a.	n.a.	1.73%
Nonaccrual loans	n.a.	n.a.	$ 5,977
Gross loan losses	$ 3,445	$ 2,707	$ 3,025
Gross loan recoveries	$ 779	$ 958	$ 1,698
Net loan losses	$ 2,666	$ 1,749	$ 1,327
Interest Sensitivity Position			
Market rate funds to total assets	n.a.	19.84%	30.48%
Market rate assets to total assets	n.a.	32.45%	34.80%
Net position in market rate assets as a percentage of total assets	n.a.	12.61%	4.32%
Maturity Distribution of Total Assets, Year-End (excludes loans to individuals and loans on one-to-four family dwelling units)			
Under one year	n.a.	32.45%	34.80%

EXHIBIT 4 (continued)

	1976	1977	1978
One to five years	n.a.	14.97	13.96
Over five years	n.a.	16.37	17.50
Total		63.79%	66.26%
Personnel			
Personnel expense per full-time-equivalent employee	$10,540	$11,130	$11,020
Full-time-equivalent employees per $1 million of assets	1.37	1.23	1.22
Deposit Service Charges			
Deposit service charges to total IPC demand deposits	0.61%	0.60%	0.63%
Rates of Cost on Bank Funds:			
All interest-bearing deposits	5.33%	5.29%	6.36%
Time certificates: $100,000 and up	5.19%	4.87%	7.65%
Federal funds purchased[a]	8.00%	6.94%	8.28%
Other borrowings	6.87%	6.78%	8.05%
Subordinated debt	—	—	—
Gross Yield on Earning Assets			
Total loans	8.95%	8.99%	9.50%
U.S. Treasury and agencies	6.92%	6.62%	6.58%
Municipal securities (FTE)	9.56%	9.51%	10.29%
Due from banks	4.21%	2.49%	7.75%
Federal funds sold[a]	3.34%	3.55%	9.62%
Growth Rates			
1. Asset growth rate	n.a.	4.07%	12.90%
2. Loan growth rate	n.a.	22.02%	19.71%
3. Investment securities growth rate	n.a.	decline	decline
4. Deposit growth rate	n.a.	4.75%	14.05%
5. Equity growth rate	n.a.	6.11%	3.96%
6. Equity growth—returned earnings	n.a.	6.11%	3.96%
7. Total capital growth rate	n.a.	6.11%	3.96%
Profit and Related Relationships			
1. Return on average equity	7.87%	6.46%	6.95%
2. Equity to assets (year-end)	7.60%	7.72%	6.57%
3. Total capital to total asset	7.68%	7.83%	7.21%
4. Assets to total capital	13.02×	12.77×	13.87×
5. Net loans to equity capital	5.34×	6.13×	7.07×
6. Net loans to total capital	5.34×	6.13×	7.07×
7. Risk assets to total equity	9.57×	9.87×	10.17×
8. Cash dividend payout ratio	38.56%	35.43%	34.97

[a]Not true representation because of correspondent transactions.

EXHIBIT 5
Peer Group Banks[a]—Asset Distribution as percentage of Average Assets

	1976	1977	1978
Assets			
Cash and due from banks	12.35%	12.64%	13.62%
Interest-bearing bank balances	4.25	4.38	4.45
Investment securities:			
U.S. Treasuries and agencies	9.27	9.79	9.03
Municipal securities	9.73	9.01	8.82
Other securities	0.77	0.82	0.67
Total investment securities	19.77	19.61	18.51
Trading account securities	.90	0.79	0.54
Federal funds sold	5.39	5.40	4.72
Loans:			
Real estate loans	12.90	12.70	13.06
Loans to financial institutions	4.29	3.96	3.79
Commercial and industrial loans	18.24	18.27	18.84
Loans to individuals	10.83	11.09	11.53
Other loans	7.31	7.41	7.11
Total loans, gross	53.57	53.43	54.33
Less:			
Unearned income	0.81	0.84	0.87
Allowance for loan losses	0.59	0.58	0.58
Total loans, net	52.17%	52.01%	52.88%
Direct-lease financing	0.59	0.64	0.73
Bank premises and equipment, net	1.69	1.61	1.60
Acceptances	0.87	0.85	0.98
Other assets	2.02	2.07	1.97
Total assets	100.00%	100.00%	100.00%
Liabilities and Capital			
Demand deposits	32.41%	31.90%	30.97%
Savings deposits	16.80	17.67	15.78
Time deposits, $100,000 and over	14.69	13.82	15.71
Time deposits, under $100,000	11.85	11.37	10.44
Deposits in foreign offices	4.73	4.98	5.52
Total time and savings deposits	47.25%	47.19%	47.06%
Total deposits	79.66%	79.09%	78.03%
Federal funds purchased and repos	9.54%	10.64%	11.15%
Other borrowed money	0.63	0.55	0.69
Acceptances	0.87	0.86	0.99
Other Liabilities	2.03	1.78	2.35
Total liabilities	92.74%	92.92%	93.20%
Subordinated debt	0.68	0.68	0.66
Equity capital	6.58	6.40	6.14
Total capital	7.26%	7.08%	6.80%
Total liabilities and capital	100.00%	100.00%	100.00%
Total earning assets to average total assets	83.07%	82.83%	81.82%

[a]Peer Group Member Banks are Federal Reserve member banks with assets between $1 billion and $5 billion.

EXHIBIT 6
Peer Group Banks[a]—Income Statement as Percentage of Average Assets

	1976	1977	1978
Interest income:			
Interest and fees on loans	4.65%	4.73%	5.52%
U.S. Treasuries and agencies	0.62	0.65	0.66
Municipal securities (FTE)	0.96	0.87	0.92
Other securities	0.05	0.06	0.01
Total investment interest	1.63%	1.58%	1.59%
Interest on due from banks	0.24	0.25	0.35
Federal funds sold and resales	0.26	0.30	0.39
Direct-lease financing	0.01	0.01	0.01
Trading account securities	0.01	0.01	0.01
Total interest income (FTE)	6.80%	6.88%	7.87%
Interest expense:			
Time certificates, $100,000 and over	0.84%	0.76%	1.19%
Other deposits	1.44	1.51	1.38
Foreign office deposits	0.30	0.29	0.44
Total interest bearing deposits	2.58%	2.56%	3.01%
Federal funds purchased and repos	0.49%	0.60%	0.88%
Borrowed money	0.06	0.08	0.05
Subordinated debt	0.04	0.04	0.05
Total interest expense	3.17%	3.28%	4.07%
Net interest margin (FTE)	3.63%	3.60%	3.80%
Other income, total	0.76%	0.84%	0.85%
Noninterest expenses:			
Personnel expenses	1.44%	1.44%	1.46%
Occupancy expenses, net of rental income	0.46	0.46	0.45
Other operating expenses	0.88	0.91	0.94
Total operating expenses	2.78%	2.81%	2.85%
Provision for loan losses	0.35%	0.31%	0.28%
Pretax net operating income (FTE)	1.31%	1.32%	1.51%
Applicable income taxes (including municipal security tax benefit)	0.63	0.63	0.72
After-tax net operating income	0.68%	0.69%	0.79%
Net security gains (losses)	0.00	0.01	(0.03)
Net income (return on average total assets)	0.68%	0.70%	0.76%

[a]Peer Group Banks include all Federal Reserve member banks with assets between $1 billion and $5 billion.

EXHIBIT 7
Peer Group Banks—Other Information

	1976	1977	1978
Earning Assets.			
As a percentage of average total assets	83.07%	82.83%	81.82%
Investment Portfolio			
Maturity distribution of investment securities:			
One year or less	26.92%	24.64%	22.42%
One to five years	36.72	37.17	35.68
Five to 10 years	16.97	18.34	19.48
Over 10 years	19.39	19.85	22.41
Total	100.00%	100.00%	100.00%
Investment securities appreciation (depreciation) to total capital	2.68%	(1.75)%	(12.17)%
Taxable securities: market to book value	101.24%	98.97%	95.00%
Nontaxable securities: market to book value	99.86%	99.67%	93.81%
Loan Portfolio			
Standby letters of credit to average assets	0.85%	0.90%	1.05%
Past due loan analysis: as percentage of loans in category:			
Real estate	n.a.	6.34%	4.97%
Commercial and industrial loans	n.a.	3.35	3.21
Loans to individuals	n.a.	2.82	2.83
Other loans	n.a.	4.07	3.66
Foreign loans	n.a.	n.a.	1.06
Total	n.a.	3.86%	3.38%
Income earned not collected to gross loans	n.a.	1.58%	1.63%
Provision for loan losses to average assets	0.35%	0.31%	0.28%
Provision for loan losses to average gross loans	0.68%	0.58%	0.51%
Gross loan losses to average gross loans	0.80%	0.60%	0.51%
Net loan losses to average gross loans	0.67%	0.47%	0.39%
Earnings coverage of net loan losses	6.30×	8.27×	9.58×
Interest Sensitivity Position			
Market rate funds to total assets	n.a.	29.96%	32.09%
Market rate assets to total assets	n.a.	43.65%	41.12%
Net position in market rate assets to total assets	n.a.	13.69%	9.03%

EXHIBIT 7 (continued)

	1976	1977	1978
Maturity Distribution of Total Assets			
(excludes loans to individuals and loans on one-to-four-family dwelling units)			
Under one year	n.a.	43.65%	41.12%
One to five years	n.a.	16.11	15.56
Over five years	n.a.	11.56	11.89
Total	n.a.	71.32%	68.57%
Personnel			
Personnel expense per full-time-equivalent employee	$12,540	$13,420	$14,730
Full-time-equivalent employees per $1 million of assets	1.16	1.12	1.02
Deposit Service Charges			
Deposit service charges to total IPC demand deposits	0.60%	0.63%	0.62%
Rates of Cost on Bank Funds			
All interest-bearing deposits	5.46%	5.43%	6.28%
Time certificates, $100,000 and up	5.71%	5.53%	7.60%
Federal funds purchased	4.97%	5.43%	7.93%
Other borrowings	6.85%	6.74%	7.51%
Subordinated debt	6.33%	6.54%	6.96%
Gross Yields on Earning Assets			
Total loans	8.76%	8.87%	10.09%
U.S. Treasuries and agencies	6.74%	6.64%	7.11%
Municipal securities (FTE)	10.03%	9.89%	10.28%
Due from banks	6.20%	6.00%	7.87%
Federal funds sold	5.13%	5.66%	8.10%
Growth Rates			
Asset growth rate	7.75%	11.48%	13.81%
Loan growth rate	5.08%	13.36%	15.39%
Investment securities growth rate	12.27%	8.23%	11.39%
Deposit growth rate	7.44%	11.41%	10.78%
Equity growth rate	10.07%	7.70%	8.81%
Equity growth from retained earnings	6.60%	6.01%	7.32%
Total capital growth rate	9.72%	7.98%	8.30%
Profit and Related Relationships			
Return on average equity	10.21%	10.93%	12.15%
Equity to assets (year-end)	6.37%	6.14%	5.87%

EXHIBIT 7 (continued)

	1976	1977	1978
Total capital to total assets	7.04%	6.81%	6.49%
Assets to total capital	14.63×	15.10×	15.84×
Net loans to equity capital	8.26×	8.76×	9.20×
Net loans to total capital	7.45×	7.78×	8.19×
Risk assets to total equity	10.11×	10.48×	10.63×
Cash dividend payout ratio	49.13%	47.66%	43.36%

CASE 17
Saline Bank of Commerce

BACKGROUND

In the year since Preston Cooper took the presidency of Saline Bank of Commerce, Saline, Missouri's, third largest bank, he had successfully implemented a wide range of progressive policies. SBC had a reputation for being a lethargic bank, so Cooper's aggressive influence was badly needed (see Exhibit 1).

His first major move was to reorganize the bank into a one-bank holding company. The board allowed this on the condition that no bank or nonbank acquisition be made in the immediate future. Considering this a partial victory from a very "stodgy" board of directors, he turned to the basic question: What kind of bank do we want to be?

Because SBC was located in the heart of downtown Saline and had no branches, Cooper decided SBC should continue to concentrate on commercial lending. He was concerned, however, that the commercial lending officers typified SBC's lethargic reputation. Cooper decided to bring into the bank an aggressive lending officer who could also help in a major way in aligning the bank with modern operating procedures. His search lead him to June Watkins.

June, we'd like you to come aboard as vice-president in our commercial lending division. But I've *got to lay it on the line; we've got our share of problems. For one thing, our customer base is getting smaller as a result of movement to the suburbs. We're also much smaller than the two other downtown banks which are lead banks in statewide multibank holding companies. It has been our philosophy to capitalize on the strong independent banker tradition in Missouri and to actively solicit correspondent bank accounts across the state. It has also been our philosophy to concentrate on commercial lending and to have commercial lending officers who are strong general bankers.*

June Watkins was not the sort of person to make snap decisions. She weighed carefully the words of Preston Cooper. Going with SBC would mean losing the security of working for a stable bank but would offer the challenge and opportunity of solving major problems. In the end June Watkins decided to accept the challenge.

Immediately upon going to work for SBC, Watkins and Cooper developed a list of four current problem areas at the bank:

1 Written lending policies.

2 Knowledge of costs (to be used in pricing).

3 Customer profitability analysis.

4 Loan profitability analysis.

The first task Watkins tackled was the drafting of written lending policies (see Exhibit 2). After completing this much needed job, Watkins asked the bank's controller, Carol Denton, to develop a study of bank expenses (see Exhibit 3). This was the first step in profitability analysis Preston Cooper wanted her to study next.

MEMORANDUM

To: June Watkins, Vice-President–Commercial Lending

From: Preston Cooper, President

June, our bank has a profit plan objective of 7.5 percent net yield on loans during 1974. Carol Denton and I feel that to make adequate use of this goal we must tie it directly to a customer profitability standard. We would use such a standard to determine if historical or projected profitability is above or below this standard.

We would like you to develop a system for analysis of customer profitability in the Commercial Lending Division. In order to test your system on a typical customer relationship, I suggest that you analyse the historical profitability of one of our most valued customers—Thomas Insurance Company.

Carol Denton has compiled the accounts and activities of Thomas Insurance and its president during 1973. I am sending you this along with a recent summary of Thomas Insurance, prepared by one of our credit trainees.

Credit Review of: Thomas Insurance Company
Prepared by: Dick Rogers, Credit Analyst
Date: January 10, 1974

Thomas had been a valued bank customer for the past 20 years. Its president, George C. Jones, is a member of the board of directors of Saline Bank of Commerce. Two months ago, Larimer Incorporated acquired all of the outstanding stock of Thomas Insurance Company. Larimer is a holding company located in Chicago and is engaged principally in consumer lending. It has other subsidiaries in the life insurance and manufacturing industries, but none is located in Saline. The Financial Vice-President has asked Saline Bank of Commerce for a $1 million unsecured line of credit. Larimer's policy is to carry 15 percent compensating balances regardless of line usage. During 1973, Larimer utilized their lines for about 270 days.

Thomas maintained average ledger balances of $710,013 (excluding Treasury tax and loan deposits) during 1973. Outstanding debt to Thomas during 1973 averaged $1 million and was secured by $1,500,000 (market value) in stocks listed on the New York Stock Exchange. Thomas has agreed to maintain 10 percent compensating balances. The loan has been outstanding for seven years and has always been renewed for one year.

Additionally, the bank has a $200,000 home loan outstanding to the president of Thomas at 8.5 percent. The original loan was for $250,000 and was granted on April 15, 1970, for a term of 10 years. It is secured by a first lien on his home having a current appraised value of $300,000 and $100,000 (market value) of stocks listed on the New York Stock Exchange. The personal financial statement of the president shows a net worth of $2 million after sale of the company.

Exhibit 4 shows the accounts and activity of Thomas Insurance and its president during 1973. Exhibit 5 shows some representative interest rates for 1973 and projected average rates for 1974. All income and financial statements were audited by a nationally recognized accounting firm.

EXHIBIT 1
Saline Bank of Commerce—Statements of Condition December 31, 1973 and 1972 (dollars in thousands)

	1973	1972	Percent change
Cash and due from banks	$ 62,470	$ 46,043	+36
Investment securities:			
United States Treasury securities	30,026	23,620	+27
Agency and corporate securities	500	1,000	−50

EXHIBIT 1 (continued)

	1973	1972	Percent change
Obligations of states and political subdivisions	50,025	31,285	+60
Other securities	431	400	+ 8
Trading account securities	3,006	2,627	+14
Federal funds sold	4,655	8,500	−45
Loans	152,921	142,246	+ 8
Bank premises and equipment	5,113	5,143	− 1
Other assets	4,881	8,403	−42
Total assets	$314,028	$269,267	+17
Demand deposits	$135,148	$114,533	+18
Time deposits	137,104	109,337	+25
Total deposits	$272,252	$223,870	+22
Federal funds purchased	21,086	25,726	−18
Other liabilities	3,978	3,369	+18
Total liabilities	$297,316	$252,965	+18
Reserve for possible loan losses	1,984	1,984	0
Capital notes and debentures	2,775	2,850	− 3
Common stock	4,400	4,400	0
Capital surplus	4,640	4,640	0
Undivided profits	2,913	2,428	+20
Total shareholders equity	$ 16,712	$ 16,302	+ 3
	$314,028	$269,267	+17

EXHIBIT 2
Saline Bank of Commerce—Lending Policies and Procedures

The officers of this bank, in making loans, shall be guided by the following policies.

1   The management of the bank believes that sound loans are a desirable and profitable means of employing funds available for investment. Authorized bank employees are expected to make, and seek to develop, all of the sound loans that the resources of the bank permit and that opportunity affords. In the allocation of resources available for loans, primary consideration shall be given to existing or potential customers with economic interests in the Saline area.

2   The board of directors realizes that the lending of money by the bank necessarily includes reasonable business risks. Some losses are to be expected in the lending program, and it is the policy of the board of directors to maintain a reserve for future loan losses as large as is allowed by pertinent banking and tax laws. Any officer may request of the senior loan officer that a loan be charged off, but such credits shall be reduced to judgment on or before the decision to charge off when such action is consistent with good banking practice. It shall be the responsibility of the officers who approved the credits to continue to follow their loans after chargeoff proceedings.

3   The administration of the bank's lending activities will be supervised by the senior loan officer of the bank, and he or she shall follow the policies set forth in this resolution. The senior loan officer shall seek the advice

EXHIBIT 2 (continued)

and counsel of the executive committee of the board of directors, when in doubt, as to credit decisions on questions involving the interpretation or application of loan policies.

4 All loans in excess of the limits hereinafter provided for the various lending officers, and not to exceed the legal limit of the bank, shall be approved prior to consummation by one or more of the following:
   (a) The executive committee of the board of directors.
   (b) An officer whose authorized limit is great enough to allow his or her individual approval of the loan.
   (c) The officers loan committee.

5 All loans shall be reported to the executive committee following disbursement and, in addition, loans and credit lines of $50,000.00 and over, not specifically approved by the executive committee, shall be reported to the executive committee at its next meeting following such approval. Any loan to an individual or company that would place the total credit extended to a related group of individuals and/or companies in excess of the bank's legal lending limit must receive approval of the executive committee prior to disbursement.

6 The members and responsibilities of the officers loan committee are set forth in Exhibit A, which is attached hereto. The executive committee of the board of directors shall review these responsibilities no less than one time during each calendar year and the executive committee is authorized to make such changes in the loan committee and its responsibilities as it may consider prudent.

7 The lending representatives of the bank shall have the authority up to the amount as is indicated by their titles, without the approval of any committee, provided such loans are in accordance with the policies and principals herein expressed. It is intended that the total liabilities of a borrower to the bank, including real estate, installment, and commercial loans, are not to exceed the authority of the lending representative approving the loan.

8 The chief executive officer of the bank may, without specific authorization of the board of directors, grant lending authority on secured loans of not more than $450,000.00 and on unsecured loans of not more than $150,000.00 to officers and/or employees. Such action must be reported to the executive committee at its next meeting and recorded in the minutes.

9 Loans of the following types are considered desirable by this bank. Each loan must meet the tests of a prudent loan:
   (a) Unsecured loans to business concerns and individuals on a short-term basis, supported by a satisfactory balance sheet and earnings statement, usually for a term not to exceed 90 days.
   (b) Loans to business concerns and individuals secured by a security interest in marketable equipment, such loan to be amortized over a period of time generally not to exceed 36 months.
   (c) Loans to companies against assignment of accounts receivable. Loans against assigned accounts receivable shall be supervised by an officer of the bank appointed by the officers loan committee, and the procedures for servicing the loan must be approved in advance by the officers loan committee.
   (d) Loans collaterally secured by marketable bonds.
   (e) Loans collaterally secured by securities listed on a recognized stock exchange; such loans must comply in *all respects* with Regulation U of the Federal Reserve system.
   (f) Loans collaterally secured by unlisted securities that are readily marketable in the "over-the-counter" market.
   (g) Loans against the cash surrender value of life insurance, such loans not to exceed the cash surrender value plus the accumulated dividends.
   (h) Loans secured by the assignment of savings accounts in the bank, or other banks, or secured by savings accounts or share accounts of federally insured savings and loan associations.
   (i) Loans under $100,000.00 in amount secured by first liens on improved business or residential properties, such loans to qualify as follows:
       (1) Real estate loans shall be in the form of an obligation secured by a first mortgage.

EXHIBIT 2 (continued)

    (2) Real estate loans shall generally not exceed, in amount, 75 percent of the appraised value of the real estate offered as security.

    (3) Real estate loans shall generally not exceed a term of fifteen years, amortized in equal installment payments.

    (4) Real estate appraisals on which mortgage loans are based shall be made by appraisers who are approved by the executive committee.

(j) Real estate loans, in excess of $100,000.00 governed by the principles as set forth in Section i, above, and approved in advance by the executive committee.

(k) Installment loans, governed by Exhibit B of this "Statement of Lending Policies."

(l) Commodity loans secured by warehouse receipts in bonded warehouses or by field warehouse receipts.

It should be recognized by each lending representative of the bank that it is to the advantage of the borrower and to the bank that each loan have a program of repayment, agreed upon at the time the loan is made.

It is evident that certain loans—due to the nature of supporting collateral—may, in reality, be less liquid than others. All loans, excluding real estate loans, shall be reviewed at least each quarter by the lending representative who initiated the loan, and when changes in the economy, the securities market, or the commodities market warrant, loans shall be reviewed more often.

All loans shall have an ample margin of safety between the advance and the current market value of the collateral. When insurance on the collateral or on the life of the borrower is warranted, it shall be obtained and periodically reviewed by the officer initiating the loan.

10 Loans of the following type are not considered desirable loans for the purposes of the bank. Such loans will ordinarily be declined unless they are specifically approved by the officers loan committee or the executive committee of the board of directors for reasons that appear to justify an exception to the bank's general policy:

(a) Capital loans to a business enterprise where the loan cannot be repaid within a reasonable period except by borrowing elsewhere or by liquidating the business.

(b) Loans to a new enterprise if the repayment of the loan is dependent on the profitable operation of the enterprise.

(c) Loans to parties whose integrity or honesty is questionable.

(d) Real estate mortgage loans secured by property out of the bank's recognized trade area.

(e) Construction mortgage loans, except in cases where the building is being supervised by an architect and/or a contractor having financial responsibility and where the borrower has produced a satisfactory take-out commitment.

(f) Loans to be paid from the proceeds of the settlement of an estate, unless these loans are fully collateralized or guaranteed by the estate and approved by bank counsel.

(g) Loans secured by stock in a closed corporation which has no ready market.

(h) Loans for the purpose of enabling the borrower to speculate on the future market of securities or commodities.

11 A written application must be prepared for all loans, in order for the bank to have a written record of the representation on which the loan was based and the agreed upon term of repayment.

12 Interest rates shall be in accordance with the schedule adopted by the officers loan committee. The officers loan committee shall review the interest rate schedule when deemed appropriate and shall make required changes.

13 All unsecured loans in excess of $1,000 must be supported by a current financial statement. Such financial statements shall contain sufficient information to support the loan, shall be signed by the borrower, or shall be certified by an acceptable independent public or certified public accountant to the extent determined by the officers loan committee and/or the approving loan officer. Whenever possible, fiscal statements are to be supplemented by interim statements and other financial information.

EXHIBIT 2 (continued)

14 It shall be the duty of the credit manager to see that an appropriate memorandum for the credit file is prepared on each loan. The memorandum shall recite the circumstance under which the loan was made, the factors that justify it, and the borrower's plan of repayment.

15 Description and classification of collateral. (Note: The state of the economy and the susceptibility of the stock market to change may make the following advances imprudent. Each member of the lending staff shall take the full responsibility for appraising the original and continuing advisability of certain percentage advances against the following types of collateral. The following percentage advances are subject to change by the executive committee.)

Description and Classification of Collateral

Class A

1 U.S. government securities (90 percent of market).

2 Securities of federal agencies (90 percent of market).

3 Stocks listed on New York Stock Exchange or American Stock Exchange (50 percent of market).

4 Municipal bonds rated by Moody's "A" or better (80 percent of market).

5 Cash surrender value of life insurance (full cash surrender value including accrued dividends).

6 Savings accounts in our bank (100 percent of amount on deposit).

Class B

1 Stocks listed on other security exchanges (40 percent of market).

2 Other bonds rated by Moody's or listed on a security exchange, or quoted in the *Wall Street Journal* (50 percent of market).

3 Mutual funds (50 percent of market).

4 Stocks quoted over the counter (40 percent of market).

5 Savings accounts of other banks, or share accounts of insured building and loans (100 percent of account).

6 F.H.A. Title I—maximum to any one borrower (including spouse) limited by law.

Class C

1 Chattel mortgage and/or security agreement with appropriate filings.

2 Assigned accounts receivable.

3 Warehouse receipts on marketable commodities.

4 Unquoted stocks.

5 Real estate mortgages.

6 All other collateral.

EXHIBIT 2A
Saline Bank of Commerce—Officers Loan Committee

1 The committee shall consist of the following members:
       Executive Vice-President, Chair
       Senior Vice-President, Vice Chair
       All Commercial Loan Vice-Presidents and Assistant Vice-Presidents
       Manager of Installment Loan Department

EXHIBIT 2A (continued)

The executive vice-president–lending of the bank shall be chair of the committee and the senior lending officer shall serve as vice-chair. Five members of the committee shall constitute a quorum, and one of the five members shall act as chair in the absence of the executive vice-president and the senior lending officer.

2 All commercial loans and approvals of credit shall be reviewed or approved by the committee. The officers loan committee shall meet each business day at 8:30 A.M.

3 The authority of the committee shall be $600,000 secured and $300,000 unsecured.

4 All loans in excess of $300,000 unsecured ($600,000 secured) or increases in total indebtedness resulting in loans in excess of $300,000 unsecured ($600,000 secured) must have the approval of the committee and have the subsequent approval of the chair of the board before the extension of credit is made.

5 The credit manager or his or her appointed representative will act as secretary of the committee and will be responsible for arranging the flow of material to meetings. Officers wishing to present matters to the committee should so notify the credit department in advance.

EXHIBIT 2B
Saline Bank of Commerce—Installment Loans

It is the purpose of this exhibit to establish a uniform and proved approach to installment lending. The following comments and point evaluations will offer guidance and set standards for the granting of such credit. All consumer loans *MUST* be evaluated according to the point system currently in use and wherever possible the signatures of both husband and wife should be obtained. Any loan made where the total points indicate excessive risk must be fully justified *in writing* at the time the loan is made. All installment loans made which do not conform to both the bank's "Statement of Lending Policies" and this Exhibit B shall be reviewed by the officer in charge of installment loans. If the loan does not conform, the member of the lending staff approving the loan shall so indicate on the application.

1 *All loans*, both direct and dealer, will be point scored using the current tables as approved by the installment loan department. Any loan not meeting the score requirements will be rejected unless written reasons for approval are shown on the application or investigation sheet.

2 Personal Loans.
   (a) Must score 60 points [on Point System, Exhibit C].
   (b) Get complete listing of all debts.
   (c) *NO* personal loans to be extended to individuals having household goods loans at loan companies.
   (d) No personal loans if the total of *all* monthly payments (excluding home mortgage) will exceed 25 percent of net income.
   (e) Get signatures of *both* husband and wife on note.

3 Automobile Loans.
   (a) Must score 50 points.
   (b) Complete description of car, including engine and major accessories, must be on application or investigation sheet.
   (c) Yegen Guide Figure or Red Book Loan Value must be shown.
   (d) Advances on new cars—Yegen Guide with 10 percent leeway.
   (e) Advances on used—Loan Value with 10 percent leeway subject to inspection of car.
   (f) All used cars to be inspected on direct loans and on indirect where advisable.
   (g) Maximum maturities—new cars, 36 months; used cars, 30 months. Loans must be fully amortized in substantially equal payments. *NO BALLOONS.*

EXHIBIT 2B (continued)

4 Collateral Loans on Household Goods:
  (a) Must score 60 points.
  (b) Get signatures of *both* husband and wife on note and security agreement.

5 Property Improvement Loans:
  (a) Must score 60 points.
  (b) Applications must be complete in every detail.
  (c) No advances for funds to be used for purposes other than improvement of the subject property.
  (d) No mortgages.
  (e) Husbands and wives must sign the note.

EXHIBIT 2C
Saline National Bank—Point System: Credit Evaluation Factors for Installment Loans

Telephone

−10	No telephone

Homeowners

10	Mortgage—equity unknown
20	Mortgage—substantial equity or owning five years or more
30	Home clear

Renters

−10	Renting—less than one year at present address, or if renting room or furnished apartment.
0	Renting—one to five years at present address; if length of residence is unknown; or is living with relatives
10	Renting—living at present address five years or longer

Income

	Weekly	*Monthly*	*Annually*
15	$100–$135	$433–$583	$5,200–$7,000
20	Over $135	Over $583	Over $7,000
−5	If income is on commission basis or if self-employed in marginal business.		

Employment

10	1–3 years
15	4–10 years
25	Over 10 years
5	If *both* husband and wife are employed

Occupation

−10	If application is employed in marginal and/or high-risk job

Age and Marital Status

−10	If single, male, and under 26; or if divorced or separated

EXHIBIT 2C (continued)

Credit
Background

25	Satisfactory reference from recognized credit source, with six months' or more experience
10	Satisfactory reference from specialty source (high credit over $100) with six months' or more experience
10	Bonus points for good Saline Bank of Commerce reference
−10	If monthly payments exceed weekly income from primary source
−10	Poor reports or evidence of slow pay (one fourth of payments made late, or if currently one month behind)

Downpayment

0	Less than 10%
10	10–33%
20	More than 33%

REJECT ALL APPLICATIONS FOR CREDIT *WITHOUT POINTING* IF THERE IS EVIDENCE OF OVERLOADING, REPOSSESSIONS, CHARGEOFFS OR EXCEPTIONALLY BAD PAY RECORD.

EXHIBIT 3
Saline Bank of Commerce—Miscellaneous Cost Data, 1973

Time deposit reserve requirement	3%
Certificate of deposit reserve requirement	5%
Demand deposit reserve requirement	15.6%
Commercial loan handling cost	0.0003 of loan amount
Commercial loan risk factor	0.0005 of loan amount
Real estate loan handling cost	0.0009 of loan amount
Real estate loan risk factor	0.0005 of loan amount
Ledger entries (paid checks)	$0.10/Item
Demand deposit account maintenance fee	$3.50/Month/Account
Deposited item (encoded)	$0.01
Deposited item (unencoded)	$0.05
Lockbox item (cost)	$0.06/Item
Lockbox item (price)	$0.10/Item
Monthly lockbox fee	$50.00
Wire transfer	$2.50/Transfer
Certificate of deposit handling cost	0.0001 of CD amount
Earnings credit rate	6.5%
Cost of funds	6.5%
1973 profitability standard	5.8% on net funds used

EXHIBIT 4
Thomas Insurance Company—1973 Accounts

Item	President's account	Company accounts					Treasury tax and loan
		1	2	3	4	5	
Average demand deposit ledger balances	$20,000	$11,378	$64,502	$84,280	($37,556)	$587,409	$16,900
Ledger entries in 1973	1,000	18,048	16,248	11,364	91,284	29,100	12
Checks deposited (encoded) in 1973	0	0	0	0	0	0	
Checks deposited (unencoded) in 1973	51	1,056	48	91,428	0	447,324	
Number of wire transfers processed in 1973		0	0	135	0	329	
Number of lockbox items processed in 1973		0	0	0	0	116,241	
Service charges in 1973	0	0	0	0	0	0	
Average float	$ 2,000	0	0	$35,191	0	$272,426	

	President	Company	
Certificates of deposit	$20,000	$60,000	$132,000[a]
Average CD interest rate paid	7.25%	7.25%	7.25%

[a] Pension and profit-sharing trust.

EXHIBIT 5
Saline Bank of Commerce—Average Rates for 1973 and Projected Average Rates for 1974

	1973 Rate	1974 Projected rate
National prime	8.50	9.00
Saline Bank of Commerce prime	9.00	9.50
Federal funds	9.00	9.50
Treasury bills	7.00	7.50
90-day certificates of deposit	7.25	7.75
Federal Reserve discount rate	7.00	
Saline Bank of Commerce's cost of funds:		
Pooled (excluding capital)	5.80	6.30
Pooled (including capital)	6.50	7.00
Consumer deposits	5.50	6.00
Consumer deposits and federal funds	6.60	7.10
Earnings credit rate		8.00
Cost of funds for use in profitability analysis		8.00
Profitability standard		7.50

EXHIBIT 6
Saline Bank of Commerce—Source and Use of Funds

Funds provided:		
Usable demand deposits	$0	
Usable time deposits	0	
Usable certificates of deposit	0	
Usable treasury tax and loan	0	
Other funds sources	0	
Total funds provided		$0
Funds used:		
Commercial loans	$0	
Installment loans	0	
Mortgage loans	0	
Other funds uses	0	
Total funds used		$0
Net funds provided (used)		$0
Float		
Demand Deposits		$0
Reserves		
Demand	0	
Time	0	
CD	0	
Total reserves		$0
Total float and reserves		$0
Investable comp balances required on loans		$0

EXHIBIT 6 (continued)

Income/Profit Statement

Income:		
Loan interest	$0	
Loan fees	0	
Service fees		
Payroll accounting	0	
Lockbox	0	
Other income	0	
Total income		$0
Expense:		
Demand deposit activity		
Items deposited	0	
Checks paid	0	
Maintenance	0	
Time deposits	0	
Certificates of deposit	0	
Interest expense	0	
Credit and loan administration	0	
Other services		
Payroll	0	
Lockbox	0	
ARP	0	
Wire transfer	0	
Coin and currency	0	
Risk expense	0	
Total expense		$0
Spread:		
Gross spread		$0
Credit (cost) for net funds provided (used)		$0
Net spread		$0
Net yield on net funds used	0.00%	
Profitability required	5.80%	
Profit index		

CASE 18
Bandera Oil Corporation

HISTORY

Bandera Oil was incorporated in 1965 under the state laws of Delaware. Since its inception, the company has been headquartered in Denver, Colorado. Predecessor companies to Bandera were predominantly four drilling and production joint ventures involving wealthy individuals from various parts of the United States. There were some common ties among these major investors through business associations, marriages, and social organizations. Samuel A. Barton, a third-generation New Yorker, was the principal investor in two of the joint programs and a substantial investor in another. He had proposed that a corporation be formed and that the individual investors sell their interest in oil and gas properties to the corporation in exchange for common stock, which in turn would provide an excellent vehicle for long-term appreciation.

The four joint ventures also had some common ties, since the managements of two of them were identical, and this management group also acted as a consultant to each of the other two programs. Thus, with the common ties in both investor and management groups, the idea proposed by Samuel Barton was consummated, and in 1965 the new corporation was formed. Samuel Barton was chosen as chairman, and the five individuals in the management group assumed the roles of president and vice-president for exploration, production, land, and finance. The five officers forming the new management group received adequate salaries and liberal stock options. The investors received common stock for their oil and gas interests and would also participate in any future drilling programs, if they so desired. As such programs were completed, the company would attempt to acquire the successful properties from the investors at a later date through the exchange of stock.

The original stockholders intended long-term capital appreciation to be their primary goal—capital appreciation that would benefit their children and grandchildren, not themselves. Thus, it became readily apparent that the company would not in the foreseeable future pay cash dividends, but would reinvest all funds in additional properties, through either drilling prospects or property purchase.

At its inception, Bandera was capitalized at $15 million and it had no debt. As it began operations, Bandera had gross revenues of $5.5 million. During the initial states of the corporation,

not all individuals in the various joint ventures exchanged their interest for stock in Bandera, but elected instead to retain their oil and gas revenues. Management believed that these remaining interests could possibly be exchanged for stock as time progressed and that it would also have the opportunity to purchase other oil and gas properties through an exchange of stock.

During the company's earlier years, it developed its properties and took varying amounts of interest in others. Depending on the estimated total cost, Bandera remained the operator when at all possible. The company prospered during its early years, while experiencing the usual struggles and setbacks. Later it expanded into other forms of energy, mainly hard minerals and oil and gas exploration in Canada.

MANAGEMENT

Bandera's initial management continued in office until 1974. At that time, it became clear to Barton that a change was necessary and the other principal investors agreed. In Barton's view, the president had allowed expenses to get out of control due to a rather flat reserve position and somewhat stagnant daily production. The president eventually resigned, and Barton assumed the responsibilities of chairman, president, and chief executive officer.

Barton was 61 years old and he had over 20 years' experience in the oil and gas business. He held a master's degree in business administration from New York University. Barton had a number of financial interests in addition to Bandera and served on the board of directors of three New York City-based corporations.

Janet W. Elliott, vice-president for exploration and production, was 46 years old and had been in the field for 25 years. She was with Mobil Oil for 15 years before joining Bandera in 1974.

Payson M. Sommers, age 43, had served as financial vice-president since 1974. Prior to that time he was a certified public accountant employed by one of the New York firms in which Barton was a director. Sommers held an M.B.A.

in accounting from State University of New York (SUNY)–Buffalo.

BANK RELATIONSHIPS

Bandera Oil Corporation had been a customer of Rocky Mountain National Bank in Denver for the past 14 years. The relationship between Bandera and Rocky Mountain had been a very satisfactory and profitable one to the bank. Since Samuel Barton resided near New York and commuted every other week to Bandera's headquarters in Denver, a New York bank, First Mutual Trust, was considered the company's lead bank. It had been a long-term goal of Rocky Mountain National Bank, however, to replace First Mutual as lead bank.

In January 1979, Bandera requested a substantial increase in its line of credit from First Mutual Trust. The bank was hesitant, however, to increase Bandera's revolving credit line from its present $55 million to a proposed $85 million. During 1977 and 1978 and into early 1979 (when the credit increase was requested), Barton had continued a vigorous program of expense reduction. In accomplishing this task, he had concentrated on some obvious loose control over operating expenses and staff overhead. As a result of these much tighter expense controls, he was able to strengthen significantly his geology department as well as to establish a property acquisition division. To complete a more ambitious exploration program, however, additional funds were required. Although the company would not retain 100 percent of each exploration project, it did plan to retain interests varying between 25 and 50 percent, depending on the particular projects and management's assessment of the probable risks involved.

Although the relationship at First Mutual Trust had proven a good one, Samuel Barton nonetheless concluded that this might be an opportune time to contact Rocky Mountain National Bank to ask that institution to assume the lead bank's role and thus to arrange for the additional funds needed by Bandera. In early 1979 there were six banks participating in the credit (Exhibit 5), and the increased amount of the loan would not present any legal lending limit problems. The participating banks were all experienced in petroleum lending and the Bandera relationship was an important one for them.

FINANCIAL INFORMATION

Financial data for Bandera are summarized in Exhibits 1 through 4. Income from operations exceeded $15 million in 1978, or twice the level of the prior year. Five-year trends in working capital and other balance sheet data are presented in Exhibit 4.

When Barton began his discussions in January 1979, with First Mutual Trust, the bank proposed a "loan request memorandum" which summarized some of the terms and conditions that had been discussed between Barton and the officers responsible for the Bandera account. This information is included in Exhibit 5.

EXHIBIT 1
Bandera Oil Corporation—Balance Sheets,
December 31, 1977, and 1978 (in thousands of dollars)

	1978	1977
Assets		
Current assets:		
Cash	$ 10,841	$ 6,752
Accounts receivable	16,432	13,021
Inventories	3,975	7,024

EXHIBIT 1 (continued)

	1978	1977
Prepayments and other	1,136	754
Total current assets	$ 32,384	$ 27,551
Property and equipment, at cost		
Producing and nonproducing oil and gas properties, wells and equipment	228,463	173,561
Nonproducing mining properties	3,290	3,585
Transportation, office, and other equipment	1,981	1,696
	233,734	178,842
Less accumulated depreciation	(96,119)	(73,021)
	137,615	105,821
Other assets	—	1,027
Total assets	$169,999	$134,399
Liabilities and Stockholders' Investment		
Current liabilities:		
Short-term notes payable to a bank	$ 3,575	$ 6,000
Amount due within one year on long-term debt	226	851
Accounts payable	9,057	9,469
Accrued liabilities	4,759	5,512
Total current liabilities	$ 17,617	$ 21,832
Long-term debt, less current portion	56,066	28,542
Deferred revenue-sale of oil to be produced in the future, less unamortized imputed interest expense of $1,831,000 and $843,000, respectively	7,816	12,898
Deferred income tax	13,332	6,607
Stockholders' Investment:		
Common stock	237	236
Capital in excess of par value	41,205	40,716
Retained earnings	33,726	23,568
Shareholders' equity	75,168	64,520
Total liabilities and shareholders' equity	$169,999	$134,399

EXHIBIT 2
Bandera Oil Corporation—Income Statement Years
Ending December 31, 1977 and 1978 (in thousands of dollars)

	1978	1977
Revenues:		
Oil sales	$32,932	$36,508
Gas sales	16,292	8,255
Natural gas liquids sales	2,470	2,312
	$51,694	$47,075

EXHIBIT 2 (continued)

	1978	1977
Costs and expenses:		
Lease operating expenses	$10,816	$10,273
Depreciation, depletion and amortization	22,256	26,388
General and administrative expenses	2,992	2,890
	$36,064	39,551
Income from operations	$15,630	$ 7,524
Other income and expenses:		
Gain on sale of mining property	$ 4,239	$ —
Gain on sale of inventory	149	763
Gain on sale of airport	—	397
Interest expense	(3,806)	(2,684)
Miscellaneous	687	61
	$ 1,269	$ (1,463)
Income before income tax	16,899	6,061
Income tax	(6,741)	(1,187)
Net Income	10,158	4,874
Net income per common and common equivalent share	$ 0.86	$ 0.41

EXHIBIT 3
Bandera Oil Corporation—Notes to Financial Statements

Oil and Gas Properties

The company follows the full cost method of accounting for oil and gas properties. Under this method, all productive and nonproductive costs, including company's proportionate share of the cost of partnership properties incurred in connection with the exploration for and development of oil and gas reserves, are capitalized. Such capitalized costs include lease acquisition, geological and geophysical work, drilling, completing and equipping oil and gas wells, and other related costs together with costs applicable to the company's technical personnel directly engaged in evaluating and maintaining oil and gas prospects and drilling oil and gas wells. No gains or losses are recognized upon the sale or other disposition of oil and gas properties except in extraordinary transactions. Maintenance and repairs are charged against income when incurred. Renewals and betterments that extend the useful life of properties are capitalized.

The capitalized cost of all producing and nonproducing oil and gas properties is amortized on a composite unit-of-production method computed quarterly on a future revenue basis. This quarterly amortization provision is determined by (1) dividing oil and gas sales during each quarter by the total future revenues applicable to the aggregate proven oil and gas reserves and (2) applying such rate to the total unamortized cost of oil and gas properties. The company's oil and gas reserves are estimated semiannually by a firm of independent petroleum engineers.

	1978	1977
Average sales price:		
Oil (per barrel)	$9.10	$8.90
Gas (per mcf)	$1.05	$0.62

EXHIBIT 3 (continued)

Natural gas liquids (per barrel)	$9.09	$8.66
Expenses stated as a percentage of sales price:		
Lease operating	20.9%	21.8%
DD&A	42.8%	55.7%
Expenses per barrel and equivalent barrel:		
Lease operating	$1.99	$1.95
DD&A	$4.07	$4.99

Mining Properties

Mining properties are in the exploration state and all costs and expenses related thereto have been capitalized. Such costs will either be amortized upon the commencement of production or recognized as losses if projects are abandoned or if a decline in a project's value becomes apparent. Gains or losses are recognized upon the sale of all or a portion of any project. Although investments of this nature necessarily involve unusual risks and uncertainties, the company's management believes that the investment will be realized through successful future operations or by sale of its interests to others.

Deferred Taxes

Deferred income taxes are provided on items that are recognized for financial and tax purposes in different periods and for items that are capitalized for financial statement purposes; deferred taxes are also included on income for gains on sales of oil and gas properties which are credited to property and equipment for financial statement purposes. Investment tax credits are recorded on the flow-through method whereby tax credits are applied as a reduction in the year's provision for income taxes.

The company's long-term debt as of December 31, 1978 and 1977, is summarized below:

	1978	*1977*
Notes payable to banks, 11.75 percent (0.5 over a bank's rate as of December 31, 1978), pursuant to a revolving line of credit (see discussion below)	$55,000,000	$22,000,000
Debentures payable to a gas pipeline company, 9.75 percent (a Canadian bank's prime rate as of December 31, 1977), unsecured (see discussion below)	—	4,920,000
Notes payable to stockholders, 6 percent, unsecured, payable in monthly installments of $52,000	208,000	832,000
Other, partially secured	1,084,000	1,641,000
	56,292,000	29,393,000
Less amount due within one year	(226,000)	(851,000)
	$56,066,000	$28,542,000

Short-Term Borrowings

During 1978 the company entered into an agreement with a bank whereby it can borrow up to an amount equal to the cost of its total inventories, not to exceed $6 million. Any amounts outstanding under the agreement are due upon expiration of the agreement on July 1, 1979.

The maximum amount outstanding under the agreement during 1978 as of any month-end was $6 million, and the approximate average amount outstanding was $4,399,000. The average interest rate paid was approximately 7.5 percent. The amounts outstanding as of December 31, 1978, bear interest at 11.75 percent (0.5 percent over the bank's prime rate). There were no other short-term borrowings during 1978, and there were no short-term borrowings during 1977.

EXHIBIT 3 (continued)

Income Taxes

On December 31, 1978, the company had a federal income tax net operating loss carry-over of approximately $26,200,000 and an investment tax credit carry-over of approximately $2,900,000, which are available to reduce or eliminate future income taxes. The net operating loss carry-over resulted primarily from the deduction for income tax purposes of oil and gas exploration and development costs capitalized for financial reporting purposes. The investment tax credit has been utilized for financial reporting purposes as a reduction of deferred income taxes. The ultimate utilization of the net operating loss carry-over and the investment tax credit carry-over will therefore not result in a reduction of income tax expense in the period utilized but will be credited to deferred income taxes. No material amount of investment tax credit will expire within the next three years. If not utilized, the net operating loss carry-over will expire as follows:

	Net Operating Loss	Investment Tax Credit
1979	$ 6,500,000	0
1980	5,600,000	100,000
1981	6,900,000	300,000
1982	0	200,000
1983	0	500,000
Remainder (1984 and 1985)	7,200,000	1,800,000
	$26,200,000	$2,900,000

The company's federal income tax returns have not been examined since the organization of the company in 1965.

Production Payments

In September 1975, the company sold 6 million barrels of oil from a certain producing field for an advance payment of $30 million. Deliveries of such oil began November 1, 1975, and have amounted to 4,556,883 barrels through December 31, 1978. Deferred revenue from the sale is being included in income as the oil is produced. The imputed interest expense is being charged to income as the 6 million-barrel repayment obligation is liquidated. The purchaser also has an option to purchase all other crude oil purchased or produced by the company at a defined "free market price" until the total contract amount of oil is delivered.

Commitments and Contingencies

Noncancellable Leases

The minimum rental commitments under long-term noncancellable leases for office space and data processing equipment approximate $3,190,000 and are payable as follows:

1979	$ 524,000
1980	464,000
1981	433,000
1982	416,000
1983	416,000
Remainder (1984 through 1987)	937,000
	$3,190,000

Rentals under such leases charged to administrative and technical expenses before reduction for amounts capitalized as oil and gas properties and charged to managed partnerships were $574,000 and $530,000 for 1978 and 1977, respectively.

EXHIBIT 4

Bandera Oil Corporation—Review of Operations, 1974–1978

	1978	1977	1976	1975	1974
Annual production:					
Liquid hydrocarbons (thousand barrels)					
Crude oil	3,618	4,100	4,192	3,947	3,114
Natural gas liquids	272	267	189	239	278
Total liquid hydrocarbons	3,890	4,367	4,381	4,186	3,392
Natural gas (million cubic feet)	15,406	13,320	13,089	14,548	12,509
Daily average net production:					
Liquid hydrocarbons (barrels)					
Crude oil	9,885	11,234	11,484	10,812	8,508
Natural gas liquids	742	731	518	655	760
Total liquid hydrocarbons	10,627	11,965	12,002	11,467	9,268
Natural gas (thousand cubic feet)	42,092	36,494	35,860	39,858	34,178
Reserves:					
Liquid hydrocarbons (thousand barrels)					
Crude oil	10,397	11,895	11,370	11,929	15,892
Natural gas liquids	1,235	1,509	953	1,128	1,050
Total liquid hydrocarbons	11,632	13,404	12,323	13,057	16,942
Natural gas (million cubic feet)	186,566	93,932	74,322	75,020	110,746
Wells completed:					
Gross exploratory wells completed	30	26	34	18	70
Gross development wells completed	76	97	128	64	76
Total gross wells completed	106	123	162	82	146
Total net wells completed	56	62	59	53	35
Exploratory wells as a percentage of total	28	21	21	22	48
Percentage of exploratory wells productive	33	27	12	33	14
Percentage of development wells productive	86	91	81	84	74
Undeveloped oil and gas acreage					
(thousand acres)					
Gross	2,506	3,942	6,070	8,040	7,180
Net	1,139	1,552	3,513	2,563	2,141
Capital expenditures:					
Oil and gas properties					
Exploratory	$ 27,669	$18,644	$ 21,470	$ 16,434	$ 11,917
Development	24,313	22,334	14,143	8,230	7,566
Acquisitions	2,468	7,149	6,525	2,874	7,247
Mining properties	2,464	568	595	540	459
Other	460	212	880	585	714
	$ 57,374	$48,907	$ 43,613	$ 28,663	$27,903
Year-end financial data:					
Working capital	$ 14,767	$ 5,719	$ 6,057	$ 29,762	$ 1,135
Property and equipment, net	137,615	105,821	87,467	69,903	49,846

EXHIBIT 4 (continued)

	1978	1977	1976	1975	1974
Total assets	169,999	134,399	109,804	110,144	68,689
Long-term debt	56,066	28,542	9,282	10,265	20,374
Deferred revenue	7,816	12,898	20,179	28,599	—
Deferred income taxes	13,332	6,607	5,525	6,855	5,090
Stockholders' investment	75,168	64,520	59,558	53,542	26,763
Common shares outstanding (in thousands)	11,852	11,778	11,761	11,340	9,272

EXHIBIT 5
Bandera Oil Corporation—Loan Presentation Data

Name:	Bandera Oil Corp.	*Division:* Energy
	Rocky Mountain Center	*Section:* Petroleum
	Denver, Colorado	*Officer:* FEZ/JAH

**Action
Requested:** Approval of an $8 million participation in a $85,000 resolving credit and term loan headed by First Mutual Trust Bank. Participants are as follows:

	Amount
First Mutual Trust	$52,000,000
Rocky Mountain National	8,000,000
Western States National	7,000,000
Fort William National	7,000,000
Commercial National	7,000,000
Fortson State	4,000,000
	$85,000,000

Rate: First Mutual prime plus 0.5 percent, as it changes. Spread above prime remains constant during both revolving and term period. Interest is due on the first of each month.

**Commitment
Fee:** 0.5 percent on the unused balance during the revolving period, payable quarterly

**Balance
Agreement:** 10 percent of unused portion of the commitment plus 20 percent of the outstanding amount

Maturity: The revolving period will end on January 1, 1980, and the final payment on the term loan will be due on January 1, 1983, provided that:

1 The semiannual consultant's reserve evaluation report indicates to the satisfaction of the agent bank that the present value of future net income of the company from "proved producing reserves" is at least 200 percent of the total long-term debt on Bandera's balance sheet, including the current portion of long-term debt.

2 If the above test *is not* met, the note will convert to a term credit payable in 12 consecutive equal quarterly installments.

EXHIBIT 5 (continued)

3 If the test *is* met, then the revolving credit will convert to term on January 1, 1980, and any outstanding balance at that time, if not paid in full, will be payable in 12 consecutive equal quarterly installments through January 1, 1983.

Security: This is an unsecured credit; however, a loan agreement does govern and, in addition to the usual provisions, provides for the company to:

1 Maintain a current ratio of at least 125 percent.

2 Maintain a working capital position of not less than $5 million.

Account Relationship: Average collected balances

	1978	1977	1976
Bandera	$1,692,000	$1,736,000	$1,447,000

Loan Relationship: Average amounts outstanding

	1978	1977	1976
Bandera	$5,000,000	$1,400,000	$1,400,000
	750,000	2,675,000	900,000
	$5,750,000	$4,075,000	$2,300,000

CASE 19
George Harris

BACKGROUND

George Harris, who was 32 years old in 1977, farmed approximately 1300 acres near Rye, Arkansas. His major crops were cotton (65 percent) and soybeans (35 percent). Harris had leased the farm from a relative for the past five years. He lived in Rye, some 22 miles from the farm, with his wife and three children. Harris was considered to be an excellent young farmer, a hard worker, and of very good moral character.

Harris had expanded the farm substantially over the past two years, and he hoped to add for the new growing season approximately 200 acres of rice to his other crops. He also was planning in the near future to build a $75,000 home on some lakefront property he owned.

BANK RELATIONSHIP

Harris had been a customer of the National Bank of Commerce in Pine Bluff, Arkansas, for the past four years. His credit record is summarized in Exhibit 1.

For 1979 Harris proposed to plant 1,000 acres of cotton and 335 acres of soybeans. He estimated that he would need a minimum loan of $200,000, which included $20,000 which he needed to pay his federal and state income taxes.

He believed that his production cost this year would be above that of the previous year because of the increased cotton acreage. In addition, the cost of most labor and material was continuing to increase.

Harris's loan requirements had increased at a much greater rate than his equity in the operation. He believed, however, that he would not have any difficulty repaying the loan. He had contracted to sell 50 percent of his cotton in 1979 for $0.60 per pound. The balance of the cotton and the soybeans were as yet unpriced.

With regard to the possibility of planting a rice crop this year, Harris thought that the current rice law would be extended and marketing quotas would not be in effect for the next four or five years. Rice production would, however, be outside the farm program, since he did not have a rice allotment. Harris had indicated to the bank that planting the rice crop would necessitate an-

other $50,000 loan. This amount would go toward the installation of an irrigation well, the purchase of seed, and other production costs. Harris did not anticipate that the rice crop would require buying major items of equipment.

Harris had asked the bank to consider the rice loan as a separate request from his regular crop loan and to advise him of its attitude toward this new venture.

Harris also advised the bank that he had 2,200 bushels of soybeans on hand. These should net him about $14,000. Harris wanted to reserve funds from the sale of these soybeans to use for partial financing of the home he planned to build. He intended to discuss home financing with the bank later in the year.

Harris's loan application is summarized in Exhibit 2, and supporting financial data on the farm are included in Exhibits 3 through 6.

EXHIBIT 1
National Bank of Commerce—Loan Memorandum

Name___George Harris___	Date___January 19, 1979___
Address___Rye, Arkansas___	Rate_____
Business___Farming___	
Application for Loan $___200,000.00___	FINANCIAL STATEMENT
Present Debt, Direct $___22,400.00 (on equip.)___	As of___January 19, 1979___
Indirect . . . . $_____	_____

Complete information regarding applicant and/or endorser, description of collateral, agreement as to payment accruements, affiliations, deposit balances, etc., to be accompanied by financial statements and all data known.

Officer:

Our past experience with Mr. Harris is as follows:

1975—Our first loan with Mr. Harris was in January 1975, when we agreed to finance him for the current crop year and to lend him an additional $30,000 to take up equipment notes with PCA. He had been with the PCA for five years, and his record with that organization was apparently good. His 1975 crop was good, and he repaid his production loan and made a satisfactory reduction in his equipment notes.

1976—We advanced Mr. Harris $126,000 for productuion purposes, and due to a short crop, he was unable to repay his crop loan. He ended the crop year owing $41,600 on his production loan plus some equipment payments.

1977—Mr. Harris stated that he would need a minimum of $100,000 to produce the 1977 crop plus the $41,600 carry-over. We agreed to put this new money into the crop provided his landlord (also a relative) would guarantee the $41,600 carry-over. This arrangement was worked out, and a total of $126,800 in crop money

EXHIBIT 1 (continued)

was advanced. Mr. Harris's crop was fairly good in 1977, and he repaid his crop loan plus $20,000 on his carry-over.

1978—Mr. Harris proposed to make a sizable increase in the acreage planted to cotton, and requested his crop loan be increased to $165,000. The $21,000 balance on the 1977 carry-over would continue to be guaranteed by his relative; however, the relative indicated that while she was guaranteeing the balance of the carry-over this year, she would not guarantee any additional amounts in the future. Mr. Harris had another good crop in 1978 and was able to meet most of his obligations. He repaid his crop loan, his carry-over, and the equipment notes due our bank.

Approved:_____   Date_____19_____

EXHIBIT 2
Application for Loan

TO:_____National Bank of Commerce of Pine Bluff, Pine Bluff, Arkansas_____

NAME OF   NAME OF WIFE
APPLICANT:_George Harris_____ AGE:_32_ (OR HUSBAND)_____
Nancy

ADDRESS:_Rye, Arkansas_____

I/We hereby make application for a loan of $___200,000.00___, or such amount as may be approved by you, the proceeds to be used (except as otherwise indicated) in planting, cultivating, and harvesting _1979_ crops or for livestock breeding, feeding or marketing on land described below:

(a) 1,050 acres rented from Mrs. John Harris
(b) 450 acres rented from L. James

Terms of rent: (a) 1/4 crops produced, payable as crops are sold.
               (b) $12,000.00, payable November 15, 1979.
               Landlord will not waive lien.

I/We have cultivated above lands for __9__ years. Production record last 3 years:

	1975	1976	1977	1978
Acres cotton planted	594	585	650	850
Bales harvested	904	565	828	962
Acres Soybeans planted		650	375	480
Bushels harvested		9,376	3,400	10,560

1979 Proposed Crops—Acreage

Crop	Harris	James	Total	Net
Cotton	720	280	1,000	820
Soybeans	200	135	335	285
Cotton				
Allotment	370	110		
Projected Yield	610#	560#		

Note: 1/2 of 1979 cotton crop sold on contract for 60¢ per pound.

EXHIBIT 2 (continued)

DISBURSEMENT SCHEDULE

	Total	Immediate	
1978 income taxes	$ 20,000	$20,000	
To produce 1979 crop	180,000	60,000	Balance to be disbursed as needed.
TOTALS	$200,000	$80,000	

EXHIBIT 3
Financial History

BORROWER: ___George Harris___   AGE: _32_ DATE OF FIRST LOAN: ___January 18, 1975___

ADDRESS:_____

	1/18/75	1/14/76	1/16/77	1/30/78	1/19/79
Assets					
Livestock	5,380	15,000	23,500	12,000	16,100
Farm Products	1,880	300	1,800	2,300	19,250
Accounts Owed Me—Good	3,000	500	1,000	800	
Stocks and Bonds	15,000	8,500	8,500	23,500	23,500
Cash on Hand and in Bank	10,000	7,500	900	1,000	1,400
Machinery, Equipment, Cars, and Trucks	120,000	123,800	126,500	145,250	162,000
City Real Estate (home)	18,000	18,000	18,000	18,000	18,000
Other Assets:					
Lakefront Property			11,000	11,000	12,000
Building Material				6,250	10,000
Total Assets	173,260	173,600	191,200	222,200	263,750
Liabilities					
Accounts I Owe (open)		3,000	4,600	28,435	32,651
Notes I Owe	38,700	58,100	88,400	81,500	78,150
Unpaid Taxes (income)					20,000
Total Liabilities	38,700	61,100	93,000	109,935	130,801
Net Worth	134,560	112,500	98,200	112,265	132,949
Total Amount Advanced	140,000	126,000	168,400	186,600	
Carryover (operating funds)		41,600	21,600	000	
Acres Rented	1,500	1,350	1,500	1,500	1,500

CREDIT STATEMENT—AGRICULTURAL

TO THE ___National Bank of Commerce of Pine Bluff___ OF ___Pine Bluff, Arkansas___

SUBMITTED
BY ___George Harris___   ADDRESS ___Rye, Arkansas___

For the purpose of borrowing money, or otherwise obtaining accommodations from time to time, I hereby make the following statement of my financial condition on the 19th day of January 1979; and it is agreed that notice in writing will be given you immediately of any materially unfavorable change in my financial condition. In the ab-

EXHIBIT 3 (continued)

sence of such notice or a new and full written financial statement, you may consider this statement as continuing and substantially correct and having the same force and effect as if delivered as an original statement of my financial condition upon application for further borrowings or accommodations.

Assets (What I Own)			Liabilities (What I Owe)		
Livestock (Schedule A)		$ 16,100	Accounts I Owe (No. _19_)		$ 32,651
Farm Products (Schedule B)		19,250	Notes I Owe (Schedule G)		78,150
Notes Owed Me—Good		1,500	1978 fed. and state income		
Stocks and Bonds (Schedule C)		23,500	taxes		20,000
Cash on Hand and in Bank		1,400			
Cash Value Life Insurance	$2,100				
Less: Borrowed on Policies	2,100	000			
Machinery, Equipment, Cars					
and Trucks (Schedule D)					
2 automobiles, 3 2-way radios		162,000			
Farm Real Estate (Schedule E)					
City Real Estate (Schedule F) (home)		18,000			
Other Assets:					
Lake property (2 lots)		12,000	Total Debts		$130,801
Building material on hand		10,000	Net Worth		$132,949
TOTAL		$263,750	TOTAL		$263,750

Schedule A—Livestock		Schedule B—Farm Products	
2 horses	$1,000	50 tons Hay	1,250
63 cows	12,600	2,200 bushels Soybeans	14,000
2 bulls	2,500	Silage	4,000
TOTAL	$16,100	TOTAL	$19,250

Schedule C—Stocks and Bonds Owned

Name	Present Value	Registered in Name of
10 shares Drew County Flying Service	$ 6,000	George Harris
Arkansas Grain Assn.	2,500	George Harris
15 shares Farmers Gin Co.	15,000	George Harris

Schedule D—Machinery, Equipment, Cars, and Trucks
(Listed on Credit Statement under ASSETS)

Schedule E—Farm Real Estate
None

Land Use—Crops Growing or to be Grown

1979 Crops	Acres	Estimated Yield	Borrower's Share
Cotton	1,000	1,250 B/C	1,025 B/C
Soybeans	335	8,375 bu.	7,125 bu.
Milo	50	75 tons	All

EXHIBIT 3 (continued)

Schedule F—City Real Estate

City and Street No.	Nature (residence, commercial, etc.)	Present Value	Amount of Mortgage
Rye, Arkansas	Residence	$18,000	$000

Schedule G—Notes I Owe

Payable To	Amount	Maturity	Secured by
This bank NBC	$ 9,800	December 1, 1979	
NBC	12,600	2 fall payments	J. D. Combine
Other banks			
First State Bank	2,100	December 1, 1979	Automobile
Relatives	10,000		
Others			
Deere & Co.	16,900		2-row Cotton Picker
I.H. Finance Co.	18,750	3 fall payments	1976 Diesel Tractor
Farmers Gin Co.	8,000	4 annual payments	Gin Stock

Do you own full interest in property in financial statement? _Yes_

Income from sources other than farming: Amount $ _None_

Life Insurance in Force _$50,000_ Beneficiary _Wife_

Insurance on Buildings $_____ Insurance on Livestock and Equipment $_____

I have never made a compromise settlement with creditors or been adjudged a bankrupt except _____ ------

Amount and details of judgments or suits pending against me _____ None _____

State when farms owned were acquired and purchase price of each _____

Amount of mortgage principal and/or interest past due $_____ Since _____

Are you cooperating with Soil Conservations Program? _Yes_

Signature _/s/ George Harris_

Signature _____

Date signed __January 19, 1979__

EXHIBIT 4
George Harris—Operation Statement

	1975	1976	1977	1978
Farm Income				
ASCS—Cotton price support	$ 48,312	$ 000	$ 000	$ 000
Sales—Cotton and seed	98,720	117,898	136,448	207,600
Sales—Soybeans	16,833	24,612	15,110	41,601
Sales—Cattle	3,148	6,100	7,863	4,120
Gin rebate	2,008	1,618	1,856	4,810
Custom work	972	3,612	198	000
Total farm income	$169,993	$153,840	$161,475	$258,131

EXHIBIT 4 (continued)

	1975	1976	1977	1978
Expenses				
Labor	$ 23,872	$ 28,372	$ 31,040	$ 38,330
Planting seed	5,180	4,650	6,238	9,200
Fertilizer	16,300	18,780	12,320	26,040
Herbicides and poison	14,800	16,470	14,790	23,600
Fuel and oil	9,431	10,632	10,800	15,600
Repairs and maintenance, equipment	15,637	14,300	16,438	19,330
Conservation work	4,260	3,000	000	5,300
Insurance	695	728	792	1,280
Interest	5,360	6,660	7,410	8,600
Cash rent	10,000	8,000	10,000	10,000
Depreciation	16,280	17,434	17,820	27,600
Equipment rentals	8,400	4,550	2,712	3,600
Miscellaneous	9,260	9,870	8,442	5,000
Total expenses	$139,475	$143,446	$138,802	$193,480
Net income before taxes	$ 30,518	$ 10,394	$ 22,673	$ 64,651

EXHIBIT 5
George Harris—Machinery and Equipment, January 19, 1979

1—International Model 1206 tractor, S/N 12688SY
1—1972 International Model 1466D tractor, S/N 15873, w/cab
1—John Deere Model 730D tractor, S/N 58732
1—Case Model 830C tractor, S/N 3872
1—1965 John Deere Model 4020 LP tractor, S/N 7383
1—1963 John Deere Model 5010 tractor, S/N 2732
1—International Model H tractor, S/N 10777
1—1969 John Deere Model 4020 tractor, S/N 142528
1—1969 John Deere Model 4520 tractor, S/N 3623
1—1970 International Model 1256D tractor, S/N 13702
1—M.R.S. UD-18A wheel tractor, S/N 1516
1—1968 John Deere Model 299 LP cotton picker, S/N 1314
10—4-wheel cotton trailers
2—6-row set Dickey fenders
3—6-row John Deere cultivators
1—By-hoe power-driven cultivator
2—John Deere 6-row Hippin Bedders
2—International 4-row cultivators
1—John Deere 6-row planter
1—Barrentine 4-row bed knocker
1—Rotary hoe tiller
1—Afco flame cultivator

1—John Deere Model 600 hicycle-12-row
3,000 ft. of 8 in. aluminum irrigation pipe
1—Relift pump
1—Power unit
1—6-row planter
1—Burch 6-row planter
1—John Deere off-set disc
4—International Model 480 discs
1—Purdy land plane
2—6-yard Reynolds dirt buckets
1—Forrest City 6-row Do-All
2—W&A 4-row mix-mizer
2—W&A 6-row heavy duty incorporators
1—Graham chisel plow
1973 Chevrolet pickup truck
1976 Ford pickup truck
1968 Ford 2-ton truck
3—Motorola 2-way radios
1—Motorola base station
Various other farm and shop equipment

The following equipment subject to prior lien:
1—John Deere Model 699H cotton picker
1—1976 IHC Model 1566 diesel tractor

EXHIBIT 6
George Harris—Yield Records

Year	United States	Arkansas	Jefferson County
Cotton (pounds per acre)			
1975	519	500	638
1976	442	513	638
1977	453	374	426
1978	465	378	488
Soybeans (bushels per acre)			
1975	27.8	25.0	25.0
1976	23.7	16.0	20.0
1977	28.4	19.0	18.1
1978	25.2	20.0	19.0

CASE 20
Watson E. Williams, Inc.

THE BANK

The Northwest Commerce Bank in Dallas, Texas, had deposits of $600 million, loans of $400 million, and capital accounts totaling $50 million. It had been the bank's practice to make construction loans to qualified and experienced builders if the terms and conditions were reasonable and if the project appeared well conceived. Loan officers' personal loan limits for this type of lending were $200,000. Any loan over $200,000 required the approval of the bank's senior loan committee.

Northwest Commerce Bank had recently received a request from a new customer for a construction loan on a retail shopping center soon to be built in the bank's trade area.

THE CUSTOMER

Watson E. Williams had been a general contractor for the past 10 years. During that time he had built a large number of "strip" shopping centers for joint ventures and other investors. He was well regarded in the construction business and he had maintained a good reputation among financial people familiar with his activities. Recent credit reports indicated that payments were prompt and that there were no legal actions pending against the company or its principal officers. In consulting with other lenders, the bank learned that Watson E. Williams was apparently an honest, hard-working, competitive contractor. He had a reputation for building quality projects and being able to lease projects in a timely manner. He had also been successful in obtaining attractive permanent financing to replace the interim construction funds used during building.

THE LOAN REQUEST

Williams was requesting a construction loan in the amount of $540,000. Interest would be 10 percent over a term of 24 months. The loan proceeds would be used to construct a 19,024 ft^2 strip shopping center and free-standing fast food restaurant (2,040 ft²) on 108,445 ft² of land. The source of repayment for this loan would be a stand-by takeout commitment. The project would be named the "Northwest Center."

Although most of his business was handled through two other competing banks, Williams believed that each project should stand on its own and he had financed several joint venture projects at various institutions in the past. Each project was incorporated as a single-purpose corporation; that is, the only corporate assets and liabilities would be those associated with the project's construction and ownership.

The individuals who would own this single-purpose corporation would be Watson Williams (60 percent) and Trudy Shelton (40 percent). Personal financial statements for these individuals are summarized in Exhibits 1 and 2. The bank had reviewed the cost estimates for this owner-

contractor project and they appeared consistent with known costs of recently completed comparable projects. Project descriptions and financial data are given in Exhibits 3 through 9, and the standby takeout commitment appears in Exhibit 10.

After providing this information to the bank, Williams was told he could expect a prompt decision on his request. He was also advised that the material he had prepared would be studied carefully and that there might be a need for at least one more meeting with the loan officer if, after thorough study of the application, there were additional questions that could not be answered from Williams's data. Other than a promise to examine the loan request quickly but carefully, no other commitments were made or implied to Watson Williams.

EXHIBIT 1
Watson E. Williams—Financial Statement, January 1, 1979

Assets		
Cash on Hand		$ 50,000.00
Commission due		150,000.00
Long-term notes receivable secured by land		100,000.00
Stocks & Bonds		
Listed stock	109,739.47	
Closely held companies	108,136.00	
		217,875.47
Real Estate		
17 acres	250,000.00	
Interest in joint ventures at cost	10,000.00	
11 acres	400,000.00	
3 acres	133,000.00	
House	125,000.00	
2 acres and house, ½ interest	12,500.00	
Vacant lot	50,000.00	
		980,500.00
Other Assets		
Office furniture and equipment	14,533.27	
Autos	13,000.00	
		27,533.27
Total assets		$1,525,908.74

EXHIBIT 1 (continued)

Liabilities

Banks
Bank notes secured	$ 4,640.00	
Bank notes unsecured	167,500.00	
Bank notes secured by real estate	353,000.00	
		$ 525,140.00

Long-Term Notes
House mortgage	79,844.30	
11 acres	387,923.70	
		$ 467,768.00
Total liabilities		$ 992,908.00
Net worth—January 1, 1979		$ 533,000.74

EXHIBIT 2
Trudy Shelton, Realtor, Real Estate Investments and Development—Financial Statement, March 1, 1979

Assets

Cash on hand and in bank	$ 33,400
Listed stocks (partially pledged)	139,180
Real estate (see schedule)	5,663,755
Autos	12,000
Commission receivables	93,826
Personal effects	90,000
Total assets	$6,032,161

Liabilities

Lien on real estate (see schedule)	3,890,931
Bank debt (partially secured)	109,000
Total liabilities	$3,999,931
Net worth	$2,032,230

Income

Salary	36,000
Bonuses and commissions	80,000
Dividends and interest	500
Real estate income	3,600
Income from deferred commissions	25,000
Total income	$ 145,100

Schedule of Real Estate, March 1, 1979

Description	Share	Market value share	Debt	Equity value
Shopping centers	20%	$3,578,000	$2,443,677	$1,134,323
Shopping centers	30	1,311,000	934,002	376,998
Land	50	549,755	428,033	121,722
Residence	100%	225,000	85,219	139,781
		$5,663,755	$3,890,931	$1,772,824

EXHIBIT 3

Northwest Center—Adjoining K-Mart, Northwest Highway, Dallas, Texas

Location

On Northwest Highway, about 6 miles northwest of downtown Dallas. Site adjoins large K-Mart family food/drug/home center.

Site

About 108,445 ft² tract with approximately 271 ft frontage on Northwest Highway. Terrain is irregular.

Improvements

See site plan following. Proposed development includes 19,024-ft² structures in "ell" configuration; steel frame, concrete block, and face material construction; asphaltic concrete parking area. Proposed parking 119 spaces.

Leasing

Developer has surveyed trading area to confirm market demand exists for convenience, service, and specialty-type tenants to occupy 1,200 to 3,000 ft² spaces. Store spaces would be only 60 to 70 ft deep. Space should lease (readily) in $4.00 to $4.50 per ft² range.

Developer wishes to reserve portion of frontage for fast food operation.

Northwest Center would "feed" off K-Mart by a connecting approach.

EXHIBIT 4
Watson E. Williams, Inc.—Northwest Shopping Center

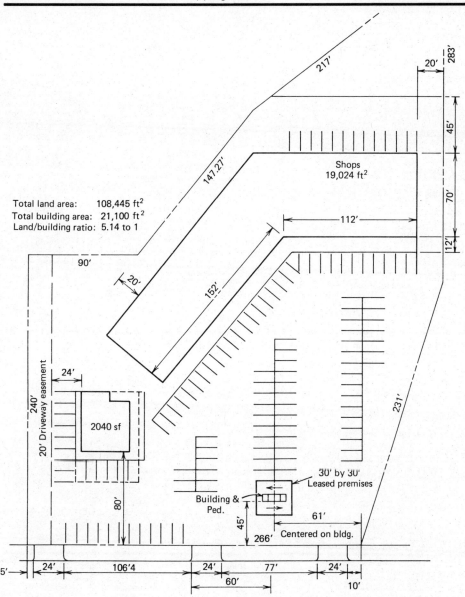

Total land area:　108,445 ft^2
Total building area:　21,100 ft^2
Land/building ratio: 5.14 to 1

Shops
19,024 ft^2

2040 sf

30' by 30'
Leased premises

Building &
Ped.

Centered on bldg.

EXHIBIT 5
Northwest Center, Dallas, Texas—Income and Expense

McDonald's (net)		11,400
Quick Photo (net)		2,400
Shops 19,024 ft²	at 4.00	76,096
		$89,896
Common area maintenance 19,024 ft²	at $0.12	2,283
		$92,179
10% vacancy excluding McDonald's		8,078
Effective gross income		$84,101
Taxes at $0.45 per ft²		8,561
Insurance at $0.07 per ft²		1,332
Maintenance at $0.10 per ft²		1,902
Management at 5% (effective gross income)		4,205
Total operating		$16,000
Expense, at $0.84 per ft²		
Net operating income		$68,101

EXHIBIT 6
Existing Retail Space in Area

Name	Approximate size[a] (ft²)	Approximate age
Ridgeview Center	66,000	8
Lakeview Center	44,000	4
Strip Center No. 1	55,000	12
Northcliff Mall	170,000	10
Strip Center No. 2	40,000	4
TG&Y Center	171,845	1
Safeway Center and Strip	50,000	12

[a]Size includes major tenants such as supermarket, drugs, and department stores. Excludes designed office space.

EXHIBIT 7
Rental Comparables—Small Tenants in Large Centers in Immediate Vicinity

	Size (ft²)	Term (years)	Rent per foot²
Beauty shop	1,000	4	$3.20
Pizza parlor	3,280	4	3.75
Various	900–3,000	3 plus	3.25–3.75
Barber	700	2	6.50
TV sales/service	2,000	2	3.00
Realtors office	1,000	2	3.50
With air conditioning	2,400	1	4.25
Various asking without air conditioning	900–3,000	—	3.75–4.25

EXHIBIT 7 (continued)

	Size (ft²)	Term (years)	Rent per foot[4]
Various	900–2,000	3 plus	2.25
Various	1,200–3,000	1	4.50–5.00

Rentals in the immediate vicinity of the site are in the $3.25 to $3.75 range on leases that average 3 years in age currently. There has been no observed vacancy in the area over the past 10 months excepting the theater at Ridgeview Center and two small lease spaces, which are ascribed to normal tenant turnover.

Older centers to the east (1–2 miles) have had long-term (6–12 years) stable occupancy. The only problem vacancy within 3 miles of the site appears at the Safeway Center. One space of 2,000 ft² at $2.25 with air conditioning has been vacant 6 months and one space of 1,000 ft² with air conditioning has been vacant 8 months. This is ascribed to traffic and general inferiority of the location.

Newer centers at the west have no vacancy or are in successful initial lease up, at rents in the $4.00 range.

Sources: Information concerning existing rentals in the area come from tenants and shopping center leasing agents and managers.

EXHIBIT 8
Cost Breakdown Summary as Submitted by Owner-Contractor

	Original loan allocation
Land (108,445 ft²)	$108,445
Architecture/Engineering	8,000
Contractors overhead and profit	10,555
Leasing	15,000
Subtotal	$142,000
Construction	
Building shell	$248,000
Tenant finishes	105,000
Subtotal	$353,000
Financing (estimated at 9% per net dollars outstanding)	45,000
Total	$540,000

EXHIBIT 9
Comparable Land Sales in Area

Date	Size	Tenant	Sale price per foot²
8/71	4.6 acres	K mart	$1.50
5/69	15,000 ft²	KFC	$2.80
9/68	10,600 ft²	Retail development	$2.27
4/67	30,400 ft²	Retail development	$1.70
11/67	22,400 ft²	Retail development	$1.33
1/71	1.5 acres	Brake check	$2.50
Asking	2.1 acres	Vacant 660 ft front	$2.22 net
12/74	1 acre	Vacant 55 ft front	$2.00
Asking	2 acres	Vacant	$2.00

EXHIBIT 10
Big Mortgage Company—Standby Takeout Commitment

Dallas, Texas

June 1, 1979

Watson E. Williams, Inc.

RE: Northwest Shopping Center Project

Gentlemen:

Big Mortgage Company (hereinafter referred to as "Lender"), hereby agrees to make a $500,000 loan secured by certain real property located in Dallas County, Texas to Watson E. Williams, Inc., a Texas corporation (hereinafter referred to as "Borrower"), subject to the following terms and conditions:

A. *Terms:*

    1. *Amount of Loan:* $500,000

    2. *Term of Commitment:*   Twenty-four (24) months. This commitment shall expire on June 1, 1981, and we may not be required to fund the loan until May 1, 1981.

    3. *Term of Loan:*   Twelve (12) months.

    4. *Interest Rate:*   The rate of interest shall be adjusted as of the first day of each calendar month so that at all times during such month the applicable interest rate shall be a rate which is 4% in excess of (a) the prime interest rate of Second National Bank charged to large commercial borrowers on the first day of such month, or (b) the 90-day dealer commercial paper rate, but not in excess of the highest lawful rate.

    5. *Repayment of Loan:*   Interest only shall be payable monthly on the first day of the month, commencing with the second month after that month in which the funding of this loan occurs and continuing until maturity when the entire outstanding principal balance and all accrued interest thereon will be due and payable in full, twelve months from the date of the first advance of our loan.

    6. *Prepayment:*   The borrower shall have the privilege of prepaying the loan in whole or in part at any time without penalty.

    7. *Guarantors:*   The loan will be personally guaranteed, jointly and severally, by Watson E. Williams and Trudy Shelton.

    8. *Security:*   Lender is to have an insurable first deed of trust lien upon Borrower's fee simple interest in real estate fronting approximately 271 feet on Northwest Highway, containing approximately 108,445 square feet together with the improvements to be constructed thereon of 19,024 square feet of new rentable area for shopping center use with lighted paved parking area for 119 automobiles. In addition, there will be a free-standing McDonald's building of 2,040 square feet, and a free-standing Quick Photo Products kiosk at the front of the site with their respective leases in place and in full force and effect.

                All improvements shall be completed in accordance with plans and specifications to be approved by Lender prior to commencement of construction.

EXHIBIT 10 (continued)

9. *Additional Parking:*   If the real estate to be encumbered has or needs easement rights for ingress, egress, or parking over other real estate or if a lease to be assigned as security requires additional rights, then the mortgage or deed of trust must likewise cover them and Lender must be furnished acceptable title evidence of same.

10. *Commitment Fee:*   Borrower shall pay to Big Mortgage Company commitment fee in the amount of $15,000.00 at the time of your acceptance hereof. This fee is deemed to have been earned upon the issuance of this commitment and shall not be refundable.

B. *Conditions:*

1. *Inspection:*   Inspection by designated representatives of the Lender may be made at any and all times during construction and throughout the life of the loan.

2. *Rents and Leases:*   Lender is to be provided with a general assignment of rents to be operative in the event of default. Unless otherwise specified by the Lender, all present and future leases are to be approved by Lender and shall be subordinate to the Lender's lien. Throughout the life of the loan, the Lender reserves the right to require specific leases be made superior to its lien at the expense of the Borrower.

Lender is to be provided with a Specific assignment of such present or future leases as Lender may require. Lender shall be authorized to notify Lessees of the existence of such assignments, but agrees not to exercise its right to collect rents until a default exists in the terms of the loan or the assignments.

Any standard lease forms to be used by the Borrower shall be submitted to and approved by the Lender.

As a condition of closing the loan, Lender is to be furnished with a satisfactory lease ratification agreement executed by both Lessee and Lessor for all superior and/or specifically assigned leases including the McDonald's and Quick Photo Products leases. This agreement shall show that the lease is in full force and effect, that the Lessee is in possession of its premises, paying the full lease rental, that no rental payments have been made in advance except as approved by the Lender, and stating the commencement date of the original term of said lease.

3. *Disbursement Contingent Upon Leasing:*   Prior to the closing of the loan, Lender must approve a net lease from McDonald's for minimum annual rents of $11,400 for a term of 20 years and a net ground lease from Quick Photo Products for a kiosk location for a minimum annual rental of $2,400 for a term of 10 years, which leases must be in full force and effect.

Upon full compliance with all other conditions of this commitment, Lender will disburse an amount equal to $395,000 when the entire shell of the center has been completed plus an additional $105,000 will be disbursed on the basis of $5.50 per square foot for tenant finish on rental space leased under leases satisfactory to Lender and finished as to tenant improvements in a manner satisfactory to Lender. Borrower will have six (6) months from

EXHIBIT 10 (continued)

date of initial funding to complete tenant finish and qualify for the total loan amount of $500,000.

4.	*Destruction:*	If on the closing date the mortgaged premises shall have suffered any material damage or destruction, Lender shall not be obligated to disburse the proceeds of the mortgage loan until the damaged or destroyed mortage premises shall have been restored or replaced or arrangements satisfactory to Lender shall have been made for such restoration or replacement.
5.	*Taxes:*	All assessments and real estate taxes which are due and payable are to be paid in full on or before the closing date.
6.	*Assignability:*	Neither this commitment nor the loan proceeds are assignable without the prior written consent of Lender.
7.	*Soil Tests:*	Borrower shall provide results from a subsurface soil test by a qualified engineer or firm certifying that the soil is suitable to support the proposed improvements.
8.	*Closing:*	There has been no adverse change in the financial condition of any of the makers of the note prior to closing. The loan is further conditioned on a reaffirmation of the appraised value after completion.

The borrowers and the guarantors indemnify us against all claims by any brokers for a commission in connection with the issuance of this commitment or the making of the loan contemplated hereby, and by their acceptance hereof, borrowers and guarantors acknowledge that we have not agreed to pay any fee or commission to any broker in connection herewith.

Our obligations set forth herein shall cease on the expiration date of June 1, 1981, unless this commitment is extended by us in writing.

This commitment shall not be binding upon us unless and until the attached copy is signed by you and the guarantors and returned to this office. This Commitment shall expire on June 10, 1979, if not so signed and returned on or before that date.

Very truly yours,

BIG MORTGAGE COMPANY

_____

ACCEPTED_____1979

_____
WATSON E. WILLIAMS, INC.
Company

_____
WATSON E. WILLIAMS
Guarantor

_____
TRUDY SHELTON
Guarantor

CASE 21
Questor, Inc.

Questor, Inc., has been a customer at a major San Francisco bank for the past 10 years. For some time, the Business Development Department at Golden West National Bank in San Francisco had called on Questor to solicit the account. These efforts had proven partially successful by obtaining the corporation's payroll account, although this did not represent particularly profitable business. Until recently, however, Golden West National had not been presented with any credit requests.

In April 1980, Catherine Logan, president of Questor Corporation, approached Lyman Porter, a Golden West loan officer, with a significant loan proposal. Logan also brought with her financial statements covering the past three calendar years, as well as an interim dated March 31, 1980.

Logan indicated that she wanted to shift all her business to Golden West, explaining with evident disapproval, that her present bank had become rather careless in handling the account. She cited, as an example, some operational errors that had resulted in improperly crediting another customer with Questor funds which had been wired to the bank for credit to Questor. The misdirection of this deposit resulted in several overdrafts for which the company had been charged. Only after considerable effort did she get "that mess straightened out and the charges reversed." At the same time, Questor's line of credit was up for renewal and Logan's request for a moderate increase was not receiving the prompt attention she thought it deserved.

Logan commented that she "just didn't understand the bank any longer" and, since she was dealing with her third loan officer in a year, she was sure the bank didn't understand her or her company either!! Finally, she decided she would discuss the company's affairs with Golden West National Bank and, accordingly, she had made

an appointment to review the firm's credit needs with Lyman Porter.

Questor, Inc., was a manufacturer of valves and pipe fittings (SIC 3494) and according to Logan would need upwards of $500,000 during the next 12 months. Logan suggested that she would like part of the credit on 90-day notes with the remainder on an intermediate-term basis. "Volume continues to grow and profits are good," she commented during her discussion with Porter. "We've been in business for 15 years and have made a profit every year. Our equipment is in good shape and the plant is adequate for at least three more years," said Logan.

Catherine Logan suggested as references her current bank together with Fairview Savings & Loan Association, a San Francisco institution. She also indicated that among her major suppliers were U.S. Steel, Armco, Davidson Co., and Acme Bolt.

Later, Lyman Porter made credit checks with these suppliers which showed a pattern of generally prompt payment. Slowness in meeting credit obligations was reported as only occasional. High credit from any one supplier was listed as $75,000. A trade report from other minor suppliers showed incidental slowness up to 30 days. Questor did not, however, take discounts on a 2/10 net 30 basis available from all suppliers.

Fairview Savings & Loan reported a balance of $137,500 owing on an original $250,000 loan. Payments of $12,500 per quarter were made on time. The loan from Fairview was secured by land and buildings owned by Questor.

Lyman Porter had not yet checked with Questor's current bank to learn of their experience and, since Golden West was anxious to establish this new account, he was unsure how far to go in checking with Questor's present bank.

At the end of her second meeting at Golden

State, Logan asked for a $500,000 loan. She had already provided the financial data shown in Exhibits 1 through 5. She also provided a personal financial statement (Exhibit 6). Logan further noted that about 40 percent of inventory represented finished goods, 20 percent was work in process, and 40 percent included raw materials.

As he reviewed the information available on Questor, Porter was somewhat uncertain about the value and the potential problems associated with accounts receivable and inventory for a company such as Questor. He realized that he probably would need to raise questions with Catherine Logan about these assets to try to understand better the potential risks related to their collateral value.

Finally, Porter sensed from his discussions that the pricing and terms of the proposed loan might prove sensitive matters to Logan. Although Golden West was anxious to obtain the Questor account, Porter was unsure how "aggressive" or competitive his bank should be in this situation given the risks involved. Porter had promised to give Logan a final decision within the week with specific details on terms if the loan were granted.

EXHIBIT 1

Questor, Inc., Financial Statements, Year Ending December 31 (unaudited)—Income and Expense

	Three months 1980	1979	1978	1977
Sales	$939,000	$3,200,000	$3,050,500	$2,700,000
Cost of goods	666,690	2,240,000	2,104,500	1,890,000
Gross	272,310	960,000	946,000	810,000
Operating expense	225,360	736,000	732,000	621,000
Net before tax	46,950	224,000	214,000	189,000
Other expenses	7,512	32,000	27,450	27,000
Tax	13,803	67,200	65,292	56,700
Profit after tax	$ 25,635	$ 124,800	$ 121,258	$ 105,300

EXHIBIT 2

Questor, Inc., Financial Statements, Year Ended December 31 (unaudited)—Balance Sheet

	Three months 1980	1979	1978	1977
Cash	$ 33,900	$ 56,500	$ 69,660	$ 65,300
Receivables	504,980	457,142	429,600	391,300
Inventory	890,000	678,800	657,600	555,900
Current assets	1,428,880	1,192,442	1,156,860	1,012,500
Land	50,000	50,000	50,000	50,000
Plant/Equipment	275,000	275,000	275,000	275,000
Depreciation	(140,000)	(135,000)	(115,000)	(95,000)
Net	135,000	140,000	160,000	180,000
C/S/V (life insurance)	22,000	20,000	16,350	14,000
Investment	10,000	10,000	10,000	10,000
Total assets	1,645,880	1,412,442	1,393,210	1,266,500
Notes payable (including current portion long-term)	450,000	450,000	375,000	375,000

EXHIBIT 2 (continued)

	Three months 1980	1979	1978	1977
Accounts payable	320,417	95,114	233,682	185,230
Accruals	35,000	40,000	32,000	25,000
Current liabilities	805,417	585,114	640,682	585,230
Long-term debt	87,500	100,000	150,000	200,000
Capital	100,000	100,000	100,000	100,000
Retained earnings	652,963	627,328	502,528	381,270
Total liabilities & net worth	$1,645,880	$1,412,442	$1,393,210	$1,266,500

EXHIBIT 3
Questor, Inc.—Receivables, January 31, 1980

			Days		
Customer	Current	1–30	31–60	61–90	Over 90
ABC Company	12,500	2,500			
Dalton Co.	10,000				
Davidson Co.	26,000	5,000			
Fredrick Co.	7,500	3,000			
Gaston, Inc.	17,800	2,200			
Hardy Sons			12,500		
Ivor		5,000	7,500		
Logan, Inc.	21,800				
Kessel Sons	30,000	3,000	1,000		
Lamont Co.	28,000	5,000	7,500		
Massey Inc.	15,000			7,000	10,000
Nestor	1,000		500		
Olympia	35,000		12,000	7,500	
Pinocle Co.	5,000	5,000			5,000
Trilogy	17,250	2,500			
Watson	8,000	2,000	5,000		
Other	20,000				
Total	254,850	35,200	46,000	14,500	15,000
Total of all receivables	365,550				

EXHIBIT 4
Questor, Inc.—Receivables, February 28, 1980

			Days		
Customer	Current	1–30	31–60	61–90	Over 90
ABC Company	15,000	6,250			
Bunson, J. C.	33,000				
Dalton Co.		10,000			
Davidson Co.	17,000	26,000			
Fredrick Co.		7,500	3,000		

EXHIBIT 4 (continued)

Customer	Current	1–30	31–60	61–90	Over 90
			Days		
Gaston Inc.	16,800				
Hardy Sons				12,500	
Ivor	2,500		5,000		
Logan, Inc.	40,000				
Jefferson Inc.	23,800				
Kessel Sons	15,000	30,000	3,000	1,000	
Lamont Co.	16,000	28,000			
Massey Inc.	7,500	15,000			17,000
Nestor	2,500				
Olympia	37,500				
Pinocle Co.	2,000	5,000	5,000		5,000
Trenton Inc.	17,800				
Trilogy	15,000		2,500		
Watson	6,000	8,000			
Other	20,000				
Total	287,400	135,750	18,500	13,500	22,000
Total of all receivables	477,150				

EXHIBIT 5
Questor, Inc.—Receivables, March 31, 1980

Customer	Current	1–30	31–60	61–90	Over 90
			Days		
Bunson, J. C.	16,500	33,000			
Carpenter Co.	22,000				
Dalton Co.			10,000		
Davidson Co.	7,500				
Fredrick Co.			7,500	3,000	
Gaston Inc.	22,500				
Hardy Sons					12,500
Ivor	3,000	2,500		5,000	
Logan, Inc.	52,000				
Jefferson Inc.	26,000	1,800			
Kessel Sons	27,000	15,000	30,000	3,000	1,000
Lamont Co.	5,000				
Lawrence Sons	17,800				
Massey Inc.		7,500	15,000		17,000
Nestor	6,000				
Olympia	42,000				
Pinocle Co.		2,000	5,000	5,000	5,000
Trenton Inc.	22,500	4,000			
Trilogy	13,000	15,000		2,500	

EXHIBIT 5 (continued)

Customer	Current	Days 1-30	31-60	61-90	Over 90
Watson	(120)				
Other	20,000				
Total	302,680	80,800	67,500	18,500	35,500
Total of all receivables	504,980				

EXHIBIT 6
Catherine and Cyril Logan—Personal Financial Statement, April 1, 1980

Assets		Liabilities and Net Worth	
Cash	$ 12,000	Notes payable—banks	$ 75,000
Marketable securities	26,000	Note payable—Questor, Inc.	20,000
Loan receivable from Logan, Inc.	40,000	Mortgage on home	167,500
Residence	275,000	Loan on life insurance	22,500
Automobiles	22,000	Total Liabilities	$ 285,000
Personal property	40,000	Net worth	910,963
Stock of Questor, Inc. (book value)	752,963	Total liabilities and net worth	$1,195,963
C/S/V Life insurance	28,000		
	$1,195,963	Salary (1979)	$ 125,000
		Bonus (estimated)	20,000
		Other	1,400
		Total income	$ 146,400

CASE 22
Edward Edwards Company

BACKGROUND

Edward Edwards was a manufacturer's representative acting on a commission basis only. He sold decorative accessories, pictures, lamps, and garden accessories and he also engaged in direct importing of similar items for his own account. His territory covered Texas, Oklahoma, New Mexico, Missouri, Arkansas, Mississippi, Tennessee, and Louisiana. Edwards's business was not seasonal, and he had two employees in addition to himself. His business was located in rented showroom space in a multistory building in Dallas' industrial section. The showrooms covered 2,000 ft², and the premises were orderly.

The business had been started 22 years ago in Oklahoma City and was moved to Dallas in 1973. Edwards was 50 years old in 1978. He had worked for his father, who was also a manufacturer's representative, for about eight years prior to forming his own company.

BANK RELATIONSHIP

Edwards had been a customer at Third Bank of Dallas for the past 10 years. Since that time he had steadily used the letter-of-credit services in the bank's international department. Third Bank of Dallas had issued its first letter of credit to Edwards some eight years ago for $1,600 on a 100 percent cash secured basis. Additional letters of credit were issued that same year on the same collateral basis, none of which individually exceeded $2,500. No more than that amount was outstanding at any time during the year.

The following year, Third Bank continued to service Edwards's letter of credit requirements covering his foreign purchases but changed its collateral position to one of security solely by shipping documents, including full sets of clean on board ocean bills of lading drawn to shipper's order and blank endorsed. Under this arrangement, individual letters of credit up to $4,000 were issued, all payable against shipping documents and sight drafts. At no time did such outstanding credits exceed $6,000 in the aggregate.

Beginning in 1972, individual credits up to $5,000 were issued and aggregate outstandings reached $12,000, all on the same basis as noted above.

Due to projected sales increases for the period 1975–1977, Edwards requested a $20,000 line to cover letters of credit payable against sight drafts when accompanied by ocean shipping documents, including bills of lading as noted above. Such bank credits would be secured by control of documents. This line would also cover financing of sight draft letter of credit payments for up to 120 days. The line of credit was granted, and the bank's experience with Edwards proved entirely satisfactory.

Edwards continued to operate under this line from 1975 to 1977. In 1978, he again asked that the bank increase the line from $20,000 to $40,000 and that drafts under letters of credit be drawn payable at 120 days after sight, thus giving rise to a banker's acceptance. Edwards' request for this change in the use of drafts arose because the Japanese banks through which his sight draft letters of credit had been utilized were offering more attractive financing charges covering Japanese exports than were available in the United States.

The discount rate in Japan on acceptances of up to 120 days, together with Third Bank's acceptance commission on 120-day drafts, would be less than Edwards's borrowing rate at Third Bank. These credits would be utilized to provide the funds to meet sight draft payments under letters of credit.

Edwards's unaudited financial statements for the past three years are summarized in Exhibits 1-3.

In discussions with Edwards, the bank indicated it would study his request, including the liabilities and responsibilities that would be included in the issuance of letters of credit and the bank's subsequent acceptance of drafts associated with those letters of credit. In making a decision, the lending officer knew she must be aware of the bank's role as the issuing bank, accepting and paying letters of credit for Edwards's account.

EXHIBIT 1

Edward Edwards Company—Statement of Source and Application of Funds, Years Ended December 31, 1976, 1977, and 1978[a]

	1976		1977		1978	
Funds provided by						
Net earnings		$17,932.37		$18,519.67		$20,006.54
Adjust for depreciation charges not requiring funds		926.24		934.99		175.46
Disposition of automobile		2,411.02		0		0
Disposition of investments				291.25		0
Disposition of investments		$21,269.63		$19,745.91		$20,182.00
Funds applied to						
Increase in working capital						
Working capital, beginning of year	$23,978.94		$30,391.85		$38,083.37	
Working capital, end of year	15,333.75		23,978.94		30,391.85	
		$				7,691.52
Acquisition of automobile		3,173.42		0		0
Acquisition of equipment		405.00		350.00		646.00
Increase in other assets and investments		2,413.43		0		5,157.56
Owners net withdrawals and other		6,632.59		12,983.00		6,686.92
		$21,269.63		$19,745.91		$20,182.00

[a] All statements prepared from the books without audit.

EXHIBIT 2
Edward Edwards Company—Balance Sheet, December 31, 1976, 1977, and 1978

Assets

	1976		1977		1978	
Current Assets						
Cash—business account	$ 3,967.53		$ 5,317.44		$16,712.10	
Cash—personal account	10,421.00	$14,388.53	13,010.00	$18,327.44	11,847.92	$28,560.02
Trade accounts receivable		5,628.37		5,667.55		6,056.24
Merchandise inventory		15,500.42		17,502.28		22,309.56
Prepaid expenses		60.00		73.30		0
Total current assets		$35,577.32		$41,570.57		$56,925.82
Fixed Assets						
Automobile—business	3,173.42		3,173.42		3,173.42	
Automobile—personal	2,751.00		2,751.00		2,751.00	
Office and showroom equipment	2,287.19		2,637.19		3,283.19	
Total—at cost	8,211.61		8,561.61		9,207.61	
Less accumulated depreciation	2,549.95	5,661.66	3,484.94	5,076.67	3,660.40	5,547.21
Other Assets and Investments						
Cash value of life insurance in force	3,744.68		3,744.68		4,195.48	
Contributions to retirement plan—General Motors	1,400.00		1,400.00		1,400.00	
Contributions to self-employed retirement plan	500.00		1,500.00		3,871.07	
Corporation stocks and bonds	11,780.00		9,495.00		13,300.00	
Deposits	35.00		35.00		35.00	
U.S. savings bonds	2,551.59		1,745.34		0	
United Science Fund Plan	0	20,011.27	1,800.00	19,720.02	2,076.03	24,877.58
Total assets		$61,250.25		$66,367.26		$87,350.61

Liabilities and Owner's Equity

Current Liabilities

Trade accounts payable	$ 1,383.50	$ 972.39	$18,005.80
Insurance loan payable	376.53	376.53	275.59
Notes payable—bank	6,192.69	6,612.96	0
Payroll taxes	36.36	217.82	167.10
Income and self-employment taxes payable	3,609.30	2,999.02	393.96
Total current liabilities	11,598.38	11,178.72	18,842.45

Owner's Equity

Balance, January 1	$38,352.09	$49,651.87	$55,188.54
Net income	17,932.37	18,519.67	20,006.54
Total	56,284.46	68,171.54	75,195.08
Less owner's withdrawal and other	6,632.59	12,983.00	6,686.92
	49,651.87	55,188.54	68,508.16
Total liabilities and owner's equity	$61,250.25	$66,367.26	$87,350.61

EXHIBIT 3

Edward Edwards Company[a]—Statement of Earnings, Years Ended 1976, 1977, and 1978

	1976		1977		1978	
Net sales		$50,186.37		$81,420.00		$102,572.00
Cost of sales:						
Inventory—beginning	$ 8,654.77		$15,500.42		$17,502.28	
Purchases	35,139.65		49,828.67		67,878.56	
Merchandise available for sale	43,794.42		65,329.09		85,380.84	
Less inventory—ending	15,500.42		17,502.28		22,309.56	
Cost of sales		28,294.00		47,826.81		63,071.28
Gross profit		21,892.37		33,593.19		39,501.62
Commission income		19,363.72		21,736.15		22,976.39
Rent subsidy		1,200.00		1,200.00		1,200.00
Miscellaneous income				114.18		
Gross income		$42,456.09		$56,643.52		$63,678.01
Expenses:						
Accounting and legal	600.00		1,260.00		825.00	
Advertising	320.58		960.79		1,209.64	
Automobile expenses	735.53		692.19		573.62	
Bad debts charged off	497.55		1,171.44		329.91	

Customer contact	197.86	298.62	219.71
Depreciation	926.24	934.99	175.46
Dues and subscriptions	91.36	174.75	0
Insurance	294.09	568.35	533.88
Interest	438.06	709.90	702.30
Office supplies	570.58	1,429.40	1,009.86
Office and showroom rent	8,238.03	7,619.91	8,793.72
Payroll taxes	178.10	155.61	311.01
Repairs and maintenance	0	47.50	139.72
Salaries	4,289.96	4,701.76	7,635.59
Sales commissions	6,877.41	10,550.00	14,716.26
Telephone	664.47	597.10	656.19
Taxes—general	65.10	351.46	320.79
Travel—lodging, meals, tips	861.77	891.53	1,106.00
Travel—commercial fares	343.87	4,209.50	3,266.39
Utilities	588.15	566.37	567.49
Miscellaneous	50.83	233.04	578.93
	26,829.54	38,123.85	43,671.47
Net operating income	15,626.55	18,159.67	20,006.54
Extraordinary income (expense)	2,305.82		
Net earnings	$17,932.37	$18,159.67	$20,006.54

aNote: No provision has been made in this statement for income taxes accruing on the proprietor.

V

INTEGRATIVE ASSET/LIABILITY MANAGEMENT TECHNIQUES

12

MANAGING INTEREST SENSITIVITY AND MARGIN

In preceding chapters we have discussed policies and management techniques for most of the key assets and liabilities areas. We have discussed in detail attracting deposits, borrowed funds, and capital. We have also introduced and evaluated policies and techniques for managing the money position, providing liquidity, lending profitability, and investing rationally in securities. The theme in all of these areas of bank management has been consistent with the framework of maximizing returns consistent with a reasonable level of risk discussed in Chapter 2. The remaining link is to integrate these areas into a system of asset and liability management. This task is undertaken in this chapter, which emphasizes managing interest sensitivity and the interest margin, and the following chapter, which emphasizes the planning process as a method for tying together asset and liability management.

DEFINITIONS, OBJECTIVES, AND RELEVANCY

The first concern is to define interest margin and interest sensitivity and explain how these concepts are measured. Next come concerns about management objectives related to interest sensitivity and margin. We then discuss why this area seems so important in the predicted future environment. Finally, the heart of the chapter is the concepts and techniques for managing a bank's interest sensitivity and margin.

Interest margin for a bank is the difference between all interest revenues on bank assets and all interest expenses on bank funds. Separate interest margins on specific types of assets or liabilities may also be calculated but are often determined by subjective allocations of revenues or expenses. The major emphasis in this chapter is on the overall interest margin. The three most common measures of a bank's overall interest margin are dollar net interest margin, percent net interest margin, and spread. All of these terms appear in literature on bank management. They are often used interchangeably; however, the distinctions may be important and should be understood by serious students of banking. Table 12-1 confirms a simplified balance sheet and income statement to illustrate these measures.

The dollar net interest margin is the difference between all interest revenues (ad-

TABLE 12-1
Measures of Interest Margin at Sixth State Bank

Average Balances, 1982
(in thousands of dollars)

Cash and Due From	$ 20,000	Demand Deposits	$ 40,000
Fed Funds Sold	5,000	Now Accounts	40,000
Securities	40,000	Savings and Time Deposits	100,000
Loans	130,000	Borrowings	8,000
Other Assets	5,000	Equity Capital	12,000
	$200,000		$200,000

Income Statement, 1982
(in thousands of dollars)

Interest Revenues taxable equivalent	$23,000	$ —
Other Revenues — fee income	1,000	24,000
Less: Interest Expenses	16,000	
Other Expenses	5,000	21,000
Operating Income		$ 3,000
Taxes		1,000
Net Income		$ 2,000

Interest Margin Measures

Dollar Net Interest Margin: Interest revenue − Interest expense
$23,000 − $16,000 = $7,000

Percent Net Interest Margin:

$$\frac{\text{Interest revenue} - \text{Interest expense}}{\text{Earning assets}}$$

$$\frac{\$23,000 - \$16,000}{175,000} = 4.00\%$$

Spread:

$$\frac{\text{Interest revenues}}{\text{Earning assets}} - \frac{\text{Interest expenses}}{\text{Interest-bearing funds}}$$

$$\frac{23,000}{175,000} - \frac{16,000}{148,000}$$

$$13.14\% - 10.81\% = 2.33\%$$

justed to a tax equivalent basis) and all interest expenses. This dollar figure is helpful in ascertaining how well the bank can cover its other expenses. The net interest margin in percentage terms is the dollar net interest cost divided by the bank's earning assets. Since this is a relative term, it is much more helpful in measuring the changes and trends in interest margin and in comparing interest margins among banks. Spread is a relative measure, which is the difference between interest returns (interest revenues divided by earning assets) and interest costs (interest expenses divided by interest-bearing funds). Advocates of spread as a measure of interest sensitivity believe that spread measures trends, swings, and relative margins as well as percentage net interest margin and that spread is a superior measure when a bank wants to investigate reasons for good or bad margin performances.

Interest sensitivity refers to the sensitivity of or fluctuations in interest margin because of endogenous and exogenous factors. Endogenous factors include the composition of a bank's assets and liability, the quality and maturity of loans, and the cost and maturity of attracted funds. Exogenous factors include general economic conditions and the level of interest rates. A bank can attempt to manage the endogenous factors, but it can only try to anticipate the exogenous factors.

As previously discussed, the overall objective of a bank should be to balance its return and risks in a way that maximizes the bank's market value to its owners. Relating this objective to interest margin and sensitivity, a bank should try to earn the highest margin it can which is consistent with the reasonable stability in the interest margin. Although this has been a primary banking objective for many years, managing interest sensitivity and the interest margin only began receiving prime attention in the late 1970s and early 1980s. This increased attention has been caused by strongly increased competition, which has narrowed margins, and by external economic conditions, particularly fluctuating interest rates, which may cause bank earnings to become relatively more volatile. It seems likely that both of these conditions will continue to affect interest sensitivity and margins in the future. Managing interest sensitivity is covered in the next section. This is followed by a discussion of a technique for understanding and improving interest margins.

MANAGING INTEREST SENSITIVITY

As stated earlier, the causes of fluctuations in interest margins are classified broadly into endogenous or internal factors and exogenous or external factors. The exogenous factors are examined first. Banks have little control over cyclical movement in savings or credit demands, fiscal and monetary policy, and the resulting fluctuations in interest rates. Although the resulting economic fluctuations never follow exactly the same pattern, market analysts have conceived a useful, if highly simplified, scenario of the typical economic cycle. Business borrowing is said to be weak in the beginning of an economic cycle upturn and strong in the final stages. Household borrowing spurts ahead in the beginning of the cycle but peaks well before business borrowing. Monetary policy and tightness mostly influence household borrowing behavior. As the availability of funds tightens, borrowing terms tighten and interest rates rise, producing a decline in household borrowing. Business, on the other hand, finds it profitable to borrow at progressively higher rates because of perceived market opportunities that persist late into the economic expansion. With a downturn in the business cycle, demand for business output and, thus, business borrowing eventually declines. Federal deficit financing increases in this stage in order to sustain or increase planned government expenditures in the face of shortfall in tax revenues.

From a banking perspective, this scenario holds profound implications. The acceleration in household and, especially, business borrowing during economic expansion, coupled with rising interest rates, ought to have an abnormal effect on banks' interest margin. The sources of such an effect can be summarized in terms of rate, volume, and mix.

Volume effects occur simply because intense credit demands during periods of rapid economic growth typically force a higher rate of credit production and, therefore, higher levels of bank assets and liabilities. Mix effects usually stem from the shift in most bank portfolios toward high-yield assets (e.g., loans) and away from low-yield assets (e.g., U.S. Treasury securities) whereas the mix of most bank resources shifts toward relatively more purchased funds in the form of either large CDs or short-term borrowed funds. Rate effects in economic expansions tend to benefit net interest margins as assets yields rise, but this benefit is reduced by negative rate effects as the marginal cost of funds rise.[1]

Table 12-2 presents data that demonstrate volume, rate, and mix effects on the banking system over two recent rate cycles. Although rate cycles tend to lag slightly behind general economic cycles, rate cycles are more relevant to bank interest sensitivity because they have more significant effects on most banks. The rate cycles are delineated by the movement of market interest rates (represented by the four to six month prime commercial paper rate) from peak-to-trough and trough-to-peak. The peaks and troughs are assumed to coincide approximately with year-ends 1969 (peak), 1971 (trough), 1974 (peak), 1976 (trough), 1979 (peak), and an undetermined period of fluctuating rates in 1980 and 1981.

Table 12-2 shows that aggregate cyclical movements in dollar interest margin were fairly consistent with the rate cycle scenario. Dollar interest margin tended to grow slightly more rapidly in periods of rising rates. Earning assets, proportions of loans to earning assets, and proportions of purchased funds to earning assets tended to increase during boom periods when rates increased and to decline during slow periods when rates fell.

The net effect of these influences on interest margin is a little more ambiguous. For example, the 13.2 percent rise in net interest margin as the cycle peaked in 1974 was virtually matched by the 12.6 percent rise as the cycle bottomed out in 1976. The explanation for this ambiguity may lie in Cates[2] finding that, within the banking system as a whole, some individual banks perform best in the increasing-rate stage of the cycle and others perform best in the decreasing-rate stage. Alternatively, the roughly equivalent performances of 1974 and 1976 may indicate that banks, in general, manage their net interest margins in such a way that results are similar at both extremes of the cycle. The

---

[1] Volume, rate, and mix effects are discussed in greater detail in Ron Olson, Don Simonson, Stan Reber, and George Hempel, "Management of Bank Interest Margins in the 1980's," *Magazine of Bank Administration* (March and April 1980).

[2] David C. Cates, "Interest Sensitivity in Banking," *The Bankers Magazine* (Jan.–Feb. 1978), pp. 23–27.

TABLE 12-2
Volume, Rate, and Mix Effects Over Credit Cycles

	Annual growth rate of dollar interest margin[a]	Volume effect: percentage change in earning assets[a]	Rate effect basis point change in 4–6 month commercial paper rate[b]	Mix effect[a]	
				Percentage change in ratio of loans/earning assets	Percentage change in purchased funds/earning assets[c]
Falling rates					
1970–1971	7.0	10.6	−340	−6.5	+15.0
Rising rates					
1972–1974	13.2	12.9	+456	+7.8	+29.0
Falling rates					
1975–1976	12.6	5.5	−441	−6.7	−4.7
Rising rates					
1977–1979	15.8	10.3	+553	+8.1	+18.9
Fluctuating rates					
1980–1981	9.8	10.8	−102	−0.8	+6.1

[a]*Source: Assets and Liabilities, Commercial and Mutual Savings Banks* (various years), a joint publication of the Board of Governors of the Federal Reserve System, the Federal Deposit Insurance Corporation, and the Comptroller of Currency.
[b]Average commercial paper rate change as defined and published by the Federal Reserve Bank of New York, release H.9 (various dates).
[c]Purchased funds are defined as total liabilities less demand deposits and IPC savings deposits. This definition is not the most satisfactory but is based on the available data and is used here only to help generalize a concept.

latest fluctuating-rate period during 1980 and 1981 produced a limited increase in net interest margin; time will tell whether banks can improve this performance in coming years.

The net influence of rate, volume, and mix effects on interest margins is not completely clear for the banking system as a whole; however, it is clear from Table 12-2 that these effects are powerful. If individual banks can harness such powerful effects, the benefits to their interest margins ought to be impressive. It is crucial, therefore, that in managing its asset and liabilities bank management knows how to analyze and understand the volume, rate, and mix linkages to interest margin.

The interest margin performance of individual banks varies greatly during such cyclical periods. These differences in interest margin performance appear to be explained primarily by endogenous factors such as the nature of the bank's assets and liabilities and the reaction of the bank to expected exogenous factors.

Differences in the interest margin performance among banks in Cates study of the 1972–1976 period are summarized in Table 12-3. In Table 12-3 the net interest margin (NIM) column shows the 1976 level of the percent net interest margin. The adjacent column shows the rise or fall in this margin from 1972 through 1976, and the final two columns show the margin during a roughly two-and-a-half-year period of rising rates and the margin during subsequent two-and-a-half-year period of falling rates.

The 60-company composite is made up of larger bank holding companies in various parts of the United States. The median percentage NIM for this composite was an increase of 0.08 (8 basis points) from 1972 through 1976. In the 1972–1974 period of ris-

TABLE 12-3
Net Interest Margin Shift Measured in Basis Points

Entity	NIM	1976/1972	1974/1972	1976/1974
60-company composite	4.01%	+ 8	− 15	+ 23
Alabama Bancorp.	4.42	+ 23	+ 33	− 10
Barnett	5.15	+ 25	+ 55	− 30
Bay Banks	5.40	− 6	+ 66	− 72
Pittsburgh National	4.21	+ 34	+ 54	− 21
Republic New York Corp.	3.76	+ 10	+125	−115
First Bank System	4.07	− 20	− 52	+ 32
Northwest Bancorp.	4.24	+ 16	− 14	+ 30
NCNB	4.09	− 55	−120	+ 65
Philadelphia National	4.41	+ 13	− 14	+ 27
BankAmerica	3.18	+ 40	+ 25	+ 15
Morgan	2.95	+ 20	− 7	+ 27
Citicorp	3.80	+ 71	+ 21	+ 50
Chase	3.21	+ 18	− 12	+ 30
Bankers Trust	2.68	− 18	− 44	+ 26
Detroitbank	3.76	+ 54	+ 49	+ 5
National City Corp.	4.67	+ 31	+ 17	+ 14
Rainier	4.50	+132	+ 45	+ 87

Source: David C. Cates, "Interest Sensitivity in Banking," *The Bankers Magazine* (Jan.–Feb. 1978), p. 24.

ing rates, the median NIM change was a decline of 15 basis points, whereas in the 1974–1976 period of falling rates, the median NIM among these 60 companies increased 23 basis points. These results were surprising in that they indicated a slight tendency for this group's liabilities to be more rate-sensitive than its assets. Cates points out that many of these 60 large bank holding companies used purchased funds extensively but that only one fifth could properly be called "wholesale" banks.[3]

The sample of individual bank holding companies in Table 12-3 illustrates the diversity of interest margin performance among banks. The first five bank holding companies, headed by Alabama Bancorporation, are strongly asset sensitive. With only one exception (Bay Banks, probably as a result of NOW account expense), the NIM increased from 1972 through 1976. More important, each of these holding companies had NIM gains from 1972 through 1974 and margin declines thereafter. Assets were clearly repriced more quickly than liabilities.

The next group of four holding companies, headed by First Bank System, is again very different in type. The common denominator here is the 1974/1972 *fall* in margins and the 1976/1974 *rise* in margins, pointing to an imbalance toward liability sensitivity. This may seem a curious conclusion in the case of the two Minneapolis-based bank holding companies (First Bank System and Northwest Bancorporation), since neither of these companies is noted for aggressive use of borrowed funds and large-denomination CDs. Yet despite limited use of purchased money, the asset yields are remarkably insensitive, perhaps reflecting the large number of mortgages and "country prime"

[3] Ibid.

loans written by the rural affiliates of these companies. NCNB and Philadelphia National were known for their aggressive use of purchased funds in the mid-1970s.

The third group is a selection of money center banks. Here the differences among companies are dramatic, with wide gains and significant losses of margin in the 1976/ 1972 period, and especially wide differences in the 1974/1972 period. Though it is presumptuous from this data alone to impute causes to each company's performance, the differences within the group suggest that there is indeed plenty of room for control of the margin process through deliberate imbalance (much like the ballast system of an efficient submarine), with rewards for successful planners and penalties for the less successful. In spite of the absolute size of these money center banks, they probably have the greatest potential for margin control. This is because they source and fund so many markets, most of which are relatively impersonal, with a variety of instruments whose maturities are short.

The final group contains three regional companies whose margins rose in both periods. The outstanding performer is Rainier. Perhaps the best explanation is that asset and liability management strategies at this company have undergone profound upgrading, including new policies toward funding, pricing, investment portfolio enrichment, and higher yield lending. To some extent, all companies are working toward these goals, and accordingly, any analysis of interest margin performance cannot overlook the potential role of management in improving efficiency, realigning the mix and maturities of assets and liabilities, raising yields, and lowering funding costs.

Fund Gap as a Method for Managing Interest Sensitivity

The wide disparity in interest margin performance among individual banks and predictions that interest rates may have relatively large and rapid fluctuations in coming years indicate that most banks should develop a system to manage their interest sensitivity. The most widely used system in the early 1980s is the so-called funds gap management. The system is a management tool which has been designed in recent years for the purpose of maintaining a high and relatively stable interest margin through the entire rate cycle.

In the typical funds gap management system, management is asked to dichotomize all items on each side of the bank's balance sheet into groups of items whose cash flows are sensitive and those whose cash flows are insensitive to changes in short-term interest rates.[4] Thus, an asset or liability is identified as sensitive if cash flows from the asset or liability change in the same direction and general magnitude as the change in short-term rates. The cash flows of insensitive (or nonsensitive) assets or liabilities do not change within the relevant time period. Some of these insensitive assets or liabilities do not have interest payments or costs at all.

Figure 12-1 illustrates this system and gives examples of sensitive and nonsensitive assets and liabilities. It is important to remember that interest sensitivity is the distinction, not maturity. A 10-year note where the rate changes with the prime would be in-

---

[4] Matched transactions, the dollar amount of assets that corresponds to specific liabilities equal in amount and having identical maturity are deducted from both sides of the balance sheet. These items, which are significant for some larger banks, are eliminated because they tend to be self-liquidating and should prove to be profitable since they were acquired on the basis of a predetermined rate spread.

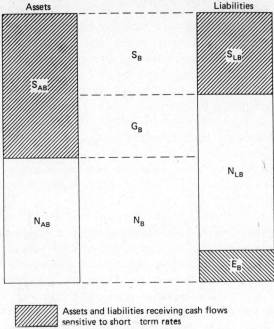

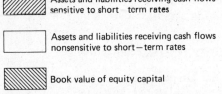

Sensitive assets (SAB) include Fed Funds sold, short-term securities, and variable-rate loans.

Sensitive liabilities (SLB) include short-maturity CDs and Fed Funds purchased.

Nonsensitive assets (NAB) include fixed-rate loans, long-term securities, and bank premises.

Nonsensitive liabilities (NLB) include long-term CDs and debt capital.

Equity capital (EB) includes common stock, surplus, undivided profits, and equity reserves.

FIGURE 12-1 Illustration of Traditional Group Management

terest sensitive. There are three basic financing relationships illustrated by Figure 12-1: S_B represents sensitive assets financed by sensitive liabilities. G_B represents sensitive assets financed by nonsensitive liabilities, and N_B represents nonsensitive assets financed by nonsensitive liabilities and common equity. Typically, assets, liabilities, and equity are valued in book value terms and the interest sensitivity of cash flows is used to classify assets and liabilities. Common equity is usually treated as nonsensitive liabilities.

There are several measures obtainable from Figure 12-1 that can be useful to bank management. The most common measure is the "funds gap" or "gap," which refers to the dollar amount by which sensitive assets exceed sensitive liabilities. The gap is negative if sensitive liabilities exceed sensitive assets. The ratio of sensitive assets divided by sensitive liabilities is also widely used. A ratio above 1.0 indicates that sensitive assets exceed sensitive liabilities. The reverse is true for a ratio below 1.0. A balance interest-sensitivity position would be a zero dollar gap or a sensitivity ratio of 1.0. The final measure is a comparison of sensitive assets as a percentage of total assets with sensitive liabilities as a percentage of total liabilities and net worth.

Figure 12-1 illustrates a bank with a positive funds gap (G_B), that is, one whose sensitive assets exceed its sensitive liabilities. Under rising short-term rates, this positive gap would increase the interest margin (the difference between interest income and interest expense). Declining short-term rates, with a positive gap, would exert downward pressure on the interest margin. On the other hand, if sensitive assets were less than sensitive liabilities, there would be a negative funds gap. With a negative gap, the interest margin would decline if short-term rates rose and increase if short-term rates fell.

The implications for bank management seem straightforward. If management expects interest rates to rise, it should widen the funds gap. On the other hand, management should narrow the bank's funds gap if interest rates are expected to decline. If used effectively, such gap management decisions should lead to higher returns for a given interest-rate risk level or reduced interest rate risk for a given return level.

Concerns About Funds Gap Management

There are four categories of concerns as to whether gap management can achieve such lofty goals. First is the concern about which time period is appropriate to use in determining whether assets and liabilities are rate sensitive. Second, there are concerns about the ability of bank management to predict the direction, magnitude, and timing of interest rate movements. Third, there are doubts about bank management's ability to flexibly adjust assets and liabilities to obtain the desired gap. Fourth, there are concerns that gap management is myopic because it focuses only on the interest sensitivity due to current flows and ignores potentially significant changes in the values of bank assets and liabilities usually deemed to be insensitive from a cash flow standpoint. Each of these concerns will be discussed in the following paragraphs.

The concern about the relevant period in which asset and liabilities are sensitive to rate changes is an important one. A bank which uses six-month money market certificates extensively may have a large positive gap if the time period is one month and may have a negative gap if the time period is six months. A bank that reprices loans annually and has significant amounts of sensitive liabilities may have a balanced sensitivity position for a year but substantial changes in its interest margin during years in which rates change substantially.

Table 12-4 illustrates an interest-sensitivity worksheet, which many banks have begun using to overcome the deficiency of selecting just one time period. Such worksheets present an interest-sensitivity profile for the bank at a given point of time. The bank used as an example in Table 12-4 is very asset sensitive during the first three months. An increase in rates would help this bank's interest margin in a short period of time, whereas a decrease in rates would similarly hurt its interest margin. One warning in using such a worksheet is that the interest-sensitivity profile can change rapidly if maturing securities are invested in assets with different sensitivity or if maturing deposits are funded from sources with different sensitivity. Thus, a new worksheet should be prepared at least monthly and more often if substantial amounts of assets or liabilities mature during a month.

The concern about the ability of bankers, or anyone else for that matter, to predict

TABLE 12-4

Community National Bank—Interest-Sensitivity Worksheet as of January 31, 1982 (in thousands of dollars)

| | Cumulative | | | | | |
	Within one month	Within three months	Within six months	Within one year	Nonsensitive	Total
Assets						
Cash and due from	$ 0	$ 0	$ 0	$ 0	$ 8,000	$ 8,000
Fed Funds and repos	1,000	1,000	1,000	1,000	0	1,000
Gov't and agency securities	1,000	1,000	3,000	4,000	4,000	8,000
Other securities	0	1,000	2,000	2,000	10,000	12,000
Commercial seasonal loans	8,000	12,000	13,000	14,000	0	14,000
Commercial term loans	1,000	6,000	8,000	9,000	4,000	13,000
Installment loans	500	1,500	3,000	6,000	12,000	18,000
Mortgage loans	0	500	1,000	2,000	14,000	16,000
Other loans	0	0	0	500	500	1,000
Other assets	0	0	0	0	1,000	1,000
Total assets	$11,500	$23,000	$31,000	$38,500	$53,500	$92,000
Liabilities and Capital						
Demand deposits	$ 0	$ 0	$ 0	$ 0	$30,000	$30,000
NOW deposits	0	0	0	0	10,000	10,000
Savings deposits	0	0	0	0	10,000	10,000
Consumer CDs	2,000	6,000	13,000	16,000	2,000	18,000
Commercial CDs	2,000	5,000	8,000	12,000	1,000	13,000
Public deposits	0	1,000	2,000	2,000	0	2,000
Other deposits	0	0	0	0	500	500
Fed Funds and repos	0	0	0	0	0	0
Other borrowings	500	500	500	500	0	500
Other liabilities	0	0	0	1,000	0	1,000
Capital notes	0	0	0	0	1,000	1,000
Equity capital	0	0	0	0	6,000	6,000
Total liabilities and capital	$ 4,500	$12,500	$24,500	$31,500	$60,500	$92,000

Measures of Interest Sensitivity

In One Month

Interest-sensitivity ratio $= \dfrac{\text{Sensitive assets}}{\text{Sensitive liabilities}} = \dfrac{11,500}{4,500} = 2.56 \times$

Dollar Interest sensitivity gap = Sensitive assets − Sensitive liabilities = 11,500 − 4,500 = $7,000

In Three Months

Interest-sensitivity ratio $= \dfrac{\text{Sensitive assets}}{\text{Sensitive liabilities}} = \dfrac{23,000}{12,500} = 1.84 \times$

Dollar interest sensitivity gap = Sensitive assets − Sensitive liabilities = 23,000 − 12,500 = $10,500

In Six Months

Interest-sensitivity ratio $= \dfrac{\text{Sensitive assets}}{\text{Sensitive liabilities}} = \dfrac{31,000}{24,500} = 1.27 \times$

Dollar interest sensitivity gap = Sensitive assets − Sensitive liabilities = 31,000 − 24,500 = $6,500

In One Year

Interest-sensitivity ratio $= \dfrac{\text{Sensitive assets}}{\text{Sensitive liabilities}} = \dfrac{38,500}{31,500} = 1.22$

Dollar interest sensitivity gap = Sensitive assets−Sensitive libilities = 38,500–31,500 = $7,000

Nonsensitive (until over a year)

Nonsensitive ratio $= \dfrac{\text{Nonsensitive assets}}{\text{Nonsensitive liabilities}} = \dfrac{53,500}{60,500} = 0.88 \times$

Dollar nonsensitive gap = Nonsensitive assets − Nonsensitive liabilities = 53,500 − 60,500 = − $7,000 interest rates is a very real one. In effect, advocates of gap management are arguing that bank managers can outpredict the market on the future course of interest rates. The authors question this assertion. However, a cause for equal, if not greater, concern is the corollary assertion that, particularly for banks that do not believe they can outpredict the market on interest rates, interest rate risk is minimized when interest-sensitive assets equal interest-sensitive liabilities. The fallacy of this assumption is discussed in the paragraphs covering the fourth concern.

A bank's flexibility in adjusting its assets and liabilities to achieve its desired gap position can also be questioned. For example, can a community bank located in a particular market rapidly change the mix of either its assets or liabilities to achieve a desired position? Also, there is the question of the effects on a bank's customers. Successful gap management by a bank means that the bank's customers have positioned themselves improperly for interest rate movements.

Finally, the interest rate risk of gap management appears to be the variability in interest margin produced by the gap. In valuation terms, however, this view of risk is incomplete because it focuses on "current" flows resulting from the funds gap and abstracts from the present value of longer term, so-called nonsensitive flows. Yield curve movements that occur over the credit cycle can profoundly affect the latter. Recent research, utilizing duration[5] of nonsensitive asset and nonsensitive liability portfolios has indicated that the changing level, volatility, and shape of yield curves have had a large effect on the value of various asset and liabilities usually deemed to be insensitive from a cash flow standpoint.[6] It is concluded that both the gap and changes in the nonsensitive portion of a bank's assets and liabilities can affect a bank's value. Even if there is no funds gap, the bank still may be subject to substantial interest rate risk. Furthermore, it may be possible to offset a mismatch in sensitive assets and liabilities by a carefully designed position in nonsensitive assets and liabilities.

Management Use of the Fund Gap

Although these concerns are real, gap management still appears to be a helpful tool. This is particularly true if a frequently updated interest-sensitivity profile is used, if management is aware of practical problems in predicting rates and managing the interest position of borrowers and depositors, and if management keeps track of changes in values. Given these conditions, funds gap measures are good indicators of the direction and possibly the size of interest margin for a given increase or decrease in interest rates. With this in mind, four potential management strategies utilizing gap management— accepting margin fluctuations, managing the gap over rate cycles, achieving gap targets with typical assets or liabilities, and achieving gap targets using financial futures—are briefly evaluated. The strategies are not mutually exclusive, and therefore some banks may use two or more strategies.

The first strategy is to accept fluctuation in interest margins as one of the risks of banking and go on about a bank's business of filling depositors' and borrowers' needs.

[5] Duration, which was discussed in the chapter on bank investments, is a proportionality constant that links changes in the present value of the stream of future cash flows to changes in market rates of interest.

[6] Donald Simonson and George H. Hempel, "Improving Gap Management as a Technique for Controlling Interest Rate Risk," *Journal of Bank Research* (Summer 1982).

Such a strategy implies that a bank's market should control the destiny of the bank's interest sensitivity. A bank in a suburban community might have a large negative gap because of nonsensitive mortgage dominating assets and short-term certificates of deposits dominating liabilities. A "wholesale" bank might have a large positive gap if nearly all of its asset were priced with the LIBOR,[7] whereas many of its deposits are demand deposits and long-term CDs. The loan and deposit markets of these two banks practically force them to hope rates will fall or rise, respectively. Movements in the opposite direction would be the bank's interest rate risk. This strategy was used successfully by many banks during the 1950s and 1960s because rate fluctuations were moderate. However, the increased volatility of interest rates in the late 1970s and early 1980s and the expectation for continued volatility in the 1980s made this strategy questionable. Most banks cannot afford the sizable rate risk often inherent in the practice of letting the market determine the bank's interest-sensitivity position.

The second strategy emphasizes managing the funds gap over the rate cycle. Such a strategy would indicate positive movement in the gap—more sensitive assets or less sensitive liabilities, or both—when rates are expected to increase. When rate declines are anticipated, the funds gap should narrow or become more negative—less sensitive asset or more sensitive liabilities, or both. Problems with implementing this strategy include the questionable ability to out predict the market on interest rate movement and the ability to and the desirability of managing borrowers and depositors to achieve the bank's objectives at the borrower's or depositor's expense. In general, this strategy is used by some larger banks that have large staffs responsible for economic and rate predictions and have entry into a large variety of impersonal financial markets. Some of these banks have publicly stated they must use gap management based on their expectations for interest rates because they are unable to earn a high enough margin on many of their loans to large, multinational companies. One way in which some of these banks try to control the risks of gap strategies is to maintain gaps for short periods, then shut down the gaps quickly if the interest rate scenario does not work out as anticipated.

The third strategy is to achieve the targeted gap level by managing typical bank assets and liabilities. This strategy could be used in conjunction with gap targets from the preceding strategy or to achieve a balanced gap position. For example, a medium-sized bank with limited staff and limited access to financial markets may decide not to take interest rate risk by seeking a balanced gap position. If, in order to remain competitive, such a bank is forced to use six-month money market certificates extensively, it may jeopardize its balance gap position. Using this strategy, the bank would, or should, adjust its asset structure to match the interest sensitivity of its liabilities. Such actions may be difficult for a bank with limited access to other markets.

The final strategy is to use financial futures to achieve the funds gap target. With financial futures, a bank can shift some of the risk of variable interest rates to the futures market. In effect, the use of financial futures enables the bank to establish interest rates on a futures instrument in advance. Financial futures are commodity contracts to take or make future delivery of a financial instrument such as U.S. Treasury securities, certificates of deposit, or Government National Mortgage Association (Ginnie Mae) se-

---

[7] This stands for the London International Borrowing Rate, which is being used more and more as the basis for variable rate borrowing by larger corporations.

curities. Delivery occurs at the date on which the instrument is issued and at a price set when the contract is executed. Contracts are executed for standardized amounts. U.S. Treasury bill and certificates of deposit contracts are for $1 million in face value of the securities; U.S. bonds and Ginnie Mae contracts are for $100,000. Dealings in financial futures involve contracts and not the actual underlying security; the latter is scheduled for future issuance and does not yet exist.

Only a few futures contracts are settled by actually making or taking delivery of the underlying security. Most futures contracts are settled or closed when holders execute an offsetting futures contract well in advance of the delivery date. For example, a holder of a contract to take future delivery of a given 90-day T-bill (a buy or "long" contract) usually closes his or her position later by selling (or going "short") a contract on the identical T-bill. The two transactions are fully offsetting.

The profitability of the combined transactions depends on the price movement of the original futures contract while the holder's position is open. In turn, the price movement is determined by the expectation for the forward interest rate on the underlying security. For example, if the interest rate expected to prevail when the security is issued falls, the futures contract price rises. The holder of a buy contract profits from this price rise because he or she is assured of the opportunity to take delivery of the underlying security at a contract price below the current market price; that is, the holder closes his or her position by buying at the earlier low contract price and selling at the present high price. Figure 12-2 illustrates these transactions. A 90-day Treasury bill *buy* contract for delivery on September 24, 1981, is executed on July 24, 1981, at a contract price of $85.45. During the ensuing weeks the forward rate on September 1981 90-day bills falls roughly in concert with the fall in the 90-day spot rate and, therefore, the price on the September 1981 futures contract rises. The holder elects to close his or her position on September 1 (well before delivery) by executing an offsetting *sell* contract at $88.00. Considering the nominal $1 million contract values, the profit would be $6,375.[8]

The workings of the futures market makes it a useful hedging tool for banks. Because the price of the futures contract moves with current and expected interest rate movements, a bank can buy or sell a futures contract to offset much of the impact a change in interest rates would have because of the bank's funds gap position. In the previous example, a long position in 90-day T-bill futures under an expected decline in interest rates would hedge some losses associated with a positive funds gap. Of course, if interest rates unexpectedly rose, the futures position would incur a loss, but this would be more or less offset by a gain from the positive funds gap. This exemplifies a true hedge in which one of two outcomes occur: (1) expected losses are partly offset by gains in the futures position, or (2) unexpected gains are partly offset by losses in the futures position. True hedges are defensive actions against losses and they preclude

---

[8] Treasury bill futures contracts are quoted according to an index equal to 100 minus the futures annual discount rate. In the above, a quote of 85.45 connotes a discount rate of 14.55 percent (100 − 85.45). On the 90-day T-bill futures, the actual transactions price is based on approximately one quarter of the annual discount or 100 − (14.55)/4 = 96.3625. In the above example, the profit equalled (97.0000 − 96.3625)/100 × $1 million = $6,375. The value 97,0000 is the selling price as derived from [100.000 − (12/4)], where the closing annual discount is 12 percent.

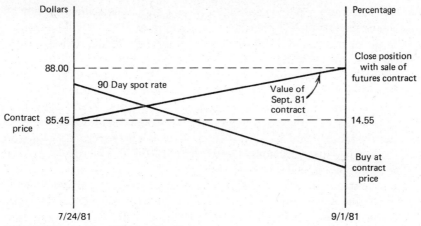

FIGURE 12-2 Value of Futures Position

speculative gains. A perfect offset is hard to achieve because of some differences in the price movements of actual financial assets or liabilities and of futures contract prices.[9]

Two conclusions from recent research about the use of futures contracts to achieve a desired interest-sensitivity position are pertinent. First, hedging of the complete asset/liability portfolio is preferable to hedging individual asset or liability contracts. Second, an adjusted duration measure of net asset/liability volatility with respect to interest rates can be used to determine how much of a single futures contract will be needed to approximately offset the bank's portfolio position.[10]

Immunization: The Key to Managing Interest Sensitivity?

It is generally recognized that there are two primary classifications of interest rate risk, changing reinvestment rates and changing market prices. Conventional gap management emphasizes cash flows (hence the changing reinvestment rate) and ignores changing market security prices. "Immunization" is the term coined to describe the design of portfolios that can achieve a target level of return for a specific future period in the face of changing reinvestment rates and security price levels. Specifically, with an increase in interest, security prices fall below expectations, but the income from reinvesting cash flows will exceed expectations. A decline in interest rates will provide higher than expected security prices but lower than expected income from reinvesting interim cash flows. A portfolio is immunized if its value at a specified future period, regardless of the course of interest rates, is at least as large as it would have been if interest rates would have been constant.

---

[9] This differential movement in prices constitutes "basic risk."

[10] Dwight Grant and George Hempel, "Bank Portfolio Management: The Role of Financial Futures," *Proceedings of 1982 Chicago Federal Reserve Conference.* This article purports that futures can be used to separate the bank's exposure to business risk and interest rate risk, permitting unconstrained optimal decisions with respect to each.

The immunization concept has been tested both mathematically and theoretically. Under the assumption that the changes in interest rates will be the same for all future rates—that is, parallel shifts in the yield curve—Fisher and Weil proved that duration is the investment horizon for which the reinvestment risk and price risk of a portfolio of banks have equal magnitudes but opposite directions. Thus, a portfolio of bonds should be immunized from interest rate risk if the duration of the portfolio equals the desired investment horizon. Empirically, Fisher and Weil tested their proof by using simulations to compare strategies with the investment horizon the same as (1) the portfolio's maturity and (2) the portfolio's duration for several time horizons. The duration strategy results were consistently closer to the promised yield, although the results were not perfect because the real-world interest rates in the simulation did not change by the same amount at all maturities.[11] Numerous minor refinements have improved the ability to immunize portfolios. Unless there are very large changes in the yield curve, it seems reasonable to conclude that a portfolio can be immunized so that the interest rate risk is minimal.[12]

Commercial banks have begun using immunization techniques in their trust department extensively and, in a few instances, with the bank's security portfolio. It seems meaningful to ask if the concept of immunization can be used to manage the interest sensitivity of the total bank asset and liability portfolios. For example, if the return on assets is relatively assured for a time period and the costs (negative returns) of liabilities relatively assured for the same time period, can a bank be reasonably assured of a constant interest margin for the period? There is not a definitive answer to this question at this time; however, there are some signs that immunization can make important contributions to bank asset/liability management.

The following are some practical problems in using immunization for asset/liability management: nonparallel shifts in the yield curve are particularly important since bank assets and liabilities are typically dominated by short maturities; treatment of variable-rate (either long or nonmaturing) assets and liabilities is controversial; the maturity of some assets (e.g., lines of credit) and liabilities (deposits that can be claimed before stated maturity) is uncertain; and rapid growth in total size and rapid changes in asset/liability composition (often out of the control of the bank) change the appropriate immunization strategy. In spite of these problems, prospects are good that immunization techniques can be used to understand and at least partially moderate interest rate risk.

Simonson and Hempel have introduced a system incorporating immunization into gap management. Sensitive assets financed by sensitive liabilities are treated as not subject to interest rate risk. The reinvestment effects of the funds gap (negative or positive)

---

[11] Lawrence Fisher and Roman L. Weil, "Coping with Interest Rate Fluctuations," *Journal of Business* (Oct. 1971), pp. 408–31.

[12] The problems of assuming parallel shifts in yield curves are summarized in Jess B. Yawitz, George H. Hempel, and William B. Marshall, "The Use of Average Maturity as a Risk Proxy in Investment Portfolios," *Journal of Finance* (May 1975), pp. 325–33. The idea that the basic framework of duration can be maintained if enhanced with simple parameters that capture to more typical nonparallel movements of the yield curve is in Jan A. Cooper, "Asset Values, Interest Rate Changes, and Duration," *Journal of Financial and Quantitative Analysis* (Dec. 1977), pp. 701–23. Some useful refinements appear in G. O. Bierwag and G. G. Kaufman, "Coping with the Risk of Interest Rate Fluctuations: A Note," *Journal of Finance* (Dec. 1977), pp. 1360–65.

and nonsensitive assets and liabilities are offset by the net market price effects of non-sensitive assets and liabilities. For example, a bank with a large positive gap may offset the large reinvestment effect with a highly reactive market price effect of long-duration nonsensitive assets financed by short-duration nonsensitive liabilities. Analytical tests of such a strategy are impressive, but data suitable for empirical testing is not available prior to 1980.[13] Immunization has at least the potential to become increasingly important in managing interest sensitivity in coming years.

OBTAINING AN ADEQUATE INTEREST MARGIN

Obtaining an interest margin adequate to cover other expenses and to earn a satisfactory return on the owner's investment in the bank is as important as, if not more important than, reasonable stability in the interest margin. A stable interest margin at a low level is certainly not consistent with the banking objective of maximizing the value of the owner's investment in the bank. Management should seek to obtain the highest interest margin possible within credit risk, liquidity risk, and capital risk constraints as well as the interest rate risk considerations discussed in the preceding section.

Competitive markets for both sources of funds and uses of funds also constrain the bank's ability to earn a higher return. For example, assume that a bank has a target "spread" of 4 percent but its average return on earning assets is 13 percent and its average cost of funds is 10 percent. The bank can obtain its target spread by increasing its average return on assets or decreasing its cost of funds or some combination thereof by 1 percent. This may be difficult if competitive returns on acceptable composition and risk asset alternatives are 13 percent and competitive costs of acceptable composition and risk alternatives are 10 percent. Either the bank has to increase the risks associated with its assets or liabilities or it has to accept the spread at least partially dictated by the competitive markets.

An Example of Yields Necessary for an Adequate Margin

Community National Bank, which was used as an example in Chapters 2 and 3, serves here as a simplified example of a model starting with the return on equity, recognizing the interest sensitivity of assets and liabilities, and showing the yield necessary on loans that will be repriced in the coming year. Table 12-5 presents the necessary information for estimating the required yields on sensitive assets for the Community National Bank. Data on the past performance of this bank appear in Tables 2-11 through 2-14 but are not essential.

The typical starting point of such an analysis is to estimate the required overall returns based on the projected cost of funds figures in Table 12-5. The estimated interest cost figures should recognize the sensitivity or nonsensitivity to interest rates in these cost figures. For example, in 1982 when rates tended to decline, average rates on non-sensitive sources such as demand deposits or passbook savings did not change, but av-

---

[13] Donald Simonson and George H. Hempel, "Improving Gap Management as a Technique for Controlling Interest Rate Risk," *Journal of Bank Research* (Summer 1982), pp. 109–115.

TABLE 12-5
Information for Estimating Required Yields on Sensitive
Assets for Community National Bank (in millions of dollars)

1. The bank's holdings of vault cash, deposits with the Federal Reserve and other banks, and other cash items in 1982 are expected to be:

> 26 percent of noninterest-bearing demand deposits
> 20 percent of interest-bearing demand deposits
> 5 percent of all time and savings deposits

2. The bank's investment in premises and equipment and other nonearning assets is expected to be 4 percent in 1982.

3. During 1982, the bank expects its net resources will average $200 million. The average amount and investable amount of the various fund sources are projected as follows (amounts in millions of dollars):

	Average Amount	Percentage Usable	Amount Investable
Demand deposits, noninterest	$ 60	70%	$ 42.00
Demand deposits, interest-bearing	18	76	13.68
Passbook savings	12	91	10.92
Savings certificates	7	91	6.37
Money market certificates	27	91	24.57
All savers certificates	6	91	5.46
CDs, $100,000 and over	32	91	29.12
Public and other time deposits	8	91	7.28
Short-term borrowing	12	96	11.52
Other liabilities	6	96	5.76
Stockholder equity	12	96	11.52
Total sources of funds	$200		$168.20

4. The bank's target rate of return on equity is 16 percent after taxes. Its marginal income tax rate is 45 percent; therefore, the pretax return is $16/1 - 0.45$ or 29 percent.

erage rates on sensitive sources such as money market certificates or larger CDs declined considerably. The decline in such average rates would depend on the old rate, the maturity of liabilities (sources) outstanding at the end of 1981, and the new rates when the liabilities matured.

Table 12-6 illustrates the calculation of the required overall returns on earning assets based on the projected average cost of funds for 1982. The overall cost of acquiring funds can be estimated by dividing the summation of total dollar acquisition cost, $21.619 million (in Column 3) in this example, by the amount investable, $168.2 million (Column 4) in this example. The percentage return required to cover interest assets on separate sources of funds (Column 5) is calculated by dividing the dollar cost of each source (Column 3) by the amount investable from each source (Column 4). The relative weighting in Column 6 was obtained by dividing the amount investable for each source (Column 4) by the amount investable, $168.2 million. Finally, each seg-

TABLE 12-5 (continued)
Information for Estimating Required Yields on Sensitive
Assets for Community National Bank (in millions of dollars)

5. Costs of each type of funding (percentage):

	Interest Cost 1981	Estimated Interest Cost 1982	Net Processing Cost 1982
Demand deposits, noninterest	0%	0%	4.6%
Demand deposits, interest-bearing	5.2	5.3	2.3
Passbook savings	5.4	5.5	1.1
Savings certificates	14.4	12.0	0.2
Money market certificates	15.7	13.5	0.4
All savers certificates	12.2	10.2	0.4
CDs, $100,000 and over	18.0	15.0	0.1
Public and other time deposits	13.3	12.1	0.2
Short-term borrowing	16.5	14.0	0.1
Other liabilities	7.1	7.0	0.1
Stockholders equity	29.1	29.1	0.1

6. Expenses other than interest for 1982 are estimated to be $3.5 million in net processing costs and $4.0 million in net other costs (other expenses of $5.5 million less other income of $1.5 million) for total net noninterest expenses of $7.5 million.

7. Forecast average assets for 1982 (in millions of dollars):

	Interest Sensitive	Nonsensitive	Total
Cash and due from banks			23.8
Short-term securities	14.2		14.2
Long-term securities		28.0	28.0
Loans	80.0	46.0	126.0
Bank premise and equipment		5.0	5.0
Other assets (nonearning)		3.0	3.0
Total			200.0

8. Projected returns on short-term securities purchased in 1982 is 12.0 percent and projected returns on loans is 16 percent.

ment's contribution to the weighted return required on investable assets (Column 7) was calculated by multiplying the return required on each source (Column 5) by its relative weighting (Column 6). The total of the contributions to weighted required returns is, of course, equal to the returns required on earning assets, which was previously calculated from the totals.

The stated objective is to obtain an interest margin adequate to cover other costs and to earn an adequate return on the owner's investment, however, costs other than those required to attract funds and income other than interest income have been ignored in the calculations. These cost and income figures can be incorporated by adding in all costs other than the acquisition costs already incorporated, net of all noninterest income items ($5.5 million less $1.5 million) divided by noncash assets ($168.2 million) to the previously calculated required return (12.85 percent).

This resulting required return to cover total net costs of 15.23 percent includes an

TABLE 12-6
Required Overall Returns Based on Projected Cost of Funds (in millions of dollars)

Types of funds	(1) Average amount	(2) Interest and net acquisition costs	(3) Total cost	(4) Amount investable	(5) Return on sources	(6) Relative weight	(7) Contribution to weighted returns
Demand deposits, noninterest	$ 60	4.6%	$ 2.760	$ 42.00	6.57%	24.97%	1.64%
Demand deposits, interest-bearing	18	7.6	1.386	13.68	10.13	8.13	0.82
Passbook savings	12	6.6	0.792	10.92	7.25	6.49	0.47
Savings certificates	7	12.2	0.854	6.37	13.41	3.79	0.51
Money market certificates	27	13.9	3.753	24.57	15.27	14.61	2.23
All savers certificates	6	10.6	0.636	5.46	11.65	3.25	0.38
CDs, $100,000 and over	32	15.1	4.832	29.12	16.59	17.31	2.87
Public and other time deposits	8	12.3	0.984	7.28	13.52	4.33	0.59
Short-term borrowing	12	14.1	1.692	11.52	14.68	6.85	1.01
Other liabilities	6	7.1	0.426	5.76	7.40	3.42	0.25
Stockholder equity	12	29.2	3.504	11.52	30.42	6.85	2.08
	$200		$21.619	$168.20		100.00%	12.85%

Return required on noncash assets to cover cost of acquiring funds: $\dfrac{\$\,21.619}{\$163.200} = 12.85\%$

Return required on noncash assets to cover total net cost of funds: $12.85\% + \dfrac{4.0}{168.2} = 15.23\%$

after-tax return to equity holders of 16 percent. This return, adjusted to a before-tax rate by dividing by 1 minus the marginal bank income tax rate, was treated as a cost of funds similar to other sources. If the forecasted interest rates were approximately correct and the bank earned above 15.23 percent on its assets, the residual return on equity would be above 16 percent and vice versa. The concern is now to employ earning assets, which are a mixture of sensitive and nonsensitive assets, so that they will yield an average of 15.23 percent or above.

Community National Bank is used in Table 12-7 to demonstrate a simplified worksheet that can be used to calculate the yields required on newly priced sensitive assets. The key characteristic of the worksheet is that to obtain the targeted return on equity the bank must earn 15.23 percent on its earning asset of $168.2 million, or $25.619 million. The yields on nonsensitive loans and long-term securities are known and the dollar returns of $6,440,000 and $3,080,000 respectively, should be reasonable estimates. Estimated dollar returns on rate-sensitive loans and short-term securities are more complex. In the case of short-term securities, Community National felt their securities, which were yielding 14 percent at the start of the year, would mature about evenly during the year and that the average yield on newly purchased securities would be 12 percent. The average yield on the $14.2 million of short-term securities would then be 13 percent, or $1,846,000.

A calculation similar to that performed on short-term securities could be performed for rate-sensitive loans if the rates on currently outstanding loans are known, if there are reasonable estimates of the repricing, renewal, and maturity profiles of these loans, and if the average rate on newly priced loans can be forecast. A slightly different approach is taken—the current rate and repricing profile are estimated and the required yield on newly priced sensitive loans to earn 16 percent on equity is calculated. Table 12-8 shows that the calculations can be made by first finding the required dollar yield on sensitive loans by subtracting the returns on short- and long-term securities and nonsensitive loans from the total return required on all assets. The required average yield on sensitive loans then can be calculated by dividing the required dollar yields on sensitive loans by the average amount of sensitive loans. Finally, if sensitive loans will

TABLE 12-7

Worksheet for Calculation of Yield Required on Newly Priced Sensitive Loans (in thousands of dollars)

Asset category	Forecasted average for 1982	Yield on nonsensitive assets	Yield on sensitive assets (old)	Yield on sensitive assets (new)	Average yield	Returns (dollars)
Short-term securities	$ 14,200		14.0%	12.0%	13.0%	$ 1,846
Long-term securities	28,000	11.0%			11.0	3,080
Loans (nonsensitive)	46,000	14.0			14.0	6,440
Loans (sensitive)	80,000		18.0	(3)[a]	(2)[a]	(1)[a]
Total earning assets	$168,200				15.23	$25,619
Nonearning assets	31,800	—	—	—	—	0
Total assets	$200,000				12.81%	$25,619

[a]Number in parentheses refers to calculation of answer in Table 12-8.

TABLE 12-8
Calculation of Yield Required on Newly
Priced Sensitive Loans (in thousands of dollars)

1. Total dollar return on all assets		$25,619
Dollar returns on:		
Short-term securities	$1,846	
Long-term securities	3,080	
Nonsensitive loans	6,440	
Cash, premises, etc.	0	11,366
Required dollar return on sensitive loans		$14,253 (1)

2. Required average yield on all sensitive loans: $\dfrac{14,253}{80,000} = 17.81\%$ (2)

3. Required yield on newly priced sensitive loans:
$$\frac{14,253 - 7,200}{80,000 - 40,000} = \frac{7,053}{40,000} = 17.63\% \qquad (3)$$

be repriced about evenly during the year, the required yield on newly priced sensitive loans can be calculated by subtracting the dollar yield at the old sensitive rate and the average amount at the old rate from the numerator and denominator, respectively. The resulting dollar amount divided by the average amount repriced during the year is the average required percentage yield on newly priced sensitive loans (17.63 percent for Community National).

Two final comments about using this type of model seem appropriate. First, the real world is more complex than this simplified model. For example, loans grow or decline, types of loans grow at different rates, prepayments and extensions occur, and so on. This type of model, however, may be made considerably more complex than this simplified example. The authors have worked with banks that have considerably more complex models (generally on microcomputers), which are based on the same basic ideas. Second, even the simplified model in this chapter can be flexibly used in numerous ways. For example, a bank can forecast all rates for the coming year and see what the resulting rate of return on equity will be. Or a bank can leave the new rate on sensitive short-term securities as an unknown to see if the rate calculated by dividing the dollar return on sensitive securities by the forecasted amount of sensitive securities is reasonable in the expected environment. The required yield on newly priced sensitive loans can then be calculated by dividing the dollar return on all sensitive loans less the dollar yield on sensitive loans at the previous yield by the average newly priced, sensitive loans.

The required yield on newly priced, sensitive loans can then be compared with the bank's estimates of competitive market rates for the coming year. If market rates are expected to be lower than the required yield, the bank will probably earn less than the targeted 16 percent on equity, unless the asset/liability structure is changed or more risk is taken to get returns higher. The bank is likely to earn above 16 percent on equity if expected market rates exceed the required yield on newly priced sensitive loans.

SUMMARY

This chapter has tried to tie together the management of both assets and liabilities to achieve the highest interest margin without taking excessive interest rate risk. The first part of the chapter presented the cause for fluctuations in interest margins and introduced methods banks could use to try to anticipate and control interest fluctuations. The second part of the chapter discussed the importance of maintaining an interest margin high enough to cover other expenses and to earn satisfactory return on the owner's investment in the bank. A method, incorporating the interest sensitivity of assets and liabilities, was outlined which would indicate the returns a bank must earn on sensitive assets in order to earn a satisfactory return to owners.

13

LONG-RANGE PLANNING FOR FUTURE RETURN-RISK TRADEOFFS

The primary function of this final chapter is to unify the material presented in earlier chapters. This function is accomplished through the longer term planning process described in this chapter. In the banking world of the past, bank managers tended to spend most of their time dealing with short-term and often nonintegrated problems, such as attracting loans, measuring seasonal deposit movements, and estimating the liquidity of the securities portfolio. Since the banking environment was relatively static, most banks did not have much incentive to look beyond the annual budget or profit plan. As pointed out in Chapter 1, this static environment no longer exists. Continuing rapid changes in economic, technological, regulatory, and competitive factors have and seem likely to continue to make banks subject to continuing dynamic change. It can now be concluded that successful bank managers cannot sit back and let the future happen to them but must implement longer term planning that will help them successfully move in a dynamic future environment while incorporating short-run operating decisions into their long-run plans.

The long-term planning described in this chapter implies looking as far as necessary into the future to accomplish two basic objectives: first, to decide among probable future return-risk tradeoffs so as to maximize the value of the bank to its owners, and, second, to determine what the bank wants to be like in the future (strategic planning). The first section of this chapter discusses some of the return-risk tradeoffs that may exist in the future (mid-1980s) and how banks may choose among these. The second section discusses how a bank's management should determine what the bank wants to be like and how the bank should try to achieve these objectives. The chapter closes with a brief section describing the current state of the art of planning in banking.

MANAGING RETURN-RISK TRADEOFFS TO MAXIMIZE OWNER'S POSITION

Once a bank has decided what markets it wants to serve—that is, what the bank wants to be—it must make policy-level decisions as to its return targets and the risks it is willing to take to achieve these targets. These so-called return-risk tradeoffs should be made so as to maximize the value of the bank to its owners. In this section we will summarize the previously discussed measures of return and risks, review the interrelationships between returns and risks, discuss the setting of objectives for returns and risks, present the effect of the predicted future environment on return-risk tradeoffs, and enumerate the key steps in making future return-risks decisions.

Measuring Returns and Risks

The primary measures of returns and risks were introduced in Chapter 2 and more sophisticated measures were discussed in subsequent chapters. The purpose here is to summarize the beginning measures a bank may use. Readers interested in greater detail on measures can turn back to the relevant chapter.

The return on equity model provides the primary return measures. The first return measure is the interest margin in percentage terms, which is interest income minus interest expense divided by earning assets. Interest income less both interest expense and other expenses divided by revenues is labeled net margin. This net margin times asset utilization (revenues divided by assets) equals the return on assets. When the return on assets is multiplied by the leverage multiplier (assets divided by equity) the result is the return on equity. The return on equity (net income divided by equity capital) is the most important measure of banking returns because it is influenced by how well the bank has performed on all other return categories and because it indicates whether a bank can compete for private sources of capital in the U.S. economy. More detail on these and other return measures can be found in Chapters, 2, 3, and 12.

The risk measures are related to the return measures because, in order to earn adequate returns, a bank must take risks. A beginning measure of the liquidity risk of a bank is approximated by comparing a proxy for the bank's liquidity needs, its deposits, with a proxy for the bank's liquidity sources, its short-term securities. Though both variables are only rough approximations—funding loans may be a major liquidity need and purchasing liabilities may be an important source of liquidity—the relationship is an indicator of many banks' liquidity risk. More sophisticated measures of liquidity risk, for example, liquidity needs based on predicted fluctuations of loans and deposits compared with sources of liquidity or a liquidity profile of all assets and liabilities compared with the projected growth of loans and deposits, appear in Chapter 5.

The ratio of interest-sensitive assets to interest-sensitive liabilities can be used as a first approximation of a bank's interest rate risk. Particularly in periods of wide interest rate movements, this ratio reflects the risk of lower returns. If a bank has a ratio above 1.0, the bank's returns will usually be lower if interest rates decline. On the other hand, a bank's returns will be lower if the bank has a ratio below 1.0 and interest rates increase. Given the difficulty of predicting interest rates, at least some banks have concluded that the way to minimize interest rate risk is to have an interest-sensitivity ratio of close to 1.0. Such a ratio may be hard for some banks to achieve and often may be reached only at the cost of lower returns on assets such as short-term securities or variable-rate loans. More sophisticated measures of interest rate risk, such as a monthly interest-sensitivity profile, were discussed in detail in Chapter 12.

The credit risk of a bank is often estimated by looking at the relationship between the loans and either the provision for loan losses or the loan loss reserve. The credit risk in the loan portfolio may also be estimated by looking at loans classified as below average by the bank's examiners or management. Credit risk in the security portfolio may be estimated by looking at bond ratings. More sophisticated measures of credit risk appear in Chapters 6 and 8.

The capital risk of a bank can be measured by examining what percentage of the bank's risk assets are covered by its capital. More sophisticated measures of a bank's capital risk are described in Chapter 4. The capital risk is inversely related to the leverage multiplier and, therefore, to the return on equity. When a bank chooses (assuming this is allowed by its regulators) to take more capital risk, its leverage multiplier and return on equity, *ceteris paribus*, is higher. If the bank chooses (or is forced to choose) lower capital risk, its leverage multiplier and return on equity are lower.

Interrelationships Between Returns and Risks

Commercial banks must take some risks in order to earn acceptable returns for their stockholders. Banks' primary final product, usable funds, has to be in a form or provide utility that direct or indirect borrowers could not obtain directly from savers. For example, a bank might buy substantial amounts of short-term funds, which it would lend longer term at a higher rate. The bank would be taking liquidity risk (the inability to meet short-term fund demands) and interest rate risk (the threat of large earning fluctuations because interest costs would change more rapidly than interest returns) in order to earn acceptable returns. The bank might take more credit risk (an increase in the probability the borrower will be unable to pay as promised) to increase returns. Or a bank might take more capital risk (a decline in the capital cushion by which assets exceed liabilities) to leverage earnings so that the return to common stockholders is higher.

Table 13-1 summarizes the impact of increasing each of the primary risk categories on the typical earnings categories. Although it is difficult to estimate the exact path and magnitude of increasing these categories of risks, there is little doubt that the return on equity will usually be higher, other things being equal, by increasing the risk taken in any of the categories. One exception would be that the bank would take so many risks that it would have declining returns and possibly fail. The reverse will also usually be true—if a bank decreases the risk taken in one of the risk categories, return on equity will be lower. It is essential to review the environment expected in the 1980s, its effects on return-risk tradeoffs, and the bank's current position before deciding which categories of risk a bank should increase or decrease.

TABLE 13-1
The Impact of Increasing Risks on Returns

Return measures	Effect of increasing risks in primary categories			
	Interest-rate risk	Credit risk	Liquidity risk	Capital risk
Interest margin	+[a]	0[b]	+	
Net margin	+	0	+	
Asset utilization		+	+	
Return of assets	+	+	+	
Leverage multiplier				+
Return on equity	+	+	+	+

[a] + = High probability that increased risk will increase return category.
[b] 0 = Medium probability that increased risk will increase return category.

Setting Objectives for Returns and Risks

Clearly returns are increased by increasing one or more of the four primary risks a bank might take. It is obvious that a bank's managers would prefer the highest returns for a given level of risks and the lowest risks for a given level of returns. Two questions remain for the managers. What degree of total risks should a bank take in order to increase returns? How much of which type of risks should a bank take? The answers to these questions are difficult and not exact. For assistance, a bank can look at its own past performance and ask if it is satisfied with the returns obtained and risks taken. Return and risk measures for similar individual banks or peer groups of banks can be compared with similar measures for the bank. But exact answers are hard to come by. Constraints, such as the nature of a bank's market, the level of competition it faces, the areas in which it has special management expertise, and the stance of its regulators, mean that each bank has individual characteristics that affect its desired return-risk tradeoffs.

The first step for bank managers is to look at how other similar individual banks and groupings of banks have made their risk-return decisions. Any bank can obtain such information on other individual banks or peer groupings from the Federal Deposit Insurance Corporation, Federal Reserve, Comptroller's Office, or numerous private bank service companies. Many banks' regulatory reports include a comparison with peer-group banks. The second step is to compare a bank's performance (return and risk) measures with those of selected similar banks. Significant variances between a bank's performance measures and those of similar banks should be justified. There are many justifiable reasons for differences—different markets, different management philosophies, and so on—however, many banks may find one or several areas for improvement. The final step is to set reasonable (challenging but attainable) objectives, given a bank's past performance, the performance of its peers, and its environment.

Prediction About the Environment in the 1980s

No one is sure about the environment banks will be facing in the 1980s. The following material summarizes the authors' predictions, which are discussed in detail in Chapter 1. The coming economic environment promises to be challenging for bank management. It appears likely that management decisions for the next few years will have to be made in an environment of slow real economic growth and continuing inflation. This slow growth and inflation will probably be accompanied by continued relatively high levels of interest rates and wide and rapid fluctuations in interest rates. High and fluctuating rates may present some profitable opportunities, but the dominant effect would seem to be an increase in the risk level for a given interest-rate-sensitivity position. Thus, for a given interest-sensitivity position, a bank is taking greater interest rate risk.

The Depository Institutions Deregulation and Money Control Act of 1980 and the Garn-St. Germain Depository Institution Act of 1982 were important legislative actions that will affect bank management appreciably in the next few years. The lower reserve requirements applied to most banks and the greater limitations in the types of deposits covered means most banks will have increased earning assets and hopefully increased earnings. The required explicit pricing for Federal Reserve services, on the other hand, will probably increase expenses and reduce earnings for most banks. The approval of nationwide NOW accounts will probably lead to higher interest expense for transaction-type deposits and lower bank earnings. The insured money market deposits should enable banks to compete with money market mutual funds, but will probably raise interest expenses appreciably. Finally, the phaseout of Regulation Q interest ceilings will probably cause a gradual increase in the interest costs of many types of bank funds and a narrowing of bank margins. Inherent in the last three changes is that emphasis in bank management will probably shift from managing the quantity of funds obtained to managing the pricing of bank funds. This change in emphasis may, *ceteris paribus*, lower liquidity risk but increase interest rate risk.

Other changes also seem likely to affect returns and risks in banking in the next few years. For example, before the mid-1980s at least regional, and probably nationwide, banking may be permitted. The banking industry is at the threshold of a veritable revolution in the electronic delivery system of bank services which has significant implications for bank management. Nondepository corporations, such as money market funds, large retail chains, and brokerage firms, will use their substantial competitive edge—fewer restrictions, no reserves, no capital requirements, less regulation—to offer more and more banklike financial services. Finally, regulatory positions on how much and what forms of capital are needed to support increasingly risky bank assets seem in a state of flux. While changes cannot be exactly predicted, the net result of these and possible other changes would seem to be a squeeze on banking returns, so that in order to make returns acceptable to owners, many banks may have to take additional risks.

Illustrating Potential Changes in Return-Risk Tradeoffs

Figure 13-1 graphically presents the changes in conceptual return-risk tradeoffs that are likely to occur in coming years. The return on equity is used as the return measure on the vertical axis. The risk measure on the horizontal axis remains the same, even if the actual risk may change as the environment changes. In Graph A, under current conditions, the return on equity rises slowly, then at an inceasing rate, until the risk of substantial credit failures causes the return to fall.[1] In the predicted future environment,

---

[1] The optimal solution is usually not where return is highest because the bank needs flexibility and the other risks mean that the return-risk line is really the mean of a probability distribution that widens as credit risk itself increases or as the other risks increase. This is true for all four risk categories.

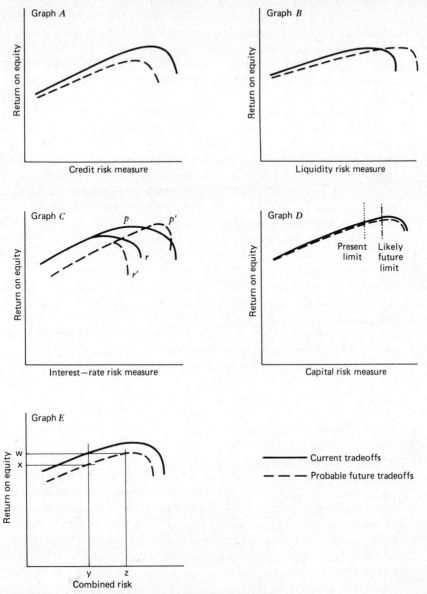

FIGURE 13-1 Shape of Changing Return-Risk Tradeoffs

however, returns are likely to be lower for each credit risk level, and the point at which returns decline, even though credit risk increases, will probably occur at a lower credit risk. Primary reasons for these predictions are an economic environment of slow growth and inflation accompanied by greater competition among banks (e.g., nationwide banking) and between banks and nonfinancial companies. To keep returns at their current level, a bank may have to increase its credit risk.

The return-liquidity risk tradeoffs appear in Graph B. Currently, the return on equity increases until the bank begins facing a serious liquidity problem. Under deregulation, when pricing will probably be more of a funds management problem than quantity, returns tend to be about the same or slightly higher for a given risk level, and the liquidity risk (measured in a consistent manner) will be higher before the bank faces a serious liquidity problem. This is an area in which the risk measure and return may increase, but the bank will not be taking additional risk because of the predicted environment.

The return-interest-rate risk tradeoffs are traced in Graph C of Figure 13-1. In the current environment, banks are often able to increase their return on equity by taking greater interest-rate risk. The increase in returns also depends on the ability of the bank to predict interest rates. As a bank increases its interest rate risk, its success or failure in increasing returns will be more and more dependent on its ability to outguess the general market on rate movements. As illustrated by line p in Graph C, a bank that actively manages its interest rate risk and successfully predicts interest rates may increase return over a broader risk range. The cost of incorrect rate predictions becomes greater as interest rate risk is increased, and a bank with only average rate-predictive abilities (depicted by r) will find returns declining considerably earlier. If predictions of greater interest rate fluctuations and a narrowing interest margin are correct for the future, management of interest rate risk becomes even more complex. The most likely scenario is that if a bank decides to take more interest rate risk to try to maintain returns, it will face a higher probability of declining returns. Another way of saying this is that the cost of not predicting interest rates correctly (so that the bank stays on line p') will be greater (line r') because of the changed environment.

There will probably not be substantial changes in the return-capital risk tradeoffs depicted in Graph D. By increasing capital risk a bank will increase its leverage multiplier and resulting return on equity, for a given return on assets, about as much in the future as now. The typical management goal seems to be to take about as much capital risk as regulators will allow (possibly allowing some flexibility for future growth); however, two conflicting pressures may occur in the next few years. As returns on assets decline due to pressures of the coming environment, bank management may want to increase the leverage multiplier (by increasing capital risk) to try to maintain the bank's return on equity. On the other hand, there are indications that regulators want to see capital risk increased only slightly (with the biggest increase in capital risk being allowed to smaller banks), which will probably lead only to a slightly higher leverage multiplier. The vertical lines in Graph D reflect these potential regulatory limits.

Finally, Graph E illustrates the effects on returns of the four risk measures combined. Over most of the potential risk range, as combined risks increase, returns increase. At some point, the risk of wide fluctuations in earnings, and possible failure, becomes great enough that returns may actually decline. Generally, bank management does not go to the point where the return on equity is highest because the bank needs flexibility and the return-risk line is really the mean of a probability distribution that widens as risks become higher. In the next few years, the predicted environment will cause the return-risk tradeoff curve to shift downward and to the left. Returns will be lower for a given level of risk and returns will begin declining at a lower risk level. For example, a bank taking y risks to obtain w return on equity would see its return on equity fall to x. The only way to maintain the bank's return on equity at w would be for it to increase the risks it takes to z.

Assuming w is at, or is close to, the minimum acceptable return level of a bank, the bank faces some difficult management decisions in the coming environment. For most banks, the same level of credit risk and interest-rate risk will cause returns to fall. Some banks may be able to recover some of this decline by increasing liquidity risk; however, because of regulatory pressures, the leverage multiplier resulting from capital risk is likely to fall slightly, or at best remain the same. In order to keep returns at or close to their current levels, banks may have to seek higher returns by taking greater credit or interest-rate risk. The actions to be taken depend heavily on the current position and the areas of management expertise of the individual bank.

Key Steps in Making Future Return-Risk Decisions

Successful integrative bank management in the 1980s will require at least three substantive steps. The first step is to measure the return-risk tradeoffs for each of the four risk categories. This step would include accurate measurement of each of the four risk categories and reasonable estimates of how increasing or reducing that risk category would affect returns. A bank cannot make rational management decisions without this information. The authors were shocked when fewer than 20 percent of the attendees at a recent bank executive seminar believed that their bank knew its interest-rate-sensitivity position.

The second step is to evaluate honestly and accurately the bank's management and market strengths and weaknesess. For example, a bank should recognize that it has a strong commercial lending department but a weak location for consumer lending. Another bank may find that because of its location, its major market and management strength is in consumer lending. A large bank located in a financial center may have the ability and staff to predict interest rates, to conduct interest arbitrages, and so on, whereas a smaller rural bank's activity in these areas should probably be limited. The primary conclusion is that a bank should take relatively more risks in those areas in which it believes its greatest management and market strengths lie.

The final step is for the bank, after considering its current return-risk positions and its areas of management and market strengths, to determine its target mix of risk objectives for the environment expected in the next few years. The basic constraint on this mix is that the combined risk should produce an acceptable return on equity. For example, determinants of the future credit risk include the bank's current credit risk, the effect of the future environment on its market location, and its management expertise in credit analysis. Future liquidity risk should probably depend on its current liquidity position, its ability to borrow liquidity, and possible declining liquidity needs as banks are able to increase their control over attracting funds.

Future interest-rate risk is difficult to control because a bank can be substantially constrained by its current net interest-sensitivity position and wide future fluctuations in rates may make a given net interest-sensitivity position even more risky. Nevertheless, a bank should have a target that is affected by its current interest rate risk, its managerial expertise in predicting rates, and its predictions about future rate fluctuations. If its target differs significantly from its current interest-sensitivity position, the bank can do one of three things: (1) accept that its target position is unattainable in the near future and try to live with its current position; (2) try to move rapidly toward its target by making substantial changes, such as selling most of the mortgage portfolio or only making new installment loans at variable rates; or (3) use financial futures to move the bank to its targeted interest rate risk position.

The determinants of future capital risk include management's desire for a larger equity multiplier, the bank's current capital risk position, and coming regulatory decisions about the allowable amount of capital risk. Although this is a potential area for improving bank returns, it seems likely that inflation-fed growth, narrower profit margins, and regulatory toughness will limit meaningful return improvement for most banks in the next few years.

Case Situations Illustrating Return-Risk Choices

The following situations are a few examples of how different individual banks must take different types of risks in order to obtain acceptable returns in the 1980s. Bank A is an approximately $20 billion asset bank located in a money center city. The majority of its loans are to good quality national corporations at very competitive rates, and its leverage multiplier exceeds 20 times. It has a large "portfolio management" group that spends considerable time looking at rate trends and special security opportunities. A bank like Bank A may have to extend its liquidity risk and capital risk as far as permissible by management and the bank's regulators. The bank's access to many markets and continued easing of Regulation Q make liability management the bank's major source of liquidity. If returns are still below an acceptable level, Bank A may also be justified in taking some additional interest rate risks by actively managing its interest-sensitivity gap. In spite of increasing rate fluctuations the probability of higher returns in this area of management strength may be higher than in the competitive national loan market.

Bank B is a slightly over $50 million asset community bank that emphasizes small business, agricultural, and individual loans in its community. Bank B has a substantially larger margin and return on assets than Bank A; however, Bank B's leverage multiplier is only 12, so its return on equity is only slightly above A's. Bank B also has lower liquidity risk and capital risk than A. Bank B believes that the effects of deregulation will include a lower profit margin and greater interest rate risk for the bank because more of its liabilities will be interest sensitive. Suggestions for Bank B would include (1) to take somewhat greater liquidity risk and capital risk, (2) to reduce interest rate risk by increasing rate sensitivity on assets or using financial futures, and (3) to increase credit risk in those areas in which the bank has a competitive advantage. Bank B probably has no business hoping to take advantage of rate movements, and it should maintain the ratio of interest-sensitive assets to interest-sensitive liabilities as close to 1.0 as possible. If the bank has to take additional risks to earn an acceptable return, these risks should be taken in the areas of the bank's greatest management and locational strength.

Bank C is a regional bank that has grown to approximately $1 billion in total assets. Its margin, return on assets, and return of equity have suffered in the last few years because the bank has a large, fixed-return mortgage portfolio. Bank C wonders what to do particularly because the bank seems to be taking as much risk as it wants in all categories and will have substantial earnings fluctuations if its liabilities become more rate sensitive and if interest rates fluctuate even more in the coming environment. Advice is easy, action difficult. For example, it is easy to say the bank should sell much of its mortgage portfolio. However, the losses on the portfolio and the fact that many of the mortgages may be in a nonsellable form may make this suggestion impossible to implement. Suggestions would include an investigation of the possibilities of (1) increasing the bank's liquidity risk, (2) making only variable-rate mortgages in the future, and (3) using financial futures to attain the bank's desired interest-sensitivity position.

Bank D is a $300 million retail-oriented commercial bank in a suburban community. The bank believes its earnings have suffered because it has substantial amounts of fixed-rate consumer installment loans and because many of the liabilities it has used to match its interest-sensitive assets are six-month certificates of deposit, which pay approximately the Treasury bill rate at the time the certificates are issued. Bank D states its consumer installment loans are earning less than its current marginal costs of funds. Furthermore, the bank was hurt in the early summer of 1980, when its returns on interest-sensitive assets fell with prime but its six-month CDs remained at February-March rates. The suggestion to this bank is to price its consumer installment loans at variable rates (probably by using fixed payments but varying principal repaid and maturity according to existing rates). Bank D may also want to refine its interest-sensitivity measure to pick up the difference between immediate and six-month rate adjustments. It could try to match the six-month CDs with similar maturity loans or securities or by using financial futures.

There are probably as many different case situations as there are banks. The primary task of a bank's managers is to measure accurately the risks the bank is currently taking to obtain returns. The bank's managers can then make rational decisions, in the light of their prediction for the future environment and their assessment of the bank's strengths and weaknesses, about which risks must be taken in order to earn acceptable returns.

STRATEGIC PLANNING

Strategic planning is that portion of long-range planning in which management determines what the bank will be like in the future. Strategic planning involves developing a set of objectives the bank wants to attain and the means with which to achieve these desired results. Although forecasting may be part of strategic planning, it is not the same as strategic planning. Forecasting attempts to measure the most probable course of future events, or more typically probability ranges of future events, based on assumptions and judgment as well as objective methods. It says where the bank is most likely to be, not where it wants to be. There are two other things often associated with strategic planning that are also misconceptions. First, strategic planning does not deal with future bank decisions, it deals with the futurity of present decisions. The primary question facing the bank planner is not what should the bank do tomorrow; it is what should the bank do today to achieve its objectives in an uncertain tomorrow. Second, strategic planning is not an attempt to eliminate or even minimize risk. Instead, strategic planning should enable the bank to rationally choose among risk-taking courses of action.

Strategic planning can probably be best achieved by looking at four basic questions:

Where is the bank now?

What are the bank's objectives in the future?

What does management want the bank to be like in about five years?

How will management get to this desired position?

Although such questions at first seem trite, if broadly applied, they form four bases for strategic planning.

Analysis of Past Performance

A system for analyzing past performance was introduced in Chapter 2. Many of the subsequent chapters also discussed more sophisticated measures of performance for specific areas of bank management. In addition to the more formal fianancial measures discussed in these chapters, in order to answer the basic question of where the bank is now, the bank also needs to ask more general questions of itself. What is the scope of its business? What markets is it in? Has it identified those markets on which it hopes to focus? How is it perceived by its community, by its competitors, and by its customers? What areas of strength and weakness can be identified in its organization? What provisions have been made for management succession? Answers to such questions as well as a thorough analysis of financial performance are the first steps in strategic planning. A bank must know where it has been and is before it can say where it wants to be.

Setting Objectives

The next step in strategic planning is a statement of the objectives the bank wants to achieve in roughly the next five years. The formulation of objectives can take place either by top management alone or by top management in conjunction with bank personnel. The more involved the personnel are, the more likely the plan is to gain greater commitment by the entire bank. To be effective, the strategic plan must have a detail implementation procedure as well as analysis and forecasting. All management levels must be wholeheartedly committed to the plan for its implementation to be successful.

Objectives should be clear-cut and as definitive as possible. Objectives such as increased growth, a gain in market share, and improved efficiency are inappropriate. Objectives should be stated in terms that are quantifiable and measurable, and thus capable of providing a check on performance. Obviously, statements for the first year will be more precise than for the later years because of the greater degree of certainty and greater ease of predictability of events in the earlier years. Planning may become too broad in scope, dealing with what may happen in the future rather than being specific about what management goals are and how to achieve them. Certain areas and key issues must be identified, and plans must be able to respond to these areas. Objectives should be selective in nature and pertain to those areas that are most relevant to management considerations. The key objective of managing risk-returns so as to maximize the value of the bank to its shareholders was discussed separately in the preceding section. Other important areas in which to set objectives appear in the following sections.

Corporate Objectives. Corporate objectives comprise the broadest area to consider: What kind of bank do we want to be? What should our community image be? And, finally, why are we in business? These are questions that, though broad in nature, can be answered in specific terms.

Management Development Objectives. Areas that are weak in leadership abilities must be determined and steps must be taken to develop expertise in these areas. If promotion and training can be made from within, it should be done; if not, outside training or new experts should be investigated.

Organizational Structure Objectives. The number of organizational units should be in proportion to asset size and earnings capabilities. Having too few departments results in a volume too large to handle and having too many results in loss of efficiency due to bureaucratic excesses of paperwork and high costs of excess personnel.

Operational Objectives. Increased operational efficiency can be viewed from personnel and equipment standpoints. Teller, proof, bookkeeping, new accounts, and other heavily personnel-oriented departments would benefit from review. Workload and staffing requirements must be consistent with customer service, scheduling, and output needs. Data processing and proof-transit operations should be consistent with the workload and amount of data flow. Examples of possible problems in this area include revision of computer and data processing equipment, personnel turnover, and communications between staff and management.

Marketing Objectives. Marketing programs have become increasingly important in bank planning. Analysis of competition and market share can develop facts that are relevant to creating marketing objectives. Customer analysis provides an important key to what kinds of services can and should be offered. Marketing mix must be defined, and higher or lower levels of concentration in each area must be determined.

Financial Objectives. Traditional objectives of planning have centered on financial objectives. Evaluation of deposit growth, revenue growth, loan volume, and earnings growth are the key factors to consider. Responsibility may be assigned to profit areas, and measurement of results must be accurate. Economic factors and conditions will be guides to how much to expect realistically from profit areas such as the lending function.

Capital Objectives. Need for bank capital should be anticipated in light of the projected growth in resources and the ability of the bank to generate funds internally.

The Bank in the Future

After establishing its future objectives, the bank needs to determine what filling these objectives will make the bank like in the future. A key concern has to be the implications of the bank's future customer base. This customer base consists of businesses, governmental units, and individuals to whom the bank lends and from whom it borrows. A bank's customer base goes a long way in determining what the bank will be like.

One approach to answering what the bank wants to be like in five years is to start with a forecast that assumes the bank will keep its current customer base and, given the anticipated environment, projects what the bank will be like in five years. Then, using assumptions about policies on the bank's risk-return tradeoff, the bank should construct a rough pro forma balance sheet. Based on the proposed balance sheet and rate forecasts, projected income statements could also be prepared. Usually the items on the pro forma balance sheet constructed in this manner will not balance, bank returns will not be high enough, and the bank's top management will not be pleased with the results. Therefore, additional efforts must be made to restructure the bank to meet the anticipated future environment and to do better than the "do nothing" forecast.

The response to this original forecast should be to ask what the bank can do or what it needs to do to get its performance to the desired level. For example, can the bank change its relative prices within its existing customer base to change the magnitude of the funding it receives or of the loans it makes. Alternatively, the bank may seek to change its customer base. In a growth situation, the bank may want to increase the number of markets within which it operates. On the other hand, if loan demand is predicted not to grow sufficiently to justify the quantity of funds the bank forecasts it will attract, the bank may have to get out of some liability markets. Changes such as these must be run through the forecasting process to see that the new results come closer to the balance sheet and profit figures desired by the bank. Several repetitions of this process may be necessary before management feels comfortable with the plan and the customer base implied by the plan.

The second approach is nearly the reverse of the first. The first step is for top management to declare where they would like the bank to be at the end of five years. Because management has chosen the plan, the bank's customer base should be as desired, the resulting balance sheet should be in balance, and the anticipated income statement should be consistent with the bank's return objectives. The second step is to determine whether this final position and desired return figures are attainable, that is, whether the bank's current position and the expected future environment will allow such results. This step is usually achieved by putting together a forecast assuming that the bank changed nothing but just passively responded to the expected environment.

The effort in this approach should be to discern how much the forecasted results differed from the desired plan. If, as is likely, the proposed plan is different from the forecast, then the bank must go back to the drawing board to determine what changes must be made to achieve the desired position. The effort, therefore, must be one of gradually approaching the position desired by the bank, whereas the first approach involves rearranging to arrive at the bank's desired position.

Achieving the Desired Position

The final step in strategic planning is to convert the chosen objectives and strategies into specific assignments and responsibilities. A desirable way to accomplish this may be through a group of activities designated as action programs. Action programs are communicated in the bank through specific assignments that identify specific projects, assign responsibilities, identify resources required, establish steps to be taken, and set completion dates. These action programs should answer the question: What is the bank going to do today that will enable it to meet its objectives for the future? The action programs are developed through the joint efforts of the planning committee, top management, and managers. The board and top management review and approve the finalized action programs. As a result, commitments are made at all levels of responsibility within the organization.

One characteristic of these action plans is that they should be flexible enough to allow bank managers to consider alternative methods and courses of action to achieve the desired results. One of the major criticisms of bank managers has been that they are afraid to try something new or different. Bank managers are finding that the challenging economy, competitive environment, and changing nature of technology are forcing them to try new and different ideas and courses of action. This does not mean managers should discard proven practices and give in to change in an indiscriminate fashion; however, as the banking industry moves further into the 1980s, it must plan change and do so in a manner that will preserve the position of banks as providers of financial services.

In addition to management direction, the establishment of action programs provides specific numbers for activities undertaken that can be used to monitor performance. The measurement of variance from plans provides the basis for a periodic review of progress toward established objectives. The essence of control for strategies is the ability to establish reasonable standards of performance expected from each department or division of the bank. Standards are forthcoming from the sequential steps stated as part of the action programs and from targets in budgets and strategies. Performance can be measured against the standards established and corrective action undertaken.

Tracking performance is difficult because the assumed environment underlying the action programs have changed and the bank manager has adjusted to match the current expectations for the future environment. Sometimes organizational changes can cause difficulty with the new manager being assigned the problems or reaping benefits not of his or her planning. To track performance accurately, a sophisticated, flexible accounting system is needed to keep up with all of the changes in plans. But some tracking system is needed to provide the base for a periodic review of progress. The control phase that is part of the review is based on setting standards for the sequence of steps in action programs, measuring performance against those standards, and taking corrective action to regain the planned position.

CURRENT EXTENT OF LONG-RANGE PLANNING IN BANKING IN THE EARLY 1980s

The preceding sections on return-risk tradeoffs to maximize the market value of the owner's investment and on strategic planning describe how banks should conduct long-range planning. It is also relevant to see how banks are applying these basic planning principles in the early 1980s. Several widely publicized recent developments have brought the concept of bank planning into the public eye. For example, Bankers Trust Company received widespread public attention when it announced its decision to focus on the corporate, institutional, government, and correspondent markets and to sell off the majority of its retail branches. Such a decision obviously reflects top management's judgment as to the means that are to be used to reach the bank's objectives.

Also, in the early 1980s, Bank of America and Citibank are looking to the nationwide commercial and consumer market as the areas through which their long-range objectives will be fulfilled. In anticipation of a possible repeal of existing regulations prohibiting interstate banking, both banks have established a presence in over 40 states through offices that generate loans, handle foreign transactions, and perform other bank-oriented functions not involving direct acceptance of deposits. First Interstate Bankcorp has used its advantage of owning banks in 15 states prior to interstate restrictions to have banks with similar names in these states. In early 1982, First Interstate announced that it would franchise banks in other states in order to move toward its long-range objectives.

Such cases are impressive, but a recent study indicates that in most banks the concept of long-range planning may be given a great deal of lip service but relatively little actual implementation. Sapp received 302 responses from a random sample selected from all insured commercial banks with assets of more than $10 million. The responses showed a strong emphasis on forward planning on a one-year basis; three fourths of the respondents said that they prepared operating budgets covering one year or less. The other fourth admitted that they never planned ahead one year. When the time frame was extended to two years, the percentage of the banks preparing plans fell to approximately three fifths of the respondents. However, if the term *long-range planning* is construed to mean the setting of targets on a basis beyond two years, slightly over two thirds admitted they did not include long-range planning in their management functions. Even among the largest banks in Sapp's respondees—those with assets in excess of $500 million—roughly two fifths stated that their planning process did not extend beyond a two-year time frame.[2]

There is a strong element of irony in such figures on bank planning. Any credit officer of one of those major banks, when approached with a loan request by a commercial customer, would insist on some pro forma balance sheets and income or cash flows showing the business' plans for future growth and profitability and reflecting known and projected industry conditions and trends. Yet in two out of five cases, that officer represents a major bank that does not plan beyond a two-year time frame. Is it logical for banks to demand more from their customers than they expect of themselves and provide through their own internal management system?

SUMMARY

Probably the most important decision most banks have to make in the challenging environment of the 1980s is how much and what types of risks the bank must take to earn a satisfactory return. Successful bank management in the 1980s will require at least three substantive steps. First, management must measure the bank's current return-risk

---

[2] Richard W. Sapp, "Banks Look Ahead: A Survey of Bank Planning," *The Magazine of Bank Administration* (July 1980).

tradeoffs for each of the four risk categories. Second, strengths and weaknesses in management talents and market position must be honestly and accurately evaluated. Third, the bank's board and top management must determine its target level and mix of risks for the environment expected in the next few years. The basic constraint is that the combined risk should produce acceptable returns and the highest value for the owner's investment in the bank.

Strategic planning is necessary for achieving the desired return risk-position in that it provides a means to deal with change. The change in economic conditions, growth and diversification, and increased competition must be projected and dealt with effectively. If change is allowed to sneak up on bank management, the bank has little chance to utilize the change to any extent and will in all probability be overwhelmed. One warning concerning strategic planning is that it must be reassessed with some degree of regularity. Plans must be flexible enough to adapt to external or internal conditions that had not been anticipated. Knowing that change is a given element, the bank can exercise some degree of control if management is forced to think about change and its implications for the future.

Strategic planning is not a mechanistic procedure but rather a highly creative process. It requires imaginative thought for implementing plans and requires continuous examination of future trends through historical perspective. The bank's directions must be defined in specific terms, the future predicted, and a means to reach these objectives determined—all of which require careful management analysis and sound judgment.

CASE 23
Fourth State Bank

Steve Fisher sat at his desk wondering if long-range planning was really worth the effort. It was early 1981 and Fourth State Bank was trying to establish what kind of bank it might become by 1986. As he reflected on the very great changes in banking in recent years, Fisher, the executive vice-president of Fourth State, was not fully convinced that a long-range plan was actually possible. As he considered a long-range strategy, he had available to him extensive information on his bank's community, its organization and officers, and financial information on Fourth National and its "peer" banks for 1979 and 1980.

The chair of Fourth State's board of directors had sent a memorandum to Fisher asking him to prepare a long-range plan including four specific areas:

1 Write a statement of Fourth State Bank's operating objectives in the following areas:
   (a) Marketing and competitive objectives: market share, specific segments or overall; new markets; services; and so on. Develop a complete marketing plan and be able to explain how it will be implemented.
   (b) Financial objectives: loan volume and deposit growth, revenue growth, cost control, earnings growth.
   (c) Operational objectives: new procedures, increased efficiency, and organizational structure changes. Implications for operating performance.
   (d) Management development objectives: specific skills as well as general management ability required.

(e) Overall corporate objectives: why are we in business, what should our mission be, what kind of bank do we want to become?

2 Evaluate the bank's sources and uses of funds during the last two years and formulate policies and objectives to guide the five-year plan with respect to asset and liability management. The analysis should include an evaluation of the structural changes taking place in banking and their possible effects on Fourth State Bank, that is, NOW Accounts, possible (probable?) interstate banking, high interest rates, dependence on large CDs and purchased money, and so forth.

3 Consider changes desirable in the bank's capitalization to permit achievement of objectives while sustaining an adequate capital position. The report should state capital objectives, with supporting explanation as well as indications of how any required strengthening of capital could be accomplished.

4 Suggest an effective organizational structure for Fourth State Bank to use over the next three to five years. The structure should attempt to correct reporting or line of authority problems you may identify, ensure proper controls and work flow, and reflect the type of bank management anticipated in future years.

COMMUNITY BACKGROUND

Economic Developments

Smithville is a county seat in the state of Oklahoma. Its economic base consists of metals, oil and gas refining, petrochemicals and related products, agriculturally oriented industry, and farming and ranching. There were approximately 100 manufacturing firms employing in excess of 17,000 persons in Smithville. The town's population exceeded 125,000; Smith County had a population of about 162,000.

Transportation facilities were excellent and

included air service by 4 carriers, railway service via 8 main-line routes, and 5 bus lines. Additionally, there were 18 motor freight lines and 4 express carriers.

There were 40 public schools in the city with an enrollment of approximately 24,000 students. Smithville had both a two-year community college (enrollment: 7,000 degree students and 11,000 nondegree students) and an upper-level university (enrollment: 6,000 students).

Economic Growth

Selected economic indicators for the greater Smithville area (Smith County) are presented in Exhibit 1. The area's population had increased from the 1970 census population base of 134,087 to 162,000—a 21.0 percent increase. This growth was expected to accelerate during the 1980s. Total employment for the county at year-end 1980 was 74,500.

Construction reflected an increased pace of activity. Total housing units constructed between 1970 and 1980 were 11,711. Building permits issued during the same period reached 27,327. The value of building permits issued in 1980 set a new annual record for the area—$103,829,009. Construction activity (new and renovation/remodeling) was currently high in the core downtown area. Work in progress included a new main post office, remodeling of the federal office building, complete rehabilitation of a department store building to include retail outlets and office space, renovation of a three-story structure to contain 17,500 ft² of office space, and a new glassware manufacturing facility that would employ approximately 500 persons. Plans were nearing completion for a new medical center complex. Five new housing subdivisions were also planned. New housing starts were the highest in history for Smithville during 1980, as was construction generally.

Economic growth was expected to continue at a somewhat higher rate than that of the last five years because of aggressive efforts by the city to attract new investment and the stimulus provided by the oil and gas industry. Many sites were available for industrial use—from small lots to sections of land owned by the city, individuals, or developers. Retail sales in Smith County had more than doubled since 1970, reaching an estimated level of $775 million in 1980.

Demographic Growth

Population projections for Smithville and Smith County are shown in Exhibit 2. The city of Smithville was projected to grow in population from 125,000 currently to 142,750 (approximately 14.2 percent) in 1985, and to 187,800 (approximately 50.2 percent) by the year 2000. Smith County was projected to grow in population from 160,000 currently to 186,400 (approximately 16.5 percent) in 1985, and to 254,900 (approximately 59.3 percent) by the year 2000.

Legislative and Regulatory Environment

Oklahoma had long been a unit banking state. Two bills, however, were pending before the state legislature: one provided authorization of bank holding companies (no limits on acquisitions), and the other for branching within metropolitan (SMSA) areas. Although both were opposed by Oklahoma's independent banks and had been defeated in the recent past, the possibility of at least one of these bills passing the legislature could not be discounted.

BANK ORGANIZATION AND OFFICERS

Organization

Fourth State Bank had been operating for 15 years. It was located in a free-standing downtown building across from a shopping center. The three-story building had been built approximately 12 years ago. A portion of the building was leased as office space to 10 businesses, including a law firm that served as the bank's legal counsel. The drive-up banking facilities were inadequate; this was especially apparent during the late afternoon when much of the bank's business was conducted. The senior management had been discussing construction of a new drive-in fa-

cility across the street and within the shopping center. It was expected that this proposed facility could handle a significant portion of the bank's business because of its accessibility.

Fourth State Bank had a total of 54 employees, 13 of whom were officers. It was organized by the former chair of the board, who had been a dominant figure in the bank's operation until she retired three years ago. The bank's stock was held by 150 stockholders, with the largest investor being an outside director who owned 10 percent of the outstanding stock. The bank's organization structure appears in Exhibit 3.

Board of Directors

Fourth State Bank's board of directors was composed of 15 members: the president and the executive vice-president of the bank and 13 outside directors who had business, farming, or ranching interests in Smithville or the county. The outside directors' investment in the bank was not a significant portion of their total wealth. The majority of the board members were 55 years of age or older; only one was under 40.

Board Committees

The board's committees included the executive committee, loan committee, and trust committee. These committees met once every two weeks, or on call. Other special committees were appointed as needed to handle matters of an exceptional nature.

The *executive committee* was composed of the president, executive vice-president, and two outside directors. It determined bank policy and handled matters that required attention between board meetings.

The *loan committee* consisted of the chair of the board, who also served as chair of the committee; the president; the executive vice-president; the vice-president responsible for larger loans; and an outside director. The loan committee reviewed all loans exceeding $10,000 and considered large loans or lines of credit prior to the bank's formal credit decision.

Chair of the Board

Winifred Evans was elected chair of the board three years ago at the retirement of the former chair. Evans's principal occupation was as a county judge. She presided over board meetings and chaired the loan committee. Evans was kept closely informed about bank matters by the president, Jack Tucker.

President

Jack Tucker, who served as the bank's chief executive officer, was also elected three years earlier. He had served on the board several years, and he owned about 5 percent of the bank's stock. A lawyer by training, Tucker had devoted the past five years to supervising his family's ranch and his wife's estate, which included property in Smithville.

Before assuming the presidency of Fourth State, Tucker considered the bank less aggressive in its loan policies than the expanding community justified. Nonetheless, he continued to solicit loan proposals similar to those approved by prior management, especially with loans related to construction activities. Most of these loans had been approved by the bank, including some loans from areas outside Smith County.

Certain loans during the past two years had provided opportunities for equity participation, and the president had made personal investments in these cases through partnerships, totaling approximately $100,000. Tucker believed that through these activities he had strengthened the loans and developed an improved relationship with some bank customers. The president had participated actively in many civic matters, and had been instrumental recently in raising funds for the new civic center. He was a very personable individual and was widely known throughout the community.

Executive Vice-President

The executive vice-president, Steve Fisher, was a native of Smithville and a graduate of Oklahoma State University, having joined the bank immediately after graduation. He was responsible for the bank's loan portfolio and for financial planning and marketing. The latter was of increasing importance because of Smithville's sharply increased level of economic activity. Fisher was also very active in community and civic affairs.

Vice-President

Helen Haltom, vice-president, had attended Texas A&M University, studying agricultural economics. She had joined the bank five years ago, coming from Fourth State's principal correspondent where she had been employed for about two years. At that bank she had worked in various divisions, including the credit department, but she had served primarily in the correspondent bank division during the six years before joining Fourth State. After accepting a position in the Smithville bank, she had worked closely with the president, principally devoting time to large personal loans, commercial loans, and farm and ranch lending. Haltom had also been given responsibility for the bank's investment portfolio. In this area, however, she followed rather closely the correspondent bank's advice on investment matters. She was personable, hard working, and had spent a great deal of time becoming personally acquainted with the bank's customers, especially the larger ranchers in the county.

Cashier

The cashier, Nelle Baker, had been with the bank for some 12 years. She had exhibited a strong sense of responsibility and had carried out her functions diligently. For the past three years she had supervised teller operations, bookkeeping, and proof and transit. She also supervised management areas related to personnel.

Trust Department

The Trust Department was managed by Weston Edwards, a vice-president and trust officer. The department handled primarily personal trusts. Recent tax legislation, with its revisions in estate and gift tax laws, continued to raise many questions for trust customers, creating a greater than normal demand for expert counseling from trust officers. Edwards was also actively involved in developing new business for the Trust Department and for the bank.

Financial Planning and Personnel

An annual profit plan was prepared during November each year by Steve Fisher, working with the cashier. The profit plan was submitted to the board at the January meeting. The chair of the board had also asked the bank management to begin some longer term strategic planning to develop a better sense of the bank's future potential opportunities. This function had also been assigned to Fisher.

Fourth State Bank had enjoyed good experience with its personnel. Employee turnover had decreased somewhat during recent years. Salary levels were about average in comparison with pay scales in the city. Staffing levels were adequate at the present time, although the president was currently searching for an additional loan officer at the rank of vice-president.

Personnel functions were supervised by the cashier. She initiated job evaluations and salary reviews for personnel below the officer level. A detailed record system was maintained, including time cards, personnel records, job evaluation, vacation time, and sick leave. Exit interviews were given to all persons leaving the bank.

FINANCIAL INFORMATION

Market Data

Fourth State Bank was a member of the FDIC and had deposits totaling $50.4 million at December 31, 1980. It was the fifth largest among eight banks in Smithville and had approximately 4 percent of the city's bank deposits. There were 10 banks in Smith County.

The market area served by the bank was characterized by small and medium-sized commercial and industrial businesses located around the inner city area, retail establishments in a shopping center located near the bank, residential areas to the north of the bank, extending into suburban areas, and farms and ranches throughout the county. Three other banks were located within the local market (the northwest sector of Smithville) served by Fourth State Bank. This market area had recently shown modest growth, which was expected to continue. Residential developments designed for middle- and upper-income families were being constructed in the suburbs north of the bank site. Fourth State had extended its loan market into the county by aggressively soliciting agricultural loans. Most of its commercial loans, however, were to businesses in the Smithville area.

Total deposits and loans for the banks in Fourth State's market area are listed in the following table. (These banks are designated with an asterisk in Exhibit 4.)

	12/31/80	12/31/79	12/31/78	12/31/77	12/31/76
Deposits (in thousands of dollars)	$117,416	$99,695	$86,350	$77,811	$60,636
Fourth State's market share	42.9%	43.7%	46.2%	47.3%	49.4%
Loans (in thousands of dollars)	$ 72,640	$67,001	$59,323	$55,343	$46,300
Fourth State's market share	46.8%	44.6%	47.2%	47.1%	50.2%

	12/31/80	12/31/79	12/31/78	12/31/77	12/31/76
Deposits	4.2%	3.9%	4.0%	4.2%	4.0%
Loans	4.0%	4.2%	4.5%	4.9%	5.1%

Total bank deposits in Smithville were $1,209 million at December 31, 1980; loans were $840 million. Total deposits in Smithville increased by $460 million since 1976 or 60.9 percent, while loans increased by $387 million, or 84.8 percent. Fourth State's share of total deposits and loans in Smithville are presented in the table above. Total deposits of three savings and loan associations were $337 million at year-end 1980, representing an increase of $142.6 million since 1976, or 73.2 percent (see Exhibit 5). These savings and loan associations each had their home offices in Smithville.

The Bank's Capital Structure

For some time examiners from the State Banking Commissioner's office had been suggesting that a higher level of capitalization would be appropriate. The chair and president repeatedly responded that they were doing everything possible to maintain capital ratios at a prudent level. Management had concluded that a common stock offering to strengthen bank capital was not the solution since the bank's common stock had been selling well below book value for quite some time. They cited the bank's relatively low dividend payout ratio as evidence of their effort to improve the capital position. The majority owners of the bank's common stock, which was rather closely held, clearly did not wish their ownership position diluted by a common stock sale below book value.

In an effort to satisfy the regulatory authorities, management proposed a capital note offering. The state authorities were very reluctant to approve the sale of capital notes since they believed it was the bank's equity position that needed improvement.

Management and the state banking authorities finally reached a compromise agreement in early 1980 whereby the bank would undertake a combination common stock and capital note offering. The state banking authorities clearly indicated, however, that the debt portion of the sale was only a temporary solution and that management should begin plans for an additional common stock distribution sometime in 1981 to reestablish a desirable level of equity capital. Management realized there were several serious issues to be resolved before a further significant sale of common stock could be undertaken.

The bank was able to complete a private placement totaling $900,000 in the second quarter of 1980: $300,000 in common stock and $600,000 in subordinated capital notes. There was some question in the minds of board members as to how attractive this financing was to the bank and its stockholders. Although the notes were sold at a favorable interest rate of only 8.75 percent, the 20,000 shares of common stock were sold for only $15.00 per share, and the common stock dividend had to be increased 16 percent, from $0.60 per share on an annualized basis to $0.70 per share. The common stock sales price of $15 per share was approximately 80 percent of book value at the time of sale.

After the common stock sale was completed, the bank had 170,000 shares of common stock outstanding, 39 percent of which was owned by one control group friendly to management. Management owned or controlled another 12.5 percent and three top executives had options to purchase another 25,000 shares at an exercise price of $7.50 per share.

EXHIBIT 1
Fourth State Bank—Selected Economic Indicators: Smith County, 1970–1980

Year	Population	Employment	Housing units constructed	Building permits issued	Retail sales (in thousands of dollars)	Estimated buying income (EBI) (in thousands of dollars)
1980	162,000[a]	74,520[a]	1,427	2,716	$775,615[a]	$948,091[a]
1979	160,165	73,887	1,353	3,245	686,385	869,808
1978	155,956	69,705	1,852	2,860	605,501	793,926
1977	151,539	65,759	1,321	3,008	535,068	724,984
1976	148,076	62,037	1,123	4,190	494,707	659,538
1975	144,337	58,248	1,112	1,616	445,073	586,840
1974	141,081	57,410	920	1,670	410,010	541,617
1973	139,883	56,934	887	1,697	356,018	504,892
1972	137,501	56,815	810	1,506	330,421	501,886
1971	136,723	56,106	704	1,457	303,572	497,037
1970	134,087	55,206	202	3,362	281,532	466,700

[a]Estimated.
Source: Smith County Council of Governments, Planning Department.

EXHIBIT 2
Fourth State Bank—Population Projections: City of Smithville and Smith County, 1980–2000

Year	Smithville	Smith County
1980	125,000	162,000
1985	142,750	186,398
1990	157,840	206,100
1995	171,414	229,183
2000	187,836	254,852

EXHIBIT 3
Fourth State Bank—Organizational Chart

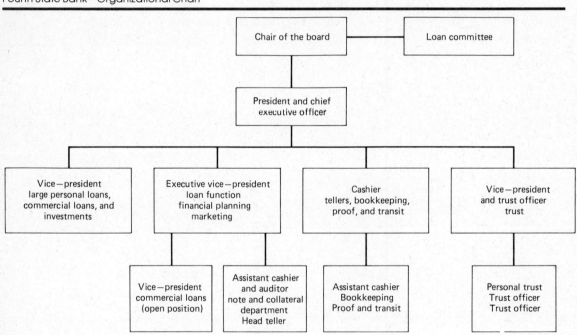

EXHIBIT 4
Fourth State Bank—Deposits and Loans of Banks in Smithville, 1976–80 (in thousands of dollars)

| | 12/31/80 | | 12/31/79 | | 12/31/78 | | 12/31/77 | | 12/31/76 | | Change 1976–1980 | | | |
| | | | | | | | | | | | Deposits | | Loans | |
	Deposits	Loans	Deposits	Loans	Deposits	Loans	Deposits	Loans	Deposits	Loans	Absolute	%	Absolute	%
Fourth State Bank[a]	$ 50,420	$ 33,975	$ 43,560	$ 29,910	$ 39,896	$ 27,978	$ 36,797	$ 26,041	$ 29,944	$ 23,225	$ 20,476	68.4	$ 10,750	46.3
City National Bank	328,091	245,066	322,162	206,833	289,018	180,337	259,021	144,022	220,205	122,102	107,886	48.9	122,964	109.7
Merchants Bank & Trust	190,931	121,482	169,968	108,393	158,888	103,381	138,914	87,301	116,134	73,889	74,797	64.4	47,593	64.4
Metropolitan National Bank	515,519	358,919	476,924	295,968	413,886	246,000	373,733	216,664	328,018	190,951	187,501	57.2	167,968	87.7
Mustang State Bank[a]	46,330	26,072	37,322	23,432	31,237	20,528	27,894	21,054	20,446	16,546	25,884	126.6	9,526	57.6
Commercial National Bank	57,053	42,319	49,939	32,987	37,835	28,312	29,902	24,121	22,525	19,115	34,528	153.3	23,204	121.4
Exchange Bank[a]	6,335	4,696	3,925	3,152	1,147	937	b	b	b	b	b	b	b	b
National Bank of Smithville[a]	14,331	7,897	14,888	10,507	14,070	9,880	13,120	8,248	10,246	6,529	4,085	39.9	1,368	20.9
TOTAL	$1,209,010	$840,426	$1,118,688	$711,182	$985,977	$617,353	$879,381	$527,451	$747,518	$452,357	$455,157	60.9	$383,373	84.8
Fourth State's Market Share	4.2%	4.0%	3.9%	4.2%	4.0%	4.5%	4.2%	4.9%	4.0%	5.1%				

[a]Banks located within Fourth State's local market area.
[b]Exchange Bank not included.

EXHIBIT 5
Fourth State Bank—Savings and Loan Deposits: Smith County, 1976–1980 (in thousands of dollars)

| | 1980 | 1979 | 1978 | 1977 | 1976 | Change 1976–1980 | |
						Absolute	Percent
Smithville Savings and Loan Association	$149,006	$140,323	$124,108	$106,241	$ 97,074	$ 51,932	53.5%
Oklahoma Savings and Loan Association	83,272	73,692	64,642	53,636	46,586	36,686	78.7
American Savings and Loan Association	105,091	96,997	82,620	65,714	51,109	53,982	105.6
Total	$337,369	$311,012	$271,370	$225,591	$194,769	$142,600	73.2%

EXHIBIT 6

Fourth State Bank—Comparative Average Statement of Condition

	1980 Actual	1979 Actual	Difference	Percent
Assets				
Cash and due from banks	$ 7735.	$ 5966.	$ 1768.	29.6
U.S. government securities	7226.	5720.	1506.	26.3
Tax-exempt securities	3392.	2110.	1282.	60.8
Other securities	1749.	755.	994.	131.7
Securities	12367.	8585.	3782.	44.1
Short-term investments	0.	0.	0.	0.
Commercial loans	22939.	20187.	2752.	13.6
Agricultural loans	1796.	1406.	390.	27.8
Real estate loans	2922.	2217.	704.	31.8
Installment loans	4047.	3979.	68.	1.7
Credit card loans	197.	170.	27.	15.9
Other loans	250.	250.	0.	0.
Gross loans	32151.	28210.	3941.	14.0
Less: valuation reserve	−159.	−162.	4.	2.3
Net loans	31993.	28048.	3945.	14.1
Fixed and other assets	2347.	1786.	561.	31.4
Total assets	$54441.	$44385.	$10056.	22.7
Liabilities and Equity				
Noninterest demand	$22036.	$19850.	$ 2186.	11.0
Interest-bearing demand	0.	0.	0.	0.
Total demand deposits	22036.	19850.	2186.	11.0
Savings	5004.	5570.	−566.	−10.2
Savings certificates	2281.	2395.	−114.	−4.7
Money market certificates	6443.	3475.	2968.	85.4
CDs over $100,000	8026.	6055.	1971.	32.5
IRA and club accounts	1671.	1144.	527.	46.1
Other time	1216.	657.	559.	85.2
Total time	24641.	19296.	5345.	27.7
Total deposits	46677.	39146.	7531.	19.2
Short-term borrowing	3136.	1949.	1187.	60.9
Other liabilities	1213.	975.	238.	24.5
Long-term debt	451.	0.	451.	0.
Stockholders equity	2964.	2315.	648.	28.0
Total liabilities and equity	$54441.	$44385.	$10056.	22.7
Total earning assets	44518.	36795.	7724.	21.0

EXHIBIT 7
Fourth State Bank–Income Statement (in thousands of dollars)

Income	Q1/80–Q4/80 Actual	Q1/79–Q4/79 Actual	Difference	Percent
Interest income—U.S. government securities	$1040.	$ 642.	$ 398.	62.0
Interest income—tax exempt securities	178.	110.	68.	61.8
Interest income—other securites	227.	96.	131.	136.0
Total securities	1445.	848.	596.	70.3
Interest income—short term investments	0.	0.	0.	0.
Interest income—commercial loans	3956.	2932.	1024.	34.9
Interest income—agriculture loans	300.	192.	108.	56.1
Interest income—real estate loans	373.	248.	125.	50.5
Interest income—installment loans	562.	518.	44.	8.5
Interest income—credit card loans	33.	29.	4.	15.4
Interest income—other loans	36.	36.	0.	0.7
Total loans	5260.	3955.	1305.	33.0
Total interest income	6705.	4803.	1902.	39.6
Interest expenses—interest-bearing DDA	0.	0.	0.	0.
Interest expenses—savings	266.	295.	−29.	−9.8
Interest expenses—savings certificate	364.	325.	39.	12.0
Interest expenses—money market	983.	530.	453.	85.5
Interest expenses—CDs over $100,000	1381.	853.	528.	61.9
Interest expenses—IRA and club	136.	86.	50.	57.9
Interest expenses—other time	138.	73.	65.	88.8
Total time	3268.	2162.	1106.	51.2
Interest expenses—short-term	499.	293.	206.	70.4
Interest expenses—long-term debt	39.	0.	39.	0.
Total interest expenses	3807.	2455.	1352.	55.1
Net interest margin	2898.	2348.	550.	23.4
Less: provision for loan loss	100.	99.	1.	1.0
Margin net of provision	2798.	2249.	549.	24.4
Service charges	174.	154.	20.	13.0
Fee income	75.	65.	10.	15.4
Other income	83.	103.	−20.	−19.4
Total noninterest income	332.	322.	10.	3.1
Salaries	908.	736.	172.	23.4
Employee benefits	99.	99.	0.	0.
Occupancy and equipment	461.	402.	59.	14.7
Advertising and sales promotion	156.	117.	39.	33.3
Supplies, postage and freight	112.	112.	0.	0.
EDP and other services	203.	165.	38.	23.0
Other expense	284.	241.	43.	17.8
Total operating expenses	2223.	1872.	351.	18.7
Net income before taxes	$ 907.	$ 699.	$ 208.	29.7
Income taxes	335.	273.	62.	22.8
Income before nonoperating	572.	426.	146.	34.2
Nonoperating G/L	0.	−29.	29.	100.0
Net income	$ 572.	$ 397.	$ 175.	44.0

EXHIBIT 8
Fourth State Bank—Interest Rate Report

	1980 Actual	1979 Actual	Difference	Percent
Earning Asset Yields				
Securities				
U.S. government securities	14.39	11.22	3.17	28.2
Tax-exempt securities	5.25	5.21	0.03	0.6
Tax-exempt—tax equivalent	9.71	9.65	0.06	0.6
Other securities	12.97	12.72	0.24	1.9
Total securities—FTE	12.91	10.97	1.94	17.6
Short-term investments	0.	0.	0.	0.
Loans				
Commercial loans	17.24	14.52	2.72	18.7
Agricultural loans	16.70	13.65	3.05	22.3
Real estate loans	12.77	11.19	1.59	14.2
Installment loans	13.89	13.02	0.87	6.7
Credit card loans	16.75	17.06	−0.31	−1.8
Other loans	14.4	14.40	0.	0.
Total loans	16.36	14.02	2.34	16.7
Total earning assets—FTE	15.40	13.31	2.09	15.7
Cost of Funds Rates				
Interest-bearing demand	0.	0.	0.	0.
Savings	5.32	5.30	0.02	0.5
Savings certificates	15.95	13.57	2.38	17.5
Money market certificates	15.26	15.25	0.00	0.
CDs over $100,000	17.21	14.09	3.12	22.2
IRA and club accounts	8.13	7.52	0.61	8.1
Other time	11.34	11.12	0.22	2.0
Total time	13.26	11.20	2.06	18.4
Short-term borrowing	15.92	15.03	0.89	5.9
Long-term debt	8.73	0.00	8.73	0.0
Total cost of funds	13.49	11.56	1.93	16.7
Net interest spread	1.92	1.75	0.16	9.3
Net interest margin	6.85	6.64	0.21	3.2

EXHIBIT 9
Fourth State Bank—Comparative Key Ratios

	1980 Actual	1979 Actual	Difference	Percent
Per Share				
Net operating income	3.46	2.84	0.62	21.9
Net income	3.46	2.65	0.82	30.9
Book value	17.96	15.44	2.52	16.3

EXHIBIT 9 (continued)

	1980 Actual	1979 Actual	Difference	Percent
Performance				
Return on equity (%)	19.29	17.15	2.14	12.5
Return on assets (%)	1.05	0.89	0.16	17.4
Equity multiplier—A/E (×)	18.37	19.17	−0.80	−4.2
Liquidity Position				
Cash to total deposits (%)	16.57	15.24	1.33	8.7
Time to total deposits (%)	52.79	49.29	3.50	7.1
Gross loans/total deposits (%)	68.88	72.06	−3.18	−4.4
Loans/Earning assets (%)	72.22	76.67	−4.45	−5.8
Earning asset mix (%)	81.77	82.90	−1.13	−1.4
Capital Adequacy				
Deposits/Equity capital (×)	15.75	16.91	−1.16	−6.8
Net loans/Equity capital (×)	10.80	12.11	−1.32	−10.9
Risk asset/Equity capital (×)	12.58	13.42	−0.84	−6.2
Loan Position				
Valuation reserve/Gross loans (%)	0.49	0.58	−0.08	−14.3
Provision/Gross loans (%)	0.31	0.35	−0.04	−11.4
Net charge-off/Gross loans (%)	0.36	0.54	−0.18	−32.9
Per Employee				
Salaries and benefits	20235.	19994.	241.	1.2
Total assets	1093962.	1062813.	31149.	2.9

EXHIBIT 10
Fourth State Bank—Reconciliation of Loan Loss Reserve, 1979–1980 (in thousands of dollars)

	1980	1979
Beginning balance	$110	$174
Plus: Provision for loan losses	100	99
Recoveries on loans previously charged off	63	56
Less: Loans charged off	79	219
Net loans charged off (recovered)	16	163
Ending balance	$194	$110
Memo: Average balance	$159	$162

EXHIBIT 11
Fourth State Bank—Reconciliation of Stockholders' Equity, 1979–1980 (dollar figures in thousands)

	1980	1979
Beginning balance	$ 2,500	$ 2,163
Plus: Net income	572	397
Sale of common stock	300	—
Less: Dividends	(75)	(60)
Ending balance	$ 3,297	$ 2,500
Memo: Average balance	$ 2,964	$ 2,315
Dividend payout ratio	13.11%	15.11%

EXHIBIT 12
Fourth State Bank—Interest Variance Analysis, 1978 (dollar figures in thousands)

	Total volume	Rate	Total change
Interest Income Change Due To:			
Interest income—U.S. government securities	43	209	252
Interest income—Tax exempt securities	−12	−0	−12
Interest income—other securities	88	34	122
Total securities	120	243	363
Interest income—short term investments	0	0	0
Interest income—commercial loans	−149	744	595
Interest income—agricultural loans	6	75	81
Interest income—real estate loans	−21	37	17
Interest income—installment loans	−31	−45	−75
Interest income—credit card loans	−184	−2	−166
Interest income—other loans	0	−1	−1
Total loans	−359	809	449
Total interest income	−240	1051	812
Interest Expense Change Due To:			
Interest expenses—interest-bearing DDA	0	0	0
Interest expenses—savings	−34	−0	−34
Interest expenses—savings certificates	−22	67	45
Interest expenses—money market	218	178	395
Interest expenses—CDs over $100,000	143	258	401
Interest expenses—IRA and Club	2	2	4
Interest expenses—other time	12	16	28
Total time	318	521	839
Interest expenses—short-term	22	92	113
Interest expenses—long-term debt	39	0	39
Total interest expenses	379	613	992
Interest margin	−619	439	−180

Under 50 Million	1971	1972	1973	1974	1975	1976	1977	1978	1979	1980
State of Condition										
Gross loans	54.1	52.4	53.2	54.9	51.4	52.4	53.1	55.1	57.4	55.6
Reserve for loan losses	−0.7	−0.6	−0.6	−0.7	−0.5	−0.5	−0.5	−0.6	−0.6	−0.6
Net loans	53.4	51.8	52.6	54.2	50.8	51.9	52.6	54.5	56.8	55.0
Securities portfolio	33.1	34.4	28.9	27.8	28.3	27.2	31.9	29.8	28.5	28.0
Short-term investments	3.4	4.1	9.0	8.6	8.3	7.7	4.1	4.7	4.6	6.4
Total earning assets	89.9	90.3	90.6	90.6	87.4	86.8	88.6	89.0	89.9	89.4
Cash	7.3	7.3	7.2	7.4	9.1	9.4	8.3	7.7	6.9	6.8
Fixed and other assets	2.9	2.4	2.2	2.0	3.5	3.8	3.1	3.3	3.2	3.8
Total assets	100.0	100.0	100.0	100.0	100.0	100.0	100.0	100.0	100.0	100.0
Demand deposits	23.5	22.4	22.9	21.6	28.6	27.9	27.4	27.9	26.8	25.7
Time deposits	68.0	70.1	69.5	70.5	61.3	62.6	63.4	62.5	62.3	63.5
Total deposits	91.5	92.5	92.4	92.0	89.9	90.6	90.8	90.4	89.1	89.2
Borrowed funds	0.0	0.0	0.0	0.0	0.6	0.5	0.4	0.8	1.4	1.4
Other liabilities	0.5	0.3	0.4	0.6	1.3	1.2	1.1	1.1	1.6	1.7
Long-term debt	0.0	0.0	0.0	0.0	0.3	0.3	0.4	0.4	0.3	0.2
Stockholders equity	8.0	7.2	7.2	7.4	7.8	7.5	7.3	7.2	7.5	7.4
Total liabilities and capital	100.0	100.0	100.0	100.0	100.0	100.0	100.0	100.0	100.0	100.0
Statement of Income										
Total interest income	94.1	95.2	95.8	95.9	89.9	90.3	89.5	90.3	90.0	90.7
Noninterest income	5.9	4.8	4.2	4.1	10.1	9.7	10.5	9.7	10.0	9.3
Total income	100.0	100.0	100.0	100.0	100.0	100.0	100.0	100.0	100.0	100.0
Interest expense	46.9	51.3	49.8	53.0	43.9	43.3	42.3	43.7	46.7	51.5
Loan loss provision	0.9	1.1	0.7	1.2	2.5	3.2	4.0	2.4	2.8	2.3
Other expenses	36.5	36.1	32.4	29.5	42.7	42.9	43.5	40.4	36.6	34.4
Total expenses	84.3	88.6	82.9	83.7	89.1	89.5	89.8	86.5	86.1	88.1
Net before taxes	15.7	11.4	17.1	16.3	10.9	10.5	10.2	13.5	13.9	11.9
Income taxes	2.6	0.2	4.3	4.0	0.4	0.6	1.3	1.9	2.7	1.8
Net before security G&L	13.0	11.2	12.8	12.3	10.5	10.0	8.9	11.6	11.2	10.1
Security G&L	0.0	0.1	−0.4	−0.9	0.3	0.6	0.4	−0.4	0.0	0.1
Net income	13.1	11.4	12.4	11.5	10.8	10.6	9.3	11.1	11.2	10.2
Statement of Margin										
Interest income—TE	182.5	194.9	192.0	202.5	180.3	179.0	177.8	181.9	196.2	215.0
Interest expense	82.5	94.9	92.0	102.5	80.3	79.0	77.8	81.9	96.2	115.0
Net interest margin—TE	100.0	100.0	100.0	100.0	100.0	100.0	100.0	100.0	100.0	100.0
Loan loss provision	1.6	2.0	1.2	2.3	4.6	5.9	7.3	4.5	5.7	5.0
Margin net of provision	98.4	98.0	98.8	97.7	95.4	94.1	92.7	95.5	94.3	95.0
Noninterest income	10.4	8.9	7.8	8.0	18.5	17.7	19.3	18.3	20.7	20.7
Other expenses	64.2	66.8	59.8	57.1	78.0	78.3	79.9	75.8	75.4	76.9
Net overhead	53.9	57.9	52.0	49.2	59.5	60.5	60.6	57.6	54.7	56.2
Net before taxes—TE	44.6	40.1	46.8	48.5	35.9	33.5	32.1	37.9	39.6	38.8
Income taxes—TE	21.6	19.3	23.2	24.7	16.8	15.3	15.7	16.3	16.6	16.2
Net before security G&L	23.0	20.8	23.6	23.9	19.1	18.2	16.4	21.7	23.0	22.6
Security G&L	0.1	0.2	−0.8	−1.7	0.6	1.1	0.7	−0.8	0.1	0.3
Net income	23.0	21.0	22.8	22.2	19.7	19.3	17.1	20.8	23.1	22.9

EXHIBIT 14

Fourth State Bank—Peer Group Information: Key Ratios, Average Balances and Tax Equivalent Income

Under 50 Million

Key Ratio Report	1971	1972	1973	1974	1975	1976	1977	1978	1979	1980
Performance										
Return on equity (%)	10.84	9.85	11.79	11.86	10.89	11.72	10.64	13.52	14.93	15.55
Dividend payout (%)	64.75	67.05	46.55	49.16	28.38	29.94	32.89	29.61	32.91	30.32
Return on assets (%)	0.86	0.71	0.85	0.87	0.85	0.88	0.78	0.97	1.13	1.16
Equity multiplier (A/E)	12.56	13.91	13.81	13.59	12.88	13.39	13.72	13.87	13.27	13.46
Interest Margin and Overhead										
Average national prime rate (%)	5.70	5.25	8.02	10.80	7.86	6.84	6.82	9.06	12.67	15.27
Yield on earned assets (%)	7.61	7.27	7.93	8.80	8.84	9.34	9.10	9.55	10.66	12.13
Cost of funds rate (%)	4.55	4.56	4.95	5.73	5.52	5.65	5.50	6.00	7.33	8.90
Spread (%)	3.07	2.71	2.98	3.08	3.32	3.70	3.61	3.55	3.33	3.23
Margin on earned assets (%)	4.17	3.73	4.13	4.35	4.91	5.22	5.12	5.25	5.43	5.64
BPT change in margin (%)	0.54	−0.44	0.40	0.22	0.56	0.31	−0.10	0.13	0.18	0.21
Overhead to E.A. (%)	2.25	2.16	2.15	2.14	2.92	3.16	3.10	3.02	2.97	3.17
Margin after overhead (%)	1.92	1.57	1.98	2.21	1.99	2.06	2.02	2.23	2.46	2.47
Loan Position										
Loans to deposits (%)	58.33	56.03	56.97	58.88	56.53	57.32	57.93	60.31	63.75	61.67
Loans to earn assets (%)	59.41	57.41	58.12	59.84	58.18	59.78	59.37	61.29	63.20	61.51
Loss reserve to loans (%)	1.25	1.14	1.05	1.29	1.00	0.89	0.99	1.04	1.05	1.10
Loss provision to loans (%)	0.11	0.13	0.09	0.17	0.39	0.51	0.63	0.38	0.49	0.46

Leverage and Capital Adequacy

Debt to total capital (%)	0.00	0.00	0.00	0.00	3.98	4.32	5.61	5.82	4.15	3.21
Deposits to capital ratio	11.49	12.87	12.77	12.50	11.13	11.60	11.76	11.92	11.33	11.62
Loans to total capital ratio	6.70	7.21	7.27	7.36	6.29	6.65	6.81	7.13	7.22	7.17
Growth rate of assets (%)	9.81	14.52	5.82	4.46	7.93	13.14	11.23	13.72	11.65	14.43
Equity retention (%)	4.13	3.35	6.71	6.41	51.55	8.94	7.75	10.70	11.85	12.22
Rate of inflation (%)	4.99	4.16	5.69	8.73	9.25	5.22	5.84	7.31	8.48	8.99
Growth rate real GNP (%)	3.39	5.66	5.83	-0.56	-1.13	5.39	5.48	4.75	3.21	-0.08

Liquidity

Cash to total deposits (%)	7.96	7.91	7.82	8.09	10.12	10.36	9.10	8.53	7.78	7.60
Time to total deposits (%)	74.31	75.76	75.24	76.56	68.20	69.18	69.82	69.09	69.95	71.21
Core to total deposits (%)	92.97	83.90	83.74	83.97	60.73	58.85	81.29	80.81	77.89	80.17
Earning asset mix (%)	89.86	90.27	90.58	90.57	87.39	86.84	88.60	88.98	89.87	88.41
Purchase funds to earned assets (%)	7.16	11.37	16.59	16.29	41.15	43.44	19.62	20.44	23.51	21.35
Net borrowed funds to total capital (%)	-42.12	-56.73	-124.11	-116.16	-94.32	-93.38	-47.90	-49.87	-39.80	-64.86

CASE 24

Midland Bank & Trust Company*

The Midland Bank and Trust Company was the flagship bank of Mid-First Corporation, a bank holding company that owned three bank affiliates. Mid-First also operated five nonbank subsidiaries in the following areas: consumer finance; leasing; mortgage banking; credit life, accident, and health insurance; and a computer and data-processing organization.

At the end of 1980, Midland Bank and Trust had resources of just under $5 billion, and operated 236 offices throughout a major midwestern industrial state. Although the bank had maintained its position as the largest bank in the state, its profitability in recent years was well below the average earnings performance of similar "peer group" banks. (See Exhibits 1 through 4 for the 1978–1980 financial data of Midland Bank, and Exhibits 5 through 7 for the peer group banks with total assets of $1 billion to $5 billion.)

During 1980, money markets in the United States experienced one of the most violent fluctuations in American financial history. There was extraordinary volatility, especially in short-term interest rates, both up and down. The prime interest rate reached 20 percent early in the year, then abruptly fell to 11 percent, and then returned to over 21 percent by the end of 1980! These extreme movements created an exceptionally difficult situation for Midland Bank and Trust Co.

The bank's fixed-rate assets were on average about 75 percent of the total assets compared with fixed-rate sources of funds that had fallen to approximately 64 percent of assets. Primarily because of this asset and liability mismatch, and due to extremely high interest rates generally, the bank's profitability in 1980 decreased dramatically. Operating expenses exceeded the taxable

portion of total income. The bank's return on assets fell to 0.16 percent and the return on average equity to 2.73 percent. The bank paid out $1.40 in cash dividends per share in 1980 while it earned only $0.99 a share that year!

As a result of this dismal earnings performance, the bank's directors accepted the resignation of the chief executive officer early in 1981 and the board voted to reduce the quarterly cash dividend from $0.35 to $0.20 a share. Hugh Leonard, a senior officer of a large money center bank, was hired by the board of directors and elected president and chief executive officer of both the Midland Bank and the Mid-First Corporation.

At the first weekly meeting of the bank's asset and liability management committee after he had assumed his new position, Leonard reviewed the bank's situation and, though he did not minimize the difficulty of the task, he was confident the bank could achieve strong profit performance within a reasonable period of time. Leonard had told the board to assume a tentative timetable of three years to achieve at least an average earnings performance consistent with the bank's peer group. Leonard realized, nonetheless, that he would be undertaking a major "turnaround" effort at an unusually complex and difficult time. Interest rates had recently exhibited extreme movements in both directions exceeding anything heretofore experienced by even the most seasoned senior bankers. By mid-1981, some financial indicators were suggesting the possibility of a slowdown in the economy, or possibly a recession, beginning later in 1981. The real likelihood of a recession, however, was unclear as Leonard assumed his responsibilities.

If a recession of any severity did occur, this would have a possibly serious impact on future earnings, at least in the short term, thus extending the turnaround timetable. Moreover, extremely high interest rates had already seriously

---

* This case was adapted from a case by Professors Harry Blythe and David Cole of Ohio State and is used with their permission.

affected many of Midland Bank's bigger accounts, since the northern and midwestern economy was clearly suffering from the effects of high interest rates. This was especially the case for business and individuals in any way related to housing, automobiles, and heavy manufacturing.

Finally, Leonard recognized that the banking industry itself was now undergoing profound structural and regulatory change due in part to serious competitive challenges from the many "nonfinancial institutions" seeking to compete with banks. All of these major considerations must somehow be assessed as Leonard reviewed the early steps in devising and implementing a turnaround strategy for Midland Bank.

Toward this objective, however, he decided to ask each member of the asset and liability management committee to study Midland's financial data for 1978–1980 in relation to data for similar-sized banks and to come to the next meeting of the committee prepared with answers to the following problems:

1 Critically analyze and evaluate the relative profit and growth performance of Midland Bank and Trust Company for the three-year period, 1978 through 1980.

2 Critically analyze and evaluate the relative liquidity and capital positions of Midland Bank from 1978 through 1980.

3 Identify the bank's financial strengths and weaknesses.

4 Outline a suggested strategic plan of action to improve the earnings performance and financial condition of the bank.

EXHIBIT 1
Midland Bank & Trust Company—Average Balance Sheet (dollar figures in millions)

	1978		1979		1980	
	Amount	*Percent*	*Amount*	*Percent*	*Amount*	*Percent*
Cash and due from banks	413	10.13	444	9.61	445	9.12
Investment securities:						
Taxable securities	534	13.10	650	14.07	713	14.61
Tax-exempt securities	538	13.20	552	11.94	523	10.71
Total investment securities	1,072	26.30	1,202	26.01	1,236	25.32
Trading account securities	16	0.39	8	0.18	3	0.06
Interest-bearing bank balances and						
other short-term investments	282	6.92	223	4.83	201	4.12
Loans, net of unearned interest:						
Commercial, financial, agricultural	859	21.07	996	21.55	1,119	22.93
Real estate mortgage	595	14.60	706	15.28	783	16.04
Consumer	675	16.56	818	17.70	760	15.57
Total loans	2,129	52.23	2,520	54.53	2,662	54.54
Less reserve for loan losses	21	0.51	22	0.48	25	0.51
Net loans	2,108	51.72	2,498	54.05	2,637	54.03
Direct-lease financing	27	0.66	38	0.82	54	1.11
Bank premises and equipment	106	2.60	116	2.51	129	2.64
Other assets	52	1.28	92	1.99	176	3.60
Total assets	4,076	100.00	4,621	100.00	4,881	100.00
Total earning assets	3,505	85.99	3,969	85.89	4,131	84.64
Demand deposits	1,057	25.93	1,074	23.24	1,075	22.03

EXHIBIT 1 (continued)

	1978		1979		1980	
	Amount	Percent	Amount	Percent	Amount	Percent
Savings and time deposits:						
Savings deposits	1,223	30.01	1,173	25.38	1,076	22.04
Time deposits, $100,000 and over	464	11.38	579	12.53	545	11.17
Money market deposits under 100,000	24	0.59	244	5.28	590	12.09
All other time under $100,000	578	14.18	555	12.01	472	9.67
Total savings and time deposits	2,289	56.16	2,551	55.20	2,683	54.97
Total deposits	3,346	82.09	3,625	78.44	3,758	77.00
Federal funds purchased and other short-term borrowings	399	9.79	616	13.33	663	13.58
Other liabilities	63	1.54	94	2.04	171	3.50
Total liabilities	3,808	93.42	4,335	93,81	4,592	94.08
Shareholders' equity	268	6.58	286	6.19	289	5.92
Total liabilities and equity capital	4,076	100.00	4,621	100.00	4,881	100.00

EXHIBIT 2

Midland Bank & Trust Company—Income Statement Years Ended December 31 (dollar figures in millions)

	1978		1979		1980	
	Amount	Percent	Amount	Percent	Amount	Percent
Income						
Interest income						
Loans	216.4	64.75	296.1	67.08	347.3	67.87
Investment securities:						
Taxable	37.9	11.34	52.5	11.89	60.6	11.84
Tax-exempt	28.3	8.47	29.8	6.75	29.3	5.73
Interest-bearing bank balances and other short-term investments	21.1	6.31	22.4	5.08	24.5	4.79
Trading account securities	1.1	0.33	0.6	0.14	0.3	0.06
Lease financing income	3.8	1.14	5.8	1.31	8.7	1.70
Total interest income	308.6	92.34	407.2	92.25	470.7	91.99
Noninterest income						
Service charges on deposits	8.7	2.60	10.8	2.45	13.8	2.70
Trust fees	6.9	2.07	8.5	1.93	10.1	1.97
Other noninterest income	10.0	2.99	14.9	3.37	17.1	3.34
Total noninterest income	25.6	7.66	34.2	7.75	41.0	8.01
Total operating income	334.2	100.00	441.4	100.00	511.7	100.00
Total operating income—tax equivalent	360.3[a]		466.8[a]		516.5[a]	
Expenses						
Interest expense						
Savings deposits	60.8	18.19	59.0	13.37	55.1	10.77

EXHIBIT 2 (continued)

	1978		1979		1980	
	Amount	Percent	Amount	Percent	Amount	Percent
Time deposits	77.2	23.10	123.9	28.07	172.6	33.73
Total savings and time deposits	138.0	41.29	182.9	41.44	227.7	44.50
Interest on short-term borrowings	31.5	9.43	67.0	15.18	81.1	15.85
Total interest expense	169.5	50.72	249.9	56.62	308.8	60.35
Provision for loan losses	8.8	2.63	12.4	2.81	23.4	4.57
Noninterest expense						
Personnel expense	64.3	19.24	74.8	16.94	84.1	16.44
Occupancy expense	20.3	6.07	24.1	5.46	29.0	5.67
Other noninterest expense	39.8	11.91	48.5	10.99	49.8	9.73
Total noninterest expense	124.4	37.22	147.4	33.39	162.9	31.84
Total operating expense	302.7	90.57	409.7	92.82	495.1	96.76
Pretax net operating income	31.5	9.43	31.7	7.18	16.6	3.24
Applicable income taxes (tax credits)	0.8	0.24	(0.5)	(0.12)	(2.1)	(0.41)
Net operating income after taxes	30.7	9.19	32.2	7.30	18.7	3.65
Securities gains (losses) net of taxes	(1.0)	(0.30)	(2.5)	(0.57)	(10.8)	(2.11)
Net income	29.7	8.89	29.7	6.73	7.9b	1.54
Cash dividends paid	9.7		10.8		11.3	

aThe tax equivalent adjustment is generally based on the statutory federal income tax rate (48 percent through 1978, and 46 percent in 1979 and 1980). However, in 1980 the bank incurred a loss for federal income tax purposes and was unable to recognize the full amount of that loss. As a result, the tax equivalent adjustment in 1980 is based on the amount of federal income benefit recorded as a percentage of the taxable loss, which approximates 14 percent.
bThe 1980 stockholders equity on the balance sheet was further adjusted upward by approximately $6 million.

EXHIBIT 3
Midland Bank & Trust Company—Income Statement Percentage of Average Total Assets

	1978	1979	1980
Income			
Interest income:			
Loans	5.31%	6.41%	7.11%
Investment securities—tax equivalent	2.26	2.33	1.94
Interest-bearing bank balances and other			
short-term investments	0.52	0.48	0.50
Trading account securities	0.03	0.01	0.01
Lease financing	0.09	0.13	0.18
Total interest income—tax equivalent	8.21	9.36	9.74
Noninterest income:			
Service charges on deposits	0.21	0.24	0.28
Trust fees	0.17	0.18	0.21
Other noninterest income	0.25	0.32	0.35
Total noninterest income	0.63	0.74	0.84
Total operating income—tax equivalent	8.84	10.10	10.58

EXHIBIT 3 (continued)

	1978	1979	1980
Expenses			
Interest expense:			
Savings and time deposits	3.39	3.96	4.67
Short-term borrowings	0.77	1.45	1.66
Total interest expense	4.16	5.41	6.33
Provision for loan losses	0.22	0.27	0.48
Noninterest expense:			
Personnel expense	1.58	1.62	1.72
Occupancy expense	0.50	0.52	0.59
Other noninterest expense	0.97	1.05	1.02
Total noninterest expense	3.05	3.19	3.33
Total operating expense	7.43	8.87	10.14
Pretax net operating income—tax equivalent	1.41	1.23	0.44
Applicable tax-tax equivalent	0.66	0.54	0.06
Net operating income after taxes	0.75	0.69	0.38
Securities gains (losses), net of taxes	0.02	0.05	0.22
Net income (return on assets)	0.73%	0.64%	0.16%
As percentage of average earning assets:			
Total interest income—tax equivalent	9.55%	10.90%	11.51%
Interest expense	4.84	6.30	7.48
Net interest margin	4.71%	4.60%	4.03%

EXHIBIT 4
Midland Bank & Trust Company—Selected Data

	1978	1979	1980
1. Year-end maturities of investment securities:			
Under one year	10.54%	10.93%	11.06%
One to five years	33.93	34.02	34.31
Five to 10 years	15.61	15.45	15.27
Over 10 years	39.92	39.60	39.36
Total	100.00%	100.00%	100.00%
2. Year-end market value to book value:			
Taxable securities	95.06%	93.72%	88.89%
Tax-exempt securities	93.21	90.03	76.17
3. Yield on average investment securities:			
U.S. Treasuries and federal agencies	7.10%	8.08%	8.50%
State and local governments—tax equivalent	10.11	10.00	6.51
Total—tax equivalent	8.61	8.96	7.66
4. Year-end past-due loans as percentage of each loan category:			
Real estate loans	2.52%	2.93%	2.19%
Commercial, financial, agricultural	1.39	0.98	1.03
Consumer	3.01	4.86	4.24

EXHIBIT 4 (continued)

	1978	1979	1980
5. Provision for loan losses:			
Provision/Average total assets	0.22%	0.27%	0.48%
Provision/Average total loans	0.41	0.49	0.88
6. Loan losses:			
Gross loan losses/Average total loans	0.47%	0.66%	1.05%
Net loan losses/Average total loans	0.27	0.42	0.81
7. Loan loss reserve:			
Ending allowance/Total loans	0.96%	0.89%	0.93%
Ending allowance/Net loan losses	3.86×	2.23×	1.16×
8. Earnings coverage of net loan losses	6.88×	4.08×	1.81×
9. Profitability ratios:			
Profit margin—tax equivalent	8.24%	6.36%	1.53%
Asset yield or utilization—tax equivalent	8.84	10.10	10.58
Return on average assets	0.73	0.64	0.16
Leverage multiplier	15.21×	16.16×	16.89×
Return on average equity	11.08%	10.38%	2.73%
10. Cash dividends declared/Net income	32.66%	36.36%	143.04%
11. Annual growth rates:			
Total assets	9.31%	13.37%	5.63%
Total loans	21.17	18.37	5.63
Total deposits	12.13	8.34	3.67
Equity capital	7.63	6.72	1.05
12. Asset yields:			
Total loans	10.16%	11.75%	13.05%
Investment securities—tax equivalent	8.61	8.96	7.66
U.S. Treasuries and federal agencies	7.10	8.08	8.50
State and local governments—tax equivalent	10.11	10.00	6.51
Interest-bearing bank balances and other			
short-term investments	7.48	10.04	12.19
Average earning assets—tax equivalent	9.55	10.90	11.51
13. Funds costs:			
All interest-bearing deposits	6.03%	7.17%	8.49%
Domestic CDs, $100,000 or more	7.61	10.63	12.78
Short-term borrowings	7.89	10.88	12.23
All interest-bearing funds	6.31	7.89	9.23
14. Interest-rate sensitivity:			
Year-end market-rate asset/Total assets	25.42%	25.57%	29.68%
Year-end market-rate funds/Total assets	26.64	36.03	35.66
Net market-rate position/Total assets	(1.22)%	(10.46)%	(5.98)%
15. Personnel expense:			
Personnel expense per FTE employee	$11,454	$12,481	$14,038
FTE employees per $1 million average assets	1.38	1.30	1.23
16. Noninterest income:			
Noninterest income/Average total assets	0.63%	0.74%	0.84%
Deposit service charges/Average demand deposits	0.82	1.01	1.28

EXHIBIT 5

Midland Bank & Trust Company—Peer Group Data: Percentage
of Average Total Assets of All Insured Commercial Banks with Assets $1 to $5 Billion

	1978	1979	1980
Cash and due from banks	12.60%	12.56%	12.73%
Investment securities:			
U.S. Treasuries and federal agencies	9.59	8.83	8.29
State and local governments	9.29	9.41	9.53
Other securities	0.71	0.63	0.69
Total investment securites	19.59	18.87	18.51
Trading account securities	0.41	0.41	0.44
Interest-bearing bank balances	3.34	3.42	4.66
Federal Funds sold and resales	4.72	4.75	4.63
Loans:			
Real estate loans	14.75	15.42	15.36
To financial institutions	3.26	2.96	2.59
For purchasing and carrying securities	1.19	0.94	0.75
Farm	0.71	0.68	0.62
Commercial	18.26	18.14	17.76
Individuals	12.70	13.21	12.46
Other loans	4.07	3.89	4.14
Total loans	54.94	55.24	53.68
Less reserve for loan losses	0.60	0.61	0.63
Net loans	54.34	54.63	53.05
Direct-lease financing	0.60	0.74	0.81
Acceptances	0.75	1.01	1.43
Bank premises and equipment	1.63	1.58	1.59
Other assets	2.02	2.03	2.15
Total assets	100.00%	100.00%	100.00%
Total earning assets	83.00%	82.82%	82.10%
Demand deposits	30.94%	29.48%	29.27%
Savings and time deposits:			
Savings deposits	17.08	13.99	11.58
Time deposits, $100,000 and over	16.67	16.98	15.85
Money market time deposits under $100,000	0.36	3.82	8.02
All other time deposits under $100,000	10.82	8.55	6.67
Total savings and time deposits	44.93	43.34	42.12
Deposits in foreign offices	3.50	4.52	5.12
Total deposits	79.37	77.34	76.51
Federal Funds purchased and repos	10.03	10.72	11.39
Other borrowings	1.02	2.12	1.93
Acceptances	0.75	1.01	1.43
Other liabilities	1.90	2.14	2.15
Total short-term liabilities	93.07	93.33	93.41
Subordinated debt	0.71	0.66	0.60
Equity capital	6.22	6.01	5.99
Total liabilities and equity capital	100.00%	100.00%	100.00%

EXHIBIT 6
Midland Bank & Trust Company—Peer Group Data: Percentage
of Average Total Assets of All Insured Commercial Banks with Assets $1 to $5 Billion

	1978	1979	1980
Interest income:			
Loans	5.68%	6.67%	7.23%
Investment securities—tax equivalent	1.71	1.85	1.97
Federal Funds sold and resales	0.39	0.55	0.62
Interest-bearing bank balances	0.27	0.38	0.63
Other earning assets	0.14	0.17	0.17
Total interest income—tax equivalent	8.19	9.62	10.62
Noninterest income	0.88	0.91	1.02
Total operating income—tax equivalent	9.07	10.53	11.64
Interest expense	4.14	5.50	6.53
Provision for loan losses	0.32	0.31	0.31
Noninterest expense:			
Personnel expense	1.56	1.60	1.66
Occupancy expense	0.49	0.49	0.51
Other noninterest expense	1.02	1.03	1.04
Total noninterest expense	3.07	3.12	3.21
Total operating expense	7.53	8.93	10.05
Pretax net operating income—tax equivalent	1.54	1.60	1.59
Applicable income taxes—tax equivalent	0.73	0.75	0.74
Net operating income after taxes	0.81	0.85	0.85
Securities gains (losses), net of taxes	(0.02)	(0.03)	(0.05)
Net income (return on assets)	0.79%	0.82%	.80%
As percentage of average earning assets:			
Total interest income—tax equivalent	9.87%	11.62%	12.94%
Interest expense	4.99	6.64	7.95
Net interest margin	4.88%	4.98%	4.99%

EXHIBIT 7
Midland Bank & Trust Company—Peer Group Data: All Insured Commercial Banks with Assets $1 to $5 Billion

	1978	1979	1980
1. Year-end maturities of investment securities:			
Under one year	21.91%	19.03%	20.70%
One to five years	36.40	36.67	38.01
Five to 10 years	20.12	21.04	18.99
Over 10 years	21.57	23.26	22.29
Total	100.00%	100.00%	100.00%
2. Year-end market value to book value:			
Taxable securities	95.95%	94.27%	92.75%
Tax-exempt securities	94.69	92.10	83.73

EXHIBIT 7 (continued)

	1978	1979	1980
3. Yield on average investment securities:			
U.S. Treasuries and federal agencies	7.25%	8.36%	9.07%
State and local governments—tax equivalent	10.33	11.15	11.86
Total—tax equivalent	8.73	9.82	10.62
4. Year-end past-due loans as percentage of each loan category:			
Real estate loans	5.06%	4.50%	4.37%
Commercial and industrial	3.27	3.76	4.12
Loans to individuals	2.99	3.28	3.38
All other domestic loans	3.74	3.83	3.70
Foreign loans	1.08	1.27	1.49
5. Provision for loan losses:			
Provision/Average total assets	0.32%	0.31%	0.31%
Provision/Average total loans	0.56	0.54	0.57
6. Loan losses:			
Gross loan losses/Average total loans	0.55%	0.55%	0.62%
Net loan losses/Average total loans	0.42	0.40	0.46
7. Loan loss reserve:			
Ending allowance/Total loans	1.09%	1.10%	1.17%
Ending allowance/Net loan losses	6.83×	5.24×	5.11×
8. Earnings coverage of net loan losses	13.84×	11.42×	9.39×
9. Profitability ratios:			
Profit margin—tax equivalent	8.71%	7.79%	6.87%
Asset yield or utilization—tax equivalent	9.07	10.53	11.64
Return on average assets	0.79	0.82	0.80
Leverage multiplier	16.08×	16.64×	16.69×
Return on average equity	12.70%	13.64%	13.36%
10. Cash dividends declared/Net income	41.27%	44.81%	43.12%
11. Annual growth rates:			
Total assets	13.90%	11.86%	8.58%
Total loans	15.08	12.82	4.77
Total deposits	11.05	10.51	7.02
Equity capital	11.74	12.37	8.39
12. Asset yields:			
Total loans	10.34%	12.08%	13.47%
Investment securities—tax equivalent	8.73	9.82	10.62
U.S. Treasuries and federal agencies	7.25	8.36	9.07
State and local governments—tax equivalent	10.33	11.15	11.86
Interest-bearing bank balances	8.08	11.11	13.52
Federal Funds sold and resales	8.20	11.58	13.39
Average earning assets—tax equivalent	9.87	11.62	12.94
13. Funds costs:			
All interest-bearing deposits	6.47%	8.13%	9.57%

EXHIBIT 7 (continued)

	1978	1979	1980
Domestic CDs, $100,000 or more	7.61	10.47	12.35
All domestic interest-bearing deposits	6.23	7.92	9.28
Foreign office deposits	7.83	11.10	12.72
Short-term borrowings	7.66	10.17	12.00
Subordinated debt	7.05	7.48	7.75
All interest-bearing funds	6.69	8.57	10.11
14. Interest-rate sensitivity:			
Year-end market-rate assets/Total assets	39.25%	·38.56%	40.30%
Year-end market-rate funds/Total assets	33.75	38.86	42.60
Net market-rate position/Total assets	5.50%	(0.30)%	(2.30)%
15. Personnel expense:			
Personnel expense per FTE employee	$14,290	$15,620	$17,280
FTE employees per $1 million average assets	1.12	1.06	0.99
16. Noninterest income:			
Noninterest income/Average total assets	0.88%	0.91%	1.02%
Deposit service charges/Average demand deposits	0.67	0.77	0.91

CASE 25

Western National Bank*

On February 20, 1980, Mr. John Hambros, senior vice-president and manager of the Hong Kong branch of Western National Bank (WNB), was gathering his thoughts about an upcoming decision on two large international loans. The situation was complicated by the fact that he had been actively pursuing business from both borrowers for over a year and the decision, pro or con, would have to be explained fully either to the head office in Los Angeles or to the borrowers. When the loans finally presented themselves within a single day, the profitability and risks of each credit made him unsure just what position WNB should take. On the one hand, there was opportunity to expand significantly the assets of his branch if he made the loans. On the other hand, since both credits were substantial commitments for five years, he realized he would be making a decision that had more than a temporary impact.

THE LOANS

Both loans were essentially government credits. The first was an invitation to participate in a $100 million syndicate led by Bank of America for the Republic of Korea. Participation could range from $1 million to $20 million with the remainder of the loan taken by the Bank of America and other U.S. and European banks. The rate

* This case was written by George G. C. Parker, Senior Lecturer in Management, Graduate School of Business, Stanford University. Copyright © 1980 by the Board of Trustees of the Leland Stanford Junior University. Used by permission.

was ⅝ percent over LIBOR[1] for five years with other terms described in Exhibit 1. Proceeds were to be used to finance the state-owned Korea Power Company.

The second credit was to the Taiwan Power Company (guaranteed by the Government of Taiwan) for $75 million with Western National Bank as the syndicate manager. The rate was also ⅝ percent over LIBOR for five years with other terms as described in Exhibit 2.

The management fee was of particular interest on both loans. Hambros recognized that the difference between a profitable and unprofitable credit could often be determined by extra fees. Analysis of loan fees would be one area to consider before deciding how to proceed.

Hambros was not concerned about the credit or "default" risk of either country. Both countries had Aa[2] ratings and had never failed to meet a financial obligation on time.

Because of the credit quality, Hambros was most concerned about the implications of his decision on the bank's lending strategy and overall profitability. The present dilemma came at a time of increasing competitive pressures and rising costs of doing business.

U.S. INTERNATIONAL BANKING BACKGROUND

Prior to World War I, U.S. banks were sufficiently occupied with domestic business that they felt little pressure to expand overseas. However, accelerating export trade and foreign investment prior to, during, and just after WW I stimulated the growth of overseas branch banking. From 1914 to 1920, U.S. banks increased the number of their foreign branches sixfold from 26 to 181

[1] LIBOR stands for the London Interbank Borrowing Rate used in virtually all international lending agreements as a base lending rate. It is analogous to the U.S. Federal Funds rate used in pricing domestic lending transactions. Generally, term loans of more than one year are priced every six months on the 180-day LIBOR rate in effect at that time. Thus, loans are essentially "floating rate loans" with the *spread* remaining fixed.

[2] The rating of "Aa" for a country is analogous to the same risk rating for a corporation or municipal bond.

(see Exhibit 3). Excessive speculation and overexpansion in the 1920s, followed by the depression in the 1930s and World War II reduced U.S. foreign banking presence significantly. By 1945 there were only 72 U.S. overseas branch offices after what was sometimes called the "great international banking retreat."

Despite the fact that the United States emerged from World War II as the leader of the Free World, American banks turned inward after the war, focusing their attention on the tremendous prosperity at home. Recurring wars in Asia and the "Cold War" in Europe constantly reminded U.S. bankers of the fragile international marketplace. Consequently, foreign branch banking expanded slowly through the 1950s. By 1957, there were still only 117 U.S. branch banks abroad.

THE RUSH OVERSEAS

Compelled by legal restrictions on interstate branch banking and a slowdown in the domestic economy in the late fifties, many U.S. banks once again looked abroad for banking opportunities. Between 1957 and 1972, foreign branches increased from 117 to 627. By 1977, their number had increased to 730.

As international competition intensified, U.S. banks began aggressive marketing programs seeking local business and individual customers. They also began participating vigorously in short term loans to developing countries experiencing "temporary disequilibrium" in their international balance of payments.

By the mid-1970s, international lending activities had become an important source of income to the banking industry and some of the major money center banks earned 50–60 percent of their income from nondomestic sources.

EVALUATING BANK PERFORMANCE

Hambros recognized that capital was a big constraint at Western National Bank. Equity capital (basically the excess of a bank's assets over liabilities) was critical to the bank's day-to-day and long-term performance. Hambros knew that investors and depositors traditionally looked at a bank's capital as their protection against the risk of insolvency.

Hambros recalled a recent conversation with John Frank, the bank's vice-president in charge of planning, about capital and required rates of return. In the conversation, Frank had summarized for Hambros a presentation that he had made in September 1979 to the bank's board of directors about the financial variables he used in formulating WNB's strategy. Frank explained that both the growth of the bank and the ability to pay dividends were fundamentally dependent on the bank's ROE. He further pointed out the ROE was really a function of two separate components, specifically ROA and leverage. Thus if the bank could earn an ROA of 0.80 percent and was leveraged 25 times (meaning Assets/Equity=25), the resulting ROE would be 20 percent.

Frank went on to note that ROA could be broken down into eight separate calculations:

$$\frac{\text{Interest income}}{\text{Assets}} - \frac{\text{Interest expenses}}{\text{Assets}} = \frac{\text{Net interest income}}{\text{Assets}} + \frac{\text{Non-interest income}}{\text{Assets}} - \frac{\text{Non-interest expenses}}{\text{Assets}} - \frac{\text{Loan loss provision}}{\text{Assets}} = \frac{\text{Pretax income}}{\text{Assets}} - \frac{\text{Accrued taxes}}{\text{Assets}} = \text{ROA}$$

Upon evaluation of the two loans in light of the above ROA equation, it was clear that both credits were very close to the indifference point in terms of what they might do for the stockholders.

Many international banking experts believed spreads below ¾ percent were insufficient to cover the bank's costs. But pricing was not the only issue. Acceptance of either loan was complicated by a series of complex considerations:

1 What is the minimum loan spread required for the bank as a whole? What does this imply in terms of ROE.

2 Should the bank be willing to accept narrower spreads on international loans?

3 Does Western National's presence in an important international money center like Hong Kong really improve domestic business and overall bank profitability?

4 How much profitability would the bank be willing to compromise over the short term to build market share?

These issues highlighted the importance of the fees associated with the loan to Taiwan in which Western National was to be the syndicate manager. While both loans were similar in size, the additional fees on the Taiwan loan made it appear more attractive relative to the bank's cost of processing the loan. In addition, the fee was to be received when the loan was funded, tentatively scheduled for April 1980. Hambros also realized that the tax liability on the income from the two loans was considerably lower in Hong Kong than for loans booked in the United States. Last year his branch's effective tax rate equaled 15 percent, almost half the bank's reported tax rate. Although he doubted either loan would default, he noted the impact loan losses had on the bank's profitability and rate of return. He had to consider all these factors before deciding whether he should accept either or both loans.

The cost of six-month LIBOR funds over the next five years was expected to average 14 percent. There was some possibility that rates could go to the low 20s, and another possibility of a dramatic reduction to single digits. He wondered what the effect of this uncertainty might be on equity returns.

Hambros glanced out his office window at the spreading shadows of dusk. Hong Kong always seemed beautiful at night. He turned purposefully toward his desk to concentrate again on his answer. Both credits required an immediate decision.

EXHIBIT 1
Western National Bank—Loan Transaction Summary
(Bank of America) Government of the Republic of Korea, U.S. $100 Million

---

I. **Summary of Terms**

Borrower: The Republic of South Korea.

Rate: ⅝ percent over LIBOR adjusted each six months.

Proceeds: Proceeds of loan shall be used for financing expansion of Korean Power Company.

Repayment: Five-year term from the date of the signature on loan agreement and funding. No amortization for 3 years with 20 percent amortization each six months commencing at the end of third year.

Prepayment: On any interest payment date in minimum amounts of $5 million U.S. with a 30-day written notice.

Participation fee: For banks participating in amounts of:

$1 million U.S.	¼ percent
$3–5 million U.S.	⅜ percent
$5 million U.S. and up	½ percent

Expense coverage: Up to a maximum of $25,000 will be covered by the borrower; any expenses over $25,000 will be paid by Bank of America.

II. **Management Group**

The sole lead manager is Bank of America with banks being appointed comanagers if they participate in amounts of $5 million U.S. or more.

III. **Syndication**

The government of the Republic of South Korea has mandated that this transaction be placed with leading U.S. and international banks.

IV. **Response Requested**

We would appreciate your answer to this transaction no later than December 13, 1979. We look forward to your acceptance.

John Nizziel
General Manager
Bank of America
Far East Division

Addendum

Republic of Korea Loan
The Republic of Korea will use the $100 million loan for financing a major expansion (12%) to the Korean Power Company (KPC), the only power utility operating in Korea. Drawdown of the loan proceeds was expected to commence 30 days after the signing and would take place in two installments of $50 million—one at 30 days, and one at 60 days.

KPC is 100 percent owned by the government of Korea. Audited financial statements for the past five years ending 6/30/79 are available upon request. Recent audited figures indicate that total assets and total paid-in capital equaled $5.2 billion and $2.9 billion, respectively, on 6/30/79. Net income for the three months ending 9/30/79 was $99.2 million, 21 percent above the prior year's quarterly performance.

Net operating cash flow has grown at a compounded annual rate of 20 percent over the last five years, slightly higher than the 18 percent growth in revenues. For the year ending 9/30/79, net operating cash flow equaled

EXHIBIT 1 (continued)

$615.2 million, 3.5 times higher than 1979's interest and debt payment of $174.2 million. The company's five-year cash flow pro forma indicates this ratio will be maintained, permitting payment loan interest and prepayment of loan principal from net operating cash flow. However, the loan is guaranteed by the government of the Republic of Korea.

Audited financial statements and the company's five-year pro forma cash flow are available upon request.

Bank of America
Far East Division

EXHIBIT 2
Western National Bank—Loan Transaction Summary
(Western National Bank) Government of Taiwan, U.S. $75 Million

I. **Summary of Terms**

Borrower: Taiwan Power Company (loan guaranteed by the Government of Taiwan).

Term: Five years; no amortization for 3 years with 20 percent amortization each six months commencing at the end of the third year.

Rate: Five-eighths percent over LIBOR adjusted each six months.

Purpose: Finance expansion of Taiwan Power Co.

Prepayment: On any semiannual interest date in minimum amounts of $100,000 (U.S.) (60-day written notice of repayment required).

Management fee: Five-eighths percent on the total loan amount payable on date of loan agreement and loan's funding.

Participating fee: For banks participating in amounts of (paid out of lead bank's management fee):

$1 million U.S.	¼ percent
$2 million U.S.	⅜ percent
$5 million U.S. and up	½ percent

Expense coverage: Up to a maximum of $20,000 will be covered by the borrower; any expenses over $20,000 will be split evenly between borrower and Western National Bank.

II. **Management Group**

The sole lead manager is Western National Bank with banks being appointed comanagers if they participate in amounts of $5 million U.S. or more.

III. **Syndication**

The government of Taiwan has requested this transaction be placed with regional U.S. banks and foreign agencies in the United States.

IV. **Response Requested**

We would appreciate your answer to this transaction no later than February 20, 1980. We look forward to your interest.

John Hambros
General Manager, Asia
Western National Bank

EXHIBIT 2 (continued)

Addendum

Additional Comments on Loan to Taiwan Power Company

Loan proceeds will be used to finance the expansion of the borrower's power-generating and distributing capacity. Taiwan Power Company (TPC) is owned by the government of Taiwan and is the country's largest single borrower.

A financial package, including audited financial statements and cash flow for the past four years and a pro forma for the next five years, is available upon request. TPC's financial statements are current through 9/30/79. Recent audited figures reveal that total assets and total capital equal $5.7 billion U.S. and $2.1 billion, respectively. Net income for the year ending 12/31/78 was $255.5 million U.S. and $216.7 million for the previous 12 months. Net income for the most recent nine-month period ending 9/30/79 was $221.3 million, or 17 percent above the previous nine months' results. TPC's net operating cash flow in 1978 equaled $455 million, sufficient to cover total interest expense of $150 million. While interest expense is projected to rise to approximately $160 million in 1979, net operating cash flow should reach $510 million. Interest coverage of at least 3 to 1 is projected to be maintained over the next five years in the company's pro forma cash flow.

Western National Bank views the principal repayment source as being the power utility's cash flow from operations. The secondary repayment source is the government's guarantee.

EXHIBIT 3
Western National Bank—U.S. Overseas Branch Banks

	Year																
	1914	1920	1926	1939	1945	1950	1957	1960	1964	1967	1968	1969	1970	1971	1972	1976	1977
Number of branches	26	181	107	110	72	95	117	131	181	295	375	459	536	583	627	731	730

Sources: (1) The 1914–1925 figures are based on Clyde William Phelps, *The Foreign Expansion of American Banks* (New York: Ronald Press Co., 1927). (2) The 1939 figures are derived from Clyde William Phelps, *Trends in American Banking Abroad* (Chattanooga: University of Chattanooga, no date). (3) The 1960–1970 figures are provided by the Board of Governors of the Federal Reserve System, Andrew F. Brimmer, *American International Banking* (April 2, 1973), p. 57. (4) The 1976–1977 figures are from "Overseas Branches of Member Banks," *Federal Reserve Bulletin* (June 1978), p. 517.

EXHIBIT 4
Western National Bank—Consolidated Statement of Income (in thousands, except per share)

	Year ended December 31,	
	1978	*1977 (restated)*
Interest Income		
Interest and fees on loans	$1,193,972	$ 823,415
Interest on investment securities:		
Taxable	72,604	93,525
Exempt from federal income taxes	30,752	22,504
Total interest on investment securities	103,356	116,029

EXHIBIT 4 (continued)

	Year ended December 31,	
	1978	*1977 (restated)*
Interest on trading account securities	2,143	4,419
Other interest income	49,179	30,823
Lease financing	37,592	32,889
Total interest income	1,386,242	1,007,575
Interest Expense		
Interest on deposits	656,997	463,733
Interest on short-term borrowings	104,002	52,944
Interest on long-term debt	22,647	21,232
Total interest expense	783,646	537,909
Net interest income	602,596	469,666
Provision for loan losses	47,537	41,028
Net interest income after provision for loan losses	555,059	428,638
Other Income		
Trust income	24,107	21,635
Service charges on deposit accounts	27,792	25,511
International commissions, syndication fees, and foreign exchange	13,107	13,439
Service fees	13,077	11,582
Other	24,034	18,508
Total other income	102,117	90,675
Other Expense		
Salaries	203,708	168,085
Employee benefits	49,986	41,028
Net occupancy expense	39,623	36,445
Equipment expense	26,210	20,649
Other	129,208	94,331
Total other expense	448,735	360,538
Income before income taxes and securities transactions	208,441	158,775
Less applicable income taxes	92,560	72,394
Income Before Securities Transactions	115,881	86,381
Securities losses, net of income tax effect of $(6,942) in 1978 and $(1,233) in 1977	(5,735)	(1,020)
Net Income	$ 110,146	$ 85,361
Per share (based on average number of common shares outstanding):		
Income before securities transactions	$5.16	$3.99
Securities transactions, net of income tax effect	(.25)	(.05)
Net income	$4.91	$3.94

Source: Western National Bank Annual Report, 1978.

EXHIBIT 5
Western National Bank—Financial Statements as of December 31, 1977 and 1978 (in thousands of dollars)

	December 31,	
	1978	1977 (restated)
Assets		
Cash and due from banks	$2,119,702	$ 1,654,141
Overseas deposits	549,866	458,313
Investment securities, at cost (market value $1,722,025 and $1,879,637 at December 31, 1978 and 1977, respectively)	1,825,428	1,919,446
Trading account securities	35,994	14,846
Funds sold	93,900	168,600
Loans:		
Commercial loans	3,052,819	2,569,759
Real estate construction loans	787,411	574,405
Real estate mortgage loans	3,639,204	2,709,492
Consumer loans	2,911,479	1,981,878
International loans	2,504,756	2,394,605
Total loans	12,895,669	10,230,139
Less: Allowance for loan losses	(102,349)	(86,185)
Unearned discount	(250,412)	(135,163)
Total net loans	12,542,908	10,008,791
Lease financing	420,815	313,805
Premises and equipment, net	227,947	202,764
Due from customers on acceptances	420,103	372,835
Accrued interest receivable	186,266	136,344
Other assets	188,507	171,886
Total assets	$18,611,436	$15,421,771
Liabilities and Stockholders' Equity		
Deposits:		
Demand deposits	$ 3,996,618	$ 3,536,899
Savings deposits	3,459,393	3,585,643
Savings certificates	2,204,363	1,635,215
Certificates of deposit	2,956,675	1,827,170
Other time deposits	614,539	424,592
Deposits in overseas offices	1,587,083	1,468,003
Total deposits	14,818,671	12,477,522
Short-term borrowings:		
Federal funds borrowed and repurchase agreements	1,034,955	759,370
Commercial paper outstanding	251,973	178,411
Other	386,347	221,586
Total short-term borrowings	1,673,275	1,159,367
Acceptances outstanding	421,584	373,022
Accrued taxes and other expenses	284,768	177,305
4½% Capital notes due 1989	50,000	50,000

EXHIBIT 5 (continued)

	December 31,	
	1978	1977 (restated)
3¼% Convertible capital notes, due 1989	4,881	10,065
Debentures, notes and mortgages	256,388	258,986
Obligations under capital leases	76,491	77,675
Other liabilities	282,776	180,294
Total liabilities	17,868,834	14,764,236
Stockholders' equity:		
Common stock—$5 par value, authorized 30 million shares, outstanding 22,543,046 shares and 22,316,305 shares at December 31, 1978 and 1977, respectively	112,715	111,581
Additional paid-in capital	239,546	234,292
Retained earnings	390,341	311,662
Total stockholders' equity	742,602	657,535
Total liabilities and stockholders' equity	$18,611,436	$15,421,771

Source: Western National Bank Annual Report, 1978.

CASE 26
Eastern National Bank: Eurovia Branch *

INTRODUCTION

Early on January 20, 1978, Otto Harcourt, manager of the Eurovia Branch of Eastern National Bank, met with his business development officer, Lynne Osborne, to discuss a deal put together by her staff. Eurovia National Airlines, the government-owned flag carrier of a major European country, wanted to add new Boeing 747 aircraft to its fleet. This represented a $50 million financing opportunity. The airline requested a loan for 10 years, at a 9 percent per annum fixed interest rate to be collected semiannually in arrears, in addition to a $250,000 arrangement fee. A com-

* This case was written by George G. C. Parker, Senior Lecturer in Management, Graduate School of Business, Stanford University. Copyright © 1980 by the Board of Trustees of the Leland Stanford Junior University. Used by permission.

mitment fee was not considered appropriate, because takedown of the unsecured loan was to be made within two weeks of acceptance.

The decision faced by Harcourt was whether or not to accept the deal as proposed. Several conversations had been held with Eurovia Airlines, and it was apparent that the terms of the credit were nonnegotiable since the borrower believed they could obtain these terms from other bank lenders.

Eastern National Bank, headquartered in the mid-Atlantic region, was among the 10 largest banks in the United States. Total assets exceeded $41 billion. International operations accounted for approximately 55 percent of assets and 45 percent of profits. Domestic business was divided almost equally between retail and wholesale activities. Few banks in the country were as well balanced in their mix of business as Eastern National.

The Eurovia branch was among the largest in ENB's international networks. It currently had total assets of $653 million.

DISCUSSION OF THE OPPORTUNITY

To assist him in reaching a decision, Harcourt asked his chief credit officer, Lars Sunderman, and his chief money trader, Horst Meyer, to attend his meeting with Osborne.

Sunderman, known for carefully protecting the bank's portfolio, favored making the loan from a credit standpoint. Although the airline continued to generate deficits, that was not unusual under government ownership. The deficits appeared to be caused by overstaffing, since personnel expenses were 135 percent of international airline industry norms. This, Sunderman suggested, appeared to be a conscious job-generating strategy that was being subsidized by annual infusions of taxpayer-generated capital. A mix of equity and unsubordinated long-term debt provided by the government had been the usual method of covering the annual deficits. However, since the airline had considerable dollar-generating capability through its international route structure, exchange for repaying the loan was considered ample.

Meyer was not so bullish on the loan and stated that funding could be a problem. Somewhat horrified at the prospect of funding a 10-year, fixed-rate loan with short Eurodollar deposits, Meyer said the most he could realistically do was to cover the loan in tenors (maturities) of up to six months. He felt there was the possibility of a small amount, about $5 million, in up-to-1-year money. At the current Eurodollar rates (see Exhibit 1) of 8⅛ to 8¼ for these maturities, the spread was acceptable, but only barely so.

It would appear, Meyer said, that funding limitations meant a sizable mismatch would be necessary. In answer to Harcourt's question regarding the U.S. money market as a better source of funds, Meyer pointed out that U.S. money markets were also thin on longer maturities. Headquarters might be willing to supply funds

with short-term maturities. (Exhibit 2, 3, and 4 show recent and historical trends in Eurodollar and U.S. CD interest rates.)

Commenting with some cynicism about the bank's return on the loan, Meyer pointed out that the branch could purchase Eurobonds of comparable quality and tenor that had a current yield to maturity of about 9.23 percent. He also said that there was an active secondary market in such issues and that either acquisition or disposal of these types of assets could be accomplished with a simple phone call.

Despite Meyer's reservations, Osborne remained strongly in favor of the loan because it represented a measurable increase in the branch's loan totals and was well within the bounds of acceptable credit risk. Ms. Osborne had joined the bank about a year ago from a London investment bank, where she had headed their very successful loan syndication activities. While admitting that the pricing of the loan was somewhat low, she pointed out that the airlines had been a business development target for some years for Eastern National Bank. Osborne also noted that having Eurovia National Airlines on the books could lead to significant future financing opportunities, not only with government-owned agencies and companies, but with many of the country's larger corporations. Harcourt conceded Osborne's point, since he was well aware of the "clubby" nature of the local business community.

Sunderman commented that Eurovia's overall rating of 3-C was based on low growth rates in industrial productivity and chronic trade deficits (see Exhibit 5). He felt the deficits were responsible for pressure on the local currency and that the government was ingeniously using the national airline as a borrowing vehicle to build up its foreign currency reserves.

FUNDING FROM THE HEADQUARTERS POOL

After ending the discussion, and thanking his staff members, Harcourt decided to call his regional vice-president in Paris before making a final decision.

It was no surprise to Harcourt that Oscar

Schultz, the RVP, enthusiastically supported the deal since, as the former manager of the Eurovia branch, Schultz had assisted in the original solicitation of the airline. He understood the difficulty of booking local accounts in Eurovia except in small businesses peripheral to the major national accounts. This deal, Schultz suggested, was an opportunity for the branch to move into the "big leagues." However, his advice on funding the loan was somewhat vague. Schultz closed the conversation by saying he knew Harcourt "would do the right thing," leaving Harcourt rather concerned.

Mustapha Abid, ENB's European funding coordinator, later phoned Harcourt about another matter. He confirmed Meyer's facts about the U.S. money market, but he did offer Harcourt a little hope in finding funding sources. Abid said that he heard from headquarters that allocations of fixed-interest-rate funds would be made available from a "headquarters pool." Consumer deposits generated by the bank's U.S. branch banking network provided the base for this pool, but Abid didn't know the circumstances under which the funds could or would be made available to overseas units.

Harcourt called headquarters to verify the existence of the "pool." Headquarters said it could fund the loan, if approved, but it would have to charge a fixed funding rate of 8.5 percent. Surprised, he asked why the rate was so high, considering the billions of dollars in noninterest-bearing demand deposits in the retail operations at home.

The headquarters officer replied that the "pool" of checking and savings account funds did have a relatively low cost at the present time. It was estimated to be under 5 percent, taking into account the average interest rate paid on the pool, as well as acquisition and maintenance costs. However, as a matter of policy, loans from this pool would be based on the maturity of the loan. Like any other lender committing funds at a fixed rate, the pool faced cost risks such as the possibility of higher savings deposit rates and the prospect of paying interest on checking account funds. Thus, a 10-year loan would be priced using an *estimate* of what it *would cost the bank to obtain money*. As illustrated by a hypothetical example in Exhibit 6, the rate was based on the average spread between CD rates and short-term U.S. government rates. This differential was assumed to exist all along the government yield curve, so the cost of 10-year pool funds was computed at the 10-year government rate, plus the spread, plus an adjustment for CD reserve requirements. This left Harcourt with a situation in which an 8.5 percent cost of funds was the only apparent matching funding available to the branch.

As a last resort, Harcourt noted that 10-year loans secured by real estate were funded from headquarters at a fixed rate of 8.25 percent. The rationale for this lower rate was based on (1) lower credit risk due to the underlying asset value, and (2) market realities and a strategic desire to stay in real estate lending. If the airline credit could qualify for the real estate rate, this would improve things somewhat, but it was unclear how this might be argued, or how much difference this would really make in the decision.

BANK OBJECTIVES

Harcourt remembered the bank's public position stated by the president and CEO in a recent speech. It described the inflationary background of recent years and the bank's desire to maintain stable and sustainable growth. The memo emphasized targets of a 1.25 percent before-tax return on assets and a 15 percent after-tax return on equity. Those targets, plus a controlled growth mode of operations, were considered necessary to support the bank's continuing obligation to its stockholders.

The formal imposition of those targets did not alarm Harcourt. He was a careful manager and had maintained the branch's net interest spread at an average of 1.27 percent for the last six months. However, about $85 million in term loans were due to mature over the next nine months, and these loans had an average earnings rate of 9.2 percent. The branch's entire loan portfolio had an average earnings rate of 9.08 percent. The overall funding costs were 7.8 percent, including an acceptable amount of funding with short maturities.

Finally, Harcourt studied the current economic forecast of U.S. dollar interest rates. The forecast described the United State's continuing trade deficits and considerable, if not alarming, inflation rate. It also discussed the various pressures and alternatives faced by the president and the Federal Reserve. The forecast said interest rates were under fairly strong and continuing upward pressure and there was a strong possibility of a recession. The timing of the recession was expressed in vague terms like "by the middle of next year." Harcourt knew, however, that 1980 was a U.S. presidential election year, so that situation could leave everything up in the air.

With such a large transaction, Harcourt considered it unwise to accept or decline the loan on his own. Therefore, he had to make a recommendation to the regional vice-president, including a funding recommendation if he decided to go ahead. A large amount of personal credibility would be weighed with his recommendation, no matter which way he went. Harcourt also knew that he had a performance report due in about a month.

EXHIBIT 1
Eastern National Bank—Current Eurodollar Rates

	January 20, 1978
O/N	$7\frac{1}{2}-\frac{3}{8}$
T/N	$7\frac{1}{2}-\frac{3}{8}$
1 week	$7\frac{5}{8}-\frac{1}{2}$
1 month	$7\frac{7}{8}-\frac{3}{4}$
2 months	$7\frac{7}{8}-\frac{3}{4}$
3 months	$8--\frac{7}{8}$
4 months	$8--\frac{7}{8}$
5 months	$8--\frac{7}{8}$
6 months	$8\frac{1}{8}--$
9 months	$8\frac{1}{8}--$
1 year	$8\frac{1}{4}-\frac{1}{8}$

EXHIBIT 2
Eastern National Bank—Three-months Eurodollar and CD Rates

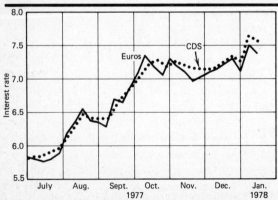

EXHIBIT 2 (continued)

	Three-months Eurodollars weekly average	90-Day CDs reserves and adjustments[a] weekly average		Three-months Eurodollars weekly average	90-Day CDs reserves and adjustments[a] weekly average
1977:26	5.844	5.799	1977:41	7.381	7.212
1977:27	5.800	5.846	1977:42	7.200	7.300
1977:28	5.775	5.872	1977:43	7.075	7.192
1977:29	5.825	5.915	1977:44	7.307	7.261
1977:30	5.900	5.945	1977:45	7.200	7.205
1977:31	6.182	6.131	1977:46	7.113	7.186
1977:32	6.319	6.303	1977:47	6.994	7.151
1977:33	6.519	6.493	1977:48	7.044	7.117
1977:34	6.388	6.444	1977:49	7.088	7.192
1977:35	6.350	6.424	1977:50	7.138	7.237
1977:36	6.288	6.437	1977:51	7.231	7.294
1977:37	6.682	6.653	1977:52	7.319	7.332
1977:38	6.663	6.761	1978:1	7.125	7.298
1977:39	6.913	6.892	1978:2	7.500	7.639
1977:40	7.094	7.063	1978:3	7.400	7.567

[a]Adjusted for 365/360-day accrual periods.

EXHIBIT 3
Eastern National Bank—Six-months Eurodollar and CD Rates

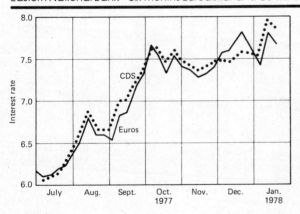

EXHIBIT 3 (continued)

	Six-months Eurodollars weekly average	180-Day CDs reserves and adjustments[a] weekly average		Six-months Eurodollars weekly average	180-Day CDs reserves and adjustments[a] weekly average
1977:26	6.156	6.047	1977:41	7.638	7.587
1977:27	6.106	6.088	1977:42	7.544	7.617
1977:28	6.125	6.120	1977:43	7.375	7.445
1977:29	6.163	6.148	1977:44	7.525	7.574
1977:30	6.206	6.241	1977:45	7.438	7.498
1977:31	6.388	6.469	1977:46	7.356	7.429
1977:32	6.525	6.681	1977:47	7.275	7.399
1977:33	6.763	6.828	1977:48	7.338	7.414
1977:34	6.613	6.731	1977:49	7.400	7.468
1977:35	6.613	6.683	1977:50	7.513	7.486
1977:36	6.525	6.685	1977:51	7.575	7.475
1977:37	6.850	6.953	1977:52	7.688	7.596
1977:38	6.882	7.017	1978:1	7.463	7.555
1977:39	7.156	7.203	1978:2	7.794	7.939
1977:40	7.363	7.375	1978:3	7.700	7.880

[a]Adjusted for 365/360-day accrual periods.

EXHIBIT 4
Quarterly Averages of Three and Six-Months Eurodollar Rates

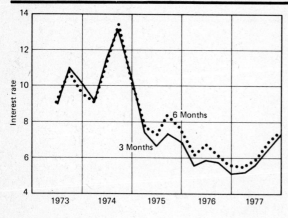

EXHIBIT 4 (continued)

	Three-month Eurodollars quarterly average	Six-month Eurodollars quarterly average		Three-month Eurodollars quarterly average	Six-month Eurodollars quarterly average
1973:2	8.825	8.890	1974:2	11.427	11.369
1973:3	10.993	10.985	1974:3	13.216	13.349
1973:4	10.079	9.748	1974:4	10.530	10.515
1974:1	9.023	9.017	1975:1	7.656	7.938

EXHIBIT 4 (continued)

	Three-month Eurodollars quarterly average	Six-month Eurodollars quarterly average		Three-month Eurodollars quarterly average	Six-month Eurodollars quarterly average
1975:2	6.519	7.426	1976:4	5.284	5.600
1975:3	7.309	8.235	1977:1	5.162	5.592
1975:4	6.837	7.595	1977:2	5.632	5.950
1976:1	5.591	6.266	1977:3	6.270	6.526
1976:2	5.935	6.583	1977:4	7.168	7.464
1976:3	5.724	6.246			

EXHIBIT 5
Explanation of the Country Rating System

The economics department has developed a Country Credit Rating System based on two rating factors:

1 The *External Debt Service* rating, which assesses the relationship between a country's current and projected external debt service and the resources that are and will be available to service that debt. The purpose of this rating factor is to determine the country's ability to fulfill those financial obligations denominated in foreign currency.

2 The *Country Assessment*, which focuses on the stability, resiliency, and adaptability of the country when confronted with shocks, incorporates both structural variables and policy-related variables in its final assessment.

The External Debt Service index consists of six rating categories (Numbers 1–6), while the Country Assessment index consists of five categories (Letters A–E). The rating descriptions attempt to give the country a rating that most nearly reflects its overall conditions.

The Country Risk Rating of 3-C reads as follows:

External Debt Service

3 The country has a relatively limited stock of financial resources and may have to rely on current flows of foreign exchange income to meet its foreign financial obligations. The country has financial authorities of demonstrated ability and can be expected to meet its foreign obligations on schedule. External funding risks are present, but not excessive.

Country Assessment

C Competent authorities are pursuing effective policies that allow for a reasonable economic performance. The country's economic, social, and political structure is not without weakness, but is basically viable. The country should be able to cope with any adverse developments without undue stress. Additional risks of doing business in that country are present, but not excessive.

EXHIBIT 6
Illustration of Pool Interest Rate Computation

	U.S. government securities	CDs	Adjusted CDs		U.S. government securities	CDs	Adjusted CDs
30 days	6.875	7.375	7.84	3 years	7.625	8.125	8.33
60 days	7.0	7.50	7.98	4 years	7.75	8.25	8.46
90 days	7.125	7.625	8.11	5 years	7.875	8.375	8.46
180 days	7.50	8.0	8.20	10 years	8.0	8.5	8.58
1 year	7.5625	8.0625	8.27	15 years	8.0	8.5	8.58
2 years	7.5625	8.0625	8.27				

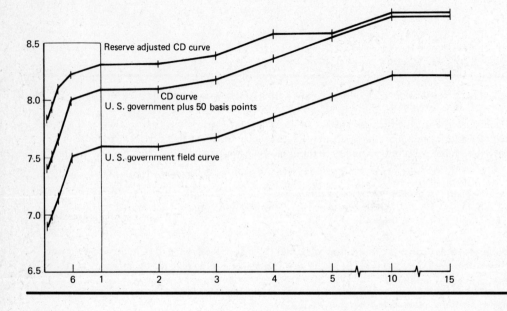

BIBLIOGRAPHY

PERIODICALS

ABA Banking Journal, American Bankers Association.

American Banker (daily banking newspaper).

Bank Marketing, Bank Marketing Association.

The Bankers Magazine, Warren, Gorham, and Lamont, Incorporated.

Federal Reserve Banks, various publications.

Financial Management, Financial Management Association.

Issues in Bank Regulation, Bank Administration Institute.

Journal of Bank Research, Bank Administration Institute.

The Journal of Commercial Bank Lending, Robert Morris Associates.

Journal of Finance, American Finance Association.

Journal of Money, Credit, and Banking (academic journal).

The Magazine of Bank Administration, Bank Administration Institute.

REFERENCE TEXTBOOKS

Baughn, William H., and Walker, Charles E., eds. *The Bankers' Handbook*, rev. ed. Homewood, Ill,: Dow Jones-Irwin, Inc., 1978.

Bowden, Elbert V. *Revolution in Banking*. Houston: Robert F. Dame, Inc., 1980.

Brick, John R. *Bank Management: Concepts and Issues*. Houston: Robert F. Dame, Inc., 1980.

Cohen, Kalman J., and Gibson, Stephen E., ed. *Managemnt Science in Banking*. Boston: Warren, Gorham, and Lamont, 1978.

Crosse, Howard D., and Hempel, George H. *Management Policies for Commercial Banks*, 3d ed. Englewood Cliffs, N.J.: Prentice-Hall, Inc., 1980.

Dougall, Herbert E., and Gaumnitz, Jack E. *Capital Markets and Institutions*, 4th ed. Englewood Cliffs, N.J.: Prentice-Hall, Inc., 1980.

Edmister, Robert O. *Financial Institutions: Markets and Management*. New York: McGraw-Hill, 1980.

Gup, Benton, E. *Financial Intermediaries: An Introduction*, 2d ed. Boston: Houghton Mifflin, 1980.

Havrilesky, Thomas M., and Boorman, John T. *Current Perspectives in Banking: Operations, Management, and Regulation*, 2d ed. Arlington Heights, Ill.: AHM Publishing Corporation, 1980.

Hayes, Douglas A. *Bank Funds Management*. Ann Arbor: University of Michigan Press, 1980.

Hempel, George H. *Bank Capital: Determining and Meeting Your Bank's Capital Needs*. Boston: Bankers Publishing Co., 1978.

Hempel, George H., Coleman, Alan B., and Simonson, Donald. *Bank Management: Text and Cases*. New York: John Wiley & Sons, 1983.

Hempel, George H., and Yawitz, Jess B. *Financial Management of Financial Institutions*. Englewood Cliffs, N.J.: Prentice-Hall, Inc., 1977.

Henning, Charles N., Pigott, William, and Scott, Robert H. *Financial Markets and the Economy*, 2d ed. Englewood Cliffs, N.J.: Prentice-Hall, Inc., 1978.

Herrick, Tracy G. *Bank Analysts' Handbook*. New York: John Wiley & Sons, Inc., 1978.

Jessup, Paul F. *Modern Bank Management*. St. Paul: West Publishing Company, 1980.

Light, J. O., and White, William L. *The Financial System*. Homewood, Ill.: Richard D. Irwin, Inc., 1979.

Mason, John M. *Financial Management of Commercial Banks*. Boston: Warren, Gorham, and Lamont, 1979.

McKinney, George W., Jr., and Brown, William J. *Management of Commercial Bank Funds*. Washington, D.C.: American Institute of Banking, 1974.

Nadler, Paul S. *Commercial Banking in the Economy*, 3d ed. New York: Random House, 1979.

Reed, Edward W., et al. *Commercial Banking*, 2d ed. Englewood Cliffs, N.J.: Prentice-Hall, Inc., 1980.

Robinson, Roland I., and Wrightsman, Dwayne. *Financial Markets: The Accumulation and Allocation of Wealth*, 2d ed. New York: McGraw-Hill, 1980.

Rose, Peter S., and Fraser, Donald R. *Financial Institutions*. Homewood, Ill.: Business Publications, Inc., 1980.

Wood, Oliver G., Jr. *Commercial Banking*. New York: D. Van Nostrand Company, 1978.

Wood, Oliver G., Jr., and Porter, Robert J. *Analysis of Bank Financial Statements*. New York: Van Nostrand Reinhold Company, 1979.

THE CHANGING NATURE OF BANK MANAGEMENT

Baker, James V., Jr. "Why You Need a Formal Asset/Liability/Management Policy." *Banking* (June 1978), pp. 33–40.

Bandel, Roland E., and Abbott, Barry A. "More Battles Ahead to Simplify Truth in Lending." *ABA Banking Journal* (May 1980), pp. 100–14.

Bruning, Charles A. "Inflation's Impact on Bank Capital: An Issue for the 1980's," *ABA Banking Journal* (Feb. 1980), pp. 76–80.

Carcione, Sandra G. "Are You Ready for Nationwide NOWs?" *Bank Marketing* (Jan. 1980), pp. 16–19.

Corrigan, Jerry. "Outlining Fed's Plans Under New Law." *ABA Banking Journal* (Aug. 1980), pp. 35–38.

Edwards, Raoul D. "Interstate Banking: The Debate Begins." *The Bankers Magazine* (Sept.–Oct. 1980), pp. 64–70.

Fraser, Donald R. "The Money Market Fund as a Financial Intermediary." *MSU Business Topics* (Spring 1977), pp. 5–11.

Gabel, Philip M. "Nondeposit Liability Management . . . In a Pressure-Laden Financial Environment." *Savings Bank Journal* (Feb. 1980), pp. 24–33.

Hempel, George H. "The Changing Environment for Bank Management Decision in the 1980's," *Review of Business and Economics* (April 1981), pp. 9–16.

Jarvis, Jay. "Thrifts Will Survive, But Not by Becoming Banks." *ABA Banking Journal* (July 1980), pp. 50–51.

Karten, Howard A. "Use of Financial Modeling Increases," *ABA Banking Journal* (Sept. 1981), pp. 88–101.

Keen, Howard. "Why Bankers Are Concerned About NOW Accounts." Federal Reserve Bank of Philadelphia, *Business Review* (Nov.–Dec. 1977), pp. 3–10.

Key, Sydney J., and Brundy, James M. "Implementation of the International Banking Act." *Federal Reserve Bulletin* (Oct. 1979), pp. 785–95.

Kimball, Ralph C. "The Maturing of the NOW Account in New England." *New England Economic Review* (July–Aug. 1978), pp. 27–42.

Kizza, Joe W. "As NOW Accounts Loom Here's Advice from Experts." *ABA Banking Journal* (Dec. 1979), pp. 45–46.

Mayes, Martin. "Merrill Lynch Quacks Like a Bank." *Fortune* (Oct. 20, 1980), pp. 134–44.

Meyer, Phillip C. "HR 4985: What It Says." *Bank Marketing* (May 1980), pp. 5–6.

Motley, Lawrence. "NOW Accounts: Profitable for Your Bank?" *Bank Marketing* (April 1979), pp. 13–17.

Raddon, Gary H. "HR 4986: What It Means." *Bank Marketing* (May 1980), pp. 9–10.

Rhoades, Stephen A. "The Competitive Effects of Interstate Banking." *Federal Reserve Bulletin* (Jan. 1980), pp. 1–8.

Rose, Sanford, "Dark Days Ahead for Banks." *Fortune* (Jan. 30, 1980), pp. 86–90.

Savage, Donald T. "CRA and Community Credit Needs." *The Bankers Magazine* (Jan.–Feb. 1979), pp. 49–53.

Segal, Robert. "The Financial Ides of March." *The Bankers Magazine* (May–June 1980), pp. 24–28.

Timlen, Thomas M. "The Eighties: The Outlook for Change." *Quarterly Review* (by Federal Reserve Bank of New York) (Spring 1980), vol. 5, no. 1, pp. 1–4.

Winningham, Scott. "The Effects of Removing Regulation Q—A Theoretical Analysis." *Economic Review* (May 1980), pp. 13–23.

Winningham, Scott, and Hagan, Donald G. "Regulation Q: An Historical Perspective." *Economic Review* (April 1980), pp. 3–17.

EVALUATING BANK PERFORMANCE: MEASURING RETURNS AND RISKS

Ahlers, David M. "A New Look at U.S. Commercial Banking." *The Executive*, Cornell University (Winter 1977).

Arahood, Dale. "NBSS Measures of Banking Industry Performance: A Long-Term View." *Magazine of Bank Administration* (Sept. 1978), pp. 40–46.

Binder, Barrett F. "A Look at 1979 Commercial Bank Performance." *Journal of Bank Administration* (Aug. 1980), pp. 20–24.

Cole, David W. "Return on Equity Model for Banks." *The Bankers Magazine* (Summer 1972).

Eisemann, Peter C. "Inflation's Impact on Bank Earnings." *The Bankers Magazine* (Jan.–Feb. 1980), pp. 47–49.

Falkenberg, John H. "Practical Profitability Analysis: Opportunities for Improvement." *Magazine of Bank Administration* (Nov. 1977), pp. 34–37.

Ford, William F. "Using 'High-Performance' Data to Plan Your Bank's Future." *Banking* (Oct. 1978), pp. 40–41, 43–44, 46, 48, 162.

Gillis, Harvey N., Lumry, Rufus W., and Oswold, Thomas J. "A New Approach to Analyzing Bank Performance." *The Bankers Magazine* (March–April 1980), pp. 67–73.

Giroux, Gary, and Grossman, Steven. "How Does Inflation Affect a Bank Holding Company's Rate of Return?" *Issues in Bank Regulation* (Winter 1981), pp. 24–31.

Gup, Benton, and Mitchusson, Linda. "Portfolios and Profits Shape Bank Attitudes." *The Bankers Magazine* (Sept.–Oct. 1978), pp. 46–49.

Howard, Timothy, and Ford, William F. "Story Behind Banking Industry's Profits and Losses, 1972–1980." *ABA Banking Journal* (July 1979), pp. 54–62.

Johnson, Bradford M. "Are Bank Stocks Undervalued?" *Magazine of Bank Administration* (April 1981), pp. 38–45.

Kimball, Ralph. "Commercial Bank Profitability in New England: A Comparative Study." *New England Economic Review* (Nov.–Dec. 1978), pp. 5–24.

Matthews, William M., and Pepin, John J. "Corporate Cash Management + Prime Pricing = Lower Regional Bank Earnings." *The Bankers Magazine* (May–June 1978), pp. 16–23.

Meyer, Philip C. "DIDC Is Off to a Stormy Start." *Bank Marketing* (Aug. 1980), pp. 5–6.

Olson, Ronald L., and Sprague, Ralph H., Jr. "Financial Planning in Action." *Magazine of Bank Administration* (Feb. 1981), pp. 54–64.

Polanis, Mark F., and Binder, Barrett F. "The Top 50 Profit Performing Banks." *Journal of Bank Administration* (Aug. 1980), pp. 25–27.

Robinson, Roland I. "Toward Improved Analysis of Bank Management." *The Bankers Magazine* (Sept.–Oct. 1980), pp. 82–87.

Spong, Kenneth, Meekr, Larry, and Myers, Forest. "The Paradox of Record Bank Earnings and Declining Capital." *Magazine of Bank Administration* (Oct. 1980), pp. 22–27.

Turner, William D. "A Better Way to Measure Retail Banking Performance." *The Bankers Magazine* (Nov.–Dec. 1978), pp. 69–75.

Wallich, Henry C. "Bank Profits and Inflation." Federal Reserve Bank of Richmond, *Economic Review* (May–June 1980), pp. 27–30.

TRENDS IN THE ACQUISITION AND COST OF BANK FUNDS

Adamson, D. Bruce. "Regional and Community Banks Moving Toward Local Base Lending Rates." *ABA Banking Journal* (June 1981), pp. 45–47.

Anderson, Paul S. "Cost and Profitability of Bank Functions." Federal Reserve Bank of Boston. *New England Economic Review* (March–April 1979), pp. 43–61.

Cocheo, Steve. "Lines for Depository Are Complex and Fast Changing." *ABA Banking Journal* (May 1981), pp. 43–50.

Crane, Dwight B., and Riley, Michael J. *NOW Accounts*. Lexington, Mass.: Lexington Books, D.C. Heath and Company, 1978.

_____."Strategies for a NOW Account Environment." *The Bankers Magazine* (Jan.–Feb. 1979), pp. 35–41.

Gilbert, Gary G., and McCall, Alan S. "The Transitional Impact of Nationwide Accounts on Bank Earnings." *Issues in Bank Regulation* (Winter 1978), pp. 20–31.

Hanks, Douglas R. "Why NOWs Will Not Replace Regular Checking." *Bank Marketing* (June 1980), pp. 9–10.

Keen, Howard. "Why Bankers Are Concerned About NOW Accounts." Federal Reserve Bank of Philadelphia. *Business Review* (Nov.–Dec. 1977), pp. 3–10.

Kelly, Charles W. *Valuing Your Money Inventory*. New York: Citicorp, 1974.

Kimball, Ralph C. "The Maturing of the NOW Account in New England." *New England Economic Review* (July–Aug. 1978), pp. 27–42.

_____. "Variations in the New England NOW Account Experiment." Federal Reserve Bank of Boston. *New England Economic Review* (Nov.–Dec. 1980), pp. 23–29.

Melton, William C. "The Market for Large Negotiable CDs." Federal Reserve Bank of New York. *Quarterly Review* (Winter 1977–1978), pp. 22–34.

Metzger, Robert O. "Coping with the Cost of NOWs." *The Bankers Magazine* (Jan.–Feb. 1981), pp. 55–58.

Motley, Lawrence. "NOW Accounts: Profitable for Your Bank?" *Bank Marketing* (April 1979), pp. 13–17.

_____. "Four Strategies for Pricing NOWs." *Bank Marketing* (April 1980), pp. 10–12.

Rhoades, Stephen A. "The Effect of Branch Banking on Purchased Money Liabilities." *The Magazine of Bank Administration* (May 1980), pp. 60–64.

Silverman, Howard B. "Judgment Considerations in Determining the Adequacy of the Loan Loss Reserve—A Banker's Point of View." *The Magazine of Bank Administration* (April 1978), pp. 26–29.

Simonson, Donald G., and Marks, Peter C. "Pricing NOW Accounts and the Cost of Bank Funds." *The Magazine of Bank Administration* (Nov.–Dec. 1980) (2-part article).

Spong, Kenneth, and Hoenig, Thomas. "Bank Examination Classifications and Loan Risk." Federal Reserve Bank of Kansas City. *Economic Review* (June 1979), pp. 15–25.

Tyler, Wat H., and Fridholm, Roger. "The Internal Transfer Price of Bank Funds." *Burroughs Clearing House* (March 1975), pp. 18–19, 56, 58–59.

Watson, Ronald, D. "Estimating the Cost of Your Bank's Funds." Federal Reserve Bank of Philadelphia. *Business Review* (May–June 1978), pp. 3–11.

_____. "How Good Are Your Marginal Cost Estimates?" *The Bankers Magazine* (Winter 1977), pp. 57–62.

_____. "The Marginal Cost of Funds Concept in Banking." *Journal of Bank Research* (Autumn 1977), pp. 136–147.

FINANCING THE BANK'S CAPITAL NEEDS

Austin, Douglas V., and Scamponi, Thomas J. "Senior Debt Securities Revisited." *The Bankers Magazine* (Nov.–Dec. 1980), pp. 73–82.

Bernon, David G. "Capacity for Asset Growth Model: A Tool for Internal Bank Managment and External Bank Analysis." *The Magazine of Bank Administration* (Aug. 1978), pp. 36–39.

Boczar, Gregory E. "External Sources of Bank Holding Company Equity." *Magazine of Bank Administration* (Feb. 1981), pp. 41–44.

Boczar, Gregory E., and Rice, R. Michael. "Stock Repurchases by Bank Holding Companies." *Magazine of Bank Administration* (Feb. 1979), pp. 38–44.

Boczar, Gregory E., and Talley, Samuel H. "Bank Holding Company Leverage." *Magazine of Bank Administration* (May 1981), pp. 53–60.

DeBussey, Fred W. "Double Leverage in Bank Holding Companies." *The Bankers Magazine* (March–April 1978), pp. 86–90.

Dince R. R., and Forston, J. C. "Bank Examination, Capital Adequacy, and Risk." *The Bankers Magazine* (May–June 1980), pp. 47–54.

Field, Andrew H., and Field, Carol. "Direct Equity Marketing for Banks." *The Bankers Magazine* (May–June 1980), pp. 77–82.

Hanweck, Gerald, A., and Mingo, John J. "External Capital Financing Requirements of Commercial Banks, 1977–1981." *Issues in Bank Regulation* (Spring 1978), pp. 27–33.

Hempel, George H. *Bank Capital: Determining and Meeting Your Capital Needs.* Boston: Bankers Publishing Company, 1978.

_____. "Bank Capital Needs in the Coming Decade." *Journal of Contemporary Business* (Summer 1977), pp. 77–93.

Isaac, William M. "A New Perspective on Capital Adequacy." *Issues in Bank Regulation* (Spring 1979), pp. 7–14.

_____. "The World Would Sleep (Or, All You Would Ever Care to Hear About Capital Adequacy)." Speech before the 85th Annual Convention, Florida Bankers Association, Boca Raton, Florida, March 16, 1979.

Keen, Howard. "Bank Dividend Cuts: Recent Experience and the Traditional View." Federal Reserve Bank of Philadelphia. *Business Review* (Nov.–Dec. 1978), pp. 5–13.

McCarthy, Michael P., and Handorf, William C. "How Requirements for Big Capital Ratios Inhibit Banks." *ABA Banking Journal* (June 1981), pp. 52–63.

Odgen, William S. "Debt Management: A Key to Capital Planning." *The Magazine of Bank Administration* (March 1981), pp. 24–31.

Pace, Edmond. "Bank Capitalization." *Journal of Commercial Bank Lending* (April–May 1980) (six-part article).

Vojta, George J. *Bank Capital Adequacy.* New York: Citicorp, 1973.

Wallich, Henry C. "Inflation Is Destroying Bank Earnings and Capital Adequacy." *The Bankers Magazine* (Autumn 1977), pp. 12–16.

Watson, Ronald D. "Insuring Some Progress in the Bank Capital Hassle." Federal Reserve Bank of Philadelphia. *Business Review* (July–Aug. 1974), pp. 3–18.

Wilbur, William L., and Brown, William J. "Bank Capital and the Spectre of Over-regulation." *The Bankers Magazine* (Nov.–Dec. 1979), pp. 82–87.

MEASURING AND PROVIDING RESERVES AND LIQUIDITY

Abken, Peter A. "Commercial Paper." Federal Reserve Bank of Richmond, *Economic Review* (March–April 1981), pp. 11–21.

Bowsher, Norman N. "Repurchase Agreements." Federal Reserve Bank of St. Louis. *Review* (Sept. 1979), pp. 17–22.

Brewer, Elijah. "Some Insights on Member Bank Borrowing." Federal Reserve Bank of Chicago. *Economic Perspectives* (Nov.–Dec. 1978), pp. 16–21.

Carlozzi, Nicholas. "Regulating the Eurocurrency Market: What Are the Prospects?" Federal Reserve Bank of Philadelphia, *Business Review* (March–April 1981), pp. 15–23.

Dince, Robert R., and Verbrugge, James A. "The Rush to Retail Repos." *The Bankers Magazine* (March–April 1981), pp. 77–82.

Gabel, Philip M "Nondeposit Liability Management . . . In a Pressure-Laden Financial Environment." *Savings Bank Journal* (Feb. 1980), pp. 24–33.

Hervey, Jack L. "Bankers Acceptances." Federal Reserve Bank of Chicago. *Business Conditions.* (May 1976), pp. 3–11.

Kaufman, Daniel J., and Lee, David R. "Planning Liquidity: A Practical Approach." *Magazine of Bank Administration* (March 1977), pp. 55–63.

Knight, Robert E. "Guidelines for Efficient Reserve Management." Federal Reserve Bank of Kansas City. *Monthly Review* (Nov. 1977), pp. 11–23.

Korell, Mark L. "Banks Can Now Tap Capital Markets Through Mortgage-Backed Conduits." *Magazine of Bank Administration* (Feb. 1981), pp. 50–52.

Kossick, Robert M. "Liquidity and the Bond Account." *The Bankers Magazine* (May–June 1981), pp. 25–26.

Lucas, Charles M., Jones, Marcos T., and Thurston, Thom B. "Federal Funds and Repurchase Agreements." Federal Reserve Bank of New York. *Quarterly Review* (Summer 1977), pp. 33–48.

Luckett, Dudley G. "Approaches to Bank Liquidity Management." Federal Reserve Bank of Kansas City. *Economic Review* (March 1980), pp. 11–27.

McKinney, George W., Jr. "Liability Management: Its Costs and Its Uses." *The Bankers Magazine* (Jan.–Feb. 1978), pp. 19–26.

Melton, William C. "The Market for Large Negotiable DCs." Federal Reserve Bank of New York. *Quarterly Review* (Winter 1977–1978), pp. 22–34.

Monhollon, Jimmy R. "Treasury Bills." Federal Reserve Bank of Richmond. *Instruments of the Money Market.* (1977), pp. 13–20.

Parthemos, James. "The Discount Window." Federal Reserve Bank of Richmond. *Instruments of the Money Market* (1977), pp. 28–37.

Rhoades, Stephen A. "The Effect of Branch Banking on Purchased Money Liabilities." *Magazine of Bank Administration* (May 1980), pp. 60–64.

Summers, Bruce J. "Negotiable Certificates of Deposit." Federal Reserve Bank of Richmond, *Economic Review* (July–Aug. 1980), pp. 8–19.

MANAGING THE SECURITIES PORTFOLIO

Brown, W. W., and Santoni, G. J. "Unreal Estimates of the Real Rate of Interest." Federal Reserve Bank of St. Louis. *Review* (Jan. 1981), pp. 18–26.

Cook, Timothy Q. "Changing Yield Spreads in the U.S. Government Bond Market." Federal Reserve Bank of Richmond. *Economic Review* (March–April 1977), pp. 3–8.

Grandstaff, Mary C. "Profitability of Bank Loan and Investment Functions: Large Variations Among Banks." Federal Reserve Bank of Dallas. *Voice* (Oct. 1979), pp. 16–23.

Hayes, Douglas A. "Bank Portfolio Management: Revolution in Portfolio Policies." *The Bankers Magazine* (Sept.–Oct. 1980), pp. 21–24.

Hempel, George H. "Basic Ingredients of Commercial Bank's Investment Policies." *The Bankers Magazine* (Autumn 1972), pp. 50–59.

_____. "Quantitative Borrower Characteristics Associated with Defaults on Municipal General Obligations." *Journal of Finance* (May 1973), pp. 523–30.

Hempel, George H., and Kretschman, Stephen R. "Comparative Performance of Portfolio Maturity Policies of Commercial Banks." *Journal of Business and Economics* (Fall 1973), pp. 55–75.

Hempel, George H., and Yawitz, Jess B. "Maximizing Bond Returns." *The Bankers Magazine* (Summer 1974), pp. 103–114.

Nelson, Jane F. "Federal Agency Securities." Federal Reserve Bank of Richmond. *Instruments of the Money Markets* (1977), pp. 85–93.

Ratti, Ronald. "Pledging Requirements and Bank Asset Portfolios." Federal Reserve Bank of Kansas City. *Economic Review* (Sept.–Oct. 1979), pp. 13–23.

Santoni, G. J., and Stone, Courtenay C. "Navigating Through the Interest Rate Morass: Some Basic Principles." Federal Reserve Bank of St. Louis. *Review* (March 1981), pp. 11–18.

Simonson, Donald G., and Hempel, George H. "Public Deposit Policies: Trends and Issues." *Issues in Bank Regulation* (Spring 1978), pp. 14–19.

Sivesind, Charles M. "Mortgage-Backed Securities: The Revolution in Real Estate Finance." Federal Reserve Bank of New York. *Quarterly Review* (Autumn 1979), pp. 1–10.

"What Markets Can Tell You About Interest Rates." *The Morgan Guaranty Survey* (July 1977), pp. 8–15.

Wood, John H. "Interest Rates and Inflation." Federal Reserve Bank of Chicago. *Economic Perspectives* (May–June 1981), pp. 3–12.

Yawitz, Jess B., Hempel, George H., and Marshall, William J. "A Risk-Return Approach to the Selection of Optimal Government Bond Portfolios." *Financial Management* (Autumn 1976), pp. 36–45.

_____. "The Use of Average Maturity as a Risk Proxy in Investment Portfolios." *Journal of Finance* (May 1975), pp. 325–33.

LENDING

Benbow, Robert F. "A New Approach for Analysis and Control of the Yield from Commercial Customers." *Journal of Bank Research* (Summer 1978), pp. 91–103.

Falkenberg, John A. "Practical Profitability Analysis: Opportunities for Improvement." *Magazine of Bank Administration* (Nov. 1977), pp. 34–37.

Furash, Edward E. "The Not-So-Obvious Impact of Inflation." *ABA Banking Journal* (July 1980), pp. 87–89.

Grandstaff, Mary G. "Profitability of Bank Loan and Investment Functions: Large Variations Among Banks." Federal Reserve Bank of Dallas. *Voice* (Oct. 1979), pp. 16–23.

Griggs, Jack, Fraser, Donald R., and Fraser, Lyn M. "A Decision Rule for IRS Loan-Loss Deductions." *Magazine of Bank Administration* (June 1980), pp. 38–42.

Hahn, William H. "Evaluating the Adequacy of Loan Loss Reserves." *The Magazine of Bank Administration* (Oct. 1977), pp. 30–35.

Hayes, Douglas A. "Commercial Loan-Pricing Policies." *The Bankers Magazine* (Jan.–Feb. 1978), pp. 45–52.

———. "Retail Banking in an Interest Sensitive World." *The Bankers Magazine* (July–Aug. 1980), pp. 37–41.

Higgins, Robert C. "Sustainable Growth: New Tool in Bank Lending." *Journal of Commercial Bank Lending* (June 1977), pp. 48–58.

Johnson, Bradford M. "An Analysis of Modern Concepts of Loan Yields." *The Magazine of Bank Administrtion* (Aug. 1977), pp. 31–36.

Lewis, James K. "Loan Pricing, Interest Margins and Inflation." *The Journal of Commercial Lending* (Sept. 1980), pp. 19–25.

Melton, William C., and Heidt, Diane L. "Variable Rate Mortgages." *Quarterly Review* (Summer 1979), pp. 23–31.

Merris, Randall C. "Loan Commitments and Facility Fees." Federal Reserve Bank of Chicago. *Economic Perspectives* (March–April 1978), pp. 14–21.

———. "The Prime Rate." Federal Reserve Bank of Chicago. *Business Conditions* (April 1975), pp. 3–12.

———. "The Prime Rate Revisited." Federal Reserve Bank of Chicago. *Economic Perspectives* (July–Aug. 1977), pp. 17–20.

———. "Prime Rate Update." Federal Reserve Bank of Chicago. *Economic Perspectives* (May–June 1978), pp. 14–16.

Sale, Alvin T. "Floating Rate Installment Loans: An Option for Increased Profitability." *Journal of Retail Banking* (Sept. 1980), pp. 1–6.

Schweitzer, Stuart A. "Bank Loan Losses: A Fresh Perspective." Federal Reserve Bank of Philadelphia. *Business Review* (Sept. 1975), pp. 18–28.

Severson, Gary R. "Determining Profitability Analysis." *Journal of Commercial Bank Lending* (Nov. 1974), pp. 2–8.

Silverman, Howard B. "Judgment Considerations in Determining the Adequacy of the Loan Loss Reserve—A Banker's Point of View." *Magazine of Bank Administration* (April 1978), pp. 26–29.

Spong, Kenneth, and Hoenig, Thomas. "Bank Examination Classifications and Loan Risk." Federal Reserve Bank of Kansas City. *Economic Review* (June 1979), pp. 15–25.

MANAGING INTEREST SENSITIVITY AND MARGIN

Allen, B. D. "Better Asset/Liability Management at Regional Banks." *The Bankers Magazine* (July–Aug. 1978), pp. 82–86.

Angotti, Arthur, A., and Maurer, Morris L. "Slope and Spread: A Tool for Strategic Performance." *Magazine of Bank Administration* (Aug. 1980), pp. 28–34.

Baker, James V. "Riding the Rates or Asset/Liability Management Revisited." *ABA Banking Journal* (Aug. 1980), pp. 57–58 +.

Bauder, Howard L. "The Short-Term Income Benefit of Long-Term NOW Account Planning." *The Magazine of Bank Administration* (July 1978), pp. 28–31.

Binder, Barrett F. "New Initiatives in Asset/Liability Management." *Magazine of Bank Administration* (June 1981), pp. 56–64.

Bonte, Eugene A., and Dieguez, Gregg A. "Spread Management: How to Maintain Profitability." *Savings and Loan News* (Nov. 1979), pp. 54–59.

———. "Spread Management: How to Evaluate Strategies for Profitability." *Savings and Loan News* (Jan. 1980), pp. 62–68.

Cates, David C. "Interest Sensitivity in Banking." *The Bankers Magazine* (Jan.–Feb. 1978), pp. 23–27.

Dieguez, Gregg A., Bonte, Eugene A., and Kinkead, Michael D. "Spread Management: How to Set Goals for Profitability." *Savings and Loan News* (Dec. 1979), pp. 54–59.

Dill, Arnold, and Gaffney, George. "The Effects and Implementation of Spread Management Banking." *Journal of Commercial Bank Lending* (April 1975), pp. 38–45.

Flannery, Mark J. "How Do Changes in Market Interest Rates Affect Bank Profits?" Federal Reserve Bank of Philadelphia. *Business Review* (Sept.–Oct. 1980), pp. 13–22.

Gilbert, Gary G., and McCall, Alan S. "The Transitional Impact of Nationwide Accounts on Bank Earnings." *Issues in Bank Regulation* (Winter 1978), pp. 20–31.

Hayes, Douglas A. "Retail Banking in an Interest-Sensitive World." *The Bankers Magazine* (July–Aug. 1980), pp. 37–41.

Heimann, John G. "How Interest Rate Risk Affects the Loan Officer." *Journal of Commercial Bank Lending* (Jan. 1981), pp. 2–7.

Lieberman, Charles. "Banking Reorganization on a Term to Maturity Basis." *Issues in Bank Regulation* (Summer 1979), pp. 16–23.

Melton, William C., and Heidt, Diane L. "Variable Rate Mortgages." Federal Reserve Bank of New York. *Quarterly Review* (Summer 1979), pp. 23–31.

Nadler, Paul S. "Spread Management—Or, Back to the Basics in Banking." *The Bankers Magazine* (Autumn 1975), pp. 11–14.

Olson, Ronald L., Simonson, Donald G., Reber, Stanley R., and Hempel, George H. "Management of Bank of Interest Margins in the 1980's." *Magazine of Bank Administration* (March–June 1980), (four-part article).

Simonson, Donald, and Hempel, George H. "Improving Gap Management as a Technique for Controlling Interest Rate Risk." *Journal of Bank Research* (Summer 1982).

Turner, William D. "On Managing Assets and Liabilities." *Burroughs Clearing House* (Oct. 1977), pp. 11–13, 45–46.

PLANNING FOR FUTURE RETURN-RISK TRADEOFFS

Ahlers, David M. "Increasing Asset-Liability Management Committee Effectiveness." *The Bankers Magazine* (July–Aug. 1980), pp. 18–22.

Arak, Marcelle, and McCurdy, Christopher J. "Interest Rate Futures." Federal Reserve Bank of New York. *Quarterly Review* (Winter 1979–1980), pp. 33–46.

Arditti, Fred D. "Interest Rate Futures: An Intermediate Stage Toward Efficient Risk Reallocation." *Journal of Bank Research* (Autumn 1978), pp. 146–50.

Baker, James V., Jr. "Statistical Relationships Are Key to Bank's Use of Interest Rate Futures." *ABA Banking Journal* (Feb.–March 1982). pp. 129–34.

Baker, James V., Jr. "Asset/Liability Management." *Banking* (June–Oct. 1978) (five-part article).

Beebe, Jack. "A Perspective on Liability Management and Bank Risk." Federal Reserve Bank of San Francisco. *Economic Review* (Winter 1977), pp. 12–24.

Binder, Barrett F. "Asset/Liability Management." *Magazine of Bank Administration* (Nov.–Dec. 1980 and Jan. 1981) (three-part article).

Brewer, Elijah. "Bank Funds Management Comes of Age." Federal Reserve Bank of Chicago. *Economic Perspectives* (March–April 1980), pp. 3–10.

Broaddus, Alfred. "Linear Programming: A New Approach to Bank Portfolio Management." Federal Reserve Bank of Richmond. *Monthly Review* (Nov. 1972), pp. 3–11.

Brodt, Abraham I. "Bank Asset and Liability Management—A Portfolio Approach." *Journal of Commercial Bank Lending* (Oct. 1980), pp. 43–52.

Buckwater, Nancy. "T-Bill Futures—The Futures in Your Present." *United States Banker* (April 1980), pp. 40–43.

Dew, James Kurt. "Bank Regulations for Futures Accounting." *Issues in Bank Regulation* (Spring 1981), pp. 16–23.

Dew, James Kurt, and Martell, Terrence F. "Treasury Bill Futures, Commercial Lending, and the Synthetic Fixed-Rate Loan." *Journal of Commercial Bank Lending* (June 1981), pp. 27–38.

Duanne, Kenneth E., and Fredman, Albert J. "How Banks Can Use Interest Rate Futures." *Bankers Monthly* (April 1979), pp. 26–29 +.

Duncan, Wallace H. "Treasury Bill Futures—Opportunities and Pitfalls." Federal Reserve Bank of Dallas. *Review* (July 1977), pp. 1–5.

Ederington, Louis. "The Hedging Performance of the New Futures Market." *Journal of Finance* (March 1979), pp. 157–70.

"Futures: More Banks Will Get In." *ABA Banking Journal* (Feb. 1981), pp. 43–46.

Grant, Dwight, and Hempel, George H. "Bank Portfolio Management: The Role of Financial Futures." *Banking Structure Conference Proceedings* (April 1982), pp. 127–139.

An Introduction to Interest Rate Futures Markets 2d rev. ed. Chicago: Chicago Board of Trade. 1980.

Opportunities in Interest Rates: Treasury Bill Futures rev. ed. Chicago: Chicago Mercantile Exchange. 1980.

INDEX